HISTORY
BEHIND THE
HEADLINES

History Behind the Headlines

The Origins of Conflicts Worldwide

VOLUME 5

Nancy Matuszak, Editor

GALE®

THOMSON

GALE

Detroit • New York • San Diego • San Francisco • Cleveland • New Haven, Conn. • Waterville, Maine • London • Munich

History Behind the Headlines, volume 5

Nancy Matuszak

Editorial
Jason M. Everett, Rachel J. Kain

Permissions
Shalice Shah-Caldwell

Imaging and Multimedia
Dean Dauphinais, Christine O'Bryan, Luke Rademacher

Product Design
Pamela A. E. Galbreath

Composition and Electronic Capture
Evi Seoud

Manufacturing
Rhonda A. Williams

ISBN 0–7876–5911–8
ISSN 1531–7307

Printed in the United States of America
10 9 8 7 6 5 4 3 2 1

TABLE OF CONTENTS

A

The hijackings of four passenger airliners in 2001 and the subsequent crashing of those planes into prominent buildings in the United States had numerous repercussions, among them the question of whether or not the skies could be secured for safe air travel.

B

Anthrax-laced letters mailed to prominent media and political figures in the United States in late 2001 raised international fears that terrorists were increasingly capable and willing to use biological weapons. What is biological terrorism and what, exactly, are the threats?

C

The use of chemical weapons in war became widespread during World War I, but was later discouraged. In the hands of terrorists, a chemical weapon could result in mass casualties to and long-ranging effects on a civilian population.

In times of war and upheaval, democratic nations may go to great—and sometimes misguided—lengths to protect national security, violating the rights of individual citizens. Do civil liberties transcend national security needs?

D

The 1995 bombing of the Oklahoma City federal building and the 2001 anthrax mail attacks are the recent and high profile domestic terrorist acts that have occurred in the United States. The threat, however, goes beyond the headline-grabbing events to smaller groups and activities that also pose a danger to domestic security.

E

The European Union responded to the terrorist attacks of September 11, 2001 with resounding support for the United States. When the United States declared its intent to engage in military reprisals against the terrorists, the EU again supported its ally—but not without reservation.

The word "extremism" is used to identify many groups and individuals whose beliefs and actions are not accepted by mainstream society. Who are extremists and how has mainstream society dealt with them?

F

Terrorist groups need money to operate. Where does this money come from and how is it routed to these secret organizations?

CONTENTS BY SUBJECT

POLITICAL

PSYCHOLOGICAL

Contents by Region

Advisory Board

Gary Ackerman is a Research Associate at the Center for Nonproliferation Studies at the Monterey Institute of International Studies, where he researches terrorism, especially terrorism involving Weapons of Mass Destruction (biological, chemical, radiological and nuclear weapons) and mass-casualty terrorism in general. Mr. Ackerman received his Master's degree in International Relations from Yale University. His work includes research on terrorism theory, empirical analysis of trends in WMD terrorism, threat assessment and government response and prevention programs.

Jerry H. Bentley is Professor of History at the University of Hawaii and editor of the *Journal of World History*. His research on the religious, moral, and political writings of Renaissance humanists led to the publication of *Humanists and Holy Writ: New Testament Scholarship in the Renaissance and Politics and Culture in Renaissance Naples*. More recently, his research has concentrated on global history and particularly on processes of cross-cultural interaction. His book *Old World Encounters: Cross-Cultural Contacts and Exchanges in Pre-Modern Times* examines processes of cultural exchange and religious conversion before the modern era, and his pamphlet "Shapes of World History in Twentieth-Century Scholarship" discusses the historiography of world history. His current interests include processes of cross-cultural interaction and cultural exchanges in modern times.

Frank J. Coppa is Professor of History at St. John's University, Director of their doctoral program, and Chair of the University's Vatican Symposium. He is also an Associate in the Columbia University Seminar on Modern Italy, and editor of the Lang Series on Studies on Modern Europe. He has published biographies on a series of European figures, written and edited more than twelve volumes, as well as publishing in a series of journals including the *Journal of Modern History* and the *Journal of Economic History*, among others. He is editor of the *Dictionary of Modern Italian History* and the *Encyclopedia of the Vatican and Papacy*.

Paul Gootenberg is a Professor of Latin American History at SUNY-Stony Brook. A graduate of the University of Chicago and of Oxford University, he specializes in the economic, social, and intellectual history of the Andes and Mexico, and more recently, the global history of drugs. He has published *Between Silver and Guano* (1989), *Imagining Development* (1993) and *Cocaine: Global Histories* (1999). Gootenberg has held many fellowships: among them, Fulbright, SSRC, ACLS, Institute for Advanced Study, Russell Sage Foundation, the Rhodes Scholarship, and a Guggenheim. He lives in Brooklyn with his wife, Laura Sainz, and son, Danyal Natan.

Margaret Hallisey is a practicing high school library media specialist in Burlington, MA. She has a B.A. in English from Regis College and a M.S. in Library and Information Science from Simmons College. A member of Beta Phi Mu, the International Library Science Honor Society, she has served on the executive Boards of the American Association of School Librarians (AASL), the Massachusetts School Library Media Association (MSLMA) and the New England Educational Media Association (NEEMA).

Donna Maier has been with the Department of History at the University of Northern Iowa since 1986. Her research interests are in nineteenth century Asante (Ghana), African Islam, and traditional African medicine. Her extensive lists of publications include "The Military Acquisition of Slaves in Asante," in *West African Economic and Social History* (1990), "Islam and the Idea of Asylum in Asante" in *The Cloths of Many-Colored Silks* (1996), and *History and Life, the World and Its Peoples* (1977- 90, with Wallbank and Shrier). She is a joint editor of the journal *African Economic History*, and a member of the African Studies Association and the Ghana Studies Council. She is currently living in Tanzania.

Philip Yockey is Social Sciences Bibliographer and Assistant Chief Librarian for Staff Training and Development at the Humanities and Social Sciences Library at The New York Public Library.

ABOUT THE SERIES

On September 11, 2001, terrorists attacked the United States, destroying the twin towers of the World Trade Center in New York City and damaging the Pentagon, near Washington, DC. More than three thousand people—from more than eighty nations—were killed in the attacks. The nation and, indeed, the world, was shocked and horrified. Who would do such a thing? Why? The U.S. government soon answered the question of "who": the Islamic extremist group al-Qaeda, led by Saudi exile Osama bin Laden. There has been no clear answer to "why," but inflicting mass casualty on the United States was undoubtedly a goal. The events of September 11 brought terrorism to international headlines and to government agendas. With the United States establishing a coalition for its "war on terror" and nations the world over reexamining their security and activating counterterrorism response teams to prepare for possible biological, chemical, nuclear, or conventional terrorist attack, the public has been bombarded with information and has often been left with more questions than answers.

How likely is it that terrorists could obtain and use a nuclear weapon? Who is Osama bin Laden and how widespread is the presence of his group, al-Qaeda? What challenges does terrorism present to the U.S. intelligence community and what must it do to meet those challenges? What motivated the hijackers who took their lives and the lives of so many others on September 11? Wading through the news and developing events to make sense of it all can be confusing and scary and, in the end, it may still not resolve all of one's questions.

History Behind the Headlines, an ongoing series from the Gale Group, strives to answer such ques-

tions in a way that television broadcasts and newspapers can not. In order to keep reports both simple and short, it is difficult for these media to give the watcher or reader enough background information to fully understand what is happening around the world today. *HBH* provides just that background, giving the general public, student, and teacher an account of each contemporary conflict, from its start to its present and even its future. This thoroughness is accomplished not just by the in-depth material covered in the main body of each essay, but also by accompanying chronologies, textual and biographical sidebars, maps, statistics, and bibliographic sources.

Not only does *HBH* provide comprehensive information on all of the conflicts it covers, it also strives to present its readers with an unbiased and inclusive perspective. Each essay, many written by an expert with a detailed knowledge of the conflict at hand, avoids taking any particular side and instead seeks to explain each vantage point. Unlike television and newspaper reports, which may only have the time, space, or even inclination to show one side of a story, *HBH* essays equally detail all sides involved.

Given the number of conflicts that beg for such fuller accounts that *History Behind the Headlines* provides, an advisory board of school and library experts helps to guide the selection process and narrow down the selection for each volume. They balance the topic lists, making sure that a proper mix of economic, political, ethnic, and geographically diverse conflicts are chosen. One to two volumes, each written in an accessible, informative way, will be released each year.

PREFACE

Selection and Arrangement

History Behind the Headlines covers twenty-five to thirty conflicts—including ethnic, religious, economic, political, territorial, and environmental conflicts—and provides an essay exploring the background to today's events. Each conflict covered in HBH is contemporary—it happened within the last several years—but the roots of today's headlines are of enduring interest.

This edition is a special volume of *History Behind the Headlines.* Devoted entirely to terrorism, it seeks to present topics such as chemical terrorism, extremism, fighting terrorism with force, and state sponsorship of terrorism to readers in a comprehensible and reasoned way. The United States and countries around the globe are on heightened alert after the September 11, 2001 terrorist attacks. Relations between Western and Islamic nations remain sensitive as the Muslim world examines the "war on terror" for anti-Islamic tendencies. Additionally, civil rights groups in the United States charge that post-September 11 legislation designed to bolster national security and immigration regulations is violating civil liberties. While not the only topic in the news, terrorism has certainly moved to center stage since September 11—and there are a lot of issues to address.

The topics in this special volume were chosen following an extensive review of the issues covered in newspapers, magazines, and on television. A large number of potential terrorism-related subjects were identified. Advisors—including academic experts, high school social study teachers, librarians, and a terrorism researcher—prioritized the list, identifying those subjects that generate the most questions. Topics were then selected to provide a balanced and comprehensive examination of the many aspects of terrorism.

The material covered is complex. Each essay discusses multiple aspects of an issue, including economic and social aspects, the interests of other countries, international organizations and businesses, and the international implication of a conflict. The entries are arranged alphabetically by a major subject, country, region, organization, or person in the conflict. Where this might not be clear in the table of contents, the keyword is placed in parentheses in front of the title.

Content

Each essay begins with a brief summary of the current situation, as well as some of the major factors in the conflict and a list of terms used in the essay with which the reader may be unfamiliar. Each essay contains the following sections:

- **Summary of the headline event.** An overview of the contemporary conflict that has brought the issue to public attention. For example, Israel's admission of an official policy of assassination toward Palestinian "threats."

- **Historical Background.** The "Historical Background" is the heart of the essay. The author provides the historical context to the contemporary conflict, summarizing the arc of the conflict throughout history. Each essay tells the "story" of the history of the conflict, capturing important events, transfers of power, interventions, treaties, and more. The author summarizes the changes in the conflict over time, describes the role of major figures in the conflict, including individuals, political organizations, and religious organizations, and provides an overview of their positions now and in the past. Where appropriate the author may draw comparisons with similar situations in the country or region in the past. In addition, the author often attempts to put the conflict in the context of global politics and to describe the impacts the conflict has had on people around the world. Finally, the author may touch on how historians' understanding of the conflict has changed over time.

- **Recent History and the Future.** The final section brings the conflict up-to-date, and may offer some projections for future resolution.

Each essay is followed by a brief bibliography that offers some suggestions of resources for further research. In addition, brief biographies may accompany the essay, profiling major figures. Sidebars may provide statistical information, a quote from a speech, a selection from a primary source document (such as a treaty), or a selection from a book or newspaper article that adds to the understanding of the conflict, or may explore an issue in greater depth (such as domestic terrorism in the United States or prosecuting terrorists).

Images may also accompany the essay, including one or more maps showing the area of conflict. A selected bibliography providing suggestions for background information and research on the nature of conflicts and a comprehensive index appear at the back of each volume.

History is to be Read Critically

Each of the talented writers (many of them subject authorities) in this volume has tried to provide an objective and comprehensive overview of the conflict and its historical context. The nature of conflict, however, involves positions strongly and passionately held; even if it were possible to write a completely objective overview of history, it would contradict with the view held by participants to the conflict. History—all history—should be read critically.

Acknowledgements

Many thanks for their help to the excellent advisors who guided this project—their ongoing attention and feedback was greatly appreciated. Thanks, also, to the thoughtful and dedicated writers who lent their expertise to help others understand the complex history behind sound bites on the news. Special thanks to Gary Ackerman, Cheryl Loeb, and Kimberly McCloud.

Comments on this volume and suggestions for future volumes are welcomed. Please direct all correspondence to:

Editor, *History Behind the Headlines*
Gale Group
27500 Drake Rd.
Farmington Hills, MI 48331-3535
(800) 877-4253

AIR SECURITY AND TERRORIST THREATS

In the weeks after the terrorist hijackings of September 11, 2001, airline traffic plummeted as potential passengers took alternate means of travel or canceled their travel plans altogether. With assurances from President George W. Bush (2001–) and Homeland Security chief Tom Ridge that air travel was safe, the airline industry staged a public relations campaign to revive its fortunes. Reassuring the public that the skies were once again safe, industry and government officials pointed to upgraded security measures, more active federal supervision, and new legislation that would help to prevent further terrorist events. By December traffic at international airports resumed its hectic pace around the busy holiday travel season; although the number of passengers was still down, it appeared that the public was once again flying and that fear had been replaced by caution. All of this progress would be called into question, however, with the bizarre and potentially devastatinghijacking/bombing attempt by Richard C. Reid on December 22, 2001.

Born in Bromley, England, a middle-class suburb southeast of London, the twenty-eight-year old Reid had a troubled youth that included several convictions for muggings. Turning to Islam during one prison stint, Reid eventually fell in with an extremist splinter group at the Brixton Mosque near London and began training as a terrorist. Presenting a valid British passport that had been issued in Belgium just three weeks previously, Reid initially attempted to board an American Airlines flight from Paris to Miami on December 21. He had missed that flight because security officers at Charles de Gaulle Airport were suspicious about his lack of luggage and other identification. Yet Reid returned the next day and made it on to American Airlines Flight 63. Once the plane was over the ocean, Reid lit a match and attempted to

THE CONFLICT

Major security lapses at American airports contributed to the terrorist attacks of September 11. To remedy some of the problems, Congress passed the Airport and Transportation Security Act in November 2001. Given the expense entailed in improving security measures, there are debates over what further actions should be taken. There are also concerns about balancing security priorities with the inconvenience to travelers and the maintenance of their privacy.

Political

- The use of the Computer Assisted Passenger Prescreening System (CAPPS) has raised concerns that the civil rights of passengers may be transgressed by the system, which uses dozens of factors to single out passengers for additional security screening.

- As part of its reforms, Congress has mandated that all security screeners hold U.S. citizenship and speak English. Employees who do not meet these requirements have argued that the new law is discriminatory.

Economic

- The cost of improving airline security is immense, with over $2 billion alone necessary to buy explosive-detection devices for U.S. airports.

- The airline industry has long argued against new security measures—such as matching each bag to each passenger on a flight before it takes off—that will add to its operating costs and fears that the inconvenience of new security measures will lead some consumers to choose other means of transportation.

Ideological

- There has been an ongoing debate over the effectiveness of contracting security responsibilities out to the private sector. In light of ongoing security problems, the U.S. federal government assumed the greater share of responsibility after November 2001.

- Experts disagree whether improved technology or improved human resources should be emphasized in the new security regime.

CHRONOLOGY

January 1973 Federal law mandates that all passengers and carryon baggage must be screened on U.S. flights.

June 27–July 4, 1976 An Air France plane is held hostage by group of Palestinian and German terrorists. The standoff ends when Israeli forces storm the plane at Entebbe, Uganda.

December 21, 1988 A bomb on Pan Am Flight 103 from London to New York City explodes over Lockerbie, Scotland, killing 259 passengers and eleven victims on the ground.

September 11, 2001 Islamic extremist terrorists hijack three aircraft—American Airlines Flight 11, United Airlines Flight 175, and United Airlines Flight 77—and attack the World Trade Center buildings in New York City and the Pentagon building in Washington, DC. A fourth hijacked plane, United Airlines Flight 93, crashes in Somerset County, Pennsylvania, after a struggle between the passengers and the terrorists.

October 8, 2001 The Office of Homeland Security is established, with Governor Tom Ridge of Pennsylvania as its first director.

October 25, 2001 After extensive controversies over security lapses at Boston's Logan Airport, the executive director of the Massachusetts Port Authority resigns.

November 19, 2001 The Aviation and Transportation Security Act is signed into law. The act creates the Transportation Security Administration within the Department of Transportation.

December 22, 2001 Al-Qaeda operative Richard C. Reid attempts to ignite a bomb hidden in his shoe on American Airlines Flight 63 from Paris to Miami. He is subdued by the flight crew and passengers.

February 17, 2002 The U.S. federal government takes over responsibility for security from airlines.

ignite a detonating device that would trigger a plastic explosives pack hidden in his shoe. The smell of burning sulfur alarmed a flight attendant, who confronted Reid. After Reid lashed back and bit the flight attendant, other passengers jumped into the fray. Some held him down while others gathered belts to tie around him. Two doctors on the flight then gave Reid shots of sedatives from the plane's emergency medical supply.

The quick response by Flight 63's crew and passengers prevented Reid from carrying out his suicide bombing, yet it revived a host of troubling questions about airline security in the wake of September 11. Why had a passenger with only one form of identification and no luggage been allowed to board the flight? Why hadn't airport screeners searched Reid more carefully, particularly in light of a Federal Aviation Authority (FAA) memo distributed earlier that month from U.S. authorities warning international airports that terrorists might plant bombs in their shoes? Finally, given his past activities, why hadn't officials been alert to Reid's terrorist ties? Despite reassurances by officials that airline security had been vastly improved, Reid's shoe-bombing attempt seemed to indicate that terrorists could still strike almost at will.

HISTORICAL BACKGROUND

A Modern Crime

The first recorded hijacking of a plane happened in Arequipa, Peru, on February 21, 1931, when rebel forces fighting in a civil war took over an American plane staffed by two pilots. The rebels ordered the pilots to fly them around Peru so that they could drop propaganda leaflets in support of their cause. The pilots refused and a ten-day standoff ensued. Eventually the abductors allowed the plane and its crew to go, but only after they agreed to fly one of the rebels to the capital, Lima. The first passenger plane to be hijacked was a Cathay Pacific plane en route from Macao to Hong Kong in July 1948. Four Chinese hijackers killed the pilot and copilot during the flight, and the plane crashed into the South China Sea along with its nineteen passengers. There were no survivors.

Plane hijackings were rare occurrences until the 1960s. The United States witnessed its first hijacking in May 1961 when a small commercial airplane flying from Miami to Key West, Florida, was diverted by a man who demanded to be taken to Cuba. That same year, three other American planes were also hijacked to Cuba; fortunately, the rash of

A SEVENTY-HOUR STANDOFF ENSUED IN FEBRUARY 2000 WHEN AN AFGHAN PASSENGER AIRCRAFT LANDED AT LONDON'S STANSTED AIRPORT. NINE HIJACKERS HELD MORE THAN ONE HUNDRED PASSENGERS CAPTIVE, DEMANDING POLITICAL ASYLUM. *(AP/Wide World Photos/Dave Caulkin. Reproduced by permission.)*

hijackings did not include any deaths. The most infamous hijacking event on U.S. soil during this period was staged on November 24, 1971, when a man abducted a Northwest Orient flight from Portland, Oregon, to Seattle, Washington. Traveling under the name D.B. Cooper, the hijacker threatened to blow up the plane unless he received US$200,000 and four parachutes. After releasing the passengers and crew in Seattle, the pilots flew Cooper and his ransom money over southwestern Washington, where Cooper jumped out of the plane. Neither Cooper nor the money was ever seen again. In the year after Cooper's leap, nineteen other people attempted to carry out extortion-style hijackings in the United States.

In contrast to D.B. Cooper's hijacking, which was monetarily motivated, most plane hijackings were carried out in order to demand political asylum or to meet political goals. In the longest hostage siege at a British airport, nine members of the Young Intellectuals of Afghanistan held more than one hundred passengers and crew members of a flight that originated in Kabul, Afghanistan, at Stansted Airport, northeast of London, in February 2000. During the seventy-hour standoff, one member of the flight crew was injured when he was thrown down some steps, and the hijackers threatened to blow up the plane before they surrendered.

Despite their insistence that they conducted the hijacking out of fear of imminent death under their country's Taliban regime, the members of the group were sentenced in January 2002 to terms ranging from twenty-seven months to five years in prison.

In contrast to the aims of extortionists and asylum seekers, other terrorists began to use hijackings as a method to achieve specific political goals in the late 1960s. Of these groups, those acting in support of Palestinian independence became the most infamous in their use of innocent passengers as political bargaining chips. In July 1968 three members of the Popular Front for the Liberation of Palestine took control of an Israeli El Al plane on its way from Rome, Italy, to Tel Aviv, Israel. For forty days the hijackers held the passengers and crew hostage until their demands for the release of Palestinian terrorists were met. In another incident that captured the world's attention, a group of Palestinian and German terrorists abducted an Air France plane in June 1976 and forced it to fly to Entebbe, Uganda. While officials negotiated over the terrorists' demands for the release of 53 Palestinian terrorists held in Israeli, European, and Kenyan jails, the standoff dragged on for eight days. On July 4 an Israeli commando squad stormed the plane and ended the siege, but four hostages were killed in the crossfire.

HIJACKING—NOT JUST A PROBLEM FOR THE AVIATION INDUSTRY

While airline hijackings command the most international headlines, other forms of public transportation—which generally have much less stringent security measures—are also targeted by criminals and terrorists. With 4,000 intercity bus stops and 140,000 miles of rail in the United States alone, it is extremely difficult for ground transportation companies to ensure passenger safety to the degree that is possible in the country's airports.

This point was driven home in October 2001 when Damir Igric, a Croatian in the United States on an expired visa, slashed the throat of the driver of a Greyhound bus bound for Orlando, Florida, and crashed the bus, killing six passengers, including himself. Due to the already tense atmosphere created by the terrorist attacks on September 11, Greyhound officials acted swiftly, shutting down its service nationwide for approximately seven hours. To the relief of everyone, the FBI determined that Igric was a disturbed individual acting alone, not a member of a terrorist network.

Similar incidents have occurred in other countries. In Taipei, Taiwan, in June 2001, a married couple angry over treatment they had received in a court dispute hijacked a bus carrying 14 passengers for four hours. Police eventually stormed the bus, and no injuries were reported. Five people in Malaysia were arrested after they hijacked an airport bus, armed with axes and machetes, and robbed passengers of passports, airplane tickets, and other valuables. The North Caucus region in Russia,

where separatists are pushing for independence in several Russian republics, including Chechnya, has also suffered numerous bus hijackings. In July 2001 a group of Chechens held 40 bus passengers hostage for 12 hours, demanding the release of five of their comrades, themselves jailed for a 1994 bus hijacking. Two people were injured when Russian commandos retook the bus.

The high seas are not exempt from hijackings, either. In May 2000 ten Haitian policemen on a ferry bound from Port-Au-Prince to the Haitian island Pestel held the crew at gunpoint and demanded the boat be sailed to the United States, where they planned to seek political asylum. U.S. federal authorities discovered the ferry near the Bahamas and reported that no one was injured.

In the United States in particular following September 11, the transportation industry was forced to take a hard look at its existing security measures. Aside from the changes made at the country's airports, Greyhound began experimenting with metal detectors, albeit at only a handful of stations. The United States' passenger rail service, Amtrak, instituted a computer program that could crosscheck ticket purchasers against FBI watch lists. Amtrak also requested US$3.2 billion from Congress for improved railroad security, specifically the hiring of more police and the repair of evacuation routes in some older tunnels. These and other safety improvements may help render ground transportation in the United States less vulnerable to attack in the future.

Terrorists have also resorted to bombing planes as a political tactic. In one of the deadliest incidents, a group of Libyan terrorists planted a bomb inside a radio carried in the cargo hold of Pan Am Flight 103. En route from London to New York City on December 21, 1988, the plane exploded over Lockerbie, Scotland. A total of 259 people on the plane and eleven on the ground were killed. Although Libyan leader Muammar Qadhafi refused to turn over the Libyan agents suspected of being responsible for the bombing, international sanctions against his country finally weakened his resolve. When the two suspects were tried in a special international court in The Hague in 2000, one was acquitted and another, Abdel Basset Ali al-Megrahi, was convicted of placing the bomb in the luggage.

Early Aviation Security Efforts

Each hijacking and bombing resulted in significant changes in air security efforts. After its 1968 hijacking—the only one in its history—El Al instituted a baggage check to match every piece of luggage on board with a passenger on the plane. D.B. Cooper's action resulted in a "Cooper Vane" put on aircraft to prevent exit stairs from being lowered during flight. A 1972 hijacking in Alabama—in which three escaped convicts threatened to crash the plane into a nuclear facility at Oak Ridge, Tennessee—led to a requirement for all baggage to be x-rayed and all passengers to be screened through metal detectors at U.S. airports. After the Pan Am 103 bombing, more advanced screening devices came into use to detect plastic and other nonmetallic explosive devices.

Despite these technical and administrative improvements against terrorism in the air, U.S. airports largely ignored security concerns in their designs. To take advantage of the soaring number of passengers since the 1970s, airport builders emphasized convenience and aesthetic appeal over more security-conscious layouts. Most airports incorporated curbside passenger and luggage drop-off areas, parking spaces near the terminal, and dining and shopping areas for passengers and the public. Before September 11 security ranked behind convenience, environmental restrictions, and the inclusion of commercial outlets in design priorities of American airports.

The Israeli Approach

With the rise of Palestinian terrorism and the hijacking of an El Al plane in July 1968, Israel's state-owned airline became the most security conscious in the world. Counterterrorist elements were built into every phase of airline travel, from the layout of airports to the screening of passengers to the design of the airplanes themselves. As everywhere in Israel, the ability of terrorists to plant bombs in cars or trucks meant that parking areas were severely restricted around airports, and vehicles were typically searched before being parked. Passengers needed to arrive two and sometimes three hours before their flights to make it through the screening process. Every passenger was personally evaluated to see whether he or she matched a profile of a potential terrorist. The evaluation included a review of the passenger's travel documents, reasons for traveling, country of origin, method of payment for the ticket, and numerous other factors. Those who raised suspicions were then drawn aside and each piece of their luggage would be searched.

Crucially, the screening process was conducted by a staff that had received extensive training in counterterrorist tactics. In contrast to the staff at American airports, Israel's security personnel were relatively well paid and the government jobs themselves were considered prestigious. The low turnover rate also ensured that an experienced security force staffed every checkpoint. This experience was especially important in screening for nonmetallic explosive devices, which had to be discerned by their shape on a scanner taking a three-dimensional picture of the interior of the baggage. Once the passengers and their luggage had cleared the screening process, every checked item also had to be matched with a passenger on the plane before it was cleared for flight. To foil terrorist attacks during flight, El Al planes featured an extra, outside cabin door that had to be locked before the cockpit door could be opened.

PUBLIC TRANSPORTATION, WHETHER IN THE AIR OR ON THE GROUND, IS VULNERABLE TO TERRORIST ATTACK. A HIJACKED BUS IS FOLLOWED BY POLICE, FIRE, AND AMBULANCE VEHICLES IN GREECE IN 1999. BUS HIJACKINGS HAVE TAKEN PLACE IN CHECHNYA, TAIWAN, AND MALAYSIA, AMONG OTHER COUNTRIES. *(AP/Wide World Photo/Giorgos Nissiotis. Reproduced by permission.)*

With only one hijacking or bombing in its history, El Al was held up as a model of airline security. Few of its security innovations, however, were adopted in the United States. Critics of Israel's system pointed out that the country was able to centralize security efforts because it had only one major international airport, Ben Gurion, to worry about. Others balked at the cost of staffing a security force with federal employees. American carriers were also adamant that a rule requiring checked bags to be matched to passengers would create unbearable delays that would hurt their profits. Most American airlines also failed to scan checked luggage in the first place, as there was no federal law requiring them to do so. By the end of the 1990s the decentralized and deregulated nature of the American airline industry, together with a push toward privatizing security measures, stood in stark contrast to the state of Israeli air security.

The BAA Approach

Air security efforts in Great Britain also differed from U.S. trends. The British Airports Authority (BAA) was founded in April 1966 by an act of Parliament that gave it operating control of four airports: Heathrow, Gatwick, and Stansted, all in the greater London metropolitan area, and Prestwick in Scotland. Over time, BAA took the operations at airports in Southampton in England, and Glasgow, Edinburgh, and Aberdeen in Scotland. By the 1990s the publicly traded company branched out to operate airports at Indianapolis, Pittsburgh, and Boston in the United States, and at Melbourne and Perth in Australia. In the aftermath of the bombing of Pan Am Flight 103 in 1988, BAA undertook an extensive reevaluation of the security measures it utilized at its British airports. By the late 1990s, BAA had set the security standard for high-volume airports in Europe.

The first area of BAA reforms focused on the screening of checked baggage. BAA developed a five-stage system that was fully operational in all of its British airports by June 1998 at a total cost of $300 million. All checked baggage passed through Level 1 security, which automatically screened the bags through x-ray machines. Those bags that were flagged at the first level—about 30 percent of the total—were then directed to a human operator for additional screening of the x-ray image in Level 2. For those bags that were still not cleared—about 3 percent of all Level 2 luggage—operators then reinspected the x-ray image a third time in Level 3. At Level 4 security, a human operator reviewed all baggage x-rays that still could not be positively cleared in the previous steps. Any remaining bags from Level 4 that were still suspicious were then sent to Level 5, staffed by a special assessment team. In the first years of operation, the need for a Level 5 threat assessment occurred fewer than ten times per year. While most airports used human operators to man the x-ray machines from Level 2 upward, Manchester's system was automated through the first two levels. At some airports, such as Stansted, the new system required an addition onto the existing facilities to make room for the equipment; at others, such as Gatwick, the modifications were built within the existing facility.

In accordance with British law, all passengers at BAA airports were screened by the same security standard. After presenting tickets and identification at an entry point, passengers were taken to a separate departure lounge, where they passed through x-ray machines and metal detectors. A predetermined number of passengers were also hand searched. All carryon items were x-rayed at the same time. Those articles that failed the inspection—about 20 percent of all carryon items—were then individually inspected. In 2000 BAA also began supplementing its x-ray machines with three-dimensional scanners and equipment that could detect trace elements of explosive devices.

About one-third of BAA's staff worked in the area of security. Those on the front lines were given a minimum of three weeks of classroom and practical training before being put to work. On the job BAA staff needed to adhere to the same security checks that passengers endured, including x-ray and metal detection screening. Ian Hutcheson, head of Group Security for BAA, noted in his December 2001 testimony to the U.S. House Subcommittee on Aviation that "The key difference between the UK approach and that of many other countries is that staff are screened to the same standard as passengers when entering airside areas." He then pointed out that many other countries rely completely on the possession of a valid ID. "Such an approach is fraught with difficulties given the typical working population of a large airport." He added, "The 'human factor' can be the weakest link in the process, leading to a lapse in security."

Despite the improved security measures, problems still cropped up at BAA airports. In October 2001 the London *Times* announced that employee background checks had not been conducted by Securicor, the private company that BAA hired to provide its security staff, although counterterrorist checks had been required by law. One undocumented worker had even provided security on a plane scheduled to fly Prime Minister Tony Blair to the Middle East. On February 11, 2002, robbers at Heathrow Airport stole £4.6 million from a British Airways van that had taken custody of the cash off of a jet from Bahrain. Just five weeks later, another robbery on March 19, 2002, netted a crew of thieves £2.1 million from a South African Airlines flight. In both cases, police declared that the robberies were likely committed with the help of security staff at Heathrow, Europe's busiest airport

ENFORCING AIR SECURITY WAS AMONG THE FIRST PRIORITIES OF THE U.S. GOVERNMENT AND ITS NEW OFFICE OF HOMELAND SECURITY AFTER THE SEPTEMBER 11 TERRORIST ATTACKS. *(AP/Wide World Photos/Mary Ann Chastain/Files. Reproduced by permission.)*

and the fifth busiest in the world. "Passengers should be extremely worried," aviation expert Chris Yates of Jane's Transport told the BBC, "If they can get airside they have access to aircraft. It only takes seconds to board an empty aircraft and plant a bomb."

Air Safety in the United States During the 1990s

In many respects, air safety in the United States lagged behind Israeli or European measures throughout the 1990s. Part of the problem stemmed from the rapid changes in the airline business after 1978's Airline Deregulation Act. Prior to that time, the Civil Aeronautics Board regulated air routes and established fares that airlines could charge. While the new economic competition was a boon to deal-seeking consumers who increasingly flew on one of the new, regional airlines, financial pressures on the industry led to aggressive cost-cutting measures on every carrier. As a group the airline industry insisted that additional security measures follow a strict cost-benefit analysis to protect the bottom line. Even measures that cost little but seemed inconvenient—such as the baggage match system—were fought by the American air industry, which feared that consumers might choose to take other means of transportation instead of flying.

Deregulation of the airline industry was followed by a similar trend in the federal government. Committed to decreasing bureaucracy, the Ronald Reagan administration (1981–89) slashed the inspection staff of the FAA by 12 percent in 1982–83 alone. Former Department of Transportation inspector general Mary Schiavo described the cumulative impact of these two trends in her 1997 book *Flying Blind, Flying Safe*: "In reality, the FAA is at a loss to know how to deal with this new style of airline business, and with new threats to airplanes. The discount airlines that appeared and grew rapidly in the late 1980s and 1990s left the FAA stunned and blinking at a whirlwind of leased and used planes, contracted and subcontracted maintenance facilities, and inexperienced pilots and flight crews."

The bombing of Pan Am Flight 103 led to a special federal inquiry on aviation security that condemned the FAA's negligence in enforcing its own rules. The public outcry over the scandal led to the 1990 Aviation Security Improvement Act. The legislation mandated criminal background checks for all security staff and specified minimum training skills and educational requirements for employees. American carriers were ordered to screen all checked baggage and match it with passengers on all flights in Europe and the Middle East. Explosive

MARY FACKLER SCHIAVO

1955– Mary Fackler Schiavo grew up on her family's farm in the small, northwestern Ohio town of Pioneer. Fascinated by aviation since childhood, she earned her pilot's license at Ohio State University in 1974 before attending Harvard University, where she completed her B.A. in 1976. She returned to Ohio State University to earn a master's degree in public administration in 1977 and completed her education with a law degree from New York University in 1980.

Schiavo initially pursued a career as an attorney. From 1982–86 she served on the U.S. Department of Justice's Organized Crime and Racketeering Task Force, where she served as an investigator and prosecutor. In 1989 Schiavo was named assistant to the secretary of labor, Elizabeth Dole, and supervised union elections. From 1990–1996 Schiavo served as the inspector general of the U.S. Department of Transportation (DOT), a position that she used to crusade for consumer safety and airline industry reforms. She was especially critical of the FAA during her tenure for its repeated failures to promote air safety. In her 1997 book *Flying Blind, Flying Safe* she wrote, "The FAA zealously guards information, deliberately burying it in suppressed reports, not because of a vague threat to passengers but because of the very real threat to profits. Informing or angering passengers with safety details is just plain bad for business."

Faced with a difficult pregnancy, Schiavo resigned from the DOT in 1996 and moved to Columbus, Ohio, with her husband and two children. Schiavo taught as a professor at Ohio State University from 1997–2001 and returned to private practice with the Washington, DC, law firm of Baum, Hedlund, Aristei, Guildord, and Schiavo. After her departure from the DOT, Congress finally enacted one of Schiavo's major reform proposals when it removed the FAA's charge to "promote" the airline industry as one of its primary mandates.

detection devices were also made mandatory for all U.S. airlines for flights originating at international airports. Despite the stringent new rules and its own past scandals, the FAA still failed to implement its legislative mandate by the mid-1990s.

Even worse than the FAA's record of safety in the air was its oversight of security measures on the ground. Between 1998 and 2000 the seven largest airlines—Delta, American, United, Northwest, Southwest, US Air, and Trans World—accumulated 1,674 security fines by the FAA for penalties totaling $11,960,225. In bomb-detection tests conducted by the Department of Transportation (DOT) in 1995–96, agents successfully took simulated bombs past screeners 40 percent of the time. While the test was an improvement over a 1993 study that found 75 percent of fake bombs making it past screeners, security at some major international airports had not improved at all. The Los Angeles (LAX) airport detected only 10 percent of simulated bombs in the DOT test, while screeners at Miami International Airport found only 15 percent of the devices. At Chicago's O'Hare Airport, the rate was 22 percent; at Boston's Logan Airport it was 23 percent. While Mary Schiavo used her tenure as DOT inspector general from 1990–96 to publicize these and other lapses in FAA supervision, the agency continued to fail in its role as a security watchdog. Even after the White House Commission on Aviation Safety and Security in 1997 reiterated the chronic problems described in prior federal studies, airlines continued to rack up hundreds of security fines each year.

Much of the problem stemmed from the subcontracting of security duties by airlines to private companies, which in turn operated with little oversight or regulatory enforcement by the FAA. One company, Argenbright Security, became a byword for corporate corruption and dereliction of duty that eventually led to criminal charges against some of its officers. The company's Philadelphia office routinely falsified background checks, educational histories, and training procedures and then certified the bogus results to comply with FAA regulations. Argenbright also continued to hire convicted criminals for security positions at the Philadelphia airport even after it had already incurred penalties for the same practice. In Phoenix and Detroit, Argenbright did not complete background checks on all of its employees, including one security officer in Detroit who was employed despite having served four years in the army in Yemen, a center of terrorist activity in the Middle East. The company racked up $1.2 million in fines by the FAA in 2000 alone.

The Argenbright scandal demonstrated the pitfalls of a privatized airline security system that strove for profitability with little regulatory supervision. In an *Aviation Today* report in March 2002, Eric Grasser and David Evans summarized the comments of one former FAA official on the shortcomings of the current system, stating that the low wages offered upon hiring created a situation in which "security is measured by cost savings." Thus, the poorly paid posts are filled by people who may have difficulty finding other jobs, and may even acquire a second job at the airport at one of its many concessionaries. The result, Grasser and Evans said, is that "some screeners end up working a second job at the airport and get little sleep before they arrive for screening duties." In contrast to Israel's emphasis on highly trained and motivated security officers, the U.S. system continued to treat human intelligence as a minor factor in its security efforts.

RECENT HISTORY AND THE FUTURE

Trouble at Logan Airport

While it is arguable whether strict enforcement of existing air security regulations could have prevented the terrorist hijackings on September 11, 2001, there is little doubt that the terrorist team planned its strategy to take advantage of known lapses in the security system. The origin of the first two hijacked aircraft was Boston's Logan Airport, which had earned a reputation for chronic corruption and mismanagement. The Massachusetts Port Authority shared 136 fines of $178,000 with American Airlines and United Airlines for security violations at Logan between 1997–99. Top positions at the Port Authority had traditionally been filled through patronage appointments without regard to any knowledge of aviation. The director of Logan Airport at the time of the hijackings, Virginia Buckingham, had served as the lieutenant governor's chief of staff, and the airport's security director, Joseph Lawless, was a former state trooper who had provided security at the Massachusetts State House.

Despite the problems at Logan, the FAA actually urged the Port Authority to be less strict in conducting its background checks on security employees. In May 2001 the FAA's chief security manager, Michael Canavan, asked Lawless to defer to airlines in making background checks, even though Lawless had discovered numerous lapses in the current system. As Sean Murphy reported in the *Boston Globe* on December 12, 2001, Canavan had issued the directive to Lawless after meeting with airline industry lobbyists who complained about the additional background checks. "It is unfortunate that such instances of noncompliance occurred," Canavan had written to Lawless, concluding, "I am asking your help in the resolution of this situation, and ask that you accept certification from U.S. air carriers that the required criminal history records check has been completed for their employees." In the wake of September 11, Canavan resigned from his position at the FAA, and both Buckingham and Lawless were ousted

AIR HIJACKINGS, 1975–2000

Year	Air Hijackings
1975-79	114
1980-84	158
1985-89	65
1990-94	130
1995-99	53
2000	20

THE GREATEST NUMBER OF AIR HIJACKINGS AROUND THE WORLD OCCURRED IN THE EARLY 1980S. AIRLINE SECURITY MEASURES ARE BEING REEVALUATED AFTER THE AIR HIJACKINGS AND TERRORIST ATTACKS OF SEPTEMBER 11, 2001. *(Gale Group.)*

from their positions in the public outrage that followed the attacks.

Renewed Vigilance at American Airports

On September 14, 2001, Congress approved a $15 billion bailout of the U.S. air industry and committed additional funds to security operations as part of a $40 billion emergency spending package. Officials also reviewed security measures at American airports during a four-day ban on air traffic imposed on September 11. After two decades of criticism of airline security during the era of deregulation, the industry and FAA could no longer duck charges that their performance had been abysmal.

The most obvious change in airline security after September 11 concerned the enforcement of existing security measures. As the September 11 terrorists had used box cutters to stage their hijackings, similar items such as scissors, pocket knives, and razors were now routinely confiscated from passengers. Flammable items such as large aerosol containers or lighter fluid were also banned from the passenger cabin. After Richard Reid's attempted bombing, passengers could also expect their shoes to be inspected before being checked in. As an additional stopgap measure, National Guard forces were placed in airports to beef up the security presence. In light of the renewed emphasis on safety, the FAA now recommended that passengers arrive two hours before their domestic flights in order to pass through more rigorous security screenings.

Other security measures were more difficult to implement. In the month after the terrorist attacks, most airlines had not complied with an FAA directive to scan all checked baggage with explosive-detection devices at the nation's highest-risk airports. The FAA came under criticism itself, however, when it was reported that the agency had failed to install about twenty of the machines that it had purchased, and that the machines it had put into service were only used part of the time. The controversies added to the perception that little progress had been made in air security in the months after September 11.

Civil rights watchdogs were also vigilant against abuses related to passenger profiling. The DOT had already implemented a Computer Assisted Passenger Prescreening System (CAPPS) that was used before September 11. Like the Israeli screening system, CAPPS selected passengers for further investigation based on factors such as flight origin and destination, method of payment, and whether the trip was one way. While the CAPPS system had been reviewed and approved by the Department of Justice, some of its screening factors were kept secret, which raised suspicions that it might actually be a racial profiling system directed at passengers of Middle Eastern descent. Even more controversial was the removal of some Middle Eastern passengers from domestic flights after other passengers voiced fears that they might be terrorists. As Sam Podberesky, assistant general counsel of the DOT, told *National Public Radio* in October 2001 after one such event, "If the decision is based solely on the fact that a person is an Arab or an Arab American or of a Muslim religion . . . if that's the sole reason for a person being selected for special security procedures or being removed from an aircraft, that's illegal. That does not preclude, however, airlines or pilots from looking for suspicious activities by anyone on board the aircraft."

Federalizing Air Security

Hoping to resolve some of the uncertainty over air security, Congress passed the Aviation and Transportation Security Act on November 19, 2001. Under the act, responsibility for screening all passengers and baggage was taken away from the airlines and put under federal authority. The act also charged the federal government to screen, hire, and train the newly federalized security work force at the nation's 429 commercial airports. The size of the work force was estimated to be between 30,000–40,000 employees, each of whom was required to be a U.S. citizen with English-language skills. After two years airports could opt out of the program and contract security services to private companies; in the interim, five airports were granted the authority to retain private security firms in pilot programs.

The new law set the date of January 18, 2002, for all checked baggage to be matched with passengers on every domestic flight, the initial step in requiring all baggage to be screened on U.S. carriers. The act also made provisions for the reinforcement of cockpit doors. Finally, the law added armed federal air marshals to many domestic flights and required them to be on flights that landed at Washington DC's Reagan National Airport. This last provision riled some Canadian officials who feared that they would also have to add armed officers on flights through American air space.

Creation of the Transportation Security Administration

In a move that recognized the FAA's abysmal record on air security supervision, the new legislation created the Transportation Security Administration (TSA) to run the federal air security force. Housed within the DOT, the TSA was charged with oversight of all the nation's transportation systems, although its creation as part of the Aviation and Transportation Security Act showed that its emphasis would be on the nation's air traffic. The new agency also assumed control of training and supervising air security staff. Despite its daunting tasks, President George W. Bush struck a hopeful note while signing the legislation that brought the TSA into being:

> Security comes first. The federal government will set high standards, and we will enforce them. These have been difficult days for Americans who fly and for American aviation. A proud industry has been hit hard. But this nation has seen the dedication and spirit of our pilots and flight crews, and the hundreds of thousands of hard-working people who keep America flying. We know they will endure. I'm confident this industry will grow and prosper.

Although many of these reforms had been advocated since deregulation in 1978, the sudden introduction of tighter security measures after September 11 caught the travel industry and government officials by surprise. In the month after the federal government took over primary responsibility for air security, forty-three airport shutdowns paralyzed air traffic across the United States. The incidents ranged from the discovery of a suspected shoe bomb in San Francisco to the realization that a screening device at LAX had been disconnected and therefore inoperable. When medical personnel responding to an emergency at New York City's LaGuardia Airport bypassed security screeners on March 2, 2002, all flights were immediately grounded and the terminal was evacuated for ninety minutes. While most travelers appreciated the vigilance that security officers now practiced, others claimed that flying had now become too inconvenient.

BIBLIOGRAPHY

"Air Security vs. Commerce." CBS News. Available online at http://cbsnews.com/stories/2002/03/22/attack/printable504442.shtml (cited March 22, 2002).

"Airline Civil Penalties for U.S. Carriers." About Airtravel. Available online at http://airtravel.about.com/library/security/nsecurityfines.htm (cited November 6, 2001).

"Analysis: Airlines Being Hit with Increasing Number of Complaints About Racial Profiling Since September 11th." *National Public Radio Morning Edition*, October 10, 2001.

Arndt, Michael. "An Airline Bailout—with Strings Attached." *Business Week Online*, October 8, 2001.

"Assessing Losses for the Airline Industry and Its Workers in the Aftermath of the Terrorist Attacks." Senate Joint Economic Committee, Democratic Staff, October 3, 2001.

"Aviation Security Act Conference Report." Republican Party Committee Central. Available online at http://www.gop.gov/committeecentral/docs/bills/107/1/bill.asp?bill=hr3150conf (cited March 13, 2002).

Begley, Sharon. "Protecting America: The Top 10 Priorities." *Newsweek*, November 5, 2001, 26.

"Big Government Is Back." *Economist*, September 29, 2001, p. 35.

British Airports Authority. "About BAA." Available online at http://www.baa.co.uk/main/corporate/about_baa/our_business/security_page.html (cited March 19, 2002).

Bush, George W. "President Signs Aviation Security Legislation." Available online at http://www.whitehouse.gov/news/releases/2001/11/print/20011119-2.html (cited March 22, 2002).

Calabresi, Mossimo, et al. "Can We Stop the Next Attack?" *Time*, March 11, 2002, p. 24.

Cordle, Ina Paiva. "Airport Law to Cut Jobs of Non-Citizens." *Miami Herald*, December 23, 2001.

Cox, Matthew, and Tom Foster. *Their Darkest Day: The Tragedy of Pan Am 103 and Its Legacy of Hope.* New York: John Wiley and Sons, 1995.

Croft, John. "Baggage Deadline to Refocus Standards." *Aviation Week and Space Technology*, January 7, 2002, p. 51.

Dorning, Mike. "Lawmakers Reach Deal on Federal Airport Security." *Chicago Tribune*, November 16, 2001.

Fairbank, Katie. "With Waits, Cutbacks, Many See Flying as Too Inconvenient." *Dallas Morning News*, December 21, 2001.

Federal Aviation Administration. "Before You Leave." Available online at http://www.faa.gov/apa/tipbroch.htm (cited March 13, 2002).

"Former Transportation Department Official Says More Needed for Air Security." *Chicago Tribune*, February 29, 2002.

Foss, Brad. "Ideologies Shape Aviation Security." Associated Press Online, October 16, 2001.

Gecker, Jocelyn. "French Increases Airport Security, Government Calls Urgent Meeting." A.P. Worldstream, December 24, 2001.

Gladwell, Malcolm. "Safety in the Skies." *New Yorker*, October 1, 2001.

Grasser, Eric and David Evans. "Special Report: Securing Passenger Confidence." *Aviation Today*. Available online at http://www.aviationtoday.com/reports/screeningprobe.htm (cited March 21, 2002).

"Grim History of Piracy in the Air." *Guardian Unlimited*. Available online at http://www.guardian.co.uk/Print/0,3858,3960251,00.html (cited March 20, 2002).

Heilprin, John. "Airlines Flunk First Security Test." Associated Press Online, October 12, 2001.

Heppenheimer, T.A. *Turbulent Skies: The History of Commercial Aviation.* New York: Avon Books, 1997.

"Hijackers Demand Release of Thirty-five Militants." *Canadian Press*, December 29, 1999.

Hutcheson, Ian. "Testimony before the Subcommittee on Aviation, Committee on Transportation and Infrastructure." FDCH Congressional Testimony, December 7, 2001.

"Interview: Sylvia Garcia Discusses Her Job as an Airport Baggage Screener." *National Public Radio Morning Edition*, November 9, 2001.

"Interview: Tom Ridge on Passage of Airline Security Bill." *National Public Radio Morning Edition*, November 16, 2001.

James, Jennie, with James Graff, Martin Penner, Ursula Sautter, and Elinor Shields. "Stuck in Traffic." *Time*, July 16, 2001.

"Lockerbie Bomber Loses Appeal, Life Sentence Stands." Canadian Broadcasting Corporation. Available online at http://cbc.ca/cgi-bin/templates/print.cgi?/2002/03/14/lockerbie_020314 (cited March 14, 2002).

Marks, Alexandra. "Latest Air Safety Thrust: Baggage." *Christian Science Monitor*, January 16, 2002.

McLughlin, Abraham. "Shoe-Bomb Incident Shows Progress, and Gaps, in Air Safety." *Christian Science Monitor*, December 24, 2001, 4.

Morris, Jim. "Israel Offers U.S. Lessons in Aviation Security." *Dallas Morning News*, November 8, 2001.

———. "FAA Stands by Bomb-Detection Devices that Some Say Are Unreliable, Underused." *Dallas Morning News*, October 22, 2001.

Morrison, Steven A., and Clifford Winston. *The Evolution of the Airline Industry.* Washington, DC: The Brookings Institution, 1995.

Murphy, Sean P. "Prior to Attacks, FAA Urged Easing Background Checks for Boston Airport Jobs." *National Public Radio Morning Edition,* December 12, 2001.

Nader, Ralph, and Wesley J. Smith. *Collision Course: The Truth About Airline Safety.* Blue Ridge Summit, PA: TAB Books, 1994.

Norfolk, Andrew, Ian Cobain, and David Charter. "Security Failures Put Heathrow at Risk." *Times* (London), October 16, 2001.

Ott, James. "Tight Security Compels Airport Design Shakeup." *Aviation Week and Space Technology,* February 18, 2002, p. 48.

Ott, James, and Raymond E. Neidl. *Airline Odyssey: The Airline Industry's Turbulent Flight into the Future.* New York: McGraw-Hill, 1995.

Petzinger, Jr., Thomas. *Hard Landing.* New York: Times Business, 1995.

Phillips, Frank, Raphael Lewis, and Glen Johnson. "Massachusetts Port Authority's Executive Director Resigns." *Boston Globe,* October 26, 2001.

"The President's Plan to Strengthen Our Homeland Security." Available online at http://www.whitehouse .gov/news/releases/2002/02/print/20020204-2.html (cited February 28, 2002).

"Preventing Terror on Land," ABC News, October 3, 2001. Available online at http://more.abcnews.go.com/ sections/us/DailyNews/WTC_busrailsafety011004 .html (cited April 24, 2002).

"Q&A: Airport Security." BBC News. Available online at http://news.bbc.co.uk/hi/english/uk/newsid_155600/ 1556974.stm (cited March 16, 2002).

Salant, Jonathan D. "Airports Using Old Equipment Against New Threats." *Los Angeles Times,* January 2, 2002.

Saporito, Bill, and Sally B. Donnelly. "Air Travel." *Time,* December 31, 2001–January 7, 2002, p. 128.

Schiavo, Mary, with Sabra Chartrand. *Flying Blind, Flying Safe.* New York: Avon Books, 1997.

Schweitzer, Yoram. "The 'Lockerbie Affair': Over but Not Done With." International Policy Institute for Counterterrorism. Available online at http://www.ict.org.il/ articles/articledet.cfm?articleid=399 (cited March 16, 2002).

"Six Killed in Greyhound Bus Crash," *Journal Sentinel* Online, October 3, 2001. Available online at http://www.jsonline.com/news/nat/ap/oct01/ ap-bus-crash100301.asp (cited April 24, 2002).

"Taiwan Bus Hijacking Ends without Injury," CNN Online, June 23, 2001. Available online at http://www.cnn .com/2001/WORLD/asiapcf/east/06/23/taiwan.bus .hijacking/ (cited April 24, 2002).

Thorne, Stephen. "Ailing Airline Industry Needs Only Minor Tinkering, Say Legislators, Analysts." *Canadian Press,* November 17, 2001.

———. "Airport, Airline Security Costs Rising 'Exponentially,' Industry Says." *Canadian Press,* October 16, 2001.

"$3 Million Heist at Heathrow." BBC News. Available online at http://news.bbc.co.uk/hi/english/uk/england/ newsid_1880000/1880953.stm (cited March 19, 2002).

Transportation Security Administration. "Transportation Security Administration." Available online at http:// www.tsa.dot.gov/main.htm (cited March 22, 2002).

"Troops Storm Hijacked Russian Bus," *Guardian Unlimited* Online, July 31, 2001. Available online at http:// www.guardian.co.uk/russia/article/0,2763,530185,00 .html (cited April 24, 2002).

U.S. Department of Transportation. "Transportation Secretary Mineta Announces $175 Million in Supplemental Funds for Airport Security." Available online at http://www.dot.gov/affairs/dot02802.htm (cited March 19, 2002).

Walters, Joanna. "British Device Sniffs Out Bombs." *Guardian* (Manchester), December 30, 2001.

Webster, Ben. "Photo ID on Internal Flights." *Times* (London), November 10, 2001.

Whittington, Les. "Ottawa Set to Tighten Airport Safety." *Toronto Star,* November 22, 2001.

"Who Is Richard Reid?" BBC News. Available online at http://news.bbc.co.uk/hi/english/uk/newsid_1731000/ 1731568.stm (cited March 20, 2002).

Williams, George. *The Airline Industry and the Impact of Deregulation.* Brookfield, Vermont: Assignee Publishing, 1994.

Wilson, Jamie. "Jail for Afghans in Stansted Hijack." *Guardian Unlimited.* Available online at http:// www.guardian.co.uk/Print/0,3858,4338846,00.html (cited March 20, 2002).

Timothy G. Borden

BIOLOGICAL THREATS
OF TERRORISM

Prior to the fall of 2001 it seemed that the only people concerned with keeping a wary eye on the threat of biological terrorism were the military, certain scientists and policy analysts, and perhaps a handful of foresighted politicians. By late October of that year, however, the world—and the United States in particular—had gained a whole new vocabulary, consisting of words such as *Bacillus anthracis*, *Variola major*, and ciprofloxacin. In the wake of the September 11 terrorist attacks in the United States, as letters tainted with deadly anthrax began arriving in offices, homes, and postal facilities across the country, what had previously been dismissed as unlikely or farfetched was suddenly all too real: the country had been targeted by bioterrorists. As the government scrambled to control the situation, emergency response teams were overwhelmed with false alarms; hospitals saw greatly increased traffic; and pharmacies ran out of antibiotics as frightened people hoarded them like gold. By mid-November, five people had died from anthrax, but the worst was over. No new cases of anthrax were being reported, but a shaken populace was left with the unwanted knowledge that they were vulnerable, not just to anthrax, but to a whole host of deadly diseases.

What is Biological Terrorism?

While no definition of terrorism is universally agreed upon, it is generally understood to be violent acts such as bombings, shootings, and even the release of biological or chemical agents on an unsuspecting public, perpetrated to achieve political or ideological goals. More recently, some terrorist actions have had no specific aim other than to inflict mass casualty and fear on a populace. This seems to have been the purpose of the terrorist attacks on September 11, 2001, in the United States,

THE CONFLICT

The anthrax mail attacks in the United States in the fall of 2001 alerted an already terrorism-sensitive world to the dangers of biological terrorist attack. A silent and deadly weapon, biological agents could potentially take a great toll on a population unprepared for and unaware that a biological attack was taking place. Several preparedness and training simulations in late 2001 and early 2002 revealed concerns about the ability of response teams and government and health officials to deal with such an attack. While the perpetrator of the U.S. anthrax attacks is unknown, the attacks themselves have raised consciousness of a population's vulnerability to biological terrorism and concerns that the mail attacks may just be a precursor to a new trend in terrorism.

Political

- While several international agreements have banned the production and use of biological weapons, monitoring compliance to these agreements has been difficult.

- Several states suspected of being state sponsors of terrorism, such as Iraq and Iran, are suspected of pursuing biological weapons programs.

Economic

- With the collapse of the Soviet Union, technicians and stockpiles from the world's largest biological weapons program have flooded the black market of terrorist resources.

- The United States has sponsored economic development programs to employ some of the Soviet scientists, but the threat persists that raw materials from Soviet labs will show up on the black market.

- While producing biological weapons is relatively inexpensive, creating relevant counterterrorist programs is expensive. In the United States, most public health systems do not have a comprehensive plan in place to deal with biological attacks, and vaccines against some of the more deadly biological agents, such as smallpox, are in chronically low supply.

CHRONOLOGY

June 17, 1925 Twenty-nine nations sign the *Protocol for the Prohibition of the Use in War of Asphyxiating, Poisonous or other Gases, and of Bacteriological Methods of Warfare* in Geneva, Switzerland.

January 17, 1972 Two college students, Allen Schwandner and Stephen Pera, are apprehended while plotting to release typhoid, botulism, meningitis, bubonic plague, anthrax, choras, and diptheria into the water supplies of Chicago and other cities. The pair had formed an extremist group, RISE, to carry out the attacks and subsequently repopulate the earth with RISE members. While on bail, the two suspects flee to Jamaica and then fly on a hijacked plane to Cuba; Schwandner dies in Cuba in 1974 and Pera returns to the United States in 1995.

April 10, 1972 The Convention on the Prohibition of the Development, Production, and Stockpiling of Bacteriological (Biological) and Toxin Weapons and on Their Destruction is signed by the United States, Great Britain, the Soviet Union, and seventy-six other nations.

March–April 1979 A major anthrax outbreak in Sverdiovsk, Soviet Union, occurs after the accidental release of the bacterium from a secret biological weapons facility.

September 1984 Rajneeshee cult members release *Salmonella typhimurium* in restaurants around The Dalles, Oregon. Approximately 750 residents are taken ill by the poisoning.

1990–91 After its invasion of Kuwait, Iraq uses its biological weapons program to assemble hundreds of biological warheads for potential use against the Gulf War Allies.

mid–September 2001 In the United States, tabloid publisher American Media receives a letter containing anthrax. Photo editor Robert Stevens later dies from the exposure.

October 15, 2001 U.S. senator Tom Daschle's office receives a letter containing anthrax; the Hart Office Building in Washington, DC, is closed for the next six weeks for decontamination.

December 2001 Twenty-three anthrax exposures are verified in the United States by the end of December, with five deaths resulting from the attacks.

January 23, 2002 The FBI and U.S. Postal Service announce a $2.5 million reward for information leading to an arrest in the anthrax exposures.

February 5, 2002 U.S. President George W. Bush announces a $4.5 billion increase in the federal budget for biological counterterrorism, for a total outlay of $5.9 billion for 2003.

---

in which more than three thousand people were killed. Biological terrorism is the use of biological agents—living organisms that cause disease—in a terrorist attack. By their very nature—silent, unseen, odorless, and tasteless—biological agents make a powerfully frightening prospect if employed by terrorists. Unlike a bombing, which it blatant and quick, a biological attack can not be so easily identified. In the time it may take to identify and mobilize against such an attack, the number of those affected may increase greatly.

The biological agents most likely to be used in a terrorist attack are bacteria and viruses, which can multiply and spread infection to others. Anthrax is a disease caused by the bacteria *Bacillus anthracis*. The people who fell ill with anthrax in the United States in the fall of 2001 became so after handling mail contaminated with anthrax causing spores, which were present in a fine, white powder included in the mailed letters. Viruses such as smallpox and Ebola are highly infectious diseases. In the case of smallpox, the disease was eradicated from the world in 1980, so a large number of vaccines were not kept in stock. Ebola, a fast-moving hemorrhagic fever that causes the victim to bleed out internally, as yet has no known cure or vaccine.

There are no universal regulatory guidelines concerning the study, possession, and use of biological agents. Thus, they are readily accessible and could conceivably be easily obtained by terrorists. In trying to trace the source of the anthrax spores used in the U.S. mail attacks, scientists examined the spores against cultures from different laboratories. Several locations were eliminated as potential sources, but nothing definitive was determined.

HISTORICAL BACKGROUND

Biological Warfare from Ancient to Modern Times

While biological agents have been used most recently in terrorist attacks, the use of weapons derived from biological agents dates back to ancient times. Many historians suspect that, around 600 BCE, Athenians poisoned the water supply of a besieged city with a biological agent to win a victory. Additionally, the practice of using arrows tipped with poison was common enough to merit mention in ancient codes of law. In one instance of disease-causing biological agents actually changing the course of world history, Tartar Mongol invaders catapulted the bodies of plague victims over the city walls of Kaffa, a Genoese trading post in the Crimea, in 1346 CE. While the precise source of the illness is debatable (from plague-ridden bodies or from plague-carrying rats) the disease quickly spread throughout Kaffa, and the Genoese traders hurried back to Italy to escape it, inadvertently taking the plague with them. The Black Death, as it was known, thus spread throughout Europe—killing half the population in some areas—and eventually heralded the end of the Middle Ages.

Because of the unpredictability of biological weaponry, however, such tactics were usually avoided in favor of conventional arms such as swords, spears, and later guns and cannons. At the same time, a greater distinction began to be drawn between military and civilian populations. With the latter being considered illegitimate targets of warfare, the indiscriminate nature of biological, as well as chemical, attacks was considered serious enough to merit condemnation at the 1899 and 1907 International Peace Conferences held in the Hague, Netherlands, which called for the prohibition of the use of poisons during war time.

The Hague Conventions soon became irrelevant with the German army's use of chemical and biological agents such as chlorine, mustard gas, glanders, and anthrax during World War I (1914–18). Revulsion over the use of chemical weapons helped contribute, in 1925, to twenty-nine nations signing the Protocol for the Prohibition of the Use in War of Asphyxiating, Poisonous or other Gases, and of Bacteriological Methods of Warfare. Like the Hague Conventions before it, however, the Geneva Protocol would almost immediately be disregarded by several signatory nations, who pursued research and testing of both chemical and biological weapons.

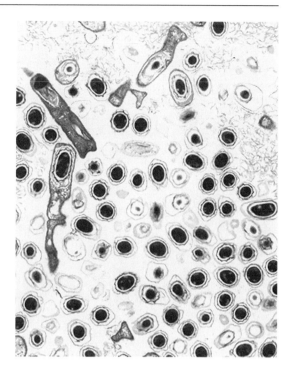

BACILLUS ANTHRACIS, A SPORE-FORMING BACTERIA, CAUSES THE INFECTIOUS DISEASE ANTHRAX. SEVERAL PEOPLE IN THE UNITED STATES WERE KILLED BY ANTHRAX AFTER HANDLING MAIL CONTAMINATED BY THE SPORES. *(AP/Wide World Photos. Reproduced by permission.)*

Modern Biological Warfare

One of the most devastating offensive biological weapons programs (1931–45) was developed by Japan as part of its strategy for domination over East Asia before and during World War II (1939–45). The crucial player in Japan's notorious agenda was Lieutenant General Shiro Ishii, who joined the military in 1920 after finishing his medical degree at Kyoto Imperial University. While in the military he focused his efforts on convincing Japan's military leadership to initiate a biological weapons program. In 1932 Ishii gained a prestigious post in occupied China with permission to inaugurate his long-anticipated biological weapons program.

Ishii's first major program began that same year. At the Zhong Ma Prison Camp in Beiyinhe, Manchuria, between 500 and 600 prisoners—typically captured communist rebels, convicts, and bandits—were routinely exposed to plague, poison gas, and frostbite to determine the effects and possible courses of treatment. While most of the subjects died in excruciating circumstances, all of the remaining prisoners were executed after the experiments. After a prison riot in 1934 the Zhong Ma facility was shut down. Word of Ishii's gruesome experiments leaked out after the riot, and he

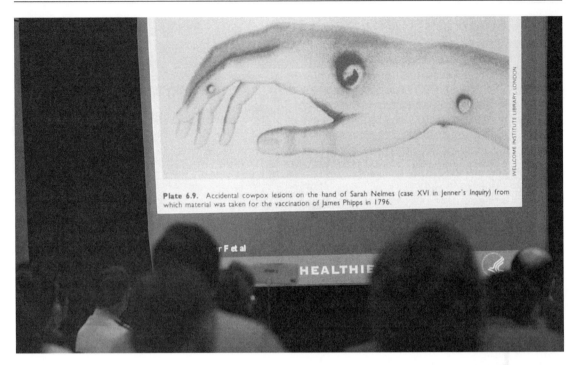

Plate 6.9. Accidental cowpox lesions on the hand of Sarah Nelmes (case XVI in Jenner's *Inquiry*) from which material was taken for the vaccination of James Phipps in 1796.

THE CENTERS FOR DISEASE CONTROL HOLDS A SMALLPOX RESPONSE AND PREPAREDNESS SESSION IN DECEMBER 2001, AFTER INCREASED CONCERNS ABOUT A BIOLOGICAL TERRORIST ATTACK. *(AP/Wide World Photos/Ric Feld. Reproduced by permission.)*

instituted even more ruthless security measures at his next biological weapons facility.

By 1939 Ishii had constructed the massive Unit 731 complex at Ping Fan near Harbin, Manchuria, where more than three thousand individuals were killed in biological experiments through 1945. In addition to weaponizing anthrax, cholera, typhoid, glanders, and the plague, Ishii's staff also conducted field experiments in nearby villages and cities. It is not known how many civilians died as a result of these tests—although thousands of such bombs were dropped—and most of the records at Ping Fan were destroyed in the closing days of World War II (1938–45). When questioned by U.S. officials after the war Ishii initially denied much of the work at Zhong Ma and Ping Fan. Later, however, he agreed to be debriefed in exchange for immunity from war crimes prosecution. Despite the horrific nature and scope of his deeds, Ishii was never punished for his experiments with biological agents.

While its Axis partners also engaged in some biological weapons studies during World War II, their programs were small in scale compared to Japan's program. Although Nazi Germany allowed numerous human experiments to be conducted in its concentration camps, the regime never officially sanctioned any coordinated offensive biological experiments. Great Britain experimented with anthrax spores by releasing them on Gruinard Island, off the northwest Scottish coast, in 1943; it took another fifty years to decontaminate the island. In the end, however, Japan was the only nation to use biological weapons on any significant scale during World War II.

In contrast, the United States was a relative latecomer to biological weapons programs. It was only in 1943, after learning details of Japan's program, that a center was established at Camp Detrick in western Maryland. While the facility produced some botulinum toxin for Great Britain in its first year, the war ended before any biological weapons were made. Although Camp Detrick's research projects were cut drastically in the aftermath of the war, Cold War tensions—including the awareness that the Soviet Union now led all other countries in biological weapons studies—ensured the facility's growth in the late 1940s and 1950s.

Superpower Biological Weapons Programs

Like Japan, the biological weapons program of the Soviet Union dated back to the 1920s and continued on through the international crises of the 1930s and 1940s. After World War II the Soviet

Union constructed its first smallpox production plant using *Variola major*, or the virus causing smallpox, just one of many biological organisms it weaponized over the years. The list of biological agents weaponized by the Soviets for possible use as biological weapons included *Coxiella burnetii*, or Q fever, a debilitating, but usually non-lethal sickness; *Bacillus anthracis*, or anthrax, typically fatal when inhaled; *Yersinia pestis*, the bacteria that causes plague; and the Marburg virus, first observed in Germany in 1967, which causes death by inducing massive internal bleeding.

While the Soviet program was well funded and attracted the elite of the country's medical and scientific corps, numerous accidents demonstrated the lethal potential of their work. The city of Kirov was contaminated by a sewer leak from a nearby anthrax facility in 1953; within a few years the city's rats had produced a new, more virulent strain of the bacterium and the area remained contaminated with *Bacillus anthracis*. Tragically, after Soviet scientists used the Kirov anthrax strain as the basis for a subsequent weapons program, another accident released the bacterium into the air in Sverdlovsk in late March or early April 1979. The incident resulted in an estimated 65 deaths and a total of close to one hundred infections. An intensive vaccination program helped stem the spread of the disease, and the government subsequently blamed the outbreak on infected meat sold on the black market.

In addition to the accidents at Kirov and Sverdlovsk, several Soviet scientists died after being exposed to toxic agents in their research labs. Yet the belief that the United States was also undertaking a biological arms race left most Soviet scientists convinced of the merit of their work. As Ken Alibek, a leading deputy chief of the Soviet's main biological weapons organization, Biopreparat, from 1988–92, explained in his memoir *Biohazard*, "We had been taught as schoolchildren and it was drummed into us as young military officers that the capitalist world was united in only one aim: to destroy the Soviet Union. It was not difficult for me to believe that the United States would use any conceivable weapon against us, and that our own survival depended on matching their duplicity."

This suspicion was not allayed by the Convention on the Prohibition of the Development, Production, and Stockpiling of Bacteriological (Biological) and Toxin Weapons and on Their Destruction, signed in 1972 by the United States, Great Britain, the Soviet Union, and 76 other nations. The convention banned all biological weapons that had no justification for prophylactic, protective, or other peaceful purposes; in other words, it banned offensive biological weapons while permitting research for defensive purposes. Additionally, it did not provide verification and monitoring provisions to ensure that states were not engaging in illegal activity. In light of the serious weaknesses of the Convention, the Soviet Union continued its biological weapons program unabated, while the United States, which had earlier decided to end its biological warfare program in 1969, complied with the agreement. Despite evidence to the contrary, Soviet officials refused to believe that the Americans had actually honored the agreement.

Indeed, the Soviets could point to numerous secret programs that the Americans had carried out over the years. In addition to a release of what they believed to be harmless organisms in San Francisco, which resulted in eleven infections caused by *Serratia marcescens* and one death, the army had also conducted numerous spraying tests of biological agents over Minneapolis and St. Louis from 1952–53 onward and released the *Bacillus subtilis variant niger*, another harmless but easily traced bacterium, in the New York City subway system in June 1966. There were an undetermined number of other similar tests that the army conducted during the height of the Cold War, but it refused to release information on them. While the United States complied with the mandates of the 1972 Convention, the Soviets remained convinced that their adversary was not above secretly violating the spirit of the agreement. In the two decades after the 1972 Convention the Soviet Union continued its aggressive production of offensive biological weapons. In 1992 Russian president Boris Yeltsin confirmed suspicions that the Soviet Union had participated in an offensive biological weapons program contrary to the 1972 Convention. After his admission in 1992 Yeltsin ordered the dismantling of the Soviet program, however, it is possible that some type of illegal activity continues in Russia.

The Turn to Terrorism

The lack of oversight concerning biological agents and the production of biological weapons is one of the contributing factors that allows terrorists such accessibility to the material. The dissolution of the Soviet Union presented the possibility that a formerly state-run program would become vulnerable to terrorist interests. Even through the final days of the Soviet Union, Biopreparat and a host of other agencies employed approximately sixty thousand workers, many recruited from the cream of the Soviet scientific community. With an annual budget that approached US$1 billion in the

BIOLOGICAL AGENTS

On September 17, 2001, only days after the terrorist attacks on New York City and Washington, DC, a letter containing anthrax spores was received by a media publishing company in Florida. The individual who opened the letter later died from the anthrax exposure. By January 2002 there were twenty-three confirmed anthrax cases, five of which resulted in death. Coming so shortly on the heels of the most stunning and casualty-laden terrorist attack in world history, the American public, media, and government voiced fears that the anthrax-laced letters were the start of a larger biological terrorist attack. The perpetrators of the anthrax attacks had yet to be determined as of May 2002, but the event has spurred greater attention to the possibilities of terrorists obtaining and using biological weapons and a greater interest in preparing for and countering such an attack.

In early 2002 U.S. President George W. Bush increased the federal budget for biological counterterrorism to US$4.5 billion. Nations around the world have initiated counterterrorism taskforces and practice preparedness responses to possible biological terrorist attacks. What, exactly, are they preparing for?

Biological or bacteriological weapons are derived from living organisms. The infectious nature of the living organisms can be manipulated and used because they can multiply in plant, animal, and human organisms, causing sickness, injury, and even death. Most biological agents are odorless and tasteless. Unlike a bomb, infection from a biological agent can be much more unassuming, as was shown in the anthrax cases of 2001, in which individuals were exposed through the simple act of opening a piece of mail. Biological and toxin weapons can be disseminated into target populations in several different ways. Technical means of delivery include the use of artillery shells and missiles. The use of such large delivery systems, however, increases the difficulty of such an attack because the launching or explosion of the weapon might kill the biological

agent. Cheaper and easy delivery methods include the use of animal vectors, crop dusters, backpack sprayers, and even postal letters.

There are four different types of biological agents: bacteria, viruses, rickettsiae, and fungi. Bacteria are single-cell organisms that cause diseases such as anthrax, tularemia, and plague. Viruses are intracellular parasites about one hundred times smaller than bacteria and can infect human beings, domestic animals, and crops. Examples include smallpox and hemorrhagic fevers like Ebola and Marburg. Bacterial and viral agents are the most commonly studied types of agents for biological weapons. They are also usually the most lethal agents.

The third type of biological agent, rickettsiae, are microorganisms. Resembling bacteria in form and structure, rickettsiae are intracellular parasites that reproduce inside animal cells. Typhus and Q fever are caused by rickettsiae. Typhus is delivered through fleas, lice, or mice. It results in fever, depression, red skin rashes, and delirium. Q fever originates with animals and can be transferred to humans through inhalation of contaminated dust (mainly on farms) or, more rarely, through ingestion of contaminated milk. It causes high fever, headache, confusion, chills, nausea, and chest and abdominal pain, among other symptoms. Finally, fungi can cause critical diseases in humans, such as histoplasmosis, a disease that primarily affects the lungs. Potato blight is a fungal disease that can destroy crops, and cause widespread food shortages and economic difficulties.

Toxins are poisonous substances created by bacteria, fungi, plants, insects, spiders, and other animals. Like biological agents, toxins are derived from living organisms. They differ, however, in that toxins are inanimate chemical derivatives and therefore can not replicate. Toxin weapons can disseminate poison, but that poison can not multiply like bacteria or viruses will. Due to the fact that toxins are chemical derivatives they also fall into the category of Chemical Weapons Conventions.

late 1980s, over one hundred research and production sites dotted the nation's landscape. Once the country collapsed into political and economic chaos, however, the biological weapons program fell apart as well. As the facilities decayed seemingly overnight, some senior scientists attempted to earn a living in the private sector before going

abroad. Others found a more lucrative pursuit when they were recruited by Iraq to bring their knowledge to that country, which is considered by the United States to be a state sponsor of terrorism. Even before 1990 Iraq had produced botulinum toxin, ricin, anthrax, and aflatoxin bombs, and it appeared the country was now poised to take over

Russia's place as the leading site of biological weapons production.

Since its defeat in the Gulf War in 1991 Iraq had delayed and obstructed inspection visits by the United Nations Special Commission (UNSCOM). Yet what little information UNSCOM had been able to glean was troubling enough. As recounted in UNSCOM chief inspector Scott Ritter's 1999 book *Endgame: Solving the Iraq Problem—Once and for All,* Iraqi capabilities included the production and weaponization of biological agents in both mobile and permanent facilities. The country had also initiated experiments with its weapons on captives at the Abu Ghraib prison, which resulted in the deaths of all fifty of the human subjects.

Even during UNSCOM's attempts at monitoring Iraq's biological weapons capability, Iraqi leader Saddam Hussein's regime pressed forward with its expansion plans for producing biological agents. In June 1995 the country arranged to purchase a factory from Biopreparat to make biological products and to pay the Russians for research and technical assistance in setting up the plant. While Iraq insisted that the facility was going to be used to make animal feed, UNSCOM officials learned that all of the Iraqis involved in the deal were part of the country's biological weapons program, and that the factory itself had been specifically designed for biological weapons production. By the time UNSCOM was ejected from Iraq in 1998 it had verified the presence of hundreds of bombs filled with anthrax and other agents, about forty separate facilities for production and storage, and about six key production facilities that were suspected of turning out weaponized biological agents.

After learning about the scope of its biological weapons program, the United States could no longer ignore the potential danger of allowing Soviet-trained scientists to work for Iraq or for any of a number of terrorist groups, most notably Osama bin Laden's al-Qaeda network. The U.S. State Department had initiated a program in 1994 to retool Soviet weapons facilities for commercial products and paid to re-train Soviet scientists as well. The U.S. Department of Defense subsequently spent tens of millions of dollars—$17 million in fiscal year 2001 alone, an amount that jumped to $55 million in the early part of 2002— to convert Soviet biological weapons facilities to nonmilitary uses. For many Soviets, however, the aid was too little and too late. As Alibek testified before a Senate Subcommittee on Funding for Bioterrorism Preparedness on November 29, 2001,

"We fear that in order to feed their families, others may offer their technical skills on the open market, which could provide our enemies with technical expertise or ready-made, engineered organisms. Some Russian microbiologists are reportedly teaching students from rogue states that are interested in this expertise. Other prominent scientists have simply dropped out of sight."

While the whereabouts of many Soviet scientists were in doubt, there was ample evidence that the products from their labs had spread throughout the black market for terrorism. A *60 Minutes II* report in late 2001 showed that biological and chemical agents formerly produced in Soviet facilities were up for sale in the chaotic North-West Frontier region of Pakistan. As the Taliban and al-Qaeda leaders were ousted from Afghanistan, they also left behind a paper trail documenting their attempts to purchase and utilize biological weapons in their war of terror. More revealing was the discovery in December 2001 of what was believed to be a rudimentary biological weapons production facility at a camp that had been under the direct control of Osama bin Laden. As Secretary of Defense Donald Rumsfeld was quoted on *60 Minutes II* in an appearance at NATO headquarters on December 18, 2001, "The nexus, between states with weapons of mass destruction and terrorist networks, raises the danger that September 11 could be a preview of what could come."

Religious Cult Attacks

The discovery of Osama bin Laden's biological weapons laboratory and Defense Secretary Rumsfeld's dire warning highlighted the growing uncertainty that characterized the United States' experience with biological terrorism. The largest biological attack on U.S. soil, in September 1984, had in fact gone undetected for more than a year. Members of the Rajneeshee cult had released *Salmonella typhimurium* bacteria in restaurants around The Dalles, Oregon, which sickened at least 750 residents. It was only after some of the participants in the attack fled the commune that public health officials were alerted to the true nature of the incident. Authorities believe that the restaurant contaminations may have been a test run for a planned follow-up attack involving the town's water supply, aimed at making residents sick in order to prevent them from going to the polls to vote in a hotly contested election with cult-endorsed candidates on the ballot.

More troubling than the Rajneeshee's plan to take control of local government, however, was the fact that it had conducted a number of other

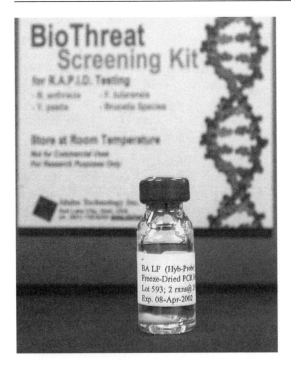

BIO-THREAT SCREENING KITS, SUCH AS A VIAL OF FREEZE-DRIED REAGENT, CAN DETECT VARIOUS BIOLOGICAL AGENTS THAT MAY BE USED IN TERRORIST ATTACKS. *(AP/Wide World Photos/Douglas C. Pizac. Reproduced by permission.)*

smaller-scale biological experiments in the region to prepare for the election-eve poisoning. After federal investigators finally entered the cult's compound, they discovered an invoice for agents ranging from *Francisella tularensis* to *Salmonella paratyphi.* The director of the cult's labs, Ma Anand Puja (also known as Diane Onang), was also said to have experimented with growing the AIDS virus as a new biological weapon in the cult's efforts. Despite the nature of the Rajneeshee attack, however, Puja and one other cult leader served less than four years in federal prison after pleading no contest to a series of murder, wiretapping, and poisoning charges. The leader of the cult, Bhagwan Shree Rajneesh himself, served no prison time and fled the United States after paying a $400,000 fine.

U.S. officials were not alone in their initial ignorance when faced with a biological attack on civilians. Like the Rajneeshees, the Aum Shinrikyo cult was ruled by a charismatic leader, Shoko Asahara, who built his organization into a billion dollar empire, much of it from mandatory donations by cult members. Asahara also warned his followers to take action against the group's enemies and ordered a series of tests involving anthrax, Q fever, and botulinum in the cult's laboratories. Eventually, the cult began to test its

weapons on the public, including a 1993 anthrax test in downtown Tokyo, which failed. A chemical attack with sarin gas in Matsumoto, Japan, was part of a plan to kill three judges who were sitting in on a case involving cult members. While the attack did not achieve its desired goal, it nonetheless illustrated Aum Shinrikyo's growing and lethal capabilities.

Once the scope of Aum Shinrikyo's chemical and biological weapons capabilities were made apparent, particularly after a 1995 sarin attack on the Tokyo subway system, U.S. authorities took steps to prepare for such a potential tragedy in the United States. Even as the threats by Aum Shinrikyo, Osama bin Laden, and Saddam Hussein became clear, however, federal efforts were still piecemeal. The Defense Against Weapons of Mass Destruction Act, passed by Congress in 1996, authorized the Department of Defense to train local- and state-level emergency response crews for biological attacks. Another 1996 federal law, the Antiterrorism and Effective Death Penalty Act, allowed the U.S. Attorney General's office to implement training and purchase equipment for emergency units. As the legislation demonstrated, counterterrorism efforts at the federal level remained fragmented and sometimes duplicated already existing programs.

Anthrax Scares

The rash of anthrax exposures beginning in September 2001 demonstrated both the progress and shortcomings of the United States' preparedness for biological assaults. Sometime around September 17, 2001, the staff at tabloid publisher American Media in Boca Raton, Florida, passed around a strange, yet seemingly harmless, fan letter written to Jennifer Lopez and sent to the publisher. The following week, photo editor Robert Stevens, who had held up the letter to take a closer look at it, came down with flu-like symptoms. By October 2, when he was admitted to the hospital, Stevens was suffering a high fever and periods of confusion. Within hours, Stevens lost consciousness and passed away on October 5. Florida authorities, working with the Centers for Disease Control in Atlanta, announced that Stevens had died from inhalation anthrax.

The success in diagnosing Stevens's fatal illness was a direct result of the 1996 legislation that increased funding for counterterrorism training. While very few doctors had ever encountered an anthrax exposure—the last inhalation anthrax case dated back to 1976 in California—Florida medical technicians had just taken courses to identify and

DURING AN ANTI-ANTHRAX TRAINING EXERCISE IN FRANCE, MUNICIPAL EMPLOYEES DON PROTECTIVE CLOTHING AND GAS MASKS AND GO THROUGH A DECONTAMINATION SHOWER. MANY NATIONS ENGAGED IN SIMILAR TRAINING EXERCISES IN AN EFFORT TO BE MORE PREPARED TO FACE A POSSIBLE TERORRIST ATTACK. *(AP/Wide World Photos/Lionel Cironneau. Reproduced by permission.)*

treat biological weapons. Despite their initial success, however, officials mismanaged the case in the days after Stevens's death. In order to allay public fears, the Florida Department of Health initially suggested that Stevens had contracted the virus from nature while vacationing in rural North Carolina, even though such an exposure was extremely unlikely. Health and Human Services Director Tommy G. Thompson also maintained that Stevens was the only victim of anthrax. Unfortunately, a second anthrax victim from American Media, mailroom employee named Ernesto Blanco, was already in the hospital with symptoms that mirrored Stevens's decline. On October 7 Blanco was diag-

nosed with inhalation anthrax; another employee tested positive for anthrax exposure a few days later. Both recovered, yet there was little comfort in the realization that the offices of American Media had been subjected to an anthrax attack.

Part of the slow response by government officials could be explained by the sheer surprise that anthrax could be used as a biological weapon in such a manner. Conventional wisdom held that even at a few millionths of a meter (or less than one-twentieth the diameter of a human hair), anthrax spores were too large to pass through sealed envelopes, and that at least eight thousand spores

BIOLOGICAL DISEASES—PRIMARY THREATS*

Common Name	Scientific Name	Description
Anthrax	*Bacillus anthracis*	Anthrax exposures can be cutaneous, inhalational, or gastrointestinal. 95% of cases are cutaneous (skin) exposures. If untreated, 20% of cutaneous anthrax exposures are fatal; gastrointestinal cases are up to 60% fatal; almost all inhalation anthrax cases are fatal. Initial symptoms mimic the onset of influenza. Anthrax is not contagious.
Botulism	*Clostridium botulinum* toxin	Botulism is typically transmitted through contaminated food and results in blurred vision, muscle weakness, and dry mouth. Although botulism can be incapacitating for several weeks, it is usually not fatal and is not contagious.
Plague	*Yersinia pestis*	The bubonic form of plague is usually transmitted by flea bites; pneumonic plague, however, can be transmitted through human contact if the plague bacterium enters the respiratory system. Antibiotic treatment can be effective if the plague is diagnosed immediately after the onset of symptoms.
Smallpox	*Variola major*	Through a global vaccination program, smallpox was eliminated as a health threat in 1977. Stores of the virus remained in research facilities and the Soviet Union attempted to develop a weaponized form of the virus in succeeding years. Fatal in about 30% of infections, there is no effective treatment regimen for individuals infected with the disease.
Tularemia	*Fracisells tularensis*	Tularemia can be contracted through contaminated food or water or by an insect bite. Although it is not contagious and can be treated with antibiotics, tularemia can be fatal.

* High-priority (or "Category A") agents are easily disseminated and cause high mortality rates. Category A agents also include viral hemorrhagic fevers such as the Marburg virus and Ebola hemorrhagic fever.

AFTER THE ANTHRAX MAIL ATTACKS IN THE UNITED STATES, MANY BEGAN TO FEAR THE POSSIBILITY OF TERRORISTS HARNESSING AND USING NATURALLY OCCURRING BIOLOGICAL AGENTS THAT CAN CAUSE HARMFUL AND EVEN DEADLY DISEASE. *(Gale Group.)*

would have to be inhaled to result in an infection. Tragically, both assumptions proved wrong when two employees at a Washington, DC, postal facility died from the disease after inhaling the anthrax laden spores. Even after U.S. Postal Service administrators learned that the exposures occurred when the facility had processed anthrax-contaminated letters, they insisted that there was no cause for greater concern. After processing centers in New Jersey, New York City, and Indianapolis were found to be contaminated, and eight employees were diagnosed with an-

thrax exposure, however, it became obvious that the there was much to learn about the disease-causing bacteria.

The anthrax attacks continued with contaminated letters sent to the offices of NBC anchor Tom Brokaw, CBS anchor Dan Rather, and U.S. senators Tom Daschle and Patrick Leahy. The letter sent to Senator Daschle, which was received in the Hart Office Building on October 15, closed the building for six weeks; the decontamination process, which had to be repeated when initial attempts to kill the anthrax failed, cost an estimated $14 million. Even more puzzling were the two anthrax deaths that seemed unrelated to the other cases. Kathy Nguyen, a New York City hospital worker, and Ottilie Lundgren, a 94-year-old widow who lived alone and rarely ventured outside her Connecticut home, were not known to have come in any direct contact with the bacteria. The letters used in each exposure were similar enough that officials decided that they had almost certainly come from the same source. In all, 23 people in the United States were confirmed with anthrax exposure during the September and October attacks, including five that resulted in death.

The United States was not alone in its fear of anthrax. Other countries were also on the alert as they experienced several scares. Spores were thought to be on a travel brochure mailed from Florida to a home in Buenos Aires, Argentina, and on a letter mailed from Atlanta, Georgia, to a doctor in Kenya, but both cases turned out to be false alarms. Similar false alarms spanned the globe from Malaysia to Brazil. In Melbourne, Australia, the passengers of a Virgin Blue flight were temporarily quarantined after a powdery substance was discovered onboard. The offices of Croatia's leading newspaper were evacuated after receiving a letter containing a white powder. Dunedin, New Zealand, mail-sorting centers reported backups after a suspicious substance spilled from a postal bag. All of these incidents were declared hoaxes, but they proved that people around the world felt vulnerable to the threat of biological terrorism.

As the anthrax exposures continued in the United States, some voiced fears that the attacks were perpetrated by the same group responsible for the September 11 terrorist attacks. U.S. president George W. Bush (2001–) himself speculated in mid-October that the two events may have been planned by Osama bin Laden, although he was careful to add that no such proof had been found. Others, such as Dr. Richard O. Spertzel, a former researcher at Camp Detrick and member of an UNSCOM inspection team, suggested that Iraq may have engineered the attacks. Testifying before the U.S. House Committee on International Relations in December 2001, Spertzel noted that the anthrax spores found in the letter sent to Senator Daschle were of higher purity and concentration than UNSCOM had found in Iraq; however, Spertzel added, "The quality [of anthrax] appeared to be such that it could be produced only by some group that was involved with a current or former state program in recent years.

The level of knowledge, expertise, and experience required and the types of special equipment required to make such quality product takes time and experimentation to develop."

In light of the poisonings by the Rajneeshee and Aum Shinrikyo cults, there was also the possibility that a well organized and militant religious or nationalist group was behind the attacks. Hate groups such as the Aryan Nations, Underground Skinhead Action, and Christian Israelite Church all advocated the use of biological weapons against their enemies. Typical of the rhetoric was one Christian Israelite Church publication (quoted in Ely Karmon's essay *The Anthrax Campaign: An Interim Analysis*) that declared, "Morality has absolutely nothing to do with the deployment of biological weaponry. The time for morality was back before the current immorality made civil war inevitable." In addition to the tension from extremist groups, 71 people were arrested between September 2001 and January 2002 for making false threats of anthrax exposure. The hoaxes were part of more than fifteen thousand anthrax scares reported across the nation.

In January 2002 the Federal Bureau of Investigation (FBI) and U.S. Postal Service indicated that they had narrowed their search for the anthrax terrorist. Creating a profile based on the anthrax letters, their intended targets, the locations where they were mailed, and other factors, officials said that the culprit was likely a single man who had extensive scientific training and possibly some military training. The suspect probably had access to a lab where anthrax was stored, possibly at a pharmaceutical company or university laboratory. Finally, given the location of the mailings, the suspect may have lived and worked in New Jersey or northeastern Pennsylvania. In the hope that an intense focus on the region would yield more clues, the U.S. Postal Service mailed out over half a million informational flyers to homes around Trenton, New Jersey. It also announced that the reward for information leading to the capture of the terrorist had been increased to $2.5 million.

RECENT HISTORY AND THE FUTURE

Testing the United States' Response

The anthrax exposures did set off some public panic and they demonstrated that there was no comprehensive response plan in place for a potential public health crisis. Such a shortcoming should not have come as a surprise. In May 2000

LARRY WAYNE HARRIS

1952– Survivalist and white supremacist Larry Wayne Harris made headlines in February 1998 when he was arrested in Henderson, Nevada, by the FBI on suspicion of carrying anthrax spores with the intent to use them. A member of the Aryan Nations, Christian Identity Church, and the National Alliance neo-Nazi group, the Lancaster, Ohio, resident was picked up after an informant tipped off federal authorities about Harris's alleged plans.

Harris had previously been arrested for fraudulently obtaining bubonic plague bacteria from a Maryland lab in 1995. After plea bargaining to one charge of wire fraud, Harris was placed on eighteen months of probation in 1997. Insisting that he had not intended to harm anyone, Harris subsequently capitalized on his notoriety to publicize his survivalist work, including a publication on bioterrorism that he sold on the Internet.

After testing the seized materials at Camp Detrick, the FBI learned that Harris had actually carried some non-lethal anthrax vaccine and dropped the charges against him. Harris cited the incident as proof of a government conspiracy against him and made a round of media appearances to promote his views. The flap over Harris's arrest and release also foreshadowed a wave of more than one hundred anthrax hoaxes bewteen October 1998 and February 1999, many of them directed at government agencies, abortion clinics and women's health centers, and high schools and universities.

federal officials had staged Operation TopOff, a seven-day, $10 million mock exercise to see how a large city would respond to a biological attack. On May 20, 2000, the first phase of Operation TopOff began with a staged chemical gas attack at an event in Portsmouth, New Hampshire. While officials were disappointed with the response time of emergency medical crews, the exercise was deemed relatively reassuring. The results of the second phase of Operation TopOff, however, were less encouraging. Simulating a biological attack of the release of the pneumonic plague virus in Denver, it took just two days after the victims started showing symptoms of the disease for the public health system to become crippled. Basic supplies needed to treat the disease ran out on the third day, and attempts to replenish the stocks utterly failed as the state's transportation system shut down. While the crisis was staged, it showed that the existing lack of coordination be-

tween the health care system and government officials would provide a crucial roadblock to dealing with any real mass emergency.

Similar conclusions were drawn from the Dark Winter exercise, a simulated smallpox attack on the United States conducted by several security and defense firms in June 2001. The study concluded that medical personnel, not the National Guard, were the vital response team to any biological attack and should be sent to the site of such an attack first—contrary to most emergency response plans. More disturbing, the health care system was found to be utterly incapable of handling the number of casualties that would occur during a mass biological attack. As a result of competition among hospitals, most had eliminated their excess capacity; as researcher Amy Smithson of the Henry L. Stimson Center told the *Economist* in October 2001, "In most of the cities that I surveyed, the central game plan for hospitals in the event of a major catastrophe was to . . . shut their doors to incoming patients."

Safeguarding Civilians

The September 11 and anthrax attacks gave renewed impetus to the government to improve upon the performances observed in Operations TopOff and Dark Winter. In February 2002 President Bush announced that the anticipated federal budget for the following year would more than quadruple spending on biological counterterrorist measures—an increase from $1.4 billion to $5.9 billion. Committing $1.6 billion of the new spending to the state and local levels, the president emphasized the need to improve regional public health systems by enhancing their ability to deal with mass disasters, creating regional planning associations, and paying for better emergency medical response training. At the federal level, Bush pledged $650 million to increase the National Pharmaceutical Stockpile and ensure sufficient antibiotics to treat twenty million people for biological attacks from anthrax, plague, and other biological agents. The National Institutes of Health was also assigned $1.75 million in the new budget to continue its research on bioterrorism and to encourage the private sector to develop vaccines for use against biological agents.

Bush's 2003 budget demonstrated that U.S. officials had recognized the crucial danger that biological weapons could present to the nation's well being. While many unanswered questions lingered—from the identity of the United States' anthrax terrorist to the capabilities of rogue groups such as al-Qaeda and states such as Iraq—the threat of biological warfare and terrorism had at least begun to be realized. In the post-September 11 world, preparedness and defense against such worst-case scenarios had become the hallmark of the United States' counterterrorist efforts.

BIBLIOGRAPHY

Alibek, Ken, with Stephen Handelman. *Biohazard: The Chilling True Story of the Largest Covert Biological Weapons Program in the World.* New York: Random House, 1999.

Alibek, Ken. "Funding for Bioterrorism Preparedness." *Congressional Testimony Before the Senate Subcommittee on Labor, Health, and Human Services, Education, and Related Agencies of the Committee on Appropriations,* November 29, 2001.

"American Anthrax Outbreak of 2001," UCLA Department of Epidemiology, School of Public Health. Available online at http://www.ph.ucla.edu/epi/bioter/detect/antdetect_list.html (cited May 8, 2002).

Annin, Peter and Tom Morganthau. "A Scare in the West." *Newsweek,* March 2, 1998, p. 26.

"Anthrax Ruled Out in Kenya, Argentina," October 24, 2001. Available online at http://iafrica.com/news/us_terror/bioterrorism/833105.htm (cited May 8, 2002)

"Appendix C: Biological Agents," Public Affairs Staff. Available online at http://www.fas.org/irp/cia/product/go_appendixc_032796.html (May 9, 2002).

Barnaby, Wendy. *The Plague Makers: The Secret World of Biological Warfare.* London: Satin Publications, Ltd., 1999.

Begley, Sharon. "Protecting America: The Top 10 Priorities." *Newsweek,* November 5, 2001, p. 26.

Begley, Sharon. "Steps Toward an 'Immune Building.'" *Newsweek,* November 5, 2001, p. 58.

Begley, Sharon. "Unmasking Bioterror." *Newsweek,* October 8, 2001, p. 20.

"Beyond Anthrax: Extremists and the Bioterrorist Threat," Anti-Defamation League Law Enforcement Agency Resource Network. Available online at http://www.adl.org/learn/Anthrax/default.asp?xpicked=1&item;=0 (cited May 13, 2002).

Carus, Seth. "RISE." In Jonathan B. Tucker, ed., *Toxic Terror: Assessing Terrorist Use of Chemical and Biological Weapons.* Cambridge: MIT Press, 2000.

Centers for Disease Control and Prevention. "FAQs About Anthrax." Centers for Disease Control and Prevention Web Site, available online at http://www.bt.cdc.gov/DocumentsApp/faqanthrax.asp (cited February 26, 2002).

Clarke, Richard A. "Finding the Right Balance Against Bioterrorism." Centers for Disease Control and Prevention Web Site, available online at http://www.cdc.gov/ncidod/EID/vol5no4/clarke.htm (cited February 26, 2002).

Cole, Leonard. *Clouds of Secrecy: The Army's Germ Warfare Tests Over Populated Areas.* Totowa, New Jersey: Rowman & Littlefield, 1988.

Edwards, Tamala M. and Elaine Lafferty. "Catching a 48-Hour Bug." *Time,* March 2, 1998, p. 56.

Frist, Bill. *When Every Moment Counts: What You Need to Know about Bioterrorism from the Senate's Only Doctor.* Lanham, Maryland: Rowman and Littlefield Publishers, 2002.

Gambardello, Joseph A. "Award Doubled in Anthrax-Mail Case." *Philadelphia Enquirer,* January 23, 2002.

Gay, Kathlyn. *Silent Death: The Threat of Biological and Chemical Warfare.* Brookfield, Connecticut: Twenty-First Century Books, 2001.

Guteri, Fred, John Barry, Warren Getler, and Christopher Dickey. "What Can Iraq Do?" *Newsweek,* November 5, 2001, p. 42.

Guterland, Fred, and Eve Conant. "In the Germ Labs." *Newsweek,* February 25, 2002, p. 26.

Hamburg, Margaret A. "Preparing For and Preventing Bioterrorism." *Issues in Science and Technology,* Winter 2001/2002, p. 27.

Harris, Sheldon H.. *Factories of Death: Japanese Biological Warfare 1932-1945 and the American Cover Up.* London: Routledge, 1994.

Henry, Larry. "Sun Profile: Harris' Troubled Past Includes Mail Fraud, White Supremacy," February 23, 1998. *Las Vegas Sun.* Available online at http://www.lasvegassun.com/dossier/crime/bio/harris.html (cited May 13, 2002).

Hoge, Jr., James F. And Gideon Rose, eds. *How Did This Happen?: Terrorism and the New War.* New York: Public Affairs, 2001.

Kaplan, David E. and Douglas Pasternak. "Terrorism's Next Wave." *U.S. News and World Report,* November 17, 1997, p. 26.

Karmon, Ely. "The Anthrax Campaign: An Interim Analysis." International Policy Institute for Counterterrorism. Available online at http://www.ict.org.il/articles/articledet.cfm?articleid=401 (cited February 22, 2002).

Lake, Anthony. *Nightmares: Real Threats in a Dangerous World and How America Can Meet Them.* Boston: Little, Brown and Company, 2000.

Lemonick, Michael D., Dan Cray, Andrea Dorfman, Alice Park, Andrew Goldstein, and Elaine Shannon. "Anthrax." *Time,* December 31, 2001-January 7, 2002, p. 126.

Levine, Herbert M. *Chemical and Biological Weapons in Our Times.* New York: Frankin Watts, 2000.

McCuen, Gary E. *Biological Terrorism and Weapons of Mass Destruction.* Hudson, WI: Gary E. McCuen Publications, 1999.

Miller, Judith, Stephen Engelberg, and William Broad. *Germs: Biological Weapons and America's Secret War.* New York: Simon and Schuster, 2001.

Osterholm, Michael T. and John Schwartz. *Living Terrors: What America Needs to Know to Survive the Coming Bioterrorist Catastrophe.* New York: Delacorte Press, 2000.

Peters, Katherine McIntire. "Behind in the Biowar." *Government Executive,* December 2001, p. 27.

Preston, Richard. *The Hot Zone.* New York: Random House, 1994.

Regis, Ed. *The Biology of Doom: The History of America's Secret Germ Warfare Project.* New York: Henry Holt and Company, 1999.

Ritter, Scott. *Endgame: Solving the Iraq Problem—Once and For All.* New York: Simon and Schuster, 1999.

Rogers, Adam, Jane Spencer, and Daniel Klaidman. "Only Questions in Connecticut." *Newsweek,* December 3, 2001, p. 8.

Schaefer, Bob. "Global Anthrax Fears Grow." ABC News Web Site. Available online at http://more .abcnews.go.com/sections/world/dailynews/ anthraxoverseas011020.html (cited April 15, 2002).

Simon, Bob. "Weapons of Mass Destruction in Pakistan." *60 Minutes II,* December 19, 2001.

Spertzel, Richard O. "Bioterrorism and Potential Sources of Anthrax." *Congressional Testimony Before the House Committee on International Relations,* December 5, 2001.

Stern, Jessica. *Chemical and Biological Weapons in Our Times.* Cambridge, Massachusetts: Harvard University Press, 1999.

U.S. State Department. "Biological Weapons Convention." U.S. State Department Web Site, available online at http://www.state.gov/www/global/arms/treaties/bwc1 .html (cited February 23, 2002).

U.S. State Department. "Fact Sheet: Bush Strategy to Defend Against Bioterrorism." Available online at http://usinfo.state.gov/topical/pol/arms/02020505 .htm (cited February 26, 2002).

"What September 11 Really Wrought." *Economist.* January 12, 2002.

Timothy G. Borden

CHEMICAL TERRORISM THREATS

The tragedy on September 11, 2001, when New York City and Washington, DC, were targeted by terrorists in hijacked commercial airliners, represented more than a terrorist attack. More American civilians died on this day than on any other single day in the nation's history, including a civil war and two world wars. The attack was a watershed event in the annals of terrorism, proving once and for all that terrorists now have both the capability and the willingness to kill or maim thousands of innocent civilians. In addition, if they are willing to cause mass casualties, then we need to ask how they might accomplish this besides using explosives and hijacked aircraft. This brings us to a consideration of terrorists' use of various unconventional weapons. (Unconventional weapons, including chemical, biological, nuclear, and radiological, are those weapons that have not been widely used throughout the history of warfare and include almost any weapons besides explosives, incendiaries, and projectile weapons.) One of the most highly feared of these potentially devastating forms of violence is chemical terrorism, the use by terrorists of toxic chemical agents to attack their targets.

In the weeks following September 11, as fears of further al-Qaeda attacks grew, the possibility of a fresh assault using toxic chemicals received much exposure. Stores nationwide began selling out of gas masks, crop dusters were grounded, and television specials instructed viewers on how to seal off their homes from poison gas. The concern over chemical terrorism was then temporarily displaced by fears of bioterrorism as the anthrax attacks via the U.S. mail came to light in October 2001. Yet even with all the attention paid to the anthrax letters and the U.S. war in Afghanistan (a response to the September attacks), the prospect of chemical terrorism on the part of extremists like

THE CONFLICT

In the past five years, and especially since the September 11 terrorist attacks in the United States, there has been a heightened awareness of all forms of terrorism, including that of chemical terrorism, which often generates more fear amongst the public due to its nature. Chemical terrorism is the use by terrorists of toxic chemical agents to attack their targets.

Military

- The use of chemicals as weapons has a long history, but their first major appearance on the battlefield was during World War I, when agents such as chlorine and mustard were used extensively.

- Chemical weapons were not used in World War II, but were used afterwards, such as during the Iran-Iraq War from 1980–88.

Security

- Although conventional explosives remain the weapon of choice for most terrorists, there are several reasons why terrorists might find chemical agents attractive, including the vulnerability of modern society to these weapons, their tactical flexibility, and the evidence that they are easier to acquire and deliver than most other unconventional weapons.

- Large-scale chemical terrorism is possible, but it is not as easy as is often assumed.

- Various measures can be taken to combat the threat, from both the prevention side, such as law enforcement and intelligence gathering, and the preparedness side, such as emergency planning and stockpiling antidotes.

Political and Religious

- The most likely perpetrators of chemical terrorism that results in mass casualties are groups or individuals with characteristics such as the lack of a need for political support and a set of moral values permitting mass murder. The most likely group type to use chemical weapons is religiously motivated terrorists, including cults.

- There have been many attempts, plots, and even several attacks using chemical agents.

CHRONOLOGY

1915–19 During World War I the first widespread use of chemicals as weapons occurs. Agents used include chlorine gas and later, mustard.

1930s Nerve agents are developed, arising out of research on organophosphates.

1946 Avenging Israel's Blood, seeking revenge for the Holocaust, poisons food eaten by German soldiers in an American prisoner of war camp in Nuremberg, Germany.

1945–1990s Both the United States and the Soviet Union produce tens of thousands of tons of chemical weapons during the Cold War, but never use them.

1980–88 During the Iran-Iraq War, Iraq uses vast amounts of chemical weapons against Iran. Later in the war, Iran retaliates with a much smaller number of chemical weapons.

1988 The government of Iraq employs chemical weapons against Kurdish civilians within Iraq. More than 4,000 people are killed in an attack on the village of Halabjah.

1991 The U.S.-led coalition forces in the Gulf War take precautions against possible chemical weapons use by Iraq.

March 1995 Aum Shinrikyo, a violent Japanese cult, releases the nerve agent sarin into the Tokyo subway system, killing 12 people and injuring about 1,000. This attack forms part of a long string of chemical attacks by the cult.

1996 The U.S. Congress approves the training and equipping of local emergency services in the country's largest cities to deal with an attack using weapons of mass destruction. This becomes known as the Nunn-Lugar-Domenici Program and includes preparation for chemical terrorism.

April 1997 The Chemical Weapons Convention comes into force, outlawing the possession, production, and use of chemical weapons and many of their direct precursors.

September 2001 Terrorists fly hijacked airplanes into the World Trade Center and the Pentagon, killing thousands of civilians. These attacks spark fears of terrorist use of weapons of mass destruction. There are concerns that al-Qaeda, the terrorist group believed to be behind the attacks, is in possession of chemical weapons.

October 2001 President George W. Bush forms the Office of Homeland Security to protect the United States against terrorism, including chemical terrorism.

the al-Qaeda organization remains a concern at the highest levels of government. President George W. Bush (2001–), in his 2002 State of the Union Address, stated emphatically that " . . . the depth of their [the terrorists'] hatred is equaled by the madness of the destruction they design. We have found . . . [in Afghanistan] detailed instructions for making chemical weapons . . . "

Chemical terrorism includes attacks with chemical agents that states have developed for use in war (high-level agents), as well as contamination with toxic chemicals used commercially (low-level agents). In either case, these substances, when used by terrorists, are intended to incapacitate, injure, or kill human beings, often on a large scale.

Chemicals, together with radioactive and biological materials, inspire a particular sense of dread that one does not encounter with even the most destructive conventional weapons. They are invisible, silent killers against which most people feel impotent. Chemical terrorism brings with it the possibility of mass casualties, panic, and even widespread hysteria. Since an individual or small terrorist group could cause so much harm using chemical agents, chemical terrorism could be considered a form of asymmetric warfare (where one side in a conflict uses unconventional tactics, weapons, or strategy to negate the military strengths of the other). As such, it poses a danger to U.S. national security, since American bombers, tanks, and soldiers can do little to protect against unconventional terrorism. The threat is also a global one, as modern terrorists like al-Qaeda and Aum Shinrikyo have been known to operate across national boundaries and often have bases and targets in several countries.

A MODEL AIRCRAFT IS USED DURING A TRAINING TEST TO DELIVER A "BIOLOGICAL" OR "CHEMICAL" WEAPON IN A SIMULATION TO CREATE REAL-LIFE SCENARIOS OF AND RESPONSES TO TERRORIST ATTACK. *(AP/Wide World Photos/Douglas C. Pizac. Reproduced by permission.)*

HISTORICAL BACKGROUND

History of Chemical Warfare

Employing chemicals as weapons is hardly a recent phenomenon. Chemicals have been used by states and other groups to hurt or incapacitate their enemies as far back as the Peloponnesian Wars (431–404 BCE) when Thucydides recorded the use of sulfur-based smokes and arsenic clouds. It was only with the technological advances of the twentieth century, however, that chemical weapons (CW) achieved the status of true weapons of mass destruction.

The first major chemical attack occurred during World War I (1914–18) at Ypres in Belgium. On April 22, 1915, the German army released copious amounts of chlorine gas from cylinders on the battlefield, causing at least 2,800 casualties. Both sides, however, quickly learned to take protective measures such as wearing gas masks, and chlorine soon became a relatively ineffective weapon. In July 1917, therefore, the Germans began to use a new agent called mustard, which after a brief delay affects the eyes and lungs, causing the skin to become extremely irritated and blister. A combination of this and similar agents and the delivery of chemicals by artillery shell made chemical warfare far more harmful than before. In total, a massive 124,000 tons of chemical agent munitions were de-livered by both sides during World War I. Yet the use of chemicals resulted in only about 1.3 percent of total battlefield deaths in the war. Chemical weapons were far more effective because of the fear, confusion, and consequent loss of morale they caused than because of their lethal effects.

Despite the scorn towards chemical weapons displayed by most nations after the World War I, Italy, under the fascists, used mustard in bombs and spray devices during its invasion of Ethiopia in 1935–36. Also during the 1930s, the lethality of chemical weapons was greatly enhanced by the de-velopment of organophosphates (phosphorus-containing compounds often used in insecticides). This led to the creation of the so-called nerve agents such as sarin, soman, and later VX. Aside from Japan's use of World War I-era chemicals in China, however, none of the aforementioned chemicals were ever used on the battlefields in World War II (1939–45). The non-use of CW in World War II probably had much to do with the threat of retaliation, although several other factors may have come into play. World War II, however, did witness the deadliest use of chemicals in hu-man history as millions of Jewish and other civil-ians were murdered by the Nazis using Zyklon B, a derivative from the civilian pesticide industry that released hydrogen cyanide gas.

POEM ON CHEMICAL ATTACKS

Gas! GAS! Quick, boys!—
  An ecstasy of fumbling
Fitting the clumsy helmets just in time,
But someone still was
  yelling out and stumbling
And flound'ring like a man in fire or lime.—
Dim through the misty panes
  and thick green light,
As under a green sea, I saw him drowning.
In all my dreams before my helpless sight
He plunges at me,
  guttering, choking, drowning.

from Dulce et Decorum Est, *by Wilfred Owen, 1918.*
Available online at http://www.hcu.ox.ac.uk/jtap/warpoems.htm#12.

During the Cold War, the United States and the Soviet Union stockpiled unprecedented amounts of chemical weapons—approximately 40,000 tons by the Soviet Union and 30,000 tons by the United States. Despite these formidable arsenals, neither superpower dared to use CW directly against one another during the Cold War, and in 1969 President Richard Nixon (1969–74) declared that the United States would not be the first side to use chemical weapons in any conflict.

Nonetheless, chemical weapons were utilized during the years of the Cold War. When Egypt intervened in the civil war in Yemen in the 1960s, it made use of chemical agents. The most widespread post-World War I use of chemical weapons against personnel occurred during the Iran-Iraq conflict from 1980 to 1988. Iraq, facing human wave attacks from neighboring Iran, used both nerve and blister agents on Iranian troops. Later in the war, Iran also employed chemical weapons, albeit minimally. Iraq found its chemical weapons fairly effective on the battlefield, but also viewed CW as a way to deter opposition to Iraqi leader Saddam Hussein's acts of intimidation towards neighbors in the Gulf region. By the time of the Gulf War of 1991 the U.S.-led coalition was extremely wary of Iraq's chemical arsenal and took measures to protect themselves through masks and protective clothing.

Whatever the present military effectiveness of chemical weapons actually is, one event showed the lethal efficiency of chemical weapons when used against civilians. In 1988 the Iraqi government used several types of chemical weapons against the Kurdish village of Halabjah. At least 4,000 civilians were killed in this attack.

Several attempts have been made by states to ban the use of chemical weapons. Both the Hague Conference of 1907 and the 1925 Geneva Protocol tried to forbid the use of chemical weapons (with various exceptions and exemptions), but these treaties did little to prevent the use or stockpiling of chemical weapons from World War I onwards. The Chemical Weapons Convention (CWC), which came into force on April 29, 1997, represents the next major step in chemical arms control in that it bans both the use and the production or possession of chemical weapons and makes provision for inspections in order to ensure compliance with the treaty. There are also voluntary efforts by like-minded states to prevent the spread of chemical weapons, such as the Australia Group, which attempts to control some of the trade in the precursors and equipment used to make chemical weapons.

Why Would Chemical Agents Be Attractive to Terrorists?

Why might terrorists find chemical weapons and agents attractive—in some cases even preferable to—conventional, nuclear, radiological, or biological weapons? Conventional weapons include almost any type of bomb or gun; nuclear weapons harness the power within atoms to cause devastating explosions; radiological weapons cause harm by emitting dangerous levels of radiation; and biological weapons use dangerous biological organisms to cause disease. Chemical agents, when used effectively, have the potential for causing far more casualties than any conventional explosive and may appear, at least on the surface, attractive to any group with this end in mind. There are, however, many reasons why terrorists would choose conventional over unconventional weapons, even if they want to cause large numbers of casualties. Explosives and hijacked planes, for instance, are cheaper, more reliable, are generally easier to acquire and use, and can cause sufficient destruction to achieve terrorist goals. Why then is there so much concern about terrorists getting their hands on chemical agents?

Three of the advantages for terrorists conducting a chemical attack will be examined: the physical and psychological vulnerability of targets; the flexibility of these weapons; and the growing ease with which these agents can be acquired and utilized.

Vulnerability. Chemical agents work best when concentrated over a limited area. Modern society

UN WORKERS IN IRAQ SEAL LEAKING ROCKETS ALLEGEDLY FILLED WITH THE CHEMICAL NERVE AGENT SARIN. IRAQ HAS LONG BEEN FEARED BY OTHER NATIONS POSSESSING CHEMICAL AND BIOLOGICAL WEAPONS. *(AP/Wide World Photos. Reproduced by permission.)*

is largely made up of densely populated areas with complex transportation networks carrying thousands of passengers at any given point in time. Large cities are thus particularly susceptible to a chemical attack, making chemical agents an ideal weapon to those terrorists seeking to maximize casualties.

On the psychological level, anthropologists have observed an almost universal loathing for poisons and impurities. People often display a disproportionate amount of fear for anything that can enter the body unnoticed and harm them from within. Historical evidence from the use of chemical weapons in war indicates that these weapons cause considerable panic and confusion. They are

also faster acting than biological agents, while inducing similar psychological effects of contamination. A significant goal of any terrorist act is to instill fear in a wider population, often referred to as the secondary target (where the primary target is the set of direct victims of an attack). Therefore, in a civilian context, where any event is magnified by the media, a chemical attack is likely to give terrorists all the terror and propaganda they seek.

Flexibility. While not nearly as wide ranging in applications, or as easy to use as conventional weapons like guns and bombs, chemical agents have certain tactical advantages over other weapons of mass destruction (WMD). First of all, they are the

BHOPAL

The Bhopal incident occurred on December 3, 1984, in Bhopal, India, when methyl isocyanate, a toxic industrial chemical used in insecticide production, leaked out of the Union Carbide plant. Jessica Stern in *The Ultimate Terrorists* (1999) lists the number of dead as 4,000 with 11,000 injuries. The Indian government alleged the incident to be an accident that was the result of inadequate safety measures on the part of the Union Carbide Company. Even though Union Carbide agreed to a settlement compensating victims, its own inquiry and a separate investigation performed on its behalf by Arthur D. Little, Inc. concluded that the toxic release was an act of sabotage. A disgruntled employee, presumably seeking only to hamper production, connected a water hose to a tank of methyl isocyanate, leading to the disaster. Although the Bhopal tragedy does not really qualify as terrorism, since the perpetrator did not intend to cause so many deaths, it does highlight the danger that even a single individual can pose when dealing with toxic chemicals.

only type of unconventional weapon which has a decent track record—military officers from World War I onwards have had substantial success causing casualties with chemical agents. While all weapons of mass destruction are inherently indiscriminate in their action, chemical agents can also be used in a more controlled fashion, involving more discriminate attacks on limited targets, such as a specific building. This would be impossible with, for instance, a nuclear explosive. Another attractive aspect is that a terrorist need not go to all the trouble of acquiring an agent that has been weaponized by states, such as VX, in order to cause mass casualties. There is a much broader range of chemicals, including certain classes of pesticides and industrial chemicals, that still have toxic effects, even if these are less than military-grade CW agents. If terrorists are already set on using unconventional weapons, the flexibility and success rate of chemical weapons may influence them to choose them over biological, nuclear, or radiological agents.

Relative Ease of Acquisition and Use. At least on a theoretical basis, chemical agents are easier to deliver to their targets than are biological or radiological agents. Certain volatile chemicals such as sarin will vaporize at room temperature and fill an enclosed space with toxic fumes. These and other natural properties of certain chemicals, combined with increases in terrorists' capability to ac-

quire and use these weapons, make chemical agents especially suitable for the terrorist who wants to cause maximum mayhem with minimal effort using a weapon of mass destruction.

One factor in the increasing chemical capability of terrorists is the access to dangerous chemicals. There is the concern that terrorists will acquire either chemical agents or completed chemical weapons from countries with unsecured storage facilities. The primary concern here is the states of the former Soviet Union, which produced thousands of tons of chemical agents and weapons. Lapses in discipline and morale of underpaid soldiers and scientists in this region since the collapse of the Soviet Union make it possible that at least small amounts of these materials have been or will be stolen and smuggled to terrorist groups. While small amounts of chemical materials and munitions are insufficient for use in a state-level program, they may be perfectly suitable for a terrorist attack. Terrorists may not even need to procure materials from state-level programs; the growth of advanced chemical industries, even in less-developed countries, means that the basic building blocks of many toxic chemical agents are easily found in any country with commercial chemical production.

Another recent development is the spread of the 'how to' of chemical weapons. The formulae and production processes for toxic chemicals have always been well known among the scientific community. The difference now is that specific details for developing these agents are being made accessible to anyone who is adept at using the Internet, and this presumably includes many terrorist groups and violent individuals. In addition to chemical materials leaking out of the former Soviet Union, there is the danger of terrorist groups recruiting or hiring chemists who used to work in the Soviet chemical weapons programs, but are now unemployed or unpaid in the cash-strapped successor republics.

Advances in technology may aid those terrorists who decide to develop their own agents. If they obtain the correct precursor chemicals, they can make use of new miniaturized chemical production equipment to produce these agents on a fairly large scale in tiny facilities like basements.

The easiest way for a terrorist group to acquire a chemical weapons capability is to be given one by a state. Several states that are known or suspected to have chemical weapons programs of their own—such as North Korea, Iran and Libya—have also been accused of sponsoring terrorism. Although there is no proof that any such transfer has occurred, government officials fear that these countries may make nuclear, chemical, or biological agents, and perhaps even operational weapons, available to their terrorist proxies.

Who Is Most Likely to Use Chemical Weapons?

It would appear that a relatively small subset of terrorists would go to all the trouble to launch a chemical attack rather than detonate a large conventional bomb. There are those for whom the factors making chemical terrorism attractive outweigh the greater ease of using conventional weapons, the moral prohibitions on mass casualties, and the costs in terms of lost support and retribution.

In the past decade, terrorist attacks seem to have become bloodier. The Tokyo subway sarin attack of 1995, the Oklahoma City (1995) and East African bombings (1998), and finally the attacks on the World Trade Center and the Pentagon in 2001 have all shown that terrorists have become more willing to cause mass casualties. In the 1980s noted terrorism scholar Brian Jenkins proclaimed that, "[t]errorists want a lot of people watching, not a lot of people dead." It seems that now they want a lot of people watching *and* a lot of people dead.

Scholars such as Bruce Hoffmann and Jessica Stern have associated this increased violence with the rise of religion-based terrorist groups. These are fundamentalist religious groups representing either extremist versions of the world's major religions or new, obscure religious beliefs, often in the form of cults. Islamic Jihad and Aum Shinrikyo are examples of such groups. Hoffmann, Stern, and others have further identified terrorist groups or individuals motivated by religion as the most likely to use weapons of mass destruction. They give various reasons for this. Religious terrorists often do not have a political constituency and are therefore less concerned about losing public support if they use weapons of mass destruction. They have radically different moral values, dehumanizing their perceived enemies and often viewing violence as a divine duty. They are sometimes even willing to inflict this violence on a large scale. Religious terrorists have also been known to seek to obliterate their enemies rather than make a symbolic point.

Several religious groups, particularly cults, have been known to display an apocalyptic outlook—they want to bring about the end of the world and may view weapons of mass destruction as the best way to do this. Certain aspects of unconventional weapons may make them especially attractive to terrorists motivated by extreme religious beliefs. For example, the very idea of bringing about death

PROPERTIES OF CHEMICAL WEAPONS

- Chemical weapons are made from more basic chemicals called **precursors**, many of which have legitimate uses in industry.

- Just possessing a chemical agent does not make it a usable weapon—the agent must be put together with a delivery system capable of causing harm. That is, it must be **weaponized**.

- The **persistence** of a chemical weapon refers to the length of time that the agent contaminates the immediate environment after release. For example, hydrogen cyanide is not very persistent in the open air, as it disperses very quickly.

- Chemical weapons are **very rarely gases** at room temperature. Rather they are often used in the form of tiny droplets of liquid called **aerosols** that float in the air. This is why we don't say 'mustard gas' or 'sarin gas' but rather mustard or sarin.

- Many chemical weapons are dangerous to make, especially in large quantities, and require specialized equipment. This, however, is not always the case for small-scale production.

and panic through a silent, invisible toxic cloud could fit a cult's vision of divine punishment better than a car bomb. Furthermore, cults often have ample resources in terms of finances and sometimes have members with technical expertise.

It may be that the most likely perpetrators of mass-casualty chemical terrorism would be religiously motivated terrorists, or terrorists who share many of the characteristics of these groups. For more limited chemical attacks, there is a much bigger pool of potential perpetrators.

Past Chemical Terrorism Incidents

The Monterey Weapons of Mass Destruction Terrorism Database records 230 politically or ideologically motivated incidents involving chemical agents from 1945 to January 2002. Only 35 of these incidents were hoaxes, pranks, or solely threats. The remaining 195 incidents include uses, possessions, and plots by subnational groups or individuals involving chemical agents. Chemical agents are by far the most common type of agent utilized

TYPES OF CHEMICAL WEAPONS

There are four classes of chemical weapons that have been used by states in the past and could be used by terrorists:

Choking Agents include: *chlorine, phosgene (CG)*

- Act on the airways and lungs, causing inflammation and in high enough doses leads to suffocation.

- Responsible for so-called 'dry land drowning' in World War I.

- Nonpersistent gases.

Blister Agents (Vesicants) include: *mustard (H, HD), Lewisite (L)*

- Act on the skin, eyes and airways, causing blisters on the skin after some delay and affecting breathing. Also affects the whole body.

- Mustard was very commonly used in World War I, causing many injuries but relatively few fatalities.

- Persistent liquid that gives off vapors.

Blood Agents include: *hydrogen cyanide (AC), cyanogen chloride (CK)*

- Usually inhaled or ingested—once absorbed into the body, it shuts down the functioning of cells and causes rapid death at low dosages.

- Nonpersistent gas or liquid giving off vapors.

Nerve Agents include: *sarin (GB), tabun (GA), soman (GD), VX*

- Most toxic agents.

- Enter the body through skin, eyes, or lungs and quickly lead to seizures, convulsions and, if untreated, death.

- G-agents: nonpersistent liquids and vapor; VX: persistent liquid.

men also took an active interest in chemical weapons. Believing they were defending the United States from a communist takeover, they gathered literature relating to producing and disseminating nerve agents, and their leader, Robert Bolivar DePugh, alleged that he had made homemade nerve 'gas' and tested it on his dog with fatal results.

An unconfirmed report notes that in Vienna in 1975, German entrepreneurs were arrested while attempting to sell the nerve agent tabun to Palestinian terrorists. The late 1970s and early 1980s also yielded two examples of deliberate chemical contamination. In 1978 the Arab Revolutionary Command used liquid mercury to contaminate Israeli citrus fruit destined for Europe, causing casualties in at least three European countries and leading to a reduction of at least 40 percent in Israeli orange exports. In September 1982 seven people died in Chicago, Illinois, from taking cyanide-laced Tylenol tablets. The culprit of this poisoning was never located, and the attacks spawned a host of copycat incidents. To some extent these attacks were responsible for the later development of tamper-resistant packaging for consumer products.

Right-wing extremists also dabbled with chemical terrorism during the 1980s. In addition to the instructive case of the Covenant, the Sword, and the Arm of the Lord (see sidebar), court testimony in 1990 by members of the skinhead organization known as the Confederate Hammerskins revealed that the group had plotted to pump cyanide into a synagogue. In Asia the Liberation Tigers of Tamil Eelam (LTTE), a rebel organization in Sri Lanka, have been accused of using 'poison gas' and other chemical agents on at least three occasions between 1990 and 1995.

Aum Shinrikyo

The event having possibly the greatest impact on the public perception of the potential for terrorist use of chemical weapons was the March 20, 1995, Tokyo subway attack by the Japanese cult Aum Shinrikyo. The attack was carried out simultaneously on five separate subway trains and the cult utilized the nerve agent sarin, which it had manufactured in its own laboratories. Cult members used sharpened umbrella tips to puncture plastic bags containing sarin and then fled. The attack brought to worldwide prominence the deadly designs of this apocalyptic organization and resulted in twelve fatalities, 1,039 injuries, and at least 4,000 people with psychosomatic symptoms (the so-called 'worried well').

when considering all similar incidents, with 195 chemical incidents compared to the mere 66 of the next most common agent type, biological agents.

The story of chemical terrorism, however, is made up of more than just numbers. The first major case of modern chemical terrorism occurred when the Avengers, a group of Jewish extremists bent on revenge, poisoned German POWs in 1945 (see sidebar "Avenging Israel's Blood"). In the 1960s the right-wing group known as the Minute-

AVENGING ISRAEL'S BLOOD

After World War II a group of Jews calling themselves Avenging Israel's Blood (*Dahm Y'Israel Nokeam* or DIN) plotted to take revenge on Germans for the murder of six million Jews during the Holocaust. Avenging Israel's Blood was led by the former partisan Abba Kovner, who formulated the group's ideology of vengeance. In 1945 DIN developed Plan A, which involved poisoning water supplies across Germany in order to kill hundreds of thousands of Germans, civilians included. Plan A was later abandoned in favor of Plan B. This called for the contamination of the food consumed by German POWs in camps holding German soldiers. Plan B was scaled down to an attack on Stalag 13, an American prisoner of war camp for SS soldiers near Nuremberg. On April 13, 1946, three members of Avenging Israel's Blood spread a mixture of glue and arsenic onto loaves of black bread eaten almost exclusively by the German inmates.

A German newspaper reported that 2,283 inmates out of 15,000 fell ill after eating the tainted bread, and 207 of those were hospitalized, with no known fatalities. DIN sources estimated that 4,300 people were sickened, 1,000 hospitalized, and that 700 to 800 of those hospitalized were paralyzed or died within weeks of the incident.

Avenging Israel's Blood is in many ways a rather unique organization in that it was not motivated by politics or religion, but solely by revenge. It did, however, share characteristics with many religious fanatics, such as seeking redemption through violence, a disregard for personal safety, and the dehumanization of its victims. All of these factors allowed it to consider inflicting mass casualties, perhaps indicating a heightened danger for mass-casualty terrorism among heavily brutalized communities.

Since the early 1990s, the cult had been attempting to overthrow the Japanese government and impose a bizarre theocratic state. The cult was dominated by Shoko Asahara, a leader who promulgated apocalyptic visions. Asahara soon became fascinated by chemical weapons and initiated a program to develop several warfare agents. Aum scientists managed to synthesize sarin, tabun, soman, VX, mustard, and hydrogen cyanide. When it came to mass production, however, their results were poor and the cult succeeded in producing only about 30 liters of sarin in total. Although Aum also pursued biological, nuclear, and conventional weapons programs, its chemical operations were by far the most successful.

It is worth noting that the group produced chemical (and other) weapons for both strategic reasons—to overthrow the state and bring about Armageddon—and also at times for tactical ones, such as to dispose of enemies and divert police from raiding Aum's headquarters.

The Tokyo attack was neither the first nor the last attempt by Aum to employ dangerous chemical agents. The Monterey Chronology of Aum Shinrikyo's CBW Activities (available online at http://cns.miis.edu/pubs/reports/pdfs/aum_chrn .pdf) reveals that between 1990 and 1995, Aum attempted several chemical attacks using sarin, VX, and phosgene. These were mostly aimed at assas-

sinating individual enemies of the cult, the results of the attacks ranging from abject failures to murder. Before the subway attack, Aum had used sarin on a larger scale in June 1994 in the town of Matsumoto, killing seven people and injuring 144 in an attempt to assassinate judges ruling against the cult. Even after the subway attack, as the cult was being hunted down by Japanese police, Aum tried to set off devices that would react to release deadly hydrogen cyanide gas.

At first glance, the case of Aum Shinrikyo has ominous implications. Aum intended to kill thousands of people and came extremely close to doing so, and had succeeded in developing a large variety of chemical and other agents. Aum's use and possession of chemical weapons came as a total surprise to Japanese law enforcement and intelligence agencies.

On closer analysis, however, the case of Aum Shinrikyo may not be the vanguard of chemical terrorism that it may at first appear. Aum was an almost unique terrorist organization. With an estimated 40,000 followers, its membership was extremely large, and it had extensive financial resources (perhaps as high as US$1 billion) and many highly skilled personnel. It invested five years' worth of research and resources into developing chemical weapons. Yet all this investment and dedication yielded surprisingly limited results with

THE COVENANT, SWORD, AND THE ARM OF THE LORD

In 1985 federal law enforcement authorities found a small survivalist group called the Covenant, Sword, and the Arm of the Lord (CSA) in possession of a drum of potassium cyanide. CSA apparently intended to poison the water supplies of major US cities. Led by James Ellison, CSA based its ideology on the Christian Identity movement, holding anti-Semitic, racist, and apocalyptic beliefs. It also plotted to overthrow the U.S. government. CSA devised the water poisoning scheme in the belief that it could bring about the return of the messiah more quickly by punishing unrepentant sinners. The plot failed when its compound was raided by U.S. government officials, although the amount of cyanide they possessed would in any case have been too small to cause any harm to the water supply of a major city.

This case has several interesting aspects with regards to the prospects for chemical terrorism. The first and perhaps most relevant point is that the group's only objective in using cyanide was mass murder rather than changing government policy. Second, the group believed it was on a divine mission and was not concerned with offending a broader constituency. Third, the CSA chose an industrial chemical (potassium cyanide) instead of trying to develop a more toxic agent like sarin. The fourth point is that the CSA was easily penetrated by law enforcement—today similar groups are far more careful.

After the first World Trade Center attack in 1993, it was widely believed that the terrorists had placed cyanide-producing compounds in their bomb. There is no evidence to suggest that this was the case, but Ramzi Yousef, the leader of the group that perpetrated the bombing, later disclosed to a U.S. Secret Service agent after he was captured that his original intent was to include cyanide in the bomb. Fortunately, according to

the testimony of Brian Parr in Yousef's trial (*United States of America v Ramzi Ahmed Yousef and Eyad Ismoil,* S1293CR.180 [KTD], October 22, 1997, pp. 4730-4731), Yousef decided that "it was going to be too expensive to implement."

The most infamous cases of chemical terrorism occurred in the mid-1990s with the actions of Aum Shinrikyo, the Japanese doomsday cult, which will be discussed in more detail later. In 1997 authorities raided the home of James Dalton Bell, an antigovernment activist, and discovered a variety of chemicals. Mr. Bell had apparently admitted to friends that he had produced a quantity of sarin nerve agent. On August 6, 1997, another lone perpetrator named Valery Borzov was arrested in Moscow, Russia, for trying to sell homemade mustard agent. Abortion clinics seem to have become popular targets for attacks using chemicals in the latter half of the 1990s, with several incidents in 1998 involving butyric acid, a mildly toxic and very foul-smelling chemical.

The cases described above are only a small percentage of the total of recorded terrorist incidents involving chemical agents, but they are sufficient to demonstrate the broad variety that exists within chemical terrorism. There are incidents involving large, military-style groups as well as those perpetrated by individual extremists. The chemicals used range from extremely lethal warfare agents like sarin to common, commercially available chemicals, like potassium cyanide. Delivery methods are diverse, from food contamination to releasing toxic vapor. It is worthwhile to note that of the groups listed that acted or plotted to bring about mass casualties with chemical agents, almost all of them were religiously motivated or shared many traits with religious terrorists.

respect to agent quality and delivery capability. Its sarin attack on March 20, 1995 used the rather crude delivery method of puncturing plastic bags filled with sarin using sharpened umbrella tips. Moreover, the attack caused limited fatalities, mostly because the sarin was diluted. While their case certainly deserves close attention, it is doubtful whether there will be many terrorist groups with the same capabilities as Aum.

Nevertheless, the Tokyo incident certainly changed the way the world viewed terrorism—no

longer were the victims of terrorist attacks limited to several unfortunate individuals or a few hundred airplane passengers. The prospect of true mass-casualty terrorism was brought home to many for the first time. It was felt by many that the Tokyo attack removed the taboo against the use of weapons of mass destruction by terrorists, thus erasing any psychological barrier to their use which had existed previously. In other words, what had once only been a possibility was now a reality. People realized that unlike states, most terrorists

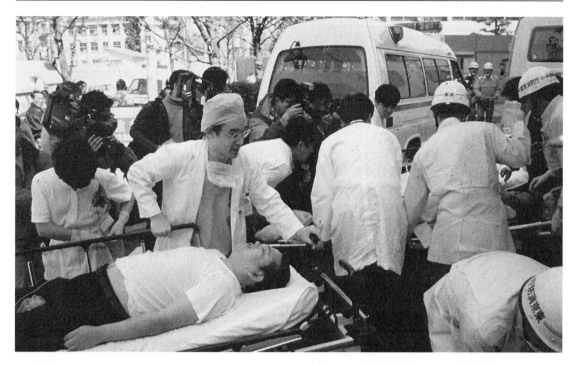

THE AUM SHINRIKYO CULT RELEASED SARIN IN A TOKYO SUBWAY ON MARCH 20, 1995. TWLEVE PEOPLE WERE KILLED AND OVER ONE THOUSAND MORE WERE INJURED IN THE FIRST SUCCESSFUL AND LARGE-SCALE CHEMICAL ATTACK BY TERRORISTS. *(AP/Wide World Photos/Chikumo Chiaki Tsukumo. Reproduced by permission.)*

have no defined "return address," and cannot be deterred from using WMD by threats of massive retaliation in kind.

The Tokyo incident arguably served as the catalyst for the widespread anxiety over terrorist use of weapons of mass destruction and led to a dramatic increase in U.S. government funding and attention to the problem. This heightened attention may also have made various governments particularly sensitive to the potential for chemical terrorism. In 1998, following the terrorist bombings of the American embassies in East Africa, the United States took the dramatic and controversial step of using cruise missiles to destroy the Al-Shaifa plant in Sudan, with the justification being that the facility was being used to produce chemical weapons destined for terrorists.

RECENT HISTORY AND THE FUTURE

Osama bin Laden, al-Qaeda, and Chemical Terrorism

The September 11 attacks in the United States focused the world's attention on one terrorist network in particular, the al-Qaeda organization, and its notoriously anti-American leader, Osama Bin

Laden. Bin Laden and the al-Qaeda network, which is an umbrella organization consisting of various groups and many largely autonomous cells, have been conducting an ongoing terrorist campaign against the West since at least 1998. Al-Qaeda has been linked with the East African embassy bombings, the assault on the USS *Cole* in Yemen in October 2000, and finally the horrendous attacks on the World Trade Center and Pentagon on September 11, 2001. Thus far, al-Qaeda has accomplished all its objectives using conventional weapons, but several concerns have been raised that it may resort to chemical terrorism.

These concerns are well founded. Bin Laden himself has on several occasions expressed his interest in acquiring weapons of mass destruction. According to a variety of newspaper reports, three meetings took place between senior members of al-Qaeda and foreign governments between 1997 and 1998, at which al-Qaeda's acquisition of chemical weapons was on the agenda. On 8 July 1999, in an article entitled "Islamic Group Said Preparing Chemical Warfare on the West," the Italian newspaper *Corriere della Serra* reported that members of the World Islamic Front Against Jews and Crusaders—which was founded by bin Laden and is part of the al-Qaeda network—had purchased three chemical and biological agent production

DESCRIPTION OF TOKYO SUBWAY ATTACK

Here is how one victim of the Tokyo subway attack describes the scene in one of the gassed train cars:

The train carries on—Shin-otsuka, Myogadani, Korakuen—and around Myogadani lots of people are beginning to cough. Of course, I'm coughing too. Everyone has his handkerchief out over his mouth or nose. A very odd scene, with everyone hacking away at the same time. As I recall, passengers started getting off at Korakuen. As if on cue, everyone was opening windows. Eyes itching, coughing, generally miserable...I didn't know what was wrong with me, it was all so strange...

Haruki Murakami. Underground: The Tokyo Gas Attack and the Japanese Psyche. *Vintage, New York: 2001.*

facilities in the former Yugoslavia in early May 1998. The article also described a similar factory that had been built near Kandahar in Afghanistan. Kenneth Katzman, a Middle East analyst and terrorism expert at the Congressional Research Service was quoted by the *Washington Post* (July 29, 1999), as saying that "we have to assume that he [Bin Laden] has some rudimentary chemical capability."

Various incidents seem to confirm these assertions. Shortly after the September 11 attack, it was reported by the *London Sunday Telegraph* (September 16, 2001) that earlier in 2001, German police had foiled a plot by an al-Qaeda cell to attack the European Parliament building in Strasbourg, France, with sarin nerve agent. al-Qaeda documents found in Afghanistan describe tests on animals with various chemical agents including cyanide gas. A group of men with possible links to al-Qaeda was also arrested in Rome, Italy, in February 2002 in possession of a cyanide-containing compound and maps of the water network in the area around the U.S. Embassy.

While there is no incontrovertible evidence that Osama bin Laden actually has the ability to conduct chemical terrorism on a large scale, there is no doubt that his organization has been exploring the possibility of conducting a chemical attack of some kind. Skeptics about the chemical threat from al-Qaeda are urged to pay heed to the recent remark by Eric Croddy in his book *Chemical and Biological Warfare: A Comprehensive Survey for the Concerned Citizen*(2002), "As recent experience has shown, however, it is dangerous to underestimate the resourcefulness of a determined adversary."

Prospects for Chemical Terrorism

From the revenge poisonings of Avenging Israel's Blood to Aum Shinrikyo's chemical attacks and al-Qaeda's quest for a toxic arsenal, chemical terrorism presents a very real and very frightening threat. Yet, in the words of Jessica Stern in her 1999 book, *The Ultimate Terrorists*, "Catastrophic risks are disproportionately feared," and in spite of the media hype and public anxiety, this threat needs to be placed in its proper context. For example, many people tend to overlook the fact that in addition to acquiring a chemical agent, a terrorist must still deliver it efficiently in order to cause mass casualties. Although crude delivery methods can be utilized—especially in enclosed areas—such as the plastic bags in the Tokyo subway attack, the most effective means of dispersal is to aerosolize the agent. This requires not only a knowledge of chemistry, but also of engineering, and took several years even for states, with all their resources, to perfect. This requires much more effort and resources than most terrorist groups have available.

While it is true that some factors, such as the dissolution of the former Soviet Union and the rise of religious groups, seem to be making chemical terrorism a slightly less challenging endeavor, this does not mean that chemical terrorism is a simple task. Even contaminating water supplies is not as simple as dumping toxic chemicals into a reservoir—dilution and water treatment will render many agents harmless and quality checks can also identify contaminants before the water gets to the public. Most experts argue that only remote water supplies, or smaller parts of a large water network, are vulnerable, lessening the chance of large numbers of casualties. As for states giving terrorists working chemical weapons, this would indeed make a chemical attack easier. The threat of retaliation from the target country and the international community, however, would dissuade all but the most foolish of states from chemical terrorism.

In the non-technical realm there are several moral obstacles that need to be dealt with before anyone will carry out a mass-casualty chemical attack, and even incentives as strong as religion may not be enough to overcome psychological restraints such as society's rejection of murder or the notion that women and children must be protected and not harmed.

The overall likelihood of chemical terrorism depends on too many factors, including unique variables like the psychological makeup of individual terrorists, to make any predictions about the prevalence of this form of terrorism in the future. Many scholars such as Jonathan Tucker and Jessica

Stern, however, believe that should terrorists engage in terrorism using unconventional weapons, they are most likely to employ chemical weapons. Furthermore, these attacks most often will be on a relatively small scale with lower-end agents. An example of this would be using a chemical agent inside a single building or contaminating individual types of foodstuffs. This does not mean that the large-scale use of a warfare agent like sarin or VX will not be seen again, but rather that this possibility is often overstated.

Combating Chemical Terrorism

The extent of the threat of chemical terrorism may not be known with any certainty, but the threat from terrorist groups is sufficiently feared that governments and the international community are devoting resources to combating it. Many of the standard counterterrorist measures apply equally well to terrorists attempting chemical attacks. These include intelligence gathering, law enforcement, diplomatic measures, and sometimes even military activities.

Some steps can be taken to combat chemical terrorism in particular. Stopping the proliferation of chemical weapons would make it more difficult for terrorists to get their hands on these agents; however, international measures such as the Chemical Weapons Convention and the Australia Group are mainly structured to prevent states from obtaining chemical weapons. They are therefore not designed to prevent or monitor the transfer of the smaller amounts of chemical agents that terrorists would seek. On the technology front, there are detectors that can provide early warning of a chemical attack, although these are not yet reliable enough for widespread use across an entire country. One of the best ways to combat chemical terrorism is to be prepared in order to minimize casualties should an attack occur. Both nerve and blood agent exposure can be treated if antidotes are administered quickly enough. Having sufficient antidotes, decontamination equipment, and trained emergency personnel in place can vastly reduce the number of fatalities in a chemical attack.

After Aum Shinrikyo's Tokyo subway attack and the Oklahoma City bombing in 1995, the U.S. government started paying much more attention to chemical and other forms of unconventional terrorism. Federal spending on defense against terrorism using weapons of mass destruction increased more than ten times from $130 million in 1997 to $1.45 billion in 2000; President Bill Clinton

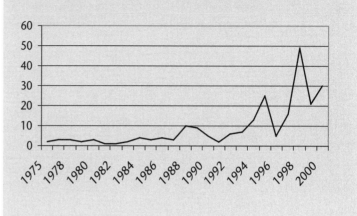

NUMBER OF CHEMICAL INCIDENTS (INCLUDING HOAXES) INVOLVING SUB-NATIONAL ACTORS, 1975–2000

NUMEROUS INCIDENTS—ACTUAL AND HOAXES—WERE CARRIED OUT BY TERRORISTS AND CRIMINALS BETWEEN 1975 AND 2000. *(Gale Group.)*

(1993–2001) issued Presidential Decision Directives (PDDs) in both 1995 and 1998 structuring government reaction to this kind of attack; in 1996 Congress passed the "Defense Against Weapons of Mass Destruction Act" (which became known as the Nunn-Lugar-Domenici Program) to train first responders to deal with a weapons of mass destruction attack; numerous organizations such as a Metropolitan Medical Response System were created to help manage the effects of an attack; and a national pharmaceutical stockpile was created, which in the event of a chemical attack would provide antidotes and medical equipment where needed. Some commentators have criticized these federal programs by calling them uncoordinated and often redundant. It is hoped that the new Office of Homeland Security, formed in reaction to the September 11 attacks, will be able to better coordinate these efforts.

Conclusion

The existence of groups and individuals who are actively pursuing a chemical capability and who seek to use it to inflict mass casualties can no longer be disputed. Eventually one of these groups may succeed in their endeavors. It is thus of little surprise that Western publics and their government officials have become particularly concerned about the threat of chemical terrorism, especially after the terrible events of September 11.

In order to develop and deliver a chemical agent that causes a large number of casualties is far more difficult than most people realize, and conventional weapons are still preferred by most terrorists. We should not, then, overstate the likelihood of chemical terrorism and cause undue alarm. Rather, we should continue the concerted effort to locate and apprehend terrorists and, in case this fails, to prepare to deal with the aftermath of a large-scale terrorist attack. In this way, we can minimize both the psychological and physical effects of this frightening form of terrorism.

BIBLIOGRAPHY

Croddy, Eric, with Clarisa Perez-Armendariz and John Hart. *Chemical and Biological Warfare: A Comprehensive Survey for the Concerned Citizen.* New York: Copernicus Books, 2002.

Falkenrath, Richard A., et al. *America's Achilles Heel: Nuclear, Biological, and Chemical Terrorism and Covert Attack.* Cambridge, MA: MIT Press, 1998.

Gurr, Nadine, and Benjamin Cole. *The New Face of Terrorism: Threats from Weapons of Mass Destruction.* London: I.B. Taurus, 2000.

Hoffmann, Bruce. "Terrorism and WMD: Some Preliminary Hypotheses," *The Nonproliferation Review.* vol. 4, no. 3 (Spring-Summer 1997).

Jenkins, Brian. *Will Terrorists Go Nuclear?* Santa Monica, CA: Rand Corporation, 1975.

Kaplan, David E. and Andrew Marshall. *The Cult at the End of the World.* New York: Crown Publishers, 1996.

Lloyd, Anthony. "Scientists Confirm bin Laden Weapons Tests," *Times* (London), December 29, 2001.

Olimpio, Guido. "Islamic Group Said Preparing Chemical Warfare on the West," *Corriere della Sera,* July 8, 1998.

Roberts, Brad, ed. *Terrorism with Chemical and Biological Weapons: Calibrating Risks and Responses.* Alexandria, VA: Free Hand Press, 1997.

Stern, Jessica. *The Ultimate Terrorists.* Cambridge, MA: Harvard University Press, 1999.

Tucker, Jonathan B., ed. *Toxic Terror: Assessing Terrorist Use of Chemical and Biological Weapons.* Cambridge, MA: MIT Press, 2000.

Zanders, Jean Pascal. "Assessing the Risk of Chemical and Biological Weapons Proliferation to Terrorists," *The Nonproliferation Review,* vol. 6, no. 4 (Fall 1999).

Gary A. Ackerman

CIVIL RIGHTS SUSPENDED

The night of January 29, 2002—just months after the most devastating terrorist attack on American soil—President George W. Bush (2001–) delivered the annual State of the Union Address to a joint session of Congress. Although he had entered office just a year earlier with an ambitious agenda of deregulation, tax cuts, and educational reform, the events of the previous September 11 had put counterterrorism at the top of the agenda. Although the president had little foreign relations experience as he began his term, his unexpected role as a wartime leader drew praise from the American public. With approval levels over 80 percent as the ground war against the al-Qaeda network, believed to be responsible for the attacks, and its supporter, the Taliban, ended in Afghanistan, Bush now called for a continuation of efforts against "an axis of evil":

> By seeking weapons of mass destruction, these regimes pose a grave and growing danger. They could provide these arms to terrorists, giving them the means to match their hatred. They could attack our allies or attempt to blackmail the United States. In any of these cases, the price of indifference would be catastrophic.

Bush then went on to detail his plans for homeland security, including more border patrols, intelligence gathering, and airport screenings.

Bush's wartime call to increased vigilance and sacrifice was the latest in a series of such presidential exhortations. During the United States' bloodiest domestic conflict, the American Civil War (1861–65), President Abraham Lincoln (1861–65) had used similar terms to explain the crackdown on Confederate sympathizers in the North. Mark E. Neely, Jr., quoted Lincoln's response to his critics in his 1991 Pulitzer Prize-winning book *The Fate of Liberty: Abraham Lincoln and Civil Liberties*: "The man who stands by and says nothing, when

THE CONFLICT

In the wake of the terrorist attacks on U.S. soil on September 11, 2001, there have been calls for increased security measures in many areas of public life. Some civil liberties and ethnic groups fear, however, that these increased security procedures may unduly infringe upon individual rights and worse, may target individuals for suspicion based solely on their ethnic background.

Political

- Both the ruling and opposition parties in any country have moved cautiously to limit civil liberties out of security concerns. In the past, political parties that have invoked limits on civil liberties have been accused of political opportunism, particularly if the limitations touch upon the right to free speech and public assembly and, therefore, political dissent. Those who have argued against curbs on civil liberties, on the other hand, have sometimes been accused of being "soft" on terrorism.

Ideological

- The conflict between individual rights and the security of a nation has increased in the age of global terrorism. While measures to keep suspected terrorists out of nations have enjoyed wide support, security measures that have an impact upon citizens' daily lives have been more controversial. Although many countries have instituted national identification cards for their citizens, such a step has not been undertaken in the United States, where political leaders are hesitant to take steps that might infringe upon one's privacy although it is currently being discussed.

Social

- Because terrorist groups in some regions draw their membership from a particular ethnic, religious, or social group, efforts to draw profiles of potential terrorists have been accused of constituting racial or ethnic profiling. In light of attacks in the U.S. by terrorists associated with the al-Qaeda group, many Arab Americans fear that they will be unfairly singled out for scrutiny by government officials looking for Islamic militant terrorists.

CHRONOLOGY

September 24, 1862 The right of *habeas corpus* is suspended by U.S. president Abraham Lincoln during the American Civil War.

1917 The Espionage Act is passed by U.S. Congress and gives federal agents broad arrest powers against individuals suspected of treason or antiwar activity. The act remains in force even after the end of World War I in November 1918.

June 2, 1919 Anarchists set off bombs in eight American cities, including one on the front porch of Attorney General A. Mitchell Palmer.

November 1919–March 1920 Palmer Raids conducted by federal agents round up thousands of suspected radicals. The raids end when Attorney General A. Mitchell Palmer predicts a general radical uprising for May 1, 1920, which does not occur.

February 19, 1942 Under Executive Order 9066, Japanese Americans on the West Coast are detained in internment camps. The internment lasts until December 1944.

1950 The McCarran Act gives the U.S. Justice Department the power to detain alien residents indefinitely during their deportation hearings and requires all Communist Party members to register with the Attorney General.

February 1950 Republican senator Joseph R. McCarthy tells a Wheeling, West Virginia, audience that the U.S. State Department is riddled with communists. A Senate hearing later labels the charge a hoax.

1974 The British Parliament passes the Prevention of Terrorism Act, granting police broad-based arrest and exclusion powers.

Late 1987 Palestinian terrorists declare the *Intifada* uprising against Israeli authority in the Occupied Territories. The *Intifada,* accompanied by suicide bombings, is renewed in late 2000.

September 11, 2001 Terrorist attacks on United States level the World Trade Center towers and nearby buildings in New York City, while the Pentagon in Arlington, Virginia, near Washington, DC, is also attacked.

October 26, 2001 President George W. Bush signs the USA Patriot Act into law, granting a wide range of new powers to domestic law enforcement and intelligence agencies.

November 13, 2001 President Bush issues a Military Order allowing summary trials by three-person military commission of noncitizens accused of terrorism.

December 13, 2001 The British Parliament passes the Anti-Terrorism, Crime, and Security Act over the objections of civil liberties groups.

January 8, 2002 U.S. Department of Justice announces the roundup of 6,000 Middle Eastern men subject to deportation hearings on visa violations.

the peril of his government is discussed, can not be misunderstood. If not hindered, he is sure to help the enemy. Much more, if he talks ambiguously— talked for his country with 'buts' and 'ifs' and 'ands.'"

From "the man who stands by" in Lincoln's day to the "price of indifference" in the contemporary United States, then, presidents have drawn on numerous images to justify aggressive wartime actions that would seem undemocratic in peacetime. Behind the stirring rhetoric, however, striking a balance between security and civil liberties has always been a challenge. Lincoln's suspension of *habeas corpus* remains one of the most controversial measures of his tenure; the internment of Japanese Americans during World War II (1939–45) has similarly been criticized as an unjustified action, despite its proponents' insistence that it was necessary in the greater fight for security. In the contemporary era, similar debates have followed the enactment of stringent security measures in efforts against terrorism, including the counterterrorism acts designed to combat the Irish Republic Army in Northern Ireland and the Palestinian Liberation Organization in the Middle East. Indeed, each of these actions has highlighted the fundamental conflict between the preservation of civil liberties and a comprehensive effort against terrorism.

HISTORICAL BACKGROUND

Suspension of Civil Liberties During the Civil War and Reconstruction

President Lincoln made a series of politically risky decisions to suspend the right of *habeas corpus* during the course of the Civil War. Enshrined in the U.S. Constitution in Article 1, *habeas corpus* ("you have the body" in Latin) protected citizens against unlawful imprisonment. In its typical invocation, a writ of *habeas corpus* was used to bring the detainee before a court or tribunal to determine whether he or she should be detained on criminal charges. Lincoln first suspended *habeas corpus* on April 27, 1861, in an area of Maryland that he feared might oppose the movement of Union troops into the capital from the north. Two weeks later, Lincoln suspended *habeas corpus* in Florida to allow Union officers to detain suspected rebels. In both cases, Lincoln cited the risks to public safety as well as the danger to life, liberty, and property of U.S. citizens. To Lincoln, the balance between civil liberties and national security could be summed up in a single question. As Lincoln asked Congress in a special joint session on July 4, 1861, just months after the outbreak of hostilities after the Southern states seceded, "Are all the laws, *but one,* to go unexecuted, and the government itself go to pieces, lest that one be violated?"

Through February 1862 almost 900 individuals were detained without hearings, many of them Southerners stranded in the North after the outbreak of war. On September 24, 1862, Lincoln took the more drastic step of suspending *habeas corpus* on a national basis. Although the president's order was later overturned by the Supreme Court as an infringement on congressional prerogatives, Congress itself later approved the measure as the Habeas Corpus Act on September 15, 1863. By the following November, as many as 14,000 individuals had been arrested and about 2,000 people had been detained in 25 federal prisons. While many had been imprisoned for supporting the Confederacy, others had been detained for fraud and corruption against the U.S. government. The latter group included several businessmen who had resorted to bribery to obtain lucrative government contracts.

Although Lincoln insisted that his actions were vital to ensuring public safety, the arrests that initially followed the suspension of *habeas corpus* caused many innocent people to be detained. Indeed, in his work *The Fate of Liberty,* Mark E. Neely, Jr. has concluded that the period "constituted the lowest point for civil liberties in the North during the Civil War . . . and one of the lowest

for civil liberties in all of American history." Yet the era of Reconstruction that followed the Civil War presented its own debates on civil liberties in a reunited United States. The Fourteenth Amendment to the Constitution, passed by Congress in 1866 and ratified in 1868, finally mandated full citizenship—including due process under the law and equal protection rights—for all Americans, regardless of race. In a section that outraged defeated Confederate leaders, however, the amendment also denied federal or state civil and military positions to high-ranking Confederates, except by a two-thirds vote of Congress.

Although President Andrew Johnson (1865–69) had proposed relatively lenient terms for readmitting the defeated Confederate states back into the Union, with few additional restrictions on civil liberties even for the rebellion's leaders, the series of racially restrictive Black Codes passed in the South spurred Congress to take more prohibitive measures. In 1870 and 1871 Congress therefore legislated the Enforcement Acts that attempted to guarantee the voting rights of newly freed African Americans. With the rise of vigilante violence by well-organized white mobs, Congress also passed the Ku Klux Klan Act in April 1871; the act federalized the crime of denying voting rights, jury service, or equal protection under the law to any individual and allowed federal officials to order military intervention—including the suspension of *habeas corpus*—in cases where state officials refused to act.

Mindful of the Supreme Court ruling that had denied the right to invoke *habeas corpus* to President Lincoln during the Civil War, Congress also debated granting such powers to the president during its 1875 legislative session. With interest in Reconstruction ebbing in northern states—and with reform-minded Republicans losing ground in Congress—the proposal withered away. The presidential election of 1876 formally ended Reconstruction when Republicans were forced to table their civil rights agenda in order to secure the presidency for Rutherford B. Hayes (1877–81) in a close and controversial election. With Reconstruction over, southern states moved quickly once again to deny African Americans their voting rights, social equality, and many other legal and economic rights. Federal laws and constitutional amendments to the contrary, it would take another century to achieve full *de facto* civil liberties for all Americans in the segregated South.

"Clear and Present Danger"

World War I (1914–18) witnessed the United States' next major confrontation over civil liberties,

HABEAS CORPUS

Habeas corpus—derived from the Latin term for "You have the body"—is specified as a right in the Constitution of the United States of America in Article I, Section 9: "The privilege of the Writ of *Habeas Corpus* shall not be suspended, unless when in Cases of Rebellion or invasion the public Safety may require it."

The most often invoked use of *habeas corpus* is to bring a prisoner before a judge or court. By safeguarding individuals from unlawful detention or imprisonment, *habeas corpus* is therefore an important part of the due process guaranteed by the Constitution. A writ of *habeas corpus* in itself, however, does not have any bearing on the final judgment of guilt or innocence, but only on the possibly unlawful imprisonment of that individual.

although the most controversial measures occurred after the war's end. As war raged on in Europe from August 1914 onward, U.S. leaders were hesitant to join the conflict. Incumbent president Woodrow Wilson (1913–21) even ran his 1916 presidential campaign on the promise to keep the United States out of the war. By April 1917, however, after widely publicized German atrocities against civilians and secret negotiations to bring Mexico into the war on the side of the Central Powers led by Germany and Austria-Hungary, became known, the United States entered the war on the side of the Allied Powers. Elected as a peace-keeper, Wilson now prepared the nation for war. In addition to instituting a military draft in July 1917, Wilson also worked with Congress to pass the Espionage Act of 1917, a law that set forth broad definitions of treason and antiwar activities. The law was later amended to include more drastic penalties under the Sedition Act of 1918. Under the acts, approximately 1,500 individuals were arrested for opposing the draft, criticizing U.S. policies, and speaking out against the war. Organizations suspected of fostering antiwar sentiments, such as the Industrial Workers of the World and the Socialist Party, were also singled out for arrests and, in some cases, vigilante violence. Socialist Party documents opposing the draft and the war were also banned from the U.S. mail; in light of the party's status as a legitimate political party with numerous elected officials across the United States, the move seemed to be a direct attack on free speech and political freedom.

In the most infamous arrest during the war, Socialist Party leader Eugene V. Debs was indicted under the Espionage Act after a speech he gave in Canton, Ohio, in June 1918. Debs had analyzed the war in terms of class conflict and the exploitation of the masses and noted the dangers to democracy that the United States' entry into war had wrought. He also commented favorably on the recent Russian Revolution (1917), which had led to that country's withdrawal from the war. Outraged at Debs's antiwar rhetoric, the U.S. Attorney for the Northern District of Ohio convened a grand jury to bring charges against Debs. Duly convicted and sentenced to a ten-year term under the Espionage Act, Debs was pardoned by President Warren G. Harding (1921–23) in December 1921. To many Americans, Debs would forever symbolize the danger to civil liberties that wartime hysteria could induce.

In one of its most celebrated cases, the Supreme Court justified the suspension of civil liberties in *Schenck v. United States.* In its unanimous 1919 ruling, authored by Justice Oliver Wendell Holmes, the court upheld the conviction of Charles T. Schenck for distributing antidraft pamphlets in violation of the 1917 Espionage Act. As future chief justice William H. Rehnquist quoted Holmes's decision in his 1998 book *All the Laws But One: Civil Liberties in Wartime,* "When a nation is at war many things which might be said in time of peace are such a hindrance to its efforts that their utterance will not be endured so long as men fight . . . . No court could regard them as protected by any constitutional right." Holmes later made reference to a "clear and present danger" standard for determining which words or actions would fall under such a prohibition, a vague guideline that offered little assistance to civil liberties advocates. Although the harsh Sedition Act was repealed in 1921, the Espionage Act remained on the books.

The Red Scare

The largest group of arrests under the Espionage Act occurred after the end of hostilities in Europe, which concluded in November 1918. Although the United States had helped to win the war in Europe, its leaders now feared an upsurge in civil unrest at home. The Russian Revolution of 1917, followed by similar uprisings and an outright communist takeover of Hungary in 1919, seemed to fulfill the Soviet's call for a global Communist revolution. Although various factions of the Communist Party numbered about 40,000 members in the United States, federal authorities perceived them as a major threat to public safety. When a series of bombs were sent by anarchists to government and business leaders in April and May 1919, those fears seemed justified. On June 2, 1919, another series of bombs were set off in eight American cities. One of them demolished the front porch of the home of Attorney General A. Mitchell Palmer. The bomb also blew up its carrier, a known anarchist from Philadelphia.

In response Palmer ordered a roundup of suspected communists and anarchists that began in November 1919 and lasted until March of the following year. An estimated 6,000 suspects were taken into custody in the Palmer Raids, as they became known, and hundreds of noncitizens were deported, even if they had no criminal record. The raids also precipitated an outpouring of vigilante violence against suspected radicals and other organizations that were perceived to favor a radical agenda. Even groups that were committed to democratic reform, such as the Socialist Party, fell under attack; in New York the legislature threw five of its members out of the chamber, simply because they were elected as candidates from the Socialist Party.

Attorney General Palmer, already under some criticism for his apparent grandstanding on the radical threat in preparation for a possible presidential run, finally overplayed his hand with the bold prediction of massive civil unrest scheduled for May Day 1920. When the day passed without major incident, Palmer's reputation was tarnished. In retrospect, the large-scale round up of citizens and noncitizens now appeared to be a hasty decision. Even after a truck loaded with bombs exploded at Broad and Wall Streets in New York City's financial district on September 16, 1920, killing 33 people, the public could not be roused to support Palmer's antiradical efforts. The incident was never solved, and no radical group took credit for the bombing; in his 1999 history of the area, *Divided We Stand: A Biography of New York's World Trade Center*, Eric Darnton has suggested that the bombing was an accident that occurred when a shipment of dynamite was set off by haphazard handling. Although investigations into the Broad Street bombing dragged on for another ten years, the United States' first Red Scare had ended.

Japanese American Internment

In many ways the United States' approach to World War II reflected its prior entry into World War I. Although the country's sympathies were with the Allied Powers and against the open aggression of the Axis Powers, the United States remained neutral after the outbreak of the war in Europe in September 1939. After the Japanese attack on Pearl Harbor on December 7, 1941, how-

ever, the country was at war again. Immediately, federal authorities were concerned about sabotage by citizens and noncitizens of Japanese, Italian, and German descent and considered various measures to counter such acts. In the first two months after Pearl Harbor, 2,192 Japanese, 1,393 German, and 264 Italian nationals were under detention by the U.S. Department of Justice. Although the government briefly considered a broader internment program for citizens who were born in Italy and Germany, the fact that there were more than one million people in such a category prevented any large-scale deportations. Instead, the government placed noncitizen Italian residents under travel restrictions and banned their use of short-wave radios, guns, and maps; once the immediate fears of sabotage abated, the order was rescinded by President Franklin D. Roosevelt (1933–45) in October 1942. Few Italian nationals faced restrictions on their civil liberties for the duration of the war, with only a handful excluded from sensitive military areas.

German-born citizens and resident aliens faced even fewer restrictions on their civil liberties during the war. With a longer history of immigration and assimilation than Italian immigrants, German Americans were perceived as somehow more "American," and therefore less threatening than their fellow immigrants and citizens. Although some German residents were ordered out of military zones in coastal areas, the number remained small; through July 1943 only 254 people were excluded from the Western, Eastern, and Southern Defense Commands. Even after two groups of German agents were apprehended after landing in New York and Florida in the fall of 1942, widespread suspicion against German Americans failed to materialize.

The internment of approximately 47,000 Japanese-born residents, called *Issei*, and formally barred from acquiring American citizenship, and their 80,000 American-born family members, known as *Nisei*, and citizens by virtue of their birth on American soil, contrasted greatly with the experience of other ethnic groups. In the wake of Pearl Harbor, the government moved quickly to remove anyone of Japanese ancestry from military service and instituted a series of increasingly restrictive curfews on Japanese Americans on the West Coast, where most of them lived. Under political pressure from congressmen in California, Oregon, and Washington, the Roosevelt administration finally resorted to a general deportation order against Japanese Americans under Executive Order 9066, signed by Roosevelt on February 19, 1942. The order covered the 110,000 Japanese

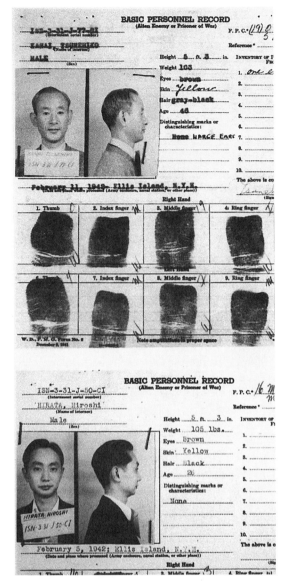

JAPANESE AMERICANS WERE CONFINED TO INTERNMENT CAMPS IN THE UNITED STATES DURING WORLD WAR II. IDENTIFICATION RECORDS LIKE THIS ONE WERE SUBTITLED "ALIEN ENEMY OR PRISONER OF WAR." FEAR OF AN ETHNIC GROUP HAS OFTEN RESULTED IN CIVIL RIGHTS VIOLATIONS FOR THOSE INDIVIDUALS—IN THE UNITED STATES AND ELSEWHERE. *(AP/Wide World Photos/Bebeto Matthews. Reproduced by permission.)*

Americans living in western states, but specifically overlooked the 158,000 ethnic Japanese living in the territory of Hawaii. Notwithstanding the Pearl Harbor attack, officials voiced their confidence in the loyalty of Japanese descendents living in Hawaii; a more realistic motivation related to the economic importance of the Japanese to the islands' economy. If any widespread internment had taken

place, Hawaii would essentially have been shut down as a staging point for the war in the Pacific. During the rest of the war, therefore, fewer than 2,000 Hawaiian Japanese were sent to internment camps, and these detainees were usually allowed to receive daily visits from their families.

While the Hawaiian Japanese were largely spared from internment due to their economic importance, Japanese living on the West Coast were targeted for internment by their business rivals. Many Japanese immigrants had built successful farming and landscaping companies, a situation that led the California Farm Bureau Federation, Western Growers Protective Association, and other business groups to lead the call for their internment. As one of the lobby stated in a *Saturday Evening Post* opinion piece reprinted in *Personal Justice Denied: Report of the Commission on Wartime Relocation and Internment of Civilians* in 1997, "We're charged with wanting to get rid of the Japs for selfish reasons. We might as well be honest. We do. It's a question of whether the white man lives on the Pacific Coast or the brown man . . . . And we don't want them back when the war ends, either."

A series of Supreme Court decisions upheld the constitutionality of the internments; although the orders were explicitly based on racial identity, they were nonetheless deemed reasonable in the interests of public safety. It was not until December 1944 that the internment order was lifted, and the over 100,000 detainees were released from the ten main relocation centers. In 1988 one of the former internees, Congressman Norman Y. Mineta, sponsored the Civil Liberties Act, which offered a formal apology by the government for its wartime actions; Congress also authorized reparation payments to detainees and their survivors of US$20,000 per individual.

The McCarthy Era: The United States' Second Red Scare

As in the wake of World War I, fears over domestic tensions characterized the post–World War II period. Once again, suspicion fell on those individuals and groups who were thought to support the Soviet Union in the nascent Cold War with the United States. As they had in the first Red Scare, labor groups were the first to feel the brunt of antiradical fears. With the passage of the Taft-Hartley Act of 1947, Communist Party members were barred from holding leadership positions in labor unions and unions themselves were banned from undertaking secondary, or "sympathy," strikes to support other unions' strikes. Although many labor leaders supported the ban on Communist Party ties, they were less than comfortable with the Taft-Hartley Act's obvious presumption that they needed to be screened for their loyalties.

While most labor unions quickly complied with the Taft-Hartley Act, fears of a communist menace soon led to investigations of the movie industry by the U.S. House Un-American Activities Committee (HUAC). Although HUAC failed to uncover any substantive communist influence in Hollywood, many writers, directors, and actors were blacklisted over their ties—real or alleged—to the Communist Party. In 1950 Congress passed the McCarran Act to force all Communist Party members to register with the U.S. Attorney General; the act also gave the Justice Department the power to detain suspect aliens during deportation hearings. Under director J. Edgar Hoover, the Federal Bureau of Investigation (FBI) also moved more aggressively to investigate alleged communist conspiracies in the United States. Invoking the 1940 Smith Act, which allowed the arrest of an individual for advocating the overthrow of the government, the FBI used its broad-based powers to begin another Red Scare similar to the one in 1919. As historian Ellen Schrecker writes in her 1998 book *Many Are the Crimes: McCarthyism in America,*" By the 1950s, American Communists had few rights that any official body had to respect. . . . They were fair game for whatever politically repressive measures ambitious politicians or right-wing ideologues might devise."

Chief among the ambitious anticommunist politicians was Wisconsin senator Joseph R. McCarthy. After declaring that the State Department was littered with communist sympathizers in a speech before a Wheeling, West Virginia, crowd in February 1950, McCarthy became the country's foremost anticommunist crusader. Although a Senate hearing later deemed McCarthy's charges bogus, his platform helped Republicans take over Congress and the White House for the first time in over twenty years. McCarthy's overblown rhetoric and outright lies, however, soon caught up with him. After opening an investigation into communist influence in the U.S. Army, it was revealed that the senator instigated the proceedings after the army had rejected one of his aides for a commissioned post. After the Army-McCarthy Hearings were televised in May and June 1954, public support for McCarthy's bullying tactics fell apart, and the country's second Red Scare faded from view. By the late 1950s, a series of Supreme Court decisions restored many of the political civil liberties

that had been suspended during the McCarthy era, and hundreds of government workers who had been suspended as a result of the loyalty investigations regained their positions.

In the decades after the McCarthy era, the Supreme Court, under Chief Justice Earl Warren, issued a number of landmark decisions that strengthened civil liberties in the United States. *Gideon v. Wainwright* (1963) established the right of an accused individual to legal counsel; *Miranda v. Arizona*, issued three years later, resulted in the well-known Miranda Rights of suspects to be informed of the charges against them, as well as their right to remain silent and to have an attorney present during police questioning. Other cases made contraceptive laws less restrictive and limited the right of the government to censor free speech. In the meantime, Congress finally acted to ensure the civil liberties of African Americans with the Civil Rights Act of 1964, which prohibited racial segregation, and the Voting Rights Act of 1965, which outlawed the literacy tests that many southern states used to keep African Americans from voting.

International Terrorism and Civil Liberties

While the United States moved to restore and safeguard civil liberties in the 1960s and 1970s, other democratic countries moved in the opposite direction in response to terrorist actions. In Northern Ireland, officials had interned suspected Irish Republican Army terrorists during their "border campaign" of bombings in the late 1950s. In the late 1960s, however, a renewed terrorist campaign commenced under the Provisional Irish Republican Army (PIRA) in support of a united Ireland free from British control. In 1970 and 1971, 199 people were killed as a result of PIRA actions, which included 153 bombings in 1970 alone. In response British authorities interned almost 2,000 suspects between August 1971 and 1975. To many observers, however, the internment of suspected PIRA members only fueled further terrorist actions; during the entire decade 2,161 people died in the violence between the PIRA and government authorities.

Of all the British policies in Northern Ireland, internment indeed caused the greatest uproar. The protests against internment led not only to violent street demonstrations—most notably the "Bloody Sunday" riots on January 30, 1972, in Derry, Northern Ireland, that left fourteen people dead—but also accusations of torture against the British government. After bombs exploded in two pubs in Birmingham, England, on November 21, 1974,

CLAIMS OF RACIAL PROFILING HAVE RISEN IN THE WAKE OF HEIGHTENED FEAR AND SECURITY EFFORTS IN THE UNITED STATES AFTER THE SEPTEMBER 11 TERRORIST ATTACKS. MANY CIVIL RIGHTS AND ETHNIC GROUPS HAVE PROTESTED THE PRACTICE. *(AP/Wide World Photos/Daniel Hulshizer. Reproduced by permission.)*

killing 21 and injuring 162 others, the British Parliament passed the Prevention of Terrorism (Temporary Provisions) Act of 1974 (PTA). The act allowed authorities to arrest suspected terrorists without a warrant and detain them for up to a week without filing charges against them. Suspected terrorists could also be deported from England to Northern Ireland. As quoted in J. Bowyer Bell's *The Irish Troubles: A Generation of Violence 1967–92* (1993), Home Secretary Roy Jenkins of Britain echoed the words of U.S. Supreme Court justice Oliver Wendell Holmes in justifying the legislation: "These powers are draconian," he admitted, "In combination, they are unprecedented in peacetime. I believe they are fully justified to meet the clear and present dangers."

The ongoing controversies over internment, however—particularly the practices of isolating detainees and forcing them to wear hoods over their heads—resulted in a formal complaint by the Republic of Ireland against the British government with the European Commission of Human Rights. Closed-door hearings began on October 25, 1973, and continued through March 1975. The final report, issued on September 3, 1976, condemned five specific practices against detainees—including deprivation of food and sleep, noise bombardment, forced standing at attention, and hooding—that

constituted torture under the European Convention on Human Rights and Fundamental Freedoms. The unanimous decision also faulted the British government for refusing to cooperate with the inquiry. There was no international legal recourse to put an end to the practices, however, and the British government ignored the commission's decision. In December 2001 the British Parliament passed updated legislation that retained many aspects of the PTA. In addition to exempting Britain from the European Convention on Human Rights with its provision for allowing indefinite detention of suspected terrorists without filing charges, the new Anti-Terrorism, Crime, and Security Act criminalized supporting, assisting, or failing to report terrorist activities.

Since its founding in 1948, the nation of Israel has also had to balance the "clear and present danger" of terrorist threats with its own democratic form of government and the guarantee of civil liberties. In addition to numerous military conflicts with its neighbors, Israel has also faced Palestine Liberation Organization (PLO) terrorists bent on achieving sovereignty over a Palestinian homeland. The PLO launched its first attacks on Israel in 1965 with a series of 35 bombings. After Israel's victory over Egypt in a brief war in 1967, Israel took control of the Gaza Strip, the West Bank, and other

BRITAIN'S NEW ANTITERROR LAWS: A THREAT TO CIVIL LIBERTIES?

In Britain, as in the United States, there has been a sharpened focus on the prevention of terrorism and the punishment of those who perpetrate it. In the same vein as the USA PATRIOT Act, Britain has developed its own antiterror legislation. The laws outline the proper avenues by which to deal with terrorists in Britain. Civil liberties organizations in Britain, however, have concerns that the new law will infringe upon the civil rights of Britain's inhabitants, particularly immigrants and naturalized citizens.

Under the new antiterror laws, British authorities are allowed to detain suspected foreign terrorists without trial for up to six months before their case is reviewed. After the six-month waiting period, the case is reviewed every six months, and the number of reviews is indefinite. This means that the period of detention prior to trial could potentially stretch on for years. Britain has similar court procedures to the United States, and one of a suspect's rights is that of a speedy trial. Many Muslims living in Britain feel that the law is a threat to

their civil rights, and due to their religious beliefs, they fear they could be considered "suspects" and subject to the new detention laws.

Although there are some concerns with the ability of British authorities to detain suspected terrorists, there are other measures that British lawmakers have taken to assure that civil rights are not infringed upon. The original bill contained a religious hatred clause, making the incitement of religious hatred a crime. That part of the bill was removed and is not expected to be reintroduced at any time. The law also limits the powers of police and other security services regarding the ability to look through confidential records.

Despite the concessions made by British lawmakers, the new laws still remain a concern. Britain, like the United States, has a balancing act to maintain between national security and the rights of individuals—protecting both, and compromising neither. Only time will tell how well the scales balance.

---

lands known as the Occupied Territories. The Occupied Territories increased the number of Palestinians living under Israeli control, and violence between the groups became an almost daily occurrence in these territories. After the PLO announced the *Intifada* (or "shaking off" of Israeli authority) in late 1987, it stepped up its terrorist campaign even as it courted legitimate recognition from the international community.

Israeli law already allowed authorities to hold suspected terrorists indefinitely without trial, and an unknown number of Palestinians (numbering at least in the thousands) were detained or deported in the first years of the *Intifada*. International observers also noted an upswing in the violence meted out by the Israeli military against Palestinian demonstrators in the Occupied Territories. Although the tensions were reduced after the withdrawal of Israeli troops from much of the Occupied Territories under a series of accords from 1993 to 1997, Israeli citizens continued to face terrorist threats on a daily basis. Indeed, with about 10 percent of the country's gross national product

spent on defense, Israel remains one of the most security-conscious places on earth.

Few aspects of everyday life in Israel—from checking into a hotel, entering an office building, visiting a shopping mall, or picking someone up at the airport—are untouched by security measures. Cars are searched for explosives before being allowed to park in some shopping areas, and regulations dictate where possible terrorist targets such as gas stations can be located. The government rigorously screens all employees who man security checkpoints, and in sensitive locations such as airports, every single employee is screened regardless of the position. Individuals at border crossings are also extensively interrogated regarding their travel plans, source of income, contacts in Israel, and many other personal issues. The government-owned airline, El Al, screens passengers according to the profiles of possible terrorists, a practice that critics liken to racial profiling. Yet Israel's leaders defend their rigorous controls as a necessity, given the region's history of terrorism. As Major General David Tsur, head of Israel's Public Security Department, told *Fortune* in Nelson D. Schwarts's

January 2002 article "Learning from Israel, "When you do security [in Israel], you take the chance you will offend people. You can invade somebody's privacy and they accept it. That's the price you pay when the cost of terrorism is so high." Israel's efforts have prevented hijackings from occurring, save for a single incident in 1968; suicide bombers, however, have continued to kill dozens of Israelis in an average of two attacks per month through the end of 2001 in a renewed *Intifada* sponsored by Palestinian terrorists.

RECENT HISTORY AND THE FUTURE

Post-September 11 security efforts in the United States adopted aspects of both the British and Israeli contemporary models, although some trends reflected the country's own prior experiences with terrorism. Through December 2001 the FBI detained 1,200 individuals for questioning—the largest roundup since the internment of Japanese Americans, and before that, the Palmer Raids—and at the end of the year 500 of the suspects remained in custody. Indeed, while the FBI's sudden sweep caused some civil libertarians to point to the Palmer Raids as a point of comparison, others noted that almost all of the detainees were from the Middle East or South Asia and questioned whether they were picked up based on the evidence or, like Japanese Americans in World War II, based on race. Federal officials reassured the public, however, that the FBI had acted on solid leads and that the racial identities of the detainees merely coincided with the fact that many terrorist groups currently operated in the Middle East and South Asia.

More controversial to civil libertarians was the suspension of some legal rights to noncitizen detainees that American citizens took for granted. Under the USA Patriot Act, passed by Congress in the wake of the September 11 attacks, immigration officials could hold suspects for a week without charging them and indefinitely if the detainee was judged to be a national security threat. In November 2001 Attorney General John Ashcroft announced that the Justice Department was allowed to listen in on conversations between attorneys and clients held in federal custody without first getting a court order to do so. Ashcroft insisted that the eavesdropping would be used only in a small number of cases.

In conjunction with the Military Order issued on November 13, 2001, by President Bush, however, the Attorney General's action seemed ominous. Under the Military Order, any noncitizen suspected of being a member of al-Qaeda, engaging in or supporting terrorist actions, or harboring a terrorist was exempt from the rules of evidence and legal framework of the U.S. criminal justice system. Instead, suspects would be held by the Department of Defense at any location, even outside of the United States, until their release or trial before a military tribunal. Unlike a criminal court, only a two-thirds majority of the three-person tribunal was necessary for conviction, and evidence could be withheld from the defense team in the interest of national security. The individual also had no right to appeal the decision after conviction.

While the Military Order guaranteed the right of detainees to humane treatment, including religious freedom, medical care, adequate food, water, and shelter, the first large group of about 150 suspected terrorists held under the order at a U.S. military base at Guantanamo Bay, Cuba, raised concerns about its implementation. Although no evidence of inhumane treatment was reported, groups such as Amnesty International labeled the government's actions a form of intimidation and humiliation, particularly after the first batch of prisoners was transported while hooded and blindfolded. The indefinite detention at Guantanamo Bay also troubled international rights activists who questioned their legal status. The U.S. government refused to grant them prisoner-of-war status—therefore exempting the detainees from the Geneva Conventions—and it remained to be seen whether the suspected terrorists would be tried before an international tribunal, in U.S. federal court, in the criminal justice systems of their home countries, or before some sort of military tribunal.

Controversies Over Profiling and Citizenship Requirements

While the Bush administration moved to allay international criticism over the detention of the prisoners at Guantanamo Bay, its popularity remained remarkably high at home. It moved gingerly, however, to avoid controversy over the increased use of the Computer Assisted Passenger Prescreening System (CAPPS), which some likened to racial profiling. The use of racial or ethnic identities to compile profiles of potential criminals had come under attack in a number of high-profile cases, including the 1999 firing of New Jersey police superintendent Colonel Carl Williams, Jr., after he stated that racial minorities were more likely to engage in drug-related crimes. Sensitive to these concerns, the U.S. Justice Department conducted a study that resulted in the 2001 ruling that CAPPS was not ethnically discriminatory—it used a number of factors in

THE USA PATRIOT ACT

On October 26, 2001, President George W. Bush signed into law the "Uniting and Strengthening America By Providing Appropriate Tools Required to Intercept and Obstruct Terrorism Act of 2001." The act, which is better known as the USA PATRIOT Act, was drafted and passed in less than five weeks, with little public debate or hearing as to its contents or effects on U.S. law. Both the House of Representatives and the Senate handily passed the bill, despite opposition and concerns about the act's ramifications regarding the civil rights of both citizens and noncitizens who are in the United States for legitimate reasons.

The act, touted as increasing the powers of the government for the strict purposes of counter- and antiterrorism measures, allows government agencies, especially the FBI and Central Intelligence Agency (CIA), significant latitude in investigations and in the sharing of previously secret information that was once difficult to obtain. The burden of law enforcement agencies to provide probable cause (provided for in the Fourth Amendment to the U.S. Constitution) and adequate evidence of criminal activity in order to conduct any type of surveillance during an investigation has been greatly reduced. It is here that the concern of the civil liberties organizations lies. They assert that the USA PATRIOT Act gives law enforcement and intelligence agencies free reign in investigations of both citizens and noncitizens as long as there is some suspicion that the person being investigated has a link to a terrorist organization. The relaxation of previously strict and specific legislation meant to protect the rights of the accused and those under investigation may have gone too far, however, allowing for the possibility of abuse and suspension of civil rights in the name of rooting out terrorism.

Title I of the USA PATRIOT Act seems to establish the act as strictly an antiterrorist bill. It provides for a new "Counterterrorism Fund" and condemns acts of violence and discrimination against Arab and Muslim Americans. Title II goes further and outlines the new requirements and abilities of law enforcement and intelligence agencies regarding surveillance. Under the act, searches can be conducted of a suspect's home without notifying the suspect or presenting the suspect with a warrant. In this case the search does not have to be limited to a person suspected of terrorist activity or af-

filiation. It applies to all criminal investigations where the law enforcement agency deems that notification would impede the search, the assumption being that a person notified of an impending search could get rid of any incriminating evidence. Title II also allows the seizure of personal records if they are deemed necessary or relevant to an investigation into terrorist activity, regardless of whether the person whose records are being seized is suspected of any crime. This type of seizure had previously been limited to foreign powers or agents of foreign powers under the Foreign Intelligence Surveillance Act (FISA). Under USA PATRIOT this type of seizure has been extended to include U.S. citizens and lawful residents.

The same title in the act also allows for greater access to phone and Internet activity. With a new computer tracking device—Carnivore, or DCS1000—government agencies can intercept all forms of Internet activity, including email messages, web page activity, and Internet phone conversations. The concern about Carnivore is that it takes all activity from a single Internet Service Provider (ISP) even if an agency was only investigating one customer, thereby allowing for the possibility that innocent users' activity could be monitored as well. The FBI claims that it has filters in place to prevent the viewing of online activity on the part of citizens who are not under investigation, though these filters have not been publicly demonstrated.

Although the new legislation of USA PATRIOT is meant, on its face, to be used only in the investigation of criminal activity—especially terrorism—there is much concern about its constitutionality and potential for abuse. Civil rights organizations feel that the surveillance of U.S. citizens and legal residents who are not under suspicion for criminal or terrorist activity is an invasion of privacy. The provisions of the act could allow for domestic surveillance of political enemies by those in power, much like the surveillance conducted by J. Edgar Hoover during his tenure as the director of the FBI. These concerns, surrounding an act that was hastily drafted and passed by Congress in reaction to the terrorist attacks of September 11, are grounded in the fear that, under the guise of a "war on terror," the rights of the citizens of the United States may ultimately be usurped.

MANY ARAB AMERICANS HAVE BEEN DETAINED BY THE U.S. GOVERNMENT SINCE SEPTEMBER 11, AND KEPT IN CUSTODY FOR MONTHS. INFORMATION ABOUT THOSE DETAINED IS FIRMLY CONTROLLED BY THE GOVERNMENT, CAUSING CONCERN ABOUT POSSIBLE CIVIL RIGHTS VIOLATIONS. *(AP/Wide World Photos/Carlos Osorio. Reproduced by permission.)*

profiling suspected terrorists, including how they bought their airline ticket, whether the ticket was one way, and where the flight had originated—and only fifteen complaints of discriminatory treatment had been filed with the Federal Aviation Administration in 2000, after CAPPS had been put into place. Nevertheless, because of the Middle Eastern origins of many suspected terrorists, CAPPS fostered resentment among some Arab Americans who felt that they were being singled out unfairly.

In his role as secretary of transportation, Norman Y. Mineta was forced to balance concerns over civil liberties with more effective screening procedures at the nation's airports. As a former Japanese American detainee, Mineta himself was acutely aware of the dangers that wartime posed to civil liberties. In an interview with MSNBC, Mineta reflected that "Now the people who look like the twenty-two [suspects on the FBI's "Most Wanted Terrorists" list] are looked upon with suspicion. I think that we are seeing shades of what we experienced in 1942." He added, hopefully, "The big difference this time is that the political leadership is responding differently, and I think that

President George W. Bush has just been terrific on this issue." Yet Mineta's cautious approach to safeguarding civil liberties had its critics. After an appearance on *60 Minutes II* in October 2001 in which he maintained that all airline passengers should be subjected to the same security procedures, some observers attacked the secretary for ignoring the obvious: because of the Middle Eastern origins of all the terrorists involved in the September 11 attacks, it seemed justifiable to heighten screening measures for individuals from those regions.

With the enactment of the Aviation and Transportation Security Act on November 19, 2001, the federal government's other attempts to strengthen airport security also stirred criticism. In taking the responsibility for airport security away from airlines and private companies working under contract, the act phased in federal control over airport security in stages through November 2002. The act mandated that all airport screeners hold United States citizenship, however, a requirement that troubled the one-fourth of security screeners nationwide who were not American citizens. At some airports, the percentage of noncitizens handling security was far higher: at San Francisco International Airport; about 80 percent of security workers were alien residents, a figure that stood at 40 percent for Los Angeles International Airport. Under the new law, screeners were also required to speak and write in English. Supporters of the law indicated that the ability to speak in a common language was not discriminatory, but rather a vital skill in the communication network to prevent terrorists from gaining access to airplanes.

Additional Roundup of Visa Violators in 2002

On January 8, 2002, the U.S. Justice Department announced a massive roundup of 6,000 Middle Eastern men who were already subject to deportation proceedings after their visas had expired. Considering the 300,000 aliens in the United States who were under deportation orders, some Muslim Americans took exception to the focus on the relatively small number of Middle Eastern men in the action. As James Zogby, president of Arab American Institute, asked *CBS News* on the day of the announcement, "Is it a profiling issue? Of course it is. Is it an effective law enforcement tool to deal with terrorism? Of course, it's not." Any connection between the 6,000 suspects and terrorist activities was indeed speculative, and the fact remained that almost all of the terrorists in the September 11 attacks were actually in the United States on valid visas.

To some, then, the announcement of another roundup of deportees symbolized the government's renewed commitment to securing its borders and the public's safety; to others, it demonstrated a threat to the civil rights of citizens and non-citizens alike. As Democratic House member John Conyers asked in a civil rights gathering in January 2002 to protest the government's counterterrorist policies, "Do we have to compromise our constitutional civil rights merely because we're trying to root out these terrorists," April Taylor's January 20, 2002, *Detroit News* article quoted the congressman, "I say no." Equating the government's use of the CAPPS system and other profiling measures with unlawful racial profiling measures, the Reverend Al Sharpton declared, "The racial profiling of anybody is wrong . . . . We are not required to agree on every issue, but we are required to protect each other's rights to survive and sustain our families and our communities."

Public support for the increased security measures remained high, however, despite the cautions of civil liberties advocates. According to a Harris poll taken after the September 11 attacks, over four-fifths of Americans supported the use of facial-recognition technology in some public areas and increased federal monitoring of banking and credit card transactions. About two-thirds of those surveyed also supported the introduction of national identification cards for American citizens, more camera surveillance in public places, and government monitoring of Internet chat room discussions. Fifty-four percent also favored a government expansion of monitoring cell phone and e-mail communications. As *Business Week* columnists noted in the November 5, 2001, article "Privacy in an Age of Terror," however, the trend toward greater government intrusion into civil society went beyond a swing in the opinion polls: " Since the forefathers, Americans have been committed to the idea that people have the right to control how much information about their thoughts, feelings, choices, and political beliefs is disclosed . . . .By reducing our commitment to privacy, we risk changing what it means to be Americans."

As the experiences of Great Britain and Israel over the past generation have shown, the balance between civil liberties and public safety is a contentious one in any democratic society. So too has the United States' historical legacy of civil liberties in wartime demonstrated the risks inherent in maintaining civil society in the face of "clear and present danger." In the months after the September 11 attacks, as in previous wartime situations, non-citizens were the first to feel the effects of expanded federal powers on their civil liberties. Whether American citizens themselves were willing to forego some of their civil liberties in the name of public safety remained to be seen.

BIBLIOGRAPHY

Armstrong, Ken. "U.S. Tries to Walk Fine Line Between Security, Ethnic Bias." *Chicago Tribune*, September 19, 2001.

Bell, J. Bowyer. *The Irish Troubles: A Generation of Violence 1967–1992.* New York: St. Martin's Press, 1993.

Bush, George W. "Military Order—Detention, Treatment, and Trial of Certain Non-Citizens in the War Against Terrorism." *Weekly Compilation of Presidential Documents*, November 13, 2001.

———. "State of the Union Address," January 29, 2002. Available online at http://www.whitehouse.gov/news/releases/2002/01/print/20020129-11.html (cited January 30, 2002).

Ciment, James. *Palestine/Israel: The Long Conflict.* New York: Facts on File, 1997.

Cohen, Adam et al. "Rough Justice." *Time*, December 10, 2001.

Conroy, John. *Unspeakable Acts: The Dynamics of Torture.* New York: Alfred A. Knopf, 2000.

Cordle, Ina Paiva. "Airport Law to Cut Jobs of Non-Citizens." *Miami Herald*, December 23, 2001.

Darnton, Eric. *Divided We Stand: A Biography of New York's World Trade Center.* New York: Basic Books, 1999.

Eichel, Larry. "Easing Rhetoric on Curbing Civil Liberties After September 11." *Philadelphia Inquirer*, December 10, 2001.

Foner, Eric. *Reconstruction: America's Unfinished Revolution 1863–1877.* New York: Harper and Row, 1988.

France, Mike et al. "Privacy in an Age of Terror." *Business Week*, November 5, 2001.

Gladwell, Malcolm. "Safety in the Skies." *New Yorker*, October 1, 2001.

Grapes, Bryan J., ed. *Japanese American Internment Camps.* San Diego: Greenhaven Press, 2001.

Hoge, Jr., James F. And Gideon Rose, eds. *How Did This Happen?: Terrorism and the New War.* New York: Public Affairs, 2001.

Holland, Jack. *Hope Against History: The Course of Conflict in Northern Ireland.* New York: Henry Holt, 1999.

Human Rights Watch. "U.K.: New Anti-Terror Law Rolls Back Rights." Available online at http://www.hrw.org/press/2001/12/UKbill1214.htm (cited February 4, 2002).

Inada, Lawson Fusao, ed. *Only What We Could Carry: The Japanese American Internment Experience.* Berkeley: Heyday Books, 2000.

Lake, Anthony. *Nightmares: Real Threats in a Dangerous World and How America Can Meet Them.* Boston: Little, Brown and Company, 2000.

Lipsitz, George. *Rainbow at Midnight: Labor and Culture in the 1940s.* Urbana: University of Illinois Press, 1994.

McDonnel, Patrick J. "Wave of U.S. Immigration Likely to Survive September 11." *Los Angeles Times,* January 10, 2002.

Miles, James. *The Legacy of Tiananmen: China in Disarray.* Ann Arbor: University of Michigan Press, 1996.

Montgomery, David. *Citizen Worker: The Experience of Workers in the United States with Democracy and the Free Market During the Nineteenth Century.* New York: Cambridge University Press, 1993.

National Public Radio. "Profile: Policies Adopted by the Bush Administration Since September 11th That Trouble Civil Liberties Groups." *Weekend All Things Considered,* December 8, 2001.

National Public Radio. "Profile: Questions of Civil Rights for Muslims in America." *Weekend All Things Considered,* January 13, 2002.

Neely, Jr., Mark E. *The Fate of Liberty: Abraham Lincoln and Civil Liberties.* New York: Oxford University Press, 1991.

"Non-Citizens and Civil Liberties." *Chicago Tribune,* December 10, 2001.

Orr, Bob. "Justice Department Seeks Arab Visa Violators." *CBS Evening News,* January 8, 2002.

Personal Justice Denied: Report of the Commission on Wartime Relocation and Internment of Civilians. Seattle: University of Washington Press, 1997.

"Questions and Answers: The Legacy of Internment Camps." *Newsweek,* October 17, 2002. Available online at http://www.msnbc.com/news/644274 .asp?cp1=1 (cited February 6, 2002).

Rehnquist, William H. *All the Laws But One: Civil Liberties in Wartime.* New York: Alfred A. Knopf, 1998.

Salvatore, Nick. *Eugene V. Debs: Citizen and Socialist.* Urbana: University of Illinois Press, 1982.

Schrecker, Ellen. *Many Are the Crimes: McCarthyism in America.* Boston: Little, Brown and Company, 1998.

Schwarts, Nelson D. "Learning from Israel." *Fortune,* January 21, 2002.

Taylor, April. "Anti-Terrorism Policies Condemned at D.C. Rally." *Detroit News,* January 20, 2002.

Tempest, Matthew. "The Issue Explained: David Blunkett's Anti-Terrorism, Crime, and Security Bill 2001." *Mancester Guardian,* November 19, 2001.

Thomas, Evan and Michael Isikoff. "Justice Kept in the Dark." *Newsweek,* December 10, 2001.

U.S. Congress Biographical Directory. "Joseph Raymond McCarthy," Washington, DC. Available online at http://bioguide.congress.gov/scripts/biodisplay .pl?index=M000315 (cited January 28, 2002).

———. "Norman Yoshio Mineta," Washington, DC. Available online at http://bioguide.congress.gov/ scripts/biodisplay.pl?index=M000794 (cited January 28, 2002).

U.S. Department of Transportation. "Norman Y. Mineta," Washington, DC. Available online at http://www.dot .gov/affairs/mineta.htm (cited January 28, 2002).

Warikoo, Niraj. "Arab Community's Complaints of Racial Profiling Surveyed at Detroit Airport." *Detroit Free Press,* June 5, 2001.

"What September 11 Really Wrought." *Economist,* January 12, 2002.

"What to Do with Al-Qaeda Prisoners." *Economist,* January 28, 2002.

Woodworth, Steven E. *Cultures in Conflict: The American Civil War.* Westport, Connecticut: Greenwood Press, 2000.

Zirin, James D. "Will U.S. Civil Liberties Be the Next Victim?" *Times* (London), December 4, 2001.

Timothy G. Borden

DOMESTIC TERRORISM: OKLAHOMA CITY TO ANTHRAX AND BEYOND

On October 2, 2001, a photo editor with American Media Inc. in Boca Raton, Florida, Robert Stevens, was admitted to the hospital with severe flu like symptoms. Diagnosed with a fatal case of inhalation anthrax, Stevens dies on October 5 as a result of the deadly disease. He is the first known person in the United States to die from inhaled anthrax since 1976. Within days more individuals tested positive for exposure to anthrax, setting off a tragic chain of events that ultimately paralyzed the country, causing disproportionate psychological effects amongst the nation's citizens, including hysteria, fear, and panic. Tragically, five people died as a result of the deadly terrorist attack.

The attempt to assign responsibility for the anthrax-contaminated letters has led to intense speculation from federal authorities and terrorism analysts alike as to the identity of the perpetrator(s) of the attack. Are they the work of an international terrorist organization harboring an intense hatred of the United States? Or is it perhaps the work of a domestic terrorist with equally nefarious motivations? To date, the investigation, dubbed *Amerithrax*, has not resulted in the definite identification of a culprit, either international or domestic. Many people were quick to assume that the September 11 terrorists, or other affiliates of the al-Qaeda terrorist organization, were responsible for these attacks against the United States. Keep in mind the first reported death from anthrax, on October 5, 2001, was less than a month after the September terrorist attacks, and many of the hijackers either lived or received flight training in Florida, where the first anthrax case was reported.

While at first it appeared as if international terrorists were responsible for the mailing of anthrax-contaminated letters that paralyzed the

THE CONFLICT

Numerous domestic terror groups are currently active in the United States. Some of these groups harbor an intense hatred and suspicion of the American government, while others follow both racist and hate based ideologies. Other groups subscribe to special interests, including animal liberation rights and anti-abortionist views. Many of these extremist groups are not only willing, but also prepared to use violence in order to achieve their radical goals. Domestic terror attacks have resulted in the disruption of social and political processes, caused widespread fear and panic, and resulted in numerous casualties

Political

- Since September 11 and the subsequent mailing of anthrax-contaminated letters, federal authorities have set in place a number of stringent domestic security measures designed to prevent further attacks. Many of these security measures may ironically serve to inflame domestic extremist groups and lead to an increase in levels of violence from this dangerous segment of American society.

- Adherents to left-wing ideologies desire to affect change in the American system through revolutionary activities, rather than through the political system, which they believe is a product of the capitalist and imperialist system they are fighting against.

- One of the most well known and active categories of terrorist groups in the United States is the extreme right. Members of the extreme right support a variety of anti-government, racist, and conspiracy theory related ideologies.

Ideological

- Special interest terrorism is different from both the extreme right-wing and left-wing movements in that the motivation behind special interest extremism is not to affect widespread social or political change, but rather to affect change on a specific interest or topic.

CHRONOLOGY

1915 A nationwide revival of the Ku Klux Klan results in an increase of violent attacks against African Americans.

February 4, 1974 The Symbionese Liberation Army kidnaps newspaper heiress Patty Hearst from her Berkley, California, apartment.

May 1980 The first FBI Joint Terrorism Task Force is established.

February 13, 1983 A member of Sheriff's Posse Comitatus kills two law enforcement officers in a shoot-out. This is the first recorded terrorist incident perpetrated by a right-wing anti-government terrorist group.

April 16, 1987 A member of Animal Liberation Front (ALF) carries out an arson fire in Davis, California. This is the first recorded special interest terrorism incident perpetrated by ALF.

August 1992 Federal authorities attempt to arrest white supremacist Randy Weaver at his rural Ruby Ridge, Idaho, home. An eleven day siege ensues, resulting in the deaths of Weaver's teenage son, his wife, and a federal officer.

February 28, 1993 Federal agents of the Bureau of Alcohol, Tobacco, and Firearms attempt to execute arrest and search warrants against David Koresh and the Branch Davidian religious compound in Waco, Texas.

April 19, 1993 A 51-day standoff comes to an end in Waco when nearly 80 Branch Davidian members are killed in a fire when buildings on the compound are set ablaze.

April 19, 1995 A truck bomb destroys the Alfred P. Murrah federal building in Oklahoma City, killing 168 people and injuring nearly 500 more.

August 10, 1995 A federal grand jury for the Western District of Oklahoma returns an indictment charging Timothy James McVeigh and Terry Lynn Nichols with the April 19, 1995 terrorist attack.

July 27, 1996 A fatal bombing occurs in Centennial Olympic Park in Atlanta, Georgia. The bombing is later attributed to Army of God activist Eric Robert Rudolph.

June 11, 2001 Timothy James McVeigh is executed by lethal injection in a federal prison in Terre Haute, Indiana.

October 5, 2001 Robert Stevens, photo editor at American Media, Inc. in Boca Raton, Florida, dies from inhalation anthrax.

December 5, 2001 Army of God member Clayton Lee Waagner is arrested by federal authorities after a ten-month nationwide manhunt.

U.S. postal service and the federal government, after a preliminary investigation and analysis of existing evidence, the Federal Bureau of Investigation (FBI) released a statement saying that it had found no direct link to organized terrorism. Linguistic and behavioral assessments of the person responsible for mailing the anthrax-laden letters indicated that it was a single individual. This led to the instant speculation that the anthrax attacks were the result of domestic terrorism, and possibly the work of a lone American.

It comes as little surprise that the person responsible for the anthrax attacks could be an American citizen. Hundreds of different domestic terror groups are currently active in the United States. Some of these groups harbor an intense hatred and suspicion of the American government, while others follow both racist and hate based ideologies. Other groups subscribe to special interests, including animal liberation rights and anti-abortionist views.

Why should the American public be concerned about such domestic terror groups? Many of these extremist groups are not only willing, but also prepared to use violence in order to achieve their radical goals. Not unlike many international terrorist organizations, adherents to these beliefs are no strangers to mass casualty terrorism, as Timothy James McVeigh and Terry Lynn Nichols so brutally demonstrated in Oklahoma City in April 1995. Even if it turns out that an American citizen is not responsible for the anthrax attacks, the overall threat from domestic terrorism is too great a danger to ignore.

HISTORICAL BACKGROUND

What is Domestic Terrorism?

While there is no single, universally accepted definition of terrorism, in the United States the Federal Bureau of Investigation (FBI) breaks terrorism down into two different categories, international and domestic. According to the FBI in *Terrorism in the United States, 1999* (p. ii), domestic terrorism is

> the unlawful use, or threatened use, of force or violence by a group or individual based and operating entirely within the United States or its territories without foreign direction committed against persons or property to intimidate or coerce a government, the civilian population, or any segment thereof, in furtherance of political or social objectives.

Within the United States, there are numerous types of active terrorist groups, representing diverse social, political, religious, and ideological perspectives. In general these groups can be broken down into three broad categories: the extreme left-wing, the extreme right-wing, and special interest.

The Extreme Left

One of the categories of domestic terrorism, as identified by the FBI, is what is known as the extreme left. Left-wing terrorist groups generally "profess a revolutionary socialist doctrine and view themselves as protectors of the people against the dehumanizing effects of capitalism and imperialism" (*Terrorism in the United States 1999*, p. 19). Adherents to left-wing ideologies desire to affect change in the American system through revolutionary activities, rather than through the political system, which they believe is a product of the capitalist and imperialist system they are fighting against.

From the 1960s until mid to late 1980s, left-wing extremism was the most prominent type of terrorism in the United States. To further their radical socialist ideologies, left-wing extremists in the continental United States and Puerto Rico planned and carried out numerous violent terrorist activities, including bombings, that claimed a number of lives and caused millions of dollars in damage. According to the FBI, from 1980–85, of 184 recorded terrorist and suspected terrorist incidents, 86 were attributed to left-wing extremists. A combination of factors in the late 1980s and early 1990s, including the collapse of the Soviet Union and infiltration of known and active groups by law enforcement officials, led to the overall decline of left-wing terrorism. In the early 1990s the extreme right-wing became the most prominent domestic terrorist threat.

The Extreme Right

By far, one of the most well known and active categories in which terrorist groups in the United States can be placed is what is known as the extreme right. Members of the extreme right support a variety of anti-government, racist, and conspiracy theory related ideologies. The most active and widely recognized subgroups in the extreme right include: Christian Identity, white supremacist, the militia movement, patriot movement, tax protest movement, and common law activists/sovereign citizens. Among the extreme right it is not uncommon for a member of one group to belong to, or subscribe to the beliefs, of another group. Some members of various militia groups in the United States, for example, adhere to the Christian Identity ideology, while also supporting various tax protest and white supremacist doctrines.

Christian Identity. Descending from British Israelism (belief that white Europeans are the descendents of the ten lost tribes of Israel), the modern American Christian Identity movement is an ideology that asserts that the white Aryan race is God's chosen race. Using the Bible to justify their hate-filled, racist-driven goals, Christian Identity followers believe that the Second Coming of Jesus Christ will lead to a violent and bloody race war between Good (white races) and Evil (Jews and non-whites). More extreme followers of the religion encourage violence against non-whites to achieve their goals. Followers of the Christian Identity movement, which is the most common unifying theology among the right-wing movement, stem from a number of diverse groups, including militias, patriot groups, and white supremacist groups.

White Supremacist. The cornerstone of the white supremacist movement is the belief in the dominance of the white race. While there are a variety of groups with different levels of belief in the movement, the more extreme followers are typically violent racists who support the establishment of a white homeland in order to maintain the purity of the white race. Traditional targets of white supremacist activity have been black Americans and Jews, although in recent years the number of hate crimes carried out against gays and lesbians and other minority and ethnic groups have been growing.

Militia Movement. Rising to prominence in the early to mid 1990s, the militia movement is based on the belief that Americans should form armed, paramilitary groups in order to protect themselves from the tyrannical and oppressive U.S. government. Some militia group members also

DOMESTIC TERRORISM PREPAREDNESS WAS DISCUSSED DURING A MAY 2001 SENATE SUBCOMMITTEE HEARING. TERRORISM PREPAREDNESS HAS RECEIVED MORE ATTENTION OVER THE YEARS, BUT NEVER MORE SO THAN AFTER SEPTEMBER 11, 2001. *(AP/Wide World Photos/Dennis Cook. Reproduced by permission.)*

subscribe to elaborate conspiracy theories, including the belief that the American government is a puppet to the New World Order. Catalysts for the militia movement stem from a number of high profile events in the early to mid 1990s, including the passage of the 1993 Brady Law (requiring a waiting period for gun purchases), fear over gun confiscation, the standoffs at Waco and Ruby Ridge, and erroneous media reports directly linking the militia movement to the 1995 bombing of the Alfred P. Murrah federal building in Oklahoma City. While the majority of active militia groups around the United States do not engage in illegal or violent activities, a small number of groups and individuals have planned and carried out violent crimes and have been responsible for a number of deadly acts of terrorism.

Patriot Movement. The patriot movement is the name given to a group of individuals or organizations who share similar societal and political beliefs. As their name suggests, followers of the patriot movement are generally united by the common conviction that the United States is not governed the way it was intended to be when it was founded, and therefore many of the local, state, and federal laws are without foundation. Many members of the patriot movement belong to other groups, including the militia movement,

the common-law movement, and the white supremacist movement.

Tax Protest Movement. The tax protest movement is an anti-government movement opposed to paying federal income tax. Originating in the 1950s, tax protestors have interpreted the law in such a way that they believe that tax laws are illegitimate and therefore argue that they have both a moral and legal right not to pay taxes. In general, tax protestors believe that filing taxes violates Fifth Amendment rights, that the Sixteenth Amendment was not ratified correctly, and that paying tax on income should be on a voluntary basis only. The Fifth Amendment, which protects against disclosing information that could be used in or lead to criminal prosecution, is claimed by those tax extremists to support their disinclination to file their income taxes. The Sixteenth Amendment gives Congress the power to lay and collect taxes on income from any source. Although the tax protest movement has not been responsible for many violent crimes or acts of terrorism, adherents to the movement also participate in the wide spectrum of other domestic groups, including militias and white supremacist groups, which have also engaged in domestic terror activities.

Sovereign Citizen. Originating in the 1970s and 1980s, sovereign citizens, also known as common law activists, are individuals who adhere to the belief that nearly all government in the United States is illegitimate, and therefore, American citizens are only subject to what they call the common law. Under common law, citizens have absolute control over their land and property, are not required to pay most taxes, and are not subject to a variety of government regulations, ordinances, and laws. Along these lines, adherents to this belief do not recognize the authority of the government and often refuse to have a social security card, a passport, or even a driver's license. Sovereign citizens have engaged in a variety of criminal activities, from minor legal offenses including fraud, to violent armed robberies and standoffs with federal authorities.

Special Interest Terrorism

The third and final category of domestic terrorism in the United States is what is known as special interest terrorism. Special interest terrorism is different from both the extreme right-wing and left-wing movements in that the motivation behind special interest extremism is not to affect widespread social or political change, but rather to affect change on a specific interest or topic. In an effort to achieve their select goals, more radical fringes of the movement attempt to force segments of society, including the general public, companies, and the government, to change their viewpoints on the issue the group is fighting for.

Some of the more prominent issues extreme special interest groups fight for include the environment, animal liberation rights, and anti-abortionism. In some cases, special interest terrorists have resorted to criminal activity including tree spiking, vandalism, bombings, killings, and in the case of some anti-abortion extremists, widespread mailing of anthrax-hoax threat letters. Special interest extremist activities have been on the rise in the past few years, with terrorist groups including the Animal Liberation Front, the Earth Liberation Front, and the Army of God planning and carrying out a number of terrorist acts in the United States.

Terrorism in the Twentieth Century

Terrorism is not a new phenomenon. Contrary to many perceptions, terrorist related activities can be traced back to ancient societies when individuals and groups struggled for land ownership, leadership rights, natural resources, and other related social and political concerns. While many of the tools of terrorism have changed over time, the results in society have remained constant. Acts of terrorism result in widespread fear, panic, violence, social and political disruption, and even death.

NEW WORLD ORDER CONSPIRACY THEORY

The New World Order is a vast global conspiracy theory rooted in the belief that in the imminent future the United Nations (UN) will lead a military coup against the nations of the world in order to establish a One World Government. The UN troops, made up of foreign nationals who, according to the theory, are not averse to killing Americans, will arrive in unmarked Black Helicopters and after a hostile military campaign, will impose a despotic rule over the United States.

Under the rule of the One World Government the U.S. Constitution will be replaced by the UN charter. American citizens will lose their right to private property and their right to own firearms, all elections will be abolished, and only UN sanctioned One World Religion churches will be allowed to operate. All individuals who oppose the many oppressive measures of the One World Government will be interned in concentration camps held throughout the United States. In some versions of the New World Order conspiracy theory, it is not the United Nations which is the invading force, but Jews, communists, and other groups.

The most prominent roots of terrorism in the United States can be traced back to the overtly racist activities of the Ku Klux Klan (KKK). Founded shortly after the Civil War (1861–65) in the mid-1860s during the Reconstruction Era, the first wave of Klan activity was relatively short-lived. Supporting virulently racist ideals, members tormented, intimidated, attacked, and murdered African Americans, predominantly in southern U.S. states. After five years of aggressive terrorist activities, around 1870 many of the active Klan chapters disbanded. From 1915 until the end of the 1920s the KKK experienced a nationwide revival, and as membership in the Klan increased, so too did the level of violent attacks.

As aggressive terror tactics against blacks increased, including mob lynching and vigilante style killings, Klan activities received nationwide press coverage. A number of high profile scandals, public condemnation of the violent racists attacks attributed to Klan members, and the onset of the Great Depression (1929–39) led to the disintegration of many Klan chapters and the overall collapse of the KKK. While Klan activity continues to persist in the United States, it is limited to a small

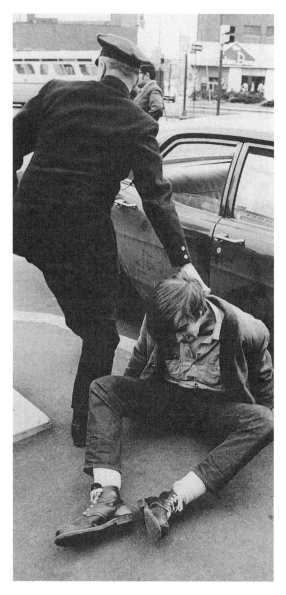

THE WEATHER UNDERGROUND, A LEFT-WING
EXTREMIST GROUP, ENGAGED IN TERRORIST
ACTIVITIES FROM THE 1960S THROUGH THE 1980S.
(© Bettman/CORBIS. Reproduced by permission.)

number of independent groups and individuals who
are largely inactive. After the breakup of the KKK
domestic terror activities remained limited and
small in scale until the emergence of the tax-protest
movement in the 1950s and the rise of left-wing
extremism in the early 1960s.

The modern era of terrorism, which began in
the late 1960s, has undeniably been the most destructive in history. Technological advances, coupled with the emergence of mass casualty and
weapons of mass destruction terrorism, have only
exacerbated this trend. From 1968–99 the FBI
recorded more than 14,000 international terrorist

attacks, resulting in over 10,000 deaths. While the
number of domestic attacks have been far fewer,
they have resulted in the disruption of social and
political processes, caused widespread fear and
panic, resulted in numerous casualties, and forced
Americans to accept domestic terrorism as an unfortunate aspect of modern-day society. Between
1980–2000 the FBI recorded 247 incidents or suspected incidents of terrorism perpetrated by domestic terrorists, and from 1980–99, 83 domestic
terrorist plots were thwarted by law enforcement
officials.

Many of the terrorist activities that took place
in the United States from the 1960s to the 1980s
were planned and carried out by left-wing extremist groups including the Weather Underground, the
Black Liberation Army, the Symbionese Liberation
Army, the United Freedom Front, and the Armed
Forces of Puerto Rico Liberation Front (FALN).
Fighting for revolutionary socialist changes to
American society, or in the case of the FALN and
other separatist groups, independence from the
United States, these left-wing groups carried out
bombings and other attacks in the United States,
primarily in New York City.

From the 1970s to the 1980s

On February 4, 1974, the Symbionese Liberation Army (SLA), a revolutionary extremist group
whose motto was "Death to the fascist insect that
preys upon the life of the people," kidnapped 19-
year old newspaper heiress Patty Hearst from her
Berkley, California, apartment. After a number of
weeks in forced confinement by her captors, Hearst
became a member of the radical leftist group, actively participating in bank robberies and other
felonies the extremist group carried out in support
of their revolutionary goals. In January 2001 she received full presidential pardon for her actions.

Other prominent left-wing terrorist activities
during this time included a fire lit by the Jewish
Defense League in Brooklyn, New York, on April
5, 1982, which resulted in one death and seven injuries. On September 16, 1983 Los Macheteros
(Popular Puerto Rican Army) stole 7.2 million
from a Wells-Fargo armored car, and on November
7, 1983, left-wing extremists bombed the U.S.
Capitol. While many of the bombings and other
terrorist attacks carried out at this time did not often result in high numbers of fatalities, they caused
widespread disruption to American society

The first recorded terrorist incident perpetrated by a right-wing anti-government group occurred on February 13, 1983, in Medina, North
Dakota, when Gordon Kahl, a member of the

Christian Identity movement and a leader of the Sheriff's Posse Comitatus, shot and killed two law enforcement officers and injured four others. The Posse Comitatus was a loosely formed, anti-government group that began in California and Oregon around 1970. Believing in an elaborate conspiracy theory whereby the legitimate American government had been replaced by an illegitimate, tyrannical one, adherents to the ideology believed in the right to bear arms and the use of force in order to protect citizens from the government. By the end of the 1980s the movement had largely died out, but the radical belief in conspiracy theories and virulent anti-government ideologies still persist in active terrorist groups, and in some aspects, heralded the rise in the right-wing and virulent anti-government extremism that currently exist in the United States.

In the late 1980s the threat from domestic terrorists came from extreme right-wing, anti-government, and white supremacist groups. One Aryan Nation affiliated organization, The Order, carried out bank robberies, armored car robberies, bombings, and murders in furtherance of their objectives. According to the FBI, in 1986 affiliates of the Aryan Nations carried out five of the eight recorded terrorist attacks in the United States.

Ruby Ridge and Waco

The early 1990s were marked by a significant decrease in the number of terrorist incidents, but saw the growth of anti-government extremism in the formation of both organized militias and patriot groups. A series of tragic and highly publicized events, including the siege at Ruby Ridge, Idaho, and the standoff near Waco, Texas, acted as catalysts to this explosion of right-wing extremism. In August 1992 federal authorities attempted to arrest white supremacist Randy Weaver on weapons charges at his rural homestead in Ruby Ridge, Idaho, where he lived with his wife, teenage son, and infant child. Weaver's fourteen-year-old son and a federal agent were killed when gunfire was exchanged when federal agents arrived on the homestead.

When Weaver refused to surrender to the authorities, more federal agents arrived, beginning a standoff that lasted eleven days. Once news of the "siege" became known, hundreds of right-wing extremists, including white supremacists and Nazi Skinheads, arrived at the scene, angrily protesting the actions taken by the federal authorities. During the siege Weaver's wife was killed by a federal sniper while Weaver and a friend were wounded. Even though Weaver was later acquitted of all charges against him stemming from the standoff, the incident became a galvanizing force among the extreme right, fueling their paranoia and anti-government convictions.

On February 28, 1993, federal agents of the Bureau of Alcohol, Tobacco, and Firearms (ATF) attempted to execute arrest and search warrants against David Koresh and the Branch Davidian religious compound in Mount Carmel, near Waco, Texas, where they believed members had stockpiled a large cache of weapons. The raid resulted in a shootout in which four ATF agents and five members of the religious group were killed. This was followed by a takeover of the operation by the FBI Hostage Rescue Team and a 51-day standoff. On April 19 the standoff came to an end when the FBI attempted to insert tear gas canisters into the compound to force Branch Davidian members to emerge from their buildings. This effort was completely unsuccessful when heavy winds ejected the tear gas from the compound as quickly as the FBI could insert them. Just hours after the failed tear gas attack, Branch Davidian members lit a number of buildings on the compound on fire, killing nearly 80 men, women, and children who became trapped inside.

The 51-day standoff at the Branch Davidian compound, which came to be referred to as the Waco standoff, made national headlines and caused outrage among the radical right. The siege at Ruby Ridge and the passage of the 1993 Brady Bill, which requires waiting periods on gun purchases, only exacerbated the perceived injustices perpetrated against American citizens by the United States government. This extreme anti-government dogma, coupled with a belief in conspiracy theories and a number of other factors led to the most destructive incident of domestic terrorism in the history of the United States, the 1995 bombing of the Alfred P. Murrah federal building in Oklahoma City.

Oklahoma City

At approximately 9:02 A.M., on the morning of April 19, 1995, an improvised explosive device made out of nearly 4,000 pounds of ammonium nitrate and diesel fuel exploded outside of the Alfred P. Murrah federal building in Oklahoma City. Placed in a rental truck, the improvised bomb destroyed the building and caused the deaths of 168 people and injured over five hundred more. Within minutes emergency crews and law enforcement officials arrived on the scene, and within eight hours of the explosion, President Bill Clinton (1993–2001) signed an Emergency Declaration, granting the Federal Emergency Management Agency

(FEMA) primary federal responsibility for the incident. Law enforcement officials immediately began searching for the perpetrators of the attack, and on April 20, Attorney General Janet Reno offered a $2 million reward for the arrest and conviction of the individuals behind the bombing.

While the country was reeling from the impact of the devastating attack in Oklahoma City, on April 19, just hours after the truck bomb exploded outside of the Alfred P. Murrah federal building, an Oklahoma Highway Patrolman pulled a car off the road for driving without a valid license plate. The driver of the vehicle, arrested for vehicle and weapons violations, was Timothy James McVeigh. On April 21, shortly before he was to make bail for the weapons and vehicle violations, authorities arrested McVeigh, charging him with maliciously damaging and destroying a federal building by mean of explosives. Terry Lynn Nichols, McVeigh's co-conspirator in the bombing, surrendered to federal authorities shortly after McVeigh was arrested and was formally charged with the same violations as McVeigh.

On August 10, 1995, a federal grand jury for the Western District of Oklahoma returned an indictment charging both men with one count of Conspiracy to Use a Weapon of Mass Destruction, one count to Use a Weapon of Mass Destruction, one count of Malicious Destruction by Explosives of Federal Property, and eight counts of First Degree Murder for the death of eight law enforcement officers. On June 2, 1997, Timothy McVeigh, who parked the truck bomb directly outside the Alfred P. Murrah federal building and was responsible for the ensuing explosion, was found guilty of all counts against him and sentenced to death by lethal injection. For his part in the terrorist attack, on December 23, 1997, Terry Lynn Nichols was convicted of conspiracy and involuntary manslaughter, and was sentenced to life imprisonment, as well as eight, six-year terms, one for each of the law enforcement officers who died in the bomb blast. A third, lesser known accomplice, Michael Fortier, who turned witness for the government, was sentenced to 12 years imprisonment for failing to warn authorities of the impending plot to blow up the building.

What motivated Timothy McVeigh and Terry Nichols to willfully and maliciously cause the deaths of 168 innocent Americans? Why should the American public be concerned about such domestic terrorists? Although not directly affiliated with any known terrorist organization, McVeigh and Nichols both believed in various anti-government and conspiracy theory related ideologies. It was these beliefs

that led them to orchestrate the worst domestic terror attack ever to occur on American soil.

Born in 1968, in Lockport, New York, Timothy McVeigh first became interested in right-wing ideologies in his teen years when he began collecting guns and reading pro-militia and survivalist literature, including the infamous anti-semantic and conspiratorial based Turner Diaries. After dropping out of college, McVeigh enlisted in the U.S. Army where he sharpened his shooting and survivalist skills, and in early 1990, served in the Gulf War (1991). Following the Gulf War, where he received a number of commendations for his superior service, he tried out for an elite special forces unit but was unable to successfully complete the rigorous battery of tests demanded of him. It was shortly after this that McVeigh dropped out of the army, bitter with his failure to make the special forces and disillusioned by his combat experience and what he believed were government improprieties in the Gulf War, and began traveling throughout the United States, selling anti-government literature and other survivalist paraphernalia at gun shows.

During his travels McVeigh spent time with two former army colleagues, Terry Lynn Nichols and Michael Fortier, both who shared his anti-government sentiments. In 1993 McVeigh traveled to Waco, Texas, to protest the federal siege of the Branch Davidian compound, becoming more enraged by what he perceived as government abuses of power and gross injustices against American citizens. Following plans set forth in the Turner Diaries, a book he carried with him and quoted from on numerous occasions, he began planning the Oklahoma City bombing—to take place on the anniversary of the Waco tragedy—as a platform for his extreme anti-government message. McVeigh believed that a high number of casualties in Oklahoma would be the best way to deliver his anti-government message.

Like Timothy McVeigh, Terry Lynn Nichols, the co-conspirator in the fatal bombing in Oklahoma City, also espoused anti-government, rightwing ideologies. Born in 1955 in Michigan, he first became interested in the survivalist movement in the early 1980s. He enlisted in the U.S. Army in 1988, where he met McVeigh. With similar interests in weapons, survivalist beliefs, and other rightwing dogma, the two became fast friends. Granted a hardship discharge in 1989 so he could look after his six-year old son, Nichols quickly became embittered with the American government when he had difficulty getting immigration clearance for his Filipino wife. His growing anti-government

TIMOTHY MCVEIGH AND CO-CONSPIRATOR TERRY NICHOLS WERE CONVICTED FOR THE 1995 BOMBING OF THE ALFRED P. MURRAH FEDERAL BUILDING IN OKLAHOMA CITY, WHICH KILLED 168 PEOPLE AND INJURED ALMOST 500. *(AP/Wide World Photos. Reproduced by permission.)*

beliefs were further reinforced when his older brother attempted to renounce his American citizenship.

Subscribing to sovereign citizen ideologies, Nichols attempted to renounce his citizenship twice, destroyed his drivers license, voter registration card, and passport. He refused to use a license plate on his vehicle, had difficulty holding work, and fell quickly into debt. In Spring 1993 McVeigh and Nichols's, along with Nichols brother, formed their own paramilitary organization they dubbed the Patriots. In 1994 Nichols moved to Kansas where he worked as a farm hand until late August of that year when McVeigh arrived at the farm. In

late September the two men left Kansas together and proceeded to carry out plans for the Oklahoma City bombing.

The Oklahoma City bombing forced many Americans to accept the unthinkable. It was the first ever mass-casualty attack against Americans in the United States, perpetrated not by foreign terrorist groups, but by domestic extremists. "Nothing compares to the Oklahoma City bombing—the senseless horror and the unnecessary loss of lives. It was not a random act of nature, but a deliberate act of man" ("One Year Later: James Lee Witt Reflects on Oklahoma City," April 19, 1996). The deadly bombing in Oklahoma City tragically exposed the

THE TURNER DIARIES

Published in 1978 by William Pierce (under the pseudonym Andrew Macdonald), leader of the neo-Nazi National Alliance, the *Turner Diaries* is a fictional novel detailing a violent overthrow of the U.S. federal government by white supremacists. Set in the 1990s during a vicious race war, the *Turner Diaries* chronicles the story of Earl Turner, a member of an underground white supremacist army known as the Organization, who wages a guerilla war against the System, which is made up of federal government and other leading social institutions.

In his battle against the corrupt government and unjust society run by Jews, Turner becomes a hero to the white race after he detonates a truck bomb filled with cases of dynamite and ammonium nitrate fertilizer outside of the FBI headquarters in Washington, DC, killing 700 people. As the race war between the Organization and the System grows more violent, Turner becomes a martyr to the people when he flies a plane equipped with a warhead into the Pentagon, causing massive damage to the center of the Systems' military and strategic operations. Due to his heroic act the Organization is able to defeat the enemy and global white domination is eventually achieved.

The *Turner Diaries* is one of the most revered and widely read books among right-wing anti-government extremists. Events in the book are chillingly familiar to real life terrorist attacks, including the 1995 Oklahoma City bombing.

vulnerability of American society to mass-casualty attack, raising the possibility of future attacks by domestic extremists. The chance that there are disaffected Americans who harbor intense hatred for their own government, who subscribe to elaborate conspiracy theories, and who are both capable and willing to express this hatred in the form of violence against national targets is too great a risk to ignore.

Special Interest Terrorism and the Army of God

While domestic terrorists who subscribe to radical anti-government beliefs are some of the most well-known extremists in the United States, there also exists a serious threat to national security from a no less dangerous quarter—special interest extremists. The motivation behind this brand of extremism is to create change in regards to a specific interest or topic that the group feels is of particular importance.

In an effort to achieve their select goals, the more radical fringes of the special interest groups attempt to force segments of society to change their viewpoints on the issue, often times through the use of violence. One of the first cases of special interest terrorism occurred on April 16, 1987, when a member of the Animal Liberation Front (ALF) carried out an arson fire in Davis, California. Since 1987 special interest terrorism has been on the rise, with animal rights, environmental, and anti-abortion groups dominating the scene. Three highly active groups include the ALF, the Earth Liberation Front (ELF), and the Army Of God.

Army of God

Since the early 1980s a number of violent events including arsons, kidnappings, bombings, murders, and anthrax-hoax threat letters have been carried out against abortion providers in the United States. Many of these attacks have been attributed to a group known as the Army of God. A loose affiliation of violent anti-abortion extremists, the Army of God has hundreds of self-proclaimed members across the United States who believe that killing abortion providers is not murder, but rather justifiable homicide. Even though it is not identified as an official terrorist organization, self-proclaimed Army of God followers, including Eric Robert Rudolph and Clayton Lee Waagner, have been responsible for a number of violent terrorist attacks across the country.

A virulently anti-abortion and anti-government activist, Eric Robert Rudolph is one of the most well-known, self-proclaimed members of the underground Army of God movement. One of the FBI's ten most wanted fugitives, Rudolph has been charged with the July 27, 1996, fatal bombing at Atlanta's Centennial Olympic Park in Georgia, which killed one person and wounded more than 100 others; as well as the double bombings at the Sandy Springs Professional Building in Atlanta on January 16, 1997; the double bombings at the Otherside Lounge in midtown Atlanta on February 21, 1997; and the January 29, 1998 fatal bombing at the New Woman All Women Health Care Clinic in Birmingham, Alabama. Letters from the Army of God, which authorities believe were written by Rudolph, claimed responsibility for all but the Atlanta Centennial Olympic Park bombing.

On May 5, 1998, the FBI announced a million dollar reward for information directly leading to the arrest of Rudolph, stating that the "bombings represent grave incidents of domestic terrorism. The FBI seeks to ensure that justice is served and that others are deterred from carrying out such senseless violence against the public." The FBI continues to search for Rudolph, but the longer that he remains at large, the more likely that he will commit another deadly terrorist attack against domestic targets.

During 2001 a second self-proclaimed member of the Army of God, Clayton Lee Waagner, was involved in a number of terrorist related activities in the United States. Believing that he was "anointed by God," in February 2001 Waagner had escaped from a county jail in Illinois where he was awaiting sentencing for a number of charges, including the unlawful possession of a firearm and the transport of a stolen vehicle across state lines. While on the run Waagner committed a number of crimes, including bank robberies in West Virginia and Pennsylvania, and frequently posted email messages condoning the killing of abortion providers on an Army of God website run by Virginian Donald Spitz. Waagner claimed responsibility for over 550 anthrax hoax threat letters that were sent to reproductive health care clinics in October and November 2001. He also claims to have compiled a list with the names, addresses, and photographs of 42 employees of abortion providers he planned on killing. After a nearly ten-month, nationwide manhunt, Waagner was arrested on December 5, 2001 by federal authorities.

RECENT HISTORY AND THE FUTURE

Even though domestic terror related activities have been of little focus in recent news, terrorist related activities continue to be a threat to national security. On March 18, 2002, two letters claiming to be from the Army of God were found in North Carolina at the *Andrews Journal* newspaper and at Roper's Boots, a shoe store where Rudolph once shopped. Each letter contained a message supporting Eric Robert Rudolph, who remains at large.

Other types of special interest terrorism are also on the rise. The FBI estimates that the ALF/ELF have committed more than 600 criminal acts in the United States since 1996, and in 2000, seven terrorist incidents occurring in the United States were attributed to special interest terrorism. In the past few years left-wing terrorism has also seen an upswing with the emergence of anarchist groups. In November and December 1999 many individuals and groups supporting anarchist ideologies publicly demonstrated against the World Trade Organization Ministerial Meeting in Seattle, Washington,

---

ARMY OF GOD LETTER

The bombing's [sic] in Sandy Spring's and midtown were carried-out by units of the Army of God.

The abortion was the target of the first device. The murder of 3.5 million children every year will not be "tolerated." Those who participate in <u>anyway</u> in the murder of children may be targeted for attack. The attack therefore serves as a warning: <u>anyone</u> in or around facilities that murder children may become victims of retribution. The next facility targeted <u>may not be empty</u>.

The second device was aimed at agent of the so-called federal government i.e. A.T.F. F.B.I. Marshall's e.t.c. We declare and will wage <u>total war</u> on the ungodly communist regime in New York and your legaslative [sic]—bureaucratic lackey's in Washington. It is you who are responsible and preside over the murder of children and issue the policy of ungodly preversion [sic] thats destroying our people. We will target all facilities and personnell [sic] of the federal government.

The attack in midtown was aimed at the sodomite bar (the Otherside). We will target sodomites, there [sic] organizations, and all those who push there [sic] agenda.

"Death to the New World Order"

Eric Robert Rudolph. "The Army of God Letter." Available online at http:// www.fbi.gov/majcases/rudolph/letters.htm (cited April 12, 2002).

---

causing damage to numerous buildings and businesses in the downtown area.

Since September 11 and the subsequent mailing of anthrax-contaminated letters, federal authorities have set in place a number of stringent domestic security measures designed to prevent further attacks. The Maryland General Assembly, for example, is negotiating nine different bills aimed at improving preparedness in the event of a terrorist attack. While the bills will give the state the broad emergency powers many believe necessary to combat a terrorist attack, several of the bills provisions curtail personal freedoms and support the expansion of, among other things, police powers to plant wiretaps.

Many of these security measures may ironically serve to inflame domestic extremist groups and lead to an increase in levels of violence from this dangerous segment of American society. The anthrax attacks serve to remind us of the possibility that a disaffected American with virulent left-wing, right-wing, or special interest beliefs may not only be willing, but also prepared to use violence in order to achieve their radical goals. Without a doubt, the threat from domestic terrorism is a possibility we dare not ignore.

BIBLIOGRAPHY

"8/95 Grand Jury Indictment of McVeigh & Nichols." Lectric Law Library. Available online at http://www.lectlaw.com/files/cas44.htm (cited April 12, 2002).

"The Militia Watchdog: Message for Students." Anti-Defamation League. Available online at http://www.adl.org/mwd/students.htm (cited April 12, 2002).

"One Year Later: James Lee Witt Reflects on Oklahoma City," Federal Emergency Management Agency, April 19, 1996. Available online at http://www.fema.gov/okc95/okcref.htm (cited April 12, 2002).

U.S. Department of Justice. Federal Bureau of Investigation. "Statement by Director Freeh regarding Top Ten Announcement: Eric Robert Rudolph," Washington, DC: May 4, 1998. Available online at http://www.fbi.gov/pressrel/pressrel98/rudpress.htm (cited April 12, 2002).

———. "Terrorism in the United States 1997," Washington, DC. Available online at http://www.fbi.gov/publications/terror/terr97.pdf (cited April 12, 2002).

———. "Terrorism in the United States 1999," Federal Bureau of Investigation, Washington, DC. Available online at http://www.fbi.gov/publications/terror/terror99.pdf (cited April 12, 2002).

Watson, Dale L. "Statement for the Record of Dale L. Watson Executive Assistant Director Counterterrorism and Counterintelligence Federal Bureau of Investigation on The Threat Confronting the United States before the Senate Select Committee on Intelligence Washington, D.C.," Federal Bureau of Investigation, Washington, DC: February 6, 2002. Available online at http://www.fbi.gov/congress/congress02/watson020602.htm (cited April 12, 2002).

Cheryl A. Loeb

THE EUROPEAN UNION'S RESPONSE TO 9/11 AND ITS AFTERMATH

Although terrorism has been a fixture of everyday life for European states since the 1960s, the attacks on September 11, 2001, against the United States shocked the European Union. Two hijacked civilian jets smashed into the World Trade Center towers in New York City, killing and injuring thousands. A third hijacked jet crashed into the Pentagon in Arlington, Virginia, near Washington, DC, while a fourth plane went down in a Pennsylvania field, further adding to the casualties. In addition to being the single deadliest terrorist episode experienced by the United States, the attack demonstrated the potential of terrorist groups to inflict massive amounts of damage on the industrialized world. The leaders of the European Union were quick to recognize that if a terrorist group could devastate the United States, the groups could just as easily conduct catastrophic attacks against the countries of Europe.

The citizens of Europe extended an outpouring of sympathy to the United States. British Prime Minister Tony Blair (1997–) stated in his speech following the September 11 attack, "The atrocity was an attack on us all." The World Trade Center was home to companies and citizens from all over the globe. Given the international composition of the World Trade Center, the attacks killed more Europeans than any previous terrorist attack on European soil. In response to the calls from U.S. president George W. Bush (2001–) for an international coalition to fight international terrorism, the members of the European Union announced their determination to assist the United States. According to Tony Blair, "The world understands that whilst, of course, there are dangers in acting the dangers of inaction are far, far greater."

Shortly after the attacks, terrorist experts pointed to exiled Saudi millionaire Osama bin

THE CONFLICT

On September 12, the day after the terrorist attacks on New York City and Washington, DC, U.S. president George W. Bush declared to the world, "Make no mistake—the United States will hunt down and punish those responsible for these cowardly acts." The European Union pledged its support. The United States, together with the European Union and other nations, responded quickly to the attacks. After defeating Afghanistan's Taliban, which had harbored Osama bin Laden and his terrorist group al-Qaeda, friction began to arise in the coalition over treatment of prisoners and continued U.S. actions.

Political

- Although the Taliban faced a massive attack by the United States and its allies, it was unwilling to hand over Osama bin Laden for his alleged participation in the September 11 attacks. Al-Qaeda was assisting the Taliban in fighting a civil war for control of Afghanistan against the Northern Alliance. Additionally, al-Qaeda remained militarily stronger than the Taliban. The Taliban feared that if it acted against bin Laden, al-Qaeda would remove it from power.

- U.S. president George W. Bush fingered North Korea, Iran, and Iraq as an "axis of evil," alarming European and other allies, who feared the United States might begin to act unilaterally in its war against terror.

Economic

- Afghanistan's economy was already devastated by Soviet occupation in the 1980s and the subsequent civil war in the 1990s. Given Afghanistan's poor economic state and the lack of central authority, terrorist groups have found the country to be an effective sanctuary from hostile governments.

- British prime minister Tony Blair argued that Afghanistan had become a terrorist haven largely because the West did not assist Afghanistan after the Soviets withdrew in the early 1990s. To prevent Afghanistan from reverting to a terrorist haven after the military campaign against the Taliban, the United States and the European Union recognized that billions of dollars would be needed to rebuild Afghanistan's infrastructure and government capacity.

CHRONOLOGY

1998 After U.S. embassies in Kenya and Tanzania are bombed by al-Qaeda, Osama bin Laden publicly issues a declaration of war against the United States and its allies for supporting Israel and "illegitimate" Arab governments.

September 11, 2001 Hijackers aboard four civilian jetliners engage in a coordinated attack on the World Trade Center in New York City and the Pentagon near Washington, DC. Although it is believed that the fourth target may have been the White House, the fourth civilian jet crashes in Pennsylvania.

September 12, 2001 U.S. president George W. Bush vows to hunt down those responsible for the attack. The members of the European Union announce that they will assist the United States in any way possible. Article Five of the NATO treaty is invoked, signifying that the attack on the United States was an attack on all of the NATO allies.

October 4, 2001 The United States presents evidence to its NATO allies that Osama bin Laden was the mastermind of the September 11 attack. The allies proceed to demand that Afghanistan's Taliban government hand over bin Laden to the United States.

October 7, 2001 The United States and the United Kingdom begin Operation Enduring Freedom, a sustained bombing campaign of Taliban targets throughout Afghanistan. U.S. and British special forces enter Afghanistan to search for al-Qaeda and Osama bin Laden.

Late October 2001 The air campaign shifts its focus from Taliban air defenses to assisting Northern Alliance commanders fighting the Taliban. U.S. and British warplanes attack Taliban troops to assist the Northern Alliance in defeating the Taliban on the ground.

November 11, 2001 Northern Alliance forces enter the Afghan capital of Kabul. The Taliban relinquishes control of the capital and flees.

December 5, 2001 Talks between Afghan political factions begin in Bonn, Germany, to discuss the future of Afghanistan and form an interim government to replace the Taliban.

Laden as the terrorist mastermind. Operating from within the borders of Afghanistan, Osama bin Laden's al-Qaeda organization had previously engaged in attacks against the U.S. military in Saudi Arabia, the U.S. embassies in Kenya and Tanzania, and the USS *Cole* in the port of Yemen. Experts argued that the only terrorist group with the capability to execute such a complicated and coordinated attack was the al-Qaeda network. Due to bin Laden's vast finances, al-Qaeda was believed to have a worldwide reach. The investigation conducted by the United States and subsequent intelligence reached similar conclusions. After receiving the evidence of bin Laden's involvement from the U.S. authorities, the European Union (EU) joined calls from the United States for Afghanistan's Taliban leadership to hand over Osama bin Laden, who was residing within that country. After the Taliban's initial refusal, the United States and its European allies threatened that if the Taliban did not hand over bin Laden, the allies would respond with military force.

Upon the Taliban's refusal, the United States and EU began a military campaign against Afghan-istan. The European Union made the pledge to stand side by side with the United States through the campaign against terrorism. In a few short weeks, Taliban and al-Qaeda forces within Afghanistan were routed by an Afghan opposition group known as the Northern Alliance. With air and ground support from allied aircraft and special forces, the Northern Alliance quickly took control of the capital city of Kabul. Peace talks soon began regarding the future reconstruction of the country and the provisions for an interim government. Though the alliance has yet to capture bin Laden himself, the United States and its allies successfully killed or captured hundreds of al-Qaeda's members.

Although the EU remained committed to fighting terrorism, EU support of U.S. actions following the victory against the Taliban began to decline. Many of the EU states were only willing to support limited action against terrorist groups. These countries believed that the fall of the Taliban would be the end of the military phase against terror. U.S. president George W. Bush, however, stated that the United States might continue the military phase of the campaign into other states sponsoring terror. In particular, the United States began suggesting that Iraq was next on the target list. The EU worried that success in the Afghan war made the United States more likely to unilaterally employ force against any state it deemed to be a supporter of terrorism. In addition, the EU grew worried about U.S. treatment of terrorist prisoners, particularly whether these prisoners may face the death penalty. Although the EU continues in its support for U.S. anti-terrorist efforts, the strength of the coalition has declined as fears of U.S. unilateralism increase on the European continent.

HISTORICAL BACKGROUND

The countries of the European Union have a long history in dealing with political terrorism. The assassination of Archduke Ferdinand of Austria by a Serbian terrorist became the catalyst for World War I (1914–18). Although terrorist events have not led to interstate wars following World War II (1939–45), terrorism has been a destabilizing force in several prominent European Union member nations.

Due to the instability in Northern Ireland, colonial legacy, and British involvement in world affairs, the United Kingdom became a frequent target of terrorism. Violence in Northern Ireland increased after 1969 as a result of increased activity by the Irish Republican Army (IRA). The IRA demanded a withdrawal of British forces from Northern Ireland and the eventual reunification of Northern Ireland with the state of Ireland. Terror tactics used by the IRA and counter-tactics used by Loyalist (pro-British) forces made terrorism a significant internal security problem for the United Kingdom. Even after a ceasefire with the IRA in the late 1990s, terrorism remains a threat in Northern Ireland due to groups such as the Real IRA, a splinter group of the IRA. The British further faced threats from abroad, particularly from the Middle East. In 1988 Pan Am Flight 103 exploded over Lockerbie, Scotland, killing hundreds of British and American citizens. It was widely believed that the Abu Nidal Organization, with ties to the Libyan government, was responsible for the deadly attack. Similarly, British citizens and peacekeepers have repeatedly been seized and taken hostage by other Middle Eastern and South Asian groups.

Though Britain remains one of Europe's most prominent targets of terrorism, France has also experienced threats from terrorism for similar reasons. French involvement in world affairs has made it a constant target for terrorist organizations. French citizens have been seized by several Middle Eastern

THE EUROPEAN UNION NUMBERS FIFTEEN MEMBERS. AS OF EARLY 2002, THIRTEEN CANDIDATE COUNTRIES WERE PREPARING TO JOIN THE ORGANIZATION. *(Gale Group.)*

terrorist organizations, including Abu Nidal, HAMAS, and Hizballah. France has also suffered attacks within its borders, however, largely as a result of continued instability in Algeria. The legacy of French colonialism in Algeria has led several extremist Islamic groups to target French citizens. In 1995 France experienced a wave of terrorist attacks by the Armed Islamic Group (GIA). The GIA attacked targets throughout Paris, resulting in hundreds of French casualties.

Although Britain and France remain prominent targets of international terrorism, the level of terrorism against other EU countries reduced following the collapse of the Soviet Union. During the Cold War, leftist groups such as the Red Army Faction in Germany and the Red Brigades in Italy engaged in repeated attacks against both European and U.S. citizens and military personnel. After the fall of the Soviet Union these groups largely died out due to declining membership and participation. Additionally, the termination of funding and political support from the Soviet Union decreased the ability of such groups to operate.

The formation of the European Union allowed the governments of Europe to coordinate efforts directed against common terrorist threats faced by all countries. Through common internal security policies, cooperation, and shared intelligence the EU became more effective at fighting terrorism within its borders. For example, both Britain and France faced potential threats from extremist Islamic groups. During the GIA campaign of 1995 the UK arrested several GIA suspects within Britain with ties to the campaign against France. Similarly, cooperation between France and Spain against the Basque Homeland and Freedom Movement (ETA) dramatically reduced the effectiveness of ETA's terrorist campaign.

Cooperation within the European Union allowed individual EU countries to get help from their fellow nations when faced with internal terrorist threats as well. Intelligence sharing between the United States, Britain, France, Italy, and Germany allowed these governments to better address threats from nation-specific groups, such as the IRA and the Red Army Faction. Cooperation and multilateral measures have become the preferred response of the European Union against hostile terrorist groups. The recent formation of EU institutions has increased the effectiveness of multilateral counterterrorist measures. The success of multilateralism would affect the European Union's reactions to the attacks on September 11 and the war that followed.

The Attack on September 11, 2001

On September 11, 2001, the world experienced the worst terrorist attack in history. The strikes against the World Trade Center in New York City and the Pentagon in Arlington, Virginia, resulted in thousands of American deaths and casualties. In addition to American casualties, a large number of European countries lost citizens in the attack. According to some estimates, the number of Europeans killed made the attacks the deadliest terror attack ever against EU countries. Like the American public, the citizens of Europe reacted to the terrorist events with shock and horror. EU external relations commissioner Chris Patten stated in the *Daily Star* on September 12, 2001, that September 11 was "one of those few days in life that one can say will change everything." The consensus of the EU was that the attack on the United States was a crime against humanity that presented a threat to the security of all states. Simply put, if the strongest power in the world could experience such devastation, a similar attack was possible against any of the European states.

The individual countries of the European Union immediately reacted to the attack with an extension of support and condolences to the United States. The majority of the countries supported the call by U.S. president George W. Bush (2001–) to hunt down and punish the terrorist perpetuators wherever they may be. Almost all of the members of the EU promised to support Bush and stand by the United States. On September 12, the members of the European Union and the United States began discussions of whether Article Five of the North Atlantic Treaty Organization (NATO) should be invoked. Article 5 stipulated that any attack against any one of the treaty's signatories represented an attack on all of the countries of NATO.

Although NATO was designed to provide common defense for the United States, Canada, and western Europe in the face of Soviet aggression, Article 5 was now being discussed in response to the September 11 attack. Soon after the meeting of NATO ministers, Article 5 was invoked, stipulating that the countries of the European Union would assist the United States against the terrorists. NATO Secretary-General George Robertson stated NATO's position, "These barbaric acts constitute intolerable aggression against democracy and underlie the need for the international community and the members of the alliance to unite their forces in fighting the scourge of terrorism." In addition to the invocation of Article 5, the United States and the European Union drafted a UN declaration condemning in strongest terms the attacks upon the United States. On September 13, the UN Security Council passed resolution 1368, condemning the attacks and authorizing all necessary steps to respond to them and to combat all forms of terrorism. EU and U.S. counterterrorist agencies began sharing intelligence and coordinating counterterrorist efforts in response to the attack.

The European response to September 11 in many ways mirrored the EU's previous efforts against terrorism. To combat the various problems experienced by each country, the EU designed institutions in which intelligence could be shared and responses could be coordinated. After September 11, the EU immediately moved to invoke Article 5 of NATO, making the response against terrorism a multilateral effort. The EU began sharing and coordinating intelligence activities with the United States. Additionally, the EU and the United States moved through the United Nations to further coordinate the campaign and establish legitimacy to the coming response. These efforts made for a truly international response to September 11, promoting multilateral measures and cooperative efforts against terrorism worldwide.

The Military Campaign and Its Aftermath

Although some early speculation existed that the hijackers of the aircraft used in the attacks were

A DEMINING VAN ARRIVES ON A PARIS STREET TO INSPECT A CAR ON SEPTEMBER 13, 2001. MANY COUNTRIES ARE ON HEIGHTENED ALERT AGAINST TERRORISM AFTER THE ATTACKS OF SEPTEMBER 11. *(AP/Wide World Photos/ Laurent Rebourts. Reproduced by permission.)*

Palestinian, U.S. officials quickly fingered exiled Saudi millionaire Osama bin Laden and his al-Qaeda network for the attacks. Bin Laden had been deemed responsible by the United States for several other attacks against Americans. U.S. officials believed bin Laden was responsible for the attacks on September 11 due to intelligence gathered shortly afterwards. The September 11 attacks involved the hijacking of four civilian aircraft. After taking control of the aircraft, the hijackers flew the passenger jets into each of the designated targets. U.S. officials believed that the attack required high level of coordination, planning, and complexity. The perpetrators needed adequate intelligence on

aviation security and pilot training to fly the commercial jetliners. The intelligence reports, as well as bin Laden's involvement in the bombing against the U.S. military at Khobar Towers in Saudi Arabia and the USS *Cole* in Yemen, the previous attacks on U.S. embassies in Kenya and Tanzania, contributed to the conclusion that the attacks on September 11 were the handiwork of al-Qaeda.

The immediate response from the EU was one of caution. EU leaders called for a thorough investigation into the attacks to determine exactly which group bore responsibility. British prime minister Tony Blair stated that any retaliation plans must

ABOUT THE EUROPEAN UNION

The European Union (EU) is a federation of 15 countries dedicated to economic integration and the strengthening of cooperation between its member states. Those member states delegate authority to common institutions representing the Union as a whole. This system is the only one of its kind in the world today.

The genesis of the EU was on May 9, 1950, with the Treaty establishing the European Coal and Steel Community (ECSC), proposed by France and also signed by Belgium, Germany, Italy, Luxembourg, and the Netherlands. The treaty dealt with tariffs and quotas on iron ore, steel, coke, and coal trade between the ratifying countries. In 1957 the participants in the ECSC signed two other treaties, the Treaty establishing the European Atomic Energy Community—commonly called Euratom, which provided for development of peaceful uses for atomic energy—and the Treaty establishing the European Economic Community (EEC).

In July 1967 the EEC, ECSC, and Euratom merged into the European Community (EC), and in 1968 all tariffs between member states were eliminated. By the mid-1980s membership in the EC had increased to 12 with the additions of Denmark, Ireland, and the United Kingdom in 1973, Greece in 1981, and Spain and Portugal in 1986. The Treaty on European Union, signed in Maastricht, the Netherlands, on February 7, 1992, transformed the EC into the EU and was intended to expand political, economic, and social integration between member states. The treaty—often referred to as the Maastricht Treaty—also committed the EU to adapting a single currency by 1999. Three years after the treaty was signed, Austria, Finland, and Sweden were accepted into the EU, bringing the total membership to 15 countries.

The EU has four principal objectives: 1) to establish European citizenship; 2) to ensure freedom, security, and justice for its members; 3) to promote economic and social progress; and 4) to assert Europe's role in the world. It seeks to attain these objectives through its five primary institutions. The European Parliament is elected by universal suffrage every five years and is the expression of the democratic will of the Union's citizens. It shares legislative and budgetary authority with the Council of the European Union, which is the EU's main decision-making body. The European Commission is the Union's executive body, upholding the general interest of the federation. The Commission is responsible for initiating draft legislation and implementing directives, decisions, budgets, and programs adopted by Parliament and the Council. The Commission also represents the Union on the national stage. The Court of Justice ensures that Community law is uniformly interpreted and effectively applied. The fifth institution, the Court of Auditors, oversees the financial management of the EU.

The two most major recent goals of the EU have been to create a single market, where the economies of the member states would be completely integrated, and to establish a universal currency for Europe. Progress has been made with both, from the signing of the Single European Act in 1986, removing physical, technical, and fiscal barriers between countries to help establish the single market, to the introduction of the euro (currency) into circulation in 1999, but coins and notes were not introduced until January 2002, when they were phased in.

---

be based on hard evidence. France and Germany also made statements suggesting that plans for retaliation did not need to be military in nature and that thorough investigations needed to be conducted. Although support for a military reprisal remained tentative in the European Union, the EU was quick to move against al-Qaeda cells operating on the continent. Hundreds of arrests were made in the UK, France, and Germany of suspected members of the terrorist organization. The governments of Europe further enacted anti-terrorist legislation to bolster the ability of the states to fight terrorist groups and outlawed some political groups associated with Islamic terror.

Although initially reluctant to release evidence against bin Laden due to concerns over intelligence breaches and conclusive evidence, the United States continued to place the blame for the attack on Osama bin Laden and al-Qaeda. In late September 2001 the United States privately released evidence of bin Laden's complicity to its European allies in NATO. After receiving the evidence, several of the European allies became convinced of bin Laden's responsibility. On October 4, the United Kingdom claimed it had reached the "clear conclusion" that al-Qaeda carried out the attacks against the United States. The U.S. report made the claim that the government of Afghanistan, known as the Taliban, had allowed bin Laden to operate within Afghanistan and therefore was partially responsible for the attacks. The United States and the international community demanded that the Taliban hand over bin Laden unconditionally to the United States or face immediate military strikes. The Taliban refused to comply with the demands, stating that bin Laden remained a guest of Afghanistan.

On October 7, 2001, the United States and the United Kingdom began Operation Enduring Freedom, the military campaign against the Taliban and al-Qaeda in Afghanistan. In the early stages of Enduring Freedom, the United States and United Kingdom attacked Afghani air defenses throughout the country. These attacks focused heavily on targets near the capital city of Kabul and Taliban strongholds in the southern city of Kandahar. Additionally, U.S. special forces and British Special Air Service (SAS) troops were deployed into Afghan territory to search for al-Qaeda forces, including Osama bin Laden.

The United States justified its attack on Afghanistan to the UN Security Council as self defense. The countries of Europe responded to the U.S. led attacks on Afghanistan with support and promises of assistance. Although European leftist parties remained critical of Operation Enduring Freedom, the governments of Europe were steadfast in their support. French president Jacques Chirac (1995–) committed France to providing military assistance to the campaign against Afghanistan. France agreed to provide fueling vessels to the campaign and announced that French ground troops would be deployed. Similarly, Germany's Chancellor Gerhard Schroder (1998–) announced that Germany would provide military support to the United States. To allow for maximum U.S. air power in the Afghan campaign, NATO agreed to provide early warning surveillance aircraft (AWACs) to the United States to monitor U.S. airspace.

Although several EU countries planned to send ground troops to assist in the war effort, the Taliban's grip on Afghanistan was cracking quickly under the U.S.-UK bombing campaign. On the ground, the Taliban was losing ground to rival political groups. The anti-Taliban United Islamic Front for the Salvation of Afghanistan, also known as the Northern Alliance, had been engaged in a civil war against the Taliban throughout much of the 1990s. After destroying the air defenses of the Taliban, the bombing campaign began assisting Northern Alliance commanders by attacking Taliban ground troops throughout Afghanistan. The air support provided by the United States and United Kingdom allowed the Northern Alliance to make

COUNTRIES OF EUROPE AND OTHER PARTS OF THE WORLD ALIGNED IN SUPPORT OF THE UNITED STATES IN THE WAKE OF THE SEPTEMBER 11 ATTACKS. THE SIGN READS, "AGAINST TERRORISM: FOR PEACE WITHIN JUSTICE." *(AP/Wide World Photos/ Claudia Gazzini. Reproduced by permission.)*

rapid advances against the Taliban army, resulting in massive Taliban defections. On November 12, Northern Alliance troops entered the capital city of Kabul. Soon after, Pashtun rebels moved against Taliban troops in the south. Despite fears that Enduring Freedom would take months and last into the summer months, the campaign had virtually ended in early December with the dramatic defeat of the Taliban at the southern city of Kandahar.

As the Taliban was collapsing, the United States and the European Union hosted a meeting of several rival Afghani political groups in Bonn,

RUSSIAN PRESIDENT VLADIMIR PUTIN (CENTER) MEETS WITH EU PRESIDENT ROMANO PRODI (LEFT), BELGIAN PRESIDENT GUY VERHOFSTADT (RIGHT), AND OTHERS DURING AN OCTOBER 2001 EU-RUSSIA SUMMIT DISCUSSING SECURITY AND COOPERATION AGAINST TERRORIST THREATS. *(AP/Wide World Photos/Thierry Charlier. Reproduced by permission.)*

Germany. On December 5, the factions agreed to the Bonn Accords to form a provisional government in Afghanistan. The factions appointed Pashtun leader Hamad Karzai as interim president. Although the Taliban had been defeated and al-Qaeda faced severe attacks from U.S. forces in the mountains of Tora Bora, the stability of Afghanistan was still in doubt. Osama bin Laden and Taliban leader Mullah Mohammed Omar remained at large. The U.S. and EU intelligence communities claimed that Taliban and al-Qaeda fighters could possibly regroup in the mountains of Afghanistan or Pakistan and attempt a guerrilla counterattack against the new government. Although the political factions agreed to Karzai's interim rule, Karzai's ability to form a successful, functioning, and viable government remained in question.

Given the unstable political situation on the ground in Afghanistan, the UN Security Council approved resolution 1386, calling for a British-led multinational peacekeeping force to be inserted into Afghanistan. Although the United States remained committed to its goal of finding bin Laden and preventing Afghanistan from reverting to a terrorist haven, President Bush was reluctant to commit U.S. troops to peacekeeping duties. One of Bush's campaign promises during the 2000 U.S. presiden-

tial election was that the involvement of the U.S. military in nation-building would decrease.

While the United States was reluctant, the countries of the European Union saw a concrete opportunity to involve themselves in the campaign against terror. Despite commitments to assist militarily in the war against terror, none of the EU, with the exception of Britain, had yet participated in the campaign due to the brevity of the military phase of the Afghan military campaign. The EU therefore decided to contribute substantially to the peacekeeping force designed to promote stability in the shattered country. Contributions of military troops were made from Belgium, Denmark, France, Germany, Italy, Greece, Portugal, and Spain.

The goals of the peacekeepers were to maintain civil peace throughout the country, assist in the establishment of authority for the new government, and continue to root out terrorist groups. A fear amongst the coalition was that if the Karzai government lacked the political capacity to monopolize the legitimate use of violence, Afghani warlords would emerge to terrorize civilians, as had happened in the past. The peacekeepers were to assist in the rebuilding of Afghanistan as well as establish authority and train an Afghan military and police force to maintain the government's strength over competing power centers, including the old tribal warlords. The peacekeepers additionally would participate in operations, such as Operation Anaconda in March 2002, designed at rooting out al-Qaeda cells remaining in Afghanistan. Anaconda consisted of U.S., Afghan, Canadian, and European troops heading into the mountains in the east of the country to attack remaining al-Qaeda pockets.

The Coalition Under Strain

By the beginning of 2002 the coalition had achieved several of its objectives in Afghanistan. The Taliban had been toppled, a new interim government was in place, and al-Qaeda was fleeing the country. Additionally, U.S. and EU police and intelligence services successfully broke up several al-Qaeda cells throughout western Europe. The cooperative efforts of NATO led Lord Robertson to conclude in his speech to American Pilgrims political group on January 31, 2002, that Operation Enduring Freedom was "a high point in the Atlantic relationship" and that the "bond between the United States and Europe was as strong as ever."

Although Robertson was correct that the coalition achieved success against the Taliban, many observers noticed the countries of the EU shifting policy lines away from the United States. One of the first areas of friction to emerge between the United States and Europe involved the treatment of Taliban and al-Qaeda prisoners. After capture, several of the prisoners under U.S. control were sent to a detention facility known as Camp X-Ray at Guantanamo Bay, a U.S. naval base in Cuba. Many EU countries believed that these prisoners should be treated under the Geneva Convention's definition of prisoners of war. Since these fighters were captured in wartime, Europeans believed the Geneva Convention was applicable to the prisoners. The United States, however, refused to classify the prisoners at Guantanamo Bay as prisoners of war. Instead, the United States used the term "detainees" to describe the prisoners' status. According to the Geneva Convention on the treatment of prisoners of war, the United States had no right to interrogate the prisoners and was obligated to send them back after the end of the war. Despite the end of the war in Afghanistan, no prisoners have been returned.

In addition to the U.S. refusal to classify the Afghan detainees as prisoners of war, the European public heard rumors of maltreatment at the prison facility at Guantanamo Bay. Several reports indicated that the prisoners had been beaten and subject to humiliation. Although the United States fervently denied these charges, U.S. commanders acknowledged that the prisoners were required to shave their beards and were subject to extensive searches. The United States claimed that since the captives were hardened fighters, such measures were necessary to protect the soldiers guarding the prisoners. The Europeans, however, believed that not only was the United States violating the Geneva Convention, but also it was subjecting the prisoners to cultural humiliation. Since growing beards was a part of the detainees' practice of Islam, the EU countries felt the United States was violating the religious rights of the prisoners. The United States countered that it allowed the prisoners access to the Qur'an, the ability to exercise and pray together, and culturally specific meals. Many Americans, including Secretary of Defense Donald Rumsfeld, argued that the prisoners were receiving better treatment at Guantanamo Bay than they would receive if they had stayed in Afghanistan.

Many European human rights groups, including the British-based Amnesty International, demanded access to the prisoners and the right to inspect the base at Guantanamo. The United States initially refused the right of any non-governmental organization to inspect the base. Under growing international pressure, however, the International Red Cross and a contingent of British inspectors were allowed into Guantanamo to inspect conditions. After making several suggestions to the U.S. command there, the Red Cross and the British inspectors concluded that no violations of human rights were taking place at the detention facility. Images of prisoners in shackles and bright red outfits walking through the barbed wire structure horrified the European public. Despite the conclusions of the inspectors, many Europeans believed that Guantanamo was a symbol of the unwillingness of the United States to comply with international law. Although the United States decried the Taliban's violations of international law, the European public perceived U.S. actions as a signal that the Bush administration felt it was above the law.

In addition to alleged human rights violations at Guantanamo, European civilians and their governments remained concerned that the United States would use the death penalty against European citizens extradited to the United States. For several years European countries had condemned the use of the death penalty in the United States. A provision for joining the EU is the abolishment of capital punishment. In particular, Europeans were disturbed at President Bush's death penalty history, which included a record number of executions while Bush served as governor of Texas.

The fears that European citizens would be subject to the death penalty were exacerbated by President Bush's call for the use of military tribunals against suspected terrorists. Military tribunals are expected to increase the speed of trials and, by reducing the evidentiary requirements for prosecution necessary in a civilian trial, decrease the possibility that terrorist suspects would escape conviction. Europeans feared that extradited suspects would face improper trials resulting in death penalty punishments.

Due to fears of the new U.S. trial system and application of the death penalty, both the United Kingdom and France called for a guarantee from the United States that suspects would not face capital punishment. To prevent its citizens from being subject to the death penalty, the United Kingdom asked that prisoners with British citizenry held at Guantanamo Bay be extradited back to the UK for trial. Similarly, France asked the United States to refrain from using the death penalty against extradited French citizens. In particular, France asked that death penalty charges against Zacarias Moussaoui, a suspected terrorist with ties to the September 11 attack, not be pursued. U.S. Attorney General John Ashcroft stated that extradition involving the possibility of the death penalty would be determined on a case by case basis. In March 2002 Ashcroft announced that if Moussaoui was convicted, prosecutors would pursue the death penalty. Ashcroft's announcement greatly disturbed the members of the European Union. Despite their repeated requests for the United States not to apply the death penalty, it indicated that it would continue to do so. Ashcroft's decision to pursue the death penalty prompted French officials to threaten to cease cooperation in the war on terror.

While the treatment of prisoners at Guantanamo and the lingering cloud of the death penalty represented the beginnings of friction between the United States and Europe, the State of the Union Address by President Bush in January of 2002 sent shock waves throughout the countries of the EU. In his address President Bush claimed that the United States would act against an "axis of evil" comprised of North Korea, Iran, and Iraq. According to President Bush these countries were active sponsors of international terrorism directed against the United States. Although Afghanistan had been defeated, Bush declared that the war was only beginning and that the United States would target any nation guilty of sponsoring international terrorism: "I will not wait on events while dangers gather. I will not stand by as peril draws closer and closer. The United States of America will not per-

mit the world's most dangerous regimes to threaten us with the world's most destructive weapons."

Although Bush did not explicitly call for military action against the "axis of evil," the governments of Iran, Iraq, and North Korea believed that Bush's statement indicated that war might be imminent. The bellicose nature of the speech greatly alarmed EU member states. Bush indicated that if the United States believed that any country sponsoring terror posed a threat to U.S. national security, the United States was prepared to destroy it as it had destroyed Afghanistan. Even more alarming, the speech indicated that the United States was prepared to act unilaterally. Given the superpower status of the United States, the EU interpreted Bush's statements as stating that the United States would attack any country it wishes if it deemed a threat was present, regardless of the views of the international community.

After the State of the Union Address the European allies were quick to challenge the Bush administration's strategy for conducting the war on terror. French prime minister Lionel Jospin and his foreign minister Hubert Vedrine criticized the simplistic nature of Bush's foreign policy. According to Jospin, all foreign policy should not be viewed according to the war on terrorism and the use of military threats. Jospin argued that instead of unilateral measures, the United States should work within a coalition to help solve the problems of the world together. In a press conference on February 8, 2002, Jospin argued that "cooperation means members of the international community can tackle together the roots of problems, since none of us can hope to resolve them alone."

Germany also indicated a growing sense of isolation from the United States and its foreign policy. Like France, Germany envisioned a more multilateral approach to solving the terrorism problem and addressing the root causes of terrorism. In response to the apparent ignoring of German viewpoints, German foreign minister Joschka Fischer argued that the United States should not treat its allies like satellite countries. Instead of expecting the EU to follow the lead of the United States, Fischer believed that the United States should consult with its allies before taking initiatives. Even the United Kingdom, the staunchest supporter of the United States, expressed reservations about classifying North Korea, Iraq, and Iran as a unified bloc of terror and using military threats to achieve foreign policy goals against terrorism. EU external affairs chief Chris Patten articulated the position of the entire European Union when he stated that the United States should curb its unilateralist instinct.

Although North Korea and Iran were also mentioned in the State of the Union Address, the EU and the nations of the Middle East were particularly worried that the State of the Union signaled the coming of a U.S. attack against Iraq. Since the Gulf War (1991) hostilities between the United States and Iraqi dictator Saddam Hussein remained extremely high. The United States and the United Kingdom remained committed to preventing Iraq from obtaining weapons of mass destruction. The United States placed Iraq on the U.S. State Department's list of sponsors of international terrorism as a result of Iraq's sponsorship of anti-Iranian groups and a failed assassination attempt against U.S. president George H. Bush (1989–93) in the early 1990s. While Iraq had no visible connections to al-Qaeda, many U.S. planners believed that the threat was too great to ignore. Although Hussein did not fit the traditional definition of a terrorist, some U.S. policymakers are presenting the issue as if he was no different from Osama bin Laden in terms of threats to the national security of the United States. As a result, some EU members felt that the United States intended to use the war on terrorism to target Iraq and end the ten-year stalemate with the Iraqi dictator.

The countries of the EU were particularly concerned about a U.S. invasion of Iraq. With the exception of Britain, the members of the EU favored beginning negotiations with Saddam Hussein. In particular, France was very critical of the U.S.-UK enforcement of the no fly zones over northern and southern Iraq and the continuation of devastating economic sanctions stemming from the 1991 war. The Europeans worried that the United States would seize the opportunity to attack Iraq under the guise of the war on terrorism. If this occurred, the United States could potentially threaten regional stability in the Middle East. The threat of U.S. force prompted many EU countries to declare that they would not support American actions against Iraq if the United States were to invade the country. Although the EU was concerned about the acquisition of weapons of mass destruction by Iraq, it remained committed to solving this problem through negotiation instead of American calls for the use of force.

Aside from fears of U.S. unilateralism, the EU believed that military action was not the most effective way of fighting international terrorism. Although it supported military action in Afghanistan, the majority of the EU felt that it was time to end the military phase of the war on terror. Instead of using military power, the EU believed that international institutions should be used to

INCIDENTS OF TERRORISM IN THE EUROPEAN UNION, 2000

Country	Terrorist Incidents
Denmark	1
England	2
France	1
Greece	2
Northern Ireland	12
Spain	21
Sweden	1

NATIONS OF THE EUROPEAN UNION ARE NO STRANGER TO TERRORISM. SPAIN EXPERIENCED THE HIGHEST NUMBER OF TERRORIST INCIDENTS IN 2000, MOST ATTRIBUTED TO THE BASQUE SEPARATIST GROUP ETA. *(Gale Group.)*

combat some of the world's problems associated with terror, such as the persistent Arab-Israeli conflict and the proliferation of weapons of mass destruction. While the United States did not believe that negotiations were possible with regimes such as Iraq and Iran, the countries of Europe were more inclined to use incentives, such as promises of investment, to induce compliance with international law. Fears of unilateralism and the continued use of military force continue to be a source of friction between the United States and the European Union to the present in the war on terrorism.

RECENT HISTORY AND THE FUTURE

After September 11, 2001, the European Union stood side by side with the United States. The EU supported U.S. efforts in Afghanistan politically and assisted in the peacekeeping efforts following the fall of the Taliban. The EU's response to the United States was one of cooperation. Currently, several observers have noticed that friction within the coalition between the EU and the United States threatens the continuation of European-American cooperation in the war on terrorism. Some have warned that increasing U.S. unilateralism threatens to damage the relationship between the United States and its European allies and threatens multilateral efforts against terrorism. A study by Jon Cauley and Todd Sandler suggests that cooperation between countries is most likely to achieve successful results in combating terrorism. If

AL-QAEDA AND THE EUROPEAN UNION

The original fatwa issued by Osama bin Laden in 1996 was only directed at the United States. However, bin Laden extended the fatwa to include the European Union in 1998. Although al-Qaeda has yet to specifically target European civilians or cities, it has used Europe as a staging ground against the United States. The investigation into the September 11 attacks revealed that several al-Qaeda activists, some of whom participated in the attacks, had European citizenry. Several al-Qaeda cells have also been found throughout the countries of western Europe, including the United Kingdom, France, and Germany, and threats have been made against American targets in Europe.

After the attacks on September 11, the European Union began actively harmonizing intelligence sharing throughout Europe and with the United States. The countries of the European Union further began passing anti-terrorism legislation to disrupt the ability of terrorist cells to operate on the continent. Additionally, European police forces became active in cracking down on European-based al-Qaeda cells. In addition to the military campaign, the European Union remains determined to prevent terrorists from using Europe as a sanctuary and denying terrorist groups the finances needed to conduct terrorist operations.

this is true, a deterioration in U.S.-EU cooperation in the war on terrorism suggests that efforts against terrorist organizations will decrease in effectiveness due to coalitional strain.

The rift between the United States and the EU is most on the question of where to use military force. While the Bush administration remained keen on applying the use of military power to defeat terrorist groups, the EU argued for the use of international institutions and multilateral agreements. The EU seemed more inclined to support diplomatic initiatives as opposed to the Bush administration's calls for military force. According to the EU, the roots of terror must be addressed before terrorism can be eradicated. The United States, on the other hand, made the case that while addressing the core factors associated with the breeding of terrorism was necessary, the danger from existing terrorist groups was too great to ignore. The United States therefore believed that to guarantee the security of the United States and the European Union, terrorist groups must first be defeated.

Although the debate over the use of force and U.S. unilateralism continues, the future of EU involvement against terrorism remains in its commitment to assist the United States in terms of intelligence and law enforcement. Following September 11, the EU and the United States took steps to share intelligence and harmonize anti-terrorism measures in order to improve coordination against terrorist groups. In several EU countries such as Britain, France, and Germany, U.S. law enforcement officials have worked with their European counterparts in an effort to destroy al-Qaeda cells operating throughout the EU. The EU countries have moved to close legal loopholes that allow suspected terrorists to escape incarceration. The EU also continues to strengthen cooperation between its police agencies EUROPOL and EUROJUST and U.S. law enforcement. Despite disagreements in the application of the death penalty, the EU remains committed to pursuing terrorist networks throughout Europe and assisting the United States in breaking up terrorist organizations.

The countries of the European Union have long experienced the consequences of terrorist activities. In addition to the current threat from al-Qaeda, several other terrorist groups and the potential for new groups remain threats to stability within the European Union. September 11 brought to the world's notice what the potential consequences of terrorism may be. After defeating the Taliban and al-Qaeda in Afghanistan, the EU discovered that al-Qaeda was attempting to acquire weapons of mass destruction. Plans were also discovered for potential attacks throughout Europe, such as an attack in the heart of London. These discoveries and the September 11 tragedy demonstrated to the EU that terrorism remains a particularly dangerous threat. Although friction exists on how to conduct the campaign against terror and on some of the methods used, the partnership of the European Union and the United States should remain through the sharing of intelligence and police coordination. Both the EU and the United States recognize the dangers of terrorism and have made commitments to work together to prevent another catastrophe like September 11.

BIBLIOGRAPHY

"Ashcroft Questioned on Death Penalty," CNN, December 12, 2001. Available online at http://www.cnn.com/2001/WORLD/europe/12/12/gen.ashcroft.blunkett/index.html (cited April 15, 2002).

Cauley, Jon, and Todd Sandler. "Fighting World War III: A Suggested Strategy," *Terrorism*, Bristol, England: Taylor and Francis, vol. 11, pp. 181–195.

European Union. Available online at http://www.europa.eu .int (cited April 27, 2002).

Ferreira, Anton, and Sayed Salahuddin. "U.S. Threatens 'Terror' States, Seeks More Arms," *World News Digest,* January 31, 2002.

"France Steps Up Criticism of the U.S.," CNN, February 8, 2002. Available online at http://www.cnn.com/2002/ WORLD/europe/02/08/france.jospin/index.html (cited April 15, 2002).

Kaniuk, Ross. "The Day the World Stood Still," *Daily Star,* September 12, 2001, p. 15.

Karon, Tony. "Why Guantanamo Has Europe Hopping Mad," *Time,* April 1, 2002.

Keesing's Record of World Events, vol. 47–48. London: Longman Press, 2001–2002.

Lesser, Ian O., Bruce Hoffman, John Arquila, David Ronfeldt, and Michele Zanini. *Countering the New Terrorism.* Santa Monica, CA: RAND Corporation, 1999.

"A Peace to Keep?" *Economist,* December 15, 2001.

Robertson, Lord. "NATO After September 11." Speech given to the Pilgrims of the United States, January 31, 2002.

"Terror Death Penalty Angers France," CNN, March 28, 2002. Available online at http://www.cnn.com/2002 WORLD/europe/03/28/inv.france.moussaoui/index .html (cited April 15, 2002).

Wright, Jonathan. "Transatlantic Rift Could Keep Growing." *World News Digest,* February 23, 2002.

Navin A. Bapat

EXTREMISM—THE FUNDAMENTALS

THE CONFLICT

The word "extremism" is used to identify people, ideologies, or organizations that differ radically from mainstream society to such an extent that they are seen as existing on the margins of that society. This term, however, is applied by those in the mainstream. "Extremists" today usually inhabit cultural worlds in which they are the center, not the margins. Disaffected, frustrated, and feeling under attack for their religion, culture, ethnicity, or other attribute, extremists may respond with violence in an attempt to change the situation or gain attention for their cause.

Social

- Extremists, once geographically isolated from one another, have used the Internet to connect physically separate communities of activists, disperse news, information, and in-group rhetoric. This both increases their interconnectedness with other extremist groups and increases their isolation from the mainstream.

- Suffering, be it human rights violations, ethnic or religious discrimination, or economic or other repression, is often a contributing factor to the formation of "extremist" groups.

Psychological

- Radical views, when joined with religion, often cast the universe in terms of a cosmic battle that depends on the actions of individuals who otherwise feel themselves a part of a faceless, meaningless society. When cosmic salvation is at stake, what does the death of one or more lives mean?

Political

- When a small peripheral population takes on the might of a major regional power, the small group is likely to suffer great casualties. With such odds, martyrdom, or dying for one's cause, may itself become a goal for many people.

- If governments push extremist groups outside the circle of potential dialogue, it isolates them entirely, ensuring no possible interchange other than a deadly one.

When we use the word "extremism," we identify persons, ideologies, or organizations, which differ so radically from mainstream society that they are seen as existing in the margins or peripheries of normalcy. This term, however, is applied by those—like most of the readers of this volume—that exist in that mainstream. Emile Durkheim, a classic theorist of sociology, proposed that every society labels some portion of its members as deviants of one sort or other, suggesting this recognition functions to keep the generally followed norms of society well-defined and strong. In this broadest level of analysis, understanding the phenomenon of terrorism today can benefit from interpretations of other extreme social institutions and responses to them from the mainstream in other times and places.

Durkheim did note, however, that under normal conditions the "extremes" a society can tolerate remain within certain proportional parameters. Durkheim also lived in a world that was relatively geographically contained, as compared with today's world in which the boundaries of "societies" cannot be drawn on a map in convenient cookie-cutter fashion. As we know, that is precisely the problem with many contemporary questions of extremism; organizations extend their reach globally, and the definition of mainstream and periphery cannot be made with Dukheimian certainty any longer. What is "extreme" to middle America may be quite the norm to another, transnationally-defined, culture. We live now in a global community of criss-crossing boundaries and overlapping units that demands far different modes of analysis.

"Extremists" today usually inhabit cultural worlds in which they are at the center, not at the margins. This is a key psychological shift one must

CHRONOLOGY

1960s A movement in northwest India supports the establishment of a new state in which the Punjabi language would be the language of the majority.

1966 The Punjab state is established in India. It has a Sikh religious majority and a Hindu minority.

1970s India's Green Revolution results in Punjab becoming "the breadbasket of India." The Indian government diverts river waters through Punjab, lowers Punjabi crop prices for sale to the rest of India, and distributes hydroelectricity to other regions over the objections and growing frustration of Punjabi farmers.

Late 1970s Nonviolent protests break out in many Punjabi cities.

1980s Sikhs in Punjab, India, experience an upsurge in religious activity. Several militant strands of Sikhism emerge. Two leaders from these militants, Jarnail Singh Bhindranwale and Babbar Khalsa, relate dis-

crimination against Punjabis with discrimination against the Sikh faith and raise fears that Sikhism may disappear within the Indian secular state.

June 1884 The Indian army launches an assault against Sikh militants, who take refuge in the Golden Temple Complex in Amritsar, Punjab.

November 1984 Indian prime minister Indira Gandhi is assassinated by two of her Sikh bodyguards.

April 1986 A Declaration of Independence of Khalistan is distributed from Amritsar, Punjab, setting out terms for the establishment of a new nation.

Late 1980s By the end of the 1980s many people involved in the movement for an independent Khalistan have fled the country. From their new homes, they develop an active community, in which they set up Khalsa schools and lobbying foreign offices for the Khalistan movement.

make when attempting to understand how groups like Aum Shinrikyo in Japan, the Khalistan Commando Force in India, or Aryan Nations in the United States, actually function. The social autonomy of the extraordinary worlds extremists inhabit is extended by technologies such as the Internet, which connects physically separated communities of activists and disperses news, information and in-group rhetoric instantaneously. Anthropologists who study these cultures note the "hothouse" atmosphere of life as a member of one of these groups; whether one lives geographically amidst "average" people or not, one can mentally and spiritually be enmeshed in a cosmic battle whose dimensions one's neighbors cannot even imagine. Likewise, desktop publishing allows an abundance of literature that previously would have been prohibitively expensive to produce; video cameras and duplication possibilities mean that cassettes featuring charismatic leaders, traumatic or victorious community events can replace conventional television just as community-produced books replace the trade market novels the rest of us read. Technology allows both unprecedented interconnectedness and unprecedented isolation, and we are seeing the advantages and disadvantages of each in the likewise unprecedented meteoric rise of extremist organizations.

Durkheim, were he alive today, would have to revise his ideas to account for these new and staggering realities. Meanwhile the cultures that flourish in pluralist democracies we have appropriately created in his time also have to cope with one other, less fortunate, reality: the availability of weapons, and the readiness of many groups to use them.

HISTORICAL BACKGROUND

Aum Shinrikyo

On March 20, 1995 the world experienced its first (and so far, only) successful, large-scale terrorist attack in which chemical weapons were used. The attack took place during the morning commute on a Tokyo subway when three young men carrying sharpened umbrellas punctured plastic bags containing liquid chemicals that released poisonous sarin gas into the crowded trains. Twelve people eventually died from the episode and thousands were affected, many suffering from permanent eye and throat disorders.

Convicted of masterminding the Tokyo attack was Shoko Asahara (born Chizuo Matsumoto), the leader of Aum Shinrikyo, a religious movement combining elements of Buddhism with millennial expectations about the end of the world and an agenda for group survival. Despite the leader's conviction to prison and the world's condemnation of the sarin gas attack, Aum Shinrikyo is continuing to grow not only in Japan but also in Russia and several other areas. One must therefore ask what it is about this organization that is appealing—particularly against the backdrop of a society typically thought to be among the best-regulated and safest in the world.

The name Aum Shinrikyo comes from the Hindu mantra *om*, followed by *shinri* meaning "supreme truth," and *kyo* or "teaching." Its founder was a charismatic individual (born in 1955) who grew up, blind in one eye, in a school in which all the other children were sightless. Failing his college entrance examinations, Asahara began a spiritual journey into the Agonshu movement, which drew from various mystic and yogic practices and focused on the prophecy of future events. By 1984 he decided to leave the group and journeyed to India and the Himalayas, where he claimed to receive mystic visions from Hindu masters. He returned to Japan in 1987 to start his own organization, called the Teaching of the Supreme Truth, "Aum Shinrikyo."

Part of Asahara's truth was the idea of an Armageddon to come, a notion he drew from the Christian Bible as well as from Nostradamus. He predicted a violent conflagration of radioactivity (far worse than the Japanese had already experienced at Hiroshima and Nagasaki), poison gas, and epidemics. Notably, there was an anti-American slant to the prophecy as well: the notion that the conflagration would begin in Tokyo, with the United States taking over the Japanese government. Ashara specifically told his members that the United States was the only military power that possessed chemical weapons, and sarin gas was named in a book of his prophecies that came out a few months before the subway attack. When the attack occurred, in trains nearing the station directly beneath Japan's parliament building, the Diet, Aum group members left in the dark about the planning assumed, when they heard the news, that Asahara's prophecy was being fulfilled. Armageddon was beginning, with an American chemical attack on the heart of the Japanese government.

Even after it became clear that Asahara and his inner circle of leaders in Aum Shinrikyo had indeed carried out the March 20 sarin gas attack, loyal members of the group found ways to understand this action consonant with their belief in the leaders' infallibility. According to scholars who have carefully studied Asahara's writings, the guru interpreted certain principles of Tibetan Buddhism to mean that a spiritually advanced individual such as himself could kill people caught in cycles of evil as an act of mercy to allow them to move on to a higher plane. They also apparently came to accept the notion that Asahara himself existed on a plane of existence not accessible to ordinary mortals, so that although he may, for example, appear to be conspiring to commit an act of terrorism and later being jailed by Japanese authorities, in reality this appearance was but the surface manifestation of some far deeper plan whose ultimate purpose most of us cannot begin to understand.

Cult scholars point out that one attraction of the Aum might be its relatively egalitarian and familial atmosphere, compared with the formal and hierarchical structure of the wider Japanese society. Like many small and communally-oriented groups, it may offer individuals a sense of "home," a place where people know one's name and face in a rapidly changing world in which the ground seems to be shifting beneath one's very feet. Yet Aum can in no way be considered anti-modern; it contained and contains among its members educated scientists and makes use of all the technology available to a technically advanced society like Japan. This presents a paradox for those who would try to dismiss these kinds of movements as nothing more than cults of the backward or ignorant. They are born of fully modern conditions. Their presence may be an indicator of wider discontents, however buried, in the societies from which they emerge.

Khalistan Commando Force

A very different sort of group is represented by separatists in the state of Punjab in India who are fighting for an independent homeland to be called Khalistan or "land of the pure." The movement for Khalistan is one of a concert of centrifugal movements in India, which is a state comprising many ethnic, linguistic, racial, and religious groups. The Kashmiris in the north, the Nagas in the east, the Tamils in the south, and the Punjabis who are agitating for a separate Khalistan, are but a sampling of the "extremists" the central government in New Delhi has had to deal with since the country's independence in 1947.

During the 1960s a movement arose in the northwestern part of India seeking a new state in which the Punjabi language would be the mother tongue of the majority. The movement succeeded, resulting by 1966 in what is today Punjab state, consisting of a Sikh majority and a Hindu minority in terms of religion. In the 1970s this state was a focus of Green Revolution technology and it became "the breadbasket of India," producing bumper

A MAN HOLDS A CONFEDERATE FLAG ALOFT AS MEMBERS OF THE WHITE SUPREMACIST GROUP ARYAN NATIONS WALK IN AN IDAHO PARADE IN 2000. *(© Reuters NewMedia Inc./CORBIS. Reproduced by permission.)*

crops of wheat and other agricultural products each year. Dependent on irrigation, however, Punjabi farmers grew resentful when plans were drawn up to divert river waters to less successful neighboring states, as well as when agricultural prices were held down by a centrally regulated economy to keep Punjab's grains and vegetables accessible to the rest of poverty-stricken India. Hydroelectricity, as well, which could have helped to nourish Punjab's underdeveloped industrial sector, was distributed to other regions. Meanwhile, newly-educated youth who had grown beyond their rural origins remained unemployed, their options in Punjab limited by the largely agricultural economy.

During the Emergency (1977–78), or period of dictatorship declared by Prime Minister Indira Gandhi in the latter part of the 1970s there were extensive nonviolent protests launched in Punjab's cities. People were arrested by the thousands and herded into jails. A resolution calling for the decentralization of authority was supported by various states that agreed that New Delhi had become overbearing in its regulation of India, but it led nowhere. By the beginning of the 1980s there was a significant upsurge of religious activity among the Sikhs who form the bulk of the rural agricultural sector of Punjab. Baptisms into the Sikh faith increased dramatically and there were calls for returns to the more orthodox or rigorous forms of Sikh tra-

dition. Several strands of militant Sikhism emerged, a major one coalesced around the charismatic preacher Jarnail Singh Bhindranwale and a second one called the Babbar Khalsa. Both of these began to equate discrimination against Punjabis with discrimination against the Sikh faith, and to predict that if Sikhism were not revitalized it might be in danger of disappearing into the Indian secular state. These militant groups began to engage in acts of violence in the early 1980s, claiming they fought in defense of Sikhism and were in line with Sikhism's command that "when all peaceful means have failed it is justified to turn to the hilt of the sword."

In June 1984 the Indian Army launched an assault on the militants, who had taken refuge at the Golden Temple Complex in the Punjabi city of Amritsar. In the battle that ensued, several thousand innocent civilians were killed and many of the sacred and historic buildings were destroyed. This apparent overreaction to the threat to national security posed by a small band of militants sparked an overwhelming turn in popular sentiment. People all across Punjab who previously had been only mildly interested in the grievances relating to economics and politics or who had been only somewhat concerned about Sikh-Hindu religious questions, now became utterly inflamed by the Indian government's actions in Amritsar. Pictures of tanks rolling across the pavements of the Golden Temple Complex and of women and children bleeding on the sidewalks were passed from hand to hand. Later that year, two Sikhs—her own bodyguards—assassinated Prime Minister Indira Gandhi, who had ordered the assault. Although across the globe people mourned her passing, in Punjab's countryside the mood was more akin to a sense of satisfaction. Had "normal" people become "extremists?"

On April 29, 1986 a Declaration of Independence of Khalistan was promulgated from Amritsar, setting out the terms of existence of what was hoped would become a new and separate nation. Of course, it is easier to declare a nation than to actually acquire one, and a decades-long period of civil unrest immediately broke out. There were several guerilla forces which made up the Khalistani insurgency, with the Khalistan Commando Force named in the Declaration of Khalistan as the core of what was envisioned as the eventual defense force of the nation of Khalistan. A brutal—and in the long term successful—counterinsurgency was launched by the Indian government, carried out by police and paramilitary forces and drawing on an extensive repertoire of legal and extralegal means of repression.

What was it actually like to be a member of the Khalistan Commando Force? Most of the participants were young, male, and Sikh. Although there is no doubt that the attractions of "heroism" and romantic dash played some role in the appeal the movement exerted on village youth, a more widespread reason for recruitment was the suffering endured by the rural population at the hands of an increasingly ruthless police force. Human rights abuses criticized by Amnesty International, Human Rights Watch, and other monitoring organizations include torture, extrajudicial execution, custodial rape, and "disappearance." It was often in response to such abuses that young people would join the Khalistan Commando Force or some other guerilla group like the Khalistan Liberation Force, the Bhindranwale Tiger Force, the Sikh Students Federation, or the Babbar Khalsa.

Once in the group, young men lived as "brothers," usually sheltering with families, on the run from house to house, village to village, field to field. Depending on the period when they entered "the struggle," life expectancy for an individual joining the Commando Force could be just a few weeks or a few months in length. Martyrdom—death in struggle—was the expected outcome of a decision to join the Khalistani freedom fighters. The freedom fighters were, of course, known as "terrorists"

in all of India, whose population could not imagine what prompted well-bred young men to throw their lives away for a cause like that of Khalistan. In the popular imagination, "the Sikh terrorist" became a dreaded figure, a likely psychopathic killer.

By the end of the 1980s many people involved in the movement for Khalistan had fled India for countries like England, Canada, or the United States, who gave them political asylum. This created a new situation for communities like that of the Khalistanis, who now found themselves scattered across several continents. Khalistanis were able to use this leverage to their advantage by creating lobbying offices in London, Ottawa, and Washington, by putting out newspapers and starting up radio stations in situations in which more freedom is allowed than in India. They also started their own "Khalsa schools" and summer camps to teach their young. Today it may well be said that the Khalistan movement is as much centered in the diaspora as in the homeland, where decades of suppression as well as disillusionment with the violence of the militants has led to a quieting of the struggle.

Aryan Nations

Aryan Nations is one among a set of white supremacist organizations in North America that came upon the scene in the 1970s. Calling for a "whites only" homeland, Richard Butler preached that the white race was in danger of being swamped by Jews, blacks, and other "mudpeople." He drew together neo-Nazis, former Klansmen, tax protesters, militiamen, and Christian Identity followers into annual Aryan Worlds Congresses, giving the white supremacist movement a unity and strength it had never seen before. In 1983 an affiliated white supremacist group known as "the Order" went on a publicized crime spree ending in a shoot-out with federal agents.

With fresh input from the youth Skinhead movement, concerts of "white power" music, media blitzes, and heavy use of electronic resources were employed to gain new supporters. Aryan Nations grew to new levels of strength in the 1990s, establishing branches in many states and in several European countries. They claim that their official website receives five hundred hits a day.

Although groups with racist ideologies often act in coalition with groups on the right-wing of the North American political spectrum, there is a special relationship between racialist thinking and the specific theology known as "Christian Identity." According to Christian Identity thinking, the people who today call themselves Jews are in fact agents of the devil, and those who would help them—such as communists or liberal democrats—are his allies. A (spurious) document titled *Protocols of the Elders of Zion*, supposed to have been produced as the result of a Jewish Congress held at Basel in 1897, is frequently cited by Christian Identity theorists as proof of a Jewish left-wing conspiracy to take over the world. To forestall this threat, militias must therefore be organized, arms collected, and white Christians trained in guerilla warfare.

The Turner Diaries, by William Pierce (writing under the pseudonym Andrew Macdonald), has now become famous as another key text of the white supremacist, ring-wing movement. It became known outside of militia circles after the Oklahoma City bombing in 1995, when Timothy McVeigh blew up the Alfred P. Murrah federal building according to almost precisely the specifications laid out in the fictional account of a revolution against U.S. government control. *The Turner Diaries* was one of Timothy McVeigh's favorite books. Not only does it detail the notion of a hero blowing up a federal building with a truckload of ammonium nitrate fertilizer and fuel oil, but it goes on to blame the failings of American society that made such an act necessary on a grand conspiracy between Jews and liberals.

Since September 11, 2001, the Federal Bureau of Investigation (FBI) has become interested in potential links between white supremacist organizations in the United States and radical Islamic groups such as al-Qaeda. Unlikely as such ties may seem on the surface, exploring the websites of hate groups and similar organizations reveals a fascination with Osama bin Laden, HAMAS, Saddam Hussein, and other diverse individuals and groups from around the extremist Islamic world. "Remember," one quote admonishes the visitor to an Aryan Nations website, "the enemy of my enemy is my friend." The quote refers to the Jews of Israel, in combination with the government of the United States with which they are seen to be in collusion.

Are men and women who seek membership in a group like Aryan Nations to be characterized as deviants? While most Americans may disapprove of racism, it is likely that they would not find anything particularly noteworthy about the individual pasts of people who become involved in white supremacist organizations. Even those who engage in extreme or criminal acts often turn out to be persons about whom neighbors say, "he was such a nice boy." Many have served their country in the armed forces and were in fact once noted for patriotism and valor. As one might expect of groups

THE NATIONAL ALLIANCE

Founded by William Pierce in 1974, the National Alliance is the largest and most active racist, neo Nazi organization active in the United States. With at least 1,500 hundred members across the United States, the organization has ties to neo Nazi, racist, and other neo fascist organizations throughout the world, including the British National Party, the German National Democratic Party, and David Duke's European-American Unity and Rights Organization (EURO).

In recent years the National Alliance has flourished when other right-wing, racist hate groups have diminished. Under the direction of William Pierce the organization has recruited new members through publications, music, use of the Internet, and other mass media tools. The National Alliance publishes numerous books and magazines, including *Resistance*, *National Alliance Bulletin*, and *The Saga of White Will!*, an anti-Semitic comic book distributed on college and university campuses. William Pierce and the National Alliance also own and operate National Vanguard Books, and the white power music company Resistance Records, which is estimated to gross more than $1 million a year with hate music record sales. Promoting its neo Nazi, anti-Semitic views, the website for Resistance Records sells a wide variety of hate related paraphernalia, including music CDs, magazines, clothing, and a video game entitled Ethnic Cleansing, "the most politically incorrect video game ever made." Pierce also owns shares in Cymophane Records, a National Socialist Black Metal (NSBM) music company.

Through the use of mass media, the publication of books and magazines, and the sales of white power music, the National Alliance is thriving, enticing disaffected individuals throughout the world to subscribe to its hate based ideologies, influencing a brand of extremism that is not well accepted by the mainstream.

linked to religion, many grew up as churchgoers. They do not typically have "shady" or alienated pasts. From their point of view, it is the wider North American society that has become extreme, in its secularism and its tolerance of contaminating diversity. From the point of view of those who believe they carry "the seed of Adam," it is they who are the norm, and the standard bearers.

The Pull of Radicalism

The three groups examined above differ in important ways. Aum Shinrikyo has its primary origins in religious mysticism, though the group

A JEWISH EXTREMIST OF THE "THIS IS OUR LAND" MOVEMENT IS DETAINED BY ISRAELI POLICE IN JERUSALEM'S OLD CITY IN JANUARY 2001. EXTREMIST GROUPS EXIST OUTSIDE OF THE MAINSTREAM AND WILL OFTEN GO TO GREAT LENGTHS FOR THEIR BELIEFS. *(AP/Wide World Photos/Laurent Rebours. Reproduced by permission.)*

developed social and political overtones to its message. The movement for Khalistan is at its heart an ethnic or national liberation movement, but has become nearly completely identified with the religion of Sikhism. Aryan Nations is defined around a racialist understanding of meaning and destiny, with links to Christian Identity teachings. All three examples illustrate organizations viewed by the governments of Japan, India, and the United States respectively as "extremist;" all three contain members who have resorted to dramatic acts of violence to achieve their aims.

As Mark Juergensmeyer notes in his book, *Terror in the Mind of God: The Global Rise of Religious Violence* (2000), it is not surprising that religion is often implicated where extremism flourishes. There is an inherent appeal, he believes, in the way in which radical views cast the universe in terms of a cosmic battle that must be won at all costs—often depending on the actions of individuals who otherwise feel themselves but cogs in a nameless, faceless, meaningless society. Each encounter becomes *the axial encounter* on which the redemption of the world could turn; what does one life more or less mean, if cosmic salvation is at

stake? Perhaps more to the point, what do secular laws mean, if one is planning one's strategy around Armageddon, or around the fulfillment of a biblically defined racial destiny?

This psychological dynamic accounts for the fact that secondary enemies of extremist movements are always secular or civil governments—whether of Japan, of India, or of the United States. Targets include moderates from among one's own community who have "sold out" to the enemy. When the stakes are so high, the danger posed by such individuals is easily magnified. Indeed, part of the attraction of an extreme view is the ease with with one can attach a label to all other positions on the sociopolitical spectrum. Complexity is eliminated when the landscape is illuminated from a single direction. Hence we find manhunts such as the Aryan Nations' focus on Southern Poverty Law Center's Morris Dees as its nemesis. (As we will note, campaigns by governments *against* "extremists" also tend to extreme personalization in this regard.)

Among Khalistani Sikhs, early calls for greater autonomy for Punjab within the Indian state were quickly eclipsed by the radical demand for total sovereignty. Additionally, the notion of the citizen-soldier, the population which resists as a whole, was replaced by the more theologically driven conception of the saint-soldier, the fighter in a state of grace, fighter in the holy war. The odds being as uneven as they are when a small peripheral population takes on the might of a major regional power, the Khalistani insurgency suffered enormous casualties right from the beginning. Thus the saint-soldiers evolved into martyrs. Eventually, martyrdom became itself a kind of goal of fighting for many young people who, in desperation, joined the guerilla organizations. We have witnessed virtually the same evolution among some of the Palestinian organizations, perhaps more widely known to Western audiences.

The combination of apocalyptic rhetoric with a rational political platform is what makes today's extremist movements difficult to pigeonhole. Gun control, for example, is one rational-level political issue in which many right-wing groups in the United States are heavily invested. One may find lucid discussions of the constitutionality of the right to bear arms side-by-side with quotations from *Mein Kampf* and imaginative reconstructions of Biblical genealogies. Aum Shinrikyo's end-of-the-world scenario was, to members, piece with its otherwise viable critique of U.S. military presence in Japan. These combinations should be kept in mind as we consider the common tendency to dismiss any individual or group engaging in apoca-

ISLAMIC EXTREMISM

"Islamic extremism" is a term usually used by people opposed to radical, anti-Western and politicized forms of Islam. For those within movements labeled "extremist," they define themselves simply as true Muslims or as those who are standing up to anti-Islamic currents in the world.

After the defeat of the Ottoman empire at the turn of the twentieth century, the world of Islam fell into a period in which Islam became not the dominant, but the subordinate religion in many countries. The humiliation of colonization by European powers was overthrown when the predominately Muslim nations of the Middle East, Africa, and Asia became independent after the World War II (1939–45). This prompted a renaissance of Islamic spirit in many regions.

Palestine was one location where Muslims remained unable to reclaim their homeland after the global sweep of de-colonization, and that is one reason why the conflict there remains central to Islamic political movements today. In other areas, the new spirit of renewal combined with global communications to forge a new, transnational identity.

Economic imbalances across the globe and the growing hegemony of Western secular culture led some in the Muslim world to feel that a new type of colonialism would lead to the ultimate decay and decline of Islamic civilization. Ideologues emerging at the end of the century held the United States—as the military, economic, and cultural superpower—responsible for this state of affairs.

Although the great majority of the world's Muslims today reject any sort of violence as a remedy to the problems they face, there is a wide sense of grievance concerning the place of Islamic civilization in world history.

lyptic rhetoric as irrational or essentially nonpolitical. Very many groups are both; they often draw people in on the political side and turn toward the cosmic as the struggle intensifies.

Osama bin Laden and al-Qaeda have often been portrayed as beyond any rational political agenda, primarily because of similar rhetoric. Analysis of documents and speeches of bin Laden and his top aides, however, reveals a distinctive political viewpoint. The fact that the battle he sees himself as fighting is couched in cosmic terms, with governments and world leaders as mere actors on a bigger stage, places him not outside of, but well within our understanding of political extremism. It is therefore possible to draw on what we have learned from attempts to grapple with other such movements—however smaller in scale—in the current crisis of "the war on terrorism."

Extreme Acts

It is not only ideologies, however, but also actions that we label as "extreme." Although some attempts to define what "terrorism" is rely solely on the issue of whether noncombatants are targeted, or not, or whether the perpetrator of the violence is a legitimately constituted authority or not, many scholars of the subject note the clearly performative and symbolic quality of many of the actions we call "terrorism." To take the most obvious example, flying two passenger airliners into the twin towers of the World Trade Center in New York City on September 11, 2001, was not the only or even the most efficient way to kill three thousand people. Nor was it the only or probably the most efficient way to scare or "terrorize" a wide swathe of the U.S. public, who could potentially be more frightened by an authentic bioterror or even realistic-seeming nuclear threat. For sheer drama, however, it could hardly be topped. Indeed, the episode had a cinematic quality remarked on by virtually everyone who watched the televised coverage—that is, virtually everyone in the industrialized world.

Joseba Zulaika and William Douglas, two anthropologists who co-authored an insightful study of terrorist violence called *Terror and Taboo: The Follies, Fables and Faces of Terrorism*, elaborate on the nonstrategic, ritual quality of many acts of violence. These acts are better grasped as elements of expression than in terms of means-toward-end military instrumentality. Sikh militants knew well, for example, that setting off bombs in crowded Hindu neighborhoods would win them the tag "communalist," discredit any legitimacy their movement may have had as a form of resistance against state oppression, and would draw criticism from human rights groups worldwide. Yet the bombings went on, and few condemned the militants who

ISLAMIC EXTREMISTS IN DHAKA, BANGLADESH, CLASH WITH POLICE AFTER THEY GATHERED TO DENOUNCE AN AUTHOR FOR BLASPHEMING ISLAM IN A NOVEL. *(AP/Wide World Photo/Pavel Rahman. Reproduced by permission.)*

committed them. Why not? Because the supporting population by that time saw such blasts as affirmations of Khalistani pride, despite the fact that they had no military target and were part of no rational or strategic plan of action. From their viewpoint—which they saw as one of extreme humiliation and extreme desperation—the expressive value of the action alone made it worthy of praise.

Franz Fanon and other anticolonial theorists of guerilla violence in fact celebrated such violence because they saw in it the capacity to jolt the silent masses into an awareness of their power. We know that although the wide majority of Muslims throughout the world thoroughly condemned the attacks of September 11, some sections felt em-

powered by them in precisely that manner. The linking of a violent act with masculine imagery, by its supporters, and with the language of cowardice and effeminacy by its detractors, is indicative of the widespread recognition of this empowering quality.

The novelist Don DeLillo commented in *Mao II* that terrorism was the language of being noticed. The Unabomber was perhaps the clearest U.S. case in which an individual used dramatic acts of violence in order to have his voice heard in the public domain. In that case, Theodore Kaczynski was an educated man who coerced the *The New York Times* into publishing his 35,000-word manifesto in exchange for ceasing his pattern of sending package bombs through the mail. Two Sikhs who assassinated a general in the Indian armed forces involved in the attack on the Golden Temple used the opportunity of their own hanging to issue a flowery statement about national liberation and martyrdom, which became staple revolutionary fare for Khalistanis to follow. Today, although the United States does not air Osama bin Laden's videotapes for fear of encoded messages, he reaches an audience of millions through the al-Jazeera television network and other media that follow him avidly.

Just as it would be misleading to suppose that only social misfits are attracted to movements that the mainstream regards as "extremist," it is not the case that people who engage in horrific acts of violence are necessarily psychopaths. The extraordinary culture inhabited by, for example, a recruit to al-Qaeda, frames a way of thinking in which actions previously unthinkable come to seem normative and even heroic relatively quickly. "Brainwashing" is not the correct word to describe the process of socialization that takes place when one enters the relatively isolated social world of a guerilla group, a militia, or an underground organization. Initiations, group exercises, and the interdependency that develops rapidly in the "cosmic war" situation perpetuated by extremist organizations all make one's new comrades seem like family within a short period. The violence in which one may have to engage in this new group may be performed with the same moral distaste—but with the same sense of duty—as others would fulfill an obligation to their country's military service during wartime.

Though everything about the discourse of terrorism and counterterrorism attempts to place these two phenomena on utterly different planes of existence, independent scholars who study them intimately find a certain mimesis, or imitation, about the way the two spheres function. Just as the dramatic violent acts of terrorism are often an overresponse to real grievances like poverty, inequality, and indignity, campaigns of counterterrorism risk prompting further extremism if they in turn overreach in their response to the real threat posed by the terrorists. Recognizing the self-perpetuating quality of cycles of extreme violence, it is critical to find ways to break out of the potentially dangerous escalation it can represent.

RECENT HISTORY AND THE FUTURE

The Importance of Measured Response

In hindsight, it appears that the Indian government's handling of the threat posed by the small band of Sikh militants in the Golden Temple Complex in 1984 exacerbated rather than muted the real danger of Sikh separatism. Indeed, it may well be that Jarnail Singh Bhindranwale, one of the key militant leaders, sought to bring down the might of the Indian military specfiically to provoke a wider uprising. "If the Indian army attacks the Golden Temple," he had said, "the foundations of Khalistan will be laid." That is precisely what happened. A massacre occurred, the sacred buildings were desecrated, and an entire population was alienated from "the largest democracy in the world." Compounding this initial debacle was the subsequent period of counterinsurgency, during which "dirty war" tactics used against the population at large persuaded average citizens that the government and its agents were as "extreme" as the "extremists" they said they were fighting. People felt they were caught in between two sets of terrorizing militias.

Timothy McVeigh specifically referred to the U.S. government's handling of the Ruby Ridge shoot-out and the seige at the Branch Davidian compound in Waco, Texas, as reasons for his mistrust of the United States government. Despite extensive public inquiries into the matter, the perception that government agencies acted in an overaggressive and inappropriate manner is one that is shared among a certain sector of the population. Were there to be a less than scrupulous attention to civil rights, this population could easily turn the way of the Sikhs. Another way of saying this is that in the face of an extreme threat, a government has to resist the temptation to respond in an extreme way lest it further encourage a dangerous and growing polarization. Evenhandedness is critical. In a new country like India, born only in 1947 and facing challenges to its integrity from multiple sides, the confidence of evenhandedness is much more difficult to maintain than in a stable country like the United States.

When we turn to the case of Japan, we can begin to understand why the Japanese government has declined to outlaw Aum Shinrikyo even though its top personnel have been convicted for committing the heinous act of the only chemical terrorist attack yet known in world history. It does not want to risk a backlash by repressing the many Aum supporters and others concerned about religious and social freedoms. The Japanese government is taking the calculated risk of allowing Aum to flourish, within legal bounds, in the public sphere where it can be monitored—rather than pushing it to an isolated underground realm where it may grow to yet more dangerous proportions.

Do the histories of these limited case studies provide any insights with regard to the current "war on terrorism?" It may be difficult to draw the appropriate analogies because the three cases we have looked at here are essentially domestic (despite the involvement of diasporan communities), while the "war on terrorism" is a virtually global phenomenon. There is no question, however, that the dramatic attacks of September 11, in addition to being intended to impress and frighten, must have had the explicit intent of provoking an extreme response. Although the World Trade Center tragedy has gotten more public attention, the attack on the Pentagon was at least as important, if not more so. No one can imagine attacking the military headquarters of the sole superpower of the world without provoking an extreme response. One may question the degree to which this was part of an explicit calculation on the part of the attackers: to prompt a wider uprising in response then to U.S. military assaults on (presumably) the Arab and Muslim world. It remains a challenge to planners of the U.S. response to September 11 to ensure that this does not become the long-term result of the current campaign.

The sociologist Robert Bellah coined the term "civil religion" to describe patriotism in the United States, complete with its rituals like the pledge of allegiance, its symbols like the stars and stripes, and its outrage at desecrations like flag burnings. He pointed out that no other industrialized democracies have such a flourishing culture of patriotism as does the United States, save countries at war such as Japan or Germany during World War II. This is an important insight given our previous discussion of the quasi-religious quality of extreme ideologies. United States culture is fertile soil for apocalyptic rhetoric of its own; U.S. citizens turn easily to grand narratives of "freedom and honor," "good versus evil," "with us or against us," and the like. These should be warning signs that the United States can easily fall into the trap of polarization that empowers the extremists who would threaten it.

The policy of nonnegotiation with those defined as terrorists is the other side of the calculated risk that Japan takes in allowing a group like Aum Shinrikyo to exist. On one hand, the United States does not want to lend any legitimacy to those it defines as terrorists by recognizing them as partners in dialogue. On the other hand, by pushing them outside the circle of potential dialogue it isolates them entirely, ensuring no possible interchange other than a deadly one. This stance is one that can be taken only by a power confident of its ultimate victory against all challengers. Others have to consider more measured and dialogical responses.

BIBLIOGRAPHY

Aho, James. *The Politics of Righteousness: Idaho Christian Patriotism.* Seattle, WA: University of Washington Press, 1990.

Brackett, D.W. *Holy Terror: Armageddon in Tokyo.* New York: Weatherhill, 1996.

Ezekiel, Raphael S. *The Racist Mind: Portraits of American Neo-Nazis and Klansmen.* New York: Viking, 1995.

Girard, Rene. *Violence and the Sacred.* Baltimore, MD: Johns Hopkins University Press, 1977.

Hoffman, Bruce. *Inside Terrorism.* New York: Columbia University Press, 1998.

Juergensmeyer, Mark. *Terror in the Mind of God: The Global Rise of Religious Violence.* Berkeley, CA: University of California Press, 2000.

Kaplan, David E. and Andrew Marshall. *The Cult at the End of the World: The Terrifying Story of the Aum Doomsday Cult.* New York: Crown, 1996.

Kapur, Rajiv. *Sikh Separatism: The Politics of Faith.* London: Allen and Unwin, 1986.

Mahmood, Cynthia Keppley. *Fighting for Faith and Nation: Dialogues With Sikh Militants.* Philadelphia, PA: University of Pennsylvania Press, 1996.

Pettigrew, Joyce. *The Sikhs of the Punjab: Unheard Voices of State and Guerilla Violence.* London: Zed Books, 1995.

Rapoport, David C., ed. *Inside Terrorist Organizations.* New York: Columbia University Press, 1988.

Reader, Ian. *Religious Violence in Contemporary Japan: The Case of Aum Shinrikyo.* Honolulu, HI: University of Hawaii Press, 2000.

Roediger, David R. *Colored White: Transcending the Racial Past.* Berkeley, CA: University of California Press, 2002.

Zulaika, Joseba and William Douglas. *Terror and Taboo: The Follies, Fables and Faces of Terrorism.* London: Routledge, 1996.

Cynthia Keppley Mahmood

FINANCING TERRORISM: MONEY FOR THE CAUSE

On June 25, 2001, two men named Mustafa Ahmed al-Hawsawi and Fayez Rashid Ahmed Hassan al-Qadi Banihammad used cash to open a bank account at a Standard Chartered Bank branch in Dubai, United Arab Emirates (UAE). From July 18 to August 1, al-Hawsawi had Visa and ATM cards sent from the UAE to Florida. On August 22, those same cards were used to withdraw almost US$5,000 in cash. At first glance, these transactions may seem innocuous, the sort of thing tourists visiting friends in the United States might arrange. That is, except for the fact that Banihammad turned out to be one of the hijackers on the plane that crashed into the south tower of the World Trade Center on September 11, 2001.

This example illustrates what intelligence agencies have known for years: the group responsible for the attacks, the al-Qaeda terrorist network, possesses a vast and highly-organized system of financing to maintain the organization and to fund attacks like those of September 11. In fact, a recent report authored by Jean-Charles Brisard estimated that Islamic terror groups receive around $5 billion annually.

Soon after these tragic events, it became clear to the U.S. administration that if the United States was going to cripple this terrorist organization and prevent it from committing further ghastly acts of terrorism, it would be just as important to dismantle its financial networks and deprive it of funding resources as to use more direct methods like military strikes. On September 24, 2001, President George W. Bush (2001–) stated that "the American people must understand this war on terrorism will be fought on a variety of fronts, in different ways" and announced "a strike on the financial foundation of the global terror network."

THE CONFLICT

Measures to deprive terrorists of their funding must be part of any effort to counter the threat of terrorism. This endeavor is complicated by financial systems, law, and the covert means often used by terrorist groups to gather and distribute money. There are four main sources of terrorist funding: state sponsorship from countries like Iran; contributions from individual supporters; criminal activities, including kidnapping, robbery, smuggling, drug trafficking, fraud, and extortion; and legitimate business activities including manufacturing, import-export, and investment companies.

Financial

- In order to move funds around undetected, terrorists use both primitive methods (hawalas or cash smuggling) and sophisticated financial techniques ("shell" banks, electronic fund transfers).

- The al-Qaeda terrorist organization, headed by Osama bin Laden, has established an extremely extensive and sophisticated financial network that operates across the globe.

Political

- There are several ways for countries to diminish terrorists' access to money: seizing the assets of organizations linked to the financing of terrorism, encouraging or requiring financial institutions such as banks to report suspicious transactions and to confirm the identities of their clients, sharing intelligence between countries and assisting other states to control international flows of funds, and monitoring informal banking networks such as hawalas.

- Before September 11, 2001, the United States did not devote significant resources to depriving terrorists of their funding. However, since the terror attacks by al-Qaeda on September 11, the U.S. government has taken the lead in international efforts to dismantle the funding network of al-Qaeda and other terrorist organizations.

CHRONOLOGY

1960s Almost all terrorists come from either left-wing or nationalist revolutionary movements. Terrorist organizations are generally small and poorly funded. They are mostly dependent on state sponsorship for funding and resources.

1970s Terrorist organizations diversify their funding sources, branching into a host of illegal activities, including bank robbery. The proportion of funding from sympathetic individuals increases, although state sponsorship from countries like Libya continues to be an important source of funding. The PLO and IRA are among the groups that establish commercial enterprises as a means of making money.

January 1976 The PLO participates in one of the largest bank robberies of all time.

1980s The Iranian revolution of 1979 leads to Iran becoming the most active sponsor of Middle Eastern terrorist groups, a position it retains to this day. Osama bin Laden gains a great deal of experience in raising money for the Islamic mujahideen in Afghanistan during their conflict with the Soviet Union. Terrorist groups such as FARC in Colombia become involved in narcotics trafficking in order to raise money.

July 1984 A right-wing American group called the Order robs an armored truck of $3.6 million.

1990s Osama bin Laden builds a worldwide terrorist network and develops a wide range of funding sources, including charity organizations, legitimate businesses and drug smuggling.

December 9, 1999 The International Convention for the Suppression of the Financing of Terrorism opens for signature.

September 11, 2001 Al-Qaeda terrorists attack the World Trade Center and Pentagon using hijacked planes. The death toll is in the thousands.

September 24, 2001 U.S. president George W. Bush issues the Executive Order on Terrorist Financing, enabling the United States Treasury Department to block the assets of various organizations and individuals associated with the financing of terrorism.

September 28, 2001 The United Nations Security Council passes Resolution 1373, which includes a requirement for all members to prevent the financing of terrorism.

October 26, 2001 The USA Patriot Act becomes law in the United States. It contains several measures designed to combat the financing of terrorism.

April 10, 2002 The International Convention for the Suppression of the Financing of Terrorism becomes international law.

Any terrorist group requires funds to increase in size and scope. The larger the group grows, the more hard currency it needs to cover costs such as travel, the purchase of weapons, the maintenance of offices or safe-houses, and even the more mundane costs of supporting members' everyday expenses. Understanding where terrorists get these funds, how they move them around the world, and how they use them is essential to denying this funding and thus decreasing their capability to perpetrate attacks on innocent civilians.

HISTORICAL BACKGROUND

Sources of Terrorist Funding

The financing methods used by the so-called first generation of modern terrorists, left-wing or nationalist groups like the Palestinian Liberation Organization (PLO) and the Irish Republican Army (IRA), set the groundwork for terrorist financing today. It is estimated that the IRA had a budget in the mid-1990s of roughly $12 million a year. The PLO succeeded during the 1970s in securing an annual income of $1.25 billion, an enormous sum at the time. Even though these groups have at least nominally declared an end to terrorism, terrorism expert Rohan Gunaratna argued in *Jane's Intelligence Review* in August 2000 that "the strategies and practices they developed to raise and manage funds are being emulated by second-generation terrorist groups" today.

So how do groups like the PLO, IRA, and al-Qaeda manage to acquire such large amounts of money? Terrorist funding is generated by a whole range of activities, which can be divided into four basic types: state sponsorship, individual contributions, criminal activities, and legitimate business activities.

State Sponsorship

In the past, certain countries have found it desirable for strategic or ideological reasons to assist various sub-national groups with their armed campaigns against a particular government. These countries then become "state sponsors" of such groups, which have included terrorist organizations. State sponsors can provide weapons and training to terrorists or give them a safe haven in their territory. Alternatively, they can simply give money. This is one of the easiest ways a terrorist group can acquire funds.

During the Cold War (which lasted from the end of World War II until the late 1980s), the United States, the Soviet Union, and China all lent support to anti-government movements. For example, the United States supported the Afghan *mujahideen* against the Soviet Union, the Soviet Union supported the African National Congress in South Africa, and the PLO against Israel. Commentators in the West repeatedly accused the Soviet Union of engaging in an international conspiracy to support terrorist organizations against Western governments. The amount of actual financing provided by the Soviet Union, however, appears to be far less than was often assumed. Reportedly, the Soviet Union more often than not offered support in terms of propaganda but charged money when it came to material assistance. James Adams, in his book *The Financing of Terror*, points out that "the PLO had to pay cash for every bullet, rocket and tank received from the Soviets since the struggle for Palestinian independence began."

In the 1970s and 1980s one of the most active state sponsors of terrorism was Libya. Fueled by revolutionary fervor, Libyan leader Muammar Qadhafi supported almost every major terrorist organization worldwide after coming to power in 1969, either with money or by other means. Recipients of Qadhafi's largesse included the IRA, ETA (Basque Fatherland and Liberty), the Red Brigades from Italy, the Japanese Red Army, and the Baader-Meinhof Gang in West Germany. Between 1982 and 1987 the IRA allegedly received $3 million in cash and gold bullion from Libya. Qadhafi's financial support for terrorist organizations, always quite capricious, declined after Libya's oil revenues began falling in the 1980s.

After the Iranian Revolution in 1979, the new extremist rulers of that country have sought to export their Islamic revolution to the countries of the Middle East. Part of this strategy has been to supply aid to terrorist groups throughout the region. Iran has been an especially active patron of those groups acting against Israel, lending support to HAMAS, Islamic Jihad, and especially Hizballah, with which Iran has especially strong influence. Iranian financial involvement has been linked to the October 20, 1983, truck bomb attack in Beirut, Lebanon, in which 241 U.S. Marines were killed. Both the truck and the explosives used in the attack were allegedly paid for from a $50,000 check that could only be cashed at the Iranian embassies in Beirut or Damascus. To this day, Iran is viewed as the most enthusiastic state sponsor of terrorism—the U.S. State Department maintains that Iran provides more than $100 million in aid per year to terrorist organizations.

Iraq has also taken on the role of a state sponsor, but not to the same extent as Iran. In March 2002 Iraqi leader Saddam Hussein increased the amount of "reward" money he gives to the families of Palestinian suicide bombers to $25,000 per bomber. In South Asia, India and Pakistan continue to fund terrorist groups in each other's territory.

There are certain disadvantages, however, to a terrorist group relying too heavily on financing from external countries. Significantly, the money may come with strings attached—state sponsors may want a say in the terrorist group's operations in exchange for funding, to such an extent that the terrorists might feel they are working for their sponsor. State sponsors can also sometimes be unreliable sources of income. For example, in 1978, ten Arab states promised $250 million to the PLO in order to fight Israel, but the bulk of this money never arrived. Nonetheless, between 1973 and 1987, the PLO always received at least $100 million a year from Arab countries.

In the 1960s and 1970s most terrorist groups were initially dependent on the support of their patron states. Many groups soon realized that they should not put all their eggs in one basket by remaining totally dependent on state sponsorship. Once they laid down a solid financial base, groups tended to develop other sources of income to sustain their campaigns and become more financially independent.

Individual Contributions

One source of funds that usually has less strings attached than state sponsorship is the financial contributions of individuals both inside and outside the target country. Most terrorist groups claim to represent a significant population—workers, the Sri Lankan Tamils, Kashmiri Muslims, and so forth. As these populations usually contain some

IRANIAN AND SAUDI REPRESENTATIVES SHAKE HANDS AFTER SIGNING AN AGREEMENT TO FIGHT CRIME AND TERRORISM. IRAN IS VIEWED BY THE UNITED STATES AS THE MOST INVOLVED STATE SPONSOR OF TERRORISM. *(© AFP/CORBIS. Reproduced by permission.)*

disaffected and sympathetic individuals, terrorists groups can appeal to their "constituents" for monetary support. Even extremist groups with a more obscure ideology are likely to find at least a few sympathizers. A large percentage of the approximately $82 million budget of the Liberation Tigers of Tamil Eelam (LTTE), for instance, is made up of contributions from Tamil expatriates living around the world.

Funds are often channeled to terrorist groups through front organizations that sometimes operate under the pretext of being charities. The motivations of donors to these organizations can not always be taken for granted—at least some of the individual donors do not know that their contributions are funding terrorism. Another factor complicating the issue is that these front organizations may in fact carry out charitable or humanitarian functions, with only a portion of their proceeds being diverted to terrorist groups. Propaganda then becomes a vital tool for terrorists wishing to gather donations, either to directly promote their cause, or to indirectly garner sympathy for the humanitarian work of the front organization.

One of the most interesting historical cases of this type of terrorist funding is that of Noraid (Irish Northern Aid), which was a key source of money

for the IRA since the beginning of its modern campaign against the British. Established in 1969 in New York City, Noraid soon possessed branches throughout the United States and in the 1970s raised enough money from sympathetic Americans (many of whom were of Irish descent), to satisfy about half of the IRA's financial requirements. Noraid was not always entirely efficient in its fundraising—in the first six months of 1981 it raised $250,000, of which only $93,000 reached Northern Ireland, with the balance spent on salaries and propaganda within the United States. Due to an FBI inspection into Noraid's connection to arms smuggling, subsequent court cases, and a decrease in U.S. sympathy for the IRA following particularly violent actions, Noraid became a less significant source of funding for the IRA by the mid-1980s. Nonetheless, the IRA has continued to receive about $3.5 million per year from sympathetic organizations since the mid-1990s.

Individual contributions to terrorist organizations are not always voluntary. Coercion is often used by terrorist groups, both domestically in the target state and in diaspora communities. For example, it has been reported that each non-fighter in the Palestinian refugee camps was required to give 5 percent of his or her salary to the PLO as a "tax" during the period when the PLO was widely regarded as a terrorist organization (1970s through early 1990s).

Criminal Activities

Terrorists engage in violence against civilians and are thus classed as dangerous criminals under most legal systems. It is therefore not surprising that they often resort to other criminal activities in order to fund their activities. Engaging in purely criminal pursuits does, however, reflect badly on the integrity of those terrorists who wish to portray themselves as noble warriors fighting oppression.

Many examples exist of terrorist groups committing robbery to gain large amounts of cash. One of the largest bank robberies of all time occurred when the PLO, a Lebanese Christian militia, and an outside group from Italy cooperated to rob the British Bank of the Middle East's Beirut branch of around $100 million in January 1976. In July 1984 a far-right American group calling itself the Order robbed a Brinks armored truck in California and made off with $3.6 million.

One of the most common crimes undertaken by terrorists is kidnapping. While kidnapping is sometimes used for ideological purposes, in order to exact concessions from a government, groups have often employed kidnapping solely for profit. For people already trained and willing to commit violent acts, kidnapping is an attractive source of funds. There are so many potential victims that law enforcement can not protect all of them. As an added incentive, terrorists often make their deals with emotionally distraught relatives who may be softer negotiators than counterterrorism professionals. In fact, kidnapping by armed groups has become so prevalent in some areas, such as South America, that an entire industry has grown up involving kidnap insurance provided by companies like Lloyds of London and retrieval professionals who handle ransoms and negotiations. This arguably only facilitates and encourages the use of kidnapping as a form of fundraising by these groups, since terrorists may expect their victim to be insured and thus have a regularized avenue for gaining a ransom.

Terrorists sometimes embark on more sophisticated crimes. The IRA, for example, made a lot of money from building fraud, unemployment benefits fraud, extortion of Northern Irish businesses, and exploitation of European subsidies through innovative smuggling operations between Northern Ireland and the Republic of Ireland. The Popular Front for the Liberation of Palestine (PFLP) at one time ran a global forgery network as a source of in-

FEDERAL AND LOCAL AUTHORITIES GATHER OUTSIDE THE OFFICES OF A FINANCIAL ORGANIZATION THE UNITED STATES HAS ACCUSED OF SUPPLYING $15 TO $20 MILLION PER YEAR TO TERRORIST ORGANIZATIONS. *(AP/Wide World Photos/ Bizuayehu Tesfaye. Reproduced by permission.)*

come. Certain groups have even resorted to human smuggling to fill their coffers.

Legitimate Business Activities

Terrorists also engage in purely legitimate business concerns in order to raise money. This practice is especially difficult for law enforcement agencies to curtail because it is necessary to prove that terrorist organizations are the beneficiaries of such businesses.

In 1970 the PLO established Samed (the Palestinian Martyr's Work Society), which provided funding and set up businesses including factories in Lebanon and elsewhere. In another case the IRA took control of the Belfast taxi business, although it is doubtful whether it intended to operate this at a profit. More recently, terrorist groups have invested in stock markets and other commercial concerns, mostly by using front companies. The IRA and LTTE are reported to have made significant returns on their investments and even to have employed professional accountants. According to James Adams, terrorists "have skillfully turned the capitalist system . . . to their own advantage."

Hawala

Hawala is the name given to an informal or "underground" system of moving money from place to place (as opposed to the international banking system, which is the formal method of conducting global transactions). The word "hawala" is derived form an Arabic word meaning "to transform" and is used in the sense of transferring or remitting money.

Hawala is used extensively by ordinary people to send money to or from different countries, especially those in South Asia, the Middle East, Africa, and North America. Transactions are often cheaper and faster than regular bank transfers and can be the only way to transfer money in countries where the formal banking system is unreliable or non-existent. The anonymous nature of hawala also makes it attractive to money-launderers, arms dealers, drug-traffickers, and terrorists. The IRA, ETA, and South American drug lords use similar systems. The hawala system has allegedly been used both to send cash funds to al-Qaeda and to distribute cash from bin Laden to other parts of the al-Qaeda network.

How hawala usually works:

- Hawala is based on trust and reputation. In our example, let us assume that the customer (whether a construction worker sending money back to his family or a terrorist moving his funds) is sending $5,000 from New York City to the town of Quetta in Pakistan.

- A customer hands the cash over to a hawala agent in New York and tells the agent where and to whom he wants the money sent. These hawala agencies are often housed in small, inconspicuous rooms, perhaps in the back of another store.

- The agent charges a small fee and gives the customer a password.

- The customer tells his friend or relative in Quetta (the recipient) the password.

- Meanwhile, the hawala agent in New York then contacts a hawala agent in Quetta by telephone, fax, or e-mail and arranges for the agent in Quetta to give the equivalent of $5,000 in Pakistani currency to the person who presents the password.

- The recipient picks up the cash from the hawala agent in Pakistan a few days later.

- The hawala agent in Quetta adds this amount to what the New York agent owes him or subtracts the amount from what he owes the New York dealer. The two hawala agents balance their accounts every now and again (perhaps by smuggling diamonds). There is reportedly little cheating because of the likelihood of a violent reaction from other parties.

- Hawala agents make their money from the fees they charge and from changes in currency exchange rates.

- The most important feature of the hawala system is that it is a cash system that leaves no paper trail and protects the identity of those who use it.

The Movement of Terrorist Finances

Once terrorists have succeeded in raising funds, they must find ways to keep those funds hidden from various law enforcement and financial regulatory agencies, while still being able to move money around the world to support their operations. This is sometimes achieved through the use of front companies that transfer funds to and between terrorists under the guise of conducting legitimate business. Occasionally, existing financial institutions have commercial or sympathetic ties to terrorist groups and will act as a conduit for terrorist funds, as the Arab Bank did for the PLO for many years.

The use of "shell banks" that have no physical presence can also help terrorists to hide their financial dealings. Offshore "tax havens" established by several countries to help companies avoid paying taxes are also useful in helping money launderers and terrorists avoid detection. Tax havens are usually created by setting up small banks that are not too particular about where the money that is deposited comes from. For example, the tiny Pacific island of Nauru has about 400 offshore banks, all registered to a single government mailbox. Terrorists also make extensive use of *hawala*, an informal system of moving money which can be used to go below the radar of financial officials (see sidebar).

Terrorist funding operations can be truly global. The *Washington Post* (October 13, 2001) published a description by an intelligence official of the triple border area between Argentina, Brazil, and Paraguay as "one of the most important financing centers for Islamic terrorists outside the Middle East."

Terrorists may be violent, but they can also be well-educated. Groups have become adept over the years at using the most modern technology to handle all their transactions, including using sophisticated computers to track investments and electronic fund transfers to conduct their international banking operations.

Financial Sophistication and Terrorist Growth

Financing has not always gone smoothly for terrorist organizations. States and donors can be fickle, corruption can set in amongst leaders, and waste and inefficiency can reduce the amount of funds that can actually be used in their campaigns. Nevertheless, it seems that terrorist groups have become more and more adept at gathering funds, from merely being dependent on handouts from sympathetic countries and individuals to actively pursuing a variety of legal and illegal commercial activities.

As terrorist groups have grown, so has their level of financial sophistication in both generating and transferring funds. Cause and effect, however, are unclear. Did the natural growth of terrorist groups require that they diversify their funding sources and adopt more advanced international banking techniques in order to cover expenses? Or did the fact that they embraced a diversity of funding methods and financial tools enable them to grow as organizations and expand their activities? The answer is most likely a little of both. The PLO, for example, had more than enough members to carry out its violent and non-violent activities— what it needed was more money than it was receiving from Arab states. For the Revolutionary Armed Forces of Colombia (FARC), involvement in a separate activity like the drug trade enabled it to expand its operations and support a larger membership.

RECENT HISTORY AND THE FUTURE

The Funding of al-Qaeda

The September 11 attacks brought about renewed interest in the subject of the financing of terrorism, especially in light of the well-developed financial networks of the perpetrators, the al-Qaeda group. Al-Qaeda has utilized all the types of funding sources described previously, as well as a variety of methods of managing and moving these funds.

To begin with, al-Qaeda's infamous leader, Osama bin Laden, has played an important part in its financial development. In 1996, the U.S. State Department, in its *Patterns of Global Terrorism* report, described bin Laden as "one of the most significant financial sponsors of Islamic extremist activities in the world today." He graduated from King Abdul Aziz University's management and economics department. In a *Los Angeles Times* article (August 22, 1998), Jack Nelson quoted a "well-placed Saudi source" that described bin Laden as "highly intelligent, one who knows how to operate in the world of finance." After the Soviet invasion of Afghanistan in 1979 bin Laden helped establish a worldwide network to finance young Arab volunteers entering the conflict to fight against the Soviets.

Much has been made of bin Laden's personal fortune (he comes from a wealthy Saudi family whose assets may go as high as US$5 billion), with Western intelligence agencies estimating his inheritance at between US$280 and $300 million. Other reports, however, put his personal wealth much lower, stating that he only received around US$27 million prior to being disowned by his family in 1993. Whatever the true size of his personal finances, these funds on their own were probably insufficient to develop and sustain al-Qaeda's large infrastructure over the last decade. That is where the other sources of al-Qaeda's funds come in.

State sponsorship does not seem to constitute a large proportion of al-Qaeda's finances. While the Taliban certainly harbored bin Laden and al-Qaeda, there is no evidence that the Taliban gave al-Qaeda significant amounts of money (if anything the relationship probably worked the other way around). There have been rumors of Iran, Iraq, and even Pakistan supporting either al-Qaeda or some of its constituent groups, but no concrete evidence of this has yet been presented.

Bin Laden has a lot of experience raising funds from his time spent assisting the Afghan mujahideen in the 1980s. Al-Qaeda has a Finance Committee that is responsible for satisfying the organization's financial needs. Al-Qaeda receives a large amount of funds from wealthy Islamic donors throughout the world, some of whom are high-level government officials. Another major funding source that has received prominence since September 11 is the channeling of individual contributions to al-Qaeda through several Muslim

COMMERCIAL ENTERPRISES REPORTED AS BEING OWNED, MANAGED BY, OR LINKED TO AL-QAEDA AND OSAMA BIN LADEN

In Sudan:

- Wadi al-Aqiq Company—holding company

- Ladin International—import/export

- Taba Investment—global stock market and currency company

- Althemar al-Mubaraka—agribusiness

- Al Hijra Construction—built the Thaadi Road (1,200 km) from Khartoum to Port Sudan, also new airport at Port Sudan

- Bareba

- Zirqani

- International al-Ikhlar Co.—manufactured sweets and honey in Kameen

- Bank of Zoological Resources—produced genes for making cattle hybrids

- Kasalla agriculture facility—produced hybrids for commercial produce

- Happ tannery in Khartoum—produced leather

- Blessed Fruits—exported fruits and vegetables

- Soba and Damazine Farms—produced white corn, peanuts, sunflower, and wheat

- Qudarat Transport—trucking company

In Yemen:

- Al Hamati Sweets— bakery

- Al-Nur Honey Press

- Al-Shifa Honey Press

In Afghanistan:

- Ariana Afghan Airlines

Export products (originating company names not specified):

- Ostriches and sheepdogs—Kenya

- Wood—Turkey

- Lemons, olives, raisins, hazelnuts, almonds—Tajikistan

- Lapis lazuli—Uganda

- Camels—Sudan

charities, done either with or without the knowledge of the contributors. U.S. Treasury officials have linked relief groups such as al-Wafa Humanitarian Organization (based in Afghanistan), Human Concern International (based in Canada), the Muwafaq Foundation (based in Saudi Arabia), and the Rabita Trust to al-Qaeda. Al-Qaeda also controls branches of some charitable organizations, such as the International Islamic Relief Organization (IIRO), whose Philippines branch is run by bin Laden's brother-in-law.

Al-Qaeda has not participated in as many illegal fund-raising activities as groups like the IRA. However, individual al-Qaeda cells have been known to generate their own finances through criminal enterprises such as credit card fraud. Al-Qaeda has also allegedly benefited handsomely by becoming involved in the opium trade and smuggling heroin out of Afghanistan.

Al-Qaeda and Osama bin Laden have been linked to a wide variety of legitimate commercial enterprises, ranging from operating a fishing business in Mombasa, Kenya, to a honey enterprise in Yemen. (See chart above for a list of some of these companies.) During his stay in Sudan bin Laden was deeply involved in the country's economy, in activities such as construction, agriculture and raw materials exports. Al-Qaeda even has links with global financial institutions. The al-Shamal Bank, for example, was allegedly set up with a $50 million investment by bin Laden in 1995, and has been implicated in making funds available for the attacks on the U.S. embassies in Kenya and Tanzania in 1998. In some cases, however, there may have been reasons for establishing these commercial enterprises other than making a profit. Some of the businesses were situated in strategic locations, and there are suggestions that certain of the al-Qaeda-owned farms doubled as terrorist training camps. Observers have suggested that many of the Sudanese projects were undertaken more for political reasons—to maintain good relations with his hosts in the Sudanese government—than for their profitability. In an interview in 1996 bin Laden himself admitted to having lost over $150 million from his businesses in Sudan.

It is one thing for al-Qaeda to raise these vast sums of money; it is quite another to be able to move them around the world and use them without drawing the attention of law enforcement officials. One avenue they have used is friendly banks like al-Shamal or the al-Taqwa financial network. Another method that has drawn much attention recently is the use of informal money transfer systems such as hawala. On occasion, even the most primitive of methods can be used—terrorist members can simply put cash in a suitcase and smuggle it across national borders. The distribution of al-Qaeda funds has apparently been managed by an exiled Saudi businessman named Sheik Mohammad Hussein al-Almadi and the Afghan-based Abu Zubayda, who was recently captured by U.S. authorities.

Most available evidence, however, shows that the actual operational cells of al-Qaeda do not always receive much funding—both the embassy bombings and the USS *Cole* attacks were carried out on shoe-string budgets. The September 11 hijackers stayed in cheap hotels and used free Internet services at the local library. Al-Qaeda operatives have been known to resort to petty crime to support themselves. The reason for this apparent miserliness at the operational level remains unclear. It could be an indication of limitations on al-Qaeda's finances, or merely a decision by its leaders to encourage self-sufficiency on the part of its terrorist cells.

Nevertheless, al-Qaeda has been able to grow as an organization and stage several high-profile attacks against American interests. During the 1990s al-Qaeda's accounts funded everything from the purchase of cars and explosives to financing hotel accommodation and safe houses.

Prospects for Curtailing the Financing of Terrorism

There are a number of measures both domestic and international that have been developed to halt, or at the very least reduce, the flow of money to terrorists. But the complex, shadowy web of terrorist financial networks presents a host of roadblocks to this effort.

Cooperation between law enforcement, intelligence, and other regulatory agencies is imperative when confronting the multi-faceted sources of terrorist funding. This needs to occur both within countries and internationally. As Kenneth Dam, a deputy secretary in the U.S. Treasury Department, put it, "You can't bomb a terrorist's bank account on foreign soil, so cooperation is extremely critical." This means that in order to combat a source of terrorist financing like the drug trade, both anti-narcotics agencies such as the Drug Enforcement Agency and counter-terrorism agencies need to work closely together.

The main vehicle for international cooperation against terrorist financing is the International Convention for the Suppression of the Financing of Terrorism, which was passed by the United Nations General Assembly on December 9, 1999. The Convention notes that "the number and seriousness of acts of international terrorism depends on the financing that terrorists may obtain" and exhorts states to identify and block (or seize) any funds connected with the commission of terrorist acts. Nations are also encouraged to cooperate with each other. Article 18 of the Convention contains guidelines for measures states should employ to curtail terrorist financing, including supervising money-transmission agencies, preventing the smuggling of funds across borders, and requiring banks to report suspicious transactions and identify their customers. Although the Convention opened for signature in January 2000, relatively few countries had both signed and ratified it by September 11, 2001. After the September 11 attacks several countries rushed to sign and ratify the Convention, bringing the number of countries who have done so above the 22 needed for the Convention to enter into force. The Convention therefore became international law on April 10, 2002. The United States has signed but has not yet ratified the Convention. It has, however, indicated its willingness to do so.

Many of the existing bodies that are now being drafted into the effort to stamp out terrorist funding were initially developed to tackle the laundering of drug money and other receipts of criminal activities. The Financial Action Task Force (FATF) was set up by the then G-7 countries more than ten years ago primarily to put a stop to money laundering. Money laundering differs from terrorist funding in that it forms only part of the terrorist financing picture. Money laundering focuses on the proceeds of illicit activities, which are often much easier to detect than the legitimate sources of income that also contribute to the funding of terrorism. It is especially important for financial regulators to bear this in mind when they try to use

TERRORISM AND THE DRUG TRADE

During the televised airing of the 2002 Superbowl in the United States, an advertising campaign was launched that asked "Where do terrorists get their money?" and answers "If you buy drugs, some of it might come from you."

The commercials have received criticism from some quarters for drawing tenuous conclusions. What is the real connection is between terrorism and drugs?

- Almost all major terrorist organizations rely on the trafficking of illegal narcotics to raise funds. This is accomplished by either providing protection for drug dealers or trafficking in drugs themselves.

- Terrorist groups involved in drug trafficking include Sendero Luminoso in Peru, Hizballah in Lebanon's Bekaa Valley, and the PKK (Kurdish Worker's Party) of Turkey who distribute heroin in Europe.

- The huge profits involved in the drug trade are an important source of funding for many groups. In Colombia, the Revolutionary Armed Forces of Colombia (FARC) and the National Liberation Army (ELN) are together believed to make between $600 and $900 million a year from "taxes" imposed on the drug cartels. In fact, drug trafficking may have put these groups on the map. FARC evolved from a struggling guerrilla movement in the 1970s with fewer than 100 fighters to having about 2,050 people under arms by 1984, arguably as a direct result of income gained from the drug trade.

- Even in the United States, extremist groups have used drugs to raise funds, mainly by producing and/or selling methamphetamines and marijuana.

This evidence suggests that the drug trade does indeed constitute a significant source of funds for terrorists and that the advertising campaign is more accurate than many people realize.

tools such as the FATF to combat terrorist funding. Much attention has also been given to shutting down offshore tax havens. While this is certainly a necessary step, it must be remembered that much terrorist financing is conducted through traditional financial centers like London and New York.

The effort to curtailing terrorist financing also requires the assistance of the private financial sector. It is one thing for countries to make laws governing bank behavior; it is another matter entirely

to convince banks and other financial institutions to do this efficiently and enthusiastically, especially when doing so will increase paperwork and business costs. In the past many banks have done the minimum necessary to avoid censure from financial regulators, although in the wake of September 11 this attitude will most likely change. The difficulty of gaining full cooperation from banks is compounded by the system of correspondent banking, in which a number of banks—often from different countries—do business with each other. This system is only as strong as the weakest link in the chain of banks. Any precautions to prevent the flow of money to terrorists are worthless if even one bank does not comply with the regulations. Governments therefore need to put a great deal of effort into monitoring the banking sector's compliance with regulations and ensuring its cooperation in the fight against terrorism.

Even when banks are willing to help, the vagueness of many regulations and the volume of international financial transactions complicate the efforts of regulators. It may sound like a good idea, for example, to require all banks to report "suspicious transactions," but these are rarely well defined, so banks are often unsure of exactly what they are supposed to report. Also, due to the massive amount of transactions internationally, U.S. authorities receive about 150,000 reports of suspicious transactions from banks each year, far too many to investigate individually. Financial regulations need to be carefully designed and clearly spelled out to yield a manageable set of anomalies. Otherwise the funding activities of terrorists will likely continue to be lost in the "background noise" of international commerce.

But these tighter regulations themselves can have negative (if unintended) political, social, and economic consequences. For example, peeking into individual accounts may lead to protests that civil liberties, especially the right to privacy, are being infringed upon. If financial regulators and counterterrorism experts restrict the search for suspicious transactions to a certain geographical region or ethnic group, they may be accused of racial profiling. Also, recent U.S. actions aimed at shutting down Barakat, a company that engaged in transferring money as a hawala to Somalia, has resulted in criticism that many innocent Somalis will now no longer be able to send money back home and that this could drive more people into the hands of Islamic extremists.

A precise sense of balance must be maintained in implementing all of the above measures. If regulations become too restrictive to the financial sector, international commerce could be obstructed, leading to adverse consequences for global economic growth. In that case, terrorists would have dealt a far more severe blow to the world's population than any single explosive. This should be kept in mind by overzealous counterterrorism officials as they craft their policies.

What is Currently Being Done?

Unfortunately, international efforts to stem the flow of funds to terrorist organizations were weak, and in some cases non-existent, prior to September 11. Lack of coordination and delays in implementing regulations were common. Within the United States, Osama bin Laden's name did not even appear on a Treasury Department's list of terrorists whose assets should be seized until after the August 1998 embassy bombings; Treasury officials claim this was because the intelligence agencies did not want to tip bin Laden off (which intelligence agencies have denied). In 1994 the Treasury Department was authorized by the U.S. Congress to require registration of hawala dealers, but foot-dragging in the implementation of these regulations meant that they were not scheduled to go into effect until the end of 2001—too late to affect the financing of attacks like September 11.

The George W. Bush administration also initially rejected the efforts of the FATF to clamp down on offshore banking centers. Reports criticized the Treasury Department's Office of Foreign Asset control for being seriously understaffed. In terms of international cooperation, performance was equally disappointing. Many states did not even sign, let alone ratify, the United Nations Convention on the Suppression of Terrorist Financing before September 11, 2001.

The attacks on September 11, however, seem to have propelled the world into action. The United States quickly made countering terrorist financing one of the pillars of its "war on terrorism." Shortly after the attacks, on September 24, 2001, President Bush issued the Executive Order on Terrorist Financing, enabling the Treasury Department to block the assets of various organizations and individuals associated with the financing of terrorism. The Executive Order also blocks donations to this same list of organizations and individuals, which includes certain Islamic charities. On October 26, 2001, the Patriot Act, designed to counter many aspects of terrorism, became law in the United States. Included in this act were provisions to increase the amount of information sharing between intelligence and law enforcement agencies with respect to the financing of terrorism and provisions

requiring securities brokers to file suspicious activity reports.

A broad range of other measures have been instituted. A special interagency task force called the Foreign Assets Tracking Center has been established to uncover terrorist assets. The Bush administration has increased the budget of the Treasury Department's Office of Foreign Assets Control, partly to provide for the development of a terrorist finance database. The U.S. Customs Service has established a financial anti-terrorism task force known as Operation GREEN QUEST, which the U.S. describes in its December 19, 2001, Report to the United Nations Counterterrorism Committee as being formed "to identify, disrupt, and dismantle the financial infrastructure of terrorist organizations." A new public-private partnership of 34 organizations known as the Intercept Forum has been formed in the United States and is working to stop the flow of funds to terrorist organizations. At last the U.S. government now has the power to clamp down on at least some aspects of terrorist financing, for example by prohibiting U.S. banks from dealing with foreign shell banks and keeping a close eye on hawalas and other informal financial networks.

As part of its crackdown on organizations linked to terrorism, the United States and its allies have frozen the accounts of Barakat, the Somali-based business group that Paul O'Neill, the U.S. Treasury Secretary, has called the "quartermasters of terror." Treasury officials estimate that Barakat could have siphoned off enough funds from its hawala transactions to supply $15 million to $20 million to terrorist organizations per year. U.S. officials, however, have been accused of acting without sufficient proof.

On the international front, a number of countries including Germany, the Philippines, Canada, the United Kingdom, Kuwait, UAE, South Korea, and Japan have instituted measures to combat terrorist financing. On September 28, 2001, the United Nations Security Council passed Resolution 1373 under Chapter VII of the UN Charter (making it binding on all member states), which includes a requirement for all members to prevent the financing of terrorism. On October 31, the FATF, the primary international group working against money laundering, extended its scope to include the financing of terrorism. The FATF agreed to a set of Special Recommendations on Terrorist Financing and a plan to implement them, even though it is only an advisory body.

These efforts seem to be yielding some results. A report issued in February 2002 stated that

SOMALI MEN STAND IN FRONT OF THE BARAKAAT HEADQUARTERS IN MOGADISHU ON NOVEMBER 9, 2001. THE
INSTITUTION'S NORTH AMERICAN OFFICES WERE CLOSED BY THE U.S. GOVERNMENT FOR ALLEGEDLY
PROVIDING FUNDING TO AL-QAEDA, MAKING IT MORE DIFFICULT FOR MANY SOMALIS ABROAD TO SEND MONEY
HOME. (© AFP/CORBIS. *Reproduced by permission.*)

in the U.S.-led campaign against terrorist financing since September 11, 149 countries had seized assets worth a total of US$104 million. Unfortunately, this probably represents only a drop in the ocean of the total sum of money possessed by terrorists around the world.

Conclusion

Something common to all terrorist groups up until now is that they require income for basic activities such as recruiting and supporting members, evading their opponents, and conducting attacks. As James Adams has observed, "In the progression from fringe radicals to recognized terrorists, all groups first have to acquire some income." Originally reliant almost completely on state sponsorship, terrorist groups soon learned to diversify their funding sources, so that today terrorist organizations like al-Qaeda use a broad range of sources to raise the funds they need. Al-Qaeda in turn funds many of its sub-groups and affiliated organizations, all of this activity creating a complex web of financial transactions.

Up until recently the world's counterterrorist campaigners have devoted the bulk of their energies towards active measures such as capturing terrorists or reacting to attacks. This has hampered efforts against the financing of terrorism, especially

in the United States, and has resulted in what the *Financial Times* (October 6, 2001) has called a "failure to enforce laws already on the books." The heinous attacks on the World Trade Center and Pentagon in September 2001 provided a catalyst for correcting this. President Bush has declared his determination to "starve the terrorists of their funding" (September 24, 2001). After the passage of UN Resolution 1373, various domestic laws, and especially the Convention for the Suppression of the Financing of Terrorism, the United States may even be willing to place sanctions on countries that don't comply with new regulations.

There will be many difficulties in stopping the flow of funds to and between terrorists. Some of these concern the practicalities of implementing regulations, as described above. Others may be more fundamental. One must not lose sight of the fact that terrorists like Osama bin Laden have shown themselves to be eminently adaptable—even if existing sources of funding are stopped, terrorists may turn to alternative means of financing, methods that have not yet even been considered. It must therefore be realized that terrorist financing is something of a "moving target" and counterterrorist efforts need to focus not only on current funding sources, but also on where the terrorists will get their money from next.

There is also the sobering thought that terrorist attacks seem to require less and less funding. Even one of Adams' "fringe radicals" is today capable of causing a large amount of destruction with surprisingly little resources, as shown by Timothy McVeigh and his simple yet effective attack on the Oklahoma City federal building. Perhaps, as their funding sources dry up, terrorists will merely make do with fewer resources. The more money they have though, the more freedom of movement they will enjoy and the greater the likelihood that they will gain access to more formidable capabilities like weapons of mass destruction. Therefore, although the fight to rein in terrorist financing is only one element in the broader struggle against terrorism, it is a vital one that must be pursued with the utmost vigor.

BIBLIOGRAPHY

Adams, James. *The Financing of Terror: How the Groups That Are Terrorizing the World Get the Money to Do It.* New York: Simon and Schuster, 1986.

Alden, Edward. "Complex Finances Defy Global Policing," *The Financial Times* (London), February 21, 2002.

Bush, George W. *Executive Order on Terrorist Financing: Blocking Property and Prohibiting Transactions With Persons Who Commit, Threaten to Commit, or Support Terrorism.* September 24, 2001. Available online at http://www.whitehouse.gov/news/releases/2001/09/20010924-1.html (cited April 22, 2002).

Carbonara, Peter. "Financing Terror," *Money,* November, 2001.

Cottle, Michelle. "Hawala v. the War on Terrorism," *The New Republic,* October 15, 2001.

Faiola, Anthony. "U.S. Terrorist Search Reaches Paraguay," *Washington Post,* October 13, 2001.

Ganguly, Meenakshi. "A Banking System Built for Terrorism," *Time,* October 5, 2001. Available online at http://www.time.com/time/world/printout/0,8816,178227,00.html (cited April 22, 2002).

Gunaratna, Rohan. "Bankrupting the Terror Business," *Jane's Intelligence Review,* August 2000.

Levin, Myron., and Josh Meyer. "Officials Fault Past Efforts on Terrorist Assets," *Los Angeles Times,* October 16, 2001.

Morais, Herbert. "Behind the Lines in the War on Terrorist Financing," *International Financial Law Review,* no. 34, December, 2001.

Pound, Edward, T. "The Root of All Evil: His Money Makes Bin Laden Dangerous. So It's Being Taken Away," *U.S. News and World Report,* December 3, 2001.

Roule, Trifin J., Jeremy Kinsell, and Brian Joyce. "Investigators Seek to Break Up Al-Qaeda's Financial Structure," *Jane's Intelligence Review,* November 2001.

Shahar, Yael. "Tracing Bin Laden's Money: Easier Said Than Done," *International Policy Institute for Counterterrorism.* September 21, 2001. Available online at http://www.ict.org.il/articles/articledet.cfm?articleid=387 (cited April 22, 2002).

Shahin, Mike. "'Banking' System Untraceable: Time to Crack Down on Ancient Method of Money Transfers, Expert Advises," *The Ottawa Citizen,* November 8, 2001.

Text and Status of United Nations Conventions on Terrorism, United Nations. Available online at http://untreaty.un.org/English/Terrorism.asp (cited April 22, 2002).

U.S. Government. *The War on Terrorism at Home & Abroad: America Responds—Financial Actions.* Available online at http://www.whitehouse.gov/response/financialresponse.html (cited April 22, 2002).

Weintraub, Sidney. "Disrupting the Financing of Terrorism," *The Washington Quarterly,* vol. 25, no. 1, Winter 2002.

Gary A. Ackerman

FIGHTING TERRORISM WITH FORCE

THE CONFLICT

The "standard" anti-terror response, honed during the era of aircraft hijacking, and hostage taking, was to calm the situation and negotiate for hostage releases or to use commando forces to raid terrorists holed up in aircraft, buildings, or outposts. This had questionable relevance, however, to the new terrorist strategies of the 1990s, in which anonymous acts of violence were staged without efforts to negotiate grievances or offer hostage releases. Military remedies in fighting terrorism are problematic for a number of reasons, including definitional and legal uncertainties about what one is fighting against, as well as tactical problems.

Political

- There is no standard definition of terrorism. The United Nations, however, has upheld notions that targeting civilians with indiscriminate violence are unacceptable and that terrorists should be apprehended, extradited, or prosecuted.

- It is difficult to gather consensus on conditions under which certain types of actions should be taken, as developing countries have generally objected to language that outlaws or condemns legitimate popular struggles.

Technological

- New technologies have afforded greater potential killing power to both authorities and terrorists alike.

- Terrorists can now operate on a more global scale, using modern technology, including the media, the Internet, and cell phones, as well as transcontinental travel.

Military

- Combating terrorism requires the cooperation or acquiescence of states and individuals actually supporting or harboring terrorist groups.

- Due to the difficulties in defining terrorism, it is inherently difficult to build and maintain an anti-terrorism coalition among cooperating states especially when relying on military force to target "terrorists."

In the aftermath of the September 11, 2001, commercial airliner attacks on the World Trade Center in New York City and the Pentagon near Washington, DC, which killed more than three thousand people, the U.S. government articulated plans for a global "war on terrorism." Immediately blaming the al-Qaeda network sponsored by the notorious Osama bin Laden and purportedly based in Afghanistan, President George W. Bush (2001–) indicated that such a war would be neither brief nor easy, and would entail military, diplomatic, intelligence, and economic components. The immediate visible preparations were in the military sphere, along with beefed up domestic security measures ranging from interrogations and deportation of certain illegal aliens and other suspected groups. These groups were comprised almost exclusively with Muslim and Arab men. Other preparations involved heightened airport security and controversial new Federal Bureau of Investigation (FBI) surveillance authority.

The U.S. response was basically supported by many governments around the world, and was legitimized by United Nations (UN) Security Council resolutions 1373 and 1377 in late 2001, recognized terrorism as a threat to international peace and security to be combated by any and all means consistent with the UN Charter. The resolution also called on states to prevent and suppress terrorism and cooperate in preventing the financial or political support of terrorists. Few if any states would condone terrorist groups commandeering airliners and flying them into public buildings. Though controversial, international law also allows states that have been attacked from the territory of another state to pursue the attackers if the government of that other state does not cooperate in stopping the attacks and apprehending

CHRONOLOGY—ATTEMPTS TO RESOLVE
THE BASQUE CONFLICT

January 12, 1999 Spain's president José Maria Aznar states that the Basque nationalist group ETA refuses to talk with the government

February 1999 A Basque national assembly is established by the Basque Nationalist Party (PNV) and Eusko Alkartasuna (EA).

March 1999 Spain's paramilitary Civil Guard searches the headquarters of the left-wing Herri Batasuna (HB), a political group seeking Basque independence. Basque political prisoners in Spain call for a renewal of the peace process.

April 1999 Talks between President Aznar and Juan José Ibarretxe, president of Baskongadak—the four provinces in Spain claimed by the Basques—toward multi-party negotiations stall after Aznar demands HB condemn ETA violence before participating.

May 1999 The ETA announces it is willing to talk with the Spanish government. A second series of meetings between Spain and Baskongadak ends without progress. At the end of the month, Basque political refugees reject Spain's offer to let them return to the country.

June 1999 President Aznar meets secretly with two ETA leaders.

August 1999 The ETA announces a suspension of talks with Spain.

October 1999 French police arrest ETA members linked to the theft of explosives and other activities. Days later, Basques in the French province of Baiona, which is claimed by the Basques, demand that France create a Basque administrative department. The ETA's proposal to the Spanish government for the renewal of talks is rejected.

November 28, 1999 One month after Spain rejected the ETA's proposal for talks, the ETA announces an end to its cease-fire.

December 1999 The PNV invites Basque nationalist parties to submit proposals for a new framework, and the Basque nationalist commission Lizarra-Garazi requests that the ETA not end the cease-fire. Spanish police seize a truck carrying a bomb heading to-

wards the capital of Madrid. The ETA is suspected to be responsible.

January 2000 An attempted car bomb linked to the ETA is stopped by Spanish police. A member of the Lizarra-Garazi commission quits in protest against other members who refuse to condemn ETA violence.

March 2000 The ETA claims responsibility for a February bomb blast that killed socialist leader Fernando Buesa.

April 2000 Iparretarrak (IK), an armed Basque organization in the three French provinces claimed by the Basques, ends its 18-month cease-fire, blaming the French government for not responding to Basque requests for an administrative department.

May 2000 Moderate Basque nationalist parties press for the ETA to enter into another cease-fire. The ETA accuses Spanish president Aznar of impairing the negotiating process, and it claims responsibility for March attacks.

July 2000 The ETA launches an offensive against Spain.

September 2000 The Spanish government approves new laws against the Basque independence movement. France arrests several people connected to the ETA.

December 2000 Spain enacts the Accord for Freedom and Against Terrorism, ruling out talks with the Basque regional government in Spain until it renounces ties with groups sharing the ETA's goals.

January 2001 ETA violence focuses on those who signed the Accord for Freedom and Against Terrorism.

February 2001 Spain's interior minister, who does not support the Basque movement, is confirmed by the government as the official Basque candidate in the Baskongadak regional elections.

March 2001 Municipal elections in France strengthen the Basque nationalist movement there.

April 2001 The ETA announces that it is optimistic in light of a plan established by left-wing Basque nationalists for Basque independence.

those responsible. Nevertheless, some groups, individuals, and even governments abroad, while condemning the massive loss of lives involved on September 11, sympathized with grievances against the United States espoused by bin Laden and others.

Styling the international community as an anti-terror coalition, President Bush authorized a major military campaign against the ruling Taliban in Afghanistan and the al-Qaeda group with which it collaborated. This took the form of massive air and missile bombardments of active or inactive training bases, military concentrations, and suspected hiding places and government facilities, conducted jointly by U.S. and British air and naval forces. In addition, U.S. and British special forces were landed in the country to link up with Afghan opposition militia, the Northern Alliance, many of which had previously participated in anti-Soviet struggles in the 1980s, a subsequent civil war, and in repressive governments ultimately overthrown by the Taliban. Faced with renewed offensives supplied by U.S. arms and logistics, Taliban forces retreated *en masse* and the opposition factions took control of Afghan cities and most of the countryside.

The ground military campaign along with the intensive U.S. bombing and intelligence efforts, however, failed to turn up either bin Laden or Mullah Mohammad Omar the Taliban leader. It was speculated that much of the top al-Qaeda and Taliban leadership disappeared over the border, perhaps into neighboring Pakistan. Hundreds of suspected terrorists were interrogated and brought to the Guantanamo Bay U.S. naval base in Cuba for incarceration, and a heated national and international controversy arose about whether they should be deemed "prisoners of war" and accorded rights and protection under the Geneva Conventions.

Therefore, while the military campaign in Afghanistan was pronounced a rousing success, despite reportedly significant civilian casualties (at least three thousand by some estimates), and while it indeed toppled Taliban leaders and offset some of their militantly religious policies (such as severely curtailing women's educational and work opportunities), it is difficult to know whether lasting progress was made in dismantling terror networks throughout the world. In addition, the military response had to pass the pragmatic test of whether it helped or hindered the campaign against terrorism. Indeed, President Bush remained cautious in noting the continued presence of terrorists in some 60 or more countries, with "tens of thousands" of trained personnel. Whether such figures are accurate, or politically self-serving in justifying an on-

going and spreading U.S. global involvement (in countries as diverse as Colombia and the Philippines) and domestic mobilization, and whether it is indeed possible to win "a war against terrorism" relying mainly on military means remains to be seen.

Thus it is important to look carefully into the question of when and under what circumstances military responses of various sorts are effective or ineffective in anti-terrorism struggles. An historical analysis can help inform such conclusions. Before we look back on the long and varied history of international terrorism and responses to it, though, we must first grapple with the definitional and conceptual problem related to anti-terrorism.

Dealing with Terrorism

The "standard" anti-terror response, honed during the era of aircraft hijacking, and hostage taking of the 1970s and 1980s was to calm the situation and negotiate for hostage releases, or to use commando forces to raid terrorists holed up in aircraft, buildings, or outposts. This had questionable relevance, however, to the new terrorist strategies of the 1990s, in which anonymous acts of violence were staged without efforts to negotiate grievances or offer hostage releases. September 11 and the preceding attempt to destroy the World Trade Center through a truck bomb in 1993 were instead meant as symbolic and integral blows against U.S. power, presumably as retribution for prior U.S. actions or policies that were considered offensive or provocative, such as stationing forces in the holy land of the Arabian Peninsula.

Other traditional anti-terror approaches, such as patiently hunting down terrorist networks through combined police and intelligence operations, although part of a prolonged global strategy, appeared too slow and indecisive to the new U.S. administration of George W. Bush in the wake of September 11. Thus, a military response was hastily prepared. It came against the backdrop of general global concerns about terrorism, reflected ultimately in similar major Israeli military attacks against the Palestinian Authority and its leader Yasser Arafat, as well as against towns, villages and refugee camps in retaliation for suicide bombings in Israel and attacks on Israeli military outposts and civilian settlements throughout the West Bank and Gaza territories.

In the Israeli-Palestinian case, as in the American case and in other countries' efforts to hunt down so-called terrorists with military force, the goals were to disrupt and "defeat terror" or eradicate "nests of terror," all rather vague notions

THE DELEGATIONS OF U.S. SECRETARY OF STATE COLIN POWELL, RIGHT, AND TURKISH FOREIGN MINISTER ISMAIL CEM, LEFT, MEET IN ANKARA, TURKEY, TO DISCUSS U.S. ANTITERRORISM EFFORTS IN AFGHANISTAN. USING FORCE AGAINST TERRORISM REQUIRES THE COOPERATION OF OTHER NATIONS AND MAY ALSO PRESENT TACTICAL PROBLEMS. *(AP/Wide World Photos/Murad Sezer. Reproduced by permission.)*

that leave the observer uncertain of when the campaign is ultimately successful. The troops seek to confiscate weapons and arrest, interrogate, or kill suspected terrorists, and attempt to discourage popular support of their movements. This is combined with efforts to intercept arms shipments and freeze economic assets of groups suspected of supporting terrorist networks. Yet the question of the ultimate "defeat" of terrorism remains. Acts of terror might cease for a period but also might reemerge or even accelerate in response to the antiterror methods.

Defining Terrorism

The vagueness surrounding the political goals of military campaigns against terrorism are compounded by the difficulty of arriving at a standard definition of the term itself. What we think of as terrorism generally consists of a set of outrageous and spectacular violent acts to achieve political, ideological, religious, or social goals through methods such as bombings, shootings. These acts spread terror and go beyond accepted limits by targeting unsuspecting victims or wreaking wanton destruction. The aim might be to convince the victims to leave an area or desist in their objectionable policies, or simply to inflict pain, suffering, and disruption on the victims who are often not the target but serve as

a tool to promote the terrorist's platform. Terrorist goals might involve political recognition, gain of power, retribution, or simply annihilation (some terrorists down through history have reputedly been anarchists, for example, seeking to wipe out a governmental system without installing an alternate system). Yet while these may be the methods and motives of those employing terror, the philosophies behind terrorist causes, philosophies ranging from revolution to revenge, might or might not be defeated through military responses. In other words, since military strategy is normally devised to defeat organized military forces on the battlefield, its use to suppress or eliminate terrorism can be questionable.

In the wake of the September 11 events, the United Nations moved much closer to consensus on defining and dealing with terrorism. Resolutions and speeches generally upheld the notions that targeting civilians with indiscriminate violence was unacceptable, and that terrorists should be apprehended, extradited, or prosecuted. As noted by international law specialist Ved P. Nanda of the University of Denver, however, a strictly law enforcement model of arrest and trial might not be sufficient to deal with well-entrenched and globally organized terrorists. Camps and training grounds would have to be destroyed, along with the terrorists' command and control infrastructure.

Military means would be necessary for such missions, although to be both legal and politically acceptable such operations should be multilateral rather than conducted by any single state alone, and the means used should be "proportional" to the task at hand and not excessively harsh.

Despite this new emerging consensus, however, the UN has had continued difficulty operationally defining terrorism and specifying the conditions under which certain types of actions should be taken. One reason for this difficulty is that developing states have generally objected to language that outlaws or condemns legitimate popular struggles against what are considered to be repressive or exploitative regimes and forces. While many states are sympathetic to fighting terrorism, since they struggle against violent opponents, many governments also hold out the possibility of supporting legitimate nationalist struggles. Palestinian leaders seek to distinguish their homeland struggle against Israeli territorial occupation in the West Bank and Gaza Strip from the indiscriminate global violence of Osama bin Laden, for example. Much the same argument was heard during the 1960s, 1970s, and 1980s in defense of liberation movements, such as those against colonialism and by the African National Congress against the minority apartheid regime in South Africa, making it difficult for the UN to codify a definition of terrorism in law. Instead the organization has fallen back on outlawing specific acts of violence, such as air hijackings.

Governments hard pressed by insurgency movements regularly refer to their opponents as "terrorists," whether or not the label really fits. It is a way of criminalizing or de-legitimizing the political movements for which the insurgents fight. This has applied to racist regimes such as South Africa's apartheid government, as well as nationalistic regimes such as Turkey and Iraq in struggles against their ethnic minorities, Israel's conflict with the Palestinians, Spain's dispute with the Basques, Russia's battles with Chechens, and Britain's century long struggle against the Irish Republican Army. Indeed, soon after the September 11 attacks and the demonstration of Washington's new resolve to fight terrorism, a number of governments called for U.S. aid in struggles against their own "terrorist" opponents, including the governments of Malaysia, Colombia, and the Philippines.

No matter how precise we aim to be about terrorism as a concept, then, there is always going to be some ambiguity about such an emotionally charged term. It can be politically useful to use such phrases as "war against terror," but it may not be very meaningful to the combatants and their beliefs. Dutch political scientist Alex Schmid and Robert J. Beck, in the 1993 book on *International Law and the Use of Force* co-authored by Anthony C. Arend, found that some 109 different definitions of terrorism appeared between 1936 and 1981 alone. In his book *Serenade of Suffering* (1999) Richard Chasdi has noted controversies about whether to include among "non-combatants" subject to terror attacks military personnel in noncombatant or peacekeeping roles as well as governmental officials not violating fundamental human rights. As peacekeeping becomes more prevalent as a military assignment, attacks on peacekeepers might increasingly become a problem of "terrorism" depending upon how one defines the concept and how one treats troops assigned to peacekeeping missions. Thus the targeted British authorities in the King David Hotel, blown up by Jewish extremists in Jerusalem during Israel's independence struggles against the British in 1947, could have been victims of terror under some definitions.

With definitional complexities such as these, it is inherently difficult to build and maintain an anti-terrorism coalition among cooperating states especially when relying on military force to target "terrorists." Some states will care about the identity of the accused terrorists for a variety of reasons, which may be political, economic, ethnic, or religious.

Despite the difficulties and complex political motives involved in defining and identifying terrorists, analysts generally distinguish terrorism from other forms of violence and from war in noting that although terrorism, like war, can involve political, ideological, religious, or social goals, terrorists target civilian populations or "non-combatants" engaged in unconventional violence such as bombings, assassinations, or the spread of toxic substances. As the author has pointed out elsewhere (Pearson and Rochester, *International Relations*, 1998, p. 448), unconventional violence is a concept implying that the acts are spectacular and violate accepted social norms while inflicting shock, fear, and severe pain on the victims and their group. Terrorists do not observe what are thought of as rules of combat. The specific targets of attack might or might not be important to the terrorist, for example in a kidnapping or assassination incident versus a random bombing in a crowded market place. In all these cases the impact of the violence is meant to go beyond the immediate target to raise fear, insecurity, and disruption among a larger "enemy" group and population.

TERRORISM TRAINING AND PREPAREDNESS BECAME A PRIMARY FOCUS OF THE U.S. ADMINISTRATION AND MILITARY AFTER THE SEPTEMBER 11, 2001 ATTACKS. *(AP/Wide World Photos/North Carolina National Guard. Reproduced by permission.)*

It has been said that terrorism tends to be a tactic of the relatively weak, i.e., those groups and individuals with political causes (though they might be marginalized groups on the fringe of politics) but lacking in standard fighting resources and weapons as compared to their opponents, or without the size of forces that would allow a conventional war campaign. Osama bin Laden, while inflicting massive civilian casualties on his "enemy," criticized the United States for supporting Israel and stationing forces in the Arabian Gulf region, as well as for past "terroristic" deeds such as the Hiroshima nuclear bombing of Japan. The terrorists who commandeered U.S. jetliners in September

2001 essentially turned the aircraft into cruise missiles to attack their targets. Presumably if the terrorists had had actual cruise missiles with the capability to reach the United States, they would have used them instead; presumably if home grown American terrorist Timothy McVeigh, the man who bombed the Alfred P. Murrah federal building in Oklahoma City in 1995, had had a conventional weapon, or a weapon of mass destruction, at his disposal, he might have used it instead of a Ryder Truck filled with fertilizer and fuel oil. In symbolically acting out a "weak attacking strong" role, terrorists often cultivate the Robin Hood or David against Goliath image. In so doing they can gain public support, admirers, and followers, but they also pick up enemies both within their movements and from those they attack.

HISTORICAL BACKGROUND

Terrorism, and therefore anti-terrorism, have been around as tactics for centuries, indeed probably going back in one form or another to the earliest days of organized human conflict. During the Middle Ages (from about the fifth century to the fifteenth century) armies reportedly sometimes launched diseased corpses into enemy towns to spread havoc and fear. Political acts of terror were seen in the so-called Reign of Terror during the French Revolution (1789–93). Acts of terror have even sparked major wars, as in World War I (1914–18) with the assassination of Austria's Archduke Franz Ferdinand by rebellious Bosnian nationalists instigated by Serbia in 1914. Nationalists, revolutionaries, "freedom fighters," zealots, heroes and scoundrels, ranging from the Irish Republican Army and their Ulster Unionist opponents in Northern Ireland, to American colonists at the Boston Tea Party, have used disruptive unorthodox violence or destruction of property to advance their causes or retaliate against their enemies.

In the modern age, new technologies have afforded greater potential killing power both to authorities and to terrorists alike, and have made our societies in a sense more vulnerable to attacks that might disrupt communication networks, contaminate water supplies, spread disease and destruction more rapidly, and gain immediate notoriety. Terrorists themselves now can operate on a more global scale, linking up in inter-group networks through the use of modern communication media such as the Internet and cell phones and through transcontinental travel. If history is any guide, however, terrorist groups are likely to be rather small and to depend on an inner core leadership network that might or might not reach out to local and international recruits.

Likewise, a number of means have been used historically to combat terrorism, including military counter-moves, police and intelligence activities, and efforts to reform or eliminate the conditions that make terrorists popular. The Cuban revolutionary Ché Guevara was hunted down captured and killed in an ambush in 1967 by Bolivian military units and U.S. advisors. The notorious international terrorist "Carlos the Jackal," leader of an international network that once kidnapped the main representatives of the Organization of Petroleum Exporting Countries (OPEC), finally was himself captured in 1994 by French intelligence agents through negotiations with the Sudanese and operating on tips from Carlos' former friends, the Central Intelligence Agency (CIA), and others. (See sidebar.) Suspects in the bombing of Pan Am flight 103 over Lockerbie, Scotland, in 1988 were finally released for trial by Scottish judges in the Netherlands through a decade long campaign of political and economic pressure brought to bear on Libyan leader Muammar Qadhafi. Crucial in these captures was the diplomatic cooperation of major powers as well as heavy economic forces such as the European Union, and the eventual willingness of those in the terror networks to betray their comrades.

The Use of Force

In a very important sense, then, combating terrorism requires the cooperation or the acquiescence of states and individuals actually supporting or harboring terrorist groups. States support such groups because they are often considered politically useful, for example to weaken an opposing state or a rival regime. Terrorist groups also receive help in the form of arms, recruits, or money, from kin or sponsors living abroad, such as those supporting Kurdishr, Albanian, or Tamil nationalists in their rebellions in Iraq/Turkey, Kosovo, and Sri Lanka respectively. Effective anti-terror approaches also require gaining the cooperation of states within which terrorists might hide or organize, as well as states that are mere bystanders. Standard exhaustive police investigative work can be just as important as military strikes in apprehending terrorists, if indeed the goal is to bring them to justice.

There are those who argue vehemently that military responses are not only appropriate to defeating the age-old terror problem, they are the most reliable means of doing so. Writing in *American Heritage* magazine in March 2002, Victor Davis-Hanson notes that Osama bin Laden comes from a long historical line of disaffected messianic zealots, including those who struggled in ancient Judea against Roman legions and ended up committing mass suicide on the heights of Masada. "Similarly, Muhammad Ahmad, the Mahdi, the 'expected Guide,' wreaked havoc in Egypt and the Sudan between 1881 and 1885" (p. 39) in a vain anti-British anti-Western struggle that ended with an estimated 27,000 of his followers killed as compared to only 48 British dead at the Battle of Omdurman. Mystical Native American Ghost Dancers "promised their followers divine invulnerability from enemy bullets and even immortality" in vainly attempting to reclaim ancestral lands in the Great Plains during the 1890s. Again vastly superior mil-

CARLOS THE JACKAL: TRAIL OF TERROR

Ilich Ramírez Sanchez, also known as "Carlos the Jackal," was one of the most feared and, in some circles, revered of all terrorists in history. Originally from Venezuela, "Carlos," as he came to be known, was raised by a staunchly communist father and a fervently Catholic mother. He came to embrace communism, ultimately graduating from Patrice Lumumba University in Moscow. After graduation he was persuaded by the views of a Palestinian friend who told him of the Palestinian/Israeli conflict. He became involved with members of the Popular Front for the Liberation of Palestine, which had communist leanings. Most of Carlos the Jackal's "work" was carried out against anticommunist groups and nations.

Carlos began terrorist training at a camp in Jordan in 1970 and participated in his first battles against the Jordanian army after a terrorist group with which he was associated bombed an airplane on Jordanian land, incurring the anger of the king of Jordan, who launched an attack on the terrorist group. Carlos soon became anxious to take on his own terrorist missions, including bombings and hijackings. His first few attempts at bombing airplanes, however, failed miserably.

Soon after, Carlos began drawing up an extensive list of names of Jews and Israeli sympathizers in Great Britain, where he spent much of his youth and where he hid his terrorist persona within the diplomatic community of London. He attempted to kill Joseph Sieff, a wealthy Jewish businessman who was the president of Marks and Spencer department stores and an honorary vice-president of the British Zionist Federation. Sieff survived the gunshot wounds, but it became clear that Carlos had a mission and intended to carry it out. He was responsible for several bombings in Paris in the 1980s, killing 13 and injuring 150. He has also been linked to Libyan president Muammar Qadhafi and Iraqi leader Saddam Hussein.

Carlos quickly became notorious. He had a reputation as a master of disguise with several different personas, complete with ID and credit cards. He was linked to several high profile terrorist attacks and assassinations, including the 1975 seizure of OPEC oil ministers and a 1976 Palestinian hijacking of an airliner that ended with an Israeli commando raid.

With the end of the Cold War, Carlos eventually "retired," due largely to the lessened importance of the threat of communism and the collapse of the Soviet Union. Additionally, with his notoriety and the scope of his activities there were increasingly fewer places safe enough to provide him refuge. He eventually went into hiding in Sudan.

The French government, however, was determined to bring Carlos to justice. It knew that he was hiding in Sudan and that the only way to apprehend him was to make a deal with the Sudanese government, which was unwilling to admit to harboring Carlos, to give him up for extradition. After much negotiation with the Sudanese government, which continuously refused to admit it harbored the terrorist, France presented irrefutable evidence of Carlos's presence.

A French intelligence officer, acting on a tip from the U.S. Central Intelligence Agency, photographed Carlos and tracked his movements in Sudan. Additionally, videotaped footage of Carlos drinking and consorting with woman at a party was shown to Sudan's negotiator Sheik Hassan al-Turabi. Al-Turabi, a devout Muslim, was disgusted by Carlos's behavior and finally acknowledged that Sudan harbored the terrorist. In exchange for loans from the International Monetary Fund and World Bank that would help erase Sudan's foreign debts, al-Turabi agreed in 1994 to release Carlos for extradition to France.

Once in France, Carlos stood trial for the shooting deaths of two French secret agents and an informer. He insisted on representing himself, claiming that he was a revolutionary and a political combatant. "There is no law for me," he said during his eight-day trial. The French court, however, disagreed, and in 1997 Carlos, aged 48, was sentenced to life in prison.

itary force crushed them, as Davis-Hanson claims it has done repeatedly to fanatical insurrectionists regardless of the legitimacy of their causes.

While he might confuse rebels, military diehards such as World War II Japanese *kamakazi* pilots, and terrorists as defined above, Davis-Hanson clearly feels that superior technology and force, most notably in the hands of "consensual" western democracies, can reliably roust such movements even if terrorists score temporary and dramatic successes. The added dimension of newly advanced military technologies such as global positioning

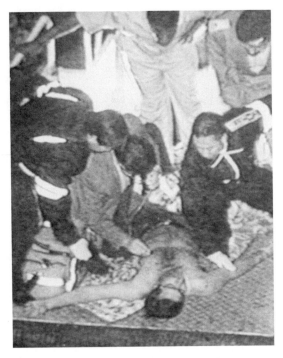

MEDICAL WORKERS EXAMINE THE BODY OF A MAN SUSPECTED OF BEING AMONG THE HIJACKERS OF AN INDIAN AIRLINES PLANE. WHILE THE CONVENTION AGAINST THE TAKING OF HOSTAGES OUTLINES HOW TO DEAL WITH AIRLINE HIJACKINGS, VIOLENCE CAN STILL RESULT. *(AP/Wide World Photo. Reproduced by permission.)*

satellites, precision munitions and guided bombs supposedly add to the ability to hit such renegades where they hide. Indeed, prior to the World Trade Center/Pentagon casualty toll and the introduction of new anti-terror military technology, most acts of terror killed relatively few people. Terrorists have seldom achieved their goals apart from gaining notoriety and avoiding apprehension.

Problems of Force as a Response

For a variety of reasons, however, the simple deduction that force trumps terror is questionable, and those who believe it might be termed just as naïve as those who believe that force is futile. The war analogy and military remedies in fighting terrorism are problematic for a number of reasons. As noted this is partly due to definitional and legal uncertainties about what one is fighting against, but history also indicates that it is due to tactical problems in fighting a set of ideas using military means.

Contrary to the relatively clear criteria set for victory against Japan in World War II (1939–45), the last time U.S. territory was successfully attacked by another country, how does one know when victory against terrorism is won? When there is no act

of terror for one week (as Israelis were demanding in 2002 during their struggles against the Palestinians), for one month, one year, one decade, ever? When an act does recur, does that mean the "war" is lost? Who exactly are the opponents? They do not wear uniforms and are not arrayed at front lines, or even in guerrilla formations ready to launch combat from hidden locations. Do they include all the states that might assist or harbor any sort of terrorists, or only states harboring the particular terrorists that have offended the states conducting the war? Terrorists can be either members of known groups or anonymous; they generally strike unexpectedly from hiding or posing as civilians. They usually use implements such as homemade bombs, small arms, or engage in hijackings or hostage takings. It is therefore easier to proceed against the terrorist enemy once he/she has been revealed through actions than in advance. Indeed, the reference to "terror" itself comes from not knowing who might be among the next victims or where the next strikes will occur.

Military campaigns against such shadowy and covert enemies are fraught with uncertainies. They often take the form of massive attacks against suspected terrorist hideouts or training grounds in mainly civilian territories—amidst towns, villages, and cities as in the crowded West Bank and Gaza Palestinian territories. Attacks meant to root out the perpetrators can, therefore, create such bitterness and vengefulness among the civilian population that terror itself can increase in response. Barbara Tuchman, in her book *The First Salute* (1988), describes such a process when British naval forces pillaged New Haven and other Connecticut towns (an act of state terror) trying to squelch the American rebellion in 1779; similar results were seen when the French tried in vain to suppress the Algerian independence uprising in the 1950s and 1960s.

The Irish writer Conor Cruise O'Brien has noted that terrorists often persist for years because they gain tremendous personal power and acclaim, and even money from the violent profession they have chosen. Therefore, if they are devoted to political causes, for example, they might not necessarily give up even if political concessions are offered and their goals or demands are met, since they would stand to lose much power and influence in the bargain. By the same token, he argues that heavy-handed and unilateral military responses also are likely to be ineffective since they play into the terrorists' hand by giving them increased notoriety and gaining them sympathizers. In O'Brien's words from his 1986 article, "Thinking About Terrorism" in *The Atlantic*, "The combating of terrorism is not helped by bombastic speeches at high levels, stressing what a monstrous evil terrorism is and that its elimination is to be given the highest priority . . . A movement that is denounced by a President is in the big time." Rather it is patient hunting, through collaboration among states who themselves reduce their own backing of violent and terror-wielding clients, along with tips and betrayals among the terrorists that often lead authorities to them.

The Recurrence and Evolution of Terrorism

Certainly at times military attacks against terrorists have been stressed. The Russians conducted a campaign of unremitting military violence against the Chechen rebels after acts of terror reached Moscow in the late 1990s. Russian troops and air attacks destroyed most Chechen towns and villages in an attempt to destroy the rebel infrastructure. The Russians succeeded at great human cost in retaining Chechnya inside the Russian Federation. Additionally, in responding to suicide bombers from the territories of the West Bank and Gaza the Israelis enjoyed enough of a fire power advantage in 2002 to dominate on questions of forming a future Palestinian state. The overall settlement of the nationalist fervor that led to the terrorism in these and other cases, however, could not be achieved by military suppression alone. As noted, though terrorists might be out for personal power, terrorism stems from political, social, or ideological cause for which people are willing to die. This is demonstrated by the increasing prevalence of incidents of suicide terrorism. Military retaliation is likely to be needed in destroying the terrorist hideouts and training grounds, but it is unlikely to wipe out the ideas behind the movement or to apprehend or deter all terrorists. In addition the terrorists' recruitment base can be diminished if political reforms and policy changes eliminate some of the grievances that drive people, especially young people, to join terrorist causes. This would require seriously heeding and addressing those grievances.

As the Palestinian example shows, terrorism also is often more complicated than merely a "good vs. evil" fight between two sides. Indeed, Yasser Arafat's religiously dogmatic rivals, the HAMAS organization of Islamic militants, was founded in the 1980s as a counterweight to the increasing power of the secular PLO after the latter group survived Israel's invasion of Lebanon in 1982. HAMAS, the more militantly anti-Israeli group during the 1990s, actually was founded with Israeli support in the 1980s to become that PLO counterweight. Similarly, Osama bin Laden emerged as a political operative in Afghanistan with U.S. and other nations' support during the 1980s in the fight of the mujahideen ("freedom fighters") against the Soviet forces supporting the leftist secular Afghani government at that time. The mujahideen, including Saudi import bin Laden, were supplied and supported by the United States, Pakistan, Saudi Arabia, and others in hopes that they would prevail against the Soviets. Indeed they did, but these same forces later both descended into a destructive Afghan civil war of their own—leaving that country essentially in ruins to be "uplifted" by the Taliban—and began to back militantly anti-Western and anti-Israeli Islamic movements in the Middle East as well.

Regional politics generally are complicated; straightforward struggles of terror and anti-terror are generally unrealistic. Iran, a country designated by George W. Bush in 2002 as part of an "axis of evil" (along with its own traditional enemy Iraq and distant North Korea) was at the very same time included among the leading regional powers with which Washington was consulting in summit meetings about the future of Afghanistan. Indeed, Iran, like the United States but for different and more ethnically related reasons, opposed the Taliban in Afghanistan. Thus to oversimplify the complexities of political conflict does little to help maintain the coalitions necessary to fight terror.

It has been glibly asserted that to fight terrorism one might have to "get in bed" with unsavory characters, who can provide the necessary information about terrorist group structure and planning to allow authorities to anticipate and counter terrorist moves. As the Carlos case showed this is true to an extent; one must maintain communication with and infiltrate terror networks, gaining information in order to eliminate the semi-independent "cell" structure that often characterizes them and allows them to continue if one cell is captured.

The notion of collaborating with the unsavory, however, is also dangerous and can be self-defeating, since these are the very people who often end up becoming and abetting terrorists. American and Saudi intelligence services were "in bed" for years during the 1980s and 1990s with bin Laden and other anti-Soviet or anti-Iranian factions in the Middle East. Similarly the CIA closely cultivated relations for years with Manuel Noriega (the former Panamanian dictator eventually tried in Florida during the 1980s on drug smuggling charges) and other Central and South American dictators. The end result was increased, not decreased, violence and terrorism in those regions. "Death squads"—militia unleashed by governments to attack their political opponents—ended up kidnapping and killing thousands, the so-called "disappeared" of the 1970s and 1980s, in Latin countries where U.S. military and intelligence agencies had trained the military. Among the victims were both nationals of those countries and foreign aid workers, nuns, and priests, and other innocent civilians. These were clearly acts of terror, the tragic and ironic result of indiscriminant "counter-terrorism" and counter-revolutionary policies conducted and largely planned through military staffs.

Thus the political story behind most terrorist movements is complex, often involving alliances of convenience between major or minor powers and dissident groups, resulting in unexpected and un-welcome later conflict between those dominant powers and the groups they once supported. The lesson is that reliance on heavy-handed violence as a counter-terror tactic is rife with dangers and can spark increased rather than decreased terrorism. From the multi-national campaigns against Carlos the Jackal and the Bader-Meinhoff and Red Brigades revolutionary groups of Germany and Italy during the 1970s, it would appear that careful study of the terrorist network links, along with tailored police and intelligence investigations exposing the likely agendas and itineraries of known terrorists, are far more effective, if less politically spectacular, than massive military assaults against so-called terrorist strongholds.

RECENT HISTORY AND THE FUTURE

Actual anti-terrorist campaigns often go through cycles of fight and negotiation, as seen in the Chronology provided by Basques in Spain and France as they took part in negotiations with re-gional and national governments, formed political parties to compete in elections, but fell back on violence such as urban bombings when they could not gain the concessions they wanted. In such cases the fighting might be out in the open, or clandestine through intelligence and police agen-cies, and the negotiations likewise might be con-ducted either openly or through cloak and dagger meetings. The Basque case reflects the disillu-sionment with negotiations brought on by acts of violence, and then the disillusionment with vio-lence that leads back to hesitant peace feelers and negotiations to apprehend the culprits or end their grievances.

In fact the political stories surrounding terror-ism are further complicated by the motives of the anti-terrorist coalition. In its struggles against al-

Qaeda and the Taliban, for example, the U.S. gov-ernment maintained that it was not fighting Islam or Arabs, but rather fighting the terrorist phe-nomenon. Yet the targets of U.S. and British mil-itary response were almost exclusively Islamic. The U.S. quandary about how to treat specific groups was reflected in its dealings with the Kurds, an Islamic group spread out among at least four coun-tries of West and Central Asia which had histori-cally used terrorist tactics and had been victimized by terrifying counter-attacks as in Iraq's use of chemical weapons in the 1980s. As Saddam Hus-sein threatened their annihilation in the 1991 Gulf War, U.S. and British forces hastily conceived of a plan to provide them sanctuary in a "no-fly" zone in northern Iraq to protect Kurds against Iraqi strikes. The United States' Turkish allies in NATO, however, also considered the Kurdish na-tionalist group the PKK as terrorists, and hunted them relentlessly both in Turkey and across the border into Iraq. Washington did little to oppose this policy or the Turks' use of U.S. supplied equip-ment in carrying it out. Thus, not for the first time in history, the United States supported both sides in a war involving terrorism. An earlier example of this behavior is during the Greek civil war (1944–49), when the Harry Truman administra-tion (1945–53) aided both the Greek right wing and the anti-Soviet Yugoslavs, even as Yugoslavia aided the Greek left wing.

Contradictions in Opposing Terrorism

In such struggles, attempting to deal with the inherent contradictions of opposing terrorism in real political circumstances where its own interests were mixed, Washington showed the cross pres-sures of an actual "war against terrorism" by pick-ing and choosing which terrorists to oppose or object to. Often this amounts to a double stan-dard, which is commonplace in politics, as nations oppose only the terrorism that seems to directly threaten one's own immediate interests or friends. It is important to identify key partners in anti-terrorism campaigns, but in doing so one might have to pay a price to each partner.

One way in which double standards are meant to be erased is in the enactment of international laws against terrorism. Effective action against ter-rorism requires the enforcement of laws and, where necessary, extradition to bring terrorists to justice for trial in appropriate civil, international, or mili-tary courts. As described by Pearson and Rochester, after outrageous acts of terror, such as the killing of Israeli athletes at the 1972 Munich Olympic Games, the international community responded by passing a series of measures designed to crack down on kidnapping, assassination, and hijacking. This included an international treaty on the Punishment of Crimes Against Internationally Protected Persons Including Diplomatic Agents, along with another convention Against the Taking of Hostages that called for the prosecution or extradition of all hostage-takers while recognizing the rights of national liberation movements. Additional measures were developed to provide for the safe release of hijacked aircraft, passengers, and crewmembers and the extradition of those suspected of terror acts against aircraft, airports, or airlines. Similar agreements were reached to cover naval vessels, stolen nuclear material, and misuse of the mails.

With the shifting of terrorist tactics and style in the 1990s to produce more destruction with less interest in negotiation or group recognition, mechanisms for international law again shifted. While no consensus could be reached on a precise definition of terrorism as a crime, Ved Nanda has pointed to agreement at the 2001 UN session to ban targeting of civilians as well as indiscriminant violence, and to apprehend, extradite, or prosecute those found responsible for such crimes.

Promoting the rule of law is crucial in combating terrorism. Commenting on future legal prospects, terrorism expert Paul Wilkinson, writing for the Canadian Security Intelligence Service ("Terrorism: Motivations and Causes," 1995), has given the following diagnosis and prescription of preparations in Europe:

> . . . .The true litmus test will be the Western states' consistency and courage in maintaining a firm and effective policy against terrorism in all its forms. They must abhor the idea that terrorism can be tolerated as long as it is only affecting someone else's democratic rights and rule of law. They must adopt the clear principle that one democracy's terrorist is another democracy's terrorist.

Wilkinson continued to note several general principles to reduce terrorism. Among them were principles to defeat terrorism democratically and "within the framework of the rule of law," a consistent policy of non-negotiation regardless of the circumstances, increased efforts to prosecute terrorists, penalizations for state sponsors who provide support to terrorist groups, and to continue "diplomatic efforts to resolve major political conflicts" without allowing terrorism to derail the process. He asserted that technology is such that, with combined and cooperative intelligence efforts, governments can establish a firm foundation for long-term success against terrorism.

Some of these strictures are, of course, controversial. There are pros and cons about whether and in what circumstances to negotiate with known terrorists, given possibilities that might produce the release of terror leaders or hostages or reduce the chances for future violence. The Basque and Palestinian conflicts illustrate clearly that violence, anti-terrorism struggles, and negotiations over issues such as cease-fires, security guarantees, and political solutions involving autonomy or independence can go on simultaneously, though the final outcome in the form of peace agreements might be uncertain at best. In all cases of violence, international and domestic, tradition has shown that there is a place for wise diplomacy to help defuse the worst situations, to get relief supplies through to endangered populations, and to create possible terms for settling the underlying political issues driving the conflict. Rewarding violent behavior is certainly to be avoided, but diplomats by definition are trained to negotiate among parties where truth and virtue might be in dispute. One can only hope that leaders come to prefer talking productively to shooting and bombing. Law and ultimate justice—for victims of all sorts of terror—are key issues in those talks.

BIBLIOGRAPHY

Antokol, Norman and Mayer Nudell. *No One a Neutral: Political Hostage Taking in the Modern World.* Medina, OH: Alpha Publications, 1990.

Arend, Anthony Clark and Robert J. Beck. *International Law and the Use of Force: Beyond the U.N. Charter Paradigm.* London: Routledge, 1993.

Campbell, Kurt M. *To Prevail: An American Strategy for the Campaign Against Terrorism.* Washington, DC: Center for Strategic and International Studies, 2001.

Chasdi, Richard J. *Serenade of Suffering.* Lanham, MD: Lexington, 1999.

Hanson, Victor Davis. "The Longest War," *American Heritage,* February/March 2002, pp. 36–46.

Laqueur, Walter. *The New Terrorism: Fanaticism and the Arms of Mass Destruction.* Oxford: Oxford University Press, 1999.

Lesser, Ian O., et. al. *Countering the New Terrorism.* Santa Monica, CA: Rand, 1999.

Martin, John R. *Defeating Terrorism: Strategic Issue Analysis.* Carlisle Barracks, PA: U.S. Army War College, 2002.

Nanda, Ved P. "Stakes in India-Pakistan Conflict Are High," *The Denver Post,* January 9, 2002.

Nanda, Ved P. "UN Must Act in Afghanistan," *The Denver Post,* October 14, 2001.

O'Brien, Conor Cruise. "Thinking About Terrorism," *The Atlantic Monthly,* June 1986.

Onwudiwe, Ihekwoaba D. *The Globalization of Terrorism.* Aldershot, UK: Ashgate, 2001.

Pearson, Frederic S. and J. Martin Rochester. *International Relations: The Global Condition in the Twenty-First Century,* 4th ed. New York: McGraw-Hill, 1998.

Pillar, Paul R. *Terrorism and U.S. Foreign Policy.* Washington, DC: Brookings, 2001.

Reeve, Simon *The New Jackals: Ramzi Yousef, Osama bin Laden and the Future of Terrorism.* Boston, MA: Northeastern University Press,1999.

Reich, Walter, ed. *Origins of Terrorism: Psychologies, Ideologies, Theologies, States of Mind.* Washington, DC: Woodrow Wilson Press Center, 1998.

Schmid, Alex. *Political Terrorism: A New Guide to Actors, Authors, Concepts, Data Bases, Theories and Literature.* Amsterdam: North-Holland, 1988

Tuchman, Barbara W. *The First Salute.* New York: Knopf, 1988.

Webster, Bobby. *Topics: Terrorism.* International Debate Education Association Database, October 31, 2000. Available online at http://www.database.org/details.pr.asp?topicID=53. (cited May 7, 2002).

World Anti-Terrorism Laws JURIST: The Legal Education Network, University of Pittsburgh School of Law. Available online at http://jurist.law.pitt.edu/terrorism/terrorism3a.htm (cited May 7, 2002).

Frederic S. Pearson

HOMELAND SECURITY: GUARDING AGAINST TERRORISM

Football fans were thrilled with the last-minute, forty-eight-yard field goal by the New England Patriots that gave them the win in the thirty-sixth Super Bowl game over the St. Louis Rams. The 73,000 spectators who witnessed the Patriots' 20–17 victory in the Louisiana Superdome on February 3, 2002, were also relieved that the suspense over the game's outcome was played out on the field and not in the stands. As one of the first National Special Security Events designated by the Office of Homeland Security and the White House, the game had received as much attention for the possibility of suffering a terrorist attack as for the storybook nature of the Patriots' comeback season. Fans were admitted five hours before the start of the game, with ticket holders subjected to a number of security screenings. Male ticket holders had to take off their shoes and reset their watches to prove that the items were not bombs. Binocular and camera bags, backpacks, and any other large bags were banned outright from the stadium, as were coolers and camera lenses longer than six inches.

The Super Bowl and the Winter Olympic Games in Salt Lake City, which began just five days later, captured the nation's attention for their heightened security efforts. Yet Office of Homeland Security director Tom Ridge cautioned that federal involvement for such major events was not realistic for every situation. "We have so many high-profile events throughout the country in all fifty states, where we literally have thousands if not hundreds of thousands of people, attracting both domestic and international visitors," Ridge told the U.S. Conference of Mayors in January 2002, adding, "We can't designate every major event as a national special security event." Emphasizing the need for state and local officials to bear the great-

THE CONFLICT

Days after the terrorist attacks of September 11, 2001, President George W. Bush announced the formation of an Office of Homeland Security. Under Director Tom Ridge, the office would coordinate the broad-based counterterrorist functions of a multitude of federal, state, and local agencies. Critics of the plan noted that without any statutory power or significant budget of its own, the Office of Homeland Security would have to rely on its persuasive power to get other agencies to cooperate on a comprehensive counterterrorist plan.

Political

- Counterterrorist spending had been greatly increased throughout the 1990s and skyrocketed after the September 11 attacks. Much of the money remained at the federal level, however, leaving state and local systems understaffed and inadequately trained. The 2003 budget for homeland security promised to address this imbalance, and Ridge staked his reputation on including state and local officials in the planning process.

Ideological

- Other nations, such as Israel and the United Kingdom, have taken strong steps to counter domestic terrorism. In instances when federal agents have taken measures against domestic fringe groups in the United States, however, the results have been controversial, including the deadly raid at the Branch Davidian compound in 1993.

CHRONOLOGY

August 1992 U.S. Marshals engage in a standoff with white supremacist Randy Weaver and his family at Ruby Ridge, Idaho.

February 28, 1993 The United States Bureau of Alcohol, Tobacco, and Firearms attempt to issue arrest and search warrants against David Koresh and the Branch Davidian compound in Waco, Texas; a fifty-one day standoff ensues.

1994–95 Aum Shinrikyo cult members stage two sarin gas attacks; the first attack kills seven people in the town of Matsumoto, and the second attack kills twelve people on the Tokyo subway.

April 19, 1995 Timothy McVeigh and Terry Lynn Nichols bomb the Alfred P. Murrah federal building in Oklahoma City, Oklahoma.

September 11, 2001 Terrorists suspected of being connected to the terrorist group al-Qaeda attack the World Trade Center buildings in New York City and the Pentagon near Washington, DC. More than three thousands people are killed.

mid-September 2001 The first of several anthrax-riddled letters sent through the U.S. mail is received in the offices of American Media in Boca Raton, Florida.

September 20, 2001 President Bush announces plans for a Homeland Security Office, the first new cabinet office since 1989.

October 8, 2001 The Office of Homeland Security is established, with Pennsylvania governor Tom Ridge as its first director.

October 11, 2001 A general terrorism alert is issued by the Office of Homeland Security. A second alert is issued on October 29, and a third alert follows on December 3.

October 17, 2001 The Financial Anti-Terrorism Act is passed by Congress.

October 26, 2001 The USA Patriot Act is enacted into law.

November 19, 2001 The Airport and Transportation Security Act is signed into law.

November 29, 2001 Congress passes the Terrorism Risk Protection Act.

December 12, 2001 The Smart Border Declaration, intended to increase security between the United States and Canada, is signed by Homeland Security Director Tom Ridge of the United States and Foreign Affairs Minister John Manley of Canada.

February 3, 2002 Super Bowl XXXVI between the New England Patriots and the St. Louis Rams is played in New Orleans, Louisiana, without any significant security threat.

February 4, 2002 President Bush announces a $37.7 billion budget for homeland security for the 2003 fiscal year.

February 8–23, 2002 The XIX Winter Games are held in Salt Lake City, Utah, without any significant security incidents.

June 6, 2002 President Bush announces a new Cabinet position, creating the Department of Homeland Security, which has far reaching implications for government.

est share of responsibility for safeguarding future events, Ridge continued to say that a security model should be applied to highly visible, broadly attended events to ensure safety. With the Office of Homeland Security created only months before, in the wake of the September 11, 2001, attacks, however, many Americans wondered what the new model of security might entail and how quickly it could be learned and applied.

HISTORICAL BACKGROUND

Controversies Over Domestic Defense

Ridge's concern over sharing responsibility with local officials stemmed not only from budgetary concerns but also from the federal government's past profile in security matters, which had often proved controversial in the era before September 11. At times the government itself was accused of acting in an aggressive, even unconstitutional, manner when confronted with extremist or terrorist groups. In one of the most contentious events, eighty agents of the Bureau of Alcohol, Tobacco, and Firearms (ATF) attempted to issue arrest and search warrants of the Branch Davidian religious compound, led by David Koresh, near Waco, Texas. After a shootout on February 28, 1993, that left four ATF agents and possibly six Branch Davidians dead, the two sides settled in for a 51-day standoff. Negotiations stalled while Federal Bureau of Investigations (FBI) agents engaged in psychological tactics—playing loud music and chants through loudspeakers, for example—and the Branch Davidians refused to surrender. After Attorney General Janet Reno received reports of a large weapons cache in the compound, on April 19 FBI agents poured tear gas into the sect's main building in the hope of ending the stalemate, but they were unsuccessful. Hours later, a massive fire blazed through the building and killed nearly 80 of the sect's members. While federal officials insisted that the Branch Davidians had set the fire themselves in a desperate and suicidal maneuver, the ensuing investigation highlighted the difficulty in balancing public safety while guaranteeing civil and religious liberties.

Convinced that the government's intervention at Waco was unjustified, Timothy McVeigh, a Gulf War (1991) veteran, and his co-conspirator Terry Nichols, decided to strike back at the government in the name of individual freedom. McVeigh had already been outraged by the U.S. Marshals Service's shootout with white supremacist Randy Weaver in August 1992 at Ruby Ridge, Idaho, which left one marshal and two members of Weaver's family dead. Feeding on the virulent racism, anti-Semitism, and antigovernment sentiments of the infamous novel by William Pierce, under the pseudonym of Andrew Macdonald, *The Turner Diaries*, McVeigh found support for his growing rage in the various militia movements that sprang up in the 1990s. Often associated with neo-Nazi, separatist, and survivalist agendas, the individual militia organizations also espoused libertarian ideals that attacked government regulation and intervention. At times their rhetoric veered into wild conspiracy theories, with the sieges of Ruby Ridge and Waco invoked as proof of a government bent on taking away all basic civil liberties. By the time McVeigh and Nichols put their plan into action, as many as two hundred small militia groups claimed as many as 100,000 members across the United States though no militia group was directly involved in the terrorist attack.

On April 19, 1995—exactly two years after the siege at Waco ended in tragedy—McVeigh parked a delivery van packed with ammonium nitrate and diesel fuel outside of the Alfred P. Murrah federal building in Oklahoma City. In the resulting explosion and rescue operations, 168 victims died. To McVeigh and Nichols—the most deadly domestic terrorists up to that point in American history—their actions were justified as a protest against the "Socialist Wannabe Slaves" of the government. As McVeigh had written to a friend in July 1994 (quoted in Lou Michel and Dan Herbeck's 2001 book *American Terrorist: Timothy McVeigh and the Oklahoma City Bombing*), "Those who betray or subvert the Constitution are guilty of sedition and/or treason, are domestic enemies and should and will be punished accordingly." He added, "Blood will flow in the streets."

The United States Before September 11

While McVeigh's actions demonstrated that government actions against perceptions of domestic groups could give rise to further violence in response, the Oklahoma City bombing was one of a handful of terrorist events that disrupted American life in the 1990s. Between 1990–95 the United States witnessed 32 separate terrorist incidents; about one-third were bombings committed by animal rights groups. Almost all of the events were staged by domestic terrorists; just two—the World Trade Center bombing in 1993 and a takeover of the Iranian Mission at the United Nations in New York in 1992;—were conducted by foreign groups. Prior to the Oklahoma City bombing, most Americans were probably more familiar with the terrorist-centered plots of movies such as *Die Hard* and *Speed* than they were with any real-life terrorist actions in the United States. Even the deadly bombing during the 1996 Summer Olympics at Atlanta's Centennial Park quickly devolved into controversies over the naming of Richard Jewell as a suspect by various media outlets. Jewell was eventually cleared of suspicion, but the investigation over the motives of indicted bomber Eric Robert Rudolph remained murky several years after the attack.

The dissolution of the Soviet Union after 1991 and the easing of Cold War tensions promised to deliver a "peace dividend" to Americans in the form of reduced spending on defense and security. With the United States standing as the world's lone superpower, it also seemed that the nation would take its place as a peace broker in places such as Bosnia and Somalia instead of the direct adversary of its former Cold War foes. Ironically, both these trends proved illusory. Within a decade the United States' status as the wealthiest and most powerful nation on earth stirred up resentment among a new generation of terrorists who used their extremist religious and cultural beliefs to begin a new war against the West, with the United States as their primary target.

Homeland Security: Comparative Perspectives

Israel. The generalized nature of the militant Islamic terrorist threats made it difficult for U.S. officials to foresee the September 11 bombings. In contrast other nations have been forced to deal with specific terrorist threats for generations. The country with perhaps the greatest experience with terrorism is Israel. Even before their nation's founding in 1948, Zionists had been targeted by their neighbors for expulsion or eradication from the Middle East. Consequently, the new State of Israel enacted broad counterterrorist measures from the start. In the Prevention of Terrorism Ordinance passed in 1948, Israel defined terrorism to include not only direct acts of violence but also *threats* of violence against a person. Members of terrorist organizations included those who directly participated in its activities, published its materials, or gave money or any other resources to the group. Terrorist organizations themselves were defined by the government, which gave it broad discretion in singling out such groups. Further, the ordinance allowed authorities to prosecute anyone who allowed a terrorist organization to meet or keep items on their property and granted broad powers to military authorities to close down any place suspected of being the center of terrorist activities.

The 1948 Ordinance was expanded in 1980 to include the offense of "manifesting identification or sympathy with a terrorist organization in a public place . . . either by flying a flag or displaying a symbol or slogan or by causing an anthem or slogan to be heard, or any other overt act clearly manifesting such identification or sympathy." In 1986 another amendment to the ordinance criminalized most contacts made abroad with terrorists, although much of this section was repealed in 1993.

The Israeli government's broad counterterrorist powers have raised numerous international controversies. The state authorized secret assassination attempts on known terrorists outside of its borders, and Shin Bet, its intelligence agency, engaged in coercive interrogation, including the use of physical force on individuals, to gather information about terrorist activities. To civil rights advocates, such activities constituted nothing less than state-sanctioned terrorism and torture. Yet Israel's leaders have consistently defended its zero-tolerance

stance against terrorism. As Benjamin Netanyahu, prime minister from 1996–99, wrote in his 1995 book *Fighting Terrorism: How Democracies Can Defeat Domestic and International Terrorism*, "Of course, there is something laudable in the efforts of Western democracies to hold their governments to the highest possible standards when it comes to respecting the rights of their citizens . . . . Yet the threat to the most basic civil rights of *not* fighting terrorism are even more debilitating to a free society."

Indeed Netanyahu fulfilled his reputation as a hardliner against the Palestinians while in office. Although he was replaced after just three years as prime minister, other officials have invoked the same outlook. After being criticized by U.S. secretary of state Colin Powell and Canadian foreign affairs minister Bill Graham in March 2002 for the use of harsh counterterrorist tactics in the face of renewed suicide bombings by Palestinian militants, President Moshe Kastav of Israel was defiant. "No one around the world has any right to condemn us if we use the right to defend ourselves," Kastav told the Canadian Broadcasting Corporation on March 7, 2002.

While Israel's counterterrorist policies stirred up criticism abroad, its citizens had long since accepted a high degree of government intervention in their daily lives. Authorities routinely searched individuals and automobiles in public places, and scrutiny at border crossings and the country's main international airport was intense. The state-owned airline El Al examined every package checked or carried onto its planes and utilized a profiling system to screen every passenger on its flights. Highly trained and well-paid security guards also questioned passengers extensively to keep terrorists from sneaking onto a flight. As he advocated such intrusive counterterrorist methods for America in his book *Fighting Terrorism*, Netanyahu admitted, "Undoubtedly the leaders of the United States in particular could be subjected to a barrage of criticism that they are curtailing civil freedoms and that they are overreacting." He added the warning that "The security of democracies and their well-being cannot be governed by the ebb and flow of local political skirmishes."

The United Kingdom. In the United Kingdom as well, the move to stronger homeland defense raised accusations of civil rights violations with the passage of the Prevention of Terrorism (Temporary Provisions) Act of 1974. Enacted to combat a rash of bombings in England perpetrated by the Irish Republican Army, the act granted broad detention powers to authorities to arrest and interrogate suspected terrorists. In conjunction with a

PEOPLE WALK THROUGH DEBRIS NEAR THE WORLD TRADE CENTER IN NEW YORK CITY ON SEPTEMBER 11, 2001. DUE TO THE HORRIFIC TERRORIST ATTACKS ON THE WORLD TRADE CENTER AND THE PENTAGON, THE GEORGE W. BUSH ADMINISTRATION ESTABLISHED THE NEW OFFICE OF HOMELAND SECURITY. *(AP/Wide World Photos/Gulnara Samoilova. Reproduced by permission.)*

number of controversial practices—including isolation, deprivation of food and sleep, and noise bombardment—however, the British government was condemned for condoning torture in a 1975 report by the European Convention on Human Rights and Fundamental Freedoms. Yet the "temporary" law remained on the books and was even strengthened in December 2001 with the Anti-Terrorism, Crime, and Security Act, which allowed authorities to detain suspected terrorists without filing charges. The 2001 act also retained provisions that made it a crime to fail to report information on terrorist activities, a device that had been used to prosecute family members of terrorists.

As in Israel, British authorities also used coercive interrogation, including the practices condemned by the European Convention, to gather information on terrorist activities. As valuable as this tactic was in the short run to prevent specific terrorist attacks, however, it may have fueled further terrorist responses in both countries. Philip B. Heymann noted in his 1998 book *Terrorism and America: A Commonsense Strategy for a Democratic Society*, that strong measures of counterterrorism have at times actually resulted in an increase in violence, "additional recruit to the terrorist cause, and reduced willingness to assist the government." In example, Heymann notes that "in Northern

TOM RIDGE, DIRECTOR OF HOMELAND SECURITY, ADDRESSES THE GOVERNMENT'S EFFORTS TO FIGHT TERRORISM. *(AP/Wide World Photos. Reproduced by permission.)*

Ireland policies allowing widespread warrantless searches of citizen houses led to increased terrorist group recruitment, especially where the searches were accompanied by excessive use of force by security personnel and extensive destruction of citizen property."

Yet countries that have taken a more cautious approach in countering terrorism have been criticized, in hindsight, for not being aggressive enough in their actions. The case of the Aum Shinrikyo religious cult, which made headlines worldwide after its sarin gas attack on the Tokyo subway on March 20, 1995, demonstrated the hesitancy of authorities in democratic countries to infringe upon religious and civil liberties. Under Japan's Religious Corporation Law of 1951, government interference in religious practices and programs was severely curtailed; only in cases where a group had clearly harmed public safety could such a group be disbanded. Unlike Israel's 1948 Ordinance, however, such a determination was not placed with the government, but rather with the judicial system. While the distinction served as an additional safeguard to religious freedom in Japan, it also slowed down attempts to deal effectively with radical fringe groups such as Aum Shinrikyo.

Japan. Beginning in the late 1980s, complaints about Aum Shinrikyo had been made to the authorities by former cult members and the families of individuals who remained with the sect. After the 1989 formation of the Aum Shinrikyo Victims' Association, the cult responded with a series of violent actions, including several abductions and murders, committed against its opponents. The group also raised suspicions with numerous incidents involving the accidental release of poisonous chemicals around its various compounds. Even after its deliberate sarin gas attack at Matsumoto, Japan, on June 27, 1994, which killed seven people, Aum Shinrikyo escaped immediate scrutiny. It was only after the accidental release of sarin gas at the cult's main compound in Kamikuishiki in July 1994 that the cult came under suspicion for terrorist activities. By January 1995 reports were made public that linked Aum Shinrikyo to the sarin gas attacks. The following month, police announced that one of the cult's leaders was wanted for the kidnapping and murder of an elderly man who helped his sister escape from the cult. Unfortunately, the announcement induced hysteria within the cult, and its apocalyptic leader, Asahara Shoko, ordered five Aum Shinrikyo members to bombard the Tokyo subway system with sarin gas.

While it operated under the cloak of religious freedom, Aum Shinrikyo's actions also demonstrated the challenge of coordinating information on terrorist activities across numerous federal and local agencies. Local authorities had little reason to suspect that the 1994 attacks were related to Aum Shinrikyo; the delay in linking the previous sarin gas attacks was crucial in permitting the cult to plan its final attack on the Tokyo subway in March 1995. Complicating matters, several years after the attacks the Public Security Agency—the intelligence arm of the Ministry of Justice—was still hampered in its efforts to monitor the cult, which the government could not ban from the country.

With the perception that the authorities had failed to deal effectively with Aum Shinrikyo, public confidence in the country's safety and welfare dropped significantly, a trend that deepened after the September 11 attacks in the United States. An AP Worldstream report in January 2002 indicated that public confidence in Japan's safety, which had already fallen to 56 percent of those polled in 1995, now stood at just 47 percent. Fully 89 percent of the Japanese public said that they worried about crime or traffic accidents. As Japanese author Haruki Murakami concluded in 2000 in his moving oral history of the Aum Shinrikyo attacks, *Underground: The Tokyo Gas Attack and the Japanese Psyche:* "The Kobe earthquake and the Tokyo gas attack of January and March 1995 are two of the gravest tragedies in Japan's postwar history. It is no exaggeration to say that there was a marked change in the Japanese consciousness 'before' and 'after' these events. These twin catastrophes will remain embedded in our psyche as two milestones in our life as a people."

Counterterrorism under the Clinton Administration

Although Aum Shinrikyo had only a minor presence in North America, its actions set off warning bells among terrorist experts in the United States. Even after the Oklahoma City bombing on April 19, 1995, however, the presidential administration of Bill Clinton (1993–2001) faced an uphill battle to pass counterterrorist legislation. The administration urged Congress to pass a comprehensive bill that included roving wiretaps that would allow authorities to track a suspect's communications regardless of location; chemical additives to explosive materials to make them easier to trace; and the criminalization of the possession of many materials used to make weapons of mass destruction, among other measures. The president's proposals were soon drowned out by partisan rhetoric, with Republican senator Orrin Hatch telling CNN in July 1996 that the provision to track explosives was "a phony issue." Hatch, along with Senate majority leader Trent Lott, also countered the administration's call for roving wiretaps. The senators then worked to tack on limitations to federal death penalty appeals as part of the bill.

As a result of the political process, the resulting Anti-Terrorism and Effective Death Penalty Act of 1996 embodied a set of measures far weaker than the administration had wanted. The 1996 legislation did, however, criminalize fund raising or providing resources to foreign terrorist groups and allowed the deportation or exclusion of terrorist agents. Further, the act banned any financial trans-

TOM RIDGE

1945– Tom Ridge was born near Pittsburgh, but grew up in the city of Erie, Pennsylvania. His family lived in a public housing project in Erie until Ridge was nine years old. An outstanding student, Ridge graduated from Harvard University in 1967; he completed a year of law school before being drafted into the U.S. Army. Ridge completed his tour of duty in Vietnam and rose to the rank of staff sergeant. He finished law school upon his return and began his political career as the assistant district attorney for Erie County before running for Congress in 1982. Ridge was reelected to the U.S. House of Representatives six times before entering the Pennsylvania governor's race in 1994. He won the race and began serving the first of his two terms as governor in 1995.

As governor, Ridge, a Republican, pressed for more stringent law-and-order measures, such as increased penalties for certain crimes, higher mandatory sentencing guidelines, and a faster process for death sentence appeals. He also delivered cuts to many social services in the state, including the public health system and welfare programs. As a Catholic who favored the maintenance of some abortion rights, Ridge drew attention from both sides of the abortion debate. While he was brought up as a potential running mate in George W. Bush's 2000 presidential bid, religious conservatives quickly denounced his stand on abortion. Despite the criticism, Ridge remained a popular chief executive in Pennsylvania, with a majority of residents routinely approving his actions in office.

actions by American citizens with any country listed as a terrorist nation by the State Department, although commercial transactions with private parties were still allowed. The act also allowed Americans to bring civil suits against terrorist nations listed by the government as state sponsors of terrorism for damages from sabotage, torture, or hostage taking.

In 1996 the Clinton administration instituted the practice of designating certain high-risk sites National Security Special Events. The policy was implemented sparingly, with just nine events earning such status between 1996–2000. Under the policy—which used undisclosed criteria to determine which events merited extra protection—National Security Special Events were given the highest level of federal assistance, comparable to the security force that accompanied any presidential appearance.

After September 11, the policy was invoked to safeguard a series of high-profile events in the United States, including the United Nations General Assembly meeting in New York City in November 2001; the State of the Union Address to Congress in January 2002; the Super Bowl in New Orleans in February 2002; and the Winter Olympic Games in Salt Lake City later that same month.

RECENT HISTORY AND THE FUTURE

Establishing the Office of Homeland Security

In his Address to a Joint Session of Congress and the American People on the night of September 20, 2001, President George W. Bush (2001–) announced the creation of a new cabinet-level agency, the Office of Homeland Security. He also introduced the office's first director, Pennsylvania governor Tom Ridge, whom he described as "a military veteran, an effective governor, a true patriot, a trusted friend." Bush charged Ridge with the mission to "oversee and coordinate a comprehensive national strategy to safeguard our country against terrorism, and respond to any attacks that may come."

Ridge, then serving his second of two terms as Pennsylvania governor, was an unfamiliar face to most Americans. Although he had been mentioned as a possible vice-presidential candidate on the Bush ticket in the 2000 presidential election, his status as a Roman Catholic who favored maintaining the status quo on abortion rights put him in disfavor with the pro-life, religious-right faction of the Republican Party. The fifty-six-year-old politician had spent almost all of his career in public service. Despite some controversies over his welfare reform program and his support for public funding of sports stadiums, Ridge had maintained his popularity in opinion polls consistently throughout his two terms in office. Although he had few other qualifications for heading a counterterrorist team, Ridge brought another intangible asset to the job: as a "trusted friend" of the president, it was clear from the start that he would have the full backing of the Bush administration to get the Office of Homeland Security off to a sound start.

Following the president's announcement on September 20, the Office of Homeland Security was officially established by an executive order on October 8, 2001. The office was described as the coordinating body for local, state, and federal counterterrorist programs. Although it would not func-

tion in itself as a response agency, the office would set priorities, announce initiatives, and oversee preparedness activities at all levels of government.

As a coordinating body of forty federal departments—including the Federal Emergency Management Agency, Department of Health and Human Services, Department of Transportation, the National Economic Council, and the Office of Management and Budget—the scope of the office's mission was broad. The office was charged not only with conducting preparedness exercises and reviewing emergency response systems across the nation, but with reviewing antiterrorist legislation and making budgetary recommendations as well. Its functions also included safeguarding the nation's agricultural sector from terrorist attacks, helping to coordinate immigration and trade policies, and improving security in the nation's airspace and along its land and sea borders. Yet it was clear that, despite the directives of the president's order, the Office of Homeland Security had little administrative or legislative power at its disposal. Ridge's role as a bureaucratic infighter with a persuasive personality and close ties to the president thus became vital to the new agency's success.

In his first month on the job Ridge learned how difficult it would be to help Americans adjust to a new level of preparedness and vigilance without causing undue panic. Just three days after the Office of Homeland Security was established, it issued a national warning to be on high alert against possible terrorist actions. Ridge did not disclose any specific threats in the October 11 warning, however, and urged people to carry on with their normal daily activities. Still, the general warning was less than reassuring to some, who wondered why the statement could not be more detailed in the nature of the threat.

The criticism continued after a second "high alert" warning on October 29, which again did not carry any specific information about a possible terrorist attack. By the time of the third warning from Ridge's office, on December 3, 2001, however, it appeared that the public had come to take such warnings in stride. A *Chicago Tribune* editorial noted on December 5, 2001, "This nation has had to learn to live with a new state of emergency . . . . This is our new reality. Ridge has become the administration's point person. He's handling the job well. Maybe his formal warning allows some citizens to feel more confident about picking up the phone to report suspicious behavior."

Ridge also faced criticism in his first month as Homeland Security chief for the federal govern-

A U.S. COAST GUARD LIFEBOAT PATROLS THE WATERS OF SAN FRANCISCO BAY. THE COAST GUARD HAS ADDED HOMELAND SECURITY TO ITS CONSIDERATIONS AS IT PATROLS THE NATION'S WATERS. *(AP/Wide World Photos/Stephan Savoia. Reproduced by permission.)*

ment's erratic response to a series of anthrax attacks in October and November of 2001. Caught by surprise over the ability of a terrorist to transmit anthrax through contaminated letters, Ridge and Secretary of Health and Human Services Tommy Thompson "often looked flummoxed and misinformed, learning medicine on the go and winging it when they didn't know," according to a January 21,2002, article in *Time* (Jeffrey Klugar, et al.), "Under Thompson and Ridge, bad—and sometimes fatal—decisions were made," the article continued, including the decision to keep a Washington, DC, mail sorting facility open even after it was known to be heavily contaminated with anthrax spores. By November 2001 five people had died from inhalation anthrax exposures, including two postal workers at the contaminated facility, with 23 confirmed anthrax cases. The attacks ceased as mysteriously as they had begun, and as the FBI and U.S. Postal Service continued their hunt for the culprit, questions about the nation's ability to deal with such a public health crisis lingered.

By the end of 2001, however, Ridge had made headway in navigating the bureaucratic channels of Washington, particularly in using his discretionary powers to influence the president's new budget. By the time the president announced his 2003 budget in a proposal announced on February 4, 2002, Ridge's authority was obvious in the US$37.3 bil-

lion devoted to homeland security. The amount nearly doubled that spent in the previous budget and reflected Ridge's recommendations on prioritizing border security, airline safety, bioterrorist defenses, emergency response training, and intelligence gathering.

Border Security: Immigration and Trade

With the advent of the North American Free Trade Agreement (NAFTA) in 1994, government officials on both sides of the border between Canada, the United States, and Mexico hailed a new era of cooperation and prosperity in the region. Sharing the longest undefended border in the world, Canada and the United States, for example, engaged in more than $1 billion in trade each day, a figure that doubled during the NAFTA era. Over 200 million people each year traveled between the two countries, with only cursory security checks on either side. After September 11, however, security concerns quickly presented roadblocks all along the border. As international shipments slowed to a standstill, factories shut down from the lack of components. Tourism also screeched to a halt as pileups at border crossings stretched into hours of waiting.

Like its American neighbor, the Canadian government quickly prioritized its response to September 11 to improve counterterrorist intelligence and prosecutions, become more engaged in international efforts to prevent terrorism, and facilitate commercial traffic across its borders. In October 2001 the Canadian government introduced legislation to broaden the number of prosecutable offenses related to terrorism, such as giving aid to terrorist groups or harboring a terrorist. The proposal also made it easier to prosecute such crimes by broadening surveillance powers and allowing authorities to keep secret some evidence of national security interest during trial.

While the counterterrorist proposals raised some criticism by civil liberties watchdogs in Canada, the introduction of new, streamlined security measures led to charges that the government risked subordinating the nation's security to economic interests. On December 12, 2001, then-Canadian foreign affairs minister John Manley and Ridge signed the Smart Border Declaration, which included thirty initiatives to facilitate trade and travel between the two countries. Under the agreement permanent residents of either country who had completed a screening process would be issued a "secure card" to allow them immediate access across the border. The new plan also outlined a system to clear goods for export at their initial shipment point instead of at the border, a system that had already been in limited use before September 11. Manley and Ridge also promised that their countries would share more of their data on customs and immigration matters.

More controversial were calls to allow customs agents to bear firearms on the Canadian side of the border. In light of the much more restrictive gun laws in Canada, some critics pointed to a creeping "Americanization" of the border. Manley rejected such assertions, telling Graham Fraser of the *Toronto Star* (December 13, 2001) the day after signing the Smart Border Declaration that "I don't believe that we have accepted the idea that our policies will be decided by the United States." He added, "The question of arming agents is something that we have not yet decided on."

Manley also refuted suggestions that the new policies were dictated by American interests rather than the security of Canada, saying that Canada's first priority was safety, with trade coming in at an important second. "[W]e lack sovereignty if we're poor," he said. Manley was also hopeful that negotiations with the United States would bring recognition of the "third country accord" principle that would allow either country to reject refugees seeking asylum after first entering the United States or Canada. If the accord were adopted as part of the security reforms, Canadian authorities would be allowed to reject those seeking asylum in their country who tried to enter the country via the United States—about half of all refugee claimants annually.

In February 2002 Canadian officials also committed themselves to increased security at the nation's ports after a U.S. Senate report documented chronic security lapses at those ports. While the greatest concern in the past had been the shipment of illicit drugs such as heroin, cocaine, hashish, and ecstasy into the country, organized crime rings such as the Hell's Angels also smuggled illegal immigrants and weapons through Canadian ports. With less than one percent of all container shipments being searched at some ports, a customs force comprised mostly of temporary workers, and a lack of information sharing among federal agencies, Canadian officials concluded that the country could no longer stint on its spending on manpower and technology at its borders. In March 2002 Ridge and Manley also announced that their countries would begin sharing teams of customs agents in the ports of Vancouver, Montreal, Halifax, Seattle-Tacoma, and Newark.

Trade and security issues also affected the post-September 11 relationship between the United States and its southern neighbor, Mexico. With a 2,000-mile-long border that had traditionally been a crossing point for millions of illegal aliens into the United States, immigration concerns jumped to the top of the agenda in talks between Ridge and Adolfo Aguilar Zinser, his Mexican counterpart. Just one week before the terrorist attacks in the United States, Mexico's president, Vincente Fox, had joined President Bush on an American tour to promote an amnesty agreement to grant permanent resident status to about three million illegal Mexican immigrants in the United States. The proposal was abruptly tabled in the aftermath of the attacks, but in November 2001 discussions resumed with broad support on both sides of the border.

Airline Security

While Ridge had forged a consensus about border security issues with officials in Canada and Mexico, the topic of domestic airline security presented an even greater challenge. As details emerged on the ease with which terrorists had hijacked four commercial flights on September 11, confidence in security measures at the nation's airports plummeted. As the public learned that security was routinely subcontracted to private firms that inadequately trained and compensated their employees and failed to conduct criminal background checks, support grew for the federal government to take over airport security. While the Bush administration at first resisted the calls to take over airport security, it eventually agreed to support the Aviation and Transportation Security Act passed by Congress on November 19, 2001. The act phased in federal control of airport security over the next year and added citizenship and English-language requirements for security employees.

Implementation of the Computer Assisted Passenger Prescreening System (CAPPS) was another controversial area of homeland security. Although CAPPS used a number of criteria to select certain passengers for in-depth searches and questioning, some regarded it as a system of racial profiling against passengers of Middle Eastern descent. When reports surfaced that several of the September 11 terrorists had been singled out by CAPPS for scrutiny—which screeners apparently failed to follow—however, there were renewed calls to strengthen the CAPPS system. Former El Al security chief Isaac Yeffet, who now worked as a security consultant in the United States, told Jim Morris of the *Dallas Morning News* in the November 8, 2001, article "Israel Offers U.S. Lessons in Aviation Security," "We have to stop relying on technology. We have to rely on qualified, well-trained human beings. The technology can help us. It cannot replace us. The enemy is sophisticated enough to know how to beat the X-ray machine."

Bioterrorism

The anthrax attacks of October and November 2001 demonstrated how ill prepared the United States was to counter a public health emergency on a significant scale. The 2003 budget thus contained a massive $4.5 billion increase in bioterrorist prevention measures, raising it to $5.9 billion. As the primary coordinating agency in this area, the Office of Homeland Security was charged with monitoring the supply of crucial vaccines; reviewing public health emergency response plans; overseeing the protection of the nation's food and water supplies; and developing a nationwide system to detect biological, chemical, and radiological threats.

Referring to the early missteps on the anthrax attacks, Ridge encouraged the public to take a long-range view of the effectiveness of the plans. In a speech given to the National Governors' Association meeting in February 2002, Ridge reflected that "We learned a lot of lessons with regard to our public health system as states and communities tried to deal with anthrax. Some of them were painful. We recognized some strengths in that system, but we saw some gaps and weaknesses . . . . So it's a

good investment for America to make. We'll be more secure against a bioterrorism attack, but we'll be a lot healthier and a lot better country, because we'll be upgrading our public health system."

Emergency Response Training

The effort to improve emergency response training at the local level was perhaps the most complex task of the Office of Homeland Security. From the start, however, the direction of the new agency represented a significant change from previous efforts, as an overwhelming percentage of past government counterterrorist funding had remained within federal agencies. As Ridge stated at the National Emergency Management Association's February 2002 meeting, "Prior to September 11, the notion that the federal government would be so involved financially with providing equipment and training and resources for local community first responders just, in the scheme of federal government, wasn't seen as a core responsibility or a federal responsibility . . . ." He went on to say that the outline of a national defense procedure will only come into clear focus once comprehensive plans from each state are integrated. Ridge reiterated the need to envision homeland defense as a coordinated effort at all levels of government, with primary efforts coming from the local level; at the National Governor's Associations meeting, he told the audience, "I have a feeling that if we make every hometown secure, the homeland will be secure."

The 2003 budget proposal included $3.5 billion in spending on "first responders," the almost two million local police, firefighters, and other emergency rescue personnel that served as the front line of assistance in a terrorist attack. The bulk of the funds was pledged to immediate training exercises and equipment for local agencies, while some was reserved for paying the overtime costs accumulated in any emergency operation. Some $230 million in the budget was marked for improving volunteer efforts against terrorism through a new Citizen Corps. Incorporating existing efforts such as the Neighborhood Watch and Community Emergency Response Team programs, the Citizen Corps would also organize Medical Reserve Corps, Volunteers in Police Service groups and Terrorist and Information and Prevention Systems throughout local communities.

Intelligence Sharing and Technology

Improving information technology was the final priority announced by the Office of Homeland Security. While the initiatives might not have made

SAFEGUARDING AMERICA'S WATER

In the wake of the September 11 attacks, concerns arose that terrorists might next target the United States' water supply, either by contaminating the water itself, or by seeking to destroy one of the nation's larger dams or aqueducts. All across the country, from large metropolitan areas like New York City to small rural towns like Greensburg, Kentucky, officials moved quickly to protect their water systems.

The threat of terrorists unleashing a biological or chemical agent into a water supply caused unease among many. Authorities at the Environmental Protection Agency (EPA) and the Centers for Disease Control (CDC) hastened to point out that it would take enormous quantities of chemical or biological agents to do any harm if introduced into a reservoir. Even if this were somehow accomplished, officials added, the contamination would most likely be detected at the water treatment plant and filtered out. The chlorine used to sterilize the water would also assist in diminishing the agent's persistence.

Of course, this scenario could change drastically if the water system in question was much smaller and more specific—for instance, one that delivered water that had already passed through treatment facilities to a particular neighborhood. The possibility of a terrorist with access to relevant areas and a basic knowledge of hydraulics succeeding in such a case as this is worth considering, and some water utility companies have taken precautions such as installing alarms in tunnels and extra locks on doors.

With water contamination a complicated and unpredictable option, some authorities fear the more straightforward possibility of an attack intended to cripple or destroy one of the United States' 58 hydroelectric dams. Immediately following September 11, security at these facilities was increased, with National Guard troops deployed and Coast Guard troops patrolling nearby. Highways that crossed dams, such as Highway 93, which traverses the Hoover Dam—a mammoth structure that holds back the nation's largest man-made reservoir—were closed to commercial vehicles and truck with trailers.

These measure seemed more than justified when federal officials announced in January 2001 that computers seized in the offensive in Afghanistan contained pictures of the Grand Coulee Dam in Washington state, the largest concrete dam in the United States and the third largest producer of electricity in the world. The Grand Coulee harnesses Lake Roosevelt and its three trillion gallons of water, which, if the Grand Coulee were destroyed, could possibly take down the nine dams downstream of it as well.

Demolishing a large dam, however, would not be an easy task. Authorities stress that as a dam is generally a solid wall of concrete, as opposed to a building which contains hollow spaces, chances are very slim that crashing a plane into the Grand Coulee, for instance, could threaten the structure's integrity to the point of collapse.

Despite the substantial obstacles faced by a terrorist organization desiring to mount an attack against the United States' water supply—in any form—September 11 taught the world that almost anything was possible. Therefore, federal assistance to secure the nation's water systems has been forthcoming. Congress has passed several bills to assist in the effort, and in October 2001 the EPA announced the formation of a water protection task force.

as many headlines as the plans for upgrading border and airline security, they represented some of the most serious behind-the-scenes challenges for Ridge. Given the traditional rivalry among the Federal Bureau of Investigation (FBI), Central Intelligence Agency (CIA), and Attorney General's Office, Ridge faced an uphill battle to get the agencies to share information. Yet almost every directive of the Office of Homeland Security depended upon doing just that. As Ridge frankly admitted to Abraham McLaughlin of the *Christian Science* *Monitor* in the December 27, 2001, article "Ridge Applies Light Touch to Weighty Task," "I don't predict smooth sailing in the future."

The 2003 budget earmarked a $50 billion investment in information technology at the federal level, with $722 million devoted specifically to new systems of intelligence gathering and sharing. The proposed Information Integration Office, housed within the Department of Commerce, would collect data on suspected terrorists and provide it to relevant governmental agencies to help prevent suspects from entering the United States. The Immigration and Naturalization Service would also receive $380 million of the new-technology funds to establish a visa-tracking system to monitor the movement of noncitizens in the United States. There had been no such system in place prior to September 11, meaning that foreign visitors could violate their visas with near impunity. The new budget also included funds for the Critical Infrastructure Protection Board, created in October 2001 to safeguard governmental information and communication during a cyberterrorist attack.

Finally, the technology initiatives included plans to establish a Uniform National Threat Advisory System to warn and advise agencies at all levels of government in the event of a terrorist threat. Under the system, the Office of Homeland Security would issue four different alerts, based on the ascending nature and risk of the threat: ready, alert, serious, and critical. An alternate plan color-coded, which was enacted, the threats into five categories. While the new system promised to remove intra-agency squabbling over making such announcements, the plans raised questions of how valuable they would be in terms of promoting homeland security. "They violate all the guidance that we've come up with from disaster research," Mike Lindell, a security expert at Texas A&M University said in an interview with the Knight Ridder Washington Bureau in February 2002. "They don't tell you what to do other than be vigilant. What's that? We don't know." Instead, Lindell and other experts suggested that a system that linked an advisory with specific directives would be more helpful in reducing the damage from a potential terrorist attack.

While his staff fine-tuned the advisory system, Ridge maintained a high profile as the administration's leading counterterrorism voice. The Super Bowl and Winter Olympic Games added to public confidence that the Office of Homeland Security was fulfilling its mission. Ridge also continued to meet with his counterparts in Canada and Mexico to ensure progress on safeguarding the region's borders. All the while, he worked to marshal the government's programs against terrorism into one coherent effort. As Ridge concluded his comments to the National Emergency Management Association members in February 2002, "It will not just be a matter of resources. It's how we plan and how we integrate and how we coordinate our activity and how we cooperate in order to create this national network." He added, "I'm confident that we'll get it done."

In June 2002, President Bush bolstered the status of the Office of Homeland Security by creating a new Cabinet position for the newly promoted Department of Homeland Security.

BIBLIOGRAPHY

Bash, Dana. "Senate Passes Anti-Terrorism Legislation." CNN. Available online at http://www.cnn.com/2001/ALLPOLITICS/10/12/ret.senate.antiterror (cited March 5, 2002).

Begley, Sharon. "Protecting America: The Top 10 Priorities." *Newsweek*, November 5, 2001, p. 26.

"Big Government Is Back." *Economist*, September 29, 2001, 35.

"Biography of Governor Tom Ridge." U.S. Office of Homeland Security. Available online at http://www.whitehouse.gov/homeland/ridgebio.html (cited February 28, 2002).

Borenstein, Seth. "Bush Administration Issues Third Terrorism Alert." Knight-Ridder Washington Bureau, December 4, 2001.

———. "Homeland Office Pondering Specific Terror Alert System." Knight-Ridder Washington Bureau, February 22, 2002.

———. "Super Bowl, Other Events Now Getting Super Security." Knight-Ridder Washington Bureau, February 1, 2002.

Bregman, Ahron, and Jihan El-Tahri. *The Fifty Years' War: Israel and the Arabs*. New York: TV Books, 1999.

Bush, George W. "Address to a Joint Session of Congress and the American People," Washington, DC: September 2001. Available online at http://www.whitehouse.gov/news/releases/2001/09/print/20010920-8.html (cited March 9, 2002).

Ciment, Jim. *Palestine/Israel: The Long Conflict*. New York: Facts on File, 1997.

Corn, David. "Ridge on the Ledge." *Nation*, November 19, 2001, p. 19.

Department of Justice Canada. "Government of Canada Introduces Anti-Terrorism Act." Available online at http://canada.justice.gc.ca/en/news/nr/2001/doc_27785.html (cited March 5, 2002).

Dotson, Ben. "Grand Coulee A Reported Terrorist Site," *Daily Barometer* Online. Available online at http://barometer.orst.edu/0102/02winter/020205/020205n3.html (cited April 26, 2002).

Dunham, Richard S. "Tom Ridge's Bureaucratic Battlefield." *Business Week Online*, February 11, 2002.

Fraser, Graham. "Border's Integrity Intact: Manley." *Toronto Star*, December 13, 2001, A17.

Geraghty, Tony. *The Irish War: The Hidden Conflict Between the IRA and British Intelligence*. Baltimore, MD: Johns Hopkins University Press, 2000.

Hall, John R., with Philip D. Schuyler and Sylvaine Trinh. *Apocalypse Observed: Religious Movements and Violence in North America, Europe, and Japan*. London: Routledge, 2000.

Harper, Tim. "Manley Pushes for Speedy Cross-Border Traffic Flow." *Toronto Star,* February 2, 2002, A2.

Heymann, Philip B. *Terrorism and America: A Commonsense Strategy for a Democratic Society.* Cambridge, MA: MIT Press, 1998.

"Israel's Homelands Minister Says Palestinian Authority Is Part of the 'Axis of Evil,'" AP Worldstream, February 5, 2002.

"Japanese Worried About Effects of Terrorism, Declining Public Safety." AP Worldstream, January 7, 2002.

Kagan, Donald, and Frederick W. Kagan. *While America Sleeps: Self-Delusion, Military Weakness, and the Threat to Peace Today.* New York: St. Martin's Press, 2000.

Kluger, Jeffrey, David Bjerklie, Andrea Dorfman, and Andrew Goldstein. "A Public Mess." *Time,* January 21, 2002, p. 92.

Koizumi, Junichiro. "Statement by Prime Minister Junichiro Koizumi on the Passing of the Anti-Terrorism Special Measures Law by the Diet of Japan." Ministry of Foreign Affairs of Japan. Available online at http://www.mofa.go.jp/region/n-america/us/terro0109/speech/pm1029.html (cited March 5, 2002).

Lake, Anthony. *Nightmares: Real Threats in a Dangerous World and How America Can Meet Them.* Boston: Little, Brown and Company, 2000.

Laquer, Walter. *The New Terrorism: Fanaticism and the Arms of Mass Destruction.* New York: Oxford University Press, 1999.

"'Lax' Port Security Focus of Senate Report." Canadian Broadcasting Corporation. Available online at http://cbc.ca/cgi-bin/templates/print.cgi?/2002/02/28/port_security020228 (cited March 3, 2002).

Lifton, Robert Jay. *Destroying the World to Save It: Aum Shinrikyo, Apocalyptic Violence, and the New Global Terrorism.* New York: Metropolitan Books, 1999.

"Living on High Alert," *Chicago Tribune,* December 6, 2001.

"Manley and Chief of American Homeland Sign Declaration on Border Issues." *Canadian Press,* December 12, 2001.

McClain, James L. *Japan: A Modern History.* New York: W.W. Norton and Company, 2002.

McCutcheon, Chuck. "Homeland Czar: Big Job, Little Power?" *Aviation Week and Space Technology,* November 26, 2001, p. 58.

McFeatters, Ann. "Unfazed by Doubters, 'Ramped-Up' Ridge Poised to Re-emerge." *Toledo Blade,* January 20, 2002, p. 1.

McLaughlin, Abraham. "Ridge Applies Light Touch to Weighty Task." *Christian Science Monitor,* December 27, 2001, p. 1.

Mello, Michael. *The United States of America Versus Theodore John Kaczynski: Ethics, Power, and the Invention of the Unabomber.* New York: Context Books, 1999.

Michel, Lou, and Dan Herbeck. *American Terrorist: Timothy McVeigh and the Oklahoma City Bombing.* New York: Regan Books, 2001.

Miller, Judith, Stephen Engelberg, and William Broad. *Germs: Biological Weapons and America's Secret War.* New York: Simon and Schuster, 2001.

Mitchell, Fred. "Safe Spot? At Your Secret Service; Super Bowl Fans Aren't Complaining About Checkpoints." *Chicago Tribune,* February 4, 2002.

Morris, Jim. "Israel Offers U.S. Lessons in Aviation Security." *Dallas Morning News,* November 8, 2001.

Murakami, Haruki. *Underground: The Tokyo Gas Attack and the Japanese Psyche.* New York: Vintage International, 2000.

Netanyahu, Benjamin. *Fighting Terrorism: How Democracies Can Defeat Domestic and International Terrorism.* New York: Farrar Straus Giroux, 1995.

"New Counterterrorism Law." United States Information Agency. Available online at http://usinfo.state.gov/journals/itgic/0297/ijge/gj-6.htm (cited March 8, 2002).

Pitzer, Gary. "Coping with the Threat of Terrorism," *Western Water* Online. Available online at http://www.water-ed.org/janfeb02.asp (cited April 26, 2002).

"President Establishes Office of Homeland Security." Washington, DC. Available online at http://www.whitehouse.gov/news/releases/2001/10/print/20011008.html (cited February 28, 2002).

"The President's Plan to Strengthen Our Homeland Security." Available online at http://www.whitehouse.gov/news/releases/2002/02/print/20020204-2.html (cited February 28, 2002).

"President Says Canada Has No Right to Condemn Israel." Canadian Broadcasting Corporation. Available online at http://cbc.ca/stories/2002/03/07/canisrael020307 (cited March 8, 2002).

"President Wants Senate to Hurry with New Anti-Terrorism Laws." CNN. Available online at http://www.cnn.com/US/9607/30/clinton.terrorism/ (cited March 8, 2002).

"Prevention of Terrorism Ordinance No. 33 of 5708-1948," September, 1948. International Policy Institute for Counterterrorism. Available online at http://www.ict.org.il/counter_ter/law/lawdet.cfm?lawid=11 (cited March 5, 2002).

Regush, Nicholas. "In Over Our Heads?" ABC News. Available online at http://more.abcnews.go.com/sections/living/dailynews/regush_watersafety011025.html (cited April 26, 2002).

Ridge, Tom. "Governor Ridge Speaks at Embassy in Mexico," March 4, 2002: United States Embassy Mexico City, Mexico. Available online at http://www.whitehouse.gov/news/releases/2002/03/print/20020304-13.html (cited March 10, 2002).

———. "Homeland Security Director Speaks at the National Governor's Association's Winter Meeting in Washington," February 26, 2002: Washington, DC. Available online at http://www.whitehouse.gov/news/releases/2002/02/print/20020224-2.html (cited February 28, 2002).

———. "Remarks at National Emergency Management Association." *FDCH Political Transcripts,* February 26, 2002.

———. "Remarks at the U.S. Conference of Mayors." *FDCH Political Transcripts,* January 23, 2002.

Ridge, Tom, and John Manley. "Joint Statement by Deputy Prime Minister of Canada and the Director of the White House Office of Homeland Security," March 8, 2002: Washington, DC. Available online at http://www.whitehouse.gov/news/releases/2002/03/20020308.html (cited March 10, 2002).

Schiavo, Mary, with Sabra Chartrand. *Flying Blind, Flying Safe.* New York: Avon Books, 1997.

Standing Senate Committee on National Security and Defense. "Canadian Security and Military Preparedness." Canadian Parliament. Available online at http://www.parl.gc.ca/37/1/parlbus/commbus/senate/com-e/defe-e/rep-e/rep05feb02-e.htm (cited March 9, 2002).

"Supporting First Responders Strengthening Homeland Security," January 24, 2002: Washington, DC. Available online at http://www.whitehouse.gov/news/releases/2002/01/print/20020124-2.html (cited March 10, 2002).

"Tom Ridge Talks: A Dispatch from the Home Front." *Business Week,* November 19, 2001, p. 37.

"Using 21st Century Technology to Defend the Homeland." Available online at http://www.whitehouse.gov/homeland/21st-technology.html (cited March 10, 2002).

"U.S.-Mexican Talks Shift to Immigration; U.S. Seeks to Tighten Border Security." AP Worldstream, November 20, 2001.

"U.S. Wants to Keep Changes to Port Security Secret." Canadian Broadcasting Corporation. Available online at http://cbc.ca/cgi-bin/templates/print.cgi?/2002/03/07/ports020307 (cited March 8, 2002).

"What September 11 Really Wrought." *Economist,* January 12, 2002.

Williams, Rhys H. "Breaching the 'Wall of Separation': The Balance Between Religious Freedom and Social Order." In Stuart A. Wright, ed., *Armageddon in Waco: Critical Perspectives on the Branch Davidian Conflict.* Chicago: University of Chicago Press, 1995, 299–322.

Timothy G. Borden

HOSTAGE TAKING AND TERRORISM: THE HUMAN BARGAINING CHIP

THE CONFLICT

The past few years have shown a noticeable increase in the number of hostage taking incidents worldwide. Motivated by the prospect of receiving money in exchange for their hostages, numerous rebel and extremist groups around the world are increasingly turning to hostage taking for ransom as a means of financing their activities, recruiting new supporters, and generating public sympathy towards their cause. Many governments are reluctant to negotiate with terrorists out of the belief that other terrorist groups may take advantage of the precedent.

Political

- A high percentage of hostage takings occur in countries with political and social unrest, a high level of inequity among the countries' citizens, and where the local law enforcement community is either corrupt or simply unable to keep the rebel groups under control.

- In countries plagued by unrest and turmoil, only a small number of terrorist groups are ever caught, further enticing rebel groups to turn to hostage taking as a means of advancing their goals.

- Few governments negotiate with terrorists, out of the belief that they will be targeted by other terrorists' in the future if they show a willingness to make concessions and meet terrorist demands.

- Without an avenue for negotiation, some terrorist groups are willing to sacrifice hostages, and even themselves, to gain publicity and support for their causes.

On May 1, 2002, a spokesman for the Abu Sayyaf Muslim extremist group operating in the southern Philippines threatened on Filipino radio to kill an American missionary couple it has been holding hostage. Philippine president Gloria Macapagal Arroyo had recently announced that the government would not negotiate with the terrorists. Kidnapped a year earlier on May 27, 2001, from a resort off the island of Palawan in the Philippines, Martin and Gracia Burnham have been held as human bargaining chips in the rebel group's campaign to create an Iranian-style Islamic state on the southern Philippine island of Mindanao.

Founded in 1991 when it split from the Moro National Liberation Front, the Abu Sayyaf group, whose name means Bearer of the Sword, has been active in various terrorist activities, including bombings, assassinations, kidnappings, and extortion. In the past two years Abu Sayyaf extremists have turned to hostage taking to further their political and religious goals. Linked to both Osama bin Ladin's al-Qaeda terrorist organization and to Ramzi Yousef, who was convicted of masterminding the 1993 World Trade Center bombing, the Abu Sayyaf group has turned hostage taking into a lucrative business, and they are not alone.

The past few years have shown a noticeable increase in the number of hostage taking incidents worldwide. Motivated by the prospect of receiving money in exchange for their hostages, numerous rebel and extremist groups around the world are increasingly turning to hostage taking for ransom as a means of financing their activities, recruiting new supporters, and generating public sympathy towards their cause. A high percentage

CHRONOLOGY

September 5, 1972 A group of Palestinian terrorists belonging to an extremist faction of the Palestinian Liberation Army known as Black September take eleven Israeli athletes hostage at the Munich Olympic Games. The terrorists demand the release of more than two hundred compatriots imprisoned in Israel in exchange for the release of their hostages. Within 24 hours all hostages, five terrorists, and one German policemen lay dead.

November 4, 1979 Iranian militants storm the American embassy in Tehran, Iran, taking 66 American diplomats hostage.

December 18, 1979 The International Convention Against the Taking of Hostages is opened for signature in New York City.

January 20, 1981 Iran releases the American hostages, who were held hostage for 444 days.

March 16, 1985 Chief Middle East correspondent for the Associated Press, Terry Anderson, is taken hostage in Beirut, Lebanon, by the Islamic extremist group Hizballah.

June 14, 1985 Lebanese terrorists hijack TWA flight 847 en route from Athens to Rome. The terrorists demand the release of 766 Shiite prisoners held in Israel in exchange for the release of the hostages.

October 7, 1985 Four Palestinian Liberation Front terrorists hijack the Italian cruise liner *Achille Lauro,* taking over seven hundred passengers hostage.

July 4, 1995 Six western tourists, including two U.S. citizens, are kidnapped and taken hostage in the Pahalgam area of the Kashmir Valley. A militant Kashmiri separatist group calling itself Al-Faran claims responsibility.

December 17, 1996 Fourteen members of the Movimiento Revolucionario Tupac Amaru (Tupac Amaru) take over five hundred people hostage during a reception at the Japanese ambassador's residence in Lima, Peru. Within days the terrorists release over four hundred of the captives, but keep nearly eighty high ranking officials as hostages.

April 22, 1997 A Peruvian special operations force storms the Japanese ambassador's residence and rescues the hostages. All fourteen Tupac Amaru terrorists are killed, as well as one hostage and two soldiers.

April 23, 2000 Abu Sayyaf rebels raid a diver's resort on Sipadan island off Malaysian Borneo and take 21 foreign tourists and resort employees hostage.

October 12, 2000 Rebels in Ecuador take ten foreigners hostage and demand $80 million in ransom in exchange for their release.

May 27, 2001 American missionary couple Martin and Gracia Burnham are kidnapped from a resort off the island of Palawan in the Philippines and held hostage by the rebel extremist group Abu Sayyaf.

January 23, 2002 *Wall Street Journal* correspondent Daniel Pearl is kidnapped and taken hostage in Karachi, Pakistan, while researching a story on the country's Islamic movement. A group calling itself "The National Movement for the Restoration of Pakistani Sovereignty" claims responsibility for the kidnapping and makes a number of demands in exchange for Pearl's release.

February 21, 2002 The U.S. government announces that it has received evidence that Daniel Pearl had been killed by his hostage takers.

of these hostage takings occur in countries where there is political and social unrest, a high level of inequity among the countries' citizens, and where the local law enforcement community is either corrupt or simply unable to keep the rebel groups under control. In countries plagued by unrest and turmoil, only a small number of these groups ever get caught, further enticing rebel groups to turn to hostage taking as a means of advancing their goals.

HISTORICAL BACKGROUND

Why Take a Hostage?

Hostage taking has been a been a popular tactic for extremists for thousands of years. As defined under international law, hostage taking is "the seizing or detaining and threatening to kill, injure, or continue to detain a person in order to compel a third party to do or abstain from doing any act as an explicit or implicit condition for the release of

INTENT TO KILL

On January 23, 2002, *Wall Street Journal* correspondent Daniel Pearl disappeared in Karachi, Pakistan, where he was researching a story on the country's Islamic movement. On January 28, 2002, a group calling itself "The National Movement for the Restoration of Pakistani Sovereignty" sent an email to the *Wall Street Journal* with a list of demands for the U.S. government. Included in the email were also pictures of Daniel Pearl in chains, and, in one photo, with a gun to his head. In its list of demands the group called for the release of a number of Pakistani nationals being held by soldiers at the U.S. military base in Guantanamo Bay, Cuba, and in the United States as terrorism suspects. The hostage takers also demanded that the United States turn over a number of F-16 fighter jets purchased by Pakistan in the late 1980s, but never delivered.

On January 29 the group sent a second email, threatening to kill Pearl if all the demands were not met within a 24-hour time period. On January 30 U.S. Secretary of State Colin Powell reiterated the U.S. policy not to negotiate with terrorists, and the terror group reacted by giving authorities one more day to respond to the hostage takers demands. Those demands were not met.

The U.S. government, on February 21, 2002, announced that it had received evidence that Daniel Pearl had been brutally killed by his hostage takers. A few days later the Department of State offered a $5 million reward under the Rewards for Justice Program for information leading to the arrest or conviction of the individuals responsible for the death of Daniel Pearl.

the seized or detained person" ("International Terrorism: American Hostage," October 17, 1995). In other words, a hostage is an individual taken by force in order to secure the taker's demands. Some of the more common objectives of hostage taking have been to make ransom demands to generate funds for the terrorists' cause, to generate sympathy for a cause, and to raise instantaneous publicity through the media. Other reasons have included the use of hostages to recruit new members, and as a means of extortion to force authorities into making compromises, including the release of imprisoned group members and other political prisoners.

If the purpose of the hostage taking is to generate sympathy for a specific cause, or to recruit new members from the publicity raised through the event, it will be in the terrorists best interest for the hostage taking incident to end peacefully. In this case, the hostages are seen as the means to an end, rather than the intended target. In many of these cases, the hostage takers are willing to negotiate with authorities.

On the other hand, if the purpose of the hostage taking is to generate massive media attention on the cause the extremists are espousing, and if the extremist is willing to die for that cause, the hostage may be seen as expendable. In such cases, hostage takers might be willing to harm or kill the hostages in order to garner the most headlines possible. Terrorists who have "nothing to lose" and are willing to die for their cause are the most dangerous types of hostage takers, and the ones most difficult with which to negotiate.

Another type of hostage taking scenario where the hostage is seen as expendable is the kidnapping and assassination scenario. Along these lines, some extremists have engaged in hostage taking with the fixed intent of killing their hostages to generate massive media attention and fear. These types of terrorists are rarely willing to negotiate with the authorities, and if and when they do, it is often only with the intent of generating media attention to the cause or to "string the authorities" along. This was the case of the recent hostage taking and brutal murder of *Wall Street Journal* news reporter and editor Daniel Pearl.

Hostage Taking Throughout History

One of the first written accounts of hostage taking can be found in the Book of Genesis, Chapter 14, in the Christian Bible. Around 1913 BCE Lot, nephew of Abram, was taken hostage along with all of his possessions by four warring kings. In an effort to rescue his nephew, Abram took a trained military force of 318 men, attacked the kings in a night raid, and rescued Lot and all of his possessions.

During the Middle Ages, where the origins of the word "hostage" are first derived (adapted from the Old French *hoste*), hostage taking was a common practice. Governed by a strict code of honor, hostages were taken to ensure that treaty obligations were fulfilled. Once the obligations were met, the hostages were returned from where they were taken. Hostage taking to fulfill treaty obligations ended in the eighteenth century.

In the late eighteenth century the practice of paying tribute to "Barbary" states become common place. The term "barbary" is derived from a sixteenth century adventurer named Barbarossa, "red beard", who, in 1510, seized Algiers and placed it under the control of the Ottoman sultan. During the eighteenth century pirates from four African countries, Algiers, Morocco, Tripoli, and Tunis, would prey on merchant ships sailing in the Mediterranean, seizing the ships, crew, and cargo, and holding them for ransom. While the United States refused to pay the ransom for the release of American hostages, many European maritime countries agreed to pay a tribute to the Barbary states to ensure that their ships passed unmolested through Mediterranean waters.

After a number of incidents with U.S. ships being taken hostage, the United States agreed to negotiate with the pirates. In 1815, however, the United States effectively ended North African piracy and the use of American hostages as bargaining chips when a fleet of U.S. ships descended upon Northern Africa and threatened to bombard Algiers. The countries agreed to immediately stop pirating American ships.

Hostage taking and the use of humans as bargaining chips continued around the world in the early twentieth century. Perhaps one of the most notable incidents of hostage taking at this time occurred in 1932 in the United States. It was in that year that the son of famous U.S. aviator Charles Lindbergh was kidnapped and held hostage. Even though Lindbergh conceded to the hostage takers' demands for ransom in exchange for his son's release, the boy was later found murdered near the family home in New Jersey.

Like the tragic Lindbergh case, a number of high profile hostage taking incidents occurred over the past thirty years, including the 1972 Munich hostage crisis, the 1979 Iran hostage crisis, the 1985 TWA flight 847 hijacking and hostage taking, and the 1996 Peruvian embassy hostage crisis. Each demonstrated that some terrorist hostage taking incidents can result in deadly and fatal outcomes.

Munich Olympic Hostage Crisis

In the early morning hours of September 5, 1972, a group of eight heavily armed Palestinian terrorists scaled the perimeter fence surrounding the Olympic Village in Munich, Germany, entered apartments housing the Israeli Olympic team, and took eleven men hostage, killing two in the initial hostage taking. After taking the Israeli athletes hostage, the terrorists, from the Black September group, demanded the release of more than two hundred political prisoners being held in Israeli jails in exchange for the release of their hostages. They said that they would execute the Israeli athletes if their demands were not met.

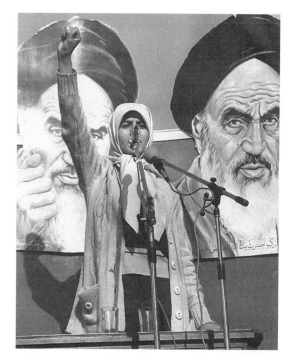

AN IRANIAN STUDENT SPEAKS FROM THE U.S. EMBASSY IN IRAN, WHICH WAS OVERTAKEN BY MILITANTS IN NOVEMBER 1979. THE FIFTY-PLUS U.S. HOSTAGES INSIDE WERE HELD FOR 444 DAYS BEFORE THEIR RELEASE. *(AP/Wide World Photos/Sayad. Reproduced by permission.)*

According to Simon Reeve in *One Day in September: The Story of the 1972 Munich Olympics Massacre* (2000), when confronted with the demands made by the terrorists, the first response of Israeli prime minister Golda Meir was that Israel would brook no deal with the terrorists. Even though the German authorities were open to compromise with the terrorists, the Israeli government adamantly refused to consider meeting any of the demands. Faced with the Israeli government's refusal to negotiate, the German authorities agreed that their initial response would be one of negotiation rather than of force.

A team of German negotiators continuously met with the Black September terrorists throughout the day. At one point during the negotiations, a number of German politicians and negotiators offered to trade themselves for the hostages, but the Black September terrorists refused, knowing that their best chance in getting Israel to concede to their demands lied with the Israeli Olympic athletes they already held. Unbeknownst to the hostage takers, Israel had no intention of meeting any of the terrorists' demands.

By early evening it became obvious to the terrorists that the Israeli government was not willing

AS MANY AS FIVE HUNDRED UN PEACEKEEPERS WERE TAKEN HOSTAGE BY REVOLUTIONARY UNITED FRONT REBELS IN SIERRA LEONE IN 2000. MOST WERE EVENTUALLY RELEASED, BUT FOUR MEN ARE BELIEVED DEAD. *(AP/Wide World Photos/Brennan Linsley. Reproduced by permission.)*

to release their list of prisoners. The hostage takers then changed tactics, demanding that the German authorities provide them with two airplanes that would take them to Cairo, Egypt. If Israel did not release the political prisoners and fly them to Cairo to meet the hostage takers, then the Israeli athletes would be executed. The German authorities had no intention of letting the Black September terrorists leave the country and devised a plan to rescue the athletes once they arrived at the local airport. In the late evening on September 5, two helicopters ferried the terrorists and their captives to an airfield outside of Munich. The rescue attempt by the German authorities failed, alerting the terrorists to the plan, and after a deadly firefight all

nine of the remaining Israeli hostages, five terrorists, and one German policeman lay dead.

The tragic deaths of the Israeli athletes at the Munich Olympic Games raised two important questions. Why did the Black September terrorists choose the 1972 Olympic Games as the venue for their hostage taking? And why did Israel adamantly refuse to negotiate with the hostage takers? The Olympic Games in Munich offered the Black September terrorists a platform through which they could broadcast their grievances. With media and camera crews from nearly every country in the world in attendance at the Games, the Palestinian terrorists were assured instant and massive media coverage of their actions. The names of the five terrorists who died during the ill fated hostage taking attempt were splashed across newspapers throughout the Arab world, giving them instant martyr status and inspiring sympathy and support for the Palestinian cause among many disaffected youth. Even though they were unsuccessful in getting the Israeli government to submit to their demands to release a number of political prisoners, the hostage takers were successful in getting instantaneous publicity for their cause.

Throughout her term as Israel's prime minister, Golda Meir had firmly stated on numerous occasions that it was Israel's policy not to negotiate with terrorists. When confronted with the Black September terrorists' demands, Meir's response was instantaneous: Israel would not give in to any concessions. If Israel had succumbed to the terrorists' demands and released the political prisoners, it is likely that other terrorist groups would have "jumped on the bandwagon" and used hostage taking as a tool from which to glean concessions from the Israeli government. Israel, like the United States and a number of other countries around the world, believe that making concessions that benefit hostage takers will only further entice other terrorists to engage in hostage taking activities.

In an effort to create a unified front against hostage taking, on December 18, 1979, the International Convention Against the Taking of Hostages was opened for signature in New York City. The United States government, a signatory to this convention, has resolutely maintained a policy of non-negotiation with terrorists, believing that making concessions to hostage takers will only further motivate terrorists to take American citizens hostage. The U.S. government policy is that it will brook no concessions to terrorists and make no deals. While many countries around the world share the same view as the United States, other countries have been willing to negotiate with terrorists, including Russia and India. This has, in part, supported the continuance of hostage taking by terrorists wishing to extract some concession from a government.

Hostage Taking in the 1970s and 1980s

A series of high profile hostage taking incidents occurred throughout the 1970s and 1980s, including a number of airplane hijackings. Following the overthrow of the shah, Mohammad Reza Pahlavi, from Iran by an Islamic revolutionary government, Iranian militants on November 4, 1979, stormed the American embassy in Tehran and took 66 American diplomats hostage. Thirteen hostages

2,454 DAYS IN CAPTIVITY

On the morning of March 16, 1985, American Terry Anderson, chief Middle East correspondent for the Associated Press, was kidnapped and taken hostage by the Islamic extremist group Hizballah as he returned home from a tennis match in Beirut, Lebanon. Held hostage for over six years, Anderson suffered frequent torture, beatings, and other abuse at the hands of his captors. Hizballah, also known as the Party of God, is a political and paramilitary terrorist organization operating out of Lebanon and supported by Iran. After spending nearly seven years—2,454 days—as a hostage in Lebanon, Anderson was released from his captivity on December 4, 1991.

The federal government in 1996 passed the Antiterrorism and Effective Death Penalty Act, allowing Americans who were victims of terrorism in foreign countries to sue those countries in American courts if the U.S. State Department listed the country as a state sponsor of terrorism. In March 1999 Terry Anderson filed a $100 million lawsuit against the Iranian government, accusing it of sponsoring the Hizballah terrorists that kept him prisoner for more than six years. One year later, in March 2000, a federal judge ordered Iran to pay $341 million to Terry Anderson and his family as restitution for this time in captivity. It is unlikely, however, that Anderson will ever receive the money from Iran.

were soon released, but the remaining 53 were held as human bargaining chips against the U.S. government. U.S. president Jimmy Carter (1977–81) responded to the hostage taking in two ways. First, he pursued the diplomatic options open to him, attempting to persuade the Iranians to release their American captives. Second, President Carter applied economic pressure on Iran by halting all oil imports from that country and freezing all Iranian assets in the United States. Both efforts failed to gain the hostages' release.

On April 24, 1980, U.S. forces mounted a rescue mission which also failed, resulting in the deaths of eight soldiers. The death of the shah in 1980, coupled with the invasion of Iran by Iraq, paved the way for negotiations between Iran and the United States. The hostage takers had less grievance with the United States after the shah's death, as they were opposed to the shah and thus to the United States' allowing him into the country in his exile. Using Algerian intermediaries, the

THE HIJACKING OF FLIGHT 847

On June 14, 1985, Trans-World Airline (TWA) flight number 847, en route from Athens to Rome, was hijacked by Lebanese terrorists associated with the Hizballah extremist organization and forced to fly to Beirut, where a number of the hostages were released. In exchange for the release of their remaining hostages, the Islamic terrorists demanded the release of 766 Shiite (Muslim) prisoners held in Israel. Over one hundred Americans were onboard the flight. The hijackers made the airline pilots fly to Algiers, Algeria, freed more hostages, and then forced the plane back to Beirut where, on June 15, they murdered a U.S. Navy diver on board. Seven American passengers were removed from the plane and taken to a secret location in Beirut, and once again the terrorists forced the airliner back to Algiers, where more hostages were freed. On June 16 the plane returned to Beirut, and after a number of days of negotiation, all the passengers were freed except for 32 Americans, who were removed from the plane by the terrorists and held hostage in Lebanon.

On June 24, after intense and complicated negotiations, the terrorists again demanded the release of the prisoners held in Israel, and also demanded that the United States remove its warships from Lebanese waters. Both the U.S. and Israeli governments refused to concede to the terrorists' demands. On June 30, however, all 39 remaining American hostages were released

and the four terrorists responsible for the hijacking successfully escaped into Beirut. The very next day, on July 1, the Israeli government announced that it was planning to release over seven hundred Shiites imprisoned in Israel, stating that the decision was independent to the hijacking of the airliner and was not related to the release of the American hostages. In response to the event, the U.S. Department of State posted a $5 million reward under the Rewards for Justice Program for information leading to the arrest of the four terrorists.

Other significant hostage taking incidents in the 1980s include the October 7, 1985, hijacking of the Italian cruise liner *Achille Lauro* by four Palestinian Liberation Front terrorists. More than seven hundred passengers on the cruise liner were taken hostage and one American passenger was killed. The hostage taking ended when the Egyptian government offered the Palestinian terrorists safe haven in return for the release of the hostages. In January 1988 Hizballah members abducted a German citizen, demanding the release of two of their compatriots in exchange for the man's freedom, and in September 1989, the Sendero Luminiso, "Shining Path," a Peruvian rebel group, held two *Newsweek* reporters hostage, but released them after three days captivity. The Shining Path, as well as other terror groups around the world, continued to use hostage taking as a means to extract concessions from governments in the 1990s.

---

two countries successfully negotiated the release of the American captives, and on January 20, 1981, 444 days after they were first taken captive, the hostages were freed. In return for the Americans' release from Iranian captivity, and on the day of newly elected President Ronald Reagan's inauguration, the United States released the nearly US$8 billion of Iranian assets it had frozen.

Other acts of hostage taking occurred throughout the world during the 1970s and 1980s. In November 1979 two hundred Islamic extremists seized the Grand Mosque in Mecca, Saudi Arabia, where hundreds of pilgrims were praying. Saudi forces decided that immediate force was necessary to resolve the situation, and after an intense battle between the Islamic terrorists and the soldiers, the security forces took control of the mosque. Tragically, the battle resulted in the deaths of more than 250 people. Nearly six hundred more were injured.

In April 1983 an American citizen was taken hostage by the Revolutionary Armed Forces of Colombia (FARC) and held for ransom, and on March 16, 1985, chief Middle East correspondent for the Associated Press, Terry Anderson, was taken hostage in Beirut, Lebanon. Held for over six years by his captors, Anderson was one of a number of Americans kidnapped and held hostage in Lebanon in the 1980s.

Hostage Taking in the 1990s

While hostage taking in the 1970s and 1980s were characterized by terrorist groups using hostages to make political statements or to extract concessions from governments, including the release of fellow compatriots, hostage taking in the 1990s has been largely characterized by hostage for ransom demands. Except for a small number of incidents, the recent upswing of hostage takings for ransom demonstrates a shifting of motivations for

HOSTAGES TAKEN BY THE PHILIPPINE GROUP ABU SAYYAF IN MAY 2000 SIT IN A HUT AS THEY AWAIT THE RESOLUTION OF THEIR SITUATION. MANY COUNTRIES REFUSE TO NEGOTIATE WITH TERRORISTS. *(AP/Wide World Photo/Enrico Soriano. Reproduced by permission.)*

some extremists groups. Out to make money rather than a political statement, hostage taking for ransom has become the dominant type of hostage taking on the world scene. In 1992, on separate occasions, two American businessmen were taken hostage in Colombia by FARC rebels; in January 1993 the FARC kidnapped three American missionaries and held them for ransom; and in September 1994 the rebels took another American citizen hostage. A deadly hostage taking incident in 1995, however, and the 1996 Peruvian embassy hostage crisis, demonstrate that not all hostage taking events in the 1990s were motivated by ransom demands.

On July 4, 1995, six western tourists, including two American citizens, were kidnapped and taken hostage in the Pahalgam area of the Kashmir Valley, a region in dispute by India and Pakistan. A militant Kashmiri separatist group calling itself Al-Faran claimed responsibility for the hostage taking and said that it would execute the hostages if the Indian government did not release 22 terrorists imprisoned in Indian jails. All of the terrorists on the Al-Faran list were members of the Pakistani based Harkat-ul-Ansar terrorist group.

Five days later, on July 9, one of the hostages, American John Childs, escaped from his captors.

On August 13 the decapitated body of one of the hostages, a Norwegian, was found with the words "Al-Faran" carved on his body. A note left at the scene from the terrorists stated that the rest of the hostages would be executed if the Indian government did not comply with the hostage takers' demands. The Indian government was adamant in its refusal to submit to the demands of the militant terrorists, accusing Pakistani intelligence of planning the operation in order to incite instability in the Kashmir Valley.

On December 4, 1995, five Al-Faran members were killed in a skirmish with Indian security forces in Kashmir, and on December 11, 1995, the group released a note in Urdu claiming that after a run-in with the Indian army, three of the tourists held captive were arrested by the army, while the fourth one went missing. In September 1997, after receiving information from imprisoned Kashmiri terrorists, authorities exhumed the body of one of the missing four tourists. Tragically, the three remaining captives were never found by authorities and are presumed dead.

Hostage Crisis in Peru

On the evening of December 17, 1996, fourteen members of the Movimiento Revolucionario Tupac Amaru, also known as Tupac Amaru, or the

MRTA, entered the Japanese ambassador's residence in Lima, Peru, during a reception and took five hundred people hostage. Among the hostages were eight American officials, a number of foreign ambassadors and diplomats, and numerous high-ranking Peruvian officials. To secure the perimeter the terrorists set up booby traps and mines around the residence. In exchange for the safe release of their hostages, the Tupac Amaru extremists demanded that the Peruvian government immediately release all imprisoned MRTA members and provide safe passage for both the freed MRTA members and the hostage takers. Within days the terrorists released over four hundred of their hostages, but kept nearly eighty high-ranking officials, including the Peruvian Foreign and Agricultural Ministers, the brother of Peruvian president Alberto Fujimori, and several supreme court justices.

A radical leftist revolutionary movement, the MRTA was formed in 1984 with the goal of replacing the established democratic system in Peru with a Marxist regime. Prior to the embassy hostage taking, Tupac Amaru rebels had been involved in a number of bombings, kidnappings, and assassinations in furtherance of their cause. One instance, uncovered in November 1995 before it could be fulfilled, resulted in the arrest of thirty extremists who had plotted to occupy the Peruvian congress with the goal of taking the members hostage in exchange for the release of imprisoned MRTA members.

During the successful hostage taking crisis at the Japanese ambassador's residence in 1996 the Peruvian government began negotiations with the hostage takers, but was unwilling to give in to their demands to release the imprisoned MTRA members. A number of governments, including the United Kingdom, Germany, and the United States, offered assistance to Peru, but President Fujimori refused all outside aid. Negotiations were further stalled when a Uruguayan court denied Peruvian and Bolivian extradition requests for two jailed MRTA militants and instead released the two terrorists from jail. The hostage takers immediately responded by releasing the Uruguayan ambassador they were holding hostage.

According to President Fujimori in a *Time Magazine* interview ("How They Did It," May 5, 1997) after the hostage crisis had been resolved, he had no intention of meeting any of the hostage takers' demands because he believed that the negotiations would prove to be unsuccessful. Unbeknownst to the guerrillas he was negotiating with, Fujimori was carefully planning a military assault against the hostage takers, while publicly showing his support

for the negotiation process. On April 22, 1997, after four fruitless months of negotiation with the Tupac Amaru rebels, a team of Peruvian special operations forces stormed the residence and rescued the hostages. All fourteen of the terrorists were killed during the raid, as well as one Peruvian hostage and two soldiers.

In the case of the Peruvian hostage crisis, the successful release of the hostages from the Japanese ambassador's residence can be attributed to the Peruvian government's policy of refusing to make concessions to terrorists. Peruvian president Alberto Fujimori's unyielding refusal to release the imprisoned MRTA members allowed him time to plan and execute the successful hostage rescue operation in April 1997.

Hostage for Ransom

Most of the hostage taking incidents after the 1996 Peruvian crisis are cases of hostage for ransom demands. Although most of the hostage for ransom demands have been for money, some hostage takers have demanded out of the ordinary ransoms. In one unusual incident, a rebel group in Sierra Leone named the West Side Boys demanded college education abroad in exchange for the release of their hostages.

From 1995–2002 FARC rebels in Colombia were responsible for hundreds of hostage taking for ransom demands. On March 7, 1997, for example, FARC guerrillas kidnapped an American mining employee and his Colombian colleague while they were searching for gold. Both men were released on November 16 after the mining company paid $50,000 for their release. In October 1997 rebels in Yemen kidnapped and held four French tourists hostage, demanding $46,000 in ransom in exchange for their release. On March 23, 1999 the National Liberation Army (ELN) in Colombia took an American citizen hostage and demanded $400,000 in exchange for his release. In July the American was released after the ELN rebels received a markedly smaller ransom payment of $48,000.

There were two hostage taking incidents in 2000 which were particularly notable, as the hostage takers demanded unusually large cash ransoms in exchange for the release of their captives. The first incident occurred in April. On April 23, 2000, a number of armed gunmen belonging to the Abu Sayyaf group raided a diver's resort on Sipadan island off Malaysian Borneo, taking 21 foreign tourists and resort employees hostage. The Sipadan raid was the first known time the rebels had ever taken any foreigners hostage outside of the Philippines. In exchange for the release of their hostages,

FOREIGN TERRORIST ORGANIZATIONS (FTOs)

In recognition of the threat to U.S. national security from international terrorist organizations, in October 1997, former secretary of state Madeleine K. Albright approved the first designation of thirty groups as foreign terrorist organizations (FTOs). Under the Anti-terrorism and Effective Death Penalty Act of 1996, which sets forth the legal guidelines of designating groups as foreign terrorist organizations, only groups that are foreign and who engage in terrorist activity that threatens the security of U.S. nationals or the national security of the United States can be placed on the list. Under legal provisions set forth in the Death Penalty Act, the secretary of state is required to designate foreign groups engaged in terrorist activity as FTOs every two years, however, organizations may be added to the list at any time.

Through placing foreign terrorist organizations on the list, the U.S. government makes it illegal for any person in the United States or anywhere under American jurisdiction to provide any type of support to these organizations, including financial assistance and material aid, such as the provision of weapons and safe houses.

Through designating groups as FTOs, the U.S. government hopes to not only increase awareness and knowledge among the general public about these groups, but also hopes that it will warn other governments and their citizens around the world of the danger these groups pose to international security. Raising awareness of these groups internationally will isolate them amongst the world community, deterring financial donations and other types of support to the organizations from their sympathizers.

Recent events in the United States following the September 11, 2001, terrorist attacks on the World Trade Center and the Pentagon illustrate the importance of this law. In late 2001 and early 2002 federal authorities froze the assets of a number of charities and groups operating in the United States who are believed to have ties to al-Qaeda, Osama bin Laden's international terrorist network, which was designated a foreign terrorist organization in 1999. Through cutting off funding and support to these terrorist organizations, it is hoped that the government can bring an end to or curb violent terrorist activities against the United States and its allies.

---

the Abu Sayyaf rebels demanded $1 million for each foreign hostage, as well as the establishment of an independent Muslim state in the southern Philippines.

The Philippine government refused to pay ransom to the terrorists, forcing the hostages to ask their respective governments to intervene on their behalf. The Libyan government intervened in the negotiations and acted as a mediator between the Abu Sayyaf terrorists and the governments of the Europeans held hostage. After a series of negotiations, Libya negotiated a reported $25 million ransom payment from the European governments to the terrorists, ultimately freeing the hostages. Abu Sayyaf used the funds to finance the groups' arms procurement and recruitment campaigns, and expanded its presence throughout the Philippines. Abu Sayyaf rebels continued to kidnap both Filipinos and foreigners throughout 2000 and 2001, issuing ransom and political demands in exchange for their release.

The second notable hostage taking in 2000 occurred in October, when a group of rebels in Ecuador took ten aviation company employees and oil

workers hostage, including five American citizens. Two hostages managed to escape, and in December the group demanded $80 million in ransom in exchange for the release of the eight remaining hostages. The oil companies began negotiations with the rebels for the release of the hostages, but the rebels executed one of the American hostages in January 2001. On March 1, 2001, representatives of the oil companies successfully negotiated the release of the seven remaining hostages. It is unknown how much ransom money the rebels received in exchange for the hostages' release.

RECENT HISTORY AND THE FUTURE

In the past ten years there has been a marked increase in the number of hostage taking incidents worldwide. While the 1970s and 1980s were often characterized by hostage taking for political and ideological motivations, present day rebel groups are increasingly turning to hostage taking to finance terror activities. Terror groups in the Philippines and in Latin and South America have turned kidnapping into a growth industry.

U.S. State Department Designated Foreign Terrorist Organizations (FTOs) as of October 5, 2001

FTO	Country/Region of Operation
Abu Nidal Organization (ANO)	Iraq, Lebanon, Middle East, Asia, Europe
Abu Sayyaf Group	Philippines
Armed Islamic Group (GIA)	Algeria
Aum Shinrikyo	Japan
Basque Fatherland and Liberty (ETA)	Spain, France
Al-Gama'a al-Islamiyya (Islamic Group)	Egypt, international
HAMAS (Islamic Resistance Movement)	Occupied Territories, Israel
Harakat ul-Mujahidin (HUM)	Pakistan, Kashmir
Hizballah (Party of God)	Lebanon, global cells
Islamic Movement of Uzbekistan (IMU)	Afghanistan, Kyrgyzstan, Tajikistan, Uzbekistan
Al-Jihad (Egyptian Islamic Jihad)	Egypt, Middle East
Kahane Chai (Kach)	Israel and West Bank settlements
Kurdistan Workers' Party (PKK)	Turkey, Middle East, Europe
Liberation Tigers of Tamil Eelam (LTTE)	Sri Lanka
Mujahedin-e Khalq Organization (MEK)	Iran
National Liberation Army (ELN)	Colombia
Palestinian Islamic Jihad (PIJ)	Israel, Occupied Territories, Middle East
Palestine Liberation Front (PLF)	Tunisia, Iraq
Popular Front for the Liberation of Palestine (PFLP)	Israel, Occupied Territories, Lebanon, Syria
PFLP-General Command (PFLP-GC)	Syria, Lebanon
Al-Qaeda	Afghanistan, global cells
Real IRA (RIRA)	Republic of Ireland, Northern Ireland, Britain
Revolutionary Armed Forces of Colombia (FARC)	Colombia
Revolutionary Nuclei (formerly ELA)	Greece
Revolutionary Organization 17 November	Greece
Revolutionary People's Liberation Army/Front (DHKP/C)	Turkey
Shining Path (Sendero Luminoso, SL)	Peru
United Self-Defense Forces of Colombia (AUC)	Colombia

THE U.S. DESIGNATION OF A FOREIGN TERRORIST ORGANIZATION MAKES IT ILLEGAL FOR ANY PERSON UNDER U.S. JURISDICTION TO PROVIDE ANY KIND OF SUPPORT TO THE ORGANIZATION, INCLUDING FINANCIAL ASSISTANCE. *(Gale Group.)*

Recognizing the threat to national and international security from terrorism in the Philippines, in January 2002, the U.S. government sent a military contingent to the Philippines to train Filipino soldiers to fight against the Abu Sayyaf group, which is believed to be linked to Osama bin Ladin's al-Qaeda terror network. Additionally, on May 7, 2002, the governments of Malaysia, Indonesia, and the Philippines signed an anti-terror pact aimed at formalizing security coordination between the three countries in order to destroy militant terrorist cells operating in the region.

Regardless of the efforts of the international community to destroy terrorism in the region, it is unclear if they will be effective in ending the high number of hostage taking incidents that take place. This raises questions of the future of hostage taking in the Philippines and around the world. Will the upswing of hostage taking for ransom demands occurring throughout the world continue to grow? How will state governments stop this trend? Will rebels groups continue to demand ransom in exchange for their hostages or will they become bold with their success and demand other concessions from governments?

As of May 10, 2002, Abu Sayyaf rebels operating in the southern Philippines continued to keep Martin and Gracia Burnham as human bargaining chips in their campaign to create an independent Muslim state on the southern Philippine island of Mindanao. With both the Philippine and U.S. governments steadfastly refusing to negotiate with the Abu Sayyaf terrorists, the future of the American missionary couple held hostage—and the future of hostage taking through out the world—remains unknown.

BIBLIOGRAPHY

Anderson, Terry. "Justice for Victims of Terrorism Act," Testimony of Terry Anderson before the United States House of Representatives Committee on the Judiciary Subcommittee on Immigration and Claims, April 13, 2000. Available online at http://www.house.gov/judiciary/ande0413.htm (cited May 3, 2002).

"Al Faran and the Hostage Crisis in Kashmir," SAPRA India, March 10, 1985. Available online at http://www.subcontinent.com/sapra/terrorism/tr_1996_03_001_s.html (cited May 4, 2002).

"International Terrorism: American Hostages," U.S. Department of State, October 17, 1995. Available online at http://www.state.gov/www/global/terrorism/fs_951017_amhostages.html (cited May 10, 2002).

Nelan, Bruce W. "How They Did It," *Time*, vol. 149, no. 18, May 5, 1997.

Reagan, Ronald. "Speech by President Ronald Reagan," June 18, 1985. Available online at http://www.stethem.navy.mil/history/presidentspeech.htm (cited May 3, 2002).

Reeve, Simon. *One Day in September: The Story of the 1972 Munich Olympics Massacre.* London, England: Faber and Faber Ltd, 2000.

"Significant Terrorist Incidents, 1961–2001: A Chronology," U.S. Department of State, October 31, 2001. Available online at http://usinfo.state.gov/topical/pol/terror/01103131.htm (cited May 3, 2002).

Cheryl A. Loeb

U.S. INTELLIGENCE IN THE TWENTY-FIRST CENTURY

THE CONFLICT

On September 11, 2001, the United States suffered a major surprise attack when terrorists hijacked and crashed four passenger airliners into buildings in New York City, Arlington, Virginia (near Washington, DC), and in a field in Pennsylvania. The U.S. intelligence community was criticized for not putting together intelligence on the planning of this most recent and deadly attack before it hit. It is commonly agreed that the U.S. intelligence community, whose legal charter dates from 1947, was created to prevent another strategic surprise like that of Pearl Harbor in 1941, to which the terrorist attack was likened. The 2001 attack raised serious questions about the capabilities of the intelligence community and its future role, giving new emphasis to a debate that began with the end of the Cold War in 1991.

Counterterrorism

- The United States has been actively engaged against international terrorism since the early 1980s, but the September 11, 2001, attacks underscored a new, more immediate threat and a higher sense of focus.

- In this struggle against a shadowy, internationally dispersed opponent, a greater burden falls on the U.S. intelligence community, which is still transforming itself from its 50-year Cold War posture to one that will be able to respond to a more diverse set of twenty-first century threats.

On September 11, 2001, the United States suffered the second major surprise attack in its history. Unlike the first attack, by Japan at Pearl Harbor, Hawaii, in December 1941, the 2001 attack was not perpetrated by a nation. This new attack was the most recent and most deadly in a series of terrorist attacks by the al-Qaeda terrorist organization, headed by Osama bin Laden. Although separated by almost sixty years, the two events are linked for U.S. intelligence. It is commonly agreed that the U.S. intelligence community, whose legal charter dates from 1947, was created to prevent another strategic surprise like Pearl Harbor. The 2001 attack raised serious questions about the capabilities of that intelligence community and its future role, giving new emphasis to a debate that had begun with the end of the Cold War in 1991. The world and the challenges facing the United States had clearly changed. After a decade in which no issue seemed paramount, terrorism became the main focus of all national security policy. How well the intelligence community responds to the post-September 11, 2001, world will have a major effect on the future role intelligence is asked or allowed to play.

HISTORICAL BACKGROUND

The Development of the U.S. Intelligence Community

As noted, the U.S. intelligence community officially dates from 1947, when the National Security Act revamped the U.S. government structure with three important changes. First, the act created a National Security Council (NSC), designed to bring together diplomatic and military policy into an advisory group under the president. The NSC currently consists of the president, vice president, and secretaries of state and defense, with the chair-

CHRONOLOGY

1940–45 Office of Strategic Services (OSS) is established as the first U.S. national (rather than military) intelligence service.

December 7, 1941 The Japanese surprise attack on Pearl Harbor is seen by many as the main cause for the creation of a post-war intelligence community.

1947 Passage of National Security Act creates the Central Intelligence Agency and gives *de jure* status to the Director of Central Intelligence.

1952–62 The U.S. intelligence community is developed with the creation of most of its major components, including the National Security Agency, State Department Bureau of Intelligence and Research, and Defense Intelligence Agency.

1947–91 The Cold War ensues between the United States and the Soviet Union, in which the U.S. intelligence community plays a major role and which also has long-lasting effects on the intelligence community.

1980s–90s U.S. counter-terrorism policy emphasizes state-sponsored terrorism.

1990s–present U.S. counter-terrorism policy emphasizes independent terrorist groups.

August 7, 1998 Al-Qaeda terrorists attack U.S. embassies in Kenya and Tanzania with bombs, killing 12 U.S. citizens and 240 Africans.

October 2, 2000 Al-Qaeda terrorists attack the USS *Cole* in Yemen, killing 17 and wounding 39.

September 11, 2001 Al-Qaeda terrorists engage in a multi-plane attack on the United States, hitting the Pentagon in Arlington, Virginia, near Washington, DC, and destroying the World Trade Center in New York.

October 7, 2001 Operation Enduring Freedom begins against al-Qaeda and the Taliban in Afghanistan.

man of the joint chiefs of staff as the military adviser and the director of central intelligence as the intelligence adviser. Second, the War and Navy Departments were merged into a new unified structure, which became the Defense Department and included a separate Air Force as well. Third, the position of Director of Central Intelligence (DCI) was given legal status (it had existed earlier by presidential order) and placed under the NSC. Further, a Central Intelligence Agency (CIA) was created under the DCI.

There had been a handful of U.S. intelligence organizations prior to 1947. Both the navy and army had created intelligence branches in the late nineteenth century, and during and after World War I (1914–18), the United States had a very successful code-breaking operation. During World War II (1939–45), President Franklin Roosevelt (1933–45) had created the Office of Strategic Services (OSS), which served both operational and analytical functions, but it was disbanded in 1945. There had never been a peacetime national intelligence organization. President Harry Truman (1945–53) had agreed to the creation of the CIA in order to coordinate better the disparate intelligence he was receiving from diplomatic and military sources. Very quickly, however, the CIA began

to fill vacuums in analysis, collection, and operations as the United States began to respond to Soviet pressure in the early days of the Cold War. By the Korean War (1950–53), the CIA was a full-blown intelligence service, not just a coordinator.

Between 1947 and 1962 the intelligence community continued to evolve and to grow. The National Security Agency (NSA) was created by presidential order in 1952, and given responsibility for collecting information from other nation's signals (that is, communications, test data, etc.) and for protecting the communications of the United States. With the advent of so-called spy satellites in the 1960s, the National Reconnaissance Office (NRO) was created, responsible for designing an array of intelligence satellites, including those that took images or photos and those that enabled the NSA to do its job. In 1962 the Defense Intelligence Agency (DIA) was formed to provide broader defense-related intelligence beyond that provided by the intelligence units of each military service for their more narrow needs. Other members of the intelligence community include four military service intelligence units: the State Department's Bureau of Intelligence and Research (INR), the Federal Bureau of Investigation's (FBI) National Security Division—responsible for counterintelligence—

IN HONOR OF THOSE MEMBERS
OF THE CENTRAL INTELLIGENCE AGENCY
WHO GAVE THEIR LIVES IN THE SERVICE OF THEIR (

PRESIDENT GEORGE W. BUSH ADDRESSES EMPLOYEES AT THE CENTRAL INTELLIGENCE AGENCY WHILE CIA DIRECTOR GEORGE TENET LOOKS ON. THE CIA DIRECTOR ALSO SERVES AS DIRECTOR OF CENTRAL INTELLIGENCE, THE NATION'S SENIOR FOREIGN INTELLIGENCE OFFICIAL. *(AP/Wide World Photos. Reproduced by permission.)*

and, most recently, the National Imagery and Mapping Agency (NIMA), created in 1996 to oversee imagery intelligence.

This is a complex and highly specialized structure. Many agencies serve similar roles, with the two dominant roles being collection or analysis. There is witting redundancy in the structure. There are many collection agencies because each one specializes in a different type of highly specialized collection. There is more obvious redundancy in analysis because of two major operational concepts. The first concept is the view that each of the senior policymakers—the president, the secretaries of state and defense—has unique intelligence needs that can best be served by a specific intelligence agency. Thus, the CIA serves the president, DIA serves the secretary of defense and the chairman of the joint chiefs, and State/INR serves the secretary of state. This does not mean that the agencies do not share analysis or do not allow others outside their agency or department to see it. It does mean that each has a "primary" policymaker customer whose needs these agencies are particularly attuned.

The second operating concept is competitive analysis. Competitive analysis is based on the view that by having many analysts with disparate viewpoints come together on a specific issue, the intel-ligence community is more likely to come to analytical conclusions that are sound because they are broadly based and of the greatest value to those same policymakers. Intelligence, more often than not, is about uncertainty and ambiguity. After all, if something were *known* to be true, we would not need intelligence to collect information about it or to decide what that information meant. It is the uncertainty that drives intelligence, along with the fact that other nations or international actors seek to deprive us of the intelligence we seek, and we, in turn, seek to keep secret how we try to obtain that same information.

When looking at the intelligence community, an obvious question is: Who is in charge of it all? There are two answers, simultaneously: the DCI, or no one. The DCI is the nation's senior foreign intelligence official and the president's senior intelligence adviser. He/she is responsible for coordinating the activities of the 14 agencies that comprise the intelligence community. However, his ability to do so is also severely limited, as the DCI has line authority and budget responsibility over only two components, the CIA and the National Intelligence Council (NIC). The bulk of the intelligence community—NSA, DIA, NIMA, and the service intelligence units—comes under the purview of the secretary of defense. Some estimate that upwards of 80 percent of the intelligence community is under the secretary of defense rather than the DCI. Thus, there is a widely acknowledged gap between the DCI's responsibilities and his authority.

The Cold War

The other important factor in the growth and development of the intelligence community was the Cold War between the United States and the Soviet Union, which lasted from the end of World War II in 1945 until the end of the Soviet Union itself in 1991. For this entire period, the intelligence community was at the center of a global struggle that was political, military, economic, scientific, and cultural. Even though the intelligence community was not created specifically to fight the Cold War, this long struggle has had lasting effects on how the intelligence community functioned far beyond the end of that struggle itself. Former DCI Robert Gates (1991–93) estimated that half of all intelligence activities during the Cold War were devoted to some aspect of the Soviet issue. First and perhaps foremost among the effects, the intelligence community emphasized a variety of national technical means by which it could remotely collect intelligence. This choice was dictated in large part by the physical and political nature of the Soviet state. The Soviet Union sprawled across the Eurasian landmass, many parts of it remote and inaccessible. It was also a police state in which everyone, foreigner and citizen alike, was under surveillance. But foreigners were also restricted to certain areas and denied access to many others. These two factors, in combination, made the usual means of intelligence collection—espionage—of only limited utility. Thus, the United States used a series of remote means—balloons, aircraft and finally satellites—to overfly Soviet territory in order to collect the needed intelligence. The two major types of technical intelligence were imagery (also called IMINT) and signals (SIGINT). There was also ongoing espionage (HUMINT), a nontechnical form of intelligence collection.

Second, the major area of emphasis was military capabilities. The Soviet Union tested its first atomic weapon in 1949 (greatly helped by Soviet espionage) and achieved the capability to launch an object into space and, by inference, the ability to hurl one across continents, in 1957. Thus, for the first time in well over a century, the United States was vulnerable to a potentially devastating attack. Even without intercontinental nuclear weapons, the vast conventional forces of the Soviet Union and its satellites in eastern and central Europe were of concern. Given the origins of the intelligence community in Pearl Harbor, this military emphasis was

THE U.S. INTELLIGENCE COMMUNITY

The intelligence community is complex and diverse. The following are the major components, listed alphabetically:

- CIA: Central Intelligence Agency, responsible for collection (espionage), analysis, and operations (known as covert actions).

- CMS: Community Management Staff, assists the DCI in carrying out his community-wide responsibilities.

- DIA: Defense Intelligence Agency, primarily responsible for analysis affecting more than one military service, and for collection (espionage) via the Defense HUMINT Service (DHS).

- INR: The State Department's Bureau of Intelligence and Research, responsible for analysis.

- Military Service Intelligence Components: army, air force, navy and marine intelligence, each serving the specific needs of their service.

- NIC: National Intelligence Council, a group of the most senior analysts (called national intelligence officers, or NIOs), who prepare and coordinate national intelligence estimates (NIEs).

- NIMA: National Imagery and Mapping Agency, responsible for imagery intelligence and for defense mapping needs.

- NRO: National Reconnaissance Office, builds and operates intelligence satellites.

- NSA: National Security Agency, responsible for all signals intelligence and for the protection of U.S. communications.

understandable. But it also led to an emphasis on studying tangible aspects of power—military forces, economic data (much of it meaningless for the Soviet Union), industrial production, and so on.

The Post-Cold War Transition

The Soviet Union collapsed in 1991, ironically driven over the brink by a failed coup staged by Soviet conservatives opposed to the reforms of the last Soviet leader, Mikhail Gorbachev. Although the United States and its allies had truly won the Cold War, there was something disquieting about the victory for the entire national security network.

SIGNALS INTELLIGENCE INCLUDES INFORMATION GATHERED FROM COMPUTERS, FAX, AND OTHER ELECTRONIC METHODS. THIS COMPUTER STORAGE ROOM AT THE CENTRAL INTELLIGENCE AGENCY HOLDS 1.2 MILLION MEGABYTES OF INFORMATION. (© *Roger Ressmeyer/CORBIS. Reproduced by permission.*)

"The enemy we had come to know and love," as one senior defense intelligence official called the Soviet Union, had ceased to exist. What would be the new area of emphasis?

In an initial attempt to answer this question, then-DCI Robert Gates asked various departments and agencies for their intelligence needs, including many agencies that had not been viewed traditionally as intelligence community customers. It is important to remember that intelligence is a service provided to policymakers, and that they are supposed to establish the intelligence agenda. Gates was sincere in his effort to canvass for requirements and priorities, but critics accused him of "shopping"

for new work to replace the lost Soviet target or of pandering to policy customers. Gates' tenure was cut short by the defeat of President George H. Bush (1989–93) by Bill Clinton in the 1992 election. The new Clinton administration (1993–2001), however, faced the same problem—what should the focus of the intelligence community be?

Some facilely answered this question by stating that the *mission* of the intelligence community had changed. This response only betrayed misunderstanding as to the purpose of the intelligence community. The mission of the intelligence community—supplying intelligence to policymakers so as to reduce their uncertainties as they make decisions—had *not* changed. What changed was the intelligence *target* and policymaker requirements. The mission was and is constant.

After several false starts in terms of his overall approach to foreign policy, in 1995 President Clinton signed Presidential Decision Directive 35 (PDD-35), which set out his administration's intelligence priorities. The first was support to military operations (SMO), meaning any and all intelligence support to the military in all of its roles. The second priority was a group of so-called Hard Targets, that is, issues that potentially threatened U.S. interests and were also difficult against which to collect intelligence. The Hard Targets included the so-called rogue states of Cuba, Libya, Iran, Iraq and North Korea; and the transnational issues. The transnational issues—proliferation of weapons of mass destruction (WMD), terrorism, crime, narcotics, and environmental issues—are not necessarily located in one nation or region and may not even involve nation states. All the other issues fell into what was called Global Coverage. It was understood that the Hard Targets would get the primary emphasis and Global Coverage less emphasis. Beyond this taxonomy, there were also tiers that described the relative priority of each issue. Issues could move up and down in the tier structure, depending on their importance. PDD-35 offered a more coherent and comprehensive outline of intelligence requirements and priorities, but the nature of international relations was such that on any given day any of several issues could claim to be the most important. The focus forced upon the intelligence community by the Soviet threat could not be recaptured, even under PDD-35.

The Terrorist Problem

Terrorism has been a recurring problem in the modern world. In the late nineteenth century, anarchists assassinated several world figures, including U.S. president William McKinley (1897–1901) in 1901. In the aftermath of World War I and the Russian Revolution, there was a new outbreak of terrorism, including bombings and assassination attempts in the United States, the so-called Red Scare.

Terrorism had been a U.S. intelligence concern for decades before the 2001 attacks. In the 1970s the focus was on independent radical groups, such as the Baader-Meinhoff gang in Germany, the Japanese Red Army Brigade, or the Italian Red Brigade, who either staged attacks for reasons of their own or allied themselves with other groups, particularly radical Arabs. During the Reagan administration (1981–89), the focus became state-sponsored terrorism. There was both the belief and intelligence to indicate that certain states were harboring terrorists, training them, and providing a range of logistical support. The United States sought to identify these states and to punish some of them for their actions. Several Soviet satellites (communist nations with ties to, and often bordering, the Soviet Union) were implicated, as were Libya and Iran.

In response to Libyan involvement in the bombing of a disco in West Berlin frequented by U.S. servicemen, the United States conducted an air raid in 1986 against the compound of Libyan leader Muammar Qadhaffi. Libya, in turn, planted a bomb on the Pan American flight 103 from London that exploded over Lockerbie, Scotland, in 1988. In the mid-1990s, however, the emphasis of U.S. policy on terrorism shifted to independent terrorist groups. Certain state sponsors were still of concern, but the emphasis had shifted to groups with increasingly potent capabilities and shifting bases of operations. For a variety of reasons, many of these groups had Arab connections, either as a direct result of the Arab-Israeli conflict or, as in the case of al-Qaeda, spawned in the successful U.S.-supported effort to force the Soviets out of Afghanistan.

Terrorism as an Intelligence Target

Several aspects of terrorism make it a difficult intelligence target. Terrorism is covert (meaning planned and carried out in secret), it is highly mobile, and it can operate with a minimum of capabilities that are distinguishable. All of these attributes run counter to the intelligence collection array that has been developed over decades, primarily to collect against the old Soviet target. Signals intelligence is usually a major means of collection against nations. Most modern states have easily identified telecommunications capabilities that provide a variety of useful intelligence. Militaries communicate regularly and extensively. They also tend to hold exercises according to a set annual schedule. Terrorist groups may rely on a variety of modern communications—cellular phones, faxes, the Internet—but these are never the same extensive networks that are found in nations. A further complication is the fact that U.S. intelligence collection capabilities are constantly becoming better known in unclassified sources, particularly the press. These revelations or leaks provide any potential target of U.S. collection with a ready-made guide on how to avoid that collection. For example, terrorists know to avoid using cell phones or faxes as much as possible to evade both yielding information and being located. Cell phones, having

TYPES OF INTELLIGENCE COLLECTION

There are a variety of means of collecting intelligence, sometimes referred to as collection disciplines or as INTs.

Imagery (IMINT or PHOTINT) is pictures, although there are a variety of ways of taking them, including electro-optical, which is akin to a standard picture; infrared, which reads the heat coming off objects and surroundings; and radar, which can locate objects through cloud cover.

Signals (SIGINT) actually has several subsets. Communications (COMINT) refers to actual exchanges between people, most often by telephone. It can mean voice, fax, or computer communications. Electronics (ELINT) refers to electronic emissions from weapons or tracking systems. Telemetry (TELINT) are the data released by weapons during tests.

Espionage (HUMINT) is the most familiar collection type, also known as spying.

Measurement and signatures (MASINT) is a somewhat obscure collection type, referring to weapons capabilities and industrial activities obtained from multispectral and hyperspectral frequencies and some fairly exotic processing.

Open source (OSINT) refers to any information that is neither classified nor proprietary and includes news media, academic papers, government reports, the World Wide Web, and so on.

---

become relatively cheap, can be used once and then discarded, which also foils collection.

Imagery, which was so useful against the Soviet Union, also suffers when used on terrorism. The Soviet Union was a large, complex, and highly visible target with a large permanent infrastructure. Military bases are often large and usually are built in familiar and recurring patterns. Military exercises often involve large units, whose deployments are observable. Many terrorist facilities have few distinguishing characteristics to assist in identifying them. Large training camps may be an exception, but these are not overly valuable targets as terrorist groups rarely have significant assets concentrated in any one place. Terrorism itself most often operates with very small groups, not large formations.

Many people familiar with intelligence capabilities argue that espionage is the best way to collect on terrorism. There has been a long, recurring debate in the U.S. intelligence community—even before the 2001 attacks—over the degree to which U.S. intelligence is dependent on technical collection when, for certain types of intelligence, espionage would be better. The basic argument runs along the following lines: technical intelligence is very useful in collecting on capabilities (IMINT and SIGINT) and can offer insights into plans (via SIGINT), but it cannot get close to its target. Moreover, all technical collection depends on there being something to collect—either something to be imaged or communications to be intercepted—both of which can be avoided. They are, in effect, "where and when" intelligence sources. Inserting a spy into an organization offers the possibility of insights into plans and also has more continuous access to the target. This debate resurfaced in the aftermath of the September 2001 attacks.

HUMINT

Generically, all of the above arguments have validity. But it is simplistic to argue that improved espionage capabilities are an easy remedy to collecting on terrorism. First, spies are not an "on the shelf" capability who can be immediately ordered to this or that part of the world to collect intelligence. Successful HUMINT requires time for preparation. The spy needs to have proficiency in the language or dialects of the place in which he or she will be operating. Combating modern terrorism, unfortunately, calls for language skills that tend to be rare in the United States, including Arabic. The spy needs to blend in with his or her surroundings in terms of ethnicity and have a plausible reason for being in the place where the espionage will take place.

Typically, there are two ways to accomplish this. Some spies are posted to an embassy, where they have a "daytime" job that provides them with official cover. In the case of terrorism, however, we are often dealing with places where there is no embassy or consulate out of which to work. The other means is what is called non-official cover (making the spy a "NOC," pronounced "knock"). The NOC usually has a job or other plausible reason for being in this location and has no overt connection to the embassy. NOCs can have a variety of jobs—lawyer, salesman, etc.—that give them a plausible reason for being in that location and has no overt connection to a foreign government. In the case of terrorism, however, this, too, can be a problem. For example, there were few, if any, plausible reasons to be in Kabul, Afghanistan, in the months preceding the terrorist attack that would have provided a NOC with cover. Two final factors also make

HUMINT more difficult. Even if one can establish a plausible reason for being in the right location, most terrorist organizations do not run major recruiting campaigns. Nor do they have an overt presence in many other states, the way nations do via their embassies. There is still the question of being able to locate and penetrate the group. Even if one penetrates the group, the inner circles tend to be very small and very well known to one another. Access to the key terrorists may still be difficult if not impossible. Finally, it is highly likely that a new recruit will be asked to prove himself. This means, in short, taking part in some sort of terrorist activity. Here we enter an ethical realm with few sure guideposts. Is there a level of activity or violence beyond which a spy should not be allowed to go? What is it—kidnapping, bombing, a single murder, multiple murders?

One means of extending HUMINT capabilities is to form partnerships with the clandestine services of other nations. This type of relationship is known as foreign liaison. Each nation has distinct HUMINT advantages in terms of regional knowledge, political relationships, history, and so on. Foreign liaison relationships are based on mutual exchanges of information, if not simultaneous, then over time. They also depend on a willingness to trust one another, given the sensitivity of the intelligence being exchanged—both requirements or actual intelligence. As useful as these foreign liaison relationships can be, their utility against terrorism may be more limited, as few intelligence organizations that are friendly to terrorists are likely to be helpful to the United States. The ambiguous stance of Pakistan's military intelligence, Inter-Service Intelligence (ISI), is a case in point. ISI had good relations with the Taliban, which should have been useful to the United States. But Pakistani president Pervez Musharraf clearly had doubts as to ISI's loyalty to the Pakistani leadership, finding it necessary to remove some senior ISI officers after he decided to support U.S. military operations responding to the September 2001 attacks. He has since taken steps to reduce greatly the size and influence of ISI.

There are also important policy issues, which must always be paramount when reviewing intelligence. As was noted above, intelligence exists solely to service policy. Intelligence exists to provide policymakers with as much information (intelligence) as possible so as to reduce the uncertainty inherent in most decisions. Intelligence officers do not, however, make policy. In U.S. practice, at least, there is a strict "line" separating intelligence from policy. The policy function is always the dominant one.

To put it in very stark terms, policymakers can exist and function without an intelligence community, but an intelligence community can not exist and function without policymakers. Intelligence has no independent function. Prior to the September 2001 attacks, the United States appeared to respond to terrorism on a local level, rather than globally. As noted, the United States staged a bombing raid against Libya. There were also several instances in which cruise missiles were used as a response to terrorism, attacking specific facilities. These included the military intelligence headquarters in Iraq in retaliation for the attempted assassination of former President George H. Bush; a suspected chemical weapons factory in Sudan; and al-Qaeda facilities in Afghanistan in retaliation for attacks prior to September 2001. This is not to suggest that the intelligence community was not active. In the mid-1990s, for example, the United States, working with France, captured the terrorist known as Carlos the Jackal. All of these responses, however, were far less than that seen after the 2001 attacks. It is also important to recognize that prior to the 2001 attacks there probably did not exist sufficient political support for a more aggressive policy against terrorism, which was another important limitation.

The political nature of terrorism also imposes limits on intelligence collection and analysis. When dealing with other nation states, there is usually the expectation of some level of give and take, or of fairly rational action/reaction. Even when dealing with states whose avowed aims are to change the international status quo, such as Nazi Germany or the Soviet Union, there was the expectation, up to a certain point, that some basis for dialogue or negotiation could be achieved. The very factor of dealing with a nation state and the possibility of dialogue predicates certain types of intelligence collection and certain lines of analysis. These might include an assumed level of rationality, the likelihood of a certain amount of give and take, an assumed unwillingness to put large portions of one's own population at risk, and so on. Little or none of this holds true when dealing with terrorist groups as opposed to their nation state supporters. Terrorists, by definition, cannot adhere to the status quo. To do so removes their very reason for being. They may issue political demands, but few states are going to be willing to meet these demands because they are either impossible, or because of the fear that this will only validate the terrorism and inspire more of it. Thus, many of the policy assumptions that may guide intelligence when dealing with nation states do not hold true for terrorists.

THE U.S. INTELLIGENCE COMMUNITY

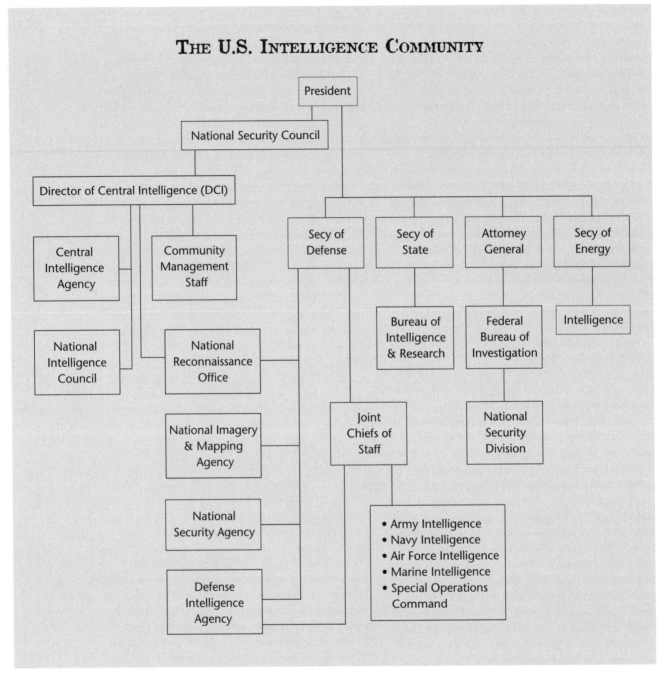

THE U.S. INTELLIGENCE COMMUNITY HAS SEVERAL LEVELS, WITH THE TOP POSITIONS INCLUDING THE PRESIDENT, THE NATIONAL SECURITY COUNCIL, AND THE DIRECTOR OF CENTRAL INTELLIGENCE. *(Gale Group.)*

The September 2001 Attacks

It is difficult to argue that the terrorist attacks in September 2001 did not represent some level of failure, but the nature of, and reasons for, that failure are important and not wholly discernable as yet. More went wrong than simply intelligence. There were flaws in airport security (the responsibility of the Federal Aviation Authority, or FAA); the Immigration and Naturalization Service (INS); and the FBI, responsible for combating terrorism within the United States. This list does not mean that there are not also responsibilities of the intelligence community. But the failure was more systemic than that.

Were the attacks a "new Pearl Harbor," as many have argued? The basis for the comparison is easy to understand, but it also ignores important differences between the two events. In both cases the hostility of the perpetrator towards the United

States was well known. U.S.-Japanese relations had been deteriorating since at least 1937, when Japan commenced its overt war in China. Similarly, Osama bin Laden had been overtly hostile to the United States since 1990, when the United States deployed troops into Saudi Arabia in reaction to Iraq's invasion of Kuwait. There had also been previous attacks by bin Laden, including the bombing of two U.S. embassies in Kenya and Tanzania in 1998 and an attack on the USS *Cole* in Yemen in 2000. In both cases there were expectations of increased hostility. In the case of Japan, U.S. policymakers widely expected some new aggression, but wrongly assumed it would be directed against vulnerable European colonies in Southeast Asia or the East Indies, not against the United States. In the case of bin Laden, DCI George Tenet issued a series of warnings of future attacks. In both events, despite these expectations, the attacker achieved surprise. At this point, however, the comparisons are no longer apt, for reasons that are also significant. Japan's attack was strategic in nature, aimed at crippling the U.S. Pacific Fleet, which had been deployed to Hawaii to deter future Japanese aggression—a classic case of a failed deterrent that became, instead, the target. Bin Laden's attack in September 2001 was mostly symbolic in nature and did not affect U.S. power. Finally, Japan and its Axis allies had the capability to defeat the United States militarily and destroy its way of life. Neither of these factors is true for al-Qaeda. This may not ameliorate all of the intelligence aspects of the September 2001 attacks, but it does place the attacks in their proper context.

As emotionally devastating as the 2001 attacks were, it is also important to keep in mind the very small number of people who had to be involved in the planning and execution of the attacks. There were 19 hijackers (with discussions as to whether or not there is a "missing" twentieth hijacker), not all of whom may have known the true nature of the operations, perhaps suspecting it was a "traditional" airplane hijacking as opposed to a suicide attack. We can assume that bin Laden and several of his chief lieutenants knew of the plan. We can even posit, solely for the sake of argument, that there may have been others in the United States in a variety of support roles who may or may not have been witting as to the attack's true nature. This still may total fewer than three dozen people, a very small number with extremely low visibility.

The intelligence community has spent decades developing the concept of indications and warning, meaning being able to detect the precursor signs of an activity. Indications and warning, or I&W as it is known to intelligence professionals, is a direct outgrowth of the origins of the intelligence community in Pearl Harbor. I&W is primarily a tool of military analysis, seeking signs that will alert one to an impending attack. During the Cold War, there was a heated debate about the I&W that might be seen before a conventional Soviet attack in central Europe. Some analysts held that there would be telltale signs: supplies moving forward, reserves being called up, and so on. Others argued that the Soviets had sufficient forces and supplies in place to attack from what was called a "standing start," without any precursor activity. Neither theory was put to the test, fortunately. But this debate does give one a feel for what is involved in I&W. For terrorism, however, there is little, if any, reliable I&W. The groups involved are small, as are the weapons of choice—previously, bombs mounted in common modes of transportation, and later the actual airplanes themselves. Thus, there is a large gap between knowing that a group is hostile to the United States, or even that it has carried out attacks and is likely to do so in the future, and knowing the location and means of the next attack. With a society as open as is that of the United States, and with as many overseas interests as the United States has (embassies, bases, military units), terrorists will always have some advantage of choosing the time, location, and means of their next attack. Which is why, after the 2001 attacks, the George W. Bush administration (2001–) decided that the best strategy was to take the war directly to the terrorists rather than to try to defeat each attack.

Intelligence and the War on Terrorism

The first two tasks of the intelligence community in the immediate aftermath of the September 2001 attacks were (1) to determine if there were more attacks coming; and (2) to determine who was responsible for the attacks. We do not know from the public record if other attacks were planned or not, or if some were thwarted either by U.S. operations or by the sudden clamp down on security in the United States. Based on the currently available information, including the tapes of bin Laden, it would seem that no immediate follow-on attacks were planned. Although the terrorists apparently did not expect the level of destruction they achieved, neither did they expect the eventual U.S. response. Intelligence linking bin Laden to the attacks apparently was established fairly quickly.

According to press accounts that relied on interviews with senior policymakers, once President Bush had decided upon a strategic—as opposed to a tactical—response, the intelligence community was quickly ready with an operational plan to link up with Afghan opposition forces and attack al-Qaeda's supporters, the Taliban. In other words, rather than launching new, limited retaliatory strikes, as had been used in the past, the Bush administration decided to destroy al-Qaeda and its supporters. This plan, which involved using U.S. paramilitary experts to link up with the Northern Alliance to provide military advice and to serve as targeteers for the bombing campaign, reveals another aspect of intelligence—the operational arm. Intelligence operations can involve a large range of types, from propaganda campaigns to economic disruption to political intervention to coups to paramilitary campaigns.

Any and all of these types of operations (also called covert actions) can be controversial, although the paramilitary operations have tended to be more so than the others. There are several reasons for this. Paramilitary operations involve sizeable armed forces and combat. They tend to take longer than other types of operations and also run a greater risk of being inconclusive. They also raise questions about the obligations of the provider of paramilitary support to the indigenous forces in the field, a key issue, especially when an operation shows no sign of success or is an actual failure. The political costs of failure in paramilitary operations are also very high. The United States has experienced paramilitary operations that failed, such as the attempted invasion of Cuba at the Bay of Pigs (1961); operations that were inconclusive, such as the Contra war in Nicaragua (1980s); and operations that were successful, such as support to Afghanistan to resist the Soviet invasion (1980s). These last two operations are interesting because they were contemporaneous, and yet one, Afghanistan, enjoyed wide political support in Congress, while the other, the Contras, was the subject of often rancorous debate. Also, one of the results of the Afghan operation was the eventual rise to power of the Taliban due to the internal fighting that erupted after the Soviets were defeated.

The CIA's operational plan for Afghanistan after September 2001, which was melded with the use of regular U.S. military Special Forces units, was tremendously successful. The Taliban was defeated with a minimum of U.S. ground force involvement and with the cooperation of indigenous troops, which is important to the political future of Afghanistan.

One interesting aspect of the post-attack debate on intelligence was a revival of the discussion over the propriety of assassination as an operational tool. This debate goes back to the mid-1970s, when a Senate select committee investigating allegations of intelligence community wrongdoing issued a report detailing U.S. government involvement in or witting knowledge of assassination attempts against foreign leaders. The targets included Fidel Castro; Patrice Lumumba, first premier of the Congo; Ngo Dinh Diem, president of South Vietnam; General Rene Schneider of Chile; and Rafael Trujillo, dictator of the Dominican Republic. The report also noted that none of the victims specifically targeted by the United States—primarily Castro—died as a result of U.S. actions. The report did result in strong public reaction and the prohibition of the use of assassination in three successive executive orders, signed by presidents Gerald Ford, Jimmy Carter, and Ronald Reagan.

The executive order signed by President Reagan in 1981 is still the governing order for the intelligence community. There was anecdotal evidence to suggest that public support for the ban had been waning. In the aftermath of the terrorist attacks, many called for a lifting of the ban, with bin Laden and his lieutenants as likely targets. In actuality, the point was moot. The United States declared itself to be at war with terrorism and under those conditions, terrorists or their leaders became legitimate military targets whose deaths would not fall under the ban. Still, the debate was an interesting indicator of one reaction to the attacks and of the greater license that many would subsequently allow intelligence operations.

Intelligence Innovations

Two intelligence innovations in the Afghan phase of the terrorism war are worth noting, both involving imagery. First, the United States continued to make advances in its use of unmanned aerial vehicles (UAVs), or drones. These pilotless aircraft, operated remotely from long distances, have the ability to fly over areas of interest for long periods of time (unlike satellites, which fly in rapid orbits), and without risk to pilots (unlike U-2s or other spy planes). Thus, UAVs can provide more continuous coverage and, when using video cameras, can supply "real-time" coverage. A second UAV innovation has been the mounting of air-to-surface missiles on the UAVs. This allows targets to be attacked as soon as they are identified, rather than waiting for aircraft to be called in and then flown to the target.

The other imagery innovation has been the greater use of commercial imagery by the intelligence community. Imagery satellites launched and flown by private companies have now achieved resolutions (that is, the ability to identify an object of a certain size in a photograph) of 0.8 meters—just over 31 inches—or better. In order to take advantage of this capability, NIMA purchased the exclusive and perpetual use of commercial images of Afghanistan taken by the Ikonos satellite, operated by Space Imaging, a private U.S. company. This not only augmented imagery collection, reserving even more powerful intelligence satellites for tasks that only they can perform, but also denied this imagery either to current or potential foes or to nations eager to assess the progress and capability of U.S. forces. This purchase also denied the use of the images to the press, which might have been eager to use them as part of its own independent analysis of the war.

The rapid success of U.S. forces in Afghanistan has, to some extent, helped to undo some of the damage done to the intelligence community's reputation by the September 2001 attacks. This is not a unique occurrence. In 1961 the CIA was badly damaged by the failure of the abortive Bay of Pigs invasion. In 1962 the intelligence community's performance in the Cuban missile crisis undid much of that damage in terms of the intelligence community's relationship with policymakers by providing sufficient warning of the emplacement of the missiles to allow President Kennedy (1961–63) to act before the missiles were operational. The intelligence community also provided U.S. policymakers with detailed intelligence about Soviet military capabilities, which also gave them greater confidence in their decisions.

RECENT HISTORY AND THE FUTURE

The Future of U.S. Intelligence

The terrorist attacks revived the ongoing but sometimes unfocused debate over the future of the intelligence community. This debate is almost as old as the intelligence community itself, and is driven by many factors. Chief among them are the relative novelty of intelligence as a permanent function of government, the levels of expectation about intelligence performance, and the inherent difficulty of managing a broad and diverse community that deals in the often intangible commodities of analysis and interpretation.

The most recent debate over intelligence had come in the mid-1990s, in the aftermath of the Cold War. As discussed above, some felt that the intelligence community's mission had changed and that it had to be re-examined. Others understood that the mission had not changed but were con-

INTELLIGENCE ISSUES FOR CONGRESS

The U.S. Intelligence Community continues to adjust to the post-Cold War environment. Congressional and executive branch initiatives have emphasized enhancing cooperation among the different agencies that comprise the Community by giving greater managerial authority to the Director of Central Intelligence (DCI).

Priority continues to be placed on intelligence support to military operations and on involvement in efforts to combat narcotics trafficking and, especially since September 11, 2001, international terrorism. Growing concerns about transnational threats are leading to increasingly close cooperation between intelligence and law enforcement agencies. This relationship is complicated, however, by differing roles and missions as well as statutory charters. The September 11, 2001 terrorist attacks, for which no specific warning was available, have led to increased emphasis on human intelligence, better cooperation between law enforcement and intelligence agencies, and on consideration of organizational changes to the Intelligence Community.

Intelligence Community leadership and congressional committees have expressed determination to enhance analytical capabilities. A major concern is an imbalance between resources devoted to collection and those allocated to analysis, with collected data much exceeding analytical capabilities.

In several regional crisis areas, the role of the U.S. Intelligence Community is especially important. Provisions for U.S. intelligence to monitor security arrangements between Israelis and Palestinians have been a significant factor in efforts to resolve Middle East tensions. Intelligence efforts have also been important in attempting to enforce U.N. sanctions on Iraq and monitoring peace agreements in Bosnia. Cruise missile and bomb attacks on Afghan targets in the campaign against the Taliban, and on Serbian targets during the Kosovo crisis have been heavily dependent upon precise targeting data provided by intelligence sensors. The mistaken attack on the Chinese Embassy in Belgrade resulted from faulty information provided by the Intelligence Community.

A particular concern for many in Congress has been the Intelligence Community's assessment of the missile attack capabilities of foreign countries, especially North Korea. Some believe that U.S. vulnerability to missile attack may arrive sooner than has been estimated by intelligence agencies.

CRS Issue Brief for Congress, received through the CRS Web. "Intelligence Issues for Congress." Updated January 8, 2002. Richard A. Best, Jr. Foreign Affairs, Defense, and Trade Division. Congressional Research Service. The Library of Congress.

cerned that the major influence of the Cold War on the intelligence community had left forms and practices that might be outmoded. Several major reviews were conducted, the two most prominent being the Commission on the Roles and Capabilities of the United States Intelligence Community, also known as the Aspin-Brown Commission after its two chairmen, former secretaries of defense Les Aspin and Harold Brown, and the House Intelligence

THE USE OF TECHNOLOGY CAN GREATLY ENHANCE INTELLIGENCE CAPABILITIES, BE IT THROUGH COMPUTERS OR SATELITE IMAGERY. (© *Roger Ressmeyer/CORBIS. Reproduced by permission.*)

Committee's study, *IC21: The Intelligence Community in the 21st Century.*

The two studies did not use similar approaches and came up with different recommendations—as well as some that agreed—but it is striking that both reports urged that the intelligence community function more like a true community, that is, one in which all the disparate agencies function as part of a more integrated whole. This remains the most central issue in what is called "intelligence reform," the degree of authority exercised by the DCI over the intelligence community. According to press reports, a study ordered by President Bush and headed by former national security adviser Brent Scowcroft recommended that the DCI have greater authority over the "national" agencies—particularly NIMA and NSA. Predictably, the intelligence staff in the Defense Department have been opposed to this concept.

The debate over the future of the intelligence community goes much further, however, than the authority of the DCI or organizational shifts. There are many other significant issues. Some argue that the intelligence community has to break away from its current bureaucratic structure—built around either geographic or topical offices—and adopt a more fluid approach, with groups of specialists coming together and disbanding as the issues require, perhaps working in "virtual" proximity rather than in the same actual building. The intelligence community began moving towards a somewhat more adaptive structure in the 1990s, when DCI Gates created a series of centers responsible for some of the more pressing transnational issues, in which analysts from several agencies could be brought together. The centers are generally seen as being successful, although some question the degree to which they are true "community" centers, given the invariable CIA dominance in them.

Such an approach also addresses the important issue of "surge," or the ability of the intelligence community to respond to sudden crises. The United States has global responsibilities and interests. The intelligence community, in theory, should be able to respond to and support any of those interests. In reality, however, all intelligence resources—like all other government resources—are finite. Therefore, the intelligence community picks and chooses among the issues it can cover in depth, those that can get some coverage and those that are largely left wanting. The choices tend to reflect policymaker requirements. When a crisis breaks, however, it often comes in one of those areas where there has been little or no coverage. The intelligence community must then "surge" resources from current coverage to this new area. During the Cold War, this was less problematic given the predominance of the Soviet issue. In the post-Cold War period, it has become more of a problem, as there has been no predominant issue. One of the other suggestions advocated to address surge is the greater use of outside experts and retirees in what would be an intelligence reserve. External regional experts, for example, could be especially useful when attention shifts to a region whose languages or cultures are not widely studied or known. Authority to use such a reserve exists, but the intelligence community's reaction has been tepid at best.

Some would take these new organizational concepts even further and treat intelligence like a commodity to be purchased by interested policymakers. Advocates of this approach believe that the introduction of "market forces," even in an economy as small and as specialized as this, would mandate changes, weeding out inefficient processes and forcing the intelligence community to focus only on those issues that really matter to policymakers. A problem with this approach is that it puts almost the entire emphasis of the intelligence community on what is called "current intelligence," that is, the issues that are on the "front burner." This flies in the face of decades of experience, which tell us that at least a few of next year's crises will come in areas that had previously been backwaters. One of the major contributions that intelligence makes at times like those is the ability to call on veteran analysts who have been following these secondary or tertiary issues for years and who can bring everyone up to speed on them. The market force model would seem to have little room for this type of background coverage, which has no immediate utility but may pay off handsomely in the years to come, reflecting the inherent uncertainty of the overall intelligence agenda. For example, as late as September 10, 2001, no U.S. policymaker would likely have been able to envision circumstances that would lead to a major U.S. military engagement in Afghanistan. This, however, is the essence of intelligence.

Intelligence Collection Issues

There are several collection issues in the reform debate. The issue of the proper balance between technical and human collection operations has already been discussed above. Another important reform collection issue is the imbalance between the amount of technical intelligence that is collected and the much smaller amount of images or signals that is processed and exploited into useable intelligence for analysts. Technical collection systems do not take a photograph or record a conversation per se. Rather, these are captured in digital form, which then must be processed into an image or audio tape. The collection systems tend to act like large vacuum cleaners, sweeping up much more than can be used. This is sometimes referred to as the TPEDs problem, which stands for tasking, processing, exploitation, and dissemination, of which the middle two—processing and exploitation—are the most problematic. Congress has been especially vocal on this issue, holding that it is difficult to allocate more funds for ever more powerful collection systems if the same levels of intelligence—or less—are ultimately made available to analysts.

Another collection issue is the internecine competition that goes on among the various collection disciplines. Although each of the INTs, or methods of intelligence collection, has its own strengths and weaknesses, there are bureaucratic and budget imperatives that foster an ultimately wasteful competition among the INTs. No one has the authority to adjudicate among the INTs, or to determine which ones should collect, or not collect, on a given issue. Some, including the House Intelligence Committee's IC21 study, have recommended that a single individual have this authority, at least for the technical collection disciplines.

This is a rich agenda and one that engages the many practitioners, students, and aficionados of intelligence. The venue in which these concepts might be debated with an eye towards reform is unclear. The only scheduled review of intelligence community performance in the events leading up to September 11, 2001, is that planned by the House and Senate Select Committees on Intelligence. The actual agenda of that investigation is not yet decided upon. The breadth or narrowness of that inquiry will determine the range of the eventual recommendations. It is also likely that there will be other investigations as well. (Pearl Harbor was the subject of multiple investigations both during and after World War II.) It will be important, in any recommendations that follow from these investigations, to be able to show how recommended changes address specific problems within the intelligence community. Pet causes or fashionable intellectual hobbyhorses will not survive without this. It is also important to work from a reasonable set of expectations about intelligence performance. Omniscience is beyond the capability of any intelligence organization. What level of success should be expected against a threat as difficult to track as terrorism? Repetitions of the September 2001 attacks are not acceptable, but a "zero tolerance" policy is also not realistic. Finally, it is important to remember that the intelligence community has to address more than terrorism. Any proposed reforms should create a more capable intelligence community across the board, rather than a response to one issue alone. After all, there are still more issues on the agenda than just terrorism.

Conclusion

The future of U.S. intelligence in the twenty-first century will depend on more than any new investigations, although these will be a factor. It will also depend on how well the intelligence community performs in the war against terrorism, while also keeping watch on the other issues on the national security agenda. It is not just a question of increased budgets, or more satellites or more spies. The intelligence community has to manage well within a fixed amount of resources, covering the necessary issues while maintaining a certain degree of flexibility. Ultimately, intelligence is one of the most difficult government functions to assess in terms of success and effectiveness. There is much about intelligence that is inefficient. The intelligence community collects more than it can process, and it tries to cover issues that, to an outsider, may look secondary or worse. Because of the requirements of security, much that goes on in intelligence is seen by very few. Finally, as noted above, it is important to have a reasonable standard of expectations for intelligence. Intelligence can perform well or poorly on the various issues it covers, but perfect knowledge or warning are not options, especially when dealing with a set of national security interests as broad and diverse as those of the United States.

BIBLIOGRAPHY

Balz, Dan and Bob Woodward. "Ten Days in September," *Washington Post,* January 27-February 3, 2002.

Berkowitz, Bruce and Allen Goodman. *BEST TRUTH: Intelligence in the Information Age.* New Haven, CT: Yale University Press, 2000.

Betts, Richard K. "Fixing Intelligence," *Foreign Affairs,* January/February 2002, vol. 81, no. 4: 43–59.

Cilluffo, Frank J., Ronald A. Marks, and George C. Salmoiraghi. "The Use and Limits of U.S. Intelligence," *The Washington Quarterly,* 25, no. 1, (Winter 2002): 61–74.

Commission on the Roles and Capabilities of the United States Intelligence Community. *Preparing for the 21st Century: An Appraisal of U.S. Intelligence.* Washington, DC: U.S. Government Printing Office, 1996.

Johnson, Loch K. *Bombs, Bugs, Drugs, and Thugs: Intelligence and America's Quest for Security.* New York: New York University Press, 2000.

Lowenthal, Mark M. *Intelligence: From Secrets to Policy.* Washington, DC: Congressional Quarterly Press, 2000.

U.S. Congress. House Permanent Select Committee on Intelligence. *IC21: The Intelligence Community in the 21st Century.* Staff Report. Washington, DC: U.S. Government Printing Office, 1996.

Mark M. Lowenthal

FORGING INTERNATIONAL RULES AGAINST TERRORISM

THE CONFLICT

Since the 1930s there has been an effort to compile international rules against terrorism. Despite the good intentions of the nations to end the threat terrorism poses to the world, there have been obstacles in the path of international agreement, such as the failure to define "terrorism," determining jurisdiction, reserving the right to rebel against oppressors, and the right to self-determination. As the global community responds to the terrorist attacks of September 11, 2001, an intensified effort, and an aggressive resolution, have attempted to force this difficult issue.

Political

- As soon as one identifies a political element in a criminal's behavior, it is very likely that some nation somewhere will sympathize with its perpetrators. This sympathetic nation will then work to prevent mistreatment of the criminal and block the approval of treaties that might criminalize his or her actions. When the goal of the international community is to draft a universally accepted standard of conduct, it only takes one country to block it.

- There was a significant change in the forms of terrorism after the end of the Cold War in the late 1980s. Democracy in many long-embattled regions replaced guerrilla or terrorist warfare. By the mid-1990s, the terrorist groups that remained tended to be more vicious and uncompromising than in the past. Those groups fanatically committed to preserving cultural and social institutions on the basis of a rigid interpretation of religion or ideology seemed to allow no possibility of dialogue or compromise.

[T]he horrifying terrorist attack against the United States sent shock waves throughout the [United Nations] . . . triggering an unprecedented outpouring of sympathy and support for the city and the country, a torrent of condemnation for the conspirators and a groundswell of resolve to bring them to justice. But if the outcry was unprecedented, it was also wholly consistent with the UN's longstanding campaign to amass a legal arsenal in the fight against terrorism . . . (UN News Center, October 6, 2001).

Diplomats and professional staff at the United Nations tend to think that most of the world's problems can be solved by bringing countries together to agree to a common set of rules. Whether it be cleaning up the environment, preventing weapons sales to revolutionaries, or keeping exchange rates stable, many hope that all that is needed is a commitment to create and keep treaty agreements. So it is no surprise that efforts have been made to formulate rules about terrorism.

As far as terrorism goes, this is easier said than done, however. Efforts to put together an international convention against terrorism began in the 1930s, when several countries agreed to a treaty that was only ratified by one of them—the Netherlands—meaning that it was not the "law of the land" anywhere but in the Netherlands. Another attempt was made in the 1970s, only to fail due to disagreements between rich and poor countries. In the 1990s the prospects for another agreement seemed good. After five years, however, disagreements on fundamental issues remain—in spite of the events of September 11 and the "groundswell of resolve" mentioned in the UN quote above—raising the questions: What seems to be holding things back? Why does there not yet exist an international convention on terrorism? Does it matter?

CHRONOLOGY

1937 The League of Nations diplomats sign the Convention for the Suppression of Terrorism.

1960 The UN General Assembly passes a resolution entitled the Declaration on the Granting of Independence to Colonies, Countries and Peoples (1514/XV).

1963 Diplomats in Tokyo sign the Convention on Offenses and Certain Other Acts Committed On Board Aircraft.

1965 The UN General Assembly passes Resolution 2105/XX, urging all states to support movements of national liberation.

1970 Diplomats in the Hague sign the Convention for the Suppression of Unlawful Seizure of Aircraft.

1971 Diplomats in Montreal sign the Convention for the Suppression of Unlawful Acts against the Safety of Civil Aviation, and the UN General Assembly approves the Declaration of Principles of International Law Concerning Friendly Relations Between States.

1972 The United States submits a Draft Convention for the Prevention and Punishment of Certain Acts of International Terrorism to the UN.

September 5, 1972 The "Black September" terrorist group attacks Israeli athletes at the Olympic Games in Munich.

1973 UN diplomats sign the Convention on the Prevention and Punishment of Crimes against Internationally Protected Persons, including Diplomatic Agents.

1976 Israel carries out a commando raid on an airport in Entebbe, Uganda.

1979 UN diplomats sign the International Convention against the Taking of Hostages.

1979 Diplomats in Vienna sign the Convention on the Physical Protection of Nuclear Material.

1988 UN diplomats sign the Protocol for the Suppression of Unlawful Acts of Violence at Airports Serving International Civil Aviation (supplementary to the Hague Convention), while diplomats in Rome sign the Protocol for the Suppression of Unlawful Acts against the Safety of Maritime Navigation and the Protocol for the Suppression of Unlawful Acts against the Safety of Fixed Platforms Located on the Continental Shelf.

1991 Diplomats in Montreal sign the Convention on the Marking of Plastic Explosives for the Purpose of Detection.

1993 A group associated with Ramzi Yousef carries out the first World Trade Center attack.

1996 The UN passes resolution 51/210, establishing four ad-hoc committees to draft international treaties on terrorism.

1997 Suspects in the World Trade Center bombing are convicted in a New York federal court.

1997 UN Diplomats sign the International Convention for the Suppression of Terrorist Bombings and the International Convention for the Suppression of Financing of Terrorism.

1998 The Good Friday accords on Northern Ireland are concluded.

August 7, 1998 U.S. embassies in Kenya and Tanzania are bombed.

September 11, 2001 Terrorists attack sites in New York City and Arlington, Virginia, near Washington, DC, killing more than three thousand people.

2001 The UN Security Council passes Resolution 1373, requiring member states to stop any support or harboring of terrorists and urging states to ratify existing antiterrorism conventions.

2001 A UN General Assembly debate on a new convention on terrorism remains mired in disagreements over scope.

2001 Suspects in the African embassy bombings are tried and convicted in New York.

2001 The IRA agrees to disarm in Northern Ireland.

Criminals and Terrorists

Crime is an essentially domestic matter, and many international rules prevent governments from imposing on each other a particular criminal code. For example, Switzerland has numbered bank accounts and strict rules on depositor confidentiality, much to the consternation of other countries. Meanwhile, the United States carries out death sentences with regularity even though they have been abolished elsewhere in the world.

Where crimes cross international boundaries, as with smuggling and drug trafficking, countries often coordinate their policing efforts. In particular many countries have signed so-called extradition treaties with each other that list crimes for which one country will surrender a suspect to another. So long as the criminal codes of both countries are fairly consistent with each other, these treaties are relatively easy to conclude. Thus, a suspect in a theft or murder in Canada who has fled to New Zealand will likely be turned over to the Canadian government by the New Zealand government.

In many extradition treaties, however, there is an escape clause known as the "political exception" provision. This exempts any crime that is inherently political, such as treason. Crimes are considered political when they only affect the power of one state and represent no real threat to any other. In fact, in some cases the other states may feel sympathy for the suspect if he or she opposes a government with which they have poor relations. For example, rather than return a treason suspect to the Soviet Union during the Cold War, the United States might well have granted him political asylum and treated him as a hero.

The same was true until recently when it came to U.S. relations with Great Britain (Britain, the United Kingdom, or UK). Many American judges interpreted the political exception provision of the U.S.–UK extradition treaty to mean that suspected members of the Irish Republican Army (IRA)—a terrorist group by British standards—need not be returned to Britain. From the British point of view, the United States was harboring terrorists.

Take a classic international crime—piracy. Until the late 1980s piracy was defined as a "private act" aimed at seizing a vessel or money and jewelry from its passengers. Politically motivated piracy was set apart as a separate problem, even if the actions were identical to those that were motivated by greed, according to Malvina Halberstam's *American Journal of International Law* article "Terrorism on the High Seas" (April 1988).

Which brings one to the basic problem of terrorism and international law. In spite of current efforts to treat all terrorism as merely an aggravated form of crime, the fact is that there would be no need for the term "terrorism" if it was merely criminal activity. (The reader may recall how important it was to law enforcement officials to know that the villains in the film *Die Hard* were merely sophisticated thieves and not the terrorists they claimed to be.) Terrorism is universally understood as violent actions intended to instill fear or create havoc with the ultimate aim of changing government policies. Consider the similarity of these definitions of terrorism gleaned from various U.S. government and academic sources, as cited in René Louis Beres's 1995 article "The Meaning of Terrorism: Jurisprudential and Definitional Clarifications," published in the *Vanderbilt Journal of Transnational Law*:

- "The unlawful use of force against persons or property to intimidate or coerce a government, the civilian population, or any segment thereof, in furtherance of political or social objectives . . . "

- "Premeditated, politically motivated violence perpetrated against noncombatant targets by subnational groups or clandestine agents . . . "

- "The unlawful use or threat of violence against persons or property to further political or social objective. It is generally intended to intimidate or coerce a government, individuals or groups or to modify their behavior or policies . . . "

In most cases terrorism is the act of an organized and politically or ideologically motivated group that is expressing its profound dissatisfaction with the order of things, whether it be the occupation of territory by a foreign power, rule of a country by a racial minority, despotic government by a dictatorial regime, or something else. Even where terrorists engage in garden-variety criminal activities, such as theft and drug running, it is oftentimes done to finance their political agenda.

Governments have long treated terrorists differently from criminals. For example, if a terrorist group becomes powerful enough, it might be necessary for a government to negotiate certain concessions, such as granting home rule to an oppressed ethnic group or releasing prisoners from jail. It is hard to imagine a government publicly carving up a piece of its territory and officially turning it over to an organized crime syndicate or street gang (not that it has not happened informally). Most important, if the terrorist group is sincere in its political demands, for example, it is conceivable that it may one day be appeased and cease terror activities. Patrick Henry, Moshe Dayan, Nelson Mandela, and Gerry Adams are among the statesmen who could have been described as terrorists in their earlier days. At this writing, the IRA has agreed to disarm and cooperate with the new joint Catholic and Protestant government of Northern Ireland. The United States has formally endorsed the creation of a Palestinian state, which, if it comes to fruition, will likely be governed by a former terrorist, Yasser Arafat.

Terrorists and Their Allies

As soon as one identifies a political element in a criminal's behavior, it is very likely that some nation somewhere will sympathize with its perpetrators. This sympathetic nation will then work to prevent mistreatment of the criminal and block the approval of treaties that might criminalize his or her actions. If the goal of the international community is to draft a universally accepted standard of conduct, it only takes one country to block it. Thus the problem becomes more clear.

HISTORICAL BACKGROUND

It is important to understand some of the types of terrorist organizations that have received international support and why. Ironically, although some groups are supported simply because they are fighting against a country's enemy, there are also good legal reasons to support terrorist groups.

To begin, during the Cold War many terrorist groups had radical ideological motivations and could therefore count on sympathy from the Soviet Union. The Japanese Red Army Brigade, the German Baader-Meinhoff Gang, and other Marxist/Maoist groups were able to receive diplomatic and logistical support from Soviet bloc countries. For that matter numerous guerrilla groups throughout the third world received direct support and training from both the United States and the Soviet Union. This is not to say that the terrorist acts of these groups were always considered legal. On the contrary, the support was more often than not provided secretly so that the sponsors could deny any link.

Self-Determination

Other groups of terrorists found that international law was at least partly on their side. This was the case for groups that were fighting for the liberation of their country from foreign domination—particularly if the foreigners were from across the sea. As early as 1919, self-determination was part of international law. U.S. President Woodrow Wilson convinced the victors of World War I (1914–18) to accept the notion that each nationality should be able to govern itself without outside interference. This contributed to the dismantling of the Austro-Hungarian and Ottoman empires and the creation of such new states as Hungary, Lithuania, Bulgaria, and Syria. It also led to the "mandates" system of the League of Nations whereby colonial powers agreed to work for the eventual independence of their colonial holdings. The organization, however, ultimately failed.

By the time the United Nations Charter was drafted in 1945, the principle of self-determination had risen to the level of a fundamental right, although it was not always clear what this implied. By the 1960s most Western powers had agreed to begin the systematic dismantling of their overseas empires, and during this decade most of the Asian and African colonies achieved independence peacefully. In 1960 the UN General Assembly passed a resolution entitled the Declaration on the Granting of Independence to Colonies, Countries and Peoples, in which it affirmed the right of all nations to self-determination. Furthermore, it declared that it is the obligation of all states, whether colonial powers or not, to accommodate the will of the people in all circumstances and prohibits the use of force to prevent their independence, if sought. In 1965 a slim majority passed an even stronger resolution, calling upon all states to provide "material and moral assistance to the national liberation movements in colonial territories." Needless to say, this statement went much farther than Western countries were willing to go.

In 1971 the Declaration of Principles of International Law Concerning Friendly Relations Between States included a specific set of provisions on self-determination that garnered near-unanimous approval. Although reiterating the obligations and rights spelled out in the 1960 declaration, the new statement does not specifically allow oppressed groups to use force, nor does it disallow colonial states to utilize force to maintain order. The declaration prohibits states from providing support for groups engaged in civil strife or terrorist acts. By now, however, the door was open for the creation of a special case for violence committed in the name of self-determination. Gradually, that exception was expanded to cover those struggling against foreign occupation (such as the Palestinians) and apartheid (such as the racial segregation system in South Africa).

Taking the Politics Out of Terrorism?

During the 1960s the number of terrorist incidents increased dramatically, involving not only organizations based in the West, but also groups from developing regions operating outside their territorial base. Airplane hijackings and bombings were becoming a common occurrence, culminating in the Black September attack on Israeli athletes at the Munich Olympic Games in 1972.

Even as the debate over the political exceptions to terrorism raged, many nations sought to take whatever steps they could to combat the danger terrorists groups posed. Two key concerns preoccupied these diplomats: how to convince countries to extradite wrongdoers regardless of ideology and politics, and how to ensure their prosecution in the absence of extradition.

Gradually, a strategy evolved centered on identifying specific acts of violence commonly perpetrated by terrorists. Efforts were made to address actions that raised questions of jurisdiction. In international law there were four well-established justifications for a country arresting, prosecuting, and convicting a suspect. First, if the crime was committed in the territory of a particular state, that state could prosecute the suspects, regardless of the nationality of either the suspect or the victim. Thus, a Palestinian attack on Israeli citizens in Germany could be tried by the German government. This is known as the "territoriality principle."

Second, if the suspect is a citizen of a particular country, that country has jurisdiction to try him or her, regardless of where the crime occurred or the nationality of its victims. When a crime takes place in the country of which the suspect is a citizen, there is no international debate. This "nationality principle," however, typically applies when the crime occurs outside the country of which the suspect is a citizen, and therefore requires his or her extradition, as in the case of Irish Republican Army (IRA) terrorists seeking refuge in the United States for crimes committed in Northern Ireland.

Third, the "protective principle" means that when a crime occurs outside of a country's territory, but was intended to disrupt the political stability of that country, then it can request extradition to prosecute the suspects. For example, the apartheid government in South Africa regularly asked neighboring states to hand over African National Congress leaders who had taken refuge there on the grounds that the ANC was planning the overthrow of the Pretoria regime. It should be noted that most of these states responded by giving ANC leaders political asylum, meaning that they were treated as special guests of the state and sheltered from criminal prosecution.

Finally, some crimes are of such character that no clear jurisdiction can be established, or else the crime is of such magnitude that it violates the ba-

A MASKED MEMBER OF BLACK SEPTEMBER APPEARS ON A BALCONY IN THE OLYMPIC VILLAGE WHERE, IN 1972, TERRORISTS TOOK HOSTAGE MEMBERS OF THE ISRAELI OLYMPIC TEAM. *(AP/Wide World Photos/Kurt Strumpf. Reproduced by permission.)*

sic principles of civilization. In either case, it may be possible for a state to prosecute a suspect on the basis of the "universality principle." For example, where a crime occurs on the high seas—where no state has territorial jurisdiction—states may allow the country best equipped to respond to arrest and try the perpetrators. Thus, piracy was one of the first crimes to come under this principle. Most international conventions against terrorism address crimes committed outside ordinary territorial jurisdiction, such as the conventions against airplane hijacking and attacks on oil platforms on the continental shelf. (See sidebar on International Conventions on Terrorism).

After World War II (1939–45), the concept of "crimes against humanity" was established and formed the basis for the prosecution of German Nazis. Since then, any individual suspected of crimes against humanity (most of which occurred in connection with the Holocaust) can be arrested and tried anywhere in the world.

In spite of this variety of coverage, a gap still existed in the rules regarding prosecution. It was determined that new treaties on terrorism should provide jurisdiction to the nation of which the victims of an attack are citizens. This principle was first enshrined in a series of treaties on airplane hijacking

STATUS OF INTERNATIONAL CONVENTIONS PERTAINING TO INTERNATIONAL TERRORISM AS OF SEPTEMBER 11, 2001

Convention	Signatures	Ratifications
1963 Tokyo Convention	41	171
1970 Hague Convention	77	173
1971 Montreal Convention	60	174
1973 Convention on Internationally Protected Persons	25	107
1979 Hostage Convention	39	95
1979 Vienna Convention	45	69
1988 Protocol to the Hague Convention	69	107
1988 Rome Convention on Maritime Navigation	41	52
1988 Protocol on Fixed Platforms	39	48
1991 Plastic Explosives Convention	51	66
1997 Convention on Terrorist Bombings	59	24
1997 Convention on Financing of Terrorism	43	3

TWELVE INTERNATIONAL CONVENTIONS REGARDING TERRORISM WERE FORMULATED BEFORE SEPTEMBER 11, 2001. NOT EVERY COUNTRY, HOWEVER, HAS SIGNED OR RATIFIED THE AGREEMENTS, WHICH LIMITS THEIR EFFECTIVENESS. *(Gale Group.)*

that were concluded in the 1960s and 1970s under the auspices of the International Civil Aviation Organization. In article 4 the 1963 Tokyo Convention declares: "A Contracting State . . . may . . . interfere with an aircraft in flight in order to exercise its criminal jurisdiction over an offense committed on board . . . in the following cases: . . . b) the offense has been committed by or against a national or permanent resident of such State . . . ."

Since then, it has become commonplace for states to take action against terrorists if their own nationals are in danger. The most dramatic example of this is the 1976 Israeli commando raid in Entebbe, Uganda, to rescue Israelis held hostage by Palestinian terrorists. In the case of the bombing by Osama bin Laden's al-Qaeda organization of U.S. embassies in Africa in 1998, local authorities and foreign governments cooperated by capturing and extraditing the suspects to the United States. They were tried in a New York federal court, convicted of numerous offenses, and sentenced to multiple life sentences in 2001. It is likewise generally understood by foreign governments that any Taliban or al-Qaeda operatives captured in Afghanistan in connection with the events of September 11, 2001, can be legitimately prosecuted by U.S. authorities.

Over time, treaties have been concluded on a wide range of terrorist offenses without much effort

given to either define terrorism or consider the root causes of the grievances. As of September 11, 2001, treaties had been concluded on three types of topics: those involving international transportation (maritime conventions, aircraft conventions), those involving specific types of attacks (hostage-taking, bombings, attacks on diplomats, and attacks on nuclear materials), and those involving the means used by terrorists to carry out their attacks (financing and plastic explosives). They fill the gaps often found in extradition treaties that make it difficult for countries to persuade other states to hand over suspects. In most cases the extradition rules of the conventions supersede existing bilateral extradition treaties—in other words, agreements between two states take a back seat to these multilateral agreements.

Domestic Laws v. International Law

A second focus of international antiterror conventions has been filling gaps in domestic law. In some countries actions that might be considered crimes overseas are not criminal. For example, U.S. laws on criminal conspiracies are not found in other countries. Since extradition treaties generally require that the offense in question be a crime under both states' laws, this gap has allowed some suspects to find refuge in spite of extradition treaties.

Antiterrorism treaties often require signatories to change their criminal code to incorporate the offenses listed. For example, under the 1988 Rome Convention on Maritime Navigation, Article 5 states: "Each State party shall make the offenses set forth in Article 3 punishable by appropriate penalties which take into account the grave nature of those offenses." Article 3 lists not only direct acts of violence against ships, but also the provision of false information aimed at endangering the ship, threatening a ship's safety with intent to intimidate, or providing assistance to anyone who does any of the above.

When a state ratifies a convention, it typically takes the steps necessary at that time to alter its domestic law to bring it into compliance with the international rules. Thus, a general provision to alter the criminal code will likely be carried out by the signers even though this may seem to be a lot to ask. As illustrated in the table entitled Status of International Conventions Pertaining to International Terrorism, a very large number of states have signed and ratified most of the antiterrorism conventions—particularly those relating to airplane safety.

With these two gaps plugged it is possible to demand that all states adopt an "extradite or prosecute" policy with respect to terrorists. Essentially, this means that a state harboring a suspected terrorist will not be able to hide behind the lack of an extradition treaty or a gap in domestic law. The hope is to extend a network of such "extradite or prosecute" commitments across topics and across countries until there is no safe haven left.

The Convention on Terrorism

The only thing that remains is to draft a treaty that is comprehensive in its scope in order to cover any terrorist acts that are not mentioned in the existing treaties. As mentioned earlier, this has proved to be extremely difficult.

During the 1970s a serious attempt was made at the UN to draft a comprehensive convention on terrorism. From 1973 until 1979, an ad-hoc committee of the General Assembly gathered periodically to review draft texts and negotiate language. The culmination of the process was a report that demonstrated a profound disagreement on the scope of terrorist crimes. Specifically, a number of states argued that terrorism was inherently political and carried with it important legal justifications in some circumstances. A concerted effort was made to exempt Palestinians fighting Israeli occupation. They hoped to include the type of language that made its way into the Hostage Convention's Article 12: " . . . [T]he present Convention shall not apply to an act of hostage-taking committed in the course of armed conflicts . . . in which people are fighting against colonial domination and alien occupation and against racist regimes in the exercise of their right of self-determination . . . "

This language is limited by the rules of the Geneva Conventions, which allow prosecution of war criminals (including hostage-takers), but represents the high-water mark of the supporters of national liberation movements, says Wil D. Verwey in the January 1981 *American Journal of International Law* article, "The International Hostages Convention and National Liberation Movements." Although the language was permitted in the Hostages Convention, the West objected to including it in an all-encompassing terrorism convention, and after a time the best the delegates could do was to agree to disagree.

Second, many developing countries have wanted to include state-sponsored terrorism as it pertains to repressive acts by governments against minorities or indigenous populations. Their argument is that far greater violence is done in the world in the name of existing states by soldiers and policemen than is done by terrorists in the name of political movements. Needless to say, the West has never wanted to include this type of behavior in conventions, mostly on the ground that humanitarian law already prohibits abuse of legal authority (note the treaties on genocide, torture, civil and political rights, and so forth).

In addition, many countries wanted to force other states to provide a once-and-for-all definition of "terrorism" in the hope that this would open up a debate on the causes of terrorism and the nature of justice in the world. Again, the West was not interested in such an exercise, which would consume a tremendous amount of time and was more than likely doomed to failure. Thus, no formal treaty was concluded.

International Resolutions and the End of the Cold War

During the next few years, the UN General Assembly passed a number of resolutions on terrorism. Although not treaties, these statements give some indication of the mood and opinion of the body and may ultimately guide the development of new laws. Common to these new resolutions was an agreement to criminalize terrorism and to specifically prevent terrorists from using political motive as an excuse, according to Ross Schreiber in his 1998 *Boston University International Law Journal* article "Ascertaining Opinio Juris of States Concerning Norms Involving the Prevention of International Terrorism."

SOME GROUPS PREFER TO TURN IN THEIR GUNS AND EFFECT CHANGE THROUGH THE BALLOT RATHER THAN CONTINUE WITH TERRORISM. THIS WAS THE CASE FOR THE CONTRA GUERRILLAS IN NICARAGUA, WHO, IN EXCHANGE FOR THEIR DISARMAMENT, RECEIVED A RETURN OF THEIR CIVILIAN STATUS. *(AP/Wide World Photos/Anita Baca. Reproduced by permission.)*

It is a bit unclear why these resolutions were successfully passed, since they were approved by countries that have since opposed this language. It is clear that international conditions and principles were evolving. The Soviet Union reversed its policy of supporting national liberation movements beginning in 1986, and by 1987 was openly critical of them. This left numerous groups without a key outside sponsor. In addition, as the Cold War climate began to thaw, it became possible for the United States to withdraw from many parts of the developing world where it had supported guerrillas and terrorists, including Central America, Afghanistan, and much of Sub-Saharan Africa. The result was the isolation of many terrorist groups, on the one hand, and the gradual emergence of democratic regimes on the other.

Where grievances had some legal basis, many groups began to find they could use the ballot rather than the bullet to achieve their ends. Note for example, the Contra guerrillas, operating in and around Nicaragua with U.S. support, disbanded as part of the Central American peace process and turning instead to campaigning in the next election, which they won. Likewise, the IRA has gradually turned away from terrorism with the loss of Soviet sponsorship and instead has pursued a negotiated settlement, culminating in the Good Friday Accords in 1998, and the establishment of a joint Catholic and Protestant government. The IRA finally announced its decision to disarm in late 2001. Most significant was the conclusion of the 1993 Oslo Accords through which Yasser Arafat and the Palestine Liberation Organization officially renounced terrorism and recognized the right of Israel to exist in peace. This led to the agreement on Israel's part to withdraw troops from numerous parts of the occupied West Bank and Gaza Strip and yield control of a few towns to the newly created Palestinian Authority. While the peace process has encountered very serious obstacles since then, the fact of the matter is that the PLO is no longer considered a terrorist organization. Finally, with the collapse of the Soviet Union, dozens of nationalities were able to secure their own state, thus resolving long-standing grievances in several regions. The number of non-self-governing territories had dwindled to a mere handful.

Terrorists of the 1990s

By the mid-1990s the terrorist groups that remained tended to be more vicious and uncompromising than in the past. Some were still traditional guerrilla-type movements with aspirations to power, such as the various groups operating in Kashmir to overturn Indian rule or the Maoist

Shining Path guerrillas in Peru that hoped to overthrow that regime in time. Still others are more clearly criminal in nature, such as the "narco-terrorist" groups in Colombia that operate like oversized street gangs.

Some groups are fanatically committed to preserving cultural and social institutions on the basis of a rigid interpretation of religion or ideology, and there appears to be no possibility of dialogue or compromise with them. Islamic extremists, in particular, have gained notoriety not only for their acts of violence and political destabilization but also for the attacks they have made against Western targets all over the world. Various extremist groups have been responsible for the assassination of Egyptian president Anwar Sadat (1918–81), ethnic cleansing in Afghanistan, bombings in Africa, and (apparently) the attacks on the United States in New York City and Arlington, Virginia, on September 11, 2001. The threat these groups pose to both developed and less-developed states has contributed to an increase in international cooperation to fight terror.

At the close of the Fifty-first General Assembly session in 1996, a resolution was passed that created a committee of all the UN's members to draft a convention on terrorism. At that time, proposals were put forward to draft treaties on four topics: financing of terrorism, terrorist bombings, preventing nuclear terrorism, and a general antiterrorism convention. Various countries drew up draft agreements, and within two years the UN negotiators were able to agree on language on the first two topics. A convention on nuclear weapons was also nearly completed, although the negotiations stalled on whether to address the question of states' use and possession of nuclear material. This treaty is still not complete.

India's 1997 Draft Text

Meanwhile, India put forward a draft text for the comprehensive convention on terrorism in 1997 in an effort to push things forward. The draft is inspired by what was becoming common language across the four conventions. In particular, it includes a now-standard phrase: "Reaffirming their unequivocal condemnation of all acts, methods and practices of terrorism as criminal and unjustifiable, wherever and by whomever committed..." (Preamble: India draft) Article 5 states:

Each State Party shall adopt such language as may be necessary, including, where appropriate, domestic legislation, to ensure that criminal acts within the scope of this Convention are under no circumstances justifiable by considerations of a political, philosophical, racial, ethnic, religious or other similar nature.

Such language is designed to force governments to commit to the criminalization of acts of terrorism once and for all—a high priority for Western countries in particular. It should be noted that India has a special concern for this topic because of its struggle against violent Kashmiri separatists, whom it brands terrorists.

Article 2 of the draft convention lists the crimes covered under the scope of the convention. They include the infliction of bodily injury or death to people, as well as damage to government property or public facilities, "when the purpose of such act, by its nature or context, is to intimidate a population, or to compel a Government or an international organization to do or abstain from doing any act." In addition, as seen in other treaties, anyone who attempts but fails to commit such an act, or aids and abets someone else in committing such an act, is guilty of terrorism.

This sweeping language seems to be exactly what the West is seeking, and, based on author interviews with UN diplomats in October 2001, the convention is in fact very popular among most governments (based on author interviews with UN diplomats, October 2001). Article 11, for example, provides for the "extradite or prosecute" rule whereby the suspect must face justice. Article 14 makes it clear that states may not apply the "political exception" rule when deciding whether to extradite someone. Article 18 clearly exempts the armed forces from prosecution under the terrorism convention on the grounds that other treaties already cover their actions.

The convention has not yet passed muster with most Arab states. In an effort to appease them, but without losing the support of Western powers, the Indian delegation inserted a number of carefully worded escape clauses. For example, Article 15 allows a government to refuse to extradite a suspect if it has a reasonable fear that the individual will be treated unfairly on the basis of his or her race, religion, political opinion, and so forth. Pakistan, for example, knows the whereabouts of many Kashmiri rebels, but chooses not to arrest or extradite them to India on these grounds. This is similar to the granting of political asylum. Most important, however, is the wording of Article 21 of the draft:

Nothing in the Convention shall affect other rights, obligations and responsibilities of States and individuals under international law, in particular the purposes of the Charter of the United Nations, international humanitarian law and other relevant conventions.

As the Indian diplomat who crafted the draft explained to the author, this article was designed to provide special treatment, if so desired, for those

UNITED NATIONS SUPPORT IN THE WAKE OF SEPTEMBER 11

On the day after the heinous September 11 terrorist attacks in Washington and New York, the General Assembly of the United Nations, by consensus of the 189 member states, called for international cooperation to prevent and eradicate acts of terrorism and to hold accountable the perpetrators and those who harbor or support them. That same day, the United Nations Security Council unanimously determined, for the first time ever, any act of international terrorism to be a threat to international peace and security. This determination laid the foundation for Security Council action to bring together the international community under a common set of obligations in the fight to end international terrorism.

On September 28, 2001, the Security Council unanimously adopted resolution 1373 under Chapter VII of the Charter of the United Nations. This historic resolution established a body of legally binding obligations on all UN member states. It defined the common core of the new international campaign to deal with international terrorists, their organizations, and those who support them.

Its provisions require, among other things, that all member states prevent the financing of terrorism and deny safe haven to terrorists. States will need to review and strengthen their border security operations, banking practices, customs and immigration procedures, law enforcement and intelligence cooperation, and arms transfer controls. All states are called upon to increase cooperation and share pertinent information with respect to these efforts. Resolution 1373 also mandated that each state report on the steps it had taken, and established a committee of the Security Council to monitor implementation. The committee will highlight best practices, identify gaps, and help coordinate advice and assistance to states that need it.

Full implementation of resolution 1373 will require each UN member state to take specific measures to combat terrorism. Most states will have to make changes in their laws, regulations, and practices. Those with the capacity to assist in these changes will be needed to help those who lack the expertise and resources to achieve full implementation.

"Report to the United Nations Security Council Counterterrorism Committee pursuant to paragraph 6 of Security Council resolution 1373 of 28 September 2001 Implementation of UNSCR 1373." December 19, 2001. Available online at http://www.fas.org/irp/threat/unsc.html (cited February 1, 2002).

who are fighting for self-determination, since this right is enshrined in numerous UN conventions and treaties. Such is the subtlety of international law!

The Process Stalls

As it turns out, the device did not work. At a session in early 2001, countries representing the Organization of the Islamic Conference (OIC) submitted a proposal to add a clause similar to Article 12 of the Hostages Convention. The proposal found very little support, but quickly became a "deal breaker" for the OIC, meaning that none of its members would approve the convention without the language in question being added. They also sought to remove the exemption for organized military forces. They stated, as did one Arab diplomat to the author, that those who live in occupied territories should be allowed to take up arms under an inherent right of rebellion just as the French did when under Nazi occupation during World War II. If the soldiers of the occupying army commit atrocities, why should this not be considered terrorism, and why shouldn't the foreign soldiers be prosecuted?

Numerous other minor amendments—over thirty in all—were on the agenda by the time the Fifty-sixth UN General Assembly was scheduled to open—on September 12, 2001.

RECENT HISTORY AND THE FUTURE

September 11, 2001, and International Law

On September 11, 2001, the terrorist attacks that took place in the United States "shook the United Nations" as well as the United States. New York's World Trade Center was less than three miles from UN headquarters, and most UN diplomats have many friends and acquaintances throughout the city. Many were personally affected by the tragedy. Secretary-General Kofi Annan labeled the event an attack on all humanity, and said that as such all humanity had a stake in finding the terrorists and bringing them to justice.

The September 11 attacks created a brand-new political climate. Both the Security Council and the General Assembly suspended business in order to issue a condemnation of the attack in the strongest language. The Security Council passed a resolution that described the attack as an act of aggression and authorized the United States to take whatever measures it saw fit to retaliate. In the days following the attack, members of the Council assured the United States that its plans to launch an attack against the Taliban regime and al-Qaeda organization in Afghanistan were consistent with the meaning of that resolution. The attack also prompted Syria, the Palestinian Authority, Iran, and other some-time supporters of terrorism to issue a formal condemnation.

It was in this environment that the United States moved to draft and pass the little-noticed Security Council resolution 1373 on September 28, 2001. It is no doubt the most powerful legal instrument on terrorism ever, and its passage represents one of the most deft diplomatic maneuvers ever executed by the United States.

Resolution 1373 targets terrorism quickly and unflinchingly. It ignores the question of defining terrorism or even terrorist acts, let alone considering political motives. It simply declares that any act like the September 11 bombings is a "threat to international peace and security" activating "the inherent right of individual or collective self-defense." This means that terrorism is an act of war and any state can retaliate militarily. Furthermore, the resolution requires all countries, under penalty of unspoken sanctions, to fight terrorism by ferreting out suspects and cutting off their funds and protection, not to mention ratifying all existing anti-terror treaties, all within ninety days. To ensure that these measures were carried out, a small committee was quickly established to monitor compliance.

In the following week, nearly every country took the microphone to speak about terrorism during a special UN meeting. Governments either specifically endorsed 1373 or were simply silent. Although a few complained later that there should have been wider consultation, only Zimbabwe expressed strong doubts about the resolution's legitimacy. Privately, most governments expressed relief that the United States was taking on al-Qaeda and the Taliban and only feared that it would stop short of completing the job.

A well-known principle in international law states that so long as no one objects to a legal claim, the claim stands. With respect to new international rules, the lack of objection also gives the rule *prima facie* (true at first appearance) validity. Beres notes that it is also true that in spite of the diplomatic support given to national liberation fronts in principle, there has always been a sense that certain violent actions against innocent victims could not be justified by any political motivation.

In early 2002 it seems the new rule was having a dramatic effect. Fidel Castro recently announced Cuba's intent to ratify all existing anti-terrorism conventions, in accordance with UN injunctions. Syria has made a similar pledge. China,

Russia, and the United States are seeing a renaissance; their usually strained relationships with one another improved thanks to unity on the terror issue. The vast majority of countries is moving quickly to comply with resolution 1373. As a gesture of good will, the United States is paying all of its back dues to the UN. It would seem a new day has dawned.

Interestingly enough, the ad-hoc committee tasked with drafting the comprehensive antiterrorism convention held its meetings in October 2001. It was clear that all the delegates felt a sense of urgency about the task at hand. Many delegations simply withdrew their earlier suggestions for amendment of the India draft on the grounds that the concerns were not significant. It is likely that they, as well as the UN staff members overseeing the negotiations, recognized that much of the work of the committee had been mooted by the Security Council's action. Because Resolution 1373 is binding, it takes on a legal status similar to a ratified convention for the UN's members. Because the subject matter of 1373 overlaps the draft conventions, many delegations felt there was simply no point in haggling over the details the treaty.

This was not the case with the OIC, however, whose members have persisted in their insistence that national liberation fronts and those fighting foreign occupation have special recognition. In spite of appeals from the secretary-general and almost all UN members, the OIC blocked adoption of a consensus document. The result is that the treaty has been simply forwarded to the General Assembly as a report. The debate has been carried over to the year 2002.

Implications and Unanswered Questions

How does all of this reflect on the war on terrorism and the place of international law? Fundamentally, it has become clear that, as former Speaker of the House Tip O'Neill used to say, "it's hard to take the politics out of politics." Terrorism is a concept, much like "assassination," that is meaningful because of its political dimension. While it is relatively easy to draft conventions to facilitate international regulation of purely criminal actions, as soon as there is a political element, there is often also someone for whom the language of a treaty is a matter of great importance—even a matter of national survival.

The West has been successful recently in persuading other states to accept the criminalization of terrorism. It has been aided in this by the end of the Cold War, decolonization, democratization, and the changing face of terror. This said, it is clear

A BRITISH SOLDIER PASSES A SINN FÉIN ELECTION CAR IN BELFAST. WHILE THE CONFLICT IN NORTHERN IRELAND ACHIEVED A POLITICAL RESOLUTION, IT IS RARE FOR TERRORISTS AND TERRORIST GROUPS TO BECOME ACCEPTED BY LEGITIMATELY RECOGNIZED GOVERNMENTS AND STATESMEN. *(AP/Wide World Photos/Paul McErlane. Reproduced by permission.)*

that in spite of this, the basic principle of self-determination is alive and well. This is clear even in the way the anti-Taliban or anti-al-Qaeda coalition has been formed. Since September 11, both India and Russia have been unable to achieve global support for labeling their long-time enemies—the Kashmiris and Chechens, respectively—as terrorists, but instead have been urged to negotiate a political settlement that honors their rights. In the Middle East, the United States and the rest of the world have put increasing pressure on Israel to withdraw from occupied territories as part of concerted drive to a lasting peace in the region. The North

Atlantic Treaty Organization (NATO) and the United Nations continue to maintain a presence in such areas as Kosovo and East Timor precisely to protect the rights of the inhabitants to self-government against the wishes of larger neighbors.

It is unlikely that the UN will ever be given the task of apprehending terrorists directly. At this point the only part of the UN that deals with terrorism is a very small UN Terrorism Prevention Branch based in Vienna, Austria, that was formed in 1999. It has roughly ten professional staff members and is devoting its time to collecting suggestions from governments on what has worked for them. It is significant that the antiterrorism unit is a part of the Center for International Crime Prevention since this reinforces the criminalization model.

It has been said that the fight for peace and the fight for justice are rarely fought in tandem. That is to say, one can maintain injustice by force and thereby create the illusion of peace, but more often than not the oppressed will find it necessary to violate the peace in order to achieve justice. You, the reader, may want to ask yourself which should come first.

BIBLIOGRAPHY

Annan, Kofi. "Fighting Terrorism on a Global Front," *New York Times,* A27, September 21, 2001.

Beres, Rene Louis. "The Meaning of Terrorism: Jurisprudential and Definitional Clarifications," *Vanderbilt Journal of Transnational Law* 28 (1995): pp. 239–250.

Crenshaw, Martha. *Terrorism and International Cooperation.* New York: Institute for East-West Security Studies, 1989.

Dean, Benjamin P. "Self-Setermination and U.S. Support of Insurgents: A Policy-Analysis Model," *Military Law Review* 122 (1988): pp. 149–220.

Halberstam, Malvina. "Terrorism on the High Seas: The Aquille Lauro, Piracy and the IMO Convention on Maritime Safety," *American Journal of International Law* 82, no. 2 (April 1988): pp. 269–310.

Morris, Virginia, and M.Christiane Bourloyannis-Vrailas. "The Work of the Sixth Committee at the Fifty-Third Session of the UN General Assembly," *American Journal of International Law* 93 (July 1999): pp. 722–732.

Paust, Jordan J. "Human Rights and Human Wrongs: Establishing a Jurisprudential Foundation for a Right to Violence," *Emory Law Journal* 32 (Spring 1983): pp. 545–581.

Petersen, Antje C. "Extradition and the Political Offense Exception in the Suppression of Terrorism," *Indiana Law Journal* 67 (Summer 1992): pp. 767–795.

Phillips, R. Stuart. "The Political Offense Exception and Terrorism: Its Place in the Current Extradition Scheme and Proposals for Its Future," *Dickinson Journal of International Law* 15 (Winter 1997): pp. 337–359.

Rosenstock, Robert. "The Declaration of Principles of International Law Concerning Friendly Relations: A Survey," *American Journal of International Law* 65, no. 4 (October 1971): pp. 713–735.

Schreiber, Ross. "Ascertaining Opinio Juris of States Concerning Norms Involving the Prevention of International Terrorism: A Focus on the UN Process," *Boston University International Law Journal* 16 (Spring 1998): pp. 309–330.

Szasz, Paul C. "The Irresistible Force of Self-Determination Meets the Impregnable Fortress of Territorial Integrity: A Cautionary Fairy Tail About Clashes in Kosovo and Elsewhere," *Georgia Journal of International and Comparative Law* 28 (Fall 1999): pp. 8,955–8,961.

Verwey, Wil D. "The International Hostages Convention and National Liberation Movements," *American Journal of International Law* 75 (January 1981): pp. 69–92.

Kendall W. Stiles

Osama bin Laden—A Face of Terrorism

The Conflict

In the 1990s Osama bin Laden and his organization al-Qaeda declared war against the United States and have been behind many of the worst terrorist acts of the last decade. On September 11, 2001, when hijackers flew passenger airliners into the World Trade Center and the Pentagon buildings, killing thousands of civilians, bin Laden was almost immediately named the number one suspect by the United States. His organization, operating in secret cells throughout the world, is a difficult enemy to fight, and bin Laden's whereabouts remained unknown in the months after the attack.

Political
- After the war in Afghanistan against the Soviet Union, a powerful new radical Islamic movement was launched, directed specifically against certain political entities, such as Western powers.

Economic
- Since bin Laden has consciously broadened his message to appeal to the poor and alienated, many of whom are furious with what they see as U.S. imperialism, he has attracted significant numbers of devotees all over the world.

Religious
- Bin Laden declared war on the United States and its people in 1996 and 1998 respectively. When Saudi Arabia invited U.S. troops into the Arabian Peninsula in 1991, bin Laden had increased his anti-Western activities, leading to the "war" declaration.

- Osama bin Laden invokes his own concept of *jihad*—in most interpretations of the Qur'an considered either a reform movement from within or a call to defend Muslim peoples against aggression—by calling for all Muslims to kill any and all Americans. Most Muslims find bin Laden's call for violence to run entirely counter to the teachings of the Qur'an and the religion of Islam.

On September 11, 2001, the United States came under terrorist attack. Two hijacked commercial airplanes were flown into the north and south towers of the World Trade Center in New York City; a third plane was flown into the Pentagon in Arlington, Virginia, near Washington, DC; and a fourth plane crashed in a Pennsylvania field. Less than two hours after the first plane hit, the twin towers of the World Trade Center collapsed. It was the single most deadly terrorist attack in history, killing thousands of people.

As people across the nation and around the world struggled to come to grips with what had happened, the question of who was responsible for the attack arose. While government officials and the media tried not to immediately cast blame, keeping in mind the erroneous early speculation in 1995 that the bombing of the Oklahoma City federal building was the work of terrorists of Middle Eastern origin, one name was consistently raised in suspicion—Osama bin Laden. (Arabic terms and names are rendered in a number of different ways in English. The transliterations here are those most commonly used in the major American news media.)

There were few terrorist organizations in the world that had the resources or the sophistication to pull off the attacks of September 11. Bin Laden's network, al-Qaeda, was the one viewed as most capable of doing so, either on its own or in conjunction with other organizations. Bin Laden, a native of Saudi Arabia, was already viewed as the world's most dangerous—and elusive—terrorist at the dawn of the twenty-first century. Whatever role he and his closest lieutenants might have played in the events of September 11, bin Laden has been involved in many of the major terrorist incidents of the last decade. An examination of his life and career will provide us with valuable insights into the

CHRONOLOGY

1957 Osama bin Laden is born in Riyadh, Saudi Arabia.

1979 The Soviet Union invades Afghanistan and war begins. Osama bin Laden travels to Pakistan to join in the fight against the Soviets.

Early 1980s Tens of thousands of Muslims from over fifty countries arrive in Afghanistan and join the *mujahideen,* the Afghan warriors, in their battle against the Soviets.

1987 Bin Laden meets members of the Egyptian Jihad group, including one of its leaders, Ayman al-Zawahiri, who would go on to help bin Laden lead al-Qaeda in international acts of terrorism.

1989 Bin Laden forms his organization, later dubbed al-Qaeda, or "the base."

1989 The Soviet Union withdraws from Afghanistan in defeat. Bin Laden returns to Saudi Arabia.

August 2, 1990 Iraq invades Kuwait, the Saudis and other moderate Arab states join in the international coalition, and Saudi Arabia allows American troops on its soil, enraging bin Laden and thousands of others.

1991 Saudi officials arrest bin Laden for smuggling weapons in from Yemen. He leaves the country, ending up in Sudan.

December 1992 Bin Laden supports fighters in the war among tribes in Somalia to interfere with the U.S. rescue mission there. They shoot down American helicopters and kill U.S. marines.

1993 A man linked to bin Laden and al-Qaeda, Ramzi Ahmad Yousef, bombs the World Trade Center for the first time, killing six and wounding more than 1,000.

1994 In what becomes known as the "Bojinka Plot," al-Qaeda is suspected of plotting multiple airliner hijackings in the Philippines.

1994 In Saudi Arabia strips bin Laden of his citizenship, and the United States and other governments freeze some of his bank accounts.

1996 Al-Qaeda is suspected of carrying out an attack on a U.S. base at Dhahran, Saudi Arabia, in which 19 U.S. military personnel are killed and 372 wounded.

1996 Bin Laden moves to Afghanistan; he issues his first "fatwa" urging Muslims to kill American officials.

1998 Bin Laden's second fatwa states that "to kill Americans and their allies—civilians and military—is an individual duty for every Muslim who can do it in any country in which it is possible to do it."

1998 Al-Qaeda is the prime suspect in the bombings of the U.S. embassies in Kenya and Tanzania, in which hundreds are killed. President Bill Clinton orders missile strikes against al-Qaeda training camps in Afghanistan.

October 15, 1999 The United Nations demands that the Taliban extradite Osama bin Laden to a country that will bring him to justice and the Afghan regime refuses.

September 11, 2001 Terrorists hijack U.S. passenger airliners and fly them into the World Trade Center and the Pentagon; another hijacked plane crashes in Pennsylvania. Over 3,000 are killed in the attack. The United States accuses Osama bin Laden and asks the Taliban to give him up or face retribution. The Taliban refuses to give up bin Laden.

October 7, 2001 The United States and Britain begin a military strike against the Taliban and al-Qaeda forces in Afghanistan.

hidden, murky world of the terrorist at the dawn of this new century and new millennium.

Qualifying terms like "alleged" appear throughout this article because it is difficult to definitively know exactly what bin Laden and his associates in al-Qaeda have done. Most Western observers see his hand in everything discussed here and many incidents have been confirmed. Others—especially outside the West—consider him to be innocent of all these charges and a hero for his

willingness to stand up to the United States. This article is based on the best information available in the West.

HISTORICAL BACKGROUND

The Making of a Terrorist

Osama bin Laden was born in 1957 in Riyadh, Saudi Arabia. His father, Mohammed, had been raised in Yemen, and moved to Saudi Arabia for

OSAMA BIN LADEN, A SAUDI EXILE, IS LEADER OF THE AL-QAEDA TERRORIST NETWORK. HE HAS BEEN LINKED TO NUMEROUS TERRORIST ATTACKS, INCLUDING THOSE OF SEPTEMBER 11, 2001. *(AP/Wide World Photos. Reproduced by permission.)*

business reasons. There he gained the backing of the Saudi royal family and became quite wealthy as the head of one of Saudi Arabia's largest construction firms. As is typical in the region, Mohammed bin Laden took several wives, and Osama was born to one of the least respected of them. His mother, a Syrian woman, divorced Mohammed bin Laden during Osama's youth and later married someone else. She always stayed close to Osama, however, and is known to have visited him in Afghanistan in 2001.

Even though Osama bin Laden was the seventeenth of a reported fifty children his father parented, he still inherited an estimated US$250 to $300 million when his father died in 1967. The estate was divided up and parceled out as shares of the very prosperous family business, which continued to thrive and grow under the eldest brother's management.

Accounts of bin Laden's life say that as a young man he joined in drunken parties (a violation of Islamic principles) with members of the royal family when they were abroad. His father was a stern parent and devoted Wahhabist Muslim, and Osama later attributed his own religious ardor to his father's influence. Additionally, he became a devout Muslim and a firm believer in the Palestinian and other Arabic causes when he was about twenty

years of age and a student at King Abdul Aziz University in Jedda, Saudi Arabia. There he became associated with an Islamic group called the Muslim Brotherhood and learned of the *jihadist* movement, a radical way of interpreting the Muslim concept of a holy war as an offensive international strike against all the perceived enemies of Islam. Bin Laden graduated from the university with a degree in economics and public administration in 1981.

The War with the Soviets in Afghanistan

While he was in school, bin Laden had become deeply influenced by one of his teachers, the Palestinian sheik Abdullah Azzam. Azzam was one of the first Palestinians to move to Pakistan to support Afghans fighting against the Soviet invasion of their country, which had begun at the end of 1979. Bin Laden followed his mentor to Pakistan. At first, bin Laden had a minor role in Azzam's Maktab al-Khidamat (MAK or Services Office). Ostensibly, the MAK raised money and volunteers for Islamic causes, but, in fact, it was used to recruit volunteers and raise money for the Afghan struggle.

Those were very different political times than ours. The United States supported the Afghan rebels because Cold War logic led Washington to back anyone taking on the Soviet Union. To that end, it allowed the MAK to set up recruiting offices in the United States in addition to those it established in the Middle East. Almost certainly with U.S. funding, the MAK helped set up training bases in both Pakistan and Afghanistan. There are also reports that the United States funded and may well have helped train bin Laden and his colleagues. By the early 1980s the MAK had built a network that brought thousands of Muslims (estimates range from 25,000 to 50,000) from over fifty countries to join the *mujahideen*, the Afghan "holy warriors," in their battle against the Soviets. These Arabs who traveled to Afghanistan to fight the Soviets were called Afghan Arabs. Peter L. Bergen, a bin Laden biographer and expert on terrorism, observes in his 2001 book *Holy War, Inc.* that the Afghan Arabs were not the major players in the Soviet-Afghan war, but that a new movement was fomenting among them in Afghanistan: " . . . [I]n the grand scheme of things, the Afghan Arabs were no more than extras in the Afghan holy war. It was the lessons they learned from the *jihad*, rather than their contribution to it, that proved significant. . . . . Those who had had their tickets punched in the Afghan conflict went back to their home countries with the ultimate credential for later holy wars. And they believed their exertions had defeated a superpower."

THE BIN LADEN FAMILY

Osama bin Laden comes from a large family—one that has not been connected with terrorism and has established its family-run business as one of the most successful in the Middle East. Mohammed bin Laden, Osama's father, was born in a poor neighborhood of Yemen. In 1930 he traveled to Saudi Arabia in search of work and new opportunities. His first employment in Saudi Arabia was with Aramco, a Saudi-American oil company. He worked there as a laborer, saving what he could of his meager wages, enough to eventually strike out on his own as a business owner.

Mohammed bin Laden became the premier builder of palaces for the Saudi royal family. He became very wealthy through his construction business, and was truly a self-made man. Bin Laden's construction business was the sole contractor in the building and restoration of Islam's second holiest site, the city of Medina and the al-Asqa mosque in Jerusalem, constructed to better serve those on pilgrimages. Bin Laden's company became the exclusive construction contractor of the Saudi royal family, and bin Laden was so wealthy that he assisted the Saudi royal family during times of financial difficulty.

Bin Laden had multiple wives, as allowed under Saudi law—three Saudi wives remained married to him throughout his life. The position of bin Laden's fourth wife was less permanent. Osama bin Laden's mother, Hamida, was one of the many wives that followed the first three. It is not known whether she was the eleventh or twelfth wife. She was unusual in comparison to his other wives. The first three "permanent" wives were all Saudi and all were members of the same devout sect of Sunni Islam as Mohammed bin Laden. Hamida was the daughter of a Syrian trader and was more Western and modern in her attitude and dress. Although Mohammed bin Laden has many former wives, they were allowed to remain in his palaces.

Mohammed bin Laden died in a helicopter crash in 1968. Although Hamida had a lower status in comparison with bin Laden's other wives—partially due to her nationality—and despite Osama being bin Laden's seventeenth son (a relatively low rank regarding inheritance and standing within the family), Osama bin Laden grew up with all of the privileges afforded to a wealthy man's son: Western-style education, expensive cars, fine clothes, and jewelry.

Although the bin Laden family is Muslim, and many members are fundamentalists—meaning they strictly adhere to the tenets of their faith—none of them (with the exception of Osama and possibly a brother) were extremists in their beliefs. Extremism in terms of religion often means that one takes tenets of faith to such an extreme that they form an ideology under which the believer may feel society should be governed. Osama bin Laden's extremism is in contrast to his mother, who was known to be loose in her adherence to Islam, refusing to wear a veil and embracing a Western lifestyle. Bin Laden's family disowned him as a result of his growing reputation as an extremist and a threat to Saudi Arabia due to his fervent opposition to the presence of U.S. troops in the area prior to the Gulf War (1991). The bin Laden family was content to maintain its business ties within Saudi Arabia and around the world rather than promote an extreme view of religion, society, and government that they likely did not believe in.

Today the bin Laden family is still very wealthy and successful. The bin Laden family owns the franchises on several popular brands in the Middle East, including Audi and Snapple. The family currently earns US$5 billion a year, and its empire runs the gamut from the original construction business of Mohammed bin Laden to financial services and biological research. Its businesses are multinational and include ties to the United States.

In the war against the Soviets, bin Laden first worked in areas in which his professional expertise with construction and heavy equipment—not to mention his millions of dollars—was most useful. In the early years of the war, he took trips back and forth from Pakistan to Saudi Arabia, raising money for the Afghans. He also brought in construction equipment and set up a hostel for men coming into Afghanistan to help fight the Soviets.

By 1986 bin Laden, who was living in Pakistan, had set up his own training camp in Afghanistan near the village of Jaji. In 1987 the Soviets attacked this base. Bin Laden and about fifty Arabs with him were outnumbered and endured nearly a week of siege before withdrawing. Bin Laden was becoming known as a hero. That year he met some members of the Egyptian Islamic Jihad group, including one of its leaders, Ayman al-Zawahiri, a

THOUGH HE DOES NOT HAVE THE SUPPORT OF MOST IN THE MUSLIM AND ARAB WORLDS, OSAMA BIN LADEN DOES HAVE FOLLOWERS WHO AGREE WITH HIS ANTI-WESTERN, ISLAMIC EXTREMIST VIEWS. *(AP/Wide World Photos/Athar Hussain. Reproduced by permission.)*

physician. Bin Laden and Zawahiri together planned to continue the holy war after the Soviets left Afghanistan and to export terrorism on an international basis. In 1989 bin Laden formed his organization, which later became known as al-Qaeda, or "the base." His earlier mentor, Azzam, who was focused primarily on the Afghan conflict, was killed by a car bomb in Peshawar, Pakistan, in 1989. The Soviets withdrew from Afghanistan in defeat around that time, and bin Laden, who split with Azzam ideologically by looking to more international concepts of jihad, chose to return to Saudi Arabia to work in the family business, seemingly putting an end to his political career, though not for long.

On August 2, 1990, Iraq invaded neighboring Kuwait and seemed poised to move on into Saudi Arabia. The Saudis and other moderate Arab states joined in the international coalition that was to win the Gulf War (1991) six months later. Saudi Arabia allowed American troops on its soil, a move that enraged bin Laden and thousands of other veterans of the Afghan and Palestinian struggles. How, they asked, could troops from the world's strongest supporter of Israel be allowed to set foot on sacred Muslim land? Bin Laden, who had worked closely with the U.S. Central Intelligence Agency during the Afghan conflict, joined those who came to see the United States as the greatest enemy of Islam. Since then, he has allegedly led al-Qaeda in a series of attacks on U.S. targets.

Al-Qaeda

In the late 1980s, bin Laden and some of his colleagues, notably in the Egyptian Islamic Jihad (which had masterminded the 1981 assassination of President Anwar Sadat) came together to form al-Qaeda, a word that means "the base." The organization's stated goal is to create a united movement of radical Islamic groups throughout the Muslim world. Among other things, it has vowed to expel non-Muslims from Muslim countries and to overthrow Muslim leaders it believes to have violated the key beliefs of Islam. Four years after it formed, the organization began preparing itself to conduct terrorist activities.

Al-Qaeda is not a single organization, but a network of cells and other bodies, some of which are very close to bin Laden, some of which are not. Several observers have compared al-Qaeda to a modern-day holding company that owns many businesses. According to the best evidence, bin Laden sits at the head of a council (*majlis al shura*) that, in turn, supervises three main committees that focus on religious policy, military affairs, and fundraising.

The key to al-Qaeda is its cells. Because secrecy and security are critical, cells are small and do not normally communicate with each other. In fact, members of one cell probably do not even know who their colleagues in other cells are. Above and beyond the cells are loosely organized groups of less committed sympathizers who carry out routine tasks, such as carrying messages and raising money. If the preliminary reports of the participants in the 2001 hijackings are correct, cells may be planted in a country and do nothing for several years before they are called on to carry out an attack.

It appears that al-Qaeda has attracted somewhere between five thousand to fifteen thousand active participants. These cells operate in as many as sixty countries. Many of the participants are drawn from Arabs and others who, like bin Laden, went to fight with the *mujahideen* in Afghanistan. Because bin Laden has consciously broadened his message to appeal to the poor and alienated throughout the Muslim world—many of whom are furious with what they see as U.S. imperialism—he has attracted support from Bosnia to the Philippines, Tanzania to Uganda. Additionally, the post-September 11 focus on al-Qaeda revealed members in the United Kingdom, Germany, Canada, and the United States.

Bin Laden has also managed a network of up to fifty training camps, at which new recruits are trained in everything from assassination to the use of rocket launchers. Al-Qaeda has maintained a shadowy network of front organizations through which it raises money to finance its operations, especially since much of bin Laden's personal wealth has been frozen by Western banks. Much of this network has also been frozen in the wake of September 11.

Terrorism expert Peter Bergen told CNN, "this organization does the unexpected." Indeed, along with conventional methods, al-Qaeda introduced new kinds of targets and used new weapons that were extremely difficult to anticipate or prevent, as will be detailed later. Each attack that was frustrated by Western intelligence services and each subsequent arrest and trial merely provided bin Laden and his colleagues with new or revised ideas for their next act of violence.

Decade of Terrorism

In 1991 bin Laden came under suspicion by Saudi officials for smuggling weapons in from Yemen and he was bribed into leaving the country. In 1994 bin Laden's Saudi citizenship was revoked. He ended up in Sudan, which welcomed him because of his money, if nothing else. It appears that, while there, he established Taba Investments, a holding company of legitimate trucking, construction, financial, and export businesses, to fund his operations and strengthen his plans for terrorism.

In December 1992 war among tribes in Somalia had grown so fierce that the United States, after much reluctance, led a rescue mission to aid the failing government and humanitarian aid missions. The U.S. marines landing in Somalia later engaged in a street battle with Somalis, including some bin Laden supporters, who were able to use skills and ammunition left over from the Soviet-Afghanistan war. In an interview with John Miller of ABC ("Greetings, America. My Name Is Osama bin Laden"), bin Laden said: "After leaving Afghanistan, the Muslim fighters headed for Somalia and prepared for a long battle . . . . The youth were surprised at the low morale of the American soldiers and realized more than before that the American soldier was a paper tiger and after a few blows ran in defeat. And America forgot all . . . about being the world leader and the leader of the New World Order, and . . . left, dragging their corpses and their shameful defeat."

Al-Qaeda gained prominence on the international scene after Ramzi Yousef, an alleged bin Laden supporter, bombed New York City's World Trade Center in 1993, in which one of the towers al-Qaeda would allegedly destroy eight years later was attacked. That first primitive bomb killed six and wounded more than 1,000. If Western analysts are to be believed, al-Qaeda has been involved in the following terrorist plots or attacks since then:

- 1994: In the "Bojinka Plot," airline hijackings in the Philippines are thwarted

- 1996: Attack on the U.S. base at Dhahran, Saudi Arabia, in which 19 U.S. military personnel were killed and 372 wounded

- 1998: Bombing of U.S. embassies in Kenya and Tanzania that killed 224 and wounded over 5,000, most of whom were not American

- 2000: Attack on the USS *Cole* in Yemen that killed 17 and hurt 39 sailors

- 2001: Attacks on the World Trade Center and the Pentagon in the United States

In 1994 Saudi Arabia stripped bin Laden of his citizenship, and the United States and other governments froze the bank accounts that held some of his wealth. No one outside his entourage knows exactly how much money he still has, though it is substantial. Whatever his exact role in any

1998 U.S. Embassy Bombings in Kenya and Tanzania

On the morning of August 7, 1998, two U.S. embassies were bombed, one in Nairobi, Kenya, and the other in Dar es Salaam, Tanzania. The blasts went off almost simultaneously, with the bomb in Nairobi the first to be detonated. Both bombs were aboard trucks occupied by drivers—suicide bombers who died along with their victims. The blast in Nairobi virtually gutted the embassy, with the embassy compound and surrounding buildings sustaining severe damage as a result. A neighboring office building, the Ufundi Cooperative Building, was completely leveled by the blast. The devastation of the explosion took 213 lives, and although the target was clearly the United States by way of its presence in Africa, the majority of the victims were Kenyan nationals in the Ufundi Building and Foreign Service nationals in the U.S. Embassy. Only 12 of the 212 victims were U.S. citizens. Nearly 5,000 others, mostly Kenyans, were wounded.

In Dar es Salaam the damage was not nearly as extensive because the U.S. Embassy there was located on the outskirts of the city proper, away from other buildings. The embassy itself suffered extensive damage. Seventy-two people were injured and eleven were killed, none of whom were U.S. citizens. Seven of those who died were Foreign Service nationals. Immediate search and rescue efforts were begun at both locations by U.S. investigators with assistance from Israel and local volunteers.

Although three Islamic extremist groups have claimed responsibility for the bombings, investigations established that Osama bin Laden's extensive terrorist network, al-Qaeda, was behind them. Ultimately, twenty-two men, including Osama bin Laden and his second-in-command, Muhammed Atef, were charged and indicted for the deaths of those killed in the bombings, conspiracy to kill American nationals abroad, and the destruction of U.S. property. Only six of the indicted were actually captured by the United States. Bin Laden and Atef were not among them.

One of the six men, Ali Mohammed, a former U.S. army sergeant who was born in Egypt, pled guilty to the charges against him. In his confession he linked al-Qaeda,

Osama bin Laden, and the other defendants to the bombings. Another defendant, Mahdouh Salim, attacked a corrections officer while in custody, and, as a result of the new charges for the attack, his case was severed from the rest of the defendants. The remaining four defendants—Wadih El-Hage, Mohamed Sadeek Odeh, Mohamed Rashid Daoud Al-'Owhali, and Khalfan Khamis Mohamed—stood trial in federal court in New York City.

The trial began on February 5, 2001, and ended on May 29, 2001, with the conviction of all four defendants. Al-'Owhali and Odeh were found guilty in the deaths of 213 people in the Nairobi bombing; Khalfan Khamis Mohamed was convicted of the deaths of eleven in the Tanzania bombing; El-Hage was convicted of perjuring himself during grand jury investigations of bin Laden's activities; and all four were convicted of conspiracy to kill Americans and destroy U.S. property.

On October 18, 2001, the sentences of all four men were handed down. Mohamed and Al-'Owhali were sentenced to life in prison without the possibility of parole. The death penalty had been an option in both of their sentencing considerations by the jury. Odeh was also sentenced to mandatory life in prison, while El-Hage was sentenced to life plus a few more years for perjuring himself. As for the rest of the indicted, thirteen are fugitives, including bin Laden and Atef. The remaining three are in England, fighting extradition to the United States.

As a result of what happened in Tanzania and Kenya, United States has made some strides toward increasing security in embassies all over the world. The U.S. State Department immediately beefed up security measures at all U.S. embassies. The amount of US$10 billion was earmarked for this purpose to be spent over five years, beginning in 1998. The new security measures utilized included anti-ramming barriers, new bomb and weapon detection equipment, video surveillance at all embassies, the construction of walls built to defend against detonations, and 4,000 local guards trained and hired as external security for U.S. embassies, all in the hope that what happened in Africa will never happen again.

attack has been, there is little doubt that he has been a major raiser and dispenser of funds to terrorist groups that strike out against Israel and the United States. As Stephen Phillip Cohen, a former State Department official, wryly put it, as quoted by Karen DeYoung and Michael Dobbs in the Sep-

tember 16, 2001, *Washington Post* article "Bin Laden: Architect of New Global Terrorism," "he's sort of the Ford Foundation of terrorists."

After the 1996 attacks on the U.S. base in Saudi Arabia, diplomatic pressure on Sudan led its government to force bin Laden to move again.

Shortly thereafter, he ended up once again in Afghanistan, where the fundamentalist Islamic group, the Taliban, had gained control of much of the country. The Taliban seem to have agreed to harbor bin Laden in exchange for financial aid and military support in its ongoing struggle to take over the rest of Afghanistan. To the best of our knowledge, bin Laden remained there until the end of 2001.

The Fatwas

If anything, al-Qaeda grew more militant in the 1990s and the first years of this century. In 1996, for instance, bin Laden issued a *fatwa*, a decree usually issued by a Muslim religious leader which bin Laden had no legitimate authority in the Muslim world to issue, declaring it to be the duty of Muslims to kill Americans. Fatwas, aside from having to be issued by one with appropriate recognition, also are not commonly "issued" without a question being asked. The initial *fatwa* limited itself to attacks on official American targets, but al-Qaeda's second *fatwa* in 1998 stated that all U.S. citizens who paid taxes were involved in their government's actions and were thus legitimate targets. Bin Laden specified that "to kill Americans and their allies—civilians and military—is an individual duty for every Muslim who can do it in any country in which it is possible to do it." In 2001 al-Qaeda circulated a videotape with a nearly two-hour interview with bin Laden in which he used religious imagery in calling for a "holy war" against the United States.

In 1998, after the bombings of the U.S. embassies in Kenya and Tanzania, President Bill Clinton (1993–2001) issued a "finding" that authorized the Central Intelligence Agency (CIA) to engage in covert activities to destroy bin Laden's network and capture him personally. The president also ordered missile strikes against suspected bin Laden training camps in Afghanistan. The United Nations, on October 15, 1999, demanded that the Taliban extradite Osama bin Laden to a country that would bring him to justice, but the Taliban refused, saying they had not seen evidence that bin Laden was responsible for the bombings.

In September 2001 rumors circulated that the CIA and other intelligence agencies had thwarted a number of other attacks, including one designed to disrupt celebrations of the new millennium, all outside the United States. As the world learned painfully on September 11, however, Western intelligence agencies had not done enough.

Responsibility for September 11?

Within days of the September 11, 2001, incidents, evidence of al-Qaeda's involvement began to mount. Few other organizations had the resources to even contemplate an operation of that magnitude. Moreover, there had been rumors of a major event in the works for some weeks, though most experts expected it to occur somewhere in the Middle East. Bin Laden had been recruiting, with a new videotape aimed at inspiring young Muslim men around the world to join his war against Americans. He made statements about an upcoming event, but nothing specific enough to prepare the United States for what was to come.

Fifteen out of nineteen hijackers who were killed on the four airplanes were from Saudi Arabia, where bin Laden is known to have done much of his recruiting. The men who died in the hijackings did not fit what many thought to be the profile of a typical suicide bomber. Most of them were older than expected. Most were well educated; some had lived in Germany or the United States for years. Some had recently had a significant religious awakening. Others blended into American suburban communities, and some had even established families and careers. The hijackers seemed to have lived quiet, unassuming lives in the months before the assault.

The day after the attacks, bin Laden issued a statement denying his involvement, but congratulating the men who staged them. This is consistent with his behavior following earlier attacks. Bin Laden has always tried to keep a veil of mystery around his personal involvement, his leverage over al-Qaeda, and its participation in any attacks.

In December 2001, however, a videotape was found in a house in Afghanistan in which bin Laden speaks about September 11. This video made it clear that bin Laden was involved in planning the attack. In the videotape, he speaks of the plans for the act: "[W]e calculated in advance the number of casualties from the enemy . . . . I was the most optimistic of them all. . . . . due to my experience in this field, I was thinking that the fire from the gas in the plane would melt the iron structure of the building and collapse the area where the plane hit and all the floors above it only. This is all that we had hoped for."

Bin Laden had earlier stated that he had no involvement with the September attacks and it has been speculated that the videotaped statement was an exaggeration. The contradiction between the videotape and bin Laden's earlier denials have led some sources, especially in the Middle East, to question the tape's authenticity.

Obrigado, Brasil,
or sua solidariedade.

INTERNATIONAL ATTENTION WAS DRAWN TO THE SEPTEMBER 11, 2001 TERRORIST ATTACKS IN THE UNITED STATES, FOR WHICH OSAMA BIN LADEN IS CREDITED WITH RESPONSIBILITY. *(AP/Wide World Photos/Eraldo Peres. Reproduced by permission.)*

RECENT HISTORY AND THE FUTURE

On October 7, 2001, the United States and Britain began a military strike against the Taliban and al-Qaeda forces in Afghanistan. With the aid of the air strikes, anti-Taliban forces were able to wrest Afghanistan's centers away from the Taliban within two months. By the beginning of 2002, U.S. and British forces finished a prolonged air strike over al-Qaeda cave complexes in the mountainous region of Tora Bora. In the network of bombed-out caves they found many dead bodies of al-Qaeda fighters along with intelligence information and weapons. U.S. officials announced that they had ef-

fectively disrupted al-Qaeda operations in Afghanistan, although there were still some pockets of Taliban and al-Qaeda resistance. Around the world, suspected al-Qaeda associates and members were questioned and/or arrested. Although the arrests were significant, they demonstrated that there remained many more terrorists still at large. The United States began to send al-Qaeda prisoners to its detention center at Guantanamo Bay, Cuba.

Early in 2002 the Arabic-language television network Al-Jazeera released an interview with bin Laden that had been recorded in October 2001. In it, bin Laden once again seemed to be acknowledging his responsibility for the September

11 attacks. He also did not appear well. In a CNN interview Peter Bergen discussed the changes in bin Laden's appearance in this October videotape and the one in December: "The big difference is that he's aged enormously between '97 and October of last year. This is a man who was clearly not well . . . . I mean, this is a man who has a number of health problems, apart from the fact that anybody running around the Afghan mountains is not going to be in great shape."

While no one knew bin Laden's whereabouts as of early 2002, and some have speculated on the possibility of his death, bin Laden himself may not be of the utmost concern in stemming the terrorist acts of al-Qaeda. In the October videotape, bin Laden's partner in terrorism, the Egyptian Ayman al-Zawahiri, is seen seated behind bin Laden. Many observers have noted that al-Zawahiri appears to be the brains and knowledge behind al-Qaeda, while bin Laden has a charismatic presence that makes him a good front man for the group. Scott Baldauf, in his October 31, 2001 *Christian Science Monitor* article, "The 'Cave Man' and Al-Qaeda", cites Pakistani journalist Hamid Mir, who interviewed bin Laden repeatedly during 1997 and 1998. Mir does not believe that bin Laden has the intellectual power or the knowledge of the Qur'an, the Muslim holy book, to have organized and led al-Qaeda in all its international complexity, while Zawahiri does. Others who have known bin Laden disagree. But all agree that there are quite a few leaders within al-Qaeda who can carry on the group's activities with or without bin Laden.

Madman or Representative of the Powerless?

The Palestinian Liberation Organization (PLO) in the 1970s and the Irish Republican Army (IRA) in the 1980s engaged in violence as a tactic to convince their stronger opponents to come to the bargaining table. If bin Laden's own statements are to be believed, he—and al-Qaeda—are not interested in any sort of negotiated settlement at all. Instead, he wants at least the departure of all vestiges of the West from all Islamic countries, if not the destruction of the United States itself.

Such extreme goals and actions have led some people to conclude that bin Laden—or whoever else might be responsible for the al-Qaeda atrocities—must be a madman. No psychologist or psychiatrist has had the opportunity to examine bin Laden or his colleagues personally. Most observers who have studied the careers of terrorists do think that many of them have had troubled pasts or bear other psychological scars. On the other hand, it is important to point out that bin Laden and others like him are motivated in large part by political and/or religious beliefs. As long as the conditions that give rise to the extreme anger and frustration in the countries in which al-Qaeda operates continue to exist, it is hard to imagine how organizations like al-Qaeda, or individuals like bin Laden, can be stopped once and for all.

BIBLIOGRAPHY

Alexander, Yonah, and Michael Swetman, *Usama bin Laden's al-Qaida.* New York: Transnational Publishers, 2002.

Baldauf, Scott. "The 'Cave Man' and Al-Qaeda," *Christian Science Monitor,* October 31, 2001. Available online at http://www.csmonitor.com/2001/1031/p6s1-wosc.html (cited February 18, 2002).

Bergen, Peter L. "Bin Laden Has Aged Enormously," CNN: February 1, 2002. Available online at http://www.cnn.com/2002/US/02/01/gen.bergen.cnna/index.html (cited February 16, 2002).

———. "Clues Lie in List Of Hijackers," CNN: January 31, 2002. Available online at http://www.cnn.com/2001/US/09/14/peter.bergen.cnna/index.html (cited February 16, 2002).

———. *Holy War, Inc.: Inside the Secret World of Osama bin Laden.* New York: The Free Press, 2001.

Bodansky, Yossef. *Bin Laden: The Man Who Declared War on America.* New York: Forum/Prima, 1999; 2001.

DeYoung, Karen, and Michael Dobbs, "Bin Laden: Architect of New Global Terrorism." *Washington Post,* September 16, 2001, A8.

eMediaMillWorks. "Text: Bin Laden Discusses Attacks on Tape," Tape released by the White House, December 13, 2001. Available online at http://www.washingtonpost.com/wp-srv/nation/specials/attacked/transcripts/binladentext_121301.html (cited February 16, 2002).

"The Jihad Against Jews and Crusaders: World Islamic Front Statement," February 23, 1998. *Washington Post* Online. Available online at http://www.washingtonpost.com/ac2/wp-dyn?pagename=article&node; =digest&contentId;=A4993-2001Sep21 (cited February 15, 2002).

Landau, Elaine. *Osama bin Laden: The War Against the West.* New York: Twenty First Century Books, 2002.

Miller, John. "Greetings, America. My Name Is Osama bin Laden," Frontline, PBS Online. Available online at http://www.pbs.org/wgbh/pages/frontline/shows/binladen/who/ (cited February 16, 2002).

Reeve, Simon. *The New Jackals: Ramzi Yousef, Osama bin Laden, and the Future of Terrorism.* Boston, MA: Northeastern University Press, 1999.

Charles Hauss

LIVING WITH TERRORISM: EVERYDAY LIFE AND THE EFFECTS OF TERROR

THE CONFLICT

Peace is a global ideal, but around the world people face violence—terrorism—on a regular basis. From Northern Ireland to Israel, Palestine, and other points on the globe, many individuals face the threat, uncertainty, and fear of terrorism every day. Newspaper headlines will report a bombing or a hijacking, quote official statements, and print pictures of the devastation, but the people who pick up their lives from the rubble around them must continue to carry on long after the media stories are written, the camera lights have faded, and the world's attention has turned. What is it like to live with terrorism as a regular presence in one's life and what are its effects?

Social

- Social norms change for people living with a consistent presence of terrorism in their lives. Conversation, daily concerns, and living with the heightened risks of sudden, violent injury or death can change people's expectations, actions, outlooks, and interactions with one another.

Psychological

- People living under conditions of regular violence must develop coping mechanisms in order to adapt to their situation. In an environment of prolonged violence, the unusual or unacceptable can become acceptable and "normal."

Political

- Frequent acts of terrorism in a society create political problems as governments struggle to maintain a semblance of order and legitimacy amidst the chaos of terror.

When a terrorist attack occurs, newspaper headlines and television news stories relay the facts, show the pictures, and report government response. Survivors of an attack may be interviewed to relay their experiences, but what about life beyond that moment? In many parts of the world, violence—be it warfare or terrorism—is an all too familiar occurrence. For the people who live with the specter of sudden violence as a daily presence in their lives, the media headlines only highlight a larger part of their everyday experiences.

The impact that living with terrorism has on individual lives is great. From giving up personal privacies in favor of greater security from checkpoints, bag searches, and armed patrols to taking an alternate route to work to avoid traffic backup from the morning bomb blast, living with terrorism as a next-door neighbor is demanding. These are not the demands made by politicians or terrorist leaders as they speak about causes, negotiations, reprisals, and responsibility. These are the demands of doing the day's grocery shopping, visiting a relative across town, and getting to work and back without ending up a part of the week's tragic toll of lives lost in a car bombing, suicide attack, or other incident of terror.

There are many places in the world where terrorism is too common an event, where the horror of sudden, violent attack has become accepted as normal. Beyond the terrorists who wage war in the name of one cause or another and the governments who respond strongly in an attempt to quell the violence and maintain order, there are the people who just want to live their lives peacefully. As the perpetrators of terrorism change, however, from primarily politically motivated groups that dominated the 1980s such as the Irish Republican Army (IRA) into the more ideologically and religiously-focused groups such as al-Qaeda emerging during the 1990s and early 2000s, the targets of terror have also changed. Walter Lacqueur, formerly of the Center for Strategic and International Studies, noted in "Postmodern Terrorism" (*Foreign Affairs*, September/October 1996) that "The trend now seems to be away from attacking specific targets like the other side's officials and toward more indiscriminate killing." What this means is that, wherever there is terrorism, there is a growing risk that anyone may be affected.

This stark reality was brought home on September 11, 2001, when terrorists hijacked four passenger airliners and crashed two of the planes into the twin towers of the World Trade Center in New York City, and one into the Pentagon in Arlington, Virginia, close to Washington, DC; the fourth plane crashed in a rural Pennsylvania field—apparently after a passenger revolt against the terrorists—before it could reach its intended target. More than three thousand people—American, Chinese, Egyptian, Kenyan, Mexican, and others from as many as eighty other countries around the world—were killed in this indiscriminate attack. The terrorists made no demands from governments and stated no purpose for the attack. It seems to have been motivated purely by the desire to inflict mass casualties and fear among the American public and, indeed, the world.

When a sudden, violent attack has no reasonable motivation, how do people cope? With the realization that such attackers could strike again, without warning, how does one continue to live beyond the specter of fear? Natural human resilience ensures that life will go on. Terror, however, always demands a toll.

HISTORICAL BACKGROUND

Israel and the Occupied Territories

In 1947 the United Nations (UN) partitioned the land of Palestine to allow for the creation of a new state, Israel. The creation of Israel was a controversial act. Jews, many of whom had survived the Holocaust of World War II (1939–45) would be returning to their ancient, ancestral homeland. In the process, however, Christian and Muslim Palestinians were uprooted from their homes as they fled the newly designated Israeli lands for the adjusted borders of Palestine. Tensions between Israel and its new neighbors were high. A series of wars were fought in 1948, 1956, 1967, and 1973. In the process, Israel occupied land not originally granted to it by the United Nations, further heightening

CHRONOLOGY

February–August 2001 Israel assassinates 15 Palestinians, including members of Islamic Jihad, HAMAS, Fatah, and the Palestinian Authority's National Security Forces. At least ten civilians are also killed, and two children are injured.

September 2001 Four people are killed and thirteen injured in two separate suicide bombings in Israel.

November 2001 At least five people are killed and two injured in suicide bombings in Hadera, Israel, and Baka al-Sharkieh, West Bank.

December 2001 Two suicide bombings result in the deaths of 27 people; one hundred are injured.

January 2002 Two people are killed in a suicide bombing.

February 2002 Bombs and suicide attacks kill seven people and injure thirty.

March 2002 In a series of suicide bombings, at least 79 men, women, and children—Israelis and Palestinians—are killed and more than one hundred are injured.

early to mid-April 2002 Fifteen people, including suicide bombers, are killed in Israel as a result of bombing attacks.

May 7, 2002 A Palestinian suicide attack kills at least sixteen people and injures more than fifty.

tensions in the region, as Palestinians living in these areas now felt under siege by the occupying force of Israel. Many left the country in a Palestinian Diaspora that reached into neighboring states and as far as Europe and North America.

Israel quickly established itself as a country with a strong military force and a readiness for action in order to preserve and protect its borders and people. The controversial nature of Israel's conception and its embattled early history as a nation, in addition to religious differences between Jewish Israel and its predominantly Muslim neighbors, meant that any peace in the region was tenuous at best. In 1987 the Palestinians living in the occupied territories of the West Bank and Gaza Strip rose up in protest of what they felt was Israel's unlawful occupation of their lands and oppression of Palestinians. This uprising, called the *intifada*, began with Palestinians, many of them children, throwing rocks at Israeli soldiers. The protest

A MASKED GUERRILLA POINTS A ROCKET-PROPELLED GRENADE LAUNCHER FROM BEHIND A TIRE. TERRORIST ATTACKS INSTILL FEAR, ANXIETY, AND INSECURITY IN A COMMUNITY. *(AP/Wide World Photos. Reproduced by permission.)*

movement took hold and grew markedly over the ensuing years. Anti-Israel groups such as the Palestine Liberation Organization (PLO), the Popular Front for the Liberation of Palestine (PFLP), HAMAS, and Islamic Jihad, many of which were based in neighboring Arab countries such as Lebanon and Jordan, supported the intifada. Some considered these groups to be freedom fighters, though Israel and much of the Western world designated them terrorists.

As Israel responded harshly to the intifada's growing violence and its threat to Israeli security, the intensity of the conflict increased. Israeli leaders Yitzhak Rabin and Shimon Peres, and PLO leader Yasser Arafat signed the landmark Oslo Accords in 1993, for which the men were honored with the 1994 Nobel Peace Prize. From that agreement, the Palestinian-run Palestinian National Authority (PA) was established to govern the West Bank and Gaza Strip. Despite these and other efforts for peace, however, the situation between Israel and the Palestinians worsened in early 2000 as the second intifada broke out. By early 2002 attacks against both Israeli soldiers and the Israeli public by Palestinian suicide bombers were occurring on an almost daily basis, as was Israeli military action in the occupied territories. As of April 2002 more than

1,140 Palestinians and over 400 Israelis had been killed since the second intifada began.

After a Palestinian suicide bombing on March 27, 2002, in which 25 Israelis were killed and more than 100 injured during the Jewish holiday of Passover, Israeli Prime Minister Ariel Sharon declared war against the terrorists. Shortly thereafter, the Israeli military surrounded Yasser Arafat's government compound in the West Bank city of Ramallah. Arafat's government was effectively made inactive as his isolation was enforced by Israeli troops for one month. Sharon declared his goal to be to "uproot the terrorists." Israeli military actions in the occupied territories, however, have been described by Palestinians as being not so much about rooting out terrorist fugitives as about instilling submission in all Palestinians.

According to the *Economist*'s "Carnage in Israel, Conquest in Palestine," (April 6–12, 2002) for several days in Ramallah, the city's residents "endured a total curfew, often without electricity, food or water; . . . Offices were shelled, homes ransacked, ambulances shot at, hospitals raided, the dead left unburied, and roads, walls and cars crushed by the marauding, unassailable [Israeli] tanks." The same scenes were carried out in other Palestinian cities as well, including Beit Jala, Tulkarm, and Jenin.

Beyond the ever more intractable politics of the situation is the suffering of both the Israeli and Palestinian publics, who have struggled with the increasingly constant and unpredictable violence that personally impacts their lives and who have lived alongside the terror and fear for many years.

Israel—"How Long Will This Madness Go On?"

A few months ago, in Milan, Italy, (I went there to visit my brother-in-law) I opened my bag at the entrance of a grocery store—as I always do—to show the guard at the door that I was not carrying any bombs. But there was no guard, and nobody cared about my bag. Only then I realized how thoroughly I had been conditioned by the atmosphere of terror in which I had been living in Israel during the last 18 months.

Last night, a Palestinian "freedom fighter" fired shots at people sitting in a restaurant in the center of Tel Aviv. He killed three and wounded 40, all civilians, most of them women who gathered for a bridal shower.

Day before yesterday, a suicide bomber pulled the switch in front of a guest house in an orthodox neighborhood in Jerusalem. He succeeded in wiping out a whole family, with friends and relatives, including two little infants (7–18 months of age) who gathered there to celebrate their son's Bar Mitzvah. Israel is a small country, everybody knows everybody. And the names of the victims are only too familiar. These people were distant relatives of my daughter-in-law. The son of a friend was killed in a terrorist attack a few months ago, and recently my granddaughter told me that the mother of a schoolmate had been killed too. So, the first thing you do as soon as you get word about a bombing or shooting, you look for the names, hoping that among the victims there is no one you know.

One of the worst effects of this situation is: we are getting unfeeling and numbed, the news of people killed, injured, and crippled does not upset us anymore, we get used to the daily terror. Except for some event that goes beyond imagination. It happened a few days ago: a husband was driving his pregnant wife to the hospital, as she was due to give birth to their first child. The car was ambushed, the husband killed, and the wife badly injured. They managed to get her to the hospital, and to deliver her child by Cesarean. By the way, the same thing happened to a Palestinian woman a few days before, when Israeli soldiers at a roadblock fired at a racing car, thinking it was a terrorist attack.

I keep asking myself: how long will this madness go on? Why can't they stop? Less than two years ago, thanks to the efforts of the American government, and especially to President Clinton's personal involvement, Israelis and Palestinians were just one inch away from a final peace treaty. But then, instead of taking the last step, the Palestinians unleashed terror. I know for sure that if they would give up bombing and firing only for a few days, the Israelis would be more than willing to restart negotiations for a settlement that both parties can live with and for peaceful coexistence. Can't they understand that they will not be able to drive away the Israelis by force? What happens is that each terrorist attack pushes the public opinion in Israel more and more towards a hard line.

Nowadays, we consider with great care an invitation to a party or to a family celebration, as one must weigh the risk of hurting the host's feelings against the risk of getting killed or injured. Every Saturday night, our children have heated arguments with their teenage children, who want to go out dancing, or to meet with friends. Usually, the parents give up, and stay awake for hours, praying that the kids come home safely. Our grandson (17) wanted to spend the weekend with a friend in Jerusalem. At first his parents—they live in Haifa—said no, then they begged him not to go, and as he went anyway, they called him every half hour on his cell phone, to make sure he was still alive. Fortunately, he came back unharmed, but the next morning a Palestinian shot several people at the very same bus station from which our grandson took the bus home.

We stopped going to the street-market, where you can get fresh fruits and vegetables at low prices. Nowadays, on market street you find more armed guards than shoppers.

When we go to work, or shopping, we look out for "suspicious objects," like a trash bag "left" on the sidewalk, or a "discarded" TV set at the street corner. Then we call the police, and they block the street,

evacuate people, and start checking on the object, which might or might not be a bomb. All activity in the area is frozen, sometimes for an hour or more. An unfamiliar car parked in front of your house makes our blood pressure rise. When we ride on a bus, we look around, to make sure that nobody "forgets" a parcel when he gets off. Roadblocks are set up everywhere to prevent terrorists from getting into our cities, but they stop Israelis too, and driving the few miles from home to the office or plant has become a major part of the workday.

Our daughter (50, four children, one grandchild) lives in a small village on the hills overlooking the coastal area. She teaches first grade in a school in Jerusalem. When I asked her the other day how she feels about her work there, she said: "You know, Daddy, every morning, on my way to school, I can't help thinking that this might be the last day of my life. And I ask myself if I am ready to die."

Yesterday, the father of a Palestinian suicide bomber was interviewed on TV. He said he was proud of what his son had done, and added that he would be glad if the rest of his children would do the same. I thought that fathers were supposed to wish their children a long and happy life . . .

Arno Baehr. Written especially for this volume of History Behind the Headlines. *March 2002.*

Palestine—"What Do They Have To Hide?"

Palestinians are not a free people. They have been ruled for decades by a foreign occupier—Israel. The Israeli army occupies their towns and villages. For years they have been humiliated on a daily basis at roadblocks and checkpoints. They are not permitted to travel, not permitted to work freely, and their land has been slowly confiscated to build new settlements for Israelis. The much talked about peace process of the mid-nineties did not bring freedom to the people; instead it brought a more rapid expansion of illegal Israeli settlements, more roadblocks, and continued humiliation. The peace process was largely made ineffective as various Israeli leaders reneged on promises to grant nationhood to the Palestinians. In their arrogance of power, they opted to pick and choose which rights and freedoms the Palestinians were worthy of. They controlled work and travel permits, they controlled access to ports and airports, they split families apart, and denied millions of refugees the right of return to their lands.

The net effect is a system very similar to apartheid in the former South Africa. The elite Israeli population claims the resources of the land, lives in freedom, and accuses the majority of Palestinians in the West Bank and Gaza of being "terrorists" to justify denying them their basic rights and freedoms. Dehumanizing the Palestinians has become the norm and indeed a necessary strategy for Israeli leaders.

The Palestinian people are disillusioned and angry. In September 2000, this anger erupted in a massive and popular uprising against the occupying foreign army. During the next eighteen months, over 1,500 people were killed, most of them Palestinian civilians. More than 20,000 Palestinians were injured.

The Israeli army continued to besiege towns and villages with troops and earth walls. The suffering was worse still for families falsely accused of supporting terrorism. Bulldozers demolished houses, forcing women and children to become homeless.

Just after midnight one night in late March 2002, the entire population of the city of Ramallah was awakened by the deafening sounds of grinding steel and gunfire. Hundreds of Israeli tanks and over 20,000 soldiers entered the city with plans to capture "wanted" Palestinians. When the tanks stopped, what you could hear were the cries of terrorized children in homes and apartments blocks, and of parents shouting at them to stop. The invasion of the Israeli army into Palestinian towns lasted almost a month, during which the entire population was under 24-hour curfew. There was no school, no work, no banking, no shopping, no ambulance or other emergency medical service; life was paralyzed for over one million people in the major cities and towns of the West Bank. The media was banned from much of the West Bank, and even Red Cross teams were shot at repeatedly and had to suspend operations. When respected human rights monitoring groups spoke out, they were simply dismissed as being anti-Israel or anti-Semitic.

Families called ambulance services for food, for water, for diapers, for medicine, for everything. When ambulances responded, they were shot at. When fires broke out, responding fire fighters were shot at by the Israeli army. Tanks drove over cars and ambulances and destroyed roads and buildings. The army took control of two local television stations, and began to broadcast pornographic films. Ambulance radios were confiscated and used to interfere with dispatch operations. Those who peeked outside their windows and balconies where shot at by Israeli snipers. Many were killed as their families watched. Soldiers broke into homes, looted money, vandalized furniture and cars, and, most seriously, dragged people from houses and marched them in front of tanks as "human shields." In short, a terror campaign was being waged by an organized Israeli army against the Palestinians.

Soldiers went house-to-house arresting grandfathers, fathers, and boys as young as fifteen by the thousands. No one was spared; doctors, nurses, professionals and students were rounded up, lined up, blindfolded, kicked and beaten in front of their families. The humiliation persisted later in large tent prison compounds. Their only crime was being Palestinian. Although many were released later, the scars they now carry from these experiences will last a lifetime.

By the time the invasion ended, over 250 Palestinians were dead, 1,000 injured, and more than 5,000 arrested and placed in newly created desert tent detention centers.

While it is true that Palestinian attacks on Israeli civilians have caused many casualties and much suffering, it is equally true that Israeli attacks on Palestinians have caused many folds the casualties and deaths. The horrors that suicide bombings have inflicted on innocent Israeli civilians can not be jus-

tified. However, it has taken over 30 years of Israeli occupation and humiliation to produce the type of despair that makes a suicide bomber. The horrors of the Holocaust and the suffering of the Jewish people in Europe is being used to justify attacks on Palestinians, as if two wrongs make a right. Incredibly, many Israeli leaders still advocate expelling the Palestinians to "any other Arab state." This is analogous to someone advocating the expulsion of Texans to a neighboring state on the basis that "Americans have so many states, and do not really need Texas."

Over three million Palestinians remain refugees in the surrounding nations of Lebanon, Syria and Jordan. These refugees are denied the right to return, or even any compensation for the lands now enjoyed by their occupiers. Legitimate resistance to this occupation is called "terrorism." While Israeli settlers in the West Bank enjoy large swimming pools and acres of land, Palestinian crops die because Palestinian farmers are prevented from digging wells for water on their own land.

Sadly, much of the Israeli public does not know about the abuses committed by their army against the Palestinian population. And unfortunately, many tend to "justify" these attacks as "necessary for Israeli security." Somehow, many Israelis and much of the world have come to accept that "Israel's need for security" must supersede "Palestinian human rights and freedoms."

Today, Palestinian suffering and pain is openly justified in much of the western media. Israel is presented as a nation that can do no wrong. Well, it has done wrong, terrible wrong. For over thirty years now, Israel has subjected the entire Palestinian population to the worst type of oppression and to systematic humiliation. This oppression and humiliation is causing an entire generation to rise up and fight back. Lies are powerful weapons of war, and the Israeli government uses them well. Consider this, why would Israel ban the world media, UN fact-finding teams, and humanitarian agencies from entering parts of the West Bank? It is worth noting that while Israel publicly proclaimed it had "nothing to hide" in the aftermath of the Israeli army's assault on the refugee camp of Jenin (in the northern West Bank), it quietly sought "immunity from prosecution" for its soldiers and officers. We all need to ask: what do they have to hide?

Peace in the Middle East will only come when justice is served; when the illegal and provocative settlements are emptied and abandoned; when refugees are allowed to return, or else are compensated for the loss of their homes; when Israel learns to share land and water with the people it occupied and forced into exile. Most Palestinians have accepted Israel as a fact. It is well past time for Israel to accept Palestine as a fact, as a nation, and as a people with a legitimate right to be here, too.

Hossam Sharkawi. Written especially for this volume of History Behind the Headlines, *May 2002.*

Northern Ireland

The conflict in Northern Ireland has centuries old roots. In 1171 English forces put down an Irish

MORE THAN EIGHT THOUSAND MOURNERS ATTENDED THE FUNERAL OF THREE CHILDREN KILLED IN THE 1998 OMAGH BOMB BLAST IN NORTHERN IRELAND. *(AP/Wide World Photos/Alastair Grant. Reproduced by permission.)*

attempt to form an independent state on the island. Ireland became part of English-administered lands, but Irish rebellion against English rule was never stamped out completely. In the mid- to late nineteenth century, Irish nationalism arose, promoting Irish culture, language, and greater Irish involvement in government and relations with Britain. First led by Isaac Butt and Charles Stewart Parnell, of the Protestant faith, the nationalist movement soon became associated with Catholics and supporters were called republicans. At the same time, an increasing number of Protestants supported a continuation of the colonial arrangement with Britain and were called unionists.

The political efforts of both sides solidified in 1905. In that year, the republican group Sinn Féin was founded, supporting an independent Irish state. Also that year, the Ulster Unionist Council was established in support of remaining with Britain. Tensions between the two camps continued to rise, and in 1916 Irish republican groups launched a rebellion against the British over Easter weekend. Called the Easter Rebellion, it was firmly put down by British forces and its leaders were executed. The rebellion marked the start of Irish republican violence against the British presence in Northern Ireland.

By 1921 the island of Ireland was partitioned. The southern part of the island received autonomy, and the six northern provinces remained under British rule. Irish republicans persisted in their efforts for a united Ireland, completely independent from Britain. Having lost the bulk of the island of Ireland to independent statehood, the unionists were now, more than ever, determined to maintain ties with Britain. Both sides developed various political parties and militant splinter groups. Violence did transpire, but it was not until the mid-twentieth century that it became an increasingly frequent occurrence.

A civil rights march in Northern Ireland on October 5, 1968, was banned by the Royal Ulster Constabulary, who stopped it and injured several marchers. In protest, two days of rioting ensued. The "Troubles," as they are called, had officially begun. More radical groups formed, violence increased, and politics between those supporting republicanism and unionism grew more protracted. Twenty-five people were killed in 1970, and 153 explosions occurred. The number of people killed jumped to 174 the next year, with 304 explosions in just the first six months of 1971. In 1972 the number of people killed grew to 467.

Early that year, on January 30, 1972, thirteen civilians were shot dead and several others injured when a civil rights march to protest the British government's practice of internment without trial turned into a clash between supporters and the British army. The violence again escalated when secret British negotiations with a republican group called the Provisional Irish Republican Army (PIRA) broke down. In response, the PIRA set off 26 car bombs in Belfast. Eleven people died as a result and 130 were injured. A unionist group quickly initiated retaliation.

THREE IRISH CATHOLIC BOYS EMULATE THE IRISH
REPUBLICAN ARMY MURAL ON THE WALL BEHIND
THEM IN BELFAST. *(AP/Wide World Photos/Peter
Morrison. Reproduced by permission.)*

Between 1970 and 1980 more than two thousand people were killed as a result of the violence
in Northern Ireland. That violence escalated
throughout the 1980s and continued into the
1990s, despite efforts at brokering peace. Catholic
leader John Hume and Protestant leader David
Trimble won the Nobel Prize for Peace in 1998
for their efforts to bring peace to the region
through the Good Friday Agreement. Peace, however, was not easily won, or kept. That same year,
on August 15, a large car bomb exploded in the
small town of Omagh in Northern Ireland, achieving the dubious status of causing the greatest number of deaths from a single event in the history of

the Troubles. Twenty-nine people were killed and
more than two hundred were injured. A hitherto
unknown group, the Real IRA, claimed responsibility for the blast, which came in the midst of a
cease-fire. Like all terrorist acts, the Omagh
bombing was horrific and terrifying, but it did not
derail efforts for peace. Unresolved issues, such as
the Irish Republican Army's decommissioning of
arms, were still to be overcome, but the process
continued to move forward.

In March 1999 an Anglo-Irish agreement was
formed that established cross-border institutions,
beginning a new relationship between the Republic
of Ireland and the six provinces of the north. Additionally, in early December power was devolved
to Belfast from the central British government in
London, allowing Northern Ireland's population to
engage in its first direct local elections in over a
generation. Responsibility for several key issues, including health and education, were now the responsibility of local leaders, who met in a new
power-sharing executive to handle these duties.
Unionists and republicans sat across the table from
one another in a landmark cooperative effort to govern—peacefully.

While peace takes hold in Northern Ireland,
its people rejoice as they move beyond the all-too-
frequent violence that has marred their lives for
decades. Unionists and republicans may continue
to snipe at each other, but they may more likely do
so now with words rather than with bullets and
bombs. The memories and effects of the Troubles'
harsh reality, however, will stay with people long
after peace becomes commonplace.

Experiencing the 'Troubles'

Various militant factions—republican and
unionist—established themselves over the course of
Northern Ireland's Troubles. As one violent attack
spawned another in what often became a series of
tit-for-tat offenses, the number of those killed and
injured increased. Despite the groups' alleged political aims, the violence itself was oftentimes indiscriminate. Belfast resident Thomas Gracey, a
Catholic, remembers in "Personal Experience," in
Laurel Holliday's *Children of 'The Troubles,'* (1997,
pp. 205–206) that his brother Paddy once had an
argument with an IRA bomber. His home was
wrecked and he was constantly harassed until the
day he was called to a meeting with the IRA to resolve the matter. Instead of a meeting, however,
Paddy faced two IRA men with guns, who shot
him in the knee. A jammed gun prevented his other
knee, and spine, from receiving the same treatment.
The men left Paddy to bleed to death, but he was

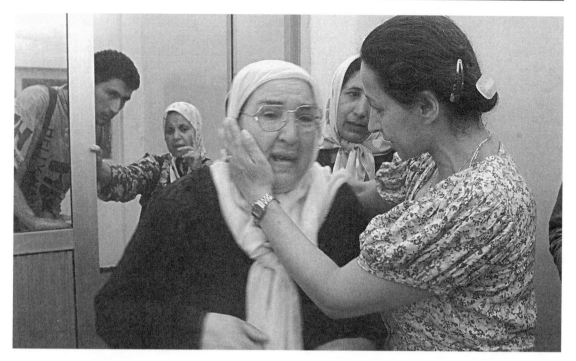

A WEEPING ALGERIAN WOMAN IS COMFORTED BY A COUNSELOR. ALGERIANS HAVE BEEN SUBJECTED TO VICIOUS TERRORIST ATTACKS BY REBEL EXTREMIST GROUPS, WHICH HAVE KILLED THOUSANDS OF PEOPLE IN THE PAST TEN YEARS. *(AP/Wide World Photos/Michel Euler. Reproduced by permission.)*

able to crawl for help. "Eventually," Gracey says, "the ambulance arrived and Paddy was rushed to hospital to begin a long and hard battle to try to regain full use of his leg. Today he walks with a permanent limp and is a totally changed person. Instead of the caring, fun-loving brother that he was, he is now a paranoid person who trusts no one—not even his family."

Protestant Mark Russell, also in Laurel Holliday's *Children of 'The Troubles,'* recalls that he "grew up in a province where murder and outrage came on a daily basis . . . ." ("The Legacy of the Past and Hope of the Future: Reflections on Growing Up in Northern Ireland," pp. 339–341). While he made Catholic friends at university and broke down walls of distrust and misunderstanding built during his childhood, Russell did not forget the capricious nature of terrorist attacks. "I can remember lying in my bed in Belfast, too terrified to sleep. I shook whenever there was a knock on the door. I thought that our house must have been the 'Heads' on a gunman's coin. And then it would turn out to be only a neighbour."

Coping with Terrorism

Terrorism instills fear, anxiety, depression, anger, frustration, and a host of other feelings in its victims. Coping with the sudden, oftentimes violent attacks and their effects is difficult. Thomas

Friedman, a journalist with the *New York Times,* was stationed in war-torn Lebanon in the 1980s. In *From Beirut to Jerusalem* (1990) he explained that "coping with the violence of Beirut . . . required a thousand little changes in one's daily habits and a thousand little mental games to avoid being overwhelmed by everything happening around you." Among the coping mechanisms employed by Beirutis, who lived among warring religious and political factions, were rationalizations for why one person was killed instead of another—it was bad luck, bad timing, or some other justification that could be reasoned out to ensure that, in the future, you did not fall into the same trap.

Taking a selective view of one's environment proved to be a highly effective coping mechanism. Friedman relayed the observation of psychologist Richard Day, who taught in Beirut in the early 1980s, on his students. "[T]hose . . . in the best physical and mental health were those who learned how to block out what was going on around them that was not under their own control and to focus instead only on their immediate environment and the things that they could control. This prevented them from suffering from 'system overload.'" It is impossible to consider all the risks and to worry about every action and every choice at every moment. By dealing with the immediate, controllable aspects of daily life, such as

STOCKHOLM SYNDROME

A terrorist attack impacts many people. The most common victim is the one killed or injured in an attack, or one who knows those killed or injured. For some, however, a far more personal relationship develops between terrorist and victim.

On August 23, 1973, three women and one man were taken hostage during a bank robbery in Stockholm, Sweden. Held captive in a bank vault for six days, the four bank employees were both threatened and treated with kindness by the two men that held them hostage. Surprisingly, the hostages resisted rescue efforts by the authorities. After they were rescued, they publicly defended their hostage takers, even raising money for the legal defense of the two men. Two of the women held hostage eventually became engaged to their captors.

After a number of similar incidents around the world during which hostages bonded with their captors, psychologists discovered that the Stockholm incident was not a lone occurrence. The emotional bonding between hostage and captor was such a common phenomenon among hostages, prisoners of war, victims of physical and emotional abuse, and cult members that scientists named the occurrence the "Stockholm Syndrome," after the 1973 incident.

In an effort to endure the violence they are subjected to by their captors, hostages and other victims bond to their abusers as a survival mechanism. One of the most famous cases of the Stockholm Syndrome occurred in February 1974, when the Symbionese Liberation Army, a revolutionary extremist group active in the United States, kidnapped 19-year old newspaper heiress Patricia Hearst. After a number of weeks of forced confinement, Hearst eventually joined the extremist group, actively participating in bank robberies and other domestic terror attacks perpetrated by the group.

what time to get up in the morning and what to have for dinner, functioning in an uncontrollable environment is, if not easier, than at least more manageable than constantly trying to predict the unpredictable.

RECENT HISTORY AND THE FUTURE

The Personal Impacts of Terrorism

For the individual and the community, terrorism can quickly erode a sense of security and safety. Brian W. Flynn noted in a speech on the psycho-logical aspects of terrorism (April 24–25, 1996) that "Nearly all terrorist attacks occur with no warning. Warning allows individuals to take psychological and physical protective action [and] allows the activation of psychological defense mechanisms . . . ." Warning also allows one to perceive some level of control over the terror attack. If you know that it is coming, you can prepare yourself to face it. In regards to terrorism, however, one rarely knows when and where it will occur. An act of terror is sudden, shocking, and unpredictable. Once it occurs, one feels vulnerable, knowing it could happen again at any time.

On April 19, 1995, an explosion wracked the Alfred P. Murrah federal building in Oklahoma City, Oklahoma. The bombing was carried out by Timothy McVeigh and his co-conspirator Terry Nichols, who were both virulently anti-government in their views. The attack came without warning and with no demands made on the government. Mass casualty was the goal. A study by the University of Oklahoma, referred to by Flynn in his speech, reported that 168 people were killed and more than 800 injured in the bombing. The victims' toll from this terrorist act, however, reaches much farther. Thirty children were orphaned; seven thousand people were left at least temporarily without a workplace, as the explosion damaged not just the federal building but several other buildings nearby; and an estimated 387,000 people knew someone who was killed or injured in the blast. For an even larger scale terrorist incident such as the attacks of September 11, 2001, the number of those personally affected is even greater.

Whether one is surviving a large-scale, high-profile terrorist attack such as that of Oklahoma City and September 11, or the almost daily suicide bombings and uncertainties of life in Israel and the occupied territories, the effects of terrorism ripple out beyond those hurt in the attack to those who know the killed and injured. In the aftermath of the September 11, 2001, attacks in the United States, concern also arose for those exposed to repeated media coverage of one of the airliners crashing into the World Trade Center, of the two towers collapsing, and the aftermath of the tragedy. Television viewers watching at home, with no friends or relatives involved in either the World Trade Center or Pentagon attacks were also traumatized.

According to the National Center for Post Traumatic Stress Disorder (PTSD), "a consistent finding is that, while most individuals exhibit resilience over time, people most directly exposed to terrorist attacks are at a higher risk to develop

ALGERIA'S DECADE OF TERROR

Over the last ten years the Algerian people have endured the most prolonged and horrific terrorist assault against a civilian population in modern times. As many as 150,000 people have been killed, most of them innocent noncombatants.

In spite of token demonstrations of democracy, Algeria's political leadership has been firmly controlled by its own military ever since it won independence from France in 1962. In 1989 the government seemed ready to attempt a more genuine democracy and lifted its ban on new political parties. Among the new parties was the fundamentalist Islamic Salvation Front (FIS). Tired of government corruption, Algerians were attracted to the party's religion and claims of populism. The FIS won the first round of parliamentary elections in December 1991 in a landslide vote. High-ranking generals declared a state of emergency, cancelled the elections, and banned the party. Although the president they subsequently appointed, Mohammed Boudiaf, was an extremely popular hero in the independence war against France, he was soon assassinated, accelerating the nation's descent into chaos.

The Armed Islamic Group (GIA) emerged as the main faction responsible for the incessant atrocities against civilians that followed. The GIA seeks to overthrow the secular government and replace it with a Taliban-like Islamic state. They have committed unspeakable acts, slaughtering entire villages with machetes, hunting down and beheading journalists, and stepping up their attacks during the Muslim holy month of Ramadan. Although most of their terrorist activities have been directed against their fellow Muslim Algerians, members of the GIA also hijacked an Air France flight in 1994 and murdered the French Archbishop of Oran in 1996. The GIA is thought to be responsible for a series of subway bombs in Paris in the mid-1990s, and Algerian suspects in a U.S. bombing plot around the time of the Millennium celebrations were found to have links to the GIA (and to al-Qaeda).

In 1997 the FIS and its armed wing, the Islamic Liberation Army (AIS), announced a unilateral cease-fire in order to distance itself from the violence. The killing, however, continued unabated. Abdelaziz Bouteflika, the latest president to be installed by Algeria's senior generals, offered a limited six-month amnesty to armed groups beginning in July 1999. He vowed to strike ruthlessly against any extremists who did not accept his offer. Around 1,500 militants turned themselves in. Unfortunately, the GIA was unresponsive, and the government's promised counterattack was largely a failure.

Throughout the conflict, allegations have arisen that some of the atrocities blamed on Islamist terrorists were actually the work of government security forces. In his book *The Dirty War* former Algerian military officer Habib Souaidia claimed that Algerian troops disguised as rebels participated in civilian massacres and tortured Islamist radicals to death. The September 11, 2001 attacks against the United States have taken the heat of these accusations off of the Algerian government. The current political climate permits Algeria to fight terrorists as it chooses, without fearing the censure of human rights groups and democracy activists.

On February 8, 2002, security forces killed Antar Zouabri, the head of the GIA since 1996. Zouabri was notorious for his role in civilian massacres and for encouraging GIA soldiers to kidnap thousands of girls to use as sex slaves in Algeria's mountainous tunnels and caves. The GIA quickly appointed a new leader, Rachid Abou Tourab, who promised to keep fighting until Algeria is an Islamist state. Despite President Bouteflika's attempts to restore peace and end his country's diplomatic and economic isolation, new attacks are reported almost daily. More encouragingly, recent global antiterrorist efforts are dismantling some of the western European Islamist networks that support Algerian terrorist groups like the GIA.

PTSD." Additionally, those affected may experience anxiety, depression, problems with substance abuse, and psychosomatic symptoms such as stomach aches and fevers, when there is nothing physically wrong. Those exposed to the chemical agent sarin in a chemical terrorism attack in the Tokyo subway in 1995 have reported fear, nightmares, insomnia, depression, and anxiety since the event, which was planned and carried out by the Aum Shinrikyo apocalyptic cult in Japan. Susan Urbach, a survivor of the Oklahoma City bombing, notes in "Ground Rules—Surviving Terrorism" that a terrorist incident "will have ramifications on every aspect of your life and you will never be like you were before—not necessarily better or worse, just different."

In Northern Ireland the government in June 2000 established a Victims Unit to help those physically or psychologically affected by the Troubles. With a goal "to raise awareness of, and co-ordinate activity on, issues affecting victims across the devolved administration and society in general," Northern Ireland is taking steps beyond the signing of peace agreements and the setting down of arms. A greater, personal reconciliation may take place by recognizing and addressing victims' needs.

While there was a resolution to the conflict in Northern Ireland, terrorism rarely ends with a political solution. The attacks of September 11, 2001 made clear that mass casualty terrorism is an increasingly real threat. Terror for the sake of terror can not be reconciled. Terror in the name of a cause is no easier for people to deal with. Whatever its brand, terrorism's impacts are personal and long lasting, something those living with it as a familiar neighbor know all too well.

BIBLIOGRAPHY

Binur, Yoram. *My Enemy, My Self.* London: Doubleday, 1989.

"Carnage in Israel, Conquest in Palestine," *Economist*, April 6–12, 2002, pp. 22–23.

"Executive Unveils Victims' Package," BBC News, April 11, 2002. Available online at http://news.bbc.co.uk/hi/english/uk/northern_ireland/newsid_1922000/1922357.stm (May 11, 2002).

Flynn, Brian W. "Psychological Aspects of Terrorism." Presented at the First Harvard Symposium on the Medical Consequences of Terrorism, April 24–25, 1996. The Center for Mental Health Services. Available online at http://www.mentalhealth.org/newsroom/speeches/terrorspeech.asp (cited May 3, 2002).

Frankel, Glenn. "A Time for Pain: Between Netanya and Tulkarm, The Short Road from Friend to Foe," *Washington Post National Weekly Edition*, April 22–28, 2002, pp. 6–8.

Friedman, Thomas L. *From Beirut to Jerusalem.* New York: Anchor Books, Doubleday, 1990.

"From Here to Palestine," *Economist*, April 13–19, 2002, p. 13.

Holliday, Laurel. *Children of 'The Troubles': Our Lives in the Crossfire of Northern Ireland.* New York: Washington Square Press (Pocket Books): 1997.

"Israel's History of Bomb Blasts," BBC News, April 12, 2002. Available online at http://news.bbc.co.uk/hi/english/world/middle_east/newsid_1197000/1197051.stm (cited May 11, 2002).

Laqueur, Walter. "Postmodern Terrorism," *Foreign Affairs*, September/October 1996.

"Northern Ireland: The Omagh Bomb, Nationalism, and Religion," in *History Behind the Headlines,* vol. 2. Farmington Hills, MI: The Gale Group, 2001.

Taylor, Peter. *Behind the Mask: The IRA and Sinn Féin.* New York: TV Books, 1997.

Tull, Muhanned. "Do You Wonder Why We're Angry? Tales from the Road to Desperation," *Washington Post National Weekly Edition*, September 3–9, 2001, p. 22.

"Under the Rubble of the Refugee Camp," *Economist*, April 20–26, 2002, pp. 41–43.

Urbach, Susan. "Ground Rules: Surviving Terrorism—A Victim's Journey to Healing and Justice." The National Center for Victims of Crime. Available online at http://www.ncvc.org/healing2.html (cited May 3, 2002).

Ventura, Raphael. "Terrorism and Public Opinion," International Policy Institute for Counter-Terrorism, August 15, 1999. Available online at http://www.ict.org.il/documents/documentdet.cfm?docid'33 (cited April 26, 2002).

Westcott, Kathryn. "Children Bear Scars of Mid-East Conflict," BBC News, April 27, 2002. Available online at http://news.bbc.co.uk/hi/english/world/middle_east/newsid_1951000/1951569.stm (cited May 11, 2002).

"What Are the Traumatic Stress Effects of Terrorism?" National Center for PTSD. Available online at http://www.ncptsd.org/facts/disasters/fs_terrorism.html (cited May 3, 2002).

Nancy Matuszak

THE MEDIA'S RELATIONSHIP WITH TERRORISM

The developments that have followed the September 11, 2001, terrorist attacks are more than a headline-making occasion. The attacks themselves, the response at home, and the deployment of forces abroad—all culminating in the first war on terrorism—may mark a turning point in world affairs. Yet if what is at hand does prove to be a watershed, it will be so for an additional reason, one that is being defined as much by television, radio, newspapers, and the Internet as by the crisis itself. Through mass media, every American not only is learning about, but is living through this terrorist event.

The crisis became a domain of the media at a very early stage, in fact at the same moment the first jetliner crashed into the World Trade Center. Morning traffic reporters for New York City radio stations had been flying in helicopters nearby. Thousands of New Yorkers had heard live, eyewitness accounts. Within minutes, wire services and each of the major television networks flashed bulletins of what first was reported as an aircraft mishap. No sooner had the second tower been struck than newscasters proclaimed a terrorist attack. By the time the third jetliner struck the Pentagon and the fourth crashed in Pennsylvania, not just the military but the media had been mobilized. News crews and equipment were dispatched to various locations, and newsrooms became command centers. Minute by minute, each new facet of the crisis was reported to a nervous world.

President George W. Bush (2001–) and administration officials went into seclusion. Their brief public statements only hinted at official options and responses. Military action, however, was already being anticipated. Public opinion was quickly consolidated by the media in support of the U.S. government and against the attackers. By

THE CONFLICT

The media played an important role in the aftermath of the September 11, 2001, terrorist attacks in the United States. As it had in the past, the media kept the public informed about what was going on, consulted with government officials, and tried to give the audience background information to better understand the perpetrators. Complaints about media-reported rumors, inaccuracies, and networks' attempts to win viewers with sensationalized coverage emerged soon after September 11. Did the media do a good job or was it carried away with the drama of the moment? Did the media relate terrorism coverage informatively or did it help promote the fear the terrorists' hoped to impart?

Media Manipulation

- Terrorists often seek to pull off high-profile attacks in an attempt to gain media coverage for their cause or their group. In reporting on an event, the media must be mindful not to legitimize the terrorists or sensationalize their attack.

- Government officials have "leaked" secret information to the media, who then report on it. Leaks such as this run the risk of compromising U.S. actions. In its quest for information, can the media go too far in reporting?

- Under the Ronald Reagan administration, government officials gave false information to the media in an attempt to achieve foreign policy goals. Rather than be the government's pawn, the media responded by initiating more investigative reports.

Social

- In its reporting, the media has the power to sway public opinion. Its treatment towards a terrorist or terrorist group, if too sympathetic, could affect support for government policies and actions.

CHRONOLOGY

1901 The media's attraction to terrorist figures is established in the assassination of President William McKinley by Leon Czolgosz. As Czolgosz awaits execution, newspaper and magazine reporters flock to interview him.

1910 The U.S. media's first major brush with terrorism occurs when two labor extremists bomb the headquarters of the *Los Angeles Times* in response to the publisher's fiercely anti-labor views.

1961 The first terrorist incident widely reported on television is the first aircraft hijacking in the United States. Although authorities regain control of the plane, filmed accounts dramatize the value of aircraft as a terrorist tool.

1967 Worldwide publicity accompanies the formation of the Popular Front for the Liberation of Palestine. Using U.S. media, leader George Habash promises terrorist action until Israel yields territory claimed in the June "Six Day War."

1968 Domestic terrorism swells with the formation of the left-wing Weather Underground. Thousands of bombings are orchestrated for filmed coverage on television newscasts.

1972 In the first global media terrorism spectacle, Israeli athletes are gunned down at the Olympic Games in Munich, Germany.

1974 The impact of live television is first demonstrated during a two-hour shootout between the Symbionese Liberation Army and Los Angeles police. The captors of heiress Patricia Hearst, SLA terrorists compete with Watergate as the period's most-covered news subject.

1979–81 The 444-day Iran Hostage Crisis marks a turning point in terrorist-media affairs. Blanket news coverage prolongs resolution. The rise of both Islamic extremism and state-sponsored terrorism begins in earnest. Iran's Ayatollah Khomeini pro-

claims the United States as the "Great Satan" of the Islamic world.

1985 The globalization of media dramatically showcases the escalation of terrorism. Spectacles include the assassination of Egypt's Anwar Sadat, the killing of 241 U.S. Marines in Beirut, a seventeen-day hijacking drama, and the killing of a wheelchair-bound passenger on the cruise ship *Achille Lauro*.

1986 Indignation in the United States over the terrorist killing of a U.S. wheelchair-bound passenger on the *Achille Lauro* speeds passage of the 1986 Antiterrorism Act. For the first time, concerns about terrorist manipulation of the media are widely expressed.

1988–89 Terrorist spectacles continue with the destruction of a Pan American jetliner over Lockerbie, Scotland. Weeks later, American networks broadcast a video showing the body of a captured U.S. Marine lieutenant colonel after his execution by hanging in Beirut.

1991 The Gulf War ends with American military based in Saudi Arabia. Saudi billionaire Osama bin Laden assembles a communication network to publicly denounce the "seizure" of his country.

1993–2000 During interviews where he invites Western media, bin Laden tells Western journalists that an attack on the United States is imminent. This furthers speculation that he is responsible for the 1993 World Trade Center bombing, the 1998 attacks on U.S. embassies in Africa, and the 2000 strike on the USS *Cole*.

September 11, 2001 The hijackings of four jetliners and the destruction of the World Trade Center and Pentagon inspire unprecedented media coverage. Instant public reaction assures the first "war on terrorism," which U.S. President George W. Bush declares the following day.

midday on September 11, 80 percent of Americans were aware of what had occurred. Through that afternoon, mixed with televised scenes of shock and destruction, calls for retaliation were voiced. That night, Americans witnessed an extraordinary scene on television. Almost every broadcast, cable, and satellite network—more than 100 in num-

ber—suspended regular programming. Most Americans tuned to news coverage either on news channels such as CNN or Fox, or the main networks of ABC, CBS, and NBC. Yet even on channels that ranged from QVC to A&E, and from Animal Planet to ESPN, terrorism was the only subject. The media had united the nation in a resolve unmatched since the invasion of Pearl Harbor (1941). Epitomizing the drawing together of Americans was the night-long appearance of aging CBS news anchor Dan Rather on MTV.

The public remained riveted both to the crisis and to the media. Through sophisticated Internet searches, newspaper reporters rather than official sources were the first to identify the hijack suspects, the first to publicly finger Osama bin Laden as being behind the attack, and the first to publicly trace bin Laden to the caves of Afghanistan. Americans were informed of recovery efforts at "Ground Zero," stepped-up security measures, and where to purchase American flags. The retaliatory U.S. invasion of Afghanistan finally began on October 7. The swift removal of Taliban leadership was covered as intensively as the September 11 attacks. This was followed by weeks of intrigue when bin Laden's whereabouts could not be pinned down.

Media Performance Under Attack

Despite unprecedented efforts to keep the public informed, concerns and critiques were soon voiced. From commentators, critics, and others who followed them closely, the media received few high marks for their performance during the crisis. First heard were complaints about rumors, inaccuracies, and network's attempts to win viewers. To surpass rival CNN, Fox had Geraldo Rivera join in the search for Osama bin Laden. Soaring above all the others, though, were two special concerns—manipulation of the media and the media's ability to inform—which are core issues in a long-standing terrorist-media relationship.

Groups such as al-Qaeda claimed not to be terrorists but rather ideological entities whose objectives were ignored by the world. Fundamental in politically-motivated terrorist strategy is holding the media "hostage" to distribute their message. This way, terrorists seize the world stage. For mass casualty terrorists, such as those who perpetrated the September 11 attacks, the media is a tool through which to create greater fear and hype over terrorist actions and threats. False reports of bombs on aircraft, biological contamination, and the destruction of bridges were ongoing after the September 11 attacks. A spectacle was made of the anthrax scare, in which contaminated letters were sent through the U.S. postal system to various people in the media and government. The mail attacks frightened millions of Americans and did take some lives, but responsibility for them has not been definitively determined. There are lingering concerns, however, that the anthrax letters and al-Qaeda are connected.

Nevertheless, the fear and confusion that arose with the anthrax scare are precisely what many terrorist groups want to instill in their targets. As much as the media has shamed bin Laden, it has also rushed to reach him. Concerns about "legitimization" of bin Laden as an acceptable ambassador of the causes he purported to support were touched off when U.S. networks televised their catches of exclusive bin Laden interviews from the Arabic news channel al-Jazeera. Every time bin Laden appeared on al-Jazeera, he also was bannered on American TV, increasing his recognition level for Americans and raising his profile to his supporters. The media, then, was caught in the middle of the problem of manipulation—report on bin Laden to inform the American public and at the same time risk increasing the terrorist's reputation with his own supporters by increased coverage.

There were also concerns, voiced by the U.S. government, that bin Laden used his videos to provide his followers with hidden or cryptic messages. On Oct. 10, 2001, Condoleezza Rice, President George Bush's national security adviser, held a telephone conference call with major television news executives. She asked them to stop airing live or unedited anti-U.S. video statements from Osama bin Laden and his lieutenants. She cautioned American television networks against being used by bin Laden and his followers for dissemination of their hidden messages and propaganda.

Equal attention grew around the other big issue: whether the media had kept Americans properly informed. In the minds of many, the shock of September 11 was a function not just of unthinkable acts but of an American public oblivious to global terrorism. Opinion polls showed that most Americans had not known of the U.S. military presence in Saudi Arabia, which dates from the Gulf War (1991). This was among the factors that bin Laden claimed as motivation for the September 11 attacks. Reports later surfaced that the hijackers had trained at flight schools in the United States. They had been welcomed into the United States by unsuspecting hosts unknowing of their guests' true motives. Reporting after the attack revealed lax airport security measures, as well as law enforcement and intelligence agencies tangled in bureaucracy. Most agreed that the media had not done enough to keep the public informed about terrorism in general and threats to U.S. interests in particular.

For example, news agencies had given little coverage to reports of an anticipated al-Qaeda strike in the United States during the millennium celebration on January 1, 2000. When al-Qaeda

AL-JAZEERA

Al-Jazeera, the pre-eminent Arab news network, may be relatively new on the media scene to those in the West, but it is already no stranger to conflict—both in the Middle East crises on which it reports and in the controversy created by what some consider its biased coverage.

In fact, while the name al-Jazeera has only been in use since 1996, most of the staff are old hands at news reporting. In April of that year, BBC Arabic Television, a BBC partnership with a Saudi Arabian company, was forced to shut down because of a Saudi attempt to censor a documentary on executions in the country. A new satellite channel, however, quickly took its place, funded by the emir of Qatar and other Arab moderates. Many of the journalists who had been with BBC Arabic began working at the new network, al-Jazeera. Broadcast uncensored except in Qatar, al-Jazeera swiftly began topping viewer ratings in the Middle East and rivaling its Western counterparts for the quality and timeliness of its reporting. It was al-Jazeera that broke the story of the April 7, 2002, ambush in the West Bank town of Jenin and broadcast the only pictures of Afghan demonstrators attacking and burning the U.S. embassy in late September 2001.

While al-Jazeera's credentials might not be in question, however, the topic of its integrity has spawned fierce debate. Some newspapers have charged al-Jazeera of being Osama bin Laden's mouthpiece, an accusation perhaps partly born of the fact that bin Laden chose al-Jazeera to broadcast his videotaped statements to the Muslim world. Other critics have likened al-Jazeera's news coverage to a rallying war cry, claiming the repetitive shots the channel airs of dead and dying Palestinians—while ignoring or impersonalising Israeli losses—stokes Arab anger. Still others denounced what they perceive as an anti-Western bias embraced by the network.

Defenders of al-Jazeera are quick to point out that Israeli authorities and journalists appear regularly on the satellite channel although they have been all but banned on other Arab networks. Al-Jazeera has also aired interviews with Western officials such as U.S. Secretary of State Colin Powell and National Security Advisor Condoleezza Rice. It should also be noted that the network doesn't shy away from controversy out of any notions of self-preservation. Al-Jazeera's bureaus around the region are periodically closed due to its insistence on broadcasting stories about government corruption in various Middle Eastern countries, such as Egypt and Saudi Arabia.

Ironically enough, in light of all this contention, al-Jazeera's motto is "We get both sides of the story." Regardless of what Western journalists may think about the veracity of this statement, it would seem that the Arab world is content enough to embrace al-Jazeera as one of its primary sources of information during these troubled times.

---

attacked the USS *Cole* nine months later in the Yemeni port of Aden, the media's interest had dissipated. Further, as President Bill Clinton prepared to leave office, members of his administration had warned of a possible terrorist action on American soil. Reduced to sound bites, these warnings had not been amplified in any sector of the general news media.

To alleviate public confusion and fear after September 11, the media began work on their own antiterrorism response. One step especially visible in the local media followed the newsroom sentiment that many news stories had done more to alarm than to inform. Through October 2001 news providers had rushed to cover all types of hijacking and bomb scares and unsubstantiated threats. Camera crews had not wanted to miss scenes of building evacuations and airport shut downs. Concerns that such coverage was adding to the public's problems reached a climax in November when California governor Grey Davis held a news conference and, based on information he said was credible, announced the possible destruction of the Golden Gate Bridge and other highway structures. After it was determined the threat was a hoax, most news media stopped covering threat spectacles. Earlier, the government had announced that the bin Laden tapes might contain hidden messages directed toward terrorist operatives still at work, which added to sentiment that editors and producers needed to demonstrate greater restraint.

The news media's efforts to increase religious and cultural awareness of Arabs and Muslims was a notable effort to prevent a backlash against Arab and Muslim Americans by other ethnic groups in the country. As a result, Americans learned that some of the most vehement anti-American Islamic leaders had condemned the September 11 attacks. By publicizing the outrage of Arabs and Muslims over the September attacks, the nonviolent doctrines of the Muslim religion, and examining the Arab and Muslim cultures the media helped alleviate what could have been a spiraling pattern of reprisals against Arab-Americans, though more than 1,500 anti-Arab and anti-Muslim attacks did take place after September 11, 2001. Even so, questions continue. The United States' "free press" tradition enabled the media to remain free to cover terrorism as they pleased.

HISTORICAL BACKGROUND

The Media and Domestic Terrorism

The media has covered terrorist activities for a longer period than most people realize. Fear of terrorism gripped the country after the assassination of President William McKinley (1897–1901) by anarchist Leon Czolgosz in 1901. Apprehended and condemned to death, Czolgosz assumed celebrity status as a martyr. Flocking to "death row" interviews, aghast yet fascinated reporters became unwitting conduits for Czolgosz's pleas for more violence.

The McKinley assassination stimulated the media's interest in what became an onslaught of organized violence. By 1920 roughly two dozen major terrorist acts had been committed by a militant pro-labor organization called the Industrial Workers of the World. These acts had included the assassinations of local political figures, the bombings of railroads, and the destruction of mines in Pennsylvania, Colorado, and Idaho. The media had a notable brush with labor terrorists in 1910, when a group that had failed to unionize the *Los Angeles Times* destroyed the headquarters of that newspaper. Although publicity had not been a main goal of these early terrorists, writers and editors remained captivated by their activities. During the so-called "Roaring '20s," newspapers reported on many of the thousands of kidnappings, bombings, and lynchings perpetrated by the Ku Klux Klan. A distant glimpse of media-directed terrorism had been coverage given to New York's so-called "Mad Bomber" in the 1930s and 1940s. Later arrested and identified as anarchist George Peter Metesky, this figure was linked to about two dozen bombings and bombing attempts that, he said, were aimed at publicity. One of his targets had been the seventy-story RCA Building, the headquarters of NBC.

It was not until the 1960s, however, that the connection between media and terrorists assumed modern form. The key development was the emergence of television (TV). Prior to the widespread popularity of TV, the public had been exposed to violent acts through still photos, newsreels, and worded accounts on radio and in print. During the 1960s TV expanded into a high percentage of American homes. With this, terrorism became a living-room experience. Two events in that decade further defined the media-terrorist relationship—the first air hijacking in the United States and the formation of the Weather Underground.

The first U.S. air hijacking occurred on August 3, 1961, when a Continental Airlines jetliner took off from Phoenix, Arizona. Communist sympathizers brandishing small knives forced their way into the cockpit and took control of the plane, and ordered the captain to fly it to Cuba. When the jetliner refueled in El Paso, Texas, and authorities stormed the plane, TV cameras recorded every detail. The reporting of the terrorists' methods was extensive. Growing numbers of successful hijackings subsequently occurred around the world. Apparent from each episode's intense publicity was the value of aircraft as a terrorist tool.

From the rise in left-wing terrorism in the late 1960s came the second event. It was the formation in the mid-1960s of a domestic terrorist organization known as the Students for a Democratic Society, comprised of college-educated radicals united in their opposition to the Vietnam War (1964–75). The group spun off from the non-violent League for Industrial Democracy, a social-democratic organization originating in the 1950s, which was the main force behind campus-based radical movements in the 1960s. The Students for a Democratic Society became increasingly revolutionary and, in 1960, split into two groups.

One of these was a radical offshoot that soon garnered more attention as a domestic terrorist group—the Weather Underground. Opposed to the Vietnam War, the U.S. invasion of Cambodia, and what they perceived as American imperialism, the so-called "Weathermen" were not only the first to recruit and train operatives within a military-like command structure, the organization's leaders were among the first to perfect a "hit-and-run" strategy that further demonstrated how news media could be lured into the coverage of terrorist acts. After planting bombs at buildings and landmarks, such as banks, courthouses, and federal buildings—all targets of U.S. authority, democracy, and power—operatives sent "communiques" to the Federal Bureau of Investigation (FBI) and

MEDIA REPORTS, WHETHER BY TELEVISION, RADIO, OR SOME OTHER MEANS, ARE RELIED ON BY MANY FOR ACCURATE, RELIABLE INFORMATION. TERRORISTS OFTEN PLAN ATTACKS TO ACHIEVE THE MOST MEDIA ATTENTION, AND THUS GAIN ATTENTION FOR THEIR CAUSE. *(AP/Wide World Photos/Peter Dejong. Reproduced by permission.)*

police. The evacuation of target locations, and often the actual explosions, became regular scenes on that period's television news.

By 1975 the Weather Underground lost impetus when each of its fugitive leaders were apprehended, and it officially disbanded in 1976. They had, however, cut a significant swath. According to official FBI reports, Weather terrorists were responsible for thirty-five bombings. Author Jay Robert Nash has written that as many as 4,000 bombings had links to the Weather Underground. The takeover of Columbia University in 1968 and a four-day rampage of riots and destruction in Chicago in 1969 were Weather-directed events. Rare was the American who had not seen these incidents depicted in the media. Also portentous had been this group's tying together of other terrorist elements in a cooperative "network" not unlike that directed by al-Qaeda. The first hint of a cooperative terrorist network beyond national borders was the Weather Underground's alliance with several terrorist groups outside the United States, including Germany's violent Baader-Meinhof gang, the Puerto Rican Armed Forces of National Liberation

(FALN), the Provisional Irish Republican Army, and the Palestinian al-Fatah.

Especially noteworthy towards bringing terrorism still further into the lap of the media was another left-wing extremist group called the Symbionese Liberation Army (SLA). The SLA began in 1972 and its activities increased dramatically in 1973 when leader Donald Freeze escaped from prison. Rather than attracting sporadic notice with hit-and-run episodes, the SLA sought to commandeer the entire media complex with a single, high profile act. This was fulfilled beginning on February 4, 1974, when the SLA kidnapped newspaper heiress Patricia Hearst, who was first confined to a closet for several weeks before she herself became active in the group. Through 1974, only one event—the Watergate scandal and the resignation of President Richard Nixon (1969–74)—surpassed the SLA in levels of coverage. Television networks interrupted programming each time a tape-recorded SLA communique was retrieved.

Further, a landmark in the media's reaction to terrorism occurred on May 18, 1974, when Los Angeles police stumbled onto an SLA hideout. Although television had made terrorism more real, Americans still were accustomed to seeing it after the fact. Coverage had consisted of filmed reports edited for the next day's news. In 1974 the Los Angeles station KNXT, however, had perfected the first "mini cam," a miniature TV camera with microwave capability that permitted live coverage from any on-the-scene location. Fifty million Americans witnessed a two-hour shootout and fire bombing exactly as it occurred. Live television brought a striking new dimension to terrorism. Hearst, who escaped the maelstrom, later affirmed in her memoir that from the perspective of her terrorist captors live coverage promised a "gripping" and "surreal" effect, just what they wanted.

The Media and Terrorism Abroad

Despite its long history, the fusion of terrorism and media at the domestic level only partially traced the direction and scale of the relationship. Conflict abroad, notably in the Middle East, had given rise to rebels whose objectives encompassed not just political discourse but social and religious revolution, the seizure of military power, and the undermining of a world order that had turned a deaf ear. Insurgent unrest had mostly only simmered as colonial rule ended in the period after World War II (1939–45). No group had had the potential for reaching the entire world, but sweeping advancements in global mass communication were soon made. A "global village" had formed from the extension of television and its worldwide linkage through instantaneous satellite delivery. With the globalization of media came the "modern era" of terrorist-media affairs.

Media and the Rise of the PFLP

This "modern" relationship between terrorism and the media began to take shape in 1967, the same year an organization known as the Popular Front for the Liberation of Palestine (PFLP) was formed. Visionary and media-minded, the PFLP was among the first groups to form in the pro-Arab underground movement. The PFLP operated under the umbrella of the Palestine Liberation Organization (PLO) and its leader Yasser Arafat until 1993, when it refused to participate in the Oslo peace accords. Unlike many other terrorist groups from the region, which are religiously organized, the PFLP operates primarily as a political organization that opposes peace with Israel.

Created by a ruthless yet educated and media savvy figure named George Habash, a Palestinian Christian, the group maintains a nationalist and Marxist-Leninist ideology. Habash, along with PLO leader Yasser Arafat, was among the first spokesmen for the hundreds of thousands of Palestinians living in the area that, after World War II, became the nation of Israel. The fortunes of these Palestinians, and their need for a homeland, was central to Arab legitimacy in the post-colonial period. Several Arab states battled Israel in 1948 and 1956, as well as later in 1967 and 1973, over the small nation's right to exist and the dispersal of the Palestinians who had once lived there. Some concerns were mollified by a 1949 treaty affirming the original 1948 United Nations (UN) partition of Israel, though many Arab states remained closed off to ties with their new neighbor. The partition allocated the land of the Golan Heights in the north, Gaza in the south, and the area in and around the holy city of Jerusalem known as the West Bank to the Palestinians.

Then in 1967 came the turning point that would herald the PFLP's formation. On June 1, Israel declared war after Egypt blocked shipping lanes and several other Arab nations took belligerent steps towards Israel. In decisive attacks over the next six days, the Israelis claimed all of the previously withheld territories. For Habash and other Arab leaders, vows by the United States that American forces would protect the new and enlarged Israel were ominous. Over impassioned Arab protests, the Israeli conquests were sanctioned by the UN. With diplomacy foreclosed and the Arab military in ruins, terrorism was considered by many to be the only potentially effective pro-Arab response.

Immediately and publicly, Habash detailed sweeping terrorist initiatives. The PFLP charter had promised a continuous "death" conflict with Israel. The role of the media simultaneously was set forth. Secretly, Habash preached expropriation of the media to Arafat and other disciples. Notably, too, the rationale for media-directed terrorism had been articulated by Habash in a 1970 article, "A Leader of the Fedayeen," in *Life* magazine (Oriana Fallaci, June 22, 1970). Habash told *Life* that "to kill a Jew far from the battleground has more effect than killing 100 of them in a battle; it attracts more attention. And when we set fire to a store in London, those few flames are worth the burning down of two kibbutzim. [Through the media] we force people to ask what is going on." Few Americans responded to what seemed to be Habash's anti-Israel diatribe.

Fatah Stages a High Publicity Event

Passing attention was given to early strikes by Fatah in Europe and at Tel Aviv's Lod Airport. Fatah is a guerrilla faction that served as the main wing of the PLO and relied on Arab support for its efforts. The PFLP formed in opposition to Fatah and pursued a strategy that included enlisting help from sources such as Russia and China, which Fatah was disinclined to do.

The world finally awakened to the growing threat of terrorism in August 1972 during the Summer Olympics in Munich, Germany. Fatah's Black September unit penetrated the dormitory that housed Israeli athletes. After murdering a coach and a weightlifter, the hostage-takers announced that they would kill an additional Israeli every hour unless their demands for the release of prisoners were met. All of this had been planned with the certainty of worldwide media publicity. More than 100 countries' radio and television networks were deployed in Munich for the Olympic Games. The episode finished with a horrific conclusion. Expecting safe passage back to the Middle East, the terrorists killed nine more Israeli athletes as they themselves were gunned down at the Munich airport.

The Munich bloodbath was the first truly global terrorist spectacle. It revealed the ease by which terrorists could manipulate not just national but multi-national media. Additionally, the intense glare of the Munich events had dramatized Habash's most chilling pronouncement: that Middle East terrorists would stop at nothing, and would sacrifice their own lives, toward bringing their demands to the attention of the world. Famed ABC sports commentator Jim McKay won that year's Emmy Award for his expert coverage of the breaking news. Again and again, McKay had emphasized that had global television not converged on Munich, the tragedy would most likely not have occurred.

The Media's Eye on the Iran Hostage Crisis

Likewise inspired by the PFLP, the next showcase was the Iran Hostage Crisis between 1979 and 1981, which began as an unauthorized hostage taking situation but later achieved the support of the Iranian government, thus becoming a state-sanctioned act. Its status as a purely terrorist event is up for debate, but again, the matter of media complicity was aired. Yet it was not this issue but rather its complement—the effectiveness of media-delivered information—that would stare back from this more precipitous event.

On November 4, 1979, armed Islamic dissidents stormed the U.S. embassy and claimed 63 people inside as hostages. What began as a publicity maneuver by the hostage-takers wound up as a protracted media melodrama. American news agencies competed with one another for "scoop" stories and the latest "hostage tapes." Nightly newscasts were headlined by the number of days the hostages had been in captivity. Ceaseless and emotional interviews with hostages' families stirred intense public concern about the hostages' safety. This had severely weakened President Jimmy Carter's (1977–81) response capability, as he could not effectively bargain with the Iranians due to the high media scrutiny and publicized fears amongst the American public that the hostages would be killed.

Among the effects of this stasis situation was an ill-fated rescue attempt. Carter's handling of the Iran Hostage Crisis was one of the main issues contributing to his 1980 presidential election defeat by Ronald Reagan (1981–88). The hostage crisis was the very first event covered by the first 24-hour television news channel, CNN. The first late-night network news broadcast, ABC's "Nightline," was another of the media's reactions to the crisis. "Nightline" evolved from terrorist updates ABC had entitled "America Held Hostage."

In the midst of this crisis, however, a gaping breakdown of understanding was observed. The public had been given little information on the rise of Islamic fundamentalism and extremism, leading to the underestimation by most Americans of the dimensions of the movement that led to the embassy takeover.

The Iran Hostage Crisis had shock value greater than Munich and was only equaled later by September 11. Most attributed the surprise to the failure of the American news media to effectively report recent changes in the Middle East. Massive U.S. arms sales to Saudi Arabia and other political developments of turmoil in the Middle East had been relegated to back page news, while the historic 1977 meetings between Egyptian President Anwar Sadat and Israeli Prime Minister Menachem Begin—engineered in part through overtures by CBS's Walter Cronkite and ABC's Barbara Walters—consumed the media and the public in an image of peace. By initiating a presence in Saudi Arabia and encouraging the softening of Egypt towards the existence of Israel, the United States had inflamed Islamic extremists who objected to the culture, politics, and style of the Western superpower.

The new leader of Iran, the Ayatollah Ruhollah Khomeini, had been swept into power by a strong surge of Islamic fundamentalist and anti-American sentiment. Still focused on the peace forged by Sadat and Begin, however, the media left the public with the impression that Middle East conflicts were on their way to resolution. In reality, a new and more frightening conflict had begun and was being left behind in many news reports—the rise of the United States as what Iran's Khomeini called the "Great Satan" of the Islamic world.

Not all of the Iranian coverage was devoted to the spectacle. An outpouring of articles, documentaries, forums, and discussions aimed at helping Americans better fathom Arab and Islamic perspectives was noteworthy. In part because they too were confused, editors, publishers, and news executives recognized a need for public education. Starting with Iran, background analysis was included in terrorist coverage. For the first time, news providers enlisted policy experts and military consultants. Through the media, Americans learned of the mix between the religion of Islam and politics in the Middle East, while news agencies placed correspondents in more Arab capitals. The media's drive for Islamic awareness did become less intense but continued after "Day 444," when the hostages were freed.

With the rise of Khomeini in Iran, however, the media-terrorism nexus entered a new phase. For groups that had included and sprung from the PFLP, terrorism was limited because money was needed. If they acted as bandits, terrorists risked discovery and destruction. Khomeini shifted the paradigm by sanctioning terrorism as an official function of the Iranian government in an attempt to export its revolution. New groups such as Hizballah received support from Iran in its formation and drew from the country's government coffers as

CONCERNS OVER GOVERNMENT LEAKS OF SENSITIVE INFORMATION TO THE MEDIA AROSE AFTER THE SEPTEMBER 11 TERRORIST ATTACKS. MEDIA REPORTING OF SUCH INFORMATION CAN SOMETIMES COMPROMISE GOVERNMENT PLANS. (*John Cole,* The Herald-Sun, Durham, NC. Reproduced by permission.)

well. It became a primary example of how terrorists were coming to operate under the protection of some governments. This concept of state-sponsored terrorism soon spread to Iraq, where Saddam Hussein had just emerged, and to Libya, where Muammar Qadhafi had consolidated control. Sudan and Afghanistan, the eventual havens for Osama bin Laden, would also join this group. For the media, the advent of state-sponsored terrorism brought a thicket of new complications.

Chief among these was an expansion in terrorist activities that left terrorism still more difficult to portray. Not only did terrorist cells thrive under protective umbrellas afforded by the governments of Iran, Iraq, Libya, and Sudan, but these societies became increasingly closed, making reporting on events within them extremely difficult. Changes in Iran were notable. Khomeini's predecessor, Mohammad Reza Shah Pahlavi, the Shah of Iran, had actively reached out to the West. Iran's domestic media system had been one of the more open and progressive among countries in that part of the world. Few restrictions were placed on Western correspondents. Through the 1970s Iraq, too, had been a relatively open nation.

Yet with the emergence of regimes like those of the Ayatollah Khomeini in Iran and Saddam Hussein in Iraq, both in 1979, flows of information deemed credible in the West ground to a halt.

Cadres of American and European journalists had sought to expose the massing of arms and the training of terrorist guerrillas. To do this, these journalists needed to penetrate terrorist enclaves, potentially facing death if they were caught. This fact was brought home in Pakistan in 2002 when *Wall Street Journal* reporter Daniel Pearl was killed while investigating a story.

Only through half-informed sources and second-hand accounts was the world aware that terrorist militants had formed. Packaged as Islamic covenants, official pronouncements had reached out to Islamic fundamentalists. Publicly, Khomeini stated: "God is our goal, the Prophet is our leader. The Koran is our Constitution, struggle is our way. Death in the service of God is the loftiest of our wishes." In the West, such rhetoric was discredited as government propaganda. Khomeini and his followers trumpeted increasing violence against the West. These claims had seemed so unlikely that they were passed off as more fundamentalist rhetoric. One of the most noteworthy of these was Khomeini's announcement that: "All the rulers of Islamic countries are servants of foreigners . . . and have left the entire Islamic heritage in the hands of foreigners. . . .We have to spread Islam everywhere, and in this path we have given a great deal of blood, and we will give more . . . .Whatever is necessary to destroy them must be carried out."

Sensitive Information and the Media

The arrival of state-sponsored terrorism in the Middle East presented new problems for U.S. policymakers that would test the relationship between the media and the U.S. government. A key issue was the media's handling of sensitive and top secret information. It was not until the increase in state-sponsored terrorism that the government formulated policies. This began in 1984 under President Ronald Reagan, whose Secretary of State, George Schultz, issued the first counterterrorism National Security Directive. This secret plan prescribed sneak attacks on terrorist bases and the uprooting of terrorist networks through covert means. Leading newspapers such as the *New York Times* and the *Washington Post* had sources inside the State Department who related what the plan entailed. Schultz met with publishers and media executives. He insisted that exposure of the plan would compromise antiterrorist action and urged the media to withhold what they knew.

For the media, this became and remains a very difficult task. Confronted on the one side by the terrorists' own secretive nature, and on the other by the public's presumed "need to know," much of what the media knew in turn became known to everybody. Although major news agencies agreed to protect most of the Schultz directive, parts of it did seep out. Then, a notable example of media exposure occurred in 1986, when in an undercover operation, U.S. warplanes struck at terrorist hideouts in Libya. CNN was on the air and detailing the attack with planes still en route. These planes would have been easy targets had Libya been forewarned by CNN's broadcast and possessed antiaircraft fire to shoot the planes down. Additionally, in 1987 and 1988 sensitive initiatives aimed at freeing U.S. hostages in Lebanon were prolonged by the media's prying reports.

An issue of increasing concern was, and still is, the "leaking" of information by the government. Versed in the media's obsession for "inside knowledge," government officials knew that they could use the media to channel counterterrorism ventures. The Reagan administration perfected this strategy. In a 1981 case, administration "insiders" leaked as "classified information" vague reports that a presidential assassination attempt by U.S.-based Libyan terrorists was imminent. American news agencies trailed this story for weeks. Although it lacked substance, the coverage helped mold public support for the passage of antiterrorist legislation. Following the U.S. strikes on Libya, insiders acted again by feeding false reports of an all-out invasion of that country. While no such plan existed, the publicity was sufficient to make Libyan leader Muammar Qadhafi back off some of his anti-American rhetoric and action and lower his profile for a while. State Department spokesperson Bernard Kalb, formerly a CBS correspondent, resigned in protest over the government's handling of terrorism with tactics such as these.

The media addressed these cases of misinformation through protest but also through a more likely and effective tactic, investigative reporting. Investigative reporters used different, more accurate "inside" sources to uncover the other "insiders" who were leaking false reports. One of these reporters was Bob Woodward of the *Washington Post*, a figure who had achieved fame for helping reveal the Watergate scandal that led to the resignation of President Richard Nixon in 1974. In 1986 Woodward published a series of scathing front-page exposés on the Reagan administration's misinformation program. These exposés, which had roused Reagan's opponents and placed the administration in a negative light, demonstrated how the media could keep the government in check.

As concerns about terrorism continued, controversies over the handling of sensitive material also continued. Policymakers still complained that prying reporters impeded antiterrorist measures, while reporters realized that their dependence on government sources made them captives of managed information.

Up Close and Personal with Terror

All of these matters bore down on the media as global terrorism became what it is today: a long chain of heinous crimes and nightmare news events. Like moths to a flame, the media was drawn to every incident. From his overtures to Israel, Egypt's Sadat won the Nobel Peace Prize in 1978, and in 1981 he was gunned down by an Islamic extremist hit squad and the assassination televised live on Egyptian TV. In 1982 Bashir Gemayal, the president-elect of Lebanon, was killed by Syrian terrorists who used a 440-pound percussion bomb to carry out their assassination. In 1983, 241 U.S. Marines stationed in Beirut were killed when a truck packed with TNT exploded. The attack is suspected to be the responsibility of Hizballah, though the group has denied involvement. Other sources allege that the group Islamic Jihad was responsible.

In June 1985, in the largest terrorist media event since the Iran Hostage Crisis, two Lebanese Hizballah terrorists hijacked a TWA jetliner en route to Rome as it took off from Athens. For seventeen days, as the plane flew between Algiers and Beirut, passengers were beaten and held at gun-

AL-JAZEERA, A PROMINENT ARAB NEWS NETWORK, HAS HAD THE INTEGRITY OF ITS NEWS CALLED INTO QUESTION BY MANY IN THE WEST AFTER THE TERRORIST ATTACKS OF SEPTEMBER 11, 2001. AL-JAZEERA WAS THE FIRST TO BROADCAST VIDEOTAPED STATEMENTS BY OSAMA BIN LADEN, THE ALLEGED MASTERMIND OF THE SEPTEMBER ATTACKS. (© *AFP/CORBIS. Reproduced by permission.*)

point. Then, in October 1985, the PFLP hijacked the Italian cruise ship *Achille Lauro*. While describing their maneuvers on radio, the terrorists seized the documents of the Americans on board. After choosing at random the passport of wheelchair-bound passenger Leon Klinghoffer, he was killed on the spot.

Indignation over the *Achille Lauro* affair sealed enactment of the 1986 Antiterrorism Act. Section 1202 of the act made it a Federal crime for a terrorist overseas to kill, attempt to murder, conspire to murder, or to engage in physical violence with the intent to cause bodily injury to a United States national. It was based on this legislation that President George W. Bush launched his "war on terrorism" after the September 11, 2001, terrorist attacks. Observers agreed that passage of the 1986 act had hinged no more on terrorist incidents than it had on the fact that through the media Americans could not escape them. The first major expressions of doubt within the media community came early on after the passage of the act.

Urging his colleagues to reconsider their fixation with the suffering of victims' families, ABC commentator George Will referred to this aspect of terrorism coverage as the "pornography of grief." Troubled that his own network had been a mari-

onette in the TWA affair, NBC anchor Tom Brokaw complained of "too much . . . unexpurgated television transmission coming from Beirut. The people were getting a kind of voyeurish experience. There was a real exploitation going on, which I don't think we should allow."

Nevertheless, whenever incidents erupted, and wherever terrorists, authorities, and victims crossed paths, the media, too, were there. In 1986, 204 revelers were injured or killed when a Libyan bomb ripped through a disco in Berlin. In 1988 a New York-bound Pan American jetliner with 259 passengers was blown up as it flew over Lockerbie, Scotland. In 1989 the world gasped again when television networks transmitted yet another hostage tape. Provided by Lebanese terrorists, this tape showed the tortured body of Marine Lieutenant Colonel William Higgins following his execution by hanging.

Known, but marginally reported in 1991, was the continued presence of half a million U.S. troops in Saudi Arabia, and their public denunciation by a Saudi millionaire named Osama bin Laden. Little attention was paid by the media and the public to bin Laden's expulsion from Saudi Arabia and his moves to Sudan and Afghanistan. At the time, he was not a known terrorist who had acted against

SEPTEMBER 11: THE MEDIA RESPOND

Swift approval of President George W. Bush's "war on terrorism" was the main outcome of the September 11 terrorist attacks on the United States. Before the president could speak to the public, television and other media had riveted Americans to the crisis. Instantaneous marshalling of public opinion cleared the way for the United States' new war. Even so, questions were raised. Issues were not new but nested in a long-standing "terrorist-media relationship."

- Notable was the mobilization of television, radio, news agencies, and Internet sources within minutes of the mid-morning September 11 attacks. Eighty percent of Americans knew of these events by noon of that day.

- Reminding many Americans of the 1941 Japanese attack on Pearl Harbor was the media's blanket response. On the night of September 11, virtually every broadcast, cable, and satellite channel suspended regular programming and provided crisis coverage, which galvanized national unity.

- Coverage peaked again on October 7, 2001, with the launch of the war in Afghanistan. Through the media, Americans followed the removal of Taliban forces, the routing of al-Qaeda, and, then, the military's search for terrorist leader Osama bin Laden.

- The first questions arose when the media fomented public fears during a purported anthrax assault by terrorists. Concerns also appeared when American networks rushed to televise interviews with bin Laden. After related concerns about threat spectacles such as airport evacuations, the coverage of such events was reduced.

- A second questionable area was the media's effectiveness in informing the American public. Several factors suggested that Americans were oblivious to global terrorism prior to September 11, 2001.

lauding their knowledge of aircraft systems, weak U.S. airport security, and his communication to the operatives during their preparation. The implications of these boasts were something that the media had yet to investigate.

RECENT HISTORY AND THE FUTURE

The history of terrorism is more than a progression of politics, ideology, and senseless events. It also is the story of normal human beings—from policymakers to people on the street—who through the media have witnessed terrorism countless times and who again and again have been struck by the next terrorist act.

This pattern has not been confined to terrorism centered in the Middle East and the regions nearby. British-controlled Northern Ireland struggles to maintain its peace accord and eliminate threats of continued violence in the region. One of the deadliest incidents perpetrated by the Irish Republican Army (IRA), a bombing near Belfast that killed or injured 250 people, occurred as recently as 1998. One of the most fearsome terrorist events of recent times occurred in 1995 in Tokyo when the radical Aum Shinrikyo cult killed 12 and injured a thousand more when it released sarin nerve agent in the Tokyo subway. The 1995 bombing of the federal building in Oklahoma City was a sure sign that American domestic terrorism was far from eliminated. Like those in the Middle East, these recent spectacles unnerved people. Yet life went on and normality returned, while terrorism continued to be a threat.

The "war on terrorism," launched against al-Qaeda and terrorism in general in the wake of September 11, finally may mark the break in this pattern. Terrorism is a top priority of the current U.S. presidential administration. For the first time, Congress has approved military intervention and homeland security and public opinion is behind these initiatives. In the past the media may have numbed the public to terrorism and over-simplified the terrorism problem. If the war on terrorism is successful, however, the media will have played a history-shaping role. The media's magnification of the September 11 events contributed significantly to the U.S. public's attitude that terrorist actions are not tolerable and should be punished. Just as the media can buoy public support, however, it remains a double-edged sword through which the terrorist's cause may be promoted or sensationalized by the same media seeking to inform and win the higher ratings.

U.S. targets, but he was a credible threat the government was watching. One of the most publicity-minded of all terrorist leaders, bin Laden granted interviews to Western journalists. He is suspected of having links to the first World Trade Center attack in 1993, the 1998 attack on U.S. embassies in Africa, and the 2000 strike on the USS *Cole*, though bin Laden himself has only talked publicly (via videotape) about the September 11 attacks. Vowing the United States "would die," bin Laden boasted of operatives in the United States after the attacks,

Questions of Time, Resolve, and Media-Terrorist Legitimacy

The "war on terrorism" will be a long and uncertain affair. After September 11, Americans braced for a terrorist assault. Terrorism, however, is often not the engagement of battle but rather of secretly planned acts spaced years, if not decades, apart.

Accordingly, a pivotal question is whether interest and national unity against terrorism can be sustained over a prolonged period of time. Experts foresee a continuation among some groups of traditional terrorist strategy, which has always assumed several objectives, including attention-grabbing attacks, demands on a government or society, and—for politically motivated terrorist groups such as the Irish Republican Army and the Basque separatists—legitimacy for their cause.

Complicating this picture is the recent increase in the number of terrorists with no immediate political demands who provoke violence from feelings of outrage and alienation. Many of these groups are more ideologically and religiously, rather than politically, based. Al-Qaeda is one such group. Although its demands have been explicit for the removal of American interests in the Middle East, al-Qaeda neither stepped forward nor voiced particular demands before or after September 11, 2001. In the meantime, the war on terrorism must address threats from individuals and groups who have no particular constituencies but whose violence can be just as, if not more, dangerous. Politically-oriented terrorist groups risk losing support if their acts kill too many, too indiscriminately. For those groups without specific political demands, there are few restrictions beyond financing and the opportunity to commit acts of mass casualty terrorism such as those seen on September 11.

Although the dimensions of terrorism are diverse, terrorist objectives will continue to involve the media. Two of these objectives are manifest in terrorist violence. First, terrorists plot incidents to arouse supporters and alert the world that causes, such as the political conflict between Protestants and Catholics in Northern Ireland, are worthy of human sacrifice. Second, terrorists have grievances and a variety of demands—among them political, ideological, and religious—that they feel can be met by holding a government or a people hostage to the threat or reality of violence.

Less visible, though—and a potential corrosive to national resolve—is what experts consider a third terrorist objective, one predominantly specific to groups with a political orientation. This is the achievement of legitimacy. Terrorists with political goals, such as Northern Ireland's IRA and the Euskadi ta Askatasuna (ETA) in northern Spain and southern France, seek independence. In the case of Northern Ireland, the IRA long sought the ousting of British control from Northern Ireland and that region's unification with the Republic of Ireland. ETA seeks a separate Basque homeland. Groups such as these exhort that they would forego violence if given a fair voice and equal seat from which to address their issues. Some observers have gone so far as to propose that if these groups and their complaints were recognized, political terrorism would become less frequent. While this view is highly uncertain and subject to debate, the political terrorist's quest for legitimacy is unquestioned—and can be helped by the media.

In sustaining the "war on terrorism" over the many years envisioned, success may rest on how well the U.S. administration continues to demonize terrorist leaders. One of its challenges will come from a media establishment whose tendency has been to portray top terrorist leaders in less-than-draconian terms, often playing up a cloak of mystery around them. Calculated public relations efforts by increasingly sophisticated terrorist groups will be encouraging the media in this regard. More of a push will be the media's own instinct to personalize figures in the news and perhaps seek to humanize a terrorist and, in the process, neglect the terror this person perpetrates on others.

This penchant was well-revealed—and the subject of much professional debate—when after September 11 the media probed every nook and cranny of Osama bin Laden's life. Portrayals, however, had negative consequences. By working in step to demystify bin Laden, the media actually raised his public profile. News reports emphasized bin Laden's family ties in the United States and that bin Laden had once helped the country as an informant for the Central Intelligence Agency (CIA). Bin Laden's videotapes were analyzed for what commentators saw as his serious, stable, and calm reactions. Background stories went on to tout bin Laden's intelligence, education, command of high technology, and that he was spiritual and worshipped by those he led. *Time* magazine even considered naming bin Laden as its 2001 "Man of the Year."

While bin Laden hardly was legitimized, the media's interest in his personal affairs was a typical reaction. In cases where terrorists seek political leverage, this practice of showcasing terrorist figures is believed by many to have significant effects. Former U.S. secretary of state Alexander Haig maintained that such treatment "risks making international outlaws seem like responsible personalities." In reporting the results of a 1994 study on the media's legitimization of terrorists, Brigitte L. Nacos concluded that it "does not make a difference whether an interviewer is tough on the terrorist or his sympathizer. The mere fact that the terrorist is interviewed by respected media representatives . . . elevates the person virtually to the level of a legitimate politician."

The PFLP's George Habash is a prime example of a terrorist leader once lambasted as the "devil" but who later thrived from his many invitations to appear in interviews and on TV talk shows. The interviews and photo opportunities given to Amal militia leader Nabih Berri during the 1985 TWA hijacking crisis is another example of media-terrorist legitimacy. Speaking for the hijackers, Berri was accorded live television interviews on at least fifty occasions. He appeared with CBS anchor Dan Rather on ten different editions of the "CBS Evening News." Additional interviews were carried on the ABC and NBC evening newscasts, ABC's "Nightline," NBC's "Today," and throughout the coverage provided by CNN.

On ABC's "Good Morning America," anchor David Hartman ended an interview by asking this terrorist, "Any final words to President Reagan this morning?" Hartman's question implied that Berri's words would be considered in official corridors, thus granting him a level of status beyond "terrorist" and closer to official spokesperson for his cause. History is rife with further examples. After the overtures for peace to Israel by Egypt's Anwar Sadat, Sadat's preceding career as one of the staunchest supporters of the PFLP, a figure vilified in the West, was expunged as the U.S. administration rushed to support Sadat's overtures and encourage peace between Egypt and Israel. The media's attempts to reach Iraq's Saddam Hussein, whose country is suspected of having biological and chemical weapons capabilities, during and since the 1991 Gulf War have also been relentless. PLO leader Yasser Arafat, a high profile individual heading the PLO for much of its history as a terrorist organization, eventually joined President Bill Clinton in strolling through the Rose Garden at the White House. The media gave little attention to Arafat's past position as the leader of a group that for years refused to recognize Israel's right to exist and refused to renounce terrorism. Indeed, under Arafat the PLO engaged in numerous terrorist acts. It finally acknowledged Israel's right to exist and renounced terrorism in December 1988.

Legitimization will not be an issue in the case of al-Qaeda. In the future, however, the government's "war on terrorism" will not target only this group. To succeed it must confront an array of leaders whose interests can be advanced by terrorism, by opportunities to be heard through the media, or by a combination of both. The media's handling and portrayal of these individuals may influence the war's direction.

Questions of Terrorist-Media Manipulation

More immediate is that question posed by the terrorist-media experience: will the media fall prey to terrorist manipulation against a backdrop of threats and violent acts? A case in point was the anthrax scare that dominated news reporting in the fall of 2001. At first, the prolonged coverage was accepted as positive because it heightened public vigilance. While few were physically affected, five victims did lose their lives. After several weeks of hearing about the dangers of biological terrorism, opinion polls suggested confusion from Americans, and a public less informed than it was disoriented. Even within the media community there were concessions that although anthrax was never traced to Osama bin Laden, the disarray in the U.S. government and public proved a major bin Laden coup. Although the anthrax attacks were considered not to be linked to bin Laden, the events as they unfolded fulfilled the terrorist determination to wreak havoc and disorder inside the United States. The degree to which the media may continue to help terrorists will depend on future events. While such events are impossible to predict, several points of interest will present themselves.

Notable among these is the handling of the media by those directing the war on terrorism. Thus far, the war has been pursued with success. At present, an overwhelming proportion of Americans both support the war and feel it is helping to address the terrorism problem. Still, the administration walks a tightrope. Through the media, the president must establish a war climate. Simultaneously, though, the president must also use the media to promote normality and alleviate fear. Adding to the president's dilemma is the abstract nature of a war against terrorism. After September 11, President Bush took forward-looking steps by declaring a "war on terrorism," having Congress approve a "war on terrorism," and vowing terrorist extermination through this "total war." Too much attention to terrorism, however, could straight-jacket the country and signal terrorist victory in paralyzing a nation with fear and uncertainty. Too little attention could lead to complacency—and another round of terrorist surprise.

Too often a more compelling reference point is not terrorism itself but anxieties inside the media community. When global terrorism rose in the 1980s, coverage was controlled by a handful of news agencies and, in the United States, just three television networks. These entities were authoritative. Today, new cable channels and Internet services have fragmented the audience and created a competitive melee. Critics fear that this "news war" will give terrorists more avenues to exploit. Not only is competition the root of "scoop" stories that lead to overtures to terrorists, but competition also feeds on sensational, attention-getting material, which fits terrorism like a hand-in-glove.

The anthrax scare was followed in the media by a ratings battle between CNN and the four-year-old Fox News Channel. Each week that the Nielsen ratings were publicized showed the Fox Channel's ratings victory. The public's window on the War on Terror will be colored by this competitive melodrama. When Fox hired Geraldo Rivera to hunt down bin Laden, ratings soared and viewers saw the gun Rivera had packed and said he was going to use. MSNBC used the war on terrorism to usher in Ashleigh Banfield a new news "star." Former presidential advisor Gary Sick has suggested that "the true genius of America [is] to transfer a political disaster into a commercial bonanza." These words have meaning as the war on terrorism moves forth with the media seeking to report all it can on the events taking place.

Finally, the media's own antiterrorism response can be followed with interest. Not since the Iran Hostage Crisis have newsroom decision-makers been more sensitive to their manipulation by terrorists. The news community continues to insist that as much as the media may be a conduit for terrorists, worse would be a world where terrorist acts go unreported. Within the bounds of this principle, however, is sentiment that the media must exert greater control on what they do report.

Centering the media's own war against terrorism is a movement to restrain and self-censor terrorist coverage. One result: within a few days of the Trade Center attacks, replays of the aircraft striking the buildings had almost disappeared. The media saw no value in indulging in this gut-wrenching event. Professionals—among them news managers and editors belonging to the Radio-Television News Directors Association (RTNDA)—now agree that if photographers should capture a gruesome scene, such as an actual terrorist strike, limits should be

JOURNALISTS FACE DAILY DEADLINES AND DANGEROUS SITUATIONS, SUCH AS THE BOMBING OF KABUL, AFGHANISTAN, TO REPORT THE NEWS. *(AP/Wide World Photos/Dimitri Messinis. Reproduced by permission.)*

placed on how it is shown. Under RTNDA guidelines affirmed in 2002, blood, bodies, and screams either are to be kept off the air or televised only with explicit preceding warnings to viewers. Moment-of-impact video is to be limited to same-day newscasts and shown only sparingly, such as in documentaries and special reports, thereafter.

Further, newsrooms are now encouraged to de-emphasize if not avoid building evacuation and airport scares. As a further step, the media endorsed the system enacted in 2002 by the Office of Homeland Security in which terrorist threats are communicated based on levels of possible danger. On the fringes of these discussions are media-terrorist laws in other countries. In Germany and Greece, excessive and overt coverage of terrorism can result in criminal prosecution. In Great Britain, antiterrorism policy contains an emergency provision that enables the government to intervene. British news providers who amplify a terrorist crisis, for example, are subject to arrest.

As for the American response, the ultimate issue is whether the threat of terrorism is sufficiently grave that it supercedes the principle of "freedom of the press." Under the First Amendment to the

U.S. Constitution, the media has extensive freedoms to publish and televise material. One limitation is cases in which reporting poses a clear and present danger to the U.S. government. Another limitation is the possibility of libel cases in which reporting that bears malicious intent falsely defames a public figure. Still, media freedoms under the First Amendment are vast. It is the First Amendment that enables the U.S. media to hold up portraits of terrorist leaders to the public and tout terrorist acts without government censorship, a freedom that is not always the case in other countries. A question for the future is whether the media will still function in a mostly open environment, or whether, with the wakening of the country to terrorism, greater restrictions will be imposed.

BIBLIOGRAPHY

Alali, A. Odasuo, and Kenoye Kelvin Eke. *Media Coverage of Terrorism*. Newbury Park, CA: Sage, 1991.

Alexander, Yonah, and Robert G. Picard. *In the Camera's Eye*. Washington, DC: Brassey's, 1991.

Altheide, David. *Creating Fear: News and the Construction of Crisis*. New York: Aldine de Gruyter, 2002.

Bremer, L. Paul. *Terrorism and the Media*. Washington, DC: U.S. Department of State, 1987.

Dobkin, Bethami A. *Tales of Terror*. New York: Praeger, 1992.

Fallaci, Oriana, "A Leader of the Fedayeen: 'We Want a War Like the Vietnam War,'" *Life*, June 22, 1970, p. 33.

Gans, Herbert J. *Deciding What's News*. New York: Pantheon, 1979.

Moaveni, Azaden. "How Images of Death Became Must-See TV," *Time*, April 29, 2002, 40.

Moran, Michael. "In Defense of al-Jazeera," NBC News Online. Available online at http://www.msnbc.com/news/643471.asp (cited April 29, 2002).

Nacos, Brigitte Lebens. *Terrorism and the Media: From the Iran Hostage Crisis to the World Trade Center Bombing*. New York: Columbia University Press, 1994.

Nash, Jay. *Terrorism in the 20th Century*. New York: Evans, 1998.

O'Neill, Michael J. *Terrorist Spectaculars*. New York: Priority, 1986.

Paletz, David, and Alex Schmid. *Terrorism and the Media*. Newbury Park, CA: Sage, 1992.

Picard, Robert G. *Media Portrayals of Terrorism*. Ames: Iowa State University Press, 1993.

Raboy, Marc, and Bernard Dagenais. *Media, Crisis, and Democracy*. Newbury Park, CA: Sage, 1992.

Rodenbeck, Max. "Broadcasting the War," *New York Times* Online, available online at http://www.nytimes.com/2002/04/17/opinion/17RODE.html?pagewanted=print&position;=top (cited April 29, 2002).

Schaffert, Richard. *Media Coverage and Political Terrorists*. New York: Praeger, 1992.

Craig Allen

The Muslim World Reacts to September 11

The attacks of September 11, 2001 against the World Trade Center and the Pentagon, two of the most visible symbols of American economic power and military might, shocked the United States and the whole world. The realization that the United States would likely retaliate for the loss of thousands of innocent civilians sent a collective shudder throughout the world, which nervously awaited news of the identity of the attackers.

World leaders immediately voiced their condemnations of the attacks, as well as their solidarity and sympathy for the suffering of the American people. Virtually every Middle Eastern state officially expressed heartfelt condolences to the American people. Iraq, however, was alone in not extending strong support to the United States. Instead Iraqi president Saddam Hussein argued that the terrorist attacks on American soil had been the inevitable "fruit" of its own foreign policy.

The deep Muslim concern for American victims on humanitarian and religious grounds was followed by a great fear that Americans would soon seek revenge against all Arabs and Muslims in response to the attack. As President George W. Bush (2001–) was deciding how to respond internationally, a backlash of anti-Arab and anti-Muslim violence inside the United States alarmed Arabsand Muslims throughout the world, as well as American policymakers. Many American Muslims and Arabs suddenly felt unwelcome in the United States, as Islamic places of worship and stores were vandalized, women wearing headdresses were harassed, and men who looked Arab were beaten, and in a few instances, killed. In response, President Bush visited mosques, reminded citizens that it was "un-American" to discriminate, and repeatedly emphasized to an American audi-

The Conflict

In order to better understand the nature of the Arab and Muslim response to the September 11 attacks, it is important to revisit what many believed to be the root causes that led to the tragedy and motivated the attackers. The reduction of complex histories and motives to pat stereotypes or phrases can be dangerously misleading and prevent the analysis necessary to halt future attacks.

Religious

- Muslim fundamentalists, as well as other religious fundamentalists, remain deeply suspicious of any new world order, and many have used religion to usher in the destruction of others to return to an idealized society. In other religions fundamentalists have provided numerous examples throughout modern and ancient history of similar such actions.

- Singling out any religious extremist group can deflect attention from the root causes of conflict, such as extreme wealth disparities, lack of economic opportunities, constant deteriorating standards of living, and the inability to protect and maintain a cohesive identity.

- Defining terms is critical to understanding the Muslim reaction to September 11. For example, how is terrorism defined? Who is a terrorist? Can a state be terrorist? Leaving such questions unanswered allowed Muslims to think that maybe this "war" is actually against Islam.

Political

- U.S. President George W. Bush has tried on several occasions to define the parties in conflict. According to him, "we're fighting evil," and there are no shades of gray. The mission of the United States, then, is to rid the world of "evildoers." Therefore the war is not against a particular country or people, but against the concept of "terrorism."

CHRONOLOGY

1095 Pope Urban preaches at Clermont sanctioning the First Crusade, which runs until 1099.

1097 The First Crusade reaches Constantinople in its first great expedition.

1100 Crusaders take control of Jerusalem.

1100–40 Crusaders and Muslims struggle for control of the region.

1144–45 The Second Crusade takes place.

1171 Saladin becomes ruler of the Turkish empire.

1174 Saladin takes Damasus.

1183 Saladin takes Aleppo.

1187–1192 The Third Crusade ensues.

May–July 1187 Saladin attacks and destroys a Crusader detachment at Tiberias, reconquering Jerusalem and a majority of Crusader territories.

October 1187 Jerusalem is captured.

1192 Richard the Lionheart makes a treaty with Saladin, recovering some land, but not the city of Jerusalem.

1193 Saladin dies; his sons enter into dispute with one another and divide his territories.

1194–1201 The Fourth and Fifth Crusades occur.

April 1204 Crusaders reach Constantinople.

1212 The Children's Crusade begins from Cologne and France.

1227 Frederick II begins the Seventh Crusade.

1229 Frederick makes a treaty with Sultan al-Kamil for Jerusalem and territories on the coast and the Seventh Crusade ends.

1245–47 The Eighth Crusade ensues.

1396 An attempt for a Crusade against the Turks is defeated decisively at the battle of Nicopolis.

1402 Tamerlane defeats the Ottoman sultan at Angora.

1422 Murad lays unsuccessful siege to Constantinople in a struggle against his challengers and begins a restoration of Ottoman power.

1443–44 A new Crusade led by King Ladislaus III of Poland and Hungary forces Murad II into a truce at Szegedin.

1444 Crusaders break a truce and are defeated at Varna.

1453 Mohammed II takes Constantinople.

---

ence unfamiliar with the religion that "Islam is a religion of peace."

Many Arab and Muslim groups felt keen frustration at not being able to communicate effectively to the American public through the media. Despite every major Muslim and Arab leader and organization's denouncement of the attack, many Americans only saw pictures of a small number of people dancing in the streets. To get their message of solidarity with the victims of the attacks across, many of these Arab and Muslim leaders and organizations relied instead on email and website postings, which reached only a limited audience.

In addition, the media drastically underreported or ignored the widespread instances of support that had sprung up all over the Arab and Muslim world. For example there were candlelight vigils from Bethlehem to Cairo, blood donation drives to help the wounded throughout the Middle East and in Muslim communities in other parts of the world, and condolence letters were sent to families of the victims. In Tehran, over 50,000 people observed a moment of silence to honor those killed, despite the intense political divisions that have long separated Iran and the United States.

Most Arabs and Muslims believed they had been doubly victimized by the September 11 tragedy. First, they felt that the attackers ignored the central messages of Islam and distorted certain verses of the Qu'ran to justify their political struggles. The hijackers were representing Islam to the world as a violent and irrational faith, leaving the majority of believers struggling to explain that "true" Islam, like Christianity, would never support violence against innocents. Secondly, the attackers also jeopardized the safety and security of many Muslim communities in the face of possible American hostility and retaliation.

While the Bush administration spoke out against discriminating against Arabs and Muslims,

Islamic charity groups were shut down under allegations of providing financial support to terrorist organizations, immigration barriers were raised, over one thousand Arabs and Muslims arrested and detained, and authorities allegedly engaged in extensive ethnic profiling. Despite the fact that over 400 Arabs and Muslims had died in the World Trade Center attack, American Arabs and Muslims feared that 'camps,' similar to Japanese internment camps following the Pearl Harbor attack during World War II (1939–45), would now be set up for them. In the information age where many in the Middle East have satellite dishes that allow viewers to see American media first-hand, anti-Arab and anti-Muslim commentaries and news broadcasts in the United States, though not widespread, caused alarm in the Muslim world.

Subsequent official announcements by President Bush did little to reassure the Arab and Muslim world. In these speeches, the president divided the world into two opposing camps: the democratic and freedom loving ("us") and the immoral and terrorist other ("them"). It would be the United States' mission to hunt down the 'barbaric' evildoers to rid the world of terrorism in whatever country it resided. For those trying to find out whether their country was on the U.S. terrorist list, President Bush gave few clues, but early comments made it clear to Muslims that in speaking of terrorism, the president had not excluded Islamic countries.

President Bush's early use of the term 'crusade' to describe the U.S. mission against the forces of evil sent chills down the spine of both Arabs and Muslims, as historically the word 'crusade' has meant the intentional mass killing of Muslims. While President Bush later regretted the use of the word, the selection of the code word "Infinite Justice" to describe the U.S. military campaign also seemed to suggest a biblical or Armageddon battle waged by Christians against non-Christians. This too was officially regretted and later replaced with "Operation Enduring Freedom," however, these two incidents, coupled with rising discrimination, left the Arab and Muslim world deeply anxious for the future.

When it became clear by early October 2001 that the United States intended to bomb Afghanistan, the Muslim world was confronted with another dilemma: how should it respond to an attack on another Muslim state? While the Taliban, like the early Puritans, were strict religious fundamentalists who had few admirers in the Middle East and the Muslim world, they were also fellow Muslims who had not directly participated in the September 11 attacks, and they governed over mil-

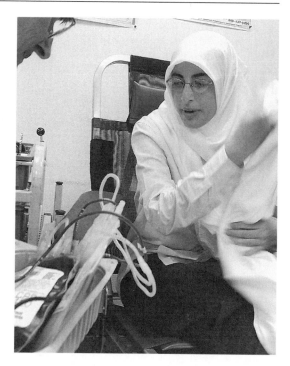

A MUSLIM AMERICAN WOMAN DONATES BLOOD TO HELP SEPTEMBER 11 RELIEF EFFORTS. MUSLIMS AND ARABS AROUND THE UNITED STATES WERE AS AFFECTED BY THE TERRORIST ATTACKS AS ANY OTHER AMERICANS. *(AP/Wide World Photos/Lucy Nicholson. Reproduced by permission.)*

lions of innocent Afghanis who would be among the victims of any attack against the Taliban regime. Was the United States really beginning a larger religious battle against all Muslims? Was it unfairly targeting an already poor and oppressed society? Many Middle Eastern countries concluded that the United States had the right to retaliate against the attackers, who had trained and had a network in Afghanistan, provided it focused solely on the culprits, avoided civilian casualties, and kept its mission narrowly defined. Aware that Muslims around the world feel a strong concern and solidarity with one another despite their many differences, and realizing the fear that Muslims had about American motives, the United States decided to launch a "Hearts and Minds" campaign to persuade Muslims and Arabs that the United States was not planning a larger war against Islam.

The audience that this campaign was directed towards was diverse. Arabs are both Christian and Muslim, while the majority of Muslims live outside of the Middle East and can be found in virtually every culture. In addition, what unites Arabs and Muslims across vast distances and cultures is a shared commitment to a just peace for the Palestinians and concern over the three holy cities of Islam: Mecca, Medina, and Jerusalem. Beyond these immediate, shared concerns, there were four distinct Arab and Muslim responses to the September 11 attacks that characterize the 'Arab street.'

On the one hand, there are those who viewed the attacks as inhumane, destructive, and unjustified. These 'moderate' Muslim voices (mainly political and religious leaders) denounced terror and violence as incompatible with the Islamic faith. A second majority group thought the attacks were wrong, but hoped that they might be a 'wake-up call' for the United States to reevaluate the effects its foreign policies may have on other nations and peoples. The third but considerably smaller group is made up of those who are supporters of Osama bin Laden and who praised the attacks on the United States as a way of fighting back against it for perceived American injustices abroad. From their point of view, the attackers were brave and honorable warriors engaged in a holy war against a Great Satan that sought to oppress and humiliate Muslims.

Unfortunately, the voices of those few are often heard the most loudly, drowning out the view of the majority of Arabs and Muslims who deeply oppose the strategies and motives of the attackers. The fourth and final group rejects that Arabs or Muslims took part in the attack at all, arguing instead that a large conspiracy against Arabs and Muslims is taking place. This comes from a belief that Islamic and Arab culture would never condone or participate in such violence and from a certain sense that much of these events are taking place beyond their ability to control them.

All of these groups experienced a general fear that the United States would begin a great war against Muslims, despite President Bush's assertions to Muslims that "we respect your faith. Its teachings are good and peaceful." President Bush went on to add that Islam itself had been hijacked by the attackers, which the majority of Muslims also believed. Part of the continuing fear in the Muslim world of American motives, however, has to do with the tendency of the media and several policymakers to repeatedly blame Islamic beliefs, culture or religion—even though they were distorted—as being responsible for motivating the attacks, rather than looking at other root causes which could have prompted them. Much of this response is rooted in long-standing misconceptions regarding Arabs, Muslims, and Islam in Western culture, which also explains the difficulty the ad-

ministration had in trying to change these negative stereotypes at home.

Muslim leaders and experts on Islam have emphasized, on numerous occasions since September 11, that unprovoked violence against innocent civilians is supported neither in the Qur'an nor in mainstream Islamic tradition, and that the majority of the world's Muslims do not support the holy war that Osama bin Laden had defined against the United States. Those leaders and experts note that even though there are some verses in the Qur'an that talk about struggle and the use of violence for self-defense, Islam remains a religion of peace and justice that prohibits mass killing, destruction of property, and mistreatment of prisoners. Bin Laden and other extremists have manipulated the faith in order to provide religious cover for their actions and to justify acts of murder against innocent civilians.

Many Americans asked the question "why do they hate us?" in trying to understand the September 11 attacks. While American media and President Bush repeated that Americans were attacked because they were free and democratic, many in the Muslim world had a different view. Whereas the vast majority of Arabs and Muslims disagree profoundly with U.S. foreign policy in the Middle East, and particularly with U.S. support for Israel, they have traditionally distinguished between a government's official policies and the people that government represents. In fact, Arab and Muslim appreciation of and attraction to American culture and spirit is evident in the consumption of Western culture, in music, food, clothes, and entertainment. Yet the attackers belonged to a minority of people who do not separate American policies from Americans themselves. They did not see themselves as attacking Americans because they hated freedom or democracy. Rather, as a Pakistani journalist wrote, the attackers believed U.S. foreign policies had denied them their freedom and dignity through keeping undemocratic regimes in power: "Those who hate America love its freedoms; they hate America not least because America's hypocritical policies deny them those freedoms."

An example of such contradictory messages that the United States has projected in the region deals with the Arabic television station *al-Jazeera*. This news organization is the first of its kind in the region to promote mostly free reporting without government interference; thus many Arabs and Muslims were upset that an advocate of free speech such as the United States wanted to shut it down or attempted to censor stories that did not support

ONLY DAYS AFTER THE SEPTEMBER 11 TERRORIST ATTACKS STUDENTS DEMONSTRATE IN SUPPORT OF ARAB AMERICAN AND MUSLIM COMMUNITIES. ARABS AND MUSLIMS HAVE BEEN UNFAIRLY TARGETED BY SOME PEOPLE IN THE UNITED STATES IN REPRISAL FOR THE 2001 ATTACKS. *(AP/Wide World Photos/Ann Heisenfelt. Reproduced by permission.)*

U.S. policies. Shortly after the airing of the first bin Laden interview after the September 11 attacks, a representative from the U.S. administration met with the Authority of Qatar, which hosts al-Jazeera, to communicate this desire. The station, however, continued to operate.

As a result of a long-standing history of rivalry and conflict between the West and Islam, the mixed messages of U.S. foreign policy in the region, such as the U.S. support for human rights, while overlooking human rights violations in friendly Gulf states such as Saudi Arabia and Kuwait, as well as continued U.S. support of Israel's policies toward the occupied territories of the Gaza Strip and West Bank despite allegations against Israel of human rights violations there, and ongoing stereotypical and generally misrepresentative depictions of Arabs and Muslims in Western media and entertainment, Muslims have been asking, "why do they hate *us*?"

Compounding this situation is the view that the growth of Western power has coincided with a decline in Islamic power, creating a sense of insecurity and sensitivity to Western claims of superiority. These feelings are closely related to a creeping anti-Americanism in the region, which

Moises Naim, in an article in *Foreign Policy*, believes can be divided into five distinct categories: politico-economic reasons which represent reactions to current U.S. foreign policies (its policy in the Middle East and its support of Israel); historical reasons, which are rooted in past U.S. behavior; religious reasons, which are expressed by fundamentalists of all faiths; cultural reasons, which resent the ability of U.S. culture to influence and displace the local indigenous cultures (through processes of globalization); and psychological factors fueled by jealousy and a loss of confidence at the strength of the West. Examples of some of the historical and politico-economic reasons include many cases in which the United Nations has passed resolutions condemning Israeli policy in the occupied territories, but the U.S. representative to the UN has opposed the resolutions and often attempted to veto such decisions in the Security Council.

As a result, in the years preceding the September 11 attacks, many in the Muslim world called for a dialogue between Islam and the West, so that each community could move away from stereotypes, fears, and insecurities with one another and begin to learn about, and value the contributions of one another. Iranian President Mohammad Khatami

OFFICIAL STATEMENTS FROM MUSLIM LEADERS CONDEMNING THE US ATTACK

Yasser Arafat, President of the Palestinian Authority: "I express my sincere condolences to the American people and the American President, not just in my name but on behalf of the Palestinian people. This crime is completely unacceptable and utterly shocking."

Hosni Mubarak, President of Egypt: "Egypt firmly and strongly condemns such attacks on civilians and soldiers that led to the deaths of large numbers of innocent victims."

Mohammad Khatami, President of Iran: We feel "deep regret and sympathy with the victims [of this crime]."

Muammar Qadhafi, President of Libya: Qadhafi stated that these attacks are "horrifying," and urged help and aid for Americans "regardless of political considerations or differences between Americans and the peoples of the world."

Sheikh Muhammad Sayed Tantawi, Imam of Al-Azhar, Egypt: "To kill innocent men, women and children is a horrible and hideous act of which no monotheist religion approves... Islam is a religion which rejects violence and bloodletting."

Organization of Islamic Conference Secretary General Abdelouhed Belkaziz: "We are shocked and deeply saddened by the news of the attacks, which led to the death and injury of a large number of innocent Americans... [We share Americans'] pain and sorrow in this terrible and devastating ordeal."

American Muslim Political Coordination Council: "American Muslims utterly condemn what are apparently vicious and cowardly acts of terrorism against innocent civilians... No political cause could ever be assisted by such immoral acts."

"axis of evil" has limited the ability of Arab and Muslim moderates to reach out to Americans and has fueled the fears of extremists.

For longstanding Arab and Muslim allies of the United States, responding to the September 11 attacks was also difficult. On the one hand, they officially support the U.S. administration's efforts in its military campaign, but on the other hand, they could not afford to be open to charges in their own countries that they were in collusion with a foreign government that was about to wage war against Muslim countries. Trying to balance sovereignty with support meant that Middle Eastern regimes tried to say little and clamped down severely on domestic dissent, particularly anti-American sentiment. This in turn generated growing resentment against Muslim and Middle Eastern regimes from the people in the street, which had the potential to destabilize some regimes.

Thus, in the aftermath of September 11, following the heavy bombardment of Afghanistan, the destruction of the Taliban regime, the collapse of the Palestinian Authority, and the continued and highly visible U.S. support for Israel, the root causes of the conflict remain to be addressed. The image of the United States in the Muslim world in general, and the Middle East in particular, remains in disarray as mistrust dominates the relationship. To understand how so much suspicion and fear came to characterize the relationship between Muslims and the West, it is important to look farther back into their history.

HISTORICAL BACKGROUND

In order to understand the roots of present conflict, it is important to look at the historical evolution in the relationship between the West and Islam in general, and between the United States and Muslim countries in particular. The United States is confronting centuries of Arab and Muslim bitterness over the violence and destruction of the Crusades in the eleventh, twelfth, and thirteenth centuries and later military campaigns, in addition to continued indignation over Western colonialism that began in the region in the early 1800s. Many Arabs and Muslims feel they experienced ten centuries of tremendous cultural achievement that collapsed with European colonialism. In *Islam: The Straight Path*, John Esposito noted that "despite their common monotheistic roots, the history of Christianity and Islam has more often than not been marked by confrontation rather than peaceful coexistence and dialogue. For the Christian West,

called for a "dialogue of civilizations" to take place in 1998 and the United Nations called 2000 the Year of the Dialogue of Civilizations. The Jordanian King Abdallah II and his brother Hassan in 1998 launched a series of conferences in London and Amman to address the relations between Islam and the West. Yet from the Muslim point of view, the U.S. division of the world between those who are good and those who are evil, and the identification of Iran, Iraq, and North Korea as belonging to the

Islam is the religion of the sword; for Muslims, the Christian West is epitomized by the armies of the Crusades."

Ever since the early decades of Islamic history, Islam presented a threat to the political and religious dominance of Christianity. From its founding in the seventh century, Islam spread rapidly, alarming the West as formerly Christian territories were falling and converting to Islam. The large numbers of Christian converts at the time were mostly due to genuine callings but also because many Christians found it easier to interact as Muslims in Islamic societies, despite the fact that their Christian status was protected in Islamic tradition. Islam's universal message invariably clashed with Christianity's universal message, as each began competing with one another for souls as well as for glory and resources in areas of the Eastern Roman Empire, Spain, and the Mediterranean from Sicily to Anatolia. The threat of Islam was even more apparent to European Christians when Islam emerged as a world power and a civilization while Christianity had begun to decline into its Dark Ages.

Beginning in the eleventh century, Christendom had mobilized beyond self-defense and launched a series of military campaigns aimed at re-conquering Spain, Italy, Sicily, and the Holy Lands up until 1492. This counter-movement initiated some of the worst religiously based violence in Western history and wreaked enormous destruction in the Muslim world. While the United States was not in existence at the time, as a symbol of Western power today the United States has inherited the legacy of these historical encounters, which were characterized by cycles of confrontation and collaboration.

Andalusia

After witnessing a short era of coexistence between Christians and Muslims, the Iberian Peninsula was split between two distinct communities in the tenth century: the Christian kingdom of Leon in the north and the larger Muslim al-Andalus (Andalusia) in the south. During the rule of Abd al-Rahman III in Cordoba, the arts, literature, medicine, science, and culture flourished, allowing the Spanish Islamic state to reach its highest level of power and fame. This period also witnessed significant tolerance and extensive social interaction between Muslims, Jews, and Christians (whom Islam refers to as "People of the Book.") A great period of scholarship, art, and learning emerged from these dynamic interactions, where Muslim scholars brought to Europe their knowledge of al-

gebra, astronomy, alchemy, and medicine. Muslim armies had saved copies of the books of Greek learning that had been burned by Christian authorities in the past, and as a consequence were directly responsible for reintroducing Europe to the works of philosophers such as Plato and Aristotle, thus ending the period known as the Dark Ages. Christians living in Andalusia became Arabized, adopting the Muslim dress code, artistic expressions, language, and styles of worship.

Although Christians were respected, tolerated, and protected, they were, to a certain extent, still considered strangers in their own society. This situation began to change with the rule of Abu Amir Al-Mansur (Almanzor) in the tenth century: Al-Rahman III's successor began a series of ruthless campaigns against Christians, who were now considered infidels. These campaigns signaled the end of the era of 'harmonious interaction' and the beginning of another dominated by intolerance, suspicion, and prejudice. In the eleventh century, the situation worsened as the rise in 'aggressive Islamic fervor' led to increasing hostility in relations with Christians. This in turn fueled and hardened Christian attitudes against Islam at a time when Christian forces were seeking to recapture Andalusian territories. By the mid-thirteenth century Christian control in Spain significantly increased, reducing Muslim rule and power. The persecution and harsh treatment of Muslims by Christians soon followed, fed by Christian fervor and the initial successes of the Crusades in the Holy Land. The final expulsion of Islam from Andalusia did not occur until the end of the fifteenth century under Ferdinand and Isabella, at the same time Christopher Columbus set sail for America.

The Crusades

The strongest reaction to the Islamic threat in the early Middle Ages was illustrated by the Christian holy wars, or crusades, that were carried out against Muslims in Europe between the eleventh and fourteenth century in the name of Christian glory. The Crusades marked a defining period in the Christian-Muslim relationship. In the areas outside of Andalusia where there was minimal contact with Muslims, widespread ignorance of the Islamic faith coupled with the active misinformation propagated by Christian religious leaders mobilized support and created a tremendous amount of fear of Islam. Instead of trying to understand the success of Islam during this period, many Christians in the West dismissed Islam as a false and rival religion. Muslims felt a strong need to prove themselves and the legitimacy of the

Qur'anic revelations to Christians, and pointed to the considerable achievements advanced by their civilization as evidence.

The first Crusade started in 1095, when Pope Urban II responding to an appeal for help from Byzantine Emperor Alexius I, who felt threatened by the Muslim Seljuk Turks, called Western Christendom to take arms in the name of Jesus and liberate the Holy Land (Jerusalem) from the Muslim infidel. This first wave of the Crusaders slaughtered thousands of Jews and Muslims en route to Jerusalem and many Crusaders became rich from their conquests. The apparent successes inspired eight major Crusades in all, but by the fourth crusade, politics and greed had replaced the intensive religious zeal of the earlier campaigns.

Overall the Crusades in the Holy Land failed in their main purpose, which was to rid the lands of Muslims and take back the Holy Land. There were no lasting results in terms of military conquest. They did, however, enrich and benefit Western civilization by bringing it more in contact with the East and its modes of living and thinking, contributing to the age of Discovery. Through extensive encounters with Islam, at home and in the Holy Land, it helped lead to the end of the Dark Ages and the Renaissance of modern Europe.

While the Crusades have a more positive connotation in the West, in the Middle East the meaning is considerably more negative, where culturally history plays an important role in understanding the world. Those who support Osama bin Laden's efforts have argued that bin Laden seems to be playing the role of a "modern-day" Saladin, a Muslim leader who fought against the second and third Crusaders.

The Ottoman Empire

The Ottoman Turkish Empire was a sign of the increase of Muslim power in the sixteenth century. It was centered in Istanbul and encompassed major portions of North Africa, the Arab world and eastern Europe. The empire was heir to the Mongol-Turkish legacy of Genghis Khan and his successors and was based on the belief in the Islamic imperative to establish a base from which to propagate and defend Islam.

By the 1600s the Ottoman Empire reached its peak and Istanbul had matured into a cosmopolitan city larger than any European capital, with a large population and an international and Islamicized center of power and culture. Political and religious institutions functioned side by side; polit-

ically, the empire was governed by a centralized administration and a well-organized bureaucracy; religiously, the *ulama*, religious schools, and the courts operated within the state's bureaucracy.

A unique feature of the Ottoman Empire was the "millet system," which regulated the rights and duties of the different religious communities, which enjoyed limited autonomy. Religion, in other words, supported the state and legitimized the rule. By the turn of the eighteenth century, the power of the Ottoman Empire was in decline, a decline that coincided with the Industrial Revolution and modernization of the West. The emergence of a strong military and economic Europe, and its quest for new markets, ushered in the era of Western colonialism. Nevertheless, the Ottoman Empire survived into the twentieth century until it collapsed during World War I (1914–18) and the following Mandate period with the Sykes-Picot Agreement of 1916. This agreement divided up Ottoman lands among the British, French, and Italians. The collapse and disintegration of the Ottoman Empire, which began in earnest in early 1800, not only brought about colonialized entities but also gave impetus to a wave of Islamic and nationalist revivalist movements that swept the Muslim world in the following centuries.

Colonialism

With the decline of the Ottoman Empire, European powers came to dominate the Middle East and penetrate Muslim areas. They established their presence and expanded it at several strategic intervals. The first turning point came in the sixteenth century when the Ottoman Empire granted European powers advantages in foreign trade in the empire. The second turning point was Napoleon Bonaparte's invasion of Egypt in 1798, which began a precedent of direct political intervention by the West in Egypt. This was followed by the Ottoman Sultan revising the entire education system to be more Westernized, while bringing technological expertise into the empire as well. The European presence in the areas originally part of the Ottoman Empire was finally legalized and took its most explicit and extended form with the establishment of the mandate system of the Sykes-Picot Agreement. Under this agreement the major European powers divided the Ottoman Empire by arbitrary boundaries, for instance France claimed Syria and Lebanon, Britain claimed Iraq, Egypt, etc. This resulted in the current Arab and Muslim states, which had not previously existed under these boundaries. This mandate system continues to generate severe territorial, political, and religious con-

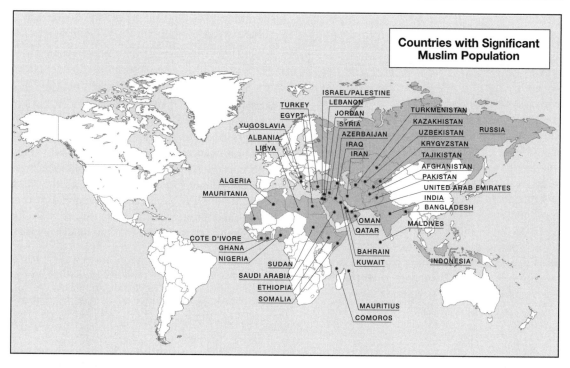

MANY OF THE WORLD'S NATIONS HAVE A SIGNIFICANT MUSLIM POPULATION, INCLUDING THE COUNTRIES IN AFRICA, EUROPE, THE MIDDLE EAST, AND ASIA. *(Gale Group.)*

flict in the Middle East today, such as those between Kuwait and Iraq and especially between Israel and the Palestinians.

The spread of Western culture was enhanced by the Western economic and political control in the region. Missionaries propagated Western ideas through education, while scientific advances allowed the West to spearhead improvements and innovations in medicine, agriculture, commerce, and industry, which devalued traditional methods and approaches. Resistance to abandoning traditional ways and insecurity brought about by rapid, foreign-induced changes that brought them few benefits prompted resistance from the colonized peoples. This resistance took several forms ranging from intellectual debates, to the reform of the Muslim educational system and reaffirming Islamic values and encouraging them to direct action.

The colonial period marks another stage of negative contact between Islam and the West. It embodies a time when the West politically, militarily, economically, and culturally dominated many Muslim lands. Edward Said, of Columbia University, writes about how colonialism plays out psychologically and the lingering effects in terms of power relations in his famous book *Orientalism*. The post-colonial Muslim world continues to

struggle with the lingering social effects of colonization, which ended in the mid-1900s. While Muslims and Arabs may enjoy much of what Europe can offer culturally, the memories of colonialism are never far from the surface.

Millions of Muslims and Arabs lost their lives in their struggles to liberate their lands from the European powers. In Algeria alone, over one million people lost their lives between 1954 and 1962 to win their freedom from French colonialism. In the process, images of Muslims and of Islam were manipulated by the French to justify increasingly aggressive policies against Algerians in the region. Muslim national and religious leaders also suspected and dehumanized Europeans and foreigners in general to mobilize popular support for their cause. The cost of decolonization was enormous for the Muslim world as it has been for many formerly colonized lands. In fact many scholars and analysts continue to argue that a great deal of the current political and economic stagnation in Arab and Muslim societies is mainly the product of colonization and the effort required to be liberated.

Islamic Revival Movements

The need for a revival and reform of Islam emerged in the eighteenth century, contributed by

WHAT IS JIHAD?

According to Karen Armstrong, a scholar of religion and the author of several books on religion, the primary meaning of the word *jihad* is not holy war but struggle, or striving. It refers to the difficult effort that is needed to put God's will into practice at every level—personal and social, as well as political. There are two kinds of jihad: *jihad al-asghar* (the lesser *jihad*), which refers to an external struggle for justice, and for implementing God's will on earth. *Jihad al-akbar* (the greater *jihad*) refers to the far more urgent and momentous task of extirpating wrongdoing from one's own society and one's own heart. A very important and much quoted Islamic tradition has Mohammed telling his companions as they go home after a battle, "We are returning from the lesser *jihad* [the battle] to the greater *jihad*."

According to John Esposito, director of the Center for Christian-Muslim Relations at Georgetown University, *jihad* means to strive or struggle in the way of God and is sometimes referred to as the 6th pillar of Islam, without actually having such official status. More generally, *jihad* refers to the "obligation incumbent on all Muslims, as individuals and as a community, to exert themselves to realize God's will, to lead virtuous lives, and to try to extend the Islamic community through preaching, education, and so on."

the growing European influence over the Muslim world, when Muslims were faced with internal as well as external challenges to 'their faith and social order.' Revivalist movements provided an answer to the question of how, after ten centuries of civilization and authority, Muslims found themselves in such dire straits. These movements encouraged a return to religious observance and extensive social and moral reform. Prior to this period Europeans themselves were also exploring and experiencing the growth of various national movements or other forms of collective identity.

A number of Islamic scholars and intellectuals voiced their concern with the subjection and weakening of the Muslim world by the Western colonial powers and called upon their fellow Muslims to unite against foreign domination and work for the rejuvenation of the entire Islamic community. Jamal al-Din-al-Afghani (1838–97) was considered the most prominent Islamic revivalist leader who spoke of the liberation and independence of Muslims as the most important of objectives.

According to al-Afghani, religion is the most important vehicle with which to achieve human progress and move humanity on its quest towards modernity.

Mohammed Abduh (1849–1905) was another influential Islamic figure who called on Muslims to reform themselves in order to meet the challenges rising from another culture. His call, however, focused on change through gradual methods rather than revolutionary ones. Abduh argued that Muslims can counter the rising threat from the West through religious, legal, and educational reform rather than through political activism. Abduh, like al-Afghani, believed that Islam and modernity were compatible.

With the continued disillusionment with colonial and authoritarian rule, another form of Islamic revivalism emerged, which took more radical and revolutionary form. Sayyid Qutb (1906–66) was the major proponent of this form of revivalism. His central claim was that both the governments and the societies of the contemporary Muslim world had fallen back into *al-jahiliyya* (unbelief and ignorance). It was therefore the duty of all true Muslims to revive the original *jihad* of Mohammed and the first Muslim community, whose efforts to drive out unbelief and establish God's work found them waging jihad against their own families. Hassan al-Banna (1906–49) was also a proponent of this form of revivalism, collapsing the Qur'anic definitions of fighting and inner spiritual struggle against evil (the inner jihad) and calls for a holy war (the outer jihad), against the infidels as well as the People of the Book (Christians and Jews). Al-Banna's position was that the crux of the problem in Muslim countries was that advances made by the Christian West and by the corruption and decadence of the Muslim elite had increasingly marginalized the role of religion in society. As a result, Islam no longer held its central position in ordering society and the lives of its members. Al-Banna urged his followers to return to the ways of Islam as the only way to begin reform.

With the continued domination of the West and through the processes of globalization, Islamic revivalist movements increased in number as well as in intensity. Calling for a return to Islamic precepts and Muslim reform is increasingly being linked with a more revolutionary Islamic activism. From this point of view, the disastrous impact that the West has had on the survival and prosperity of the Islamic tradition and way of life have left Muslims few choices besides holding more closely to Islamic teachings in order to maintain control over their own destiny.

ISLAMIC REVIVALISM VS. ISLAMIC FUNDAMENTALISM

The General or Common Ideological Framework of Islamic Revivalism:

- Islam is a total and comprehensive way of life

- The failure of Muslim communities results from their departure from the straight path of Islam and their following a Western secular path

- The renewal of society requires a return to Islam, an Islamic religio-political and social reformation or revolution, that draws its inspiration from the Qur'an and from the first great Islamic movement led by the Prophet Mohammed

- To restore God's rule and inaugurate a true Islamic social order, Western-inspired civil codes must be replaced by Islamic law

- Although the Westernization of society is condemned, modernization as such is not

- The process of Islamization, or more accurately re-Islamization, requires organizations or associations of dedicated and trained Muslims, who by their example and activities, call on others to be more observant and who are willing to struggle (jihad) against corruption and social injustice

The General or Common Ideological Framework for Radical Activists (known to some as Islamic fundamentalists)

- A crusader mentality that pits the West against the Islamic world

- Establishment of an Islamic system of government as an Islamic imperative

- Governments that do not allow the *sharia* are illegitimate and those who fail to follow Islamic law are guilty of unbelief

- Jihad against unbelief and unbelievers is a religious duty

- Radicals demand total commitment and obedience: the army of God is locked in battle or holy war with the followers of Satan

- Christians and Jews are generally regarded as unbelievers rather than "People of the Book" because of their connections with Western Christian colonialism and Zionism

The Rise of Islamic Fundamentalism

The increase in Islamic activism and Islamic discontent has, at the same time, triggered alarm in the West as this activism has become viewed as a direct challenge and threat to Western interests and security. The rising Islamic activism manifested itself with the Islamic Revolution in Iran, which toppled the Western supported regime in 1979. The United States in particular suffered a dramatic blow when its embassy personnel were taken hostage by Iranian revolutionaries. The leader of the revolution, Ayatollah Ruhollah Khomeini, called for the export of an Islamic revolution throughout the region to uproot Western control and influence, calling the United States the "Great Satan." Islam thus emerged as a new and assertive political force for change—one not well-understood in the West—posing a serious challenge to the West and to all Western established orders in Muslim areas. Although the United States was preoccupied with communism as its primary threat at the time, when the Soviet Union collapsed the direct challenge that Islam had posed to the West beginning with the Iranian revolution crystallized into a fear by some of a "clash of civilizations."

Muslim fundamentalists called for the establishment of Islamic states and the return to religion as a way to eliminate corruption and subordination and to take matters into their own hands. Islamicizing the regimes was seen as a way of liberating Muslims from Western control. While fundamentalism is always religious in form and is not confined to any particular faith or country, fundamentalist beliefs themselves do not necessarily lead directly to violence. The path that fundamentalism will take depends on the social and political context within which it emerges. Fundamentalists are not necessarily contrary to change and backward-looking. Fundamentalists are in fact often strong advocates for change in a world that they believe to be decaying from its abandonment or perversion of religion. As such, Islamic activism was not only confined to Iran and the revolution of 1979, but formed the context within which political activism took place. It is often difficult to distinguish anti-Western action from pro-Islamic action since the two have often been related as a result of colonialism and a history of violent conflict.

Throughout the Cold War, a number of attacks were carried out in various Muslim countries against Western embassies, citizens, airlines, and businesses in protest against perceived U.S. control over national resources and policies, as well as against U.S. support for the state of Israel. As a result, Americans were kidnapped by Hizballah forces in Lebanon and the Abu Sayyaf group in the Philippines. The Gulf War (1991) marked a period of brief coalition of some Muslim and Arab states in cooperation with the West when Iraq invaded Kuwait. The United States led a coalition to drive out Iraq and restore the Kuwaiti government with the active participation and support of Saudi Arabia and a number of other Arab and Muslim countries. After the war, however, the continued military presence of Western troops in the region began causing concern and alarm from many Arabs and Muslims in regard to Western motives.

While Saudi Arabia officially requested that U.S. troops continue to stay in the region and train on Saudi military bases, many Muslims disapproved of the Saudi initiatives for two reasons: first, Saudi Arabia is home to the two holiest places in Islam: Mecca and Medina. Mecca being the birthplace of the Prophet Mohammed and the place where he received his first divine revelations. So important is Mecca to Muslims that Muslims worldwide pray in the direction of Mecca five times a day. Medina is where the first Muslim community was established when Mohammed and his followers fled Mecca. Having U.S. and Western troops so close to these sites—only 30 miles away—caused great anxiety given the memories for Muslims of the Crusades and the more recent experiences with Western military colonialism.

Secondly, many Saudi political dissidents objected to the presence of U.S. troops in Saudi Arabia because they felt the United States was helping to keep an unpopular regime in power (since Saudi Arabia does not have any significant standing army of its own). It was due to the continued presence of U.S. troops in the region following the war that Saudi Arabian dissident Osama bin Laden began his militant campaign against the West. Initially his goal was to "liberate" Saudi holy land from Western "crusading" troops that he believed were also keeping a regime he opposed in power. Toward this end, bin Laden was directly connected to the bombings of U.S. training facilities and military complexes in Saudi Arabia in 1995, 1996, and the September 11 attacks in 2001.

Bin Laden later announced that he had widened his *jihad* against the West beyond military targets to include U.S. civilians, an action that Islam rejected outright. His own justification for deviating from Islamic tradition was that the United States was the first government to have "extended its war against troops to civilians" in its ongoing confrontation with Iraq, where hundreds of thousands of Iraqi children have died from starvation and disease stemming in part from U.S.-led sanctions against Saddam Hussein's regime. Furthermore, he argued that because the United States was a democracy, all American citizens were responsible for its government's policies. In an interview with CNN in 1997, he argued that "because [Americans] chose this government and voted for it despite their knowledge of its crimes in Palestine, Lebanon, and Iraq and in other places, and [because of American] support of its agent [Arab] regimes who filled our prisons with our best children and scholars," bin Laden believed he was justified in targeting American civilians. The first civilian target with ties to bin Laden was the first World Trade Center bombing in 1993.

Due to the fact that bin Laden was convinced that U.S. global policies oppressed Muslims worldwide, bin Laden began organizing a network, al-Qaeda, to challenge the West through violence against U.S. civilians and interests throughout the world. In 1998 bin Laden continued his attack, with strikes against American embassies in Nairobi and Dar es Salaam, resulting in the loss of hundreds of innocent lives, most of which were not U.S. casualties but rather Kenyan and Tanzanian citizens. The United States became increasingly alarmed at the development of bin Laden's network, which had ties to a number of different Muslim countries, and began working with Arab regimes to capture bin Laden in the years prior to 2001.

The State of Israel

Arab and Muslim reactions to the September 11 tragedy cannot be properly understood outside of the context of the Palestinian and Israeli conflict. The conflict with Israel has consistently remained the number one concern of Arabs and Muslims since the Jewish state was founded in 1948. The profound depth of feeling that Arabs and Muslims have in reaction to the establishment of Israel in-

AN INDONESIAN POLICE OFFICER GUARDS THE U.S. EMBASSY IN JAKARTA, WHERE CITIZENS HAVE LEFT FLOWER ARRANGEMENTS AND EXPRESSIONS OF SYMPATHY. INDONESIA HAS THE WORLD'S HIGHEST POPULATION OF MUSLIMS. *(AP/Wide World Photos/Dita Alangkara. Reproduced by permission.)*

volve historical fears and mistrust that a foreign, colonizing Western power, such as the nations supporting Israel's formation, might aspire to control all of the region and subvert Islam, the religious attachment to the holy land of Jerusalem (the third most sacred site in Islam), the deep social solidarity with and empathy for the uprooted Palestinian refugees, and the anger arising from perceived humiliations and dehumanization at the hands of Israelis. As a result, the conflict with Israel and the plight of the Palestinians strikes a powerful chord in the hearts and minds of Arabs and Muslims.

Longstanding U.S. support for Israel has been a vexing question for Arabs and Muslims who look to the United States for leadership in restraining or balancing Israel's relations in the region and with Palestinians in particular. The United States struggled to bring both parties to the negotiating table for years as an 'honest broker' to help each side find common ground. With the signing of the Oslo Peace Accords in 1993, many Arabs and Israelis were hopeful that a durable peace could be achieved. These hopes soon dimmed when Arabs and Muslims observed an acceleration of Jewish settlement that was slowly expanding the territory of Israel beyond agreed borders into the Occupied Territories, while neither the U.S. nor the Israeli

governments appeared able to stop them. Additionally, Arafat rejected a peace proposal at the Camp David II discussions in July 2000, which raised tensions further. While the years following the Oslo Accords witnessed the lowest levels of violence between the two sides, the controversial visit in September 2000 by the right-wing Israeli leader Ariel Sharon to the al-Haram al-Sharif ("the Noble Sanctuary"), the sacred Islamic mosque in Jerusalem, which is also an important Jewish site called the Temple Mount, triggered massive Palestinian mobilization and unrest. The visit was profoundly inflammatory to Muslims because Sharon had declared during his visit that he was walking on Israeli territory. The subsequent election of Sharon as Israeli prime minister amid a violent uprising by Palestinian groups oversaw the collapse of the Oslo peace process and brought a strong sense of frustration, anger, and despair to many Muslims.

The conflict with Israel has also contributed to the rise in Islamic activism and revivalism as religious solutions appeared to some to be the most viable way to deal with a sense of oppression and injustice. Islamic fundamentalists rely on the Palestinian conflict to describe why they need to resort to more extreme measures and beliefs to remedy their situation, and why non-Muslims

A YOUNG PALESTINIAN MAN HANGS A SIGN IN FRONT OF THE U.S. CONSULATE IN JERUSALEM TO SHOW SUPPORT FOR THOSE AFFECTED BY THE SEPTEMBER 11 TERRORIST ATTACKS. *(AP/Wide World Photos/Lefteris Pitarakis. Reproduced by permission.)*

Recent History and the Future

In the wake of the September 11 attacks, the West and Islam again find themselves estranged from one another and in conflict. Some have argued that we are entering into a "war of fundamentalisms," where extremists from all sides are engaged in a demonization process that insists that the other is out to destroy them. Is it true then that the West is really trying to take over Mecca and Medina? Is it true that Arabs and Muslims really hate democracy and freedom? Looking more closely at the context, history, and needs of the conflict itself helps us to respond in the long-term to the root causes of the conflict and not in the short-term out of fear or rage.

The relationship between the West and Islam is long, complex, and often troubled. Many historians have described it as deeply competitive and marked by periods of violent friction followed by collaboration. This is due to legitimate differences in beliefs about how to live a good and moral life as well as to competition over resources and fears about the motives of the other. Learning about the history, culture, and experiences of one another gives us the safety to value human diversity without feeling fundamentally threatened.

The factor that is continuing to aggravate the current situation is the view of Arabs and Muslims that many Western governments, and in particular the United States, refuse to acknowledge or link the impact of their foreign policies in these post-colonial countries with any of the grievances stated by radical Muslim groups, pushing them further from the accepted mainstream and into extremism. Military solutions do not begin to address the underlying causes of conflict or prevent young men and women from committing acts of destruction and suicide. Equating Islam as a religion to Islamic extremism is also aggravating the relationship between Islam and the West and adding to the misunderstandings between the two. Certain people have come to associate Islam with terrorism. For these people, Islam can then be considered a threat to Western security.

Addressing the underlying causes of conflict and mistrusts involves certain basic and necessary steps from the Arab and Muslim point of view. First, a just and peaceful solution to the Palestinian struggle must take place that allows both Israelis and Palestinians to live free from fear and to live as neighbors. The United States could more actively support human rights and the desire for democracy in the region, as these are deeply compatible with American principles and values. In ad-

threaten to undermine Islam. In addition, the religious attachment to Jerusalem gives the Israeli-Palestinian conflict a global character. Muslims around the world are deeply concerned with, and could conceivably mobilize around, the fate of Jerusalem. For all Arabs and Muslims, the struggle of the Palestinians remains one of the most powerful rallying cries that evokes profound sympathy and massive support, making this issue quite volatile in the region. It is unsurprising that in their bids for popular opinion, both Saddam Hussein and Osama bin Laden promised to deliver justice for the Palestinian people.

dition, the United States has considerable expertise in development assistance that could be used to help democratic Muslim governments adjust to globalization processes and advance the interests, health, and well-being of their peoples so that everyone is allowed to benefit.

If positive and genuine change is to ensue, this should be coupled with changes in Muslim societies and leaders; blaming only external force for the increasing use of violence by certain Muslim groups is not enough. In addition to that, more efforts should be invested in reaching out to non-Muslim audiences and media to further understanding about Islam and the Muslim world, and to reflect the complexity of opinions and positions within each Muslim society. A growing number of Muslim scholars, leaders, and activists, such as Ibrahim Musa, Farid Esack, Khalid Abu Fadel, Abdul Aziz Sachedina, Jawdat Said, Abdul Aziz Said and Mohammed Abu-Nimer, among others, have been engaged in examining frameworks for nonviolence and pluralism based on primary Islamic religious sources such as the Qur'an and the Hadith. The writings of many of those authors, in addition to promoting values of tolerance and diversity within an Islamic framework, provide many alternatives to engage in social and political change and to pursue justice by adopting Islamic values of nonviolent resistance. Such attempts can be part of a larger campaign to open channels of communication between the West and Islam (both on the level of leaders and people) that will help in breaking the negative mutual stereotypes.

These are the steps that would lead to a peaceful, just, and collectively secure future.

BIBLIOGRAPHY

Ajami, Fouad. "In Bin Laden's Mirror," *U.S. New and World Report*, December 24, 2001.

Amuzegar, Jahangir. "Islamic Fundamentalism in Action: The Case of Iran," *Middle East Policy*, vol. 4, no. 1 & 2, September 1995.

Armstrong, Karen. "The True, Peaceful Face of Islam," *Time*, October 1, 2001.

———. *Muhammad: A Biography of the Prophet.* San Francisco: Harper, 1992.

Appleby, Scott and Martin Marty. "Fundamentalism," *Foreign Policy*, January/February 2002.

Atia, Tarek. "Bruce Willis versus Bin Laden," *Al-Ahram Weekly On-Line*, November 5–11, 1998. Available online at http://www.ahram.org.eg/weekly/1998/402/focus.htm.

Betancourt, Rolando Perez. "America's Second Loss of Innocence," *World Press Review*, November 2001.

Beyer, Lisa. "Roots of Rage: Grievances Over U.S. Policy in the Middle East Combined with Islamic Triumphalism Make a Toxic Mix," *Time*, October 1, 2001.

Ehteshami, Anoushiravan and A.S. Sidahmed. *Islamic Fundamentalism.* Boulder: Westview Press, 1996.

Ergene, Bogac. "Pre-Modern Islamic Revivalism (Intellectual Roots)." University of Vermont. Available online at http://216.239.39.100/search?q=cache:FpXFUBl9AU4C:college.hmco.com/currentconflict/instructors/history/islamic_activities/pre_modern/pre_modern.pdf+Modern+Islamic+Revivalism+(Intellectual+Roots)&hl;=en&start;=1 (cited May 2, 2002).

Esposito, John. *Islam: The Straight Path.* New York: Oxford University Press, 1991.

———, ed. *The Oxford History of Islam.* New York: Oxford University Press, 1999.

"From Uncle Ben's to Uncle Sam," *The Economist*, February 23, 2002.

Gauhar, Humayun. "Reporting from Karachi: Let a Muslim Speak," *The World Paper*, March 4, 2002.

Gerges, Fawaz. *America and Political Islam: Clash of Cultures or Clash of Interests?* New York: Cambridge University Press, 1999.

Gibb, H.A.R. *Whither Islam.* London, 1932.

Huntington, Samuel. *The Clash of Civilizations and the Remaking of World Order.* New York: Touchstone, 1996.

Iglesias, Carlos Basombrio. "Feeding on Horror...and Mistakes," *World Press Review*, November 2001.

Johnson, James Turner. *The Holy War Idea in Western and Islamic Traditions.* Pennsylvania: Pennsylvania State University Press, 1997.

Mabrouk, Mirette. "Egyptians Sympathize with Americans, Not with U.S. Government," *The World Paper*, October, 2001.

Morrison, Blake. "This Time, There were Cameras." *The Guardian*, September 14, 2001.

Morrow, Lance. "Who's More Arrogant? In Islam vs. the West, What's Needed Is An Examination Of Conscience On Both Sides," *Time*, December 10, 2001.

Naim, Moises. "Anti-Americanisms: A Guide to Hating Uncle Sam," *Foreign Policy*, January/February 2002.

Saghiyeh, Hazem. "It's Not All America's Fault," *Time*, October 15, 2001.

Said, Edward. *Orientalism.* New York: Vintage, 1979.

Salem, Paul. *Bitter Legacy: Ideology and Politics in the Arab World.* New York: Syracuse University Press, 1994.

Schulze, Reinhard. *A Modern History of the Islamic World.* New York: New York University Press, 2000.

Sheler, Jeffrey. "Muslim in America: What is Islam? In this Country, There are Many Answers to That Question," *U.S. News and World Report*, October 29, 2001.

———. "Of Faith, Fear, and Fanatics: The Masterminds of Terror Are Far Removed From the Mainstream of Islam," *U.S. News and World Report*, September 24, 2001.

Simon, Roger. "A Nation, Still In Pain, Rallies: 'Now We Understand the Horrors of Terrorism Firsthand. Now, We Are All One,'" *U.S. News and World Report*, October 22, 2001.

Southern, R.W. *Western Views of Islam in the Middle Ages*. Cambridge. MA: Harvard University Press, 1962.

Tolson, Jay. "Struggle for Islam: How do the Terrorists Responsible for the Attacks on September 11 Fit Into the Muslim Faith?" *U.S. News and World Report*, October 15, 2001.

Van Biema, David. "As American As...Although Scapegoated, Muslims, Sikhs And Arabs are Patriotic, Integrated and Growing," *Time*, October 1, 2001.

Mohammed Abu-Nimer, Amal Khoury,
Lynn Kunkle

NUCLEAR TERRORISM: THREATS, CHALLENGES, AND RESPONSES

Only weeks after the devastating terrorist attacks of September 11, 2001, on the World Trade Center in New York City and the Pentagon in Arlington, Virginia, near Washington, DC, a secret intelligence alert went out to a small number of U.S. government agencies. According to the alert, terrorists were thought to have obtained a nuclear weapon from the Russian arsenal and planned to smuggle it into New York City. Allegedly, the yield of the weapon would have been equivalent to ten kilotons of TNT, a thousand times higher than the biggest conventional bomb ever exploded. In response to the threat, the Federal Bureau of Investigation (FBI) alerted a number of other federal agencies, including the Nuclear Emergency Search Team (NEST), a special unit under the control of the Energy Department's Nevada Operations Office. In the days after September 11, doomsday scenarios like a terrorist nuclear attack suddenly seemed plausible. Detonated in lower Manhattan, the effects of even a crude nuclear device would have been devastating. But in the end, the investigators found nothing and concluded that the information was false.

The possible need to track down lost, stolen, smuggled, or "improvised" nuclear devices has concerned national security agencies for as long as such weapons have existed. This time, the secret intelligence alert was a false alarm. But will this nightmare soon become reality? Since the beginning of the 1990s media have frequently reported that several portable nuclear devices were missing from the Russian stockpile and that weapons-usable nuclear material has been lost at both civilian and military facilities. Moreover, rumors have risen that the terrorist organization of Osama bin Laden, al-Qaeda,

THE CONFLICT

In the days after September 11, doomsday scenarios like a terrorist nuclear attack suddenly seemed plausible. Even the use of a crude nuclear device would have a devastating effect, both physically and psychologically. In response to these threats, governments and agencies have sought to upgrade worldwide protection against acts of terrorism involving nuclear and other radioactive materials.

Ideological

- A new breed of terrorists appears more inclined to commit acts of extreme violence. This new set of terrorists may include everything from ad hoc groups motivated by religious conviction or revenge, violent right-wing extremists, and apocalyptic cults.

Technological

- With the proliferation of nuclear weapons and materials worldwide, the possibility of terrorists obtaining nuclear weapons has increased.

- Potential nuclear weapon producers can find useful sites within the information swamp on the Internet.

Political

- Cooperation between the United States and Russia has led to security upgrades of the weapons-useable material sites in Russia.

- International cooperation is necessary to ensure the strengthening of nuclear security.

CHRONOLOGY

Late 1941 The United States establishes a secret program, which came to be known as the Manhattan Project, to develop an atomic bomb.

1992 The book *The Los Alamos Primer: The First Lectures on How to Build an Atomic Bomb,* is declassified and published. The book originated as a series of five lectures given to the physicists of the Manhattan Project at its commencement, outlining the theoretical foundations of the intended bomb-making.

1995 A container containing the radioactive substance cesium, planted by Chechen rebels, is removed from a heavily used Moscow park.

1998 A key aide of Osama bin Laden's is arrested in Germany and charged with trying to obtain nuclear material.

February 2001 After nearly a decade of cooperation, U.S.-assisted security upgrades are completed or partially completed at slightly less than one-third of the weapons-useable materials sites in Russia.

September 11, 2001 Devastating terrorist attacks take place at the World Trade Center in New York City and the Pentagon near Washington, DC. In the weeks following the attacks, a secret intelligence alert to a small number of U.S. government agencies warns that terrorists are thought to have obtained a nuclear weapon and planned to smuggle it into New York City.

has been developing a serious weapons program with a heavy emphasis on building a nuclear device.

Bin Laden has been accused of masterminding the devastating terrorist attacks September 11, 2001. The spectacular and highly publicized attacks killed more than 3,000 people from a number of countries. The attacks were all carried out with traditional terrorist means—hijacked airliners—but in the past, bin Laden has declared that acquiring weapons of mass destruction was "a religious duty." During the U.S.-led military retaliations against Afghanistan, bin Laden warned that he possesses both chemical and nuclear weapons, claiming that if the United States used such weapons, he would "reserve the right to use them" himself. Moreover, diagrams of U.S. nuclear power plants were found among al-Qaeda materials in Afghanistan. The target for the fourth plane in the September terrorist attacks, the plane that crashed in a field in Penn-

sylvania, could have been the White House, the Capitol, or Camp David—but it also could have been the Three Mile Island nuclear power plant. Alarmed by growing hints of al-Qaeda's progress toward obtaining a nuclear or radiological weapon, hundreds of new and sophisticated sensors have been deployed to U.S. borders, overseas facilities, and points around Washington, DC.

No publicly known terrorist incidents have ever involved actual nuclear weapons. The "history" of nuclear terrorism involves only *threats* of uses of nuclear arms and attacks on nuclear power plants and infrastructure. While these actions carry with them a strong potential for societal disruption, none of the attacks have resulted in releases to the environment or radioactive exposures to the public. The number of hoax incidents and threats remains classified, but approximately three to four incidents occurred annually in Germany during the 1990s. The number is likely to be higher in the United States. Nor have any large-scale acts of radiological terrorism occurred, though there have been several threats and some credible scenarios involving radioactive substances. In 1995 Chechen rebels told Russian news media that they had buried a container with the radioactive substance cesium on Russian territory. One container was identified, again without any releases to the environment. The rebels claimed to possess a total of four canisters of cesium, two of which were equipped with explosives and hidden in Moscow.

Nuclear and Radiological Terrorism

Despite some common features, nuclear and radiological terrorism are in fact quite distinct and different types of terrorism. Nuclear terrorism involves the use of nuclear weapons, where large amounts of energy are released when highly enriched uranium or plutonium atoms split during the process of fission. The consequences and destruction wrought from even a crude nuclear weapon may be incredibly devastating due to the heat, pressure and radiation generated.

Radiological dispersion devices expose people to radiation, for instance through a "dirty bomb," in which radioactive laboratory waste or civilian nuclear fuel rods would be wrapped around a conventional explosive and detonated, spreading poison and contamination. While acute deaths may occur, the primary impact on health and life would be through long-term effects like cancer development. A radiological device detonated by terrorists would require the evacuation and decontamination of the immediate area, disrupting the local economy. Given the relative simplicity of constructing a dirty bomb and the vast availability of radioactive materials, scenarios involving radioactive substances have been assumed to be more probable than acts of nuclear terrorism. The psychological impact of either type of device may be severe. Hospitals would be overrun by injured and worried people from the surrounding area.

With weapons of mass destruction, the terror may have moved from a mostly psychological level to a real threat of massive deaths and damages. Suddenly, single actors may possess striking power superseding that of many states. The search for weapons of mass destruction in Afghanistan highlights the potential dangers of terrorists getting access to weapons of mass destruction, and in particular nuclear weapon capabilities. In November 2001 apparent al-Qaeda documents describing production of weapons of mass destruction (WMDs) were found in a Kabul house. The U.S. government initiated investigations into the information found in al-Qaeda camps in Afghanistan to establish how close the group was to gaining nuclear and biological weapons capabilities. Said U.S. Undersecretary of State John Bolton, "I don't have any doubt that al-Qaeda was pursuing nuclear, biological, and chemical warfare capabilities. It's not our judgment at the moment that they were that far along, but I have no doubt that they were seeking to do so."

Bin Laden's Quest for Nukes in the 1990s

According to R. James Woolsey, former director of the U.S. Central Intelligence Agency (CIA), Osama bin Laden has been trying to get his hands on enriched uranium for seven or eight years. The trail for the bombings of the U.S. embassies in Nairobi, Kenya, and Dar al Salaam, Tanzania, in August 1998 shed new light on bin Laden's and al-Qaeda's nuclear weapon intentions. Dating back to 1993, the group tried on several occasions to acquire nuclear material. In 1998 a key aide of bin Laden's was arrested in Germany and charged with trying to obtain nuclear material. Moreover, an ex-bin Laden associate who testified for the U.S. government in the trial of the 1998 embassy bombings admitted that he had been trying to obtain highly enriched uranium for bin Laden.

Independent reviews of the documents found in Afghanistan and made available publicly did not reveal if al-Qaeda really tried to build a nuclear weapon. After reviewing several hundred pages of terrorist documents some experts believe al-Qaeda was working on a serious nuclear program. But one document labeled "super bomb" appears to be a plan for a nuclear device experts say is unworkable.

The experts added, however, that the authors behind the document clearly are knowledgeable of various ways to set off a nuclear bomb. Moreover, others warn that a dirty bomb may be within the reach of the terrorist organization. Such a device would not create a nuclear explosion, but would instead expose people to radiation and render entire city blocks uninhabitable.

In his State of the Union Address at the end of January 2002, U.S. president George W. Bush (2001–) warned of terrorists joining forces with states possessing biological, chemical, or nuclear weapons. According to the U.S. president, such an alliance would be a logical one for terrorists who have found that they are unable to purchase those weapons or their components on the black market. But after searching more than a hundred buildings, military compounds, and camps, no significant amount of radioactive material was found in the containers seized in Afghanistan. U.S. officials indicated that Osama bin Laden and al-Qaeda may have been duped by black-market weapons swindlers selling crude containers hand-painted with skulls and crossbones and dipped, perhaps, in medical waste to fool a Geiger counter. At the same time, the officials cautioned that it is impossible to make a blanket assertion that al-Qaeda possesses no nuclear material. Despite the analysis and al-Qaeda's rout from Afghanistan, the group still has the desire, resources, and global network of operatives to seek and, perhaps some day, acquire nuclear materials, or biological or chemical ones, that could be used in a terror attack, officials said.

While consensus about an increased threat thus seems to have evolved, experts still argue about the likelihood of large-scale nuclear terrorist violence. Is nuclear terrorism, as some scholars suggest, "an overrated nightmare," since the uses of nuclear weapons remain outside both the intentions and capabilities of contemporary terrorists? Or will terrorists turn to and successfully deploy crude nuclear weapons in the future?

HISTORICAL BACKGROUND

Trends and Patterns in International Terrorism

According to an official U.S. survey, there were 423 international terrorist attacks in 2000, an increase of eight percent from the 392 attacks recorded during 1999. All recorded attacks were performed with traditional terrorist means—conventional weapons and explosives. Western Europe saw the largest decrease, from 85 to 30, owing to fewer attacks in Germany, Greece, and

Italy as well as to the absence of any attacks in Turkey. While the number of terrorist attacks have declined or remained fairly constant, the terrorist mortality rate is on the rise with more indiscriminate killings. The death polls from the September 2001 attacks represented nothing less than a quantum leap in terms of terrorist casualties, in itself suggesting that there could be future weapons of mass destruction terrorism.

As clearly evidenced in Manhattan in September 2001, terrorist incidents are often high-profile events. The news media tend to focus on spectacular and negative events, and terrorism may be regarded as a way of communicating. To get attention, terrorists traditionally employ showy attacks that produce a great deal of noise. The news media, for their part, tend to focus on spectacular and negative events. The immense destructive power and the definitive "shock value" of nuclear weapons would immediately create a manifest confirmation of an attack, and, of course, wide-spread and direct attention. Moreover, the detonation of a nuclear device could set a terrorist organization apart from any other group, and could compel governments to take it seriously. The psychological impact of nuclear detonations is likely to be strong, with a radius of psychological damage far exceeding that of injury and death. The public has a greater fear of events and consequences that are catastrophic and not well understood. Past nuclear explosions and nuclear accidents, limited public understanding and knowledge of radiation, and the human inability to sense potential radiation exposure may have cultivated disproportionate fears of radiation. Terrorists who capitalize on these factors are likely to have a strong impact.

There have always been enormous gaps, however, between the potential of a weapon and the abilities and/or the will to employ it by terrorists. New means and methods of violence with unknown outcomes and new technical requirements (and thus an increased risk of failure) could be less appealing for sub-national groups. Unsuccessful or failed actions may waste resources, kill members of the terrorist groups, increase the risk of revelation and retaliation, embarrass the terrorist organization, and reduce support amongst followers—all putting the very existence of the group at stake. Terrorists operate in contexts of enormous uncertainty and anxiety, and may thus prefer known means. If a target is regarded as too challenging, other targets may be chosen, while the tactics of the group remain the same. Alternatively, well-known tactics may be further developed, as painfully evidenced on September 11, 2001. The

use of weapons of mass destruction could, moreover, stigmatize the terrorist group and render any political aspirations harder to accomplish. Conventional off-the-shelf weaponry and well-known approaches are thus likely to remain the major tools for most traditional terrorists.

Due to the range of terrorist motivations, incentives, and constraints, fulfillment of the feared nuclear super-terrorism would be highly counterproductive for nearly all terrorist groups. The constraints against the use of weapons of mass destruction are particularly severe for terrorists who are concerned with their constituents (such as social revolutionary and national separatist terrorists). While the majority of terrorist groups are likely to stick to traditional terrorist means, however, some groups may be ready to take the step up to a new level of weaponry. Weapons of mass destruction may thus again come to be used outside the sphere of state military activities, as seen in the Tokyo subway sarin attack in 1995. This was the first widely publicized large-scale attempt at using weapons of mass destruction for terrorism. Similar or related actions cannot be ruled out in the future, as several interrelated developments have increased the risk that terrorists will use weapons of mass destruction.

Terrorists and Weapons of Mass Destruction

Terrorists' motivations are changing. A new breed of terrorists appears more inclined than terrorists of the past to commit acts of extreme violence. This set of new terrorists may include everything from ad hoc groups motivated by religious conviction or revenge, violent right-wing extremists, and apocalyptic cults. Secondly, weapons of mass destruction (WMD) could be especially valuable to terrorists who have no traditional political goals, but instead seek to enact divine retribution, to display prowess, or just to perform large-scale killing. Thirdly, terrorists will generally choose their technology to exploit the vulnerabilities of a particular society. Modern societies are particularly susceptible to weapons that are capable of killing many people at one time. Additionally, as governments implement more sophisticated security measures against terrorist attacks, terrorists may find weapons of mass destruction appealing as a way to overcome such countermeasures.

Commonly, weapons of mass destruction are defined and understood as weapons capable of causing mass casualties: nuclear, biological, and chemical weapons. The three classes of weapons differ greatly, however, in lethality, destructive power, feasibility of protection and defense, and in their potential missions. While biological weapons still have to be proven efficient on a larger scale, the weapons could possess lethality comparable to a single nuclear weapon. The ultimate weapons of mass *destruction* are nuclear weapons, which have enormous destructive powers. A single modern nuclear warhead can destroy a large city. One hundred warheads are said to have the capacity to destroy the United States and civilization as we know it.

With the break-up of the Soviet Union and the resulting economic struggles and weapons security issues in that region, black markets may now offer unprecedented access to weapons, components, and know-how. Furthermore, copy-cat efforts, where groups find both inspiration and ideas from previous attempts at large-scale terrorist violence, may spur additional terrorist attacks and maybe even some level of "competition" among terrorist groups. Ever since the Tokyo subway attack, incidents involving chemical and biological weapons have been on the rise. Before the attack, the U.S. Federal Bureau of Investigation (FBI) typically encountered a dozen cases a year involving threats or actual attempts to acquire or use chemical, biological, radiological, or nuclear materials. In 1997, 71 cases were investigated; by 1999 the number had increased to 143, most of these hoaxes. Finally, advances in technology may have made terrorism with weapons of mass destruction easier to carry out. Looking at the technical history of nuclear devices, this becomes particularly evident. The first nuclear weapons, produced more than half a century ago, then represented state of the art technology and science. Today, first generation nuclear weapons are not only old, they are also regarded as primitive, with well-known designs presented in the scientific literature and physics textbooks.

Nuclear Weapon Production

To create a nuclear weapon, a designer must learn a whole set of manufacturing steps and develop confidence in the weapon's design. Any aspiring nuclear actor must be able to:

- develop a design for the nuclear device or obtain such a design from a weapon-holding state

- produce or obtain the fissile material for the nuclear core of the device

- produce or obtain the non-nuclear parts of the device, including the high-explosive elements and triggering components that will detonate the nuclear core

A SHERIFF'S DEPUTY GUARDS THE ENTRANCE TO A U.S. NUCLEAR POWER PLANT. NUCLEAR POWER PLANTS ACROSS THE UNITED STATES AND THE WORLD BOLSTERED SECURITY AFTER SEPTEMBER 11, 2001, FEARING POSSIBLE TERRORIST ATTACKS. *(AP/Wide World Photos/Chris O'Meara. Reproduced by permission.)*

- verify the reliability of these various elements individually and as a system, and finally assemble all of these elements into a deliverable nuclear armament—a process often dubbed 'weaponization'

Due to the technical challenges, first generation fission weapons of either the gun-type or implosion type are likely to be the weapon of choice for nuclear terrorists. It is considerably simpler to make a bomb using enriched uranium than to make one using plutonium, but the critical mass is larger.

THE MANHATTAN PROJECT

Alarmed by rumors that the Nazis were developing an atomic bomb, the United States initiated its own program under the Army Corps of Engineers in June 1942. Scientists needed fissionable material, which meant uranium (U-235) or plutonium (Pu-239), the only suitable substances known at the time. A large but secret crash production program was initiated at facilities at different locations in the United States.

Two types of nuclear explosives were developed in Los Alamos, New Mexico. One, nicknamed "Little Boy," was a gun-type weapon that projected a slug of uranium into the center of another piece of uranium, resulting in a nuclear explosion. The second bomb, "Fat Man," used implosion to detonate plutonium. Explosives surrounded a plutonium ball. When detonated, they would compress the plutonium, causing a nuclear explosion. In August 1945 the two weapons were dropped with devastating effects on the Japanese cities of Hiroshima and Nagasaki.

Whether terrorists choose an implosion-type or a gun-type weapon may depend on the type and quantities of fissile material they have access to. The late Luis W. Alvarez, a Nobel Laureate in Physics and a prominent nuclear weapon scientist in the Manhattan Project, has emphasized the simplicity of constructing a nuclear explosive with highly enriched uranium (HEU):

> With modern weapons-grade uranium, the background neutron rate is so low that terrorists, if they have such materials, would have a good chance of setting off a high-yield explosion simply by dropping one half of the material onto the other half. Most people seem unaware that if separated HEU is at hand it's a trivial job to set off a nuclear explosion . . . even a high school kid could make a bomb in short order.

Nuclear Production and Proliferation Concerns

The design and production of nuclear weapons today is a far simpler process than it was during the Manhattan Project in the early 1940s. Under the right set of conditions the required skills for making a crude nuclear weapon are minimal. Indeed, in a 1960s experiment conducted by the U.S. government, three newly graduated students were able to develop a workable nuclear weapon design using only publicly available information. In the years since, much more information has en-

tered the public domain. *The Los Alamos Primer: The First Lectures on How to Build an Atomic Bomb*, for example, was declassified and published in 1992. The book originated as a series of five lectures given to the physicists of the Manhattan Project at its commencement, outlining the theoretical foundations of the intended bomb-making. Potential nuclear weapon producers can find useful sites within the information swamp on the Internet. While these are not likely to be "step-by-step" descriptions for nuclear weapon acquisition, parts of the openly available information on the Internet are likely to assist and even guide potential bomb-makers in the process. There may also be lessons for new bomb makers to learn from the now abandoned and dismantled South African nuclear weapons program. South Africa indigenously produced six nuclear devices based on the simple uranium gun-type weapon principle while under the constraints of an international embargo, thus relying solely on its own domestic resources.

The Alvarez statement above illuminates the fundamental difference between a terrorist and a state nuclear weapon. While potential nuclear terrorists probably seek results no more specific than an undefined "high yield explosion," military nuclear weapons must meet an array of requirements before they are fielded. These highly different requirements for performance and delivery can make weapons designed to meet the "terrorist nuclear weapon standards" less technically challenging than traditional state nuclear weapons.

A state must be concerned with safety, so it would be at least as concerned with a nuclear device *not* going off during storage and transportation as with optimizing the yield and detonation of the weapon. Such concerns might be given less consideration by terrorists, especially groups attracted to martyrdom. Concerns for reliability may also be low among terrorists. While an ignition failure or a fizzle yield would be unfortunate from the viewpoint of terrorists, it could have profound impact on the security of a state. States want fairly accurate and known yields to predict damages and the number of weapons needed. To a terrorist, any explosion in the lower kiloton range represents an unprecedented yield, and even failed plutonium explosives may serve as radiological dispersion devices. States need reliable, conventional delivery systems such as missiles or mortars. Such slender nuclear explosives are technically challenging and expensive, and weapons for military use are usually required in fairly large numbers. Crude terrorist nuclear weapons, on the other hand, could easily fit into a van, a truck, or even a hot-air balloon.

HIROSHIMA, JAPAN, WAS DECIMATED AFTER THE UNITED STATES DROPPED AN ATOMIC BOMB ON THE CITY ON AUGUST 6, 1945, PRECIPITATING THE END OF WORLD WAR II. THE U.S. NUCLEAR PROGRAM DEVELOPED DURING WORLD WAR II UNDER THE MANHATTAN PROJECT. *(AP/Wide World Photos. Reproduced by permission.)*

The primary technical barrier to terrorist nuclear capabilities is probably the difficulty of accessing highly enriched uranium (HEU) or plutonium, the essential component of any nuclear weapon. Estimates of the quantities of fissile material needed for weapon production vary, depending on expected yield performance and technical sophistication. While the International Atomic Energy Agency's (IAEA) "Significant Quantities" (SQ) estimates are 25 kilos of HEU and eight kilos of plutonium, as little as one kilo of plutonium and 2.5 kilos of HEU may be sufficient with a highly sophisticated weapon design.

The vast production of fissile materials during the Cold War has left the world today with a staggering legacy of three million kilograms of weapons-usable material. Two-thirds of these materials are produced for military purposes, and more than half of the quantities are in excess of national security needs. Reports of lax security and accountancy of nuclear materials raise concerns about the possibility of a successful diversion of significant quantities of weapons-usable materials, particularly in the former Soviet Union. While the potential consequences of proliferation are chilling, the problems of fissile weapons-usable material management have proven anything but simple to solve.

WORKERS AT THE IZHORA NUCLEAR FACTORY IN ST. PETERSBURG, RUSSIA, ATTEND A CEREMONY DEDICATED TO THE COMPLETION OF A REACTOR BODY MADE FOR AN IRANIAN NUCLEAR POWER PLANT. WEAPONS-USABLE NUCLEAR MATERIAL HAS GONE MISSING FROM RUSSIAN STOCKPILES SINCE THE COLLAPSE OF THE SOVIET UNION. *(AP/Wide World Photos/Dmitry Lovetsky. Reproduced by permission.)*

Protecting Nuclear Materials in Russia

According to the U.S. Department of Energy (DOE), 603 metric tons of highly enriched uranium and plutonium—enough to produce almost 40,000 nuclear bombs—are at risk of nuclear material theft in Russia. This material can be used directly in a nuclear weapon without further enrichment or reprocessing. The material is considered to be highly attractive to theft because it is not very radioactive and therefore relatively safe to handle, and it can easily be carried by one or two people in portable containers or as components from dismantled weapons. As of February 2001, after nearly a decade of cooperation, U.S.-assisted security upgrades were completed or partially completed at slightly less than one-third of the weapons-useable materials sites in Russia. Internal U.S. reviews indicate that the security systems already installed do not reduce the risk of theft of nuclear material at approximately one quarter of the sites.

To protect, control, and keep track of nuclear materials, systems of so-called "MPC&A" (Material Protection, Control, and Accounting) are installed at all nuclear facilities. The systems are intended to protect material against theft or diversion, and to detect such events if they occur. To prevent the spread of nuclear materials in Russia, existing security systems at Russian facilities have been upgraded with U.S. cooperation. Under this program the U.S. Department of Energy is installing site-tailored and integrated security systems. The security enhancements include such features as entry/exit barriers, traps, personnel access control, intrusion detection, alarm communication, video surveillance, response, and computerized systems for nuclear material accounting.

The security systems installed by the DOE are reducing the risk of theft of nuclear material in Russia, but hundreds of metric tons of nuclear material still lack improved security systems. As of February 2001 the DOE had installed completed or partially completed security systems in 115 buildings, protecting about 32 percent of the 603 metric tons of weapons-usable nuclear material identified as being at risk of theft or diversion from Russia. The DOE installed completed systems in 81 buildings, protecting about 86 metric tons, or about 14 percent, of the nuclear material. It has also installed partially completed security systems, known as rapid upgrades, in 34 additional buildings, protecting about 106 metric tons, or 18 percent, of the nuclear material.

Specialists from Russian law enforcement bodies have identified poor physical protection as the primary causes of nuclear thefts, along with the acute shortage of funds allocated for nuclear material protection, control and accounting. The ratio of prevented to successful thefts remains uncertain due to insufficient accounting of nuclear material at some facilities and the failure to carry out an overall national fissile material inventory exercise. A close call apparently took place a couple of years ago, when the Russian Federal Security Services intercepted an attempt to divert 18.5 kg of "radioactive materials that might have been used in the production of nuclear weapons." Russian officials, stating that the perpetrators "could have done serious damage to the Russian state" later confirmed this attempt, making it the first confirmed case that apparently involved a conspiracy to steal enough materials for a bomb in a single stroke.

According to a research group at Stanford University, over the past 10 years at least 40 kg of weapons-usable uranium and plutonium have been stolen from poorly protected nuclear facilities in the former Soviet Union. While most of this material was subsequently retrieved, at least two kg of highly enriched uranium stolen from a reactor in Georgia remains missing. In an official Illicit Trafficking Database governed by the International Atomic Energy Agency (IAEA) about 600 illicit trafficking incidents have been recorded since January 1, 1993. Of these, about 400 incidents are confirmed by states. A little less than half of the confirmed cases (175) involve nuclear material, including 18 cases with highly enriched uranium or plutonium.

None of the quantities of seized nuclear material is enough to produce a workable nuclear explosive and no endpoint, or buyers, have been identified. Yet the seizures produce a disturbing picture—clearly, only one successful transfer of high-quality nuclear material could be one too many. The cases of HEU and plutonium theft represent as large a proportion of the total as was the case in the early 1990s, indicating a remaining market, or at least a remaining interest in fissile materials. Successful transfers will never be registered, and the identities of the smugglers remain unknown. Some of the material traveled across wide distances and through several border crossings, illustrating the difficulty of detecting illicit unirradi-

ated fissile material. The seized quantities may just be test samples for larger amount of materials available for sale.

RECENT HISTORY AND THE FUTURE

Nuclear Terrorism: Threats and Challenges

The September 11, 2001, large-scale terrorist attacks were a dire reminder of the destructive powers of terrorism. The spectacular and innovative attacks against U.S. domestic targets were performed with conventional terrorist means. The magnitude, crudeness, and the efficacy of which these actions were carried out, however, may point in the direction of future large-scale terrorist uses of weapons of mass destruction. The multiple attacks spurred a tidal wave of rumors about imminent large-scale terrorist attacks, including terrorists with low-flying crop-dusters filled with biological materials and trucks destined for city centers full of nasty toxicants. And indeed, letters containing anthrax were soon mailed to several U.S. recipients. Few were infected, but the radius of psychological damage far exceeded that of the physical impact.

Many, many questions have been raised and additional ones will evolve in the aftermath of the terrorist attacks on the United States. The more fundamental questions naturally deal with the possibility of future "superterrorism" and the new security paradigm we may be facing. Following the U.S. terrorist attacks the Secretary General of the United Nations singled out terrorists' use of nuclear, biological, and chemical weapons as the gravest threat the world faces. Former U.S. senator Sam Nunn echoed this assertion: "The most significant, clear, and present danger we face is the threat posed by nuclear, biological, and chemical weapons. The question is not whether we must prepare for terrorism or for attacks with weapons of mass destruction. These two threats . . . if joined together, become our worst nightmare." While the risk of nuclear terrorism may be remote, it cannot be excluded. Technically, crude nuclear weapon production is likely to be within range of the capabilities of some terrorist groups. Rigorous standards and means for the protection, control, and accounting of fissile materials, the essential ingredients of any nuclear device, are thus of vital importance.

Terrorist groups aspiring to weapons of mass destruction capabilities face strong practical and strategic constraints. Use of conventional weaponry is likely to remain the approach of choice for most

NUCLEAR EMERGENCY SEARCH TEAM (NEST)

The mission of the NEST is to search out and, where necessary, de-fuse or destroy nuclear material or nuclear weapons as safely as possible. It is also used in delineating the distribution of radioactive material resulting from a nuclear accident. The team is based in Nevada. Along with the ability to deploy about 600 people, it also has about 150 tons of equipment at its disposal. NEST's air force consists of four helicopters equipped with radiological search systems and three airplanes. The equipment includes various nuclear radiation detection systems developed for use in surveying an area for lost or diverted nuclear weapons and special nuclear material.

An elite group, NEST has hidden primarily behind a cloak of secrecy, so much so that while the organization's existence has been public, its activities have only been visible to those intimately involved with their operations. NEST's cooperation with first responders like police, fire and other public safety officials is close. In the last few years different governmental agencies have been banding together to train for the frightening event in which a terrorist does field a weapon of mass destruction in the United States.

Since NEST's creation, about 100 threats involving alleged nuclear devices or radioactivity have come to its attention. At least a dozen, and possibly more than twice that number, have resulted in deployment of NEST personnel. NEST, in general, will not confirm or deny when or whether it has deployed to a particular city or region. However, it has been reported that between 1975 and 1981 NEST personnel were sent to investigate threats in Boston, Los Angeles, Spokane, Pittsburgh, New York, Sacramento, Tennessee, and Reno.

terrorists. However, as the world experiences new acts of terror, provable and strong interest amongst some terrorist groups in acquiring nuclear weapon capabilities does not allow us to ignore the risk of nuclear terrorism. The use of crude (HEU) nuclear weapons provides the opportunity for distinct, original, fairly reliable, and highly visible acts of large-scale terrorism, without prior testing of the devices. The impact is likely to be strong, both physically and psychologically. Even crude nuclear explosives have the potential of introducing yields in the lower kiloton range, at least three times the magnitude of the most powerful conventional explosive ever deployed.

Nuclear Terrorism: U.S. and International Responses

Technical barriers should not be regarded as sufficient to prevent future terrorist nuclear violence. Both the flow of knowledge and general descriptions of crude weapon designs into the popular sphere has been too prominent. Terrorist nuclear weapon standards are, moreover, likely lower than state (military) nuclear weapon requirements, potentially making production of terrorist nuclear weapons less challenging. In addition, some terrorist groups now apparently possess unprecedented resources for performing their terror activities. Acquisition of sufficient qualities and quantities of fissile material is the most formidable obstacle to nuclear terrorist capabilities. It is therefore imperative that preventing terrorists from gaining access to fissile materials be a high priority component of the new global battle against terrorism. The transnational nature of contemporary international terrorism can make inadequately secured nuclear material anywhere a threat to nations everywhere.

With U.S. assistance over the past decade, Russia has made some progress in securing dangerous weapons and material, but more must be done. In January 2001 Republican Howard Baker, a former senator and White House chief of staff, and Democrat Lloyd Cutler, a former White House counsel, chaired a bipartisan panel on the security of Russia's nuclear materials. Their conclusions were not encouraging. Their report said, "The most urgent unmet national security threat to the United States today is the danger that weapons of mass destruction or weapons usable material in Russia could be stolen and sold to terrorists or hostile nation states and used against American troops abroad or citizens at home." Following a year-long review, the George W. Bush administration concluded that most of the U.S. non-proliferation assistance programs are cost-effective and beneficial to national security. But these conclusions are not properly reflected in the administration's budget proposal. Despite the threats, the assistance to Russia remains a highly politicized issue. Some programs receive small increases, others remain flat, and still others are targeted for spending cuts.

The Baker-Cutler report concludes that US$3 billion per year would go a long way to address the problem of poorly guarded fissile materials in Russia. Senator Joseph R. Biden, Jr., argues that "That's a lot of money, but we're spending $7.8 billion on national missile defense research and development in fiscal year 2002 and the administration has requested a similar amount for fiscal year 2003." According to the senator, it doesn't make sense to focus on the potential last line of defense when we need to do so much to bolster the more achievable first line of defense. The additional resources that should be allocated could be used to double the size of the U.S. Department of Energy's $174 million Materials Protection, Control and Accounting program, which safeguards Russia's nuclear materials.

Russia recently signed an agreement to open up many more nuclear sites to U.S. assistance, providing an opportunity to substantially increase the security of nuclear stockpiles guarded by little more than a chain-link fence. Another, more controversial, proposal is to reduce Russia's Soviet-era debt in return for Russian investment of the proceeds in non-proliferation programs. According to Senator Biden, debt swaps are a win-win proposition: Russia can avoid an expected payment crunch next year while bolstering security through protection of sensitive materials and technologies.

In response to the threat of nuclear terrorism, the International Atomic Energy Agency (IAEA) in March 2002 approved an action plan designed to upgrade worldwide protection against acts of terrorism involving nuclear and other radioactive materials. In approving the plan, the IAEA recognizes that the first line of defense against nuclear terrorism is the strong physical protection of nuclear facilities and materials. The plan covers eight areas: physical protection of nuclear material and nuclear facilities, detection of malicious activities (such as illicit trafficking) involving nuclear and other radioactive materials, strengthening of national state systems for nuclear material accountancy and control, security of radioactive sources, assessment of safety and security related vulnerabilities at nuclear facilities, response to malicious acts or threats thereof, adherence to international agreements and guidelines, and enhancement of program co-ordination and information management for nuclear security related matters.

These activities are not a substitute for national measures, nor can they diminish the primary responsibility of nation states on all matters of security; rather, the measures are designed to supplement and reinforce national efforts in areas where international cooperation is indispensable to the strengthening of nuclear security. These areas include better border controls and enhanced national and international mechanisms for responding to radiological emergencies. A number of states, including Australia, Great Britain, Japan, the Netherlands, Slovenia, and the United States

THE INTERNATIONAL ATOMIC ENERGY AGENCY (IAEA)

The IAEA is an independent, intergovernmental science and technology-based organization in the United Nations family that serves as the global focal point for nuclear cooperation. The agency assists national states in using nuclear science and technology for various peaceful purposes, including the generation of electricity. The IAEA develops nuclear safety standards and, based on these standards, promotes the achievement and maintenance of high levels of safety in applications of nuclear energy, as well as the protection of human health and the environment against ionizing radiation. The IAEA also verifies that states comply with their commitments under the Non-Proliferation Treaty and other non-proliferation agreements, to use nuclear material and facilities only for peaceful purposes.

pledged money to a special fund set up to support the plan. Other states have announced support for the plan. If applied, current supplies of nuclear material and other radioactive sources may be kept under firmer lock and key from terrorists.

BIBLIOGRAPHY

Alvarez, Luis W. *The Adventures of a Physicist.* New York: Basic Books Inc., 1987.

Baker, Howard, and Lloyd Cutler. *A Report Card on the Department of Energy's Non Proliferation Programs with Russia,* Secretary of Energy Advisory Board, United States Department of Energy: January 10, 2002. Available online at http://www.hr.doe.gov/seab/rusrpt.pdf (cited April 17, 2002).

Barnaby, Frank. *Issues Surrounding Crude Nuclear Explosives. Proliferation and the Terrorist Threat.* International Physicians for the Prevention of Nuclear War Global Health Watch Report, Number 1, 1996.

Boettcher, Mike, and Ingrid Arnesen. "Al-Qaeda Documents Outline Serious Weapons Program," CNN: January 25, 2002. Available online at http://www.isis-online.org/publications/terrorism/cnnstory.html (cited April 17, 2002).

Bunn, Mathew. *The Next Wave: Urgently Needed Steps to Control Warheads and Fissile Materials.* Carnegie Endowment for International Peace, 2000.

Calabresi, Massimo and Ratnesar Romesh. "Can We Stop the Next Attack?" *Time,* March 3, 2002. Available online at http://www.time.com/time/nation/printout/0,8816,214064,00.html (cited April 17, 2002).

Cameron, Gavin. "Multi-track Micro-proliferation: Lessons from Aum Shinrikyo & Al Qaida." *Studies in Conflict and Terrorism*, vol. 22, October-December, 1999.

Carnegie Analysis. *Going Nuclear: What It Takes to Build A Bomb*, November 6, 2001. Available online at http://www.ceip.org/files/nonprolif/templates/article.asp?NewsID=1732.

Cochran, T.B. and C.E. Paine. "The Amount of Plutonium and Highly-Enriched Uranium Needed for Pure Fission Nuclear Weapons," *Nuclear Weapons Databook*. Natural Resources Defense Council Inc., 1995.

Kamp, K.H. "An Overrated Nightmare," *The Bulletin of the Atomic Scientists*, vol. 52, no. 4, July/August, 1996.

Laqueur, Walter. *The New Terrorism: Fanaticism and the Arms of Mass Destruction*. New York: Oxford University Press, 1999.

Maerli, Morten Bremer. "Relearning the ABCs: Terrorists and Weapons of Mass Destruction," *The Nonproliferation Review*, vol. 7, no. 2, Summer 2000.

McCloud, Kimberly and Matthew Osborne. *WMD Terrorism and Usama Bin Laden*. Center for Nonproliferation Studies, CNS Reports, 2001. Available online at http://www.cns.miis.edu/pubs/reports/binladen.htm (cited April 17, 2002).

National Atomic Museum. Available online at http://www.atomicmuseum.com (cited April 17, 2002).

Richelson, Jeffrey T. "Defusing Nuclear Terror," *Bulletin of Atomic Scientists*, March/April 2002. Available online at http://www.thebulletin.org/issues/2002/ma02/ma02richelson.html (cited April 17, 2002).

Security of Russia's Nuclear Material Improving; Further Enhancements Needed. United States General Accounting Office, GAO-01-312, February, 2001.

Serber, Robert. *The Los Alamos Primer. The First Lectures on How to Build an Atomic Bomb*. Berkeley, CA: University of California Press, 1992.

Shanker, Thom. "U.S. Analysts Find No Sign bin Laden Had Nuclear Arms," *New York Times*, February 26, 2002. Available online at http://www.nytimes.com/2002/02/06/international/asia/26NUKE.html (cited April 17, 2002).

Stern, Jessica. *The Ultimate Terrorists*. Cambridge, MA: Harvard University Press, 1999.

Tucker, Jonathan, ed. *Toxic Terror. Assessing Terrorist Uses of Chemical and Biological Weapons*. BCSIA Studies in International Security, Cambridge, MA: MIT Press, 2000.

United States Department of State. Bureau of Public Affairs. *Patterns of Global Terrorism, 2000*. Office of the Coordinator for Counterterrorism. Washington, DC: U.S. GPO, 2000. Available online at http://www.state.gov/s/ct/rls/pgtrpt/2000 (cited April 17, 2002).

Morten Bremer Maerli

THE OLYMPICS CONFRONTS TERRORISM

The Olympic Games receive a high profile from the media and the international public. While sportsmanship receives the greatest attention, there have been times in the history of the Games where violence has taken center stage. In an arena where cooperation and goodwill are showcased, acts of terror are shocking and tragic. On heightened alert for possible terrorist acts going into the 2002 Salt Lake City Games in Utah, the Olympic organizers, participants, and audience were ready and willing to share the moment, despite the possibility of violence. While the Salt Lake City Games ended peacefully, the Olympics have been subject to increasingly higher security measures due to past events.

In the weeks before the 1996 Summer Olympic Games in Atlanta, Georgia, organizers and officials reassured the public that every precaution had been taken to abort terrorist attacks on the event. With a global audience in the billions, the Olympics had in the past presented a high-profile stage for groups attempting to broadcast their platform, and the results were sometimes lethal. In 1972 when Palestinian terrorists abducted Israeli athletes from the Olympic Village in Munich, eleven athletes died, along with one police officer and five of the terrorists. In the wake of an attack on the World Trade Center in February 1993, the Oklahoma City bombing in April 1995, and assaults on American military operations in Saudi Arabia, tensions ran even higher. Would the first Olympics held on American soil in twelve years witness another attack, possibly directed at the United States' dominant presence in world affairs?

With local, state, and federal assistance, Olympic organizers spent about US$110 million on security measures for the 1996 Games. In addition

THE CONFLICT

In the wake of the terrorist attacks on the United States on September 11, 2001, there was fear of additional strikes during the Winter Olympic Games in Salt Lake City, Utah, scheduled for February 2002. While U.S. and Olympic officials insisted that a comprehensive set of counterterrorist efforts would guarantee the safety of athletes and spectators, they also acknowledged that no event can be 100 percent safe. Given the worldwide attention that the Olympics generate, the site of the Games will continue to be a primary target for any terrorist organization with the means to carry out such an attack.

Political

- The Olympics symbolize international understanding and cooperation through sportsmanship. Despite the stated goals of the Olympic Movement, however, the games have always been inherently politicized. They were cancelled in 1916 and from 1940–44 due to the World Wars. In 1972 the Games were marred by a deadly attack against Israel's athletes by Palestinian terrorists. In 1996 a bomb allegedly planted by anti-abortion activist Eric Robert Rudolph at the Games killed one spectator and injured 111 more.

- The Olympics suffered two successive boycotts in 1980 (led by the United States in protest of the 1979 Soviet invasion of Afghanistan) and in 1984 (led by the Soviet Union). Subsequent site selections for the Games have often provoked outpourings of nationalist sentiment on the part of potential host countries. Pointing to China's poor human rights record, many observers criticized the selection of Beijing for the 2008 Games.

Ideological

- With the world's focus on the Olympic games every four years, the events are designed to promote international goodwill and understanding. For terrorist groups, however, the games present the chance to declare their presence on the global stage.

CHRONOLOGY

1896 The first Olympic Games of the modern era are held in Athens, Greece.

1968 Controversies arise over political actions of two African-American athletes at the Mexico City Summer Olympic Games.

September 5, 1972 Israeli athletes are taken hostage by Palestinian terrorists at Olympic Games in Munich, Germany. Two are killed by the terrorists and the remainder die in a rescue attempt.

1975 The Greek terrorist organization 17 November assassinates a U.S. embassy employee.

July 27, 1996 A bomb is set off in Centennial Park in Atlanta, Georgia, during XXVI Olympiad, with one spectator killed.

October 1998 Eric Robert Rudolph is charged by the FBI as being responsible for the Centennial Park bombing.

September 15–October 1, 2000 The XXVII Summer Olympiad is held in Sydney, Australia. Security is heightened in light of the Atlanta Games, but no terrorist acts occur.

September 11, 2001 Terrorist attacks on United States in New York City and Washington, DC, kill and injure thousands.

February 8–23, 2002 The XIX Olympic Winter Games are held in Salt Lake City, Utah, employing even great security measures. The Games pass without terrorist violence.

package containing the bomb not been discovered by security officer Richard Jewell, who notified an ATF agent and began to clear the area. At first Jewell was hailed as a hero, but in the weeks to come he would be named as the bombing's primary suspect. In the controversy that followed, Jewell was eventually cleared and another suspect, anti-abortion protester Eric Robert Rudolph, was charged with the attack. Six years later, Rudolph remained at-large, and troubling questions regarding security measures at the Games lingered.

HISTORICAL BACKGROUND

Taking their inspiration from the Olympic Games held in Greece from at least 776 BCE to 391 CE, organizers led by Dimitrious Vikelas of Greece (1835–1908) and Pierre de Coubertin of France (1863–1937) established the International Olympic Committee (IOC) in 1894. In 1896 the IOC inaugurated the modern era of the games with the Summer Olympiad in Athens. About 300 men participated in 42 events across nine sports; following de Coubertin's insistence that the Olympic movement hold itself apart from material considerations, competition was limited only to amateur athletes. The second Olympic Summer Games, held in Paris in 1900, were opened to women, although their numbers did not exceed one hundred participants until 1924. That year a Winter Olympiad was established; held in the same quadrennial year as the Summer Games until 1992, the Summer and Winter Games subsequently alternated in even-numbered years. By the 1996 Summer Games, 197 nations sent athletes to the event, and the 1998 Winter Games, held in Nagano, Japan, welcomed eighty nations.

Political Controversies

From the start, the modern games embodied the ideals of Olympism, a concept that urged individual athletes to excel in sports while fostering mutual understanding among competitors and their nations. As stated in the U.S. Olympic Committee's volume Olympism: A Basic Guide to the History, Ideals, and Sports of the Olympic Movement, the set of ideals "is a strong moral force that seeks and promotes: Individual well-being; National spirit; [and] International understanding and friendship." The modern Olympics faced the first challenge to these principles in 1916, when the games were canceled in light of World War I (1914–18). Four years later the Central Powers of Austria, Bulgaria, Germany, Hungary, and Turkey—named as aggressors in the war—were barred from the revived games in Antwerp. After another

to 1,000 video cameras stationed throughout the competition sites and the Olympic Village, a staff of 2,400 volunteer police officers from around the world was added to a sizable contingent from the Federal Bureau of Investigation (FBI), U.S. Bureau of Alcohol, Tobacco, and Firearms (ATF), and the U.S. Customs Service. On July 9, 1996, just ten days before the Games opened, John Gordon, a Major with the Atlanta Police Department, confidently predicted to the Emergency Net News Service that "When all is said and done, this city might be the safest place on the planet."

Tragically, Gordon's prediction proved wrong. Around 1:00 AM on July 27, during a concert in Centennial Park, a bomb exploded that killed one spectator, Alice Hawthorne, and injured 111 others. The toll might have been even higher had the

period of expansion in the 1920s and 1930s, the games were again canceled in 1940 and 1944 due to World War II (1939–45).

The 1936 Summer and Winter Games—both held in Nazi Germany—perhaps represented the most politicized games in the modern era. In a bid to avoid a boycott of the games, Third Reich Chancellor Adolf Hitler temporarily suspended some of the anti-Semitic laws enacted after the Nazi Party's rise to power. With the pageantry of the Nazi regime on full view, however, African American athlete Jesse Owens's success at the games belied the Party's racist platform. Owens began by taking the gold medal in the 100-meter dash with a time of 10.3 seconds that tied the world record, one of four gold medals he won in the games. Later Owens would claim that Hitler had refused to congratulate him after his gold-medal performances, and "Hitler's snub" became part of Olympic history; Hitler, however, had not met with any gold medal winners after the opening day and the "snub," while controversial, was not intentional. Another athlete, figure skater Cecilia Colledge of Great Britain, raised protests for another reason, as she greeted spectators with a Nazi salute before her performance. While Colledge insisted that she was simply showing respect for the host nation, the episode demonstrated the intense politicization of the 1936 games.

Terrorist Attacks in 1972

After the suspension of the games in 1940 and 1944, the politicization of the games continued. Following the Soviet invasion of Hungary in 1956, a water polo match between the two countries at the Melbourne Games left athletes bloodied. In 1968 two African American athletes, sprinters Tommie Smith and John Carlos, raised their fists in a Black Power salute on the medal stand; the protest outraged Olympic hero Jesse Owens, and the image became one of the enduring images of the Games. In 1972, however, the use of the Games as a political platform turned deadly when a group of Palestinian terrorists attacked the Israeli delegation in the Olympic Village in Munich. While the IOC had become accustomed to political turmoil surrounding the Olympics—including a threatened boycott by African nations to protest the inclusion of Rhodesia at the 1972 competition—the event was the first actual terrorist attack at the Games.

Perpetrated by a group of six Palestinians under the name Black September, with the assistance of two Palestinian workers in the Olympic village, the terrorists staged their attack in the early morning hours of September 5, 1972. Eleven hostages

INTERNATIONAL OLYMPIC COMMITTEE PRESIDENTS, 1894–2001

President	Term
Demetrius Vikelas (Greece)	1894-96
Pierre de Coubertin (France)	1896-1925
Henri Baillet-Latour (Belgium)	1925-42
J. Sigfrid Edstrøm (Sweden)	1942-46 (acting); 1946-52
Avery Brundage (United States)	1952-72
Lord Killanin (Ireland)	1972-80
Juan Antonio Samaranch (Spain)	1980-2001
Jacques Rogge (Belgium)	2001-

THE INTERNATIONAL OLYMPIC COMMITTEE, WHICH HEADS THE OLYMPIC GAMES, HAS HAD EIGHT PRESIDENTS SINCE THE GAMES BEGAN IN 1894. (Gale Group.)

were taken, two of whom were killed in the initial fighting. After demanding that 234 Palestinian prisoners in Israel be released—along with infamous leaders of Germany's Baader-Meinhof terrorist group—the terrorists negotiated with the West German Interior Minister Hans-Dietrich Genscher for a plane to fly them to an Arab country. At the airfield, however, the German police fired on the group as it attempted to board the plane; all of the hostages and five of the terrorists were killed.

While the scheduled competitions were suspended during the day-long standoff, IOC president Avery Brundage insisted that the Games resume after a memorial service on the morning of September 6. The decision had the support of the IOC governing board and Israeli prime minister Golda Meier, who believed that ending the Games would signal a surrender to the terrorists' actions. Arab delegates, however, refused to attend the memorial service, despite a storm of criticism for their apparent support for the terrorists' deeds. Adding to the tension, as recounted in Allen Guttmann's The Olympics: A History of the Modern Games (1992), Brundage kicked off another controversy by equating the threatened boycott over the Rhodesian affair with the violence of the past day. "Sadly, in this imperfect world, the greater and more important the Olympic Games become, the more they are open to commercial, political, and now criminal pressure," he stated at the memorial

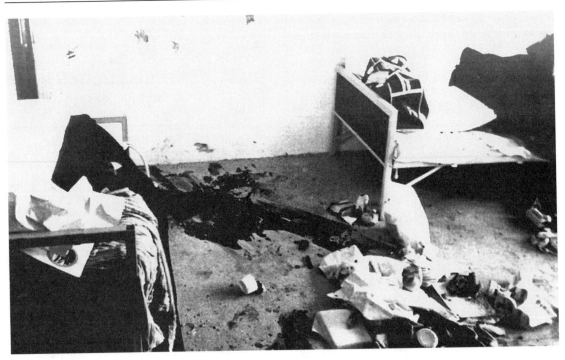

WHEN BLACK SEPTEMBER TERRORISTS TOOK THE ISRAELI OLYMPIC TEAM HOSTAGE IN 1972, TWO ATHLETES WERE KILLED IN THEIR ROOM. THE REMAINING ATHLETES AND FIVE TERRORISTS WERE LATER KILLED IN A RESCUE ATTEMPT. (AP/Wide World Photos. Reproduced by permission.)

service. " . . . I am sure that the public will agree that we cannot allow a handful of terrorists to destroy this nucleus of international cooperation and goodwill we have in the Olympic Movement."

After the 1972 Games: Politics and Security

The fact that no attack had taken place during an Olympic competitive event was little comfort for the IOC and the local Olympic Committees in charge of arranging security for future games. After 1972, security was a primary consideration in awarding the Games to any host city, a situation that the organizers of the 1976 Montreal Summer Games blamed for enormous cost overruns in hosting the event. Montreal's mayor, Jean Drapeau, had estimated that the Games would cost about $125 million; eventually, the total came to more than $2 billion. Drapeau's critics, however, pointed to corruption and inefficiency within his administration for the inflated costs. Either way, many potential host cities were scared off from submitting bids for future Olympic Games. For the 1984 Summer Olympiad, only one city, Los Angeles, completed the application process.

Stung by the criticism of the IOC's handling of political issues and security measures, Brundage's successor, Anglo-Irishman Michael Morris (better known by his royal title, Lord Killanin), faced one controversy after another during his term as IOC

president from 1972–80. At the Summer Games in Montreal in 1976, a flap over Canada's refusal to admit Taiwanese athletes under a Chinese flag in deference to the readmission of the People's Republic of China to the Olympics almost derailed the event. Despite pressure from the IOC the Canadian government refused to back down, even after it was accused of caving in to the communists' demands in order to secure a lucrative grain deal with the country.

Cold War tensions resurfaced again in 1980 when the United States organized a boycott of 56 countries to protest the Soviet Union's invasion of Afghanistan in late 1979. Although the United States, West Germany, and the People's Republic of China refused to attend the Games, 81 other countries participated in the Moscow Games; 16 nations, including Great Britain, France, and Denmark, chose to attend under the Olympic flag instead of their own national banners. Given the intense scrutiny of the Soviet secret police, the KGB, however, there were few concerns over security at the Games. If anything, the KGB's iron grip on Moscow—dissendents were ejected from the city before the Games, all public protests were quickly disbanded, and potentially controversial film footage of the Soviet Union was confiscated by the authorities—set the tone for the event.

The 1984 Los Angeles Olympic Games were also marred by a boycott, this time led by the Soviet Union. Angered by the denial of a visa to the designated Soviet Olympic representative to the Games—whom the United States suspected of being a key KGB agent—the Soviets abruptly announced in May 1984 that they would not attend the Games. Only those countries under Soviet influence in Eastern Europe, with the exception of Romania, joined the boycott, however, and the Games proceeded with 139 participating nations. Although the opening torch-lighting ceremony was almost called off because of a bomb threat, the Los Angeles Police Department quickly assured officials that it was a false alarm. From a security standpoint, the rest of the Games were uneventful.

The selection of Seoul, South Korea, as the site of the 1988 Summer Games once again raised the possibility of terrorist attacks, particularly from the country's neighbor, the Democratic People's Republic of Korea, or North Korea. The two countries shared one of the most contentious borders in the world, the heavily guarded Demilitarized Zone, where hostile exchanges sometimes occurred. Juan Antonio Samaranch, who took over the IOC presidency in 1980, deftly negotiated with the North Koreans, however, and promised to allow them to host ten individual competitions in four sports during the Games. While the offer fell short of North Korea's demand to act as a co-host, the offer greatly reduced the support of North Korea's position by other communist countries. After Samaranch traveled to the Soviet Union to bolster support for the IOC's position—he had formerly served as Spain's ambassador to the nation—North Korea's boycott was doomed.

While Samaranch expertly managed the tensions between the two Koreas, the IOC president had far less control over the turbulent domestic politics of South Korea. Student protests over the autocratic regime of Chun Doo Hwan turned violent in the spring of 1987; in response, President Chun pleaded with protesters to postpone their demands for democratization until after the Games were concluded. As the protest movement gained momentum through the summer, Chun eventually announced his resignation. His successor quickly arranged for direct presidential elections, and the Games went off without a hitch. Olympic officials proudly noted that the spirit of the Olympic Movement had actually helped to bring democracy to South Korea.

Terror Returns to the Olympics—1996

With the Soviet Union in disarray, the usual Cold War tensions abated for the 1992 Summer Games in Barcelona and the Winter Games in Albertville, France. The 1996 Summer Games in Atlanta, Georgia, however, witnessed the most destructive terrorist attack—at least in terms of injuries—that the Games had ever suffered. As a result of the Centennial Park bombing, which occurred during a free concert just after 1:00 AM on July 27, 111 spectators were injured and one woman, Alice Hawthorne, was killed. The bomb indirectly claimed another victim when a member of a Turkish television crew suffered a fatal heart attack while fleeing the area.

Even though the scheduled events went forward, the bombing cast a pall over the Atlanta Games. In the aftermath of the attack, security guard Richard Jewell, who first discovered the suspicious package containing the bomb, was named as the primary suspect after the president of Piedmont College, where Jewell had once worked, contacted the FBI to report him as a suspect. When the FBI leaked the name of Richard Jewell as the primary suspect in the bombing, it touched off a media frenzy. The Atlanta Constitution carried the headline "FBI Suspects 'Hero' May Have Planted Bomb" and alleged that Jewell fit the profile of a lone-bomber suspect. The paper also accused him of sharing characteristics with convicted child serial killer Wayne Williams. Soon every other major news organization jumped on the story. In addition to being followed by several FBI agents everywhere they went, Jewell and his mother, Barbara, were tailed by cameras and crews for weeks after the FBI's investigation was launched. It was only in October 1996 that the FBI officially cleared Jewell's name as a suspect in the case.

Two years later, Eric Robert Rudolph, already under indictment for two other bombings, was indicted for the Centennial Park attack as well as another Atlanta bombing at a gay nightclub. Rudolph, claiming to represent the "Army of God," had already gone into hiding before the indictments were issued. Officials believed that Rudolph had gone into the mountains of western North Carolina to escape capture; however, they made few comments about his possible motivation for bombing the Olympic Games. Known as a fervent opponent of abortion, Rudolph had also railed against gays; it seemed likely that his latest terrorist act was a publicity seeking gesture for his political beliefs. Rudolph was added to the FBI's Ten Most Wanted Fugitives list, but there were no reported sightings of him after his January 1998 disappearance.

The FBI's mishandling of the Centennial Park bombing investigation added to the criticism of security efforts at the Atlanta Games. Prior to

RICHARD JEWELL

1963– A native of Georgia, Richard Jewell spent most of his career in law enforcement, including a stint at Piedmont College in Demorest, Georgia, that would come back to haunt him. An avid volunteer who coached Little League football teams, Jewell signed up as a security guard during the Olympic Games, held not far from the apartment he shared with his mother in Atlanta. Around 1:00 AM on July 27, 1996, during a concert in Centennial Park, Jewell spotted a suspicious package and alerted an ATF agent. He then immediately helped clear the area of spectators. When the bomb went off, however, one woman was killed and 111 others were injured. After the Piedmont College president contacted the FBI to voice his belief that Jewell was the bomber, the security officer became the primary suspect in the bombing.

After an intensive, 88-day investigation, the FBI cleared Jewell's name in the bombing. Jewell subsequently threatened several lawsuits against various media outlets for their alleged invasion of his property, and NBC and CNN settled claims for libel before they reached court. The *New York Post* and an affiliate of ABC Radio also settled lawsuits by Jewell, who reportedly received over $2 million in settlements from the various media outlets. The *Atlanta Constitution,* however, fought Jewell's lawsuit. As the sixth anniversary of the bombing approached, the matter had not been settled.

the event, officials had widely publicized measures to keep Olympic competitive venues safe from harm. Every day before the start of any events, federal officials electronically searched the rowing courses for explosives; at the kayaking and canoeing course, about 300 agents monitored the activity 24 hours a day. Mindful of the 1972 Munich attacks, security at the Olympic Village was the tightest of any venue: only visitors with registered hand prints matching their security badges were allowed to pass into the athletes' compound. For all of the other areas—including the promenade of Centennial Park, a public gathering place of kiosks, concerts, and other attractions—a team of 2,400 volunteer security officers, working with FBI, ATF, and local and state police officials monitored the crowds.

Although the security presence was indeed massive at the Atlanta Games, coordination among the several agencies involved actually handicapped counterterrorist efforts. Instead of naming one

agency to coordinate security throughout the Games, there was only a contingency plan to put the FBI in charge "if things hit the fan," as U.S. Attorney Gil Childers, a U.S. Justice Department official, admitted to Emergency Net News in July 1996. Caught off guard when a terrorist event actually took place, the FBI's immediate response was less than reassuring to the public.

Richard Jewell later settled a number of lawsuits against media organizations for a reported $2 million settlement. The Atlanta Constitution, however, insisted that its reporting was fair and accurate and decided to fight Jewell's lawsuit in court. After five years, the case had not yet been settled. Working as a police officer in an unnamed Georgia town, Jewell remained bitter about the experience of being held up as the suspected Olympic bomber. As he told Mike Wallace in an interview on the television news show 60 Minutes II in January 2002, "No one has ever bothered to even say, 'Thank you, Mr. Jewell'. . . . People will never forget my name. People will be ninety years old that were at the Olympic Games and go, 'Do you remember when the bomb went off, that Jewell fellow that they accused of that? Do you remember that?' . . . It will never end, sir."

Lessons from the Atlanta Games

Organizers of the 2000 Sydney Olympic Summer Games heeded the lessons from the Atlanta Games and coordinated all security measures through one centralized office of the New South Wales Police Service. Officials also hoped that Australia's geographic isolation and immigration control measures would make it easier to screen out potential terrorists before they entered the Olympic sites. These factors had made Australia almost immune from attacks in the past; in the thirty years leading up to the Olympics, only a handful of attacks made the headlines. In a counterterrorist summit held in Australia in December 1995, however, security expert Bruce Hoffman warned Olympic organizers not to get too complacent. He told Emergency Net News that Australia should not "wrap itself in a fatally false blanket of security" because of its geographic isolation and immigration policies. Terrorism, Hoffman warned, is always a threat. Hoffman also predicted that the Olympics would remain an attractive target for terrorists, in part because such attacks usually attained their goal of publicizing a group's platform. "I don't think it's coincidental that a year following the 1972 Munich Olympic massacre that the PLO [Palestine Liberation Organization] was granted observer status in the United Nations and in 1974 Yasser Arafat was invited to address the General Assembly. That itself shows that although people were certainly appalled by what occurred in 1972, it was nonetheless a tremendous publicity vehicle."

In the months before the Sydney Games, authorities uncovered two potential terrorist plots directed at the Olympics. Beginning in December 1999 a series of letters was sent to the U.S., Russian, Turkish, British, and Israeli consulates in Australia. The letters demanded $50 million—later raised to $100 million—or else a terrorist team of fifteen agents with guns, chemical weapons, missiles, and explosives would be used against Centerpoint Tower in Sydney, as well as on incoming passenger planes. In staged negotiations from the Turkish embassy, New South Wales police were able to trace the threats to Mehmet Akin Kayirici, who lived in a suburb of Sydney; Kayirici's thumbprint was also found on the letter to the British consulate. Although Kayirici did not appear to have ties to any known international terrorist group, his actions resulted in an indictment on four charges of sending a letter demanding money with menacing intent and one charge of demanding money with threats of attacking an airplane.

The second terrorist plot appeared far more serious than Kayirici's attempted extortion. In March 2000 New Zealand police investigating a people-smuggling operation uncovered a plot to blow up a nuclear reactor in Sydney during the Games. Four Afghan men with suspected ties to Osama bin Laden were initially arrested for passport fraud and suspicion of people-smuggling, but a search of their home uncovered extensive planning operations for an Olympic assault. In addition to maps of the Sydney area, the group had planned entrance and exit routes to and from the reactor and had conducted its own assessment of police security measures around the site. Because the reactor itself was used only for research, and therefore presented a less devastating target than an operating power plant, officials decided not to close it down during the Games. Fortunately, there were no incidents at the Games themselves, and the enthusiastic and warm crowds made the Sydney Olympics one of the most successful of the modern era.

Preparing for the Salt Lake City Games

While the corruption scandal was an ongoing distraction for the Salt Lake City Organizing Committee (SLOC) and IOC, security concerns were once again foremost in their minds in the wake of the September 11 terrorist attacks on New York City and Washington, DC. In the wake of the attacks the Winter Games in Salt Lake City were now seen as a primary terrorist target—both as the

---

ERIC ROBERT RUDOLPH

1966– One of the FBI's Ten Most Wanted Fugitives, Eric Robert Rudolph was indicted in October 1998 for the Centennial Park bombing of July 27, 1996. Rudolph was also charged as the suspect in two other bombings in the indictment. On January 16, 1997, Rudolph was alleged to have placed two bombs at an Atlanta abortion clinic; the second of the bombs injured four people with shrapnel. In a similar incident, Rudolph was charged with placing two bombs at a gay nightclub in Atlanta; the first bomb inflicted shrapnel wounds on five people, but the second bomb was disabled before it went off.

Prior to the indictment for the three bombings, Rudolph had already been charged with a January 1998 bombing at an abortion clinic in Birmingham, Alabama. In that case, a police officer was killed and one woman was severely injured. After the bombing, as in the attack on the nightclub, letters from someone claiming to be the "Army of God" took responsibility for the bombings. The FBI believed that Rudolph and the "Army of God" were one and the same.

Rudolph, a carpenter by trade, was last seen in January 1998, shortly before he was charged with the Birmingham bombing. An experienced outdoorsman, Rudolph had prepared for a long stay in the wilderness of western North Carolina; after his disappearance, the FBI discovered that Rudolph had bought at least six-month's worth of provisions to take with him. While many believe that Rudolph is still alive in the mountainous terrain of North Carolina, there have been no confirmed reports of his whereabouts since his disappearance.

---

focus of international attention and as a symbol of the United States' power—and security measures were stepped up on every front. Not only would all of the estimated 3,500 athletes, trainers, and coaches be screened before entering the Olympic Village, but every individual article would also be examined, including food items and personal hygiene products. As Mark Camillo, coordinator of the U.S. Secret Service efforts at the Olympics told a 60 Minutes II interviewer, "Every one of those items will have been looked at to make sure there's nothing embedded or inserted in its packaging that could be harmful."

While the unprecedented security checks at the Olympic Village recalled the 1972 Munich massacre, other measures stemmed directly from the September 11 attacks. Mindful of the air assaults

VISITORS OBSERVE THE SITE OF A FATAL EXPLOSION IN CENTENNIAL OLYMPIC PARK IN ATLANTA, GEORGIA, DURING THE 1996 SUMMER GAMES. SUCCEEDING OLYMPIC GAMES HAVE TAKEN HEIGHTENED SECURITY MEASURES TO GUARD AGAINST POTENTIAL TERRORIST ATTACKS. (AP/Wide World Photos/Bob Galbraith. Reproduced by permission.)

miles away from the competition sites. And in light of the ongoing anthrax scares, special teams of agents studied possible methods of transmitting weapons of biological mass destruction at all of the Olympic venues. Governor Mike Leavitt struck a hopeful note about the possibility of preventing such an attack, telling the Chicago Tribune, "Utah has a long experience with preparation for biological warfare, or elements related to that." Mitt Romney, head of the SLOC added, "I'm sure there are a lot of Utahans saying, 'I wish right now the Games weren't on their way here,' but they are, so we will do a good job hosting them."

In addition to spending more than $300 million on security for the Salt Lake City Games—about three times the amount laid out for the Atlanta Olympics—officials hoped that the organization of security efforts had learned from past mistakes. Under Presidential Directive 62, signed by President Bill Clinton in 1998, the U.S. Secret Service was designated as the lead federal agency for Olympic security planning, with the FBI named as the intelligence unit and the Federal Emergency Management Agency (FEMA) put in charge of immediate crisis management. Each of these agencies in turn was integrated into the Utah Olympic Public Safety Command (UOPSC). With an estimated 12,000-plus security officers—ranging from U.S. military personnel to FBI, ATF, and FEMA agents to the Utah National Guard—designated for the Olympic Games, UOPSC's challenges were not insignificant. Although there would be more security officers than athletes in Salt Lake City, such a fact did not deter the Centennial Park bomber in 1996. Still, the SLOC hoped that all of its planning would not create a lock-down atmosphere at the Games. As Salt Lake City mayor Rocky Anderson told the Los Angeles Times, "What people will find is a very appropriate security presence. It's not going to be oppressive or overwhelming, but it will be conspicuous in a sense that most people would expect or even desire."

In the weeks before the Games, SLOC and UOPSC officials put their security measures on full public display. The public was also reassured by Homeland Security Director Thomas J. Ridge, who reviewed security plans and announced to the Los Angeles Times, "I believe one of the safest places on the globe from the beginning to the end of February will be Salt Lake City" (January 11, 2002). Perhaps reminded that similar comments had been made on the eve of the Atlanta Games, however, Ridge added, "There's no guarantee it is a fail-safe system." IOC officials once again restated the board's policy of carrying on with the

that damaged the Pentagon and brought down the World Trade Center buildings, much of Utah was declared a no-fly zone for the duration of the games, while air activity was banned at Salt Lake City's airport during the opening and closing ceremonies of the Games. Throughout the Olympics, all flights except commercial airliners and cargo airlines were banned outright from the airport.

To prevent a car bomb from disrupting the Games, parking for the predicted 80,000 daily spectators was also limited to a giant lot about ten

Olympics despite possible terrorist threats. Congratulating the SLOC for putting together the most comprehensive security effort in the Games' history, it reiterated in a statement in October 2001 that "The Games will go on and should go on. . . . We fully believe that the Olympic Winter Games, the celebration of the athletic pursuits and achievements of the world's youth, should be an answer to violence, not a victim to it."

RECENT HISTORY AND THE FUTURE

While the IOC was impressed with the efforts to secure the safety of the Salt Lake City Olympics, the 2004 Summer Games in Athens were a nagging concern for officials. Bitter over the awarding of the Centennial 1996 Games to Atlanta, Greece had lobbied heavily to host the 2004 Games; once the award was made, however, the Greek government failed to swing into action in preparation for the event. A series of political fiascoes followed, with the Socialist government of Premier Costas Simitis receiving much of the blame. In September 2001, new IOC president Jacques Rogge made an unexpected visit to Greece to review the progress toward the Athens Games and reportedly left with a long list of concerns about the event. Even more troubling was the Greek government's apparent unwillingness to allay security worries over its inability to suppress the domestic terrorist group 17 November, which had operated in Greece for almost thirty years.

The terrorist group 17 November took its name from the day in 1973 when the Greek government ordered a crackdown on student protests. In response, the group—claiming an anti-capitalist, anti-American, and super-nationalist platform—assassinated Richard Welch, an employee at the U.S. embassy in Athens, in 1975. In the next ten years the group carried out five more attacks. Between 1975 and 1985, 17 November killed a total of eight people in its assassination plots. Acting with apparent impunity from the Greek government, which to date has never identified even a single member of 17 November, the group stepped up its terrorist activities in 1985 with a campaign of bombings and assassinations. In December 1990 the group launched a rocket at the offices of the European Community in Athens; another rocket attack on the office of the Greek Finance Minister in Athens killed a bystander. 17 November stepped up its attacks during the Gulf War (1991) and is believed to have killed one U.S. Army sergeant in March 1991 in addition to attacking the Turkish embassy later that year.

Western observers have long contended that 17 November has strong ties to the Greek government, which is too embarrassed to conduct an effective campaign against it for fear of scandal. With the 2004 Olympics set for Athens, however, international pressure intensified for the Greek government to initiate comprehensive counterterrorist measures, including the elimination of 17 November. While the government officially denied that it had ties to 17 November, the IOC reportedly stepped up pressure in the wake of President Rogge's visit in late 2001 to bring in international counterterrorist forces to deal with the group.

In contrast to the lackluster efforts of the Athens Olympic Organizing Committee, the Summer Olympics planned for Beijing in 2008 recalled the KGB-dominated Games of Moscow in 1980. With open dissent against the ruling Chinese Communist Party outlawed, domestic surveillance—and according to international rights groups, outright repression—was the norm in Chinese society, even before the arrival of the Olympic Games. Because of China's dismal human rights record, some observers were outraged that the IOC awarded the 2008 Summer Games to Beijing, an announcement that made headlines on July 13, 2001. "The IOC didn't even try to get guarantees on human rights," complained Sidney Jones, director of Asia Human Rights Watch, in comments to the Washington Post. "If abuses take place as preparations for the Games proceed, it won't be just the Chinese authorities who will look bad; the IOC and the corporate sponsors will be complicit," Jones warned. Secretary of State Colin Powell, on the other hand, took a more encouraging view of the decision, telling the Washington Post, "I do think it provides an opportunity for China over the years to move in the direction that will create a positive environment where people will go and see more progress in China, more openness in China, more willingness to tolerate dissent." He added, "I hope China takes advantage of that opportunity."

Others rejected outright the IOC's Seoul analogy—that hosting the Olympic Games could serve as a democratizing force, as it had been in South Korea—in justifying its decision to hold the Games in Beijing. As Sally Jenkins of the Washington Post wrote the day after the announcement, "Do you really think that somehow the leaders of China care so much about being liked that they will improve their record on human rights if we come play ball with them? Not likely" (July 14, 2001). Describing the IOC as a "profiteering, junketeering cartel" in light of its ongoing bribery and corruption scandals, Jenkins went on to revive one of the sharpest

AN ARMY BLACKHAWK HELICOPTER CIRCLES STADIUM AUSTRALIA, THE MAIN VENUE FOR THE 2000 SUMMER OLYMPICS IN SYDNEY, AUSTRALIA. THE MANEUVERS WERE PART OF THE AUSTRALIAN ARMY'S ANTI-TERRORIST TRAINING. (AP/Wide World Photos/Rick Rycroft. Reproduced by permission.)

criticisms of the group: that in awarding the Games to a dictatorship, the IOC was actually rewarding a repressive regime. Jenkins ignored the secondary effect of the Seoul Olympics, however, which had also helped to reduce international tensions between South Korea and its main adversary, North Korea. In bringing North Korea into negotiations about the possibility of hosting some Olympic events, the dictatorship had been drawn into the international arena in a meaningful way for the first time in generations. While the country ended up boycotting the Games and remained relatively isolated afterwards, the threat of North Korea sponsoring a terrorist attack on the Games had been eliminated. In addition to helping democratize South Korea, then, the Olympics had eased regional tensions as well.

In the post-Cold War, post-September 11 world, however, the Olympic Movement may have more to fear from splintered, subaltern groups, not those seeking national aggrandizement, as in the case of 17 November, or international legitimacy, as in the case of Black September in Munich. As Eric Rudolph's Centennial Park bombing demonstrated, any extremist group might target the Olympics for reasons only obscurely related to the Games themselves. Despite the difficulty in predicting who

might attempt to attack the Olympics, however, the awareness of such a possibility seems to preclude any large-scale assaults in the future. As the IOC has reminded the public, the regular schedule of the Olympic Games means that security measures can be initiated years in advance of the events themselves. In addition, future Games will also take security into consideration when it comes to selecting the competition sites. For the Salt Lake City Games, numerous surveillance and security devices were built into the competition facilities; features such as sensors and cameras have become a standard part of the Olympic infrastructure.

As the best known international sports competition, however, the Olympic Games will doubtless be subjected to further political controversies and terrorist threats. Unlike soccer's World Cup matches, the Olympic Movement generates a huge interest in North America every four years, adding further to the possibility that terrorist groups might strike at the Games to publicize their anti-Western views. Despite these risks the IOC has steadfastly maintained its commitment to continue on with the Games. As it concluded in its October 2001 report after the terrorist attacks on the United States, "The world needs the display of basic human values the Olympic Games exhibit now more than ever."

BIBLIOGRAPHY

Alderman, Ellen and Caroline Kennedy. "The Legacy of Richard Jewell." Columbia Journalism Review, March/April 1997, p. 27.

Baker, William J. Jesse Owens: An American Life. New York: The Free Press, 1992.

BBC News. "Bribery Scandal Appeal Bid," January 24, 2002. Available online at http://news.bbc.co.uk/winterolympics2002/hi/english/features/newsid_1776000/1776853.stm (cited February 27, 2002).

Cannon, Angie. "Bombing Charges Filed Against Rudolph in Olympic and Two Other Bombings." Knight-Ridder Washington Bureau, October 14, 1998.

Canoe Canada. "Olympic Extortion Trial Begins," November 6, 2000. Available online at http://www.canoe.ca/2000GamesNews/nov6_trial-ap.html (cited February 27, 2002).

Chronicle of the Olympics, 1896–1996. New York: Dorling Kindersley Publishing, 1996.

Cross, Martin. "Olympics: Athens' Games Struggle," NOW Network of the World. Available online at http://www.now.com/sport/feature.now?javascript=dhtml&fid;=2361510$cid=659206 (cited January 16, 2002).

Federal Bureau of Investigation. "Eric Robert Rudolph," FBI's Ten Most Wanted Fugitive List. Available online at http://www.fbi.gov/mostwant/topten/fugitives/rudolph.htm (cited January 17, 2002).

Griffin, Anna. "As Agents Hunt Rudolph, Fear Stalks Bomb Victims." Charlotte Observer, December 14, 1998.

———. "Most People Believe that Bomb Suspect Eric Rudolph Is Alive and in the Woods." Charlotte Observer, August 26, 1999.

"Growing Concern about Security at Athens 2004 Olympics." EmergencyNet News Service, February 15, 2001, Vol. 7, No.- 046. Available online at http://www.emergency.com/2001/greece02-15-01.htm (cited January 16, 2002).

Guttman, Allen. The Olympics: A History of the Modern Games. Urbana, IL: University of Illinois Press, 1992.

Hersh, Philip. "Olympic Security Questions Mount," Chicago Tribune, October 20, 2001.

Hoge, Jr., James F. And Gideon Rose, eds. How Did This Happen?: Terrorism and the New War. New York: Public Affairs, 2001.

International Olympic Committee. "IOC Confident of Secure, Successful Olympic Winter Games." Available online at http://www.olympic.org/ioc/e/news/pressreleases/press%5F499%5Fe.html (cited January 16, 2002).

International Policy Institute for Counterterrorism. "Revolutionary Organization 17 November." Available online at http://www.olympic.org/uk/news/publications/press_uk.asp?release=40 (cited January 17, 2002).

Jenkins, Sally. "Games Put China in Glass House for the Whole World to See," Washington Post, July 14, 2001.

Lake, Anthony. Nightmares: Real Threats in a Dangerous World and How America Can Meet Them. Boston, MA: Little, Brown and Company, 2000.

Lonkevich, Dan. "Risk Managers Play Down Olympics Terrorism Threat," National Underwriter, July 15, 1996.

Lucas, John A. Future of the Olympic Games. Champaign, IL: Human Kinetics Books, 1992.

Macko, Steve. "Experts Look at Potential Terrorist Threat at the 2000 Olympics," EmergencyNet News Service, January 10, 1996. Available online at http://www.emergency.com/olym2000.htm (cited February 27, 2002).

———. "Security at the Summer Olympic Games Is Ready." EmergencyNet News Service, July 9, 1996. Available online at http://www.emergency.com/olymsec.htm (cited February 27, 2002).

Merry, E. Wayne. "Don't Ignore Greek Terrorism." Christian Science Monitor, February 14, 2001.

Mufson, Steve. "Powell Hopes Olympics Will Open Chinese Society," Washington Post, July 13, 2001.

Pelley, Scott. "Salt Lake City Olympics," 60 Minutes II, January 9, 2002.

Reaves, Jessica and Barry Hillenbrand. "Beijing Gets the Games," Time, July 13, 2001.

"Report: Police Foil Plot Against Sydney Olympics," CNN News, August 26, 2000. Available online at http://www.cnn.com/2000/ASIANOW/australasia/08/26/olympic.plot.01/ (cited January 23, 2002).

"Richard Jewell Faces Uncertain Future," CNN News, July 1997. Available online at http://www.cnn.com/US/9707/olympic.park.bombing/wrong.man/ (cited February 27, 2002).

"Rogge Wins Top Olympics Job," CNN News, July 16, 2001. Available online at http://www.cnn.com/2001/WORLD/europe/07/16/olympics.president (cited January 24, 2001).

Salt Lake City Organizing Committee. "Frequently Asked Public Safety Questions."

Senn, Alfred E. Power, Politics, and the Olympic Games: A History of the Power Brokers, Events, and Controversies that Shaped the Games. Champaign, IL: Human Kinetics Books, 1999.

Serrano, Richard A. and Julie Cart. "Response to Terror: Security Planners Building Fortress Utah for Olympics," Los Angeles Times, January 11, 2002.

United States Olympic Committee. Olympism: A Basic Guide to the History, Ideals, and Sports of the Olympic Movement. Milwaukee, WI: Griffin Publishing Group, 2001.

Wallace, Mike. "Interview with Richard Jewell," 60 Minutes II, January 2, 2002.

Wyatt, Kristen. "Five Years after Olympic Park Bombing, Still No Justice for Victims," AP Worldstream, July 27, 2001.

Timothy G. Borden

THE PLO AND YASSER ARAFAT—FROM TERRORISM TO STATESMANSHIP TO TERRORISM

THE CONFLICT

From the beginning, Yasser Arafat and the Palestine Liberation Organization (PLO) have been seen by Palestinians and other Arabs as "freedom fighters" seeking to oust the Israelis from Palestine. At the same time, there has been a more general view held outside of the Arab world that has often been less supportive of the Palestinian position. In this second group have been those such as Israel, the United States, and other portions of the international community that have seen Arafat as a terrorist who evolved to a statesman and who now seems to have reverted to the role of terrorist under the increasing violence of the second *intifada*.

Political

- A Palestinian nationalist umbrella organization—the Palestine Liberation Organization—was formed in 1964 to represent Palestinians, work for the liberation of Palestine, and establish an independent Palestinian state. Soon headed by Yasser Arafat, the group engaged in what much of the international community considered to be terrorist activities for decades before Arafat officially renounced terrorism in 1988.

- Arafat was hailed as a hero in 1994 when he was awarded a Nobel Peace Prize in Oslo, Norway, for his participation in the 1993 Oslo Accords, which established the most solid plan for peace in the region to date.

- By 2002, after renewed uprising and increasing suicide attacks by Palestinians, Arafat was regarded as a perpetrator of terrorism and an encourager of violence rather than as a statesman seeking to achieve peace in the Middle East.

- With U.S. and world attention focused on combating terrorism, Arafat's position as the legitimate leader of the Palestinians is under scrutiny while questions rise about his involvement with terrorist activities.

In the spring of 2002 the Israeli-Palestinian component of the Arab-Israeli conflict reemerged as a complex and violent issue that generated widespread international attention. The most senior United States policymakers—the president and vice president, the secretaries of state and defense, and the national security advisor—became directly engaged in this issue and it became a staple of the news listened to, watched, and read by Americans, and much of the rest of the world on a daily basis.

The conflict also seemed to affect other U.S. interests and policies. Some argued that the United States would find it more difficult to gain Arab world support for continued actions against Osama bin Ladin and al-Qaeda in retaliation for the September 11 attacks, as well as for any future steps against Iraq, as long as the Israeli-Palestinian issue remained at a high level of tension.

In the view and minds of most observers, Yasser Arafat and the Palestine Liberation Organization (PLO) are very much synonymous with the Palestine National Authority (PNA or PA) created under the terms of the 1993 Oslo Accords. At the same time there has been an evolution in the way in which these elements have been perceived. From the beginning, Arafat and the PLO have been seen by Palestinians and other Arabs as the incarnation of, and representation of, the Palestinians in their effort to achieve a state in Palestine—they were "freedom fighters" seeking to oust the Israelis from Palestine. At the same time, there has been a more general view held outside of the Arab world that has often been less supportive of the Palestinian position, and especially of the Palestinian organizations such as the PLO and the PA and of Yasser Arafat. In this second group have been those such as Israel, the United States, along

CHRONOLOGY

May 14, 1948 Israel proclaims its independence. The first Arab-Israeli War begins.

December 1949 Jordan's King Abdullah annexes the West Bank and East Jerusalem.

January 1964 The Palestine Liberation Organization (PLO) is created in Cairo, Egypt.

January 1, 1965 Fatah launches its first attack against Israel.

June 5–10, 1967 In the Six Day War, Israel captures the West Bank and East Jerusalem from Jordan, the Sinai Peninsula and Gaza Strip from Egypt, and the Golan Heights from Syria.

August 1967 An Arab Summit at Khartoum, Sudan, declares "no recognition, no negotiation, no peace with Israel."

November 22, 1967 UN Security Council Resolution 242 is adopted, designed to be the basis for an Arab-Israeli peace, emphasizing an exchange of land for peace. This has been the basis of all subsequent Arab-Israeli peace efforts.

February 1–4, 1969 Yasser Arafat is elected chairman of the PLO.

September 1970 Conflict breaks out in Jordan between the Jordanian armed forces and the PLO. The PLO is ousted from Jordan.

October 6–22, 1973 The Yom Kippur/Ramadan War begins when Syria and Egypt launch a coordinated attack on Israeli positions on the Suez Canal and Golan Heights. The war ends in a ceasefire.

October 1974 The PLO adopts a phased program for liberation of Palestine. The Arab League designates the PLO as the "sole legitimate representative of the Palestinian people."

November 13, 1974 Arafat addresses the UN General Assembly; the PLO is later granted observer status and allowed to participate in debates on the Arab-Israeli question.

September 5–17, 1978 Israeli leader Menachem Begin and Egyptian president Anwar Sadat sign the Camp David Accords.

March 26, 1979 The Egypt-Israel Peace Treaty is signed in Washington, DC.

June 6, 1982 Responding to Palestinian attacks from southern Lebanon, Israel invades Lebanon in Operation Peace for Galilee.

July–August 1982 Israel lays siege to Beirut.

August 1982 A multinational peacekeeping force enters Beirut to oversee the PLO's evacuation from Lebanon. PLO forces are dispersed to a number of Arab countries. Arafat and his aides establish themselves in Tunisia.

December 9, 1987 The first Palestinian *intifada* begins.

November 15, 1988 The Palestine National Council (PNC) in Algiers declares an independent Palestinian state.

December 1988 Arafat addresses the United Nations in Geneva. He recognizes Israel's right to exist, accepts UNSC Resolutions 242 and 338, and renounces terrorism. The United States announces that it will begin a dialogue with the PLO in Tunisia.

October 30, 1991 An Arab-Israeli peace conference begins in Madrid, Spain.

Spring 1993 Secret negotiations between Israel and the PLO occur in Oslo, Norway.

September 13, 1993 The Israel-PLO Declaration of Principles (DOP) is signed in Washington, DC.

December 10, 1994 Yasser Arafat, Shimon Peres, and Yitzhak Rabin receive the 1994 Nobel Peace Prize.

July 1, 1995 Israel and the PLO fail to meet their deadline for agreement on expansion of the Palestinian self-rule authority beyond Gaza and Jericho into other locations in the West Bank.

January 1996 Arafat is elected head of the Palestine National Authority.

1995–2000 Negotiations between Israel and the PLO continue sporadically.

Summer 2000 The Camp David II Summit fails to achieve an agreement. Soon thereafter the al-Aqsa intifada begins. Over succeeding months the violence escalates, including suicide bombing attacks against Israeli civilians.

March 2002 Israel launches Operation Defensive Shield in retaliation to Palestinian suicide bombings.

March 27, 2002 The U.S. Department of State designates the al-Aqsa Martyrs Brigade as a foreign terrorist organization.

April 1, 2002 U.S. President George W. Bush publicly encourages Arafat to denounce Palestinian attacks against Israel and take stronger leadership measures to halt violence.

with portions of the international community, that have seen Arafat as a terrorist who evolved to a statesman and who now seems to have reverted to the role of terrorist. The Yasser Arafat who was hailed by many as a hero when he was awarded a Nobel Prize in Oslo, Norway on December 10, 1994, for his participation in the Oslo Accords in 1993, was, by 2002, regarded as a perpetrator of terrorism and an encourager of violence rather than as a statesman seeking to achieve peace in the Middle East. During a press briefing on February 13, 2002, White House spokesman Ari Fleischer referred to the Palestinian Authority as one of a number of regimes that "invite terrorism and that practice terrorism." He also linked the PA to the "axis of evil" described by US President George W. Bush in his State of the Union address in January 2002.

The U.S. view of Arafat, the PA, and the PLO and its various constituent organizations was strongly suggested by the muted response of the Bush administration to Israel's assault in April 2002 on Yasser Arafat's compound in Ramallah and elsewhere in the West Bank. The administration was faced with a dilemma, given the parallels between Israel's response to Palestinian terrorist strikes which have killed Israeli civilians in Israel and the U.S. response in Afghanistan to the September 11 attacks on the United States. This followed suggestions that Israel had the right of self-defense especially when the United States had labeled the attacks against Israeli civilians as acts of terror although Palestinians civilians have also been killed by Israeli actions. After the initial Israeli assault and the siege of Arafat's headquarters, the United States noted that it was "monitoring the events very closely and assessing appropriate responses." The United States suggested that Arafat should act to stop terror and violence. Secretary Powell, on March 29, 2001, noted that "terrorism" had brought about the crisis and that it had prevented a political move in the direction of peace. Powell made it clear that opposition to and combating terrorism was the central theme of the Bush administration and that it insisted that Arafat take actions to stop terrorist bombings and implement a cease-fire. Powell made it clear that the onus was on Arafat for the deteriorating situation in the Middle East. Bush reacted similarly in comments from his Crawford, Texas, ranch on March 30.

HISTORICAL BACKGROUND

How Did this Evolution of Arafat and the PLO Occur?

The core of the Arab-Israeli conflict is more than 100 years old and focuses on the ultimate dis-

position of the territory long known as Palestine—a small piece of land located between the Mediterranean Sea and the Jordan River. This territory was contested by Palestinian Arabs and Jewish Zionists for much of the twentieth century and this conflict has continued into the twenty-first century.

The Arab-Israeli conflict as a contemporary political issue with military and para-military components began in the Palestine sector of the Ottoman Empire in the nineteenth century when the Zionist movement sought to establish a Jewish home in Palestine, where the historic Jewish state had been located. Violence in Palestine periodically broke out between the Zionist Jews and the Arabs. The Arabs of Palestine opposed the influx of Jewish immigrants and sales of land to them; the Zionists sought to purchase land and to increase Jewish immigration to the Holy Land to bolster the Jewish community already there.

Despite promises to both Arabs and Zionists made during World War I (1914–18), the British government accepted a League of Nations mandate over Palestine—control it maintained until 1948—despite sporadic violence between the communities in Palestine. It was only after World War II (1939–45), and against the background of the Holocaust, that the Zionist movement achieved a part of its goal with the United Nations decision of November 29, 1947 to partition Palestine into a Jewish state and an Arab state with the city of Jerusalem as a *corpus separatum* (a separate entity) administered by the United Nations. Israel, however, was faced with the rejection of the partition decision by the Arabs of Palestine and by the League of Arab States. When Britain terminated its Mandate over Palestine on May 14, 1948, Israel declared its independence. Despite Western hopes for peaceful coexistence with its Arab neighbors in Palestine and in the broader Middle East, the declaration of independence was greeted by a declaration of war, in effect formalizing the hostilities that followed the UN partition vote.

The first Arab-Israeli War was followed by a number of other major conflicts and thousands of less-than-war clashes and events, including guerrilla warfare and terrorist strikes. During the period between the first Arab-Israel War in 1948–49 and the Six Day War of 1967, a number of guerrilla/terrorist organizations were created whose goal was to strike at Israel and replace it with a Palestinian Arab state. Among these was Fatah, a group co-founded by Arafat and which remains a major component of the PLO and closely linked to Arafat.

At the same time the decades after 1948 were marked by strident Arab opposition to Israel's exis-

YASSER ARAFAT

1929– Yasser Arafat was born of Palestinian parentage on August 4, 1929, in Cairo, Egypt. As a boy, he ran errands and delivered messages for the Mufti of Jerusalem, and later worked as an arms smuggler for the Mufti's Arab partisans. A mufti is a Muslim expert in Islamic theology and jurisprudence. After the conclusion of the first Arab-Israeli war in 1948, Arafat enrolled in Cairo University to study engineering. There, he dedicated much of his time to the General Union of Palestinian Students (GUPS), on which he served as both president and chairman.

After graduating in 1956, Arafat moved to Kuwait, and founded the guerilla group Fatah, whose frequent cross-border attacks against Israel contributed to the outbreak of the 1967 war. Following the war, his revolutionary exploits allowed him to rise to the post of Chairman of the Palestine Liberation Organization (PLO), and he used the position to adjust the PLO's traditionally pan-Arab objectives—the aspiration for the unity of *all* the Arabs in one unit rather than a series of individual Arab national units, such as Palestine, Egypt, Syria, etc.—with those advocating Palestinian liberation. Arafat's diplomatic skills, however, were hampered by his lack of foresight and mercurial nature, which ultimately led to the PLO's forced eviction from bases in Jordan during the 1970s and Lebanon in the early 1980s.

Although Arafat's open support for Iraq's Saddam Hussein during the 1991 Gulf War marked a major diplomatic and financial mistake, his political career was saved by the historic nature of the Oslo Accord he signed with Israel less then three years later. For this, he was also awarded the Nobel Peace Prize. Under post-Oslo agreements, Israel began withdrawing from territory in the West Bank and Gaza Strip that was to be governed by the newly created Palestinian Authority (PA), to which Arafat was elected president. Palestinians accused the Israelis of failing to implement the agreements properly, pointing especially to the continuation of the building

YASSER ARAFAT, ONCE CONSIDERED THE LEADER OF A TERRORIST ORGANIZATION, SHAKES HANDS WITH UN SECRETARY-GENERAL KOFI ANNAN AS THE OFFICIALLY RECOGNIZED LEADER OF THE PALESTINIANS. CURRENT EVENTS, HOWEVER, HAVE RAISED QUESTIONS ABOUT ARAFAT'S CONTINUED INVOLVEMENT IN TERRORIST ACTIVITY. *(AP/Wide World Photo/Steve Chernin. Reproduced by permission.)*

of Jewish settlements in the Occupied Territories. Permanent status negotiations were begun at Camp David II in the summer of 2000, Arafat, however, rejected Israeli proposals on Palestinian statehood, and failed to make any counteroffers. Several months later, after a controversial visit by now Israeli prime minister Ariel Sharon to the al-Aqsa/Temple Mount site in Jerusalem, the second Palestinian uprising (*intifada*) began, and despite the US efforts of the Tenet plan and Mitchell ceasefire, Arafat has done little to quell the increasing violence and resume the peace process.

tence. Thus, for example, the Palestine National Covenant of 1964 called the creation of Israel null and void. Article 19 of the Covenant read: "The partition of Palestine in 1947 and the establishment of the State of Israel are entirely illegal . . . ." Article 20 reads: "The Balfour Declaration, the Mandate for Palestine and everything that has been based upon them, are deemed null and void." At the 1967

Arab League summit meeting in Khartoum, Sudan, after the Six Day War the Arab states adopted a resolution, which spoke of "no peace with Israel, no recognition of Israel, no negotiations with it." Israelis recall that when President Anwar Sadat of Egypt initiated peace negotiations between Egypt and Israel (1977), and later made peace with it (1979), he was assassinated by extremists and Egypt was os-

A MAN WAVES A PALESTINIAN FLAG AMIDST VIOLENCE IN THE WEST BANK. THE FIRST PALESTININIAN UPRISING, OR INTIFADA, BROKE OUT AGAINST ISRAELI OCCUPATION IN 1987. THE SECOND INTIFADA BEGAN IN 2000. (© *David and Peter Turnley/CORBIS. Reproduced by permission.*)

tracized by many in the Arab world. Arafat and the PLO opposed the Egypt-Israel Peace Treaty as a capitulation to Israeli demands and a selling-out of the Palestinians. The goal was an Arab Palestinian state in place of Israel.

Palestine Liberation Organization (PLO)

At an Arab Summit in Cairo in 1964, the Arab League decided to form a Palestinian nationalist umbrella organization—the Palestine Liberation Organization (PLO)—that would represent Palestinians and work for "the liberation of Palestine" and the establishment of an independent Palestinian state in lieu of Israel. Ahmed Shukairy was chosen to head the new organization.

The Palestine National Council (PNC) became the highest Palestinian policymaking body. In 1970, it established a Central Committee to act on its behalf when it is not in session. The Executive Committee of the PLO is akin to the executive branch of government. It implements PNC decisions and is responsible to it. It speaks for the Palestinian people and represents them internationally. The PLO includes all the Palestinian Armed Resistance (commando) groups, as well as a number of popular organizations, including the General Union of Palestinian Workers, the General Union of Palestinian Students, the General Union of Palestinian Writers and Journalists, the General Union of Palestinian Doctors, the General

Union of Palestinian Teachers, and other such groups. Additional institutions were developed over time by the PLO. These included such groups as the Palestine Red Crescent Society and the Palestinian News Agency (WAFA). The United States has considered the PLO an umbrella organization that includes several constituent groups and individuals with differing views on terrorism.

The PLO gained renewed energy after the Arab defeat in the Six Day War of 1967 and Shukairy was forced to resign in December 1967. At the Palestine National Congress held in February 1969, Yasser Arafat was elected chairman of the PLO's Executive Committee. In the 1970s and 1980s PLO elements staged a series of terrorist attacks, including airplane hijackings and the murder of Israeli athletes at the 1972 Munich Olympics, which drew world attention to the Palestinian cause. Israel responded by tracking the terrorists, both individuals and groups, by improving security in Israel and on its national airline (El Al), and by launching retaliatory raids against terrorist groups and the countries that provided safe havens and bases from which to operate against Israel.

In the 1970s and early 1980s terrorist attacks against Israel often were launched from neighboring Arab states. After being ousted from Jordan in 1970 the PLO and Arafat moved to Syria and Lebanon. Raids launched from Lebanon led to an Israeli attack against Palestinian groups in Lebanon in 1978 in Operation Litani. Their objective was to destroy bases and infrastructure of the PLO in Lebanon and to capture or destroy weapons, ammunition, and war material. Despite some success, PLO attacks against Israeli targets continued.

In June 1982 Israel launched Operation Peace for Galilee (the war in Lebanon)—a major military action against the PLO in Lebanon in order to reduce its military and terrorist threat to Israel and as a major response to years of PLO terror attacks against Israel and its people. At the end of the fighting Yasser Arafat and his associates were allowed to transfer the PLO's headquarters to Tunis, from which they operated until they moved to Jericho and Gaza after the signing of the Oslo Accords in 1993. Attacks against Israel were reduced in number and severity over the next few years.

In 1987 the first *intifada* (uprising) began in the Gaza Strip and West Bank. Palestinians saw this as a means to bring about the end to Israeli occupation of those territories that Israel captured in 1967 as a result of its successful defense in the June 1967 Arab-Israeli war and to promote an independent Palestinian state. Palestinians also sought to gain a representative role for the PLO in negotiations with Israel and the United States rather than remain isolated as a terrorist organization with which neither Israel nor the United States would deal. PLO chairman Arafat publicly renounced terrorism in December 1988 on behalf of the PLO.

U.S. Dialogue with the PLO (December 14, 1988)

As part of the Egypt-Israel Sinai II Accords negotiations in 1975, a Memorandum of Agreement between the governments of Israel and the United States spelled out the U.S. position concerning the PLO: "The United States will continue to adhere to its present policy with respect to the Palestine Liberation Organization, whereby it will not recognize or negotiate with the Palestine Liberation Organization so long as the Palestine Liberation Organization does not recognize Israel's right to exist and does not accept Security Council Resolutions 242 and 338." Later, in the Carter administration (1977–81), renunciation of terrorism was added to the requirements that the PLO would need to meet prior to a dialogue with the United States. These conditions were not accepted by the PLO until late in the second Reagan administration (1981–89).

In December 1988 Yasser Arafat, in a speech to the United Nations suggested that the PLO had decided to meet these requirements. The statement, however, was not unambiguous and, thus on December 14 Arafat, in a press conference in Geneva, Switzerland, clarified his position:

> . . . Our desire for peace is a strategy and not an interim tactic. . . . .Our statehood provides salvation to the Palestinians and peace to both Palestinians and Israelis. Self-determination means survival for the Palestinians and our survival does not destroy the survival of the Israelis as their rulers claim . . . .
>
> As for terrorism, . . . we totally and absolutely renounce all forms of terrorism, including individual, group and state terrorism.

In response to Arafat's declaration, the United States announced that it was prepared to hold a substantive dialogue through U.S. Ambassador to Tunisia, Robert Pelletreau. "The Palestine Liberation Organization today issued a statement in which it accepted U.N. Security Council Resolutions 242 and 338, recognized Israel's right to exist in peace and security and renounced terrorism. As a result, the United States is prepared for a substantive dialogue with PLO representatives." A dialogue began but no major achievements were recorded until after the Gulf War (1991). The dialogue between the United States and the PLO was

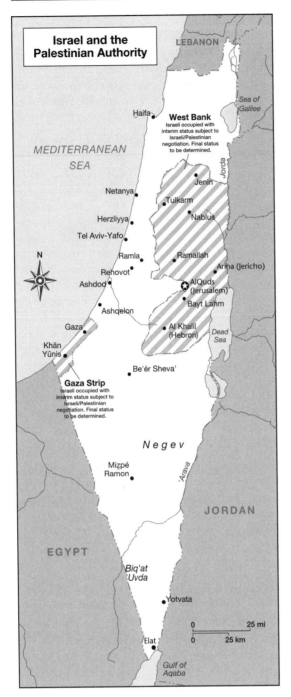

Israel and the Palestinian Authority

LEBANON

Sea of Galilee

Haifa

West Bank
Israeli occupied with interim status subject to Israeli/Palestinian negotiation. Final status to be determined.

MEDITERRANEAN SEA

Jordan

Jenin

Netanya

Tulkarm

Herzliyya

Nablus

Tel Aviv-Yafo

Ramla

Ramallah

Rehovot

Ariha (Jericho)

Ashdod

AlQuds (Jerusalem)

Bayt Lahm

Ashqelon

Al Khalil (Hebron)

Dead Sea

Gaza

Khān Yūnis

Be'ér Sheva'

Gaza Strip
Israeli occupied with interim status subject to Israeli/Palestinian negotiation. Final status to be determined.

N e g e v

Mizpé Ramon

'Arava

JORDAN

EGYPT

Biq'at Uvda

Yotvata

0   25 mi
0   25 km

Elat

Gulf of Aqaba

MAP OF ISRAEL AND THE PALESTINIAN AUTHORITY.
(*Gale Group.*)

other elements, he became the leader, duly elected, of the PA.

The Middle East Peace Process (MEPP)

The Middle East Peace Process (MEPP) had its origins in the aftermath of the Iraqi invasion of Kuwait in August 1990, which initially diverted attention from the Arab-Israeli arena to the Persian Gulf sector of the Middle East. When the Gulf War hostilities ended, the United States initiated an exploratory effort that culminated in an Arab-Israeli peace conference in Madrid, Spain, in October 1991. A brief ceremonial opening of the peace conference was followed by direct bilateral negotiations involving Israel, Lebanon, Syria, Jordan, and the Palestinians, as well as multilateral negotiations on specific functional issues such as water, refugees, economic development, and the environment. Israelis greeted this process with caution and skepticism, given Arab hostility toward Israel and the continuing Palestinian *intifada* in the West Bank and Gaza. Palestinians were also cautious. Nevertheless, the Madrid Conference marked a watershed—the major Arab confrontation states (and the Palestinians) for the first time met with Israel in direct, face-to-face negotiations to consider the substantive issues of the Arab-Israeli conflict.

The Madrid meetings were followed by several rounds of bilateral talks in Washington, DC, later in 1991 and 1992 during which the wide gap between the Israeli and Arab positions was not narrowed. In the spring of 1993 a parallel channel of discussion between Israelis and Palestinians began in Oslo, Norway, under the aegis and with the facilitation of Norway's foreign minister, Johan Jorgen Holst. The talks were secret and known to but a handful of individuals. They led to an agreement, "the Oslo Accords," that was initialed in Norway during the summer of 1993. The result of the negotiations, the Declaration of Principles (DOP), was formally signed on the White House lawn in Washington, DC, by Israeli and Palestinian representatives with Arafat and Israeli prime minister Yitzhak Rabin present on September 13, 1993, and paved the way for further Israel-PLO negotiations and accords.

As part of the arrangement, Israel recognized the PLO as the representative of the Palestinian people and the PLO recognized Israel's right to exist in peace and security, accepted UN Security Council Resolutions 242 and 338, and renounced the use of terrorism and violence. The process thus inaugurated was to culminate in a permanent peace settlement. The signing of the DOP marked the

suspended after the PLO failed to condemn the May 30, 1990, Palestine Liberation Front (PLF) attack on Israeli beaches.

In the 1990s, especially after the Oslo negotiations and the signing of the Oslo Accords on the White House lawn on September 13, 1993, Arafat seemed to be moving from terrorist to statesman—from militant to peace seeker. Among

beginning of a new period in Israel's approach to peace. The agreement also formally marked Arafat's transition from "terrorist" to statesman.

The Israelis and the Palestinians began public and formal negotiations in the fall of 1993, after the signing of the DOP. By May 1994 they had reached an agreement, signed in Cairo, that provided for negotiations to resolve the issues of the occupied territories of the West Bank and the Gaza Strip. The agreement also included how much Israel would turn over to Palestinian control, within a relatively short period. Israel and the PLO gave themselves five years (with a deadline of May 4, 1999) to negotiate the permanent (or final) status of the Israeli-Palestinian problem, on the difficult issues including Jerusalem, refugees, settlements, security arrangements, borders, regional neighborly arrangements, and other issues of common interest.

The MEPP launched at Madrid, and given impetus with the Oslo Accords, involved substantial negotiations between Israel and the PLO. During this period Arafat and the PLO were seen, formally at least, as peace partners negotiating for the termination of the conflict between Israel and the Palestinians, not as terrorists whose ultimate goal was the destruction of Israel. Nevertheless, while there was some progress toward a final settlement of the Israeli-Palestinian conflict, there were Palestinian groups that continued to engage in terrorist activity (these included HAMAS and Islamic Jihad) while Israel continued to build Jewish settlements in the occupied territories.

Camp David II and the al-Aqsa Intifada

The Israeli-Palestinian negotiations launched after the signing of the Oslo Accords were punctuated by successes, but also by failures and violence. When Ehud Barak was elected prime minister of Israel in 1999 the process was reinvigorated. His victory was seen as a repudiation of outgoing prime minister Benjamin Netanyahu, with his generally skeptical views of Arafat and of the MEPP, and as a positive omen, since Barak had run on a platform stressing peace through negotiations.

Negotiations resumed soon after Barak's election but little progress was made. Six years after the signing ceremony on the White House lawn, Israel and the PLO had yet to conclude their negotiations on territory and there was no agreement on any of the "final status" issues. Despite hope for progress, little was achieved after Barak's election. As the U.S. administration of Bill Clinton (1993–2001) entered its final year in office, accelerated efforts suggested a possible tripartite summit, bringing Clinton, Barak, and Arafat together. The objective

of the negotiations at Camp David, known as Camp David II, was to put together a package which Barak believed would generate acceptance and recognition from the Palestinians, which had eluded Israel to that point, on the basis of a two peoples, two state solution within the region. This, however, was not to be. Arafat left the negotiating table rather than respond to an offer by Barak and thereby provided the basis for the al-Aqsa intifada, which soon brought violence to the area. The al-Aqsa intifada, a violent uprising by Palestinians, broke out after a controverisal visit by Ariel Sharon to the al-Aqsa/Temple Mount site—holy to both Jews and Muslims. Sharon was subsequently elected as Israel's prime minister in February 2001.

The historic reconciliation, begun with the handshake in Washington at the signing of the DOP, would not be followed by peace. In January 2001, after meetings at Taba, Egypt, Israeli and Palestinian negotiators noted they were closer now than they have ever been to reaching an agreement, but no agreement was codified.

As the Middle East Peace Process moved along from the high point at Oslo to the low point of Camp David II the assumption underlying that process was that Arafat, the PLO, and the PA, as well as other centrist Palestinian organizations and institutions, were committed to resolving the Arab-Israeli conflict through peaceful means, that is, negotiations, not through violence and terrorism. On that basis, the PLO was no longer seen as a terrorist organization and neither was Arafat by the majority of observers. Some Israelis and others, however, never accepted that view and believed him still to be the terrorist he had been identified as in the past.

With the failure at Camp David II and the start of the al-Aqsa intifada, this perception of the PLO and Arafat as part of the terrorist camp began to grow significantly. When the U.S. State Department issued its *Patterns of Global Terrorism* report for 2000 it included, for the first time since the signing of the DOP, criticism of mainstream elements of the Palestine Liberation Organization. These included Israeli accusations that the largest PLO faction, Fatah, took part in terrorist activities.

Al-Aqsa Intifada, Suicide Bombers, and Operation Defensive Shield

The current crisis erupted in September 2000 when the second intifada began in the aftermath of the failed Camp David II summit. Israel accused Arafat of resorting to violence as a tool to achieve political objectives, in violation of the Oslo Accords, and of resorting to terrorism after rejecting

THE 1994 NOBEL PEACE PRIZE

In recognition of the protracted conflict in the Middle East and the long measures taken to move towards peace in the region, as significantly noted by the signing of the 1993 Oslo Accords, the Norwegian Nobel Committee awarded the Nobel Peace Prize for 1994 to Palestinian leader Yasser Arafat, and Israeli leaders Shimon Peres and Yitzhak Rabin. The announcement for the prize issued by the Nobel Committee in October 1994 referred to the conflict between Israel and the Palestinians, as well as Israel and its other neighbors, as "among the most irreconcilable and menacing in international politics." It further stated that, "The parties have caused each other great suffering. By concluding the Oslo Accords, and subsequently following them up, Arafat, Peres, and Rabin have made substantial contributions to a historic process through which peace and cooperation can replace war and hate."

Arafat, on behalf of the Palestine Liberation Organization (PLO), which he led, publicly renounced terrorism in 1988. The 1993 Oslo Accords were a pinnacle moment for Arafat and the PLO. In making a serious effort towards peace, Arafat succeeded in achieving legitimacy for his organization and its cause and garnered significant international approval for his peacemaking attempts in an intractable conflict. The road, for both the Palestinian and Israeli leaders, was a difficult one. Both sides had to overcome objections and criticism from extremist groups and reassure their publics that the Oslo Accords were a positive step for all sides involved.

In concluding its announcement for the peace prize, the Nobel Committee recognized the obstacles Arafat, Peres, and Rabin had faced and would continue to face, noting that the award was intended "to honor a political act which called for great courage on both sides . . . It is the Committee's hope that the award will serve as an encouragement to all the Israelis and Palestinians who are endeavoring to establish lasting peace in the region."

Israel's peace offer at Camp David, which was not wholly agreeable to the Palestinians. The Palestinian leadership argued that Israel's offers were not just and Israel remained an occupying power in the West Bank and Gaza Strip, continuing a series of illegal actions such as confiscation of Palestinian land for illegal Jewish settlements.

Since the beginning of the al-Aqsa intifada hundreds of Israelis and Palestinians have been killed. Israeli civilians have been killed by a series of Palestinian suicide bombers and Israeli soldiers and civilians have been shot by Palestinian gunmen in the West Bank and Gaza Strip. Israel's response has taken various forms including "targeted killings" of Palestinian militants, reprisal raids into West Bank cities and refugee camps, the shelling and bombing of Palestinian facilities, and other actions resulting in the destruction of Palestinian homes and the deaths of Palestinian civilians.

In the wake of the failure of the Camp David II summit and Ariel Sharon's controversial visit to the al-Aqsa/Temple Mount site, violence began in the West Bank and Gaza Strip and this soon deteriorated into suicide bombing attacks against Israeli civilian targets. These were seen within Israel, and by others, as suicide attacks against civilians, hence terrorism. In most instances the Israelis

were able to connect the terrorist bombers directly to Palestinian organizations and institutions.

As more suicide (later to be called "homicide" or "martyrdom") bombers attacked Israeli civilian targets with greater lethality, Israel began to increase its responses to these actions proclaiming its right of self-defense. Since late in 2001, when Israel destroyed his helicopters, Yasser Arafat was confined to the West Bank city of Ramallah and to his presidential compound there.

By the spring of 2002 the situation had reached a low point when Israel decided to act in self defense against the growing number of terrorist attacks and launched a military operation into the West Bank to destroy the Palestinian terrorist infrastructure. After Israel launched Operation Defensive Shield as this military operation was called and laid siege to the West Bank city of Ramallah, Arafat was further confined to his headquarters in Ramallah—effectively isolated.

On March 21, 2002, Prime Minister Ariel Sharon's bureau released the following statement:

> It is Arafat who is solely responsible for the continuation of murderous terrorist attacks. Arafat has done nothing up until now to advance the cease-fire and he is acting—whether covertly or through inability—to torpedo the mission of General (ret.) Zinni.

Israel will be unable—for long—to persist in a unilateral effort to implement the Tenet document. This must be clear to all who expect a change of direction on the part of the Palestinian Authority, i.e. a halt to violence and terror.

As the regional situation had deteriorated, there arose doubt about Arafat's ability to control terrorist attacks carried out by groups such as HAMAS and Islamic Jihad. Some questioned his motivation, some his desire, and some his ability. As the number and severity of the attacks grew, and there was a closer examination of them and the perpetrators, it was suggested that Arafat was more directly linked to the acts and those who carried them out. By early 2002 it became clear that groups connected directly to Arafat's Fatah group and especially the al-Aqsa Martyrs Brigade (added to the Foreign Terrorist Organization list by the United States in early 2002) were directly involved.

The al-Aqsa Martyrs Brigade was linked to Arafat's Fatah faction of the PLO. Some of the Brigade's leaders admitted to taking orders from Arafat, others denied the connection. Many of its members apparently were also on the payroll of the Palestinian Authority, often as members of the Palestinian security services.

The al-Aqsa Martyrs Brigade provided a specific link between terrorism and Arafat. It is a new organization that apparently was formed around the time of the outbreak of the al-Aqsa intifada. Over the ensuing months it emerged in the forefront of the organizations and has been the major perpetrator of terrorist attacks against Israel—with growing lethality. Initially it focused its attacks on soldiers and on Jewish settlers in the West Bank, but by the beginning of 2002 it struck within Israel at civilian targets. Support and financing was provided directly from Palestinian Authority resources, and from evidence gathered by Israel, it appears that Arafat had the most direct control over it.

The Brigade draws recruits from Arafat's various security services. It appears to be formally subordinate to Tanzim, the radical youth militia force of Fatah. The Tanzim leader is Marwan Barghouti, whom the Israelis captured on April 15, 2002. They had evidence that showed his involvement in financing terrorist activities in Israel, mostly through the al-Aqsa Martyrs Brigades. They also had documentation of the connection from Arafat to Barghouti and then to the al-Aqsa Brigades to fund their activities.

Arafat's link to the growing terrorism against Israel was difficult to formally prove. Nevertheless there was growing "documentation" of Arafat's role as well as that of the PLO and the PA. Israel and others saw Arafat as the man who had promised in a series of agreements and statements to abandon terrorism and to use his forces to prevent it, but he instead betrayed those pledges. The peace process that developed with the Oslo agreements ultimately depended on Arafat being a serious partner for peace, which the allegations of terrorism involvement put into doubt.

In the first months of 2002 there were a number of developments that produced a clear and specific linkage between the terrorist actions and Arafat's Palestinian Authority and related groups. In January 2002 Israeli commandos seized a boat carrying some 50 tons of weapons traveling from Iran to the Palestinian Authority. These weapons were in excess of the quantities and types of weapons approved by the Oslo Accords for the Palestinian Authority. For Israel this was proof that Arafat was preparing for a new round of violence, not trying to stem the violence that had disrupted the peace process. The Palestinians dismissed these charges as Israeli propaganda. Israel provided evidence that the Palestinian Authority owned the intercepted ship (Karine A) and that the captain was an officer in the Palestinian naval police. The weapons included long range rockets that could reach all parts of Israel from the West Bank and Gaza. U.S. President George W. Bush (2001–) noted on January 25: "Ordering up weapons that were intercepted on a boat headed for that part of the world is not part of fighting terror, that's enhancing terror, and obviously we're very disappointed in him [Arafat]." Later during Operation Defensive Shield, Israel captured documents that showed a direct link between Palestinian officials closely linked to Arafat and the terrorist operations. This included an "invoice" for funds to pay for bomb components. There was also documentation of cash payments to various members of Tanzim and Fatah, which have been involved in terrorist attacks on Israel.

The United States and Palestinian Terrorism After 9/11

As the situation deteriorated the Bush administration developed a clear perception of the connection between violence, terrorism, the PLO, the Palestinian Authority, and Arafat. U.S. Secretary of State Powell, on December 1, 2001, said:

> The United States condemns in the strongest possible terms the evil and horrific terrorist attacks in Jerusalem tonight . . . .I have spoken which Chairman Arafat and have made absolutely clear that these despicable and cowardly actions must be brought to an end . . . .through immediate, comprehensive, and sustained action by the Palestinian Authority against

FATAH

Al-Fatah, meaning "conquest," is an acronym that, when reversed, stands for Harakat al-Tahrir al-Falistin (Movement for the Liberation of Palestine). It was founded in the late 1950s by a group of Palestinian students, including Yasser Arafat, in Cairo, Egypt. Fatah is the oldest of the Palestinian organizations. From the outset it saw the liberation of Palestine as the primary task, and the victory of the Algerian revolution spurred Fatah supporters in their cause. The Algerian revolution was launched on November 1, 1954, by Algerians seeking the end of French rule in Algeria and an independent Algerian state. French President Charles de Gaulle proclaimed Algeria independent on July 3, 1962.

The first armed action by Fatah against Israel took place on January 1, 1965, a date that has since been commemorated. Only after the Six Day War of 1967, however, did Fatah became prominent in the Palestinian movement. The battle at Karameh in March 1968 between the Israeli army and Fatah forces based in Jordan enhanced Arafat's prestige. It was then that a large unit of the Israel Defense Forces (IDF) launched an assault on the Jordanian villages of Karameh and Shune in response to repeated terrorist attacks launched from bases in Jordan. Each side claimed victory in the ensuing battle. For Fatah this was a clear victory because it was able to hold its ground and inflict substantial losses on the IDF. As word of the accomplishment spread, Fatah and the PLO were elevated to the level of folk heroes, the legend grew, and Fatah membership expanded.

Headed by Yasser Arafat, Fatah joined the Palestine Liberation Organization (PLO) in 1968 and won the leadership role of the organization in 1969. Its leaders were expelled from Jordan in 1970 and 1971. After the 1967 Arab-Israeli War numerous Palestinians had moved into Jordan, from which various Palestinian organizations launched numerous raids into Israel. Their presence and actions, in addition to Israeli responses, proved destabilizing to Jordan, leading to fighting between the PLO and the Jordanian armed forces. The PLO was defeated in September 1970 and was forced to move from Jordan to Syria and then to Lebanon, which was unable to prevent the establishment of a "state-within-a-state" by the PLO and especially by Fatah in southern Lebanon. From these positions they launched attacks on Israel, to which the Israelis responded with attacks on Fatah and the PLO positions in Lebanon in 1978 and then again in 1982.

Israel's invasion of Lebanon in 1982 led to the group's dispersal to several Arab states, including Tunisia, Yemen, Algeria, and Iraq. It has several components that have been involved in terrorist attacks, including Force 17 and the Hawari Secial Operations Group. Two of its senior leaders, Abu Jihad and Abu Iyad, were assassinated. Fatah's armed wing is known as Al-Asifa ("The Storm").

both the individuals responsible and the infrastructure of the groups that support them. There can be no excuse for failure to take immediate and thorough action against the perpetrators of these vile acts.

After a major suicide bombing in Jerusalem, President Bush, on December 2, 2001, condemned the bombing in these terms:

I strongly condemn them as acts of murder that no person of conscience can tolerate and no cause can ever justify . . . .Chairman Arafat and the Palestinian Authority must immediately find and arrest those responsible for these hideous murders . . . .Now more than ever, Chairman Arafat and the Palestinian Authority must demonstrate through their actions, and not merely their words, their commitment to fight terror.

Two days later, on December 4, 2001, Bush said: "The message is this: Those who do business with terror will do no business with the United States or anywhere else the United States can reach."

The Bush Doctrine

In the wake of the September 11, 2001 attacks against the United States, President George W. Bush developed a series of new policies concerning terrorism. Slowly these evolved into what the media and the administration referred to as the Bush Doctrine. These helped to provide the framework within which the U.S. administration (and the Congress) developed its views and policies concerning the Palestinians and Arafat.

The elements of the doctrine were slow to be articulated and included the U.S. conception of the terrorist phenomenon. There was the notion that there is no such thing as a "good terrorist" although others seek exemptions for "freedom fighters." The president noted that no cause justifies attacks on civilians. At Fort Campbell, Kentucky, in November 2001, the president said: "America has a message for the nations of the world: If you harbor terrorists, you are a terrorist; if you train or arm a terrorist, you are a terrorist; if you feed a terrorist or fund a terrorist, you're a terrorist, and you will be held accountable by the United States and our friends." An indicator of the central theme was articulated by Bush on January 10, 2002 when he noted: "Our nation, in our fight against terrorism, will uphold the doctrine of either you're with us or against us."

This theme of choosing between being with the United States against terrorism or with the terrorists, was restated and elaborated in subsequent statements. In a speech at the Virginia Military Institute on April 17, 2002, Bush said (emphasis added):

> Every nation that needs our help will have it. And no nation can be neutral. Around the world, the nations must choose. They are with us, or they're with the terrorists.
>
> And in the Middle East, where acts of terror have triggered mounting violence, all parties have a choice to make. Every leader, every state must choose between two separate paths: the path of peace or the path of terror . . . .Now, every nation and every leader in the region must work to end terror.
>
> All parties have responsibilities . . . .*The Palestinian Authority must act, must act on its words of condemnation against terror . . . .All parties have a responsibility to stop funding or inciting terror. And all parties must say clearly that a murderer is not a martyr; he or she is just a murderer.*

Despite U.S. and Israeli condemnation, terrorist actions continued, often in response to Israeli efforts to crackdown on Palestinian violence. On April 12, 2002 a suicide bomber struck in Jerusalem during Secretary Powell's mission to halt the violence and restore a political process to lead to peace. A White House spokesman encouraged Arafat to publicly denounce terrorist attacks, believing that such a statement would help distance Arafat from the terrorism and garner him more international support.

In connecting Arafat to terrorism a crucial element is the parallelism between the events in Israel and those of September 11 in New York City and Washington, DC. The Bush administration made this connection on numerous occasions in several ways. In an interview on MSNBC-TV on April 12, 2002, Secretary of Defense Donald H. Rumsfeld was asked: "Is it hard for you to look at that [a suicide attack in Jerusalem] and not see what Israel is engaged in as the same war on terror that you are leading in this country?" He responded:

There's no question that terror and terrorism involves the killing of innocent men, women and children. And that's what happened in this building six months ago, that's what happened in New York at the World Trade Centers, and it clearly is what's happening in Israel. When a suicide bomber goes in and takes their own life and kills innocent men, women and children, the word "terror" is the correct word.

Arafat Redefined as "Terrorist"

Secretary of State Powell, in his April 2002 visit, was sent to the region to help the situation move toward peace. The initial emphasis of his visit was to get action to halt violence. On April 12, 2002 Powell said: "I'm not interested just in declarations; I am interested in performance and action." Arafat later issued a statement in Arabic condemning terrorism.

Whatever his formal label by mid-2002 Yasser Arafat was widely seen by virtually all Israelis, and numerous others, as a terrorist. After September 11, 2001, as the United States expanded its view and definition of terrorism, Arafat seemed to qualify. In the wake of Camp David II and the violence of the second intifada, Arafat was seen as moving from negotiations back to the violence that characterized Palestinian policy prior to the 1988 disavowal of terrorism by Arafat. Arafat was called upon by the United States to exercise leadership, to speak out, and to punish those responsible for suicide attacks. He was to bring them to justice. Failure to do so would, U.S. officials said, undermine his leadership of the Palestinian Authority and would undermine the dreams and hopes of the Palestinians for their own state and for peace in the Middle East.

President Bush has, since September 11, equated terrorists with those who harbor and support them, but has been reluctant to apply the formal label to Arafat despite his fitting the broad definition created by the administration. The primary reason for not doing so has been because Arafat, as the Palestinian leader, has been essential to the peace process to which he agreed at Madrid and Oslo.

So while Arafat has been held responsible for attacks against Israel by terrorist organizations, he was not formally labeled as a terrorist. The U.S. administration continued to make clear its view that Arafat could, at minimum, slow down, if not stop, terrorist activity. He could also condemn the actions in statements directly to the people of Palestine and the Arab world. The Bush theme could be summed up in the concept: "They're not martyrs. They're murderers." Palestinians, however, might argue that they are responding to an

PALESTINIAN REPRESENTATIVES FROM THE NEGOTIATIONS SUPPORT UNIT OF THE PLO SPEAK IN LATE 2001 BEFORE AN ISRAELI AUDIENCE IN AN ATTEMPT TO ENCOURAGE SUPPORT FOR PEACE NEGOTIATIONS DESPITE THE VIOLENCE OF RECENT SUICIDE ATTACKS AND SHOOTINGS. *(AP/Wide World Photos/Eitan Hess-Ashkenazi. Reproduced by permission.)*

oppressive, occupying force in hopes of gaining their freedom.

Arafat's condemnation of the terrorist attack in Jerusalem in April was equivocal, symptomatic of the mixed messages often provided by the Palestinian leader. In that vein it is also useful to note that his wife, Suha al-Taweel Arafat, in an interview published in the Arabic language magazine *Al Majalla* on April 12, 2002, said that she endorsed suicide attacks as legitimate actions against Israel because of its occupation of the West Bank and Gaza. She noted that if she had a son there would be "no greater honor" than to sacrifice himself for the Palestinian cause. What then is the message?

The connection of Arafat to the Bush Doctrine was articulated on a number of occasions, including the Bush statement on March 21, 2002 where he noted:

> America will fight terror wherever we find it, and as well, we will call upon leaders around the world to do so . . . Mr. Arafat must do more to stop violence in the Middle East . . . .the Secretary of State and I will remind leaders of their obligation to defend innocent people; of their obligation to stamp out terrorists wherever they light; of their obligation to make sure they uphold this doctrine: If you harbor a terrorist, if you hide a terrorist, if you feed a terrorist, you're just as guilty as the terrorists themselves.

By this construction Arafat, and his institutions and subordinates, were "just as guilty as the terrorists themselves."

RECENT HISTORY AND THE FUTURE

At the end of April 2002 Israeli and Palestinian leaders agreed to a Bush administration compromise proposal to end an armed siege of Arafat's compound in the West Bank city of Ramallah, which began on March 29, 2002. The decision by Israel to accept the compromise resulted, in part, from American pressure to do so. As part of the compromise, Israel agreed that the six Palestinians held in Palestinian custody for assassinating Israel's tourism minister would be held in Palestinian custody in Jericho, but their confinement would be monitored by British and American wardens. Israel had demanded the extradition of the men as its condition for releasing Arafat from confinement in Ramallah since December 2001, and from a portion of his compound there since March 29, 2002. President Bush welcomed the news with the observation, on April 28, that it was a "hopeful" day. He said, "Chairman Arafat is now free to move around and free to lead . . . ." Bush also made it clear that he expected Arafat to "perform" in combating violence.

In early May 2002 the United States announced that it would convene a peace conference with Russia, the European Union, and the United Nations in summer 2002 to deal with the various issues of the Arab-Israeli conflict. From the Palestinian and broader Arab perspective Arafat remained the only leader for the Palestinians and thus an essential participant in the discussions concerning the future. For Israel, Arafat was not an appropriate partner because of his role in anti-Israel violence and terror. The preliminary concept suggested bypassing the issue by holding the meeting at the level of foreign ministers and not heads of state or government. That would avoid the problem of Arafat's participation and the question of his role as a legitimate partner versus his role as an ineffectual leader of the Palestinians and his failure in preventing terrorism.

In pressing for the conference President Bush noted in a statement on May 2, 2002, after meeting with European leaders, that the goal of the conference and of his administration's efforts was: "A Palestinian state must be achieved by negotiation of an end to occupation. And such a state cannot be based on a foundation of terror or corruption." While clearly believing that the Europeans, the Russians, and the United Nations could be helpful, it was also the administration's position that the Arab states and their leaders would have to play a role in moving the process along, especially with efforts focusing on Arafat and the Palestinians. The administration clearly put much of the responsibility for the process on Israel and the Palestinians and, in the case of Arafat, stressed that much was expected of him, as Secretary Powell noted: "With respect to Chairman Arafat, it's not a question of rehabilitating him. He knows what is expected of him."

BIBLIOGRAPHY

Cobban, Helena. *The Palestinian Liberation Organization: People, Power and Politics.* New York: Cambridge University Press, 1984.

———. "Yasser Arafat," in Bernard Reich, ed., *Political Leaders of the Contemporary Middle East and North Africa.* Westport, CT: Greenwood Press, 1990, pp. 44–51.

Cooley, John. *Green March, Black September.* London: Frank Cass, 1973.

Dimbleby, Jonathan, and Don McCullin. *The Palestinians.* London: Quartet Books, 1980.

Gowers, Andrew and Tony Walker. *Behind the Myth: Yasser Arafat and the Palestinian Revolution.* New York: Olive Branch Press, 1992.

Hart, Alan. *Arafat: A Political biography.* Bloomington: Indiana University Press, 1989.

Iyad, Abou (Khalaf, Salah), with Eric Rouleau. *My Home, My Land.* New York: Times Books, 1981.

Kelman, Herbert C. "Talk with Arafat," *Foreign Policy,* No. 49 (Winter 1982–83): 119–39.

Khalidi, Rashid. *Under Siege; PLO Decisionmaking During the 1982 War.* New York: Columbia University Press, 1986.

Kiernan, Thomas. *Arafat, the Man and the Myth.* New York: Norton, 1976.

Kirisci, Kemal. *The PLO and World Politics: A Study of the Mobilization and Support for the Palestinian Cause.* London: Francis Pinter, 1986.

Livingstone, Neil C. and David Halevy. *Inside the PLO.* New York: William Morrow, 1990.

Nassar, Jamal R. *The Palestine Liberation Organization: From Armed Struggle to the Declaration of Independence.* New York: Praeger, 1991.

Reich, Bernard, ed. *An Historical Encyclopedia of the Arab-Israeli Conflict.* Westport, CT: Greenwood Press, 1996.

Rubenberg, Cheryl. *The Palestine Liberation Organization: Its Institutional Infrastructure.* Belmont, MA: Institute of Arab Studies, 1983.

Rubin, Barry. *Revolution until Victory? The Politics and History of the PLO.* Cambridge: Harvard University Press, 1994.

Sahliyeh, Emile. *The PLO After the Lebanon War.* Boulder, CO: Westview Press, 1986.

Sayigh, Rosemary. *Palestinians: From Peasants to Revolutionaries.* London: Zed Press, 1979.

Wallach, Janet and John Wallach. *Arafat in the Eyes of the Beholder.* New York: Carol Publishing Group/Lyle Stuart, 1990.

Bernard Reich, Michael Buczek

Prosecuting Terrorism

The Conflict

Throughout its long history, terrorism often has been addressed through swift violence in return, rather than through prolonged legal proceedings. Prosecution of terrorism, especially with the rise of international terrorism, involves coordination of multiple legal systems and frequently conflicting political aims.

Political

- Nations that have harbored terrorists often covertly support their acts or fear reprisals from them.

- Reluctance to extradite terrorist suspects to countries that allow capital punishment has delayed many prosecutions.

- Successful prosecution of terrorists can require years of investigation of well-hidden funds and tiny pieces of circumstantial evidence spreading across nations and continents.

Religious

- In the age of international terrorism, alliances cross national borders and frequently have been based on religious beliefs rather than national objectives.

Nations that have fallen victim to terrorism during its long history have attempted to battle it in many ways, the main approach being a violent attack in retaliation. The sad story of the Arab-Israeli conflict, with suicide bombings in Israel being countered by raids on Palestinian villages, is a prime example. In modern times, however, another method is gaining importance: prosecuting terrorists through legal systems.

The practice of trying terrorists, rather than killing them in military attacks or executing them upon capture, reaches back to the late 1700s. In Ireland, a French-supported group known as the United Irishmen rebelled against British rule, resulting in massive casualties. The British government suspended many legal protections and established new laws that carried a death penalty, such as the Insurrection Act forbidding "secret oathtaking." Trials for these crimes lacked many of the protections for defendants that are taken for granted now, and often they were stages for violence as well. After being found guilty of treason in 1795 for allegedly serving as a French agent during the Irish rebellion, for example, Reverend William Jackson committed suicide in the courtroom.

During the latter part of the twentieth century and the beginning of the twenty-first, terrorism became rampant throughout the world. While people within the United States focused their attention on the attacks on the World Trade Center and the Pentagon in September 2001, there had been many prior acts of domestic and foreign terrorism directed against the United States. At the same time, pursuit and prosecutions of captured terrorists had been ongoing in numerous other countries for attacks committed against their citizens. As terrorism took on an international focus, many experts

CHRONOLOGY

1796 The British Parliament passes the Insurrection Act, directed at Irish rebels, making secret oathtaking a capital offense.

1940 A trial of Christian Front militia members ends unsuccessfully in New York City.

1972 Palestinian terrorists murder the Israeli Olympic team in Munich; the terrorists who survive the hostage rescue operation are released a month later in exchange for hostages aboard a hijacked airliner.

1981 Ten IRA prisoners die in an Irish prison following a hunger strike aimed at achieving political status.

1985 Italian fascists accused of bombing a Milan plaza in 1980 are acquitted.

1988 Terrorists blow up Pan AM Flight 103 over Lockerbie, Scotland; one Libyan suspect is convicted twelve years later.

1995 United States student Lori Berenson is arrested in Peru and convicted of collaborating with terrorists.

1995 Unabomber Ted Kaczynski is arrested and charged with a package bomb campaign spanning two decades; he pleads guilty three years later.

1996 Islamic militants are sentenced to life imprisonment for the 1993 attack on New York City's World Trade Center.

1997 "Carlos the Jackal" is sentenced to life imprisonment following trial in France.

1998 New York obstetrician Bernard Slepian is killed; abortion opponent James Kopp is arrested in France and extradited to the United States two years later to face trial.

2001 Timothy McVeigh is executed for carrying out the Oklahoma City federal building bombing, becoming the first federal prisoner in the United States to be executed in 38 years.

2001 Four Saudi and Jordanian men are convicted of bombing United States embassies in Kenya and Tanzania; Osama bin Laden is indicted for conspiracy.

2001 The September 11 attacks on the World Trade Center and Pentagon lead to approval of military tribunals in the United States and new legal weapons against terrorism worldwide.

2002 Three ex-members of the Symbionese Liberation Army are arrested for participation in California robberies and bombings during the 1970s.

---

began to look at how nations could cooperate to battle terrorism through the courts.

HISTORICAL BACKGROUND

Domestic Terrorism in Europe

For more than 200 years various groups have rebelled violently against British rule in Ireland, and trials of captured rebels have often led to further violence. The Society of United Irishmen, founded in 1791, began as a political movement working for parliamentary reform and religious freedom. After war broke out between Britain and France, however, the United Irishmen were supported by French revolutionaries and became more violent. Many of the group's members and supporters were arrested on charges of treason or sedition, sometimes merely because they had published materials critical of British rule. In 1796 the British established the Insurrection Act, which made the crime of "secret oathtaking" punishable by death

and suspended the right of *habeas corpus* (charging someone with a crime) for prisoners, thus allowing the government to hold accused persons for long periods without bringing them to trial. After 16 leaders of the United Irishmen were arrested and the British imposed martial law, violence spread throughout Ireland and several of the leaders were sentenced to death.

Rebellion in Ireland continued for the next century and escalated after Britain partitioned Ireland in 1921, creating an independent nation in the south but keeping the north under British rule. The Irish Republican Army (IRA), which emerged after the partition, split into two groups in 1969. The "officials" worked through political means, but the "provisionals" devoted their efforts to terrorist activities in both Northern Ireland and England. In 1971 the British army arrested hundreds of suspected terrorists, many of whom were imprisoned without trials, and in the following year almost 500 people died in Northern Ireland and England.

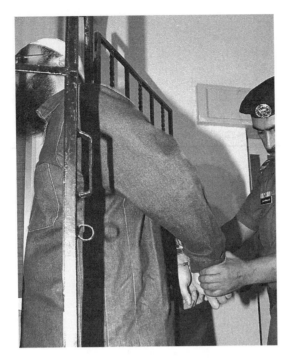

A SUSPECTED TERRORIST ACCUSED OF PLOTTING ATTACKS ON U.S. AND ISRAELI TOURISTS DURING THE 2000 NEW YEAR'S CELEBRATION IS UNCUFFED AND PLACED IN A CELL AT THE JORDAN MILITARY COURT IN AMMAN, JORDAN. *(AP/Wide World Photos/Jamal Nasrallah. Reproduced by permission.)*

Fearing that the IRA would intimidate jurors, a special court was set up to try alleged terrorists without a jury. The IRA was outlawed, resulting in many more arrests and long prison terms.

In 1981 a group of prisoners serving sentences in the Maze Prison near Belfast for firearms offenses and other crimes began a hunger strike. Led by prisoner Bobby Sands, the strike was an effort to regain political status for the IRA and to win privileges such as freedom of association among the IRA prisoners. While Sands claimed to be a political prisoner fighting an unjust occupier, not a terrorist, the British government disagreed and rejected the prisoners' demands. As quoted in Thomas Hennessey's *A History of Northern Ireland* (1997), British Prime Minister Margaret Thatcher had no intention of making concessions to the terrorists: "Crime is crime is crime; it is not political." Sands and nine other prisoners died after several weeks of starvation, touching off further violence.

By the late 1990s more than 15,000 people (both Catholic and Protestants) had served prison sentences for violent acts. As part of the peace process, the last of them was released from Maze Prison in 2000, including several convicted murderers, and the prison was closed. Nevertheless,

there still was a trial pending for a major terrorist act in Northern Ireland, the 1998 bombing in the market square of Omagh, which killed 29 people. Although prosecutors had arrested several accused participants in the bombing, they had not been able to convict anyone because witnesses were afraid to testify. The first conviction came in January 2002, when Colin Murphy, a member of a militant splinter group, the Real IRA, was found guilty of conspiracy to cause an explosion.

Several European countries experienced long and bloody domestic terrorist sieges lasting from the 1960s through the 1980s at the hands of political extremists. In Italy, for example, the reign of terror began in 1969; several bombs that exploded in Milan's Piazza Fontana and in Rome, causing numerous deaths and injuries, were blamed on leftist activists. The government arrested four thousand activists and instituted many repressive measures to control leftist groups. The violence, however, continued throughout the next decade, peaking in 1980 when more than 80 people were killed in the bombing of a train station in Bologna. During the intervening years several Italian judges (who have the responsibility under Italian law for investigating crimes) had concluded that the Piazza Fontana bombing actually had been the work of Ordine Nuovo, a right-wing fascist group, rather than leftists. But, after a long series of trials and appeals, all of the fascists arrested were acquitted in 1985. Almost fifteen years later a new investigation by Judge Guido Salvini resulted in the trial of a member of Ordine Nuovo. During his investigation Salvini uncovered a possible government cover-up of fascist involvement in the bombing, as well as the unjust arrests of many leftists.

Prosecution of Home-Grown Terrorism in the United States

There is a long history of domestic terrorism in the United States, originating at all ends of the political spectrum and involving both organized groups and individual terrorists. The Ku Klux Klan, which emerged in the years following the Civil War (1861–65), was one of the first domestic terrorist organizations, known for its intimidation of African Americans and involvement in killings of civil rights workers. Because of the secrecy surrounding the Klan's activities and the unfortunate public support of some of its actions, arrests and convictions were few and far between. Just before World War II (1938–45) began, an equally dangerous and violent group, the Christian Front, sprang up. Founded by radio personality Father Charles E. Coughlin, the Christian Front blamed Jews for the Russian Revolution (1917) and the Spanish Civil

War (1936–39). Its members believed that, if not stopped by armed force, Jews would turn the United States into a communist state. The group was thought to be linked to both the Nazi government and the IRA.

Partly out of fear of the Christian Front, Congress passed the first federal gun control law. In 1940 several of the group's leaders were arrested in New York City and charged with running a covert militia movement. Stashes of guns and ammunition, some supposedly stolen from military bases, were discovered. During their trial, the Christian Front leaders claimed that the government was trying to frame them and had encouraged them to perform violent acts. Prosecutors feared that some of the jurors were secretly Coughlin supporters. The prosecution's case crumbled and the defendants were released, with Coughlin publicly congratulating them. He continued to preach hatred until the United States entered World War II and the government shut down his newspaper and radio program. When trying terrorists in future years, the federal government had to overcome the damage to its reputation that resulted from this trial.

During the 1970s left-wing terrorist acts were rampant in the United States. One of the most notorious left-wing groups was the Symbionese Liberation Army (SLA), which became best known for kidnapping newspaper heiress Patricia Hearst. The SLA was also responsible for numerous bank robberies and attempted bombings in California. Some members of the SLA were arrested and convicted during the 1970s, including Hearst, despite her claim that she was an innocent victim who had been forced to participate in robberies under her new revolutionary identity. Other members, however, were not apprehended because they had fled and were living "underground" with new identities. Kathleen Soliah, who allegedly had been involved in a plot to kill police officers in Los Angeles with pipe bombs, was arrested in 1999 while living as a Minnesota housewife under the name of Sara Jane Olson. Although she later claimed to be innocent of any crime, Soliah entered a guilty plea in late 2001, fearing that she would receive a harsh sentence in the aftermath of the World Trade Center attack. Hearst received a pardon from outgoing president Clinton in 2001. During that year police in Los Angeles also reopened their investigation into a 1975 bank robbery in which a female customer had been killed. Three ex-SLA members, Bill and Emily Harris and Mike Bortin, were arrested in January 2002 for their participation in the robbery, but another participant, James Kilgore, still remained at large.

LORI BERENSON

In the aftermath of the 2001 World Trade Center attack, a great deal of media attention was paid to John Walker Lindh, a young American who fought with Taliban forces in Afghanistan and was returned to the United States for prosecution. Not as well known is the case of Lori Berenson, an American woman imprisoned as a terrorist in Peru. Berenson, a former student at the Massachusetts Institute of Technology, was arrested by the Peruvian government in 1995 and accused of assisting the Movimiento Revolucionario Túpac Amaru (MRTA), a guerilla organization that had plotted to take over the national congress.

Although Berenson claimed that she was merely a political activist helping the poor, a secret military tribunal ruled that she was a leader of MRTA and sentenced her to life imprisonment. The verdict was based largely on evidence that she had rented a house where police arrested a known terrorist and that she had visited the congressional building with the wife of another terrorist.

Berenson received a new trial before a civilian court in 2001, after new evidence was made public showing that she was not a leader of MRTA. Despite diplomatic pressure from the United States and protests from human rights groups, Berenson was found guilty of the lesser charge of "terrorist collaboration" and sentenced to 20 years in prison. Berenson appealed the verdict to a higher Peruvian court, saying, "It is not a crime to worry about poverty and injustice in the world." Ignoring Berenson's protests of innocence and pleas from her parents, the court upheld her sentence in February 2002.

Prosecuting the Unabomber

For almost two decades, beginning in the 1970s, a mysterious individual known only as the Unabomber was responsible for a series of package bombings that resulted in three deaths and dozens of injuries. With the Unabomber's motives and targets unclear to authorities, the FBI investigated the case as a criminal matter, though the Unabomber's actions were akin to terrorism. Despite extensive investigations involving 200 suspects, the Unabomber remained at large until 1995. After the Unabomber extorted the New York Times and the Washington Post into publishing his rambling manifesto attacking modern technology, a New York man told the FBI that he thought his brother, Theodore "Ted" Kaczynski, might be the Unabomber. When Kaczynski was arrested at his mountain cabin, the FBI found unquestionable evidence that he was indeed responsible for the attacks, including materials identical to those used in the package bombs and a draft of the manifesto.

Kaczynski, a promising scientist during his twenties, had become increasingly antisocial and eventually had retreated to a primitive cabin, leading his attorneys to argue an insanity defense in hopes of avoiding a death sentence. Kaczynski, however, frustrated their efforts on his behalf by insisting that he was not mentally ill and by refusing to allow psychiatrists to examine him. Instead, he wanted to dismiss his lawyers and represent himself during the trial. After the judge refused to allow him to represent himself unless he could convince the court that he was mentally competent to do so, Kaczynski finally agreed to be examined by a court-appointed psychiatrist. The psychiatrist determined that Kaczynski was a paranoid schizophrenic. The judge would not allow Kaczynski to represent himself and said that he would admit the psychiatric findings at the trial.

Rather than face the prospect of a trial, Kaczynski agreed to a plea bargain in which he admitted responsibility for all of the bombings and would serve four consecutive life sentences. Several of the Unabomber's surviving victims were infuriated that he had not received a death sentence. Prosecutors at the sentencing hearing described him as being motivated by personal revenge, which in turn clearly angered Kaczynski, who promised to respond to this misrepresentation at an unspecified "later date."

Oklahoma City Bombers on Trial

The trials of Timothy McVeigh and Terry Nichols for the 1995 bombing of a federal building in Oklahoma City raised international controversy and exposed gaping flaws in the Federal Bureau of Investigation's (FBI) operations. McVeigh, an army veteran who eventually admitted responsibility for the deaths of 168 people and injuries to hundreds of others, was an unrepentant and unappealing defendant. Nevertheless, the death sentence imposed on him by a federal court fanned the flames of an already heated international debate on the use of the death penalty in the United States. After the U.S. Supreme Court allowed the death penalty to be reinstated in 1976, more than 700 prisoners were executed in the United States during the next quarter century, and 3,700 more were awaiting execution on death row. According to the May 21, 2001, cover story in *Time International,* only China, Iraq, and Saudi Arabia had more executions than the United States. President

George W. Bush (2001–) himself had presided over 152 executions during his mere five years as Texas governor. At the same time, 108 other countries had banned the death penalty, including all other western industrial countries.

McVeigh's execution was scheduled for May 16, 2001. Only a few days before that date, however, a greatly embarrassed FBI disclosed that thousands of pages of documents that might have been helpful to McVeigh's defense were never given to his lawyers. The execution was postponed to give the defense team a chance to review the documents, but nothing was discovered that justified changing the verdict. On June 11, 2001, McVeigh became the first federal prisoner to be executed in 38 years.

McVeigh's co-conspirator, Terry Nichols, who had received a separate federal trial, was found not guilty of actually participating in the bombing. One mitigating circumstance was that Nichols and his wife had assisted prosecutors in the McVeigh trial. Nichols was instead convicted of manslaughter for conspiring in the bombing, a crime that did not carry a possible death sentence. After the jury became deadlocked over what sentence to impose, the judge dismissed it and sentenced Nichols to life imprisonment. The Nichols verdict caused an outcry among survivors of the bombing and the victims' families. The jury forewoman claimed that she received several bomb threats, and infuriated state prosecutors were determined to bring Nichols to trial in state court on other charges that could carry the death penalty.

Trying Antiabortion Terror

After the Supreme Court legalized a woman's right to have an abortion in the landmark case of *Roe v. Wade,* 410 U.S. 113 (1973), protests of the court's decision soon became an ongoing activity. Many of the protesters engaged in disruptive but peaceful activities, such as praying in front of women's health clinics. Others chose somewhat more drastic means, chaining themselves to clinic doors or to automobiles blocking the entrances. A few extremists, however, turned to violence as a means of protest. Bombings of women's health clinics and shootings of doctors who performed abortions led the Justice Department to launch a grand jury investigation in 1994 to determine whether there was a national conspiracy among abortion opponents. The grand jury was dissolved two years later, however, after it could find no compelling evidence of a conspiracy.

Nevertheless, violence against clinics and abortion providers continued to escalate, resulting in the

THE JUDGE VERSUS THE JACKAL

One of the most feared terrorists of the late twentieth century was "Carlos the Jackal," a Venezuelan whose real name was Ilich Ramirez Sanchez. He was linked to an international network of terrorist organizations, including the Black September group that murdered Israeli athletes at the 1972 Munich Olympics. "Carlos the Jackal" was also believed to be responsible for the 1974 attack on the French embassy at The Hague, in which 83 people were killed. His story was dramatized in the popular film *The Day of the Jackal*.

Despite a massive manhunt and a death sentence imposed at a trial at which he was not present, Carlos remained at large for another twenty years. He finally was captured in the Sudan in 1994 and tried by a French court, which sentenced him to life in prison three years later.

The French judge who tracked down and tried Carlos was Jean-Louis Brugiere, a controversial figure who began investigating terrorist activities during the 1980s. In addition to convicting Carlos, Brugiere also thwarted several Islamic extremist plots, including one directed at the soccer World Cup held in France in 1998.

Under French law, investigating judges have wide authority, such as the almost unrestricted ability to order wiretaps and search warrants or to hold suspects for questioning for as long as 96 nonstop hours without a lawyer present. Such judges can also plant infiltrators in suspected terrorist groups and can make a pretrial finding that a suspect is guilty or innocent.

Brugiere acquired his own nickname, "the Sheriff," based on his tough investigations and the handgun he carried at all times. French civil rights and human rights groups have often protested Brugiere's harsh methods, and even other French courts have found him to be out of line at times. In 1994 he ordered the arrest of 138 suspected Algerian terrorists, who were held for five years without trial until a higher court stepped in. Thirty-one were acquitted of all charges, and most of the rest were convicted of minor charges and immediately released because of the long time they had already served in prison. Nevertheless, Brugiere had support from the French public, which was relieved that he had quickly located the terrorists responsible for a series of subway bombings in 1995.

---

death or injury of several health workers. Dr. Barnett Slepian, a Buffalo, New York, obstetrician, was shot and killed through a window of his home on October 23, 1998, while his wife and children looked on.

The suspect, James Kopp, became an antiabortion activist after his girlfriend ended their relationship and had an abortion. He had been arrested numerous times since 1984 in connection with violent protests and was the suspect in three nonfatal shootings of health workers in Canada, but he remained free at the time of the Slepian murder. He finally was arrested in France more than two years later after being traced through email and money sent to him there by two antiabortion activists in New York City. Kopp's return to the United States for trial was complicated by the same anti-death penalty debate that had arisen during the McVeigh trial. The death penalty had been abolished in France in 1981, and the French government refused to extradite Kopp to the United States unless Attorney General John Ashcroft agreed not to seek a death sentence. When returned

to the United States Kopp faced federal and state charges that could lead to life imprisonment.

Ironically, just prior to Kopp's arrest, a federal court had ruled that a website called the "Nuremberg Files" was protected by the First Amendment right to free speech. The website listed names, addresses, and photographs of abortion providers; more ominously, the list contained the crossed-out names of doctors who had been killed (including Slepian). The Kopp investigation also uncovered a possible international antiabortion terrorist movement that centered around Rev. Patrick Mahoney. For several years members of Mahoney's Washington, DC-based group, the Christian Defense Coalition, had been occupying offices of the Irish Family Planning Association and teaching Irish antiabortion protesters how to blockade clinics and to intimidate women trying to enter. The day before Kopp was arrested an Irish court had issued an injunction prohibiting Mahoney from continuing this harassment. When Mahoney heard that Kopp had been arrested, according to Bruce Shapiro in the *Nation* (April 23, 2001), he warned the Bush administration not to "harass and intimidate the pro-life movement."

The Spread of International Terrorism

The year 1968 marked the beginning of widespread terrorism throughout the world. Following the "Six Day War" of 1967, some extremist Arabs began bombing and shooting raids within Israel, which responded with raids of its own. Soon this part of the Arab-Israeli conflict was out of control, and terrorist acts aimed at Israel and its allies, especially the United States, became common both inside and outside of Israel. Some groups began to form alliances based on religious bonds rather than national borders, giving rise to internationally based terrorist movements.

Domestic terrorism also escalated after 1968 in Europe, especially in France, Germany, and Italy, as leftist students conducted widespread protests against their governments; the most radical students turned to terrorism. Terrorist movements also sprang up in Latin America, often resulting in the rise of repressive governments. The Provisional IRA broke away from the main IRA movement in Northern Ireland and created the decades of violence that became known as "the Troubles."

While the countries that fell victim to these terrorists made great efforts to capture and prosecute them, governments were often forced to release them from prison when a later group of terrorists would make the release of imprisoned terrorists a condition of freeing their hostages. In 1969, for example, an El Al airliner flying from Switzerland to Israel was hijacked and several passengers were killed or wounded. Three terrorists were convicted and imprisoned, but they were all released the next year as a concession to terrorists who hijacked a Swissair plane.

Trouble Keeping Them Behind Bars

Keeping terrorists behind bars once they've been convicted in a trial has proven difficult, as terrorist groups regularly demand the release of their compatriots in exchange for a release of hostages. In September 1972 Palestinian Arabs belonging to the Black September group slipped onto the grounds of the Olympic Village in Munich, West Germany, where they killed two Israeli athletes and kidnapped nine others. They demanded the release of 200 Palestinian terrorists being held by Israel, which refused to concede to this demand. In a gunfight at the city's airport, all of the hostages and most of the terrorists were killed. The three who survived were arrested, but only a month later they were released in exchange for hostages on a hijacked Lufthansa airliner. The suspected leader of Black September, Abu Daoud, later was sentenced to death for a terrorist attack on Jordan, but eventually he too was reprieved and released.

Four years after the Munich massacre, a group of West German and Palestinian terrorists hijacked a French airliner bound for Entebbe, Uganda, and demanded the release of jailed terrorists. Although most of the hijackers were killed in a battle at the airport, they were succeeded by two other groups of terrorists, who kidnapped and later killed West German businessman Hans-Martin Schleyer and then hijacked a Lufthansa airliner. Again the terrorists' demand was that jailed terrorists be freed, among them the leaders of the Baader-Meinhof gang. The Baader-Meinhof gang, headed by Andreas Baader and Ulrike Meinhof, operated out of Germany in the early 1970s; most of Germany's terrorist activity in this time is attributed to Baader-Meinhof. Even though most of the group's leaders were captured and imprisoned in early 1972, they continued to inspire fellow terrorists from their cells.

The Lockerbie Trial

Another terrorist prosecution that spanned many years and showed the difficulty of bringing suspects to trial involved the bombing of Pan American Flight 103 over Lockerbie, Scotland, in 1988. The crash killed 259 passengers and crew members, plus another 11 residents of the small village of Lockerbie. Investigators had to search through wreckage that had been scattered over hundreds of square miles of the countryside. Their efforts led them to terrorist groups operating throughout Europe, and eventually to two Libyan suspects, Abdel Basset Ali Mohamed al-Megrahi and Lamen Khalifa Fhima, who were believed to work for Libyan intelligence. The suspects, employees of a Libyan airline, allegedly had placed a suitcase containing the bomb on a flight that connected with Flight 103.

Libyan leader Muammar Qadhafi initially fought all efforts to have the suspects extradited for trial, resulting in United Nations sanctions and blockades against Libya, but eventually he agreed to a trial with specific restrictions. The pair would not be extradited to the United States or to Scotland, and they would be tried under Scottish law, rather than American law, which provided for the death penalty. The trial finally began in 2000, at a Dutch military base that temporarily was considered Scottish territory. Prosecutors claimed that the bombing had been in revenge for a 1986 air raid on Tripoli, Libya, in which Qadhafi's adopted daughter had been killed. The air raid, in turn, had been launched in response to Libya's alleged participation in a Berlin discotheque attack that killed two American soldiers.

Despite extensive forensic evidence and testimony from 230 prosecution witnesses during the eight-month-long trial, only one of the suspects, al-Megrahi, was convicted. He was sentenced to life imprisonment. Al-Megrahi's codefendant, Fhima, was acquitted for lack of evidence.

Prelude to Prosecution: Investigation

During the 1990s terrorism became a major worldwide crisis. Networks of terrorists crossed national lines and chose targets in widespread locations. The groups responsible were often sheltered by other nations that sympathized with the political or religious aims of the terrorists, or were fearful of antagonizing terrorist sympathizers in their own countries. Israeli politician Benjamin Netanyahu, in his book *Fighting Terrorism* (1995), pointed out the importance of treating terrorism as a criminal act: "The point of departure for the domestic battle against terrorism is to treat it as a crime and terrorists as criminals. To do otherwise is to elevate both to a higher status . . . .The fact that terrorists are politically motivated criminals is irrelevant." In Israel, this approach often has been translated into mass arrests of suspected terrorists and armed retaliation.

Investigations of terrorist acts in foreign countries by the FBI or other law enforcement agencies sometimes take years; by the time that suspects are identified, they have taken refuge elsewhere. The United States investigation of the 1998 embassy bombings in Africa, for example, required review of phone messages and computer databases involving thousands of possible terrorists and organizations. In 1993 the first bombing of New York City's World Trade Center caused six deaths and hundreds of injuries. In 1995 a blind Islamic priest, Sheik Omar Abdel-Rahman, and nine of his followers were convicted of plotting to bomb various New York landmarks, but prosecutors were unable to prove that any of the defendants were linked to the 1993 World Trade Cener bombing. The sheik was sentenced to life in prison without parole, and his followers also received long sentences. The key piece of prosecution evidence, provided by an FBI informant who had infiltrated the group, was a videotape of the suspects filmed at a New Jersey mosque, showing them mixing explosives in a huge metal drum. In November 1997 the elusive terrorist Ramzi Ahmed Yousef was convicted of being

LAMEN KHALIFA FHIMAH, ONE OF TWO LIBYAN MEN TRIED FOR THE BOMBING OF PAN AM FLIGHT 103 OVER LOCKERBIE, SCOTLAND, RAISES HIS HAND IN VICTORY AFTER HIS ACQUITTAL AND RETURN HOME. CO-DEFENDANT ABDEL BASSET ALI AL-MEGRAHI WAS CONVICTED AND SENTENCED TO PRISON FOR THE BOMBING. (*AP/Wide World Photos. Reproduced by permission.*)

the mastermind behind the bombing, as well as a thwarted plan to blow up numerous airliners.

Prosecutions of later terrorist attacks in Saudi Arabia, Kenya, and Tanzania proved equally difficult. In 1996 a terrorist bombing of the Khobar Towers apartment complex in Dharhan, Saudi Arabia, killed 19 United States military personnel and injured 200 others. Although FBI director Louis Freeh believed that several Iranian officials were involved in the bombing, direct witnesses were lacking, and the George H. Bush administration (1989–1993) feared that prosecuting these men would endanger diplomatic relations in the Middle East. The capture and trial of terrorists accused of the 1998 bombings of United States embassies in Kenya and Tanzania took three years and implicated the terrorist group al-Qaeda and its leader, Osama bin Laden. Despite a massive international investigation, the case was put together by a stroke of luck. A man later arrested with a phony passport gave investigators the names of suspects and also linked al-Qaeda to the attacks. After a lengthy trial, four Saudi and Jordanian men were sentenced to life imprisonment in 2001. The judge imposing

THE U.S. EMBASSIES IN NAIROBI, KENYA, AND DAR ES SALAAM, TANZANIA, WERE BOMBED IN 1998, KILLING 224 PEOPLE, MOST OF WHOM WERE FOREIGN NATIONALS. THE UNITED STATES PURSUED PROSECUTION OF THOSE DEEMED RESPONSIBLE FOR THE TERRORIST ATTACKS. *(AP/Wide World Photos/Sayyid Azim. Reproduced by permission.)*

the sentences also ordered restitution of US$33 million, which he hoped would come from al-Qaeda bank accounts being traced. Thirteen other indicted suspects, however, including bin Laden, had not been apprehended.

RECENT HISTORY AND THE FUTURE

Within the United States recent attention to terrorist prosecutions understandably focused on the attacks that destroyed the World Trade Center and damaged the Pentagon on September 11, 2001, and their aftermath. The legal fate of suspects such as "shoe bomber" Richard Reid and "American Taliban" John Walker Lindh remained uncertain, as did that of the many Taliban fighters who were captured and imprisoned at the United States military base at Guantanamo Bay, Cuba. In the months immediately after these attacks, the United States and numerous other nations took major steps to toughen prosecution of suspected terrorists, and experts began to strategize about how best to conduct these prosecutions. The difficulty of investigating and prosecuting terrorism was apparent; by late 2001 the State Department had profiled 28 foreign terrorist organizations considered an immediate threat to United States security.

Shortly after September 11, 2001, hundreds of people (most of them of Middle Eastern ancestry) were rounded up and arrested for violations of immigration statutes. Since those arrested were not United States citizens, legal protections such as the right to a lawyer or bail often were not provided. Information provided to the public was limited, so that even the names of the people detained were kept secret. The federal government also began to interrogate thousands of Middle Eastern immigrants about their political beliefs and personal contacts. By November, Congress had passed the "USA Patriot Act," targeting terrorism within the United States. The act contained many provisions that alarmed civil rights advocates, among them reducing the requirements for obtaining search warrants and monitoring email communications without a court order.

Military Tribunals

A question also arose about how to try captured terrorists and whether a trial would even be an option, particularly in the case of suspected al-Qaeda leader Osama bin Laden and the leaders of Afghanistan's Taliban. In late 2001 President George W. Bush authorized the use of military tribunals to try suspected terrorists who were not United States citizens. Such tribunals had not been used since 1942, when German saboteurs landed

INTERNATIONAL TERRORISM CONVENTIONS

According to the U.S. Department of State's Office for Counterterrorism, a large number of international legal instruments ("conventions") exist which can be used in prosecuting terrorists. Key provisions require parties to the conventions to prosecute offenders or turn them over for prosecution to another party, and to assist in prosecutions brought by other parties. Although the United States is a party to all of these conventions, they are not binding on other nations that have not ratified them, including some nations that might harbor terrorists.

Among these conventions are several that apply to airline safety, sabotage, and hijacking: Convention on Offenses and Certain Other Acts Committed On Board Aircraft ("Tokyo Convention" of 1963); Convention for the Suppression of Unlawful Seizure of Aircraft ("Hague Convention" of 1970); Convention for the Suppression of Unlawful Acts Against the Safety of Civil Aviation ("Montreal Convention" of 1971); Protocol for the Suppression of Unlawful Acts of Violence at Airports Serving International Civil Aviation (1988); and Convention on the Marking of Plastic Explosives for the Purpose of Identification (1991), which provides for chemical marking of the plastic explosives that have been used in airplane sabotage.

The Convention on the Prevention and Punishment of Crimes Against Internationally Protected Persons (1973) protects government officials and diplomats, while the International Convention Against the Taking of Hostages (1979) applies to other victims of terrorist kidnappings or similar violence. The Convention on the Physical Protection of Nuclear Material (1979) addresses the unlawful possession and use of nuclear material. The Convention for the Suppression of Unlawful Acts Against the Safety of Maritime Navigation (1988) provides for prosecution of terrorist activities on board ships, while the Protocol for the Suppression of Unlawful Acts Against the Safety of Fixed Platforms Located on the Continental Shelf (1988) targets terrorist acts on offshore platforms such as oil rigs. The International Convention for the Suppression of Terrorist Bombing (1997) creates a system of international jurisdiction for cooperatively prosecuting the use of explosives or other lethal devices in public places. Finally the International Convention for the Suppression of the Financing of Terrorism (1999) calls for States to sieze terrorists funds and cooperate with other states to block terrorist funding.

in submarines near New York City during World War II.

The tribunals would be held in secret and presided over by military officers; a guilty verdict could be reached by a two-thirds vote of the presiding officers, rather than the unanimous jury verdict required in other criminal trials. Civil liberties advocates worried that the tribunals could be expanded to allow prosecution of United States citizens, and that the president was upsetting the balance of government power among the executive, legislative, and judicial branches of government by unilaterally establishing the tribunals. Because of the outrage over the September 11 attacks, however, there was a great deal of public support for the tribunals, as well as for military action that would kill the suspected terrorists and eliminate the need for trials altogether.

President Bush, in a speech to U.S. attorneys on November 29, 2001, voiced his support for military tribunals.

Those who plot terror and those who help them will be held accountable in America. That's what we're going to do. Protecting [the] innocent against violence is a solemn duty of this country . . . .To meet that obligation, a wartime reorganization is under way at the Justice Department. More investigators will go to front lines. The federal government will work more closely with state and local authorities . . . Agents will receive better training and new technology to help track and capture terrorists or those who support them. And these changes are essential . . .

I've also reserved the option of trial by military commission for foreign terrorists who wage war against our country . . . .Non-U.S. citizens who plan and/or commit mass murder are more than criminal suspects, they are unlawful combatants who seek to destroy our country and our way of life. And if I determine that it is in the national security interests of our great land to try by military commission those who make war on America, then we will do so.

Prosecuting Terrorism Today

The September 11 attacks launched a discussion among terrorism experts and the international community about how to join forces to prosecute terrorism. David Scheffer of the United States Institute for Peace released a report on options for prosecution in which he noted that the United States and numerous nations were using a combination of armed force and criminal justice tools to fight terrorism. Scheffer's report discussed nine possible judicial forums for trying cases, including United States federal courts and military tribunals, foreign national courts, and international courts administered by the United Nations. A group of international conventions could be invoked against suspected terrorists to support the prosecutions (see sidebar).

In the months immediately following the 2001 attacks, many nations tightened their surveillance and prosecution of terrorist activities. Some acted at the urging of the United States, while others were concerned about preventing the spread of terrorism in their own countries. In the European Union, for instance, task forces were established to trace funds that were laundered by terrorist groups. Canada and Mexico arrested dozens of people who might have been connected to the September 11 attacks and then fled the United States. In Germany, where some of the suicide terrorists involved in the September 11 attacks had lived, authorities raided several terrorist cells. International arrest warrants were issued for numerous suspected terrorists, most of whom were hiding in unknown locations.

While debate still swirls around the use of military tribunals over that of federal courts in the United States, the need to investigate and prosecute terrorists remains a worldwide problem. The methods and standards may vary and will undoubtedly change over time, but the end result will remain—to put those responsible on trial and stop their acts of terror.

BIBLIOGRAPHY

"African Embassy Bombing Trial Begins," *United Press International*, February 5, 2001.

"The Bird Has Flown; Anti-Terrorism," *Economist*, January 12, 2002.

"A Brief History of Strife," *Economist*, December 4, 1999.

Bush, George W. Speech to U.S. attorneys, November 29, 2001. "Transcript: Bush Defends Military Tribunals." Available online at http://www.washingtonpost.com/wp-srv/nation/specials/attacked/transcripts/bush_text112901.html (cited January 29, 2002).

Cohen, Adam. "Rough Justice," *Time*, December 10, 2001.

Coogan, Tim Pat. *The Troubles: Ireland's Ordeal 1966–1996 and the Search for Peace*. Boulder, CO: Roberts Rinehart, 1996.

Dickey, Christopher. "At Last, a Long Shot at Justice: Eleven Years Later, the Pan Am 103 Case Goes to Trial," *Newsweek*, May 8, 2000.

Dobbs, Michael. "In France, Judge Fights Terrorism and Critics," *Washington Post*, November 23, 2001.

Dobson, Christopher, and Ronald Payne. *The Never-Ending War: Terrorism in the 80's*. New York: Facts on File, 1987.

Edwards, Catherine, and Stephanie K. Taylor. "Terrorists Threaten United States Over World Trade Center Bomber," *Insight on the News*, May 21, 2001.

Edwards, Jim. "Attorneys Face Hidden Hurdles in September 11 Detainee Cases," *New Jersey Law Journal*, December 3, 2001.

Egendorf, Laura K., ed. *Terrorism: Opposing Viewpoints*. San Diego, CA: Greenhaven Press, 2000.

"Embassy Bomber Gets Life Imprisonment," *United Press International*, July 10, 2001.

"Far-Flung Fanaticism," *National Journal*, October 27, 2001.

Fenoglio, Gia, et al. "How Life Could Change," *National Journal*, September 22, 2001.

Foot, John. "Cross Current: Truth, Memory, and Justice in Milan," *History Today*, March 1, 2000.

Foroohar, Rana, et al. "Storming the Fortress," *Newsweek International*, October 8, 2001.

Frater, Elizabeth. "Studying Terrorists' Lessons," *National Journal*, December 1, 2001.

Gibbs, Nancy, and David S. Jackson. "In Fits and Starts; Kaczynski Throws the Unabomber Trial Into Disarray." *Time*, January 19, 1998.

Haynes, V. Dion. "Four Former SLA Members Arrested in 1975 Killing," *Knight-Ridder/Tribune News Service*, January 16, 2002.

Hennessey, Thomas. *A History of Northern Ireland*. New York: St. Martin's Press, 1997.

Hoffman, Bruce. *Inside Terrorism*. New York: Columbia University Press, 1998.

"Indictments in Saudi Bombing Pose Dilemma," *United Press International*, May 7, 2001.

"The Irish Rising of 1798," *History Today*, June 1998.

Jenkins, Philip. "Home-Grown Terror," *American Heritage*, September 1995.

Kates, Brian. "The Fates of Mass Killers," *Knight-Ridder/Tribune News Service*, October 21, 2001.

"Kopp May Not Face Death Penalty," *United Press International*, June 2, 2001.

Lancaster, John, and Susan Schmidt. "U.S. Rethinks Strategy for Coping With Terrorists," *Washington Post*, September 14, 2001.

Lasseter, Tom. "Alleged Shoe Bomber Indicted on Eight Counts," *Knight-Ridder/Tribune News Service*, January 16, 2002.

Loeb, Vernon. "Trial of Four in Alleged Bin Laden Bomb Plot Set to Begin," *Washington Post*, December 31, 2000.

"The Long Trail Twisting From Lockerbie; Lockerbie Suspect Found Guilty," *Economist*, February 3, 2001.

MacLeod, Scott, et al. "Terror in Africa," *Time*, August 17, 1998.

Maier, Timothy W. "Olympic Tragedy: 1972 Revisited," *Insight on the News*, November 12, 2001.

"A Matter of Life or Death," *Time International*, May 21, 2001.

Mintz, John. "Palestinian-Born Man Deported to Jordan," *Washington Post*, November 30, 2001.

Netanyahu, Benjamin. *Fighting Terrorism: How Democracies Can Defeat Domestic and International Terrorists*. New York: Farrar Straus Giroux, 1995.

"Never Shall Be Slaves," *Economist*, September 29, 2001.

O'Meara, Kelly Patricia. "Police State," *Insight on the News*, December 3, 2001.

"On Terrorism's Trail," *U.S. News and World Report*, November 23, 1998.

"Osama Bin Laden's Network of Influence Reaches Across Five Continents," *Time*, November 12, 2001.

Perry, Joellen. "Setting Snares on the Net," *U.S. News and World Report*, November 5, 2001.

"Peru: Lori Berenson Sentenced to 20 Years in Retrial," *NotiSur*, June 29, 2001.

Pomerantz, Steven L. "How to Tackle Terrorism," *New Republic*, August 31, 1998.

Powell, Michael. "Four Bombers Get Life Sentences," *Washington Post*, October 19, 2001.

Quindlen, Anna. "The Terrorists Here At Home," *Newsweek*, December 17, 2001.

Reid, T.R. "Militant Convicted of Conspiracy in Omagh Bombing," *Washington Post*, January 23, 2002.

Rossant, John, et al. "Now, a Different Kind of War," *Business Week*, December 3, 2001.

Samuel, Terence. "Sheik, Nine Followers Sentenced to Long Prison Terms," Knight-Ridder/Tribune News Service, January 17, 1996.

Scheffer, David. "Options for Prosecuting International Terrorists," United States Institute of Peace, Washington DC: November 14, 2001. Available online at http://www.usip.org/pubs/specialreports/sr78.html (cited January 23, 2002).

Shapiro, Ben. "The Doctor Killers," Nation, April 23, 2001.

"Sharon Aims Israel's Guns at Arafat," *Economist*, December 8, 2001.

Slevin, Peter, and George Lardner, Jr. "Bush Plan for Terrorism Trials Defended," *Washington Post*, November 15, 2001.

Sonder, Ben. *The Militia Movement*. New York: F. Watts, 2000.

"Terrorist Trials: Missing Someone?" *Christian Science Monitor*, February 8, 2001.

"Time Trip," *Current Events*, October 12, 2001.

"Toughening Up; Canada and the United States," *Economist*, December 8, 2001.

U.S. Department of State, Office for Counterterrorism. "International Terrorism Conventions," Washington, DC: August 17, 1998. Available online at http://www.state.gov/www/global/terrorism/980817_terror_conv.html (cited January 23, 2002).

"US v. Bin Laden: Is a Trial a Real Option?" *Christian Science Monitor*, December 3, 2001.

Vatz, Richard E., and Lee S. Weinberg. "The Unabomber's Twisted Saga," *USA Today Magazine*, July 1998.

Warner, Mary Beth, et al. "Beseeching the World," *National Journal*, September 22, 2001.

"A Way Out of the Maze," *Economist*, July 29, 2000.

Zengerle, Jason. "Infinite Justice; Can Courts Try Terrorists?" *New Republic*, November 19, 2001.

Gerry Azzata

(Psychology) Understanding the 9/11 Perpetrators: Crazy, Lost in Hate, or Martyred?

The Conflict

In the wake of the September 11 terrorist attacks in the United States, many people have asked the question "why?" Why did those who hijacked four passenger airliners with the intent to fly them into buildings, killing thousands—including themselves—do what they did? The question of what motivated these men to willingly, determinedly, and violently give up their lives is an important one for many seeking to understand what happened.

Psychological

- Prior to September 11, few people could imagine that such a shocking and large-scale terrorist attack could occur on U.S. soil. After September 11, few could comprehend what motivated the attackers. With responsibility linked to the Islamic extremist group al-Qaeda, possible religious motivations or hatred for the West were considered by those surviving the chaos. A manual used by the attackers reveals that hate was not a driving force behind the terrorists' actions. Rather, the hijackers focused on their belief and devotion to their cause as they carried out their plan.

Foreign Policy

- What motivated the hijackers may not be the same as what motivated their leader, Osama bin Laden, head of the al-Qaeda network. Bin Laden has a history of anti-Western, and particularly anti-American, statements and actions. In a taped video after September 11, bin Laden acknowledged that the attacks were a success. It can be guessed that causing a large number of deaths and instilling chaos and fear in the United States was part of his goal.

Social

- Most people can not fathom an environment or belief system that would support a person's desire to participate in a suicide attack. Suicide is not condoned by any of the world's major religions, including Islam. Under extremist beliefs and interpretations, however, suicide attacks—or martyrdom operations—have become increasingly common.

Four groups of Muslim Arabs hijacked four commercial aircraft on the morning of September 11, 2001. Two of these groups succeeded in flying their planes into the World Trade Center in New York City; one group succeeded in flying its plane into the Pentagon near Washington, DC; and the fourth group crashed its plane in western Pennsylvania when the passengers tried to take control of the plane back from the hijackers. About three thousand lives were lost, including the lives of nineteen hijackers.

Americans were shocked that nineteen men were willing to give their lives to kill Americans. Why did they do it? No terrorist group took credit for the attack or issued any demands. The mystery only deepened when it was learned that fifteen of the nineteen attackers had Saudi passports. Saudi Arabia has been a long-time ally of the United States; indeed the Gulf War (1991) can be seen as a response not only to Iraq's invasion of Kuwait but to the threat this invasion represented to Kuwait's neighbor Saudi Arabia. When Osama bin Laden was seen on videotape admitting that the collapse of the World Trade Center on September 11 (9/11) was more than he had hoped for, Americans finally had a clear enemy but still no clear explanation of the behavior of the nineteen attackers.

These were not men who had lost all sense of self in a cult that occupied their every waking moment; before the attack the men were dispersed, living in separate apartments in different towns. They were not living under the political power of a regime that controlled their lives; before 9/11 they spent months, even years breathing the free air of the United States. It cannot be maintained that they attacked what they did not know; their extended experience living in the United States means

CHRONOLOGY

August 1996 Osama bin Laden issues a "Declaration of War" against the United States.

February 1998 Bin Laden announces the creation of the World Islamic Front for Jihad Against Jews and Crusaders, an alliance of terrorist groups intent on attacking the United States, its allies, and civilians, wherever they can be found.

May 2000 During an investigation into Osama bin Laden, agents of the Federal Bureau of Investigation uncover a terrorist manual, "Military Studies in the Jihad Against Tyrants," in Manchester, England. Among its instructions, the manual details how to blend in while awaiting the time of attack.

September 11, 2001 Nineteen men hijack four passenger airliners. In a suicidal mission, two of the planes are flown into the towers of the World Trade Center in New York City and a third plane is flown into the Pentagon near Washington, DC; the fourth plane crashes in a Pennsylvania field after the passengers revolt against the hijackers.

September 12, 2001 A car hired by Mohammed Atta and left in the parking lot of Boston's Logan airport is found. It contains a flight manual in Arabic and a copy of the Qur'an.

September 28, 2001 Mohammed Atta's suicide letter is found; it contains a reference to shine your shoes before meeting your maker.

December 22, 2001 Richard Reid boards an American Airlines flight from Paris to Miami. He is overpowered by passengers and crew when he tries to light an explosive hidden within his shoe.

---

that they did know the country and its people. Yet they chose to die in order to kill thousands of Americans. A variety of explanations for this puzzle have been offered since 9/11: They were crazy. They were suicidal. They hated Americans. These explanations, and the attackers' view of themselves as martyrs for Islam, will be explored here from a psychological perspective.

Are They Crazy?

It is difficult to see the 9/11 attacks as an expression of mental disorder. The attacks were brilliantly planned and executed with striking coordination, and the quality of planning and execution offer a strong argument that the attackers could not be crazy in any serious sense. Crazy in a serious sense means suffering from some form of psychopathology represented in the American Psychiatric Association's *Diagnostic and Statistical Manual* (DSM-IV). Psychopathology, however, is associated with unrealistic appraisal of the world, including disturbed perceptions of self and others. In other words, psychopathology is pathology, a disease or disorder, and pathology gets in the way of effective performance rather than explaining it.

A particular kind of psychopathology might at first glance seem a more promising explanation. Sociopaths, sometimes called psychopaths, are people who do not feel guilt or shame. They do not feel normal social attachments; they use and manipulate others as means for their own ends. Such people, one might think, can kill civilians—including women, children, and the elderly—without remorse. Perhaps this kind of pathology is what makes terrorists able to do the terrible things they do. Unfortunately for this explanation, the hallmark of sociopathy or psychopathy is selfishness. No one studying this kind of pathology has ever suggested that it can be expressed in self-sacrifice or suicide. Even if the self-sacrifice is risk-taking short of self-destruction, a pathology of selfishness cannot account for the group cohesion and trust which are the essential foundations of terrorist groups.

A third kind of pathology that can be invoked to explain 9/11 is the pathology that leads to suicide. Were the attackers suicidal? Certainly they were in the sense that at least some of them, in particular the pilots who flew the planes into buildings, intended to die. But if "suicidal" is to be an explanation of their behavior, then describing the 9/11 attackers as suicidal again implies that there was something wrong with them. Suicide is usually associated with depression, a form of psychopathology recognized in the DSM-IV. Again, however, there is no reason to believe that the attackers were suffering from depression and good reason, in their success, to believe that they were normal by any psychiatric standard.

Mohammed Atta is thought to have been the leader of the 9/11 attacks and his background has been extensively investigated. His middle-class parents have been interviewed in Egypt, his schoolmates and acquaintances have been interviewed, and his German employers in Hamburg have been interviewed. None suggested that Atta showed any signs of depression or any other form of psychopathology.

In short, explanation of 9/11 as the work of nineteen crazy individuals cannot be taken seriously. Any attempt to translate this kind of talk into specific psychiatric diagnoses quickly runs into the fundamental inconsistency between disorder—any kind of mental disorder—and the demonstrated organization and effectiveness of the 9/11 attackers.

Was 9/11 a Hate Crime?

Did the attackers hate America and Americans? Osama bin Laden has issued numerous statements justifying violence against Americans, and he has consistently leveled three accusations. First, American troops have been stationed in Saudi Arabia since the Gulf War against Iraq; the presence of these "infidels" is a desecration of the Muslim holy land that includes the cities of Mecca and Medina. Second, the U.S.-led boycott of Iraq since the Gulf War has resulted in half a million Iraqis, mostly children, dying from lack of food and medicine. Third, Americans have armed and supported Israel in its domination of the Palestinians, who were forced from their lands in the founding of the Jewish state in 1948. These are grounds for anger and hatred, and many have explained the 9/11 attacks as an expression of hatred.

In a speech to his nation on September 20, 2001, U.S. President George W. Bush (2001–) asked the question, "Why do they hate us?" His answer: "They hate what they see right here in this chamber: a democratically elected government . . . . They hate our freedoms: our freedom of religion, our freedom of speech, our freedom to vote and assemble and disagree with each other."

A new organization, "Americans for Victory over Terrorism" (AVOT), has offered the same interpretation. The AVOT, chaired by William Bennett (former U.S. secretary of education), offers ten Fundamental Principles. The second principle is a confident statement of the hate-crime hypothesis: "The radical Islamists who attacked us did so because of our democratic ideals, our belief in, and practice of, liberty and equality. AVOT will take to task those who blame America first and who do not understand—or who are unwilling to defend—our fundamental principles" ("Americans for Victory over Terrorism," 2002).

A quick search of the Lexis-Nexus database of newspaper articles indicates that literally thousands of news stories since 9/11 have linked "terrorism" and "hate." Unfortunately for this kind of explanation, polling data from Muslim countries do not indicate widespread hatred of the United States. Fifteen of the nineteen men who attacked on 9/11 had Saudi passports. To the extent that these fifteen represent or draw inspiration from the opinions of other Saudis, we can learn something about their motivations from polls in Saudi Arabia. Shibley Telhami, Anwar Sadat Professor for Peace and Development at the University of Maryland, describes such polls in the *New York Times* on March 3, 2002.

In a survey last month of Saudi elites—defined as media professionals, academics and chamber of commerce members—43 percent said that their frustrations with the United States would be completely removed, and 23 percent said they would be significantly reduced, if America brokered a just and lasting peace in the Arab-Israeli conflict. This result also jibes with a general public opinion survey conducted last summer in which 63 percent of Saudis said that the Palestinian issue was 'the single most important issue' to me, personally. Other surveys, too, have confirmed the importance of the Arab-Israeli issue among the Saudi people. When asked if their attitudes toward the United States were mostly based on its policies or on its values, 86 percent answered politics. Only 6 percent said values.

A much-misunderstood Gallup poll of nine Muslim countries, released February 26, 2002, offers further evidence that Muslim views of the United States have more to do with politics than hatred. The nine countries polled were Pakistan, Iran, Indonesia, Turkey, Lebanon, Morocco, Kuwait, Jordan, and Saudi Arabia. The headline results of the poll were that 53 percent of Muslims had unfavorable views of the United States; 58 percent had unfavorable views of President Bush; 61 percent did not believe that the 9/11 attacks were carried out by Arabs; and 77 percent believe that U.S. military action in Afghanistan is morally unjustified. It is worth noting, however, that these results are not as negative as many of the headlines led readers to believe; they imply, after all, that more than 40 percent of Muslims are *not* negative towards the United States and President Bush.

By way of context, Gallup polling in the United States between March 1–3, 2002, found 41 percent of Americans unfavorable toward "Muslim countries in general." Thus Americans are nearly as unfavorable toward Muslim countries as Muslim countries are toward the United States. (41 percent of Americans unfavorable toward Muslim countries; 53 percent of Muslims unfavorable towards the United States). Asked about specific Muslim countries, Americans were most unfavorable towards Iran (72 percent) and least unfavorable towards Morocco (21 percent).

In the Gallup poll of nine Muslim countries, perhaps most important for judging hatred of the United States is the question about the 9/11 attacks. A surprisingly large 67 percent of Muslims said the 9/11 attacks were morally unjustified. That is, for two-thirds of respondents in nine Muslim countries, hatred of the United States does not rise to the level of justifying the attacks of 9/11.

Even if hatred of the United States is not widespread among Muslims, it might yet be the case that hatred motivates the few hundreds or thousands of Muslims who are members of al-Qaeda. In particular it may have been what motivated the 9/11 terrorists. To evaluate this possibility, it is necessary to be a little more specific about how hatred can explain suicide terrorism.

As an explanation of 9/11, hatred has to be stronger than fear. Hatred is a strong emotion and can perhaps be strong enough to drive out fear of death. Most of us have had the experience of being so angry that we did something stupid, something that cost us heavily. Taking a swing at someone bigger and stronger than we are, for instance. Anger and hatred are strong emotions and can overwhelm good sense and even self-interest. Anger and hatred over perceived wrongs by the United States could conceivably lead men to give up their lives for revenge. With this possibility in mind, we are fortunate to have a document that gives access to the minds and motives of the 9/11 attackers.

HISTORICAL BACKGROUND

"Atta's Manual"

Found in the personal belongings of several of the 9/11 attackers were copies of the same handwritten document, a kind of manual for the attack. The author of the document is not known with certainty, although it has sometimes been attributed to Mohammed Atta as the presumed leader of the 9/11 operation. As published by the Federal Bureau of Investigation (FBI), this document has four pages. The first page of the document does not begin with the usual Muslim invocation or prayer, however, and the first line of this page seems to refer to something earlier. Thus the published document appears to be pages two through five of an

A MAN HOLDS SOME AL-QAEDA LITERATURE AS HE WALKS OUT OF A TUNNEL FROM A TERRORIST TRAINING CAMP IN AFGHANISTAN. A MANUAL WITH INSTRUCTIONS FOR THE SEPTEMBER 11 ATTACKS IN THE UNITED STATES WAS FOUND AMIDST THE BELONGINGS OF ONE OF THE ATTACKERS. (© AFP/CORBIS. Reproduced by permission.)

original from which the first page has either not been found or has not been released by the FBI.

The "manual" has been independently translated by two scholars, Hassan Mneimneh and David Cook, each of whom has offered a discussion and interpretation of his translation (Mneimneh, 2002; Cook, in press). The discussion here is based on the work of both scholars, to whom this author owes many thanks for providing access to their work before publication.

The manual is divided into three sections: "The last night" in an apartment before the attack, "the second phase" from the taxi to the airport until boarding the plane, and "the third phase" from boarding the plane to welcoming death and the end of the mission. In each of these sections, by far the greatest attention is given to prayer; much smaller attention is given to group solidarity among the attackers and to practical details of carrying out the plan of attack; and almost no attention to the enemy or justification for the attack.

Hatred

The first and perhaps most surprising aspect of the manual is that it does not incite or even

MANUAL FOR A RAID

The handwritten manual found in the belongings of several of the September 11 attackers is not, as many may suppose, filled with talk of hate, vengeance, and death. To the contrary, the manual consistently focuses on devotion to God as it leads the reader through three phases: (1) preparations on the last night before the raid; (2) on the way to the airport; and (3) boarding the plane.

The first phase, as translated by Hassan Mniemneh in "Manual for a 'Raid'" (*New York Review of Books,* January 17, 2002) details fifteen steps discussing attitude, focus, and faith. From its first step—a mutual pledge to die and a renewal of intent—to its last—morning prayer—the manual offers encouragement to remain positive and optimistic. "God is with those who persevere." One's remaining hours should be devoted to forgetting earthly amusements and making oneself closer to God. In the face of the adversity to come, trust in God and remain steadfast. At the end of this preparation, one should make sure that everything is in order, including passports, plane tickets, clothing, and weapons. After morning prayer, phase two begins.

The manual's second phase offers spiritual encouragement and more prayer on the way to the airport. "Smile and feel secure, God is with the believers." Assurances in God, dedication and invocations to Him, and phrases supporting group cohesion are stressed throughout phase two. "[D]o not show signs of confusion or tension. Be happy and cheerful, be relaxed and feel secure because you are engaged in an action that God loves and is satisfied by it."

The third and final phase of the manual continues to focus on group cohesion, as well as the action of the attack itself. Be mindful and purposeful, it says, in taking action not for vengeance, but for the sake of God. Once the plane has boarded and taken off, the manual encourages the attackers to act against the non-believers. "Defeat them and cause them to tremble. Recite supplications that you and all your brothers be granted victory, triumph, and the hitting of the target. Do not be afraid . . . . When the moment of truth comes near, and zero hour is upon you, open your chest welcoming death on the path of God." In the final seconds before hitting the target, the attackers are advised that their last words be an invocation to God.

approve of hatred of the enemy. There is no list of outrages to justify the mission. There is no mention of infidels in Saudi Arabia, or children dying in Iraq, or U.S. support for Israel.

On the contrary, the manual argues explicitly against individual motivation based on personal feelings: "Do not act out of a desire for vengeance for yourself. Let your action instead be for the sake of God." The manual reinforces this injunction with the example of Ali ibn Abi Talib, as described in Muslim sacred writings from the seventh century. Ali was fighting with an infidel who spat on him. Rather than strike the infidel in anger, Ali held his sword until he could master himself and strike for Allah rather than for himself. The importance of this example is increased by the paraphrase that follows. "He might have said it differently. When he became sure of his intention, he struck and killed him." This reference to intention resonates with the first line of the first section, which asks for a mutual pledge to die and a renewal of intent. The intention of the attackers is crucial and is an issue that will be explored later in this essay.

Here it suffices to note that, not only does the manual *not* encourage hatred of the enemy, it actually warns against acting out of hatred or vengeance. Indeed the manual does not identify any specific enemy. There are a few general references to the "enemy" (e.g. second point in first phase), but no direct reference to the United States or to any other country. Perhaps most explicit is the reference, in the second phase, to "the followers of Satan"—"These are the admirers of Western civilization." More allusive are references to the enemy as "the factions" or "the confederates," using a term, *ahzab,* that appears in the Qur'an, Islam's holy book, and in the Hadith, the secondary literature of sayings of the Prophet Mohammed and his Companions, to refer to Mohammed's enemies. This historical term is more specific than it may appear, however, because the term is commonly used among radical Muslims to refer to the United States and the West. Beyond these indirect references are phrases even less direct: "we seek refuge from their evil, "place a bar in front of them," "blind them," "all their technology does not do benefit or harm."

The manual's references to the enemy thus do not support the idea that the 9/11 attackers were motivated by hatred of the enemy; indeed references to the enemy are relatively few, general, and indirect. Overall, the emotional quality of the manual is positive, rather than negative. Hate, anger, and vengeance are discouraged while submission to God and sacrifice in accord with God's will are encouraged. The nature of this encouragement becomes clearer in considering the importance of prayer in the manual.

Prayer

Prayer is generally understood as lifting up one's heart and mind to God, and at least ninety percent of the lines in the manual fit this description. Simply counting lines, however, will underestimate the consistency of content and style. There are many direct quotations from the Qur'an, which Muslims believe to be the word of God, and from the Hadith. There are also many paraphrases and allusions to the Qur'an and the Hadith that are easily recognized by most Muslims. Finally, there are repeated injunctions to recite "invocations" or "devotionals" in the situation of travel, entry of town or building, facing enemies, and so forth. These are formulas of brief prayer for various occasions that are widely published in Muslim countries. Likewise prayer is enjoined at every point in the manual, including the instruction to stay awake the night before the attack to spend the whole night in prayer.

In style as well as in content, the manual is a prayer and is written almost entirely in the vocabulary of the seventh century. References to modern nouns such as airport, or airplane, are given only as the first initial of the relevant modern word in Arabic. The result is that the document conveys a feeling of connection to the roots of the Muslim faith, in the same way that some Christians find the language of the King James version of the Bible more powerful than versions that use modern English.

The manual, however, is more than spiritual encouragement. It describes a contract, or at least a compact, between the attackers and their God. The attackers will be martyrs in the Muslim tradition of martyrs; one who dies with the correct intention, that is, doing the will of Allah, is brought immediately to paradise. The manual refers to this paradise in three different aspects (here this author depends particularly on Mneimneh's insight and discussion). The first aspect is social: "to start the happy God-pleasing life with the prophets, saints, and martyrs, who are the best of companions." The second aspect is a physical paradise: the beautiful garden in which "heavenly brides" await. This is the most common representation of paradise in Islamic literature. Finally, a third aspect is the meeting with God in "the highest paradise."

The alternative to paradise is hell and human weakness and sinfulness will lead to this punishment. A martyr, however, is purified of his sins and enters paradise without impediment or punishment. This may be the explanation of reports that some of the 9/11 attackers had frequented lap-dance bars and other impure places during their sojourn in the U.S. A man on his way to martyrdom need have no fear of punishment for sins. On the other hand, frequenting bars rather than mosques could be a part of the "tradecraft" by which the 9/11 attackers avoided FBI attention to pious Muslims when seeking radical Muslims. Of course it is also possible that "tradecraft" and a pass to paradise came together in the barroom.

In sum, the contract advanced in the manual is this: a man who gives his life in the path of Allah is a martyr who trades the pain and disappointments of human existence for release from sin and glory in heaven. Considered strictly as a contract, this is an attractive proposition. Life can be more difficult than death; " . . . to Some, Not to be martyrs, is a martyrdom" (John Donne). Death in the flash of impact and explosion can be easier than withstanding torture in an enemy's prison and easier than watching loved ones suffering pain, shame, or disease.

Group Cohesion

In addition to encouraging prayer, the manual aims to build group solidarity and unity among the attackers. The first line of the first section calls for a mutual oath to the death on the last night. Later the manual asks its reader to remember to pray and to remind others in the group to pray, and, at the end of the first section, directs its readers to pray the morning prayer as a group. The second section, instructions for the trip to the airport, and preparing to board the airplane, contains no explicit reference to the group. This should not be surprising because the attackers needed to avoid giving any clues to their relationship at the airport; conversation among them, mutual recognition, or even physical proximity could create the perception of a suspicious group of young Arabs. The third section, however, which dealt with taking over the plane, returns to building group solidarity and unity. The manual warns against disagreement at the point where passengers may have to be killed; rather the injunction is to "listen and obey." This warning indicates a predetermined ranking of the attackers, as to who would command and who would obey, and the ranking would need to be complete enough that loss of one or more individuals would not leave authority uncertain.

Once in control of the plane, the attackers are asked to be glad with their brothers, to make them feel secure, and to encourage them. In order to appreciate the need for this encouragement, consider the situation of the attackers at this point. For example, they are few in relation to the number of passengers and crew. They are likely to have killed in taking over the plane, probably by cutting the throat of one or more passengers, resulting in great volumes of blood around them and on them. The bodies of their victims are before them. Normal reactions to this situation might include feelings of disgust and guilt, and, in looking at the lifeless bodies of their victims, fear at the fast approach of their own deaths. In this situation some encouragement is called for, and the manual suggests something not unlike the "infield chatter" of a baseball team: praying, talking, supporting, and caring.

The manual specifically suggests that the mutual encouragement should include sharing some food or water. "Do not forget to take some of the spoils, even if only a cup of water, to drink from it and offer it to your brothers to drink, if possible." This seems at first a bizarre idea. If you are to die in a few minutes, why do you need a drink of water? As noted, however, particularly by Mneimneh in his discussion of the manual, this injunction has been prepared for in an earlier part of the third section: "If you slaughter you should plunder." This injunction appears in a context of preparing the reader to do his part in slaughtering passengers.

Despite the non-sequitur quality of sharing a drink of water while racing toward death, it is worth considering how this advice may be very practical. As the sharing of water occurs in the context of mutual encouragement, the most obvious possibility is that the sharing is a contribution to group cohesion. Sharing of food and drink is one of the strongest rituals of relationship. Another possibility is the value of distraction. Getting and sharing food or even a glass of water during the minutes approaching death offers a concrete group activity, a gesture of normalcy in an extreme situation, and a distraction from thinking about oncoming death. A third possibility is the value of decreasing fear by focusing on nurture. Psychological research indicates the incompatibility of appetitive motives and fear. Many have noticed how fear gets in the way of feeling hunger and thirst, but the reverse is also true; motives of hunger and thirst can suppress fear

in the presence of the food and drink. This is an old idea, at least as old as the antidote to fear in the twenty-third Psalm: "You prepare a table before me, under the eyes of my enemies." In short, the manual's injunction to try to share at least a glass of water in the last minutes of the mission may not be so bizarre after all. Whether by building cohesion, distracting from fear or actively inhibiting fear, this sharing can be very practical advice.

Action

In comparison with praying and supporting the group, the manual contains only a few references to the practical requirements of the plan of attack. The first section enjoins some basics for the night before the attack: knowing the plan well, checking clothes, knife, ticket, passport and other papers, and dressing neatly. The second section suggests reassuringly that, at the airport, prayer will lead to a smile and to feeling secure. This suggestion is psychologically sophisticated: the best way to look relaxed and unsuspicious is to feel secure. Trying to look relaxed is less likely to succeed. The third section contains a reminder that the critical moment in the plan is to take control of the plane after takeoff; they should strike as heroes, and shout the name of God in order to instill terror in the infidels. This last can have the practical effect of multiplying the surprise of the attack with disconcerting noise in the same way that soldiers are taught to scream through a bayonet charge. And that, surprisingly enough, is the extent to which action is discussed. Physical action of the plan is represented only in outline and in no more than a dozen lines, whereas the action and varieties of prayer appear in nearly every line.

It is possible that the lack of action detail was intended as a security precaution, in case the document were uncovered before the attack. This possibility is made less likely, however, by noting that the references to suitcase, knife, ticket, and passport should alone be enough to give away the plan if the document were found by U.S. security personnel. Having said as much as it does, why does the document not have any clue to such key pieces of coordination as what the signal will be to get out of their seats to take the plane, and who will give this signal? Why no warning against proximity or mutual recognition while waiting to board at the airport? Why nothing about whether the attack should begin with taking over from the pilots in the cockpit, or the passengers in the cabin? Why nothing about what to do with the passengers after takeover, whether to keep them in their seats or move them to the back of the plane? The most natural interpretation of this document is that it is not a manual for action but a manual for motivation and control. The author of the manual is not concerned with security and coordination among the attackers, but with strengthening their resolve when it comes to killing passengers first and then themselves.

In brief, the manual is more a manual of prayer than a manual of action. It offers several kinds of mind-control mechanisms, notably a focus of attention in prayer and the promise of martyrdom. It aims to maintain a martyr's intention, not for vengeance or hatred, but for satisfaction of God's will. These same goals and many of the same mechanisms are found in the preparation of Palestinian suicide bombers.

Palestinian Martyrs

Nasra Hassan, a Pakistani woman and a Muslim, has interviewed over 200 Palestinians involved in "martyrdom operations" against Israel ("An Arsenal of Believers," *New Yorker*, November 19, 2001). Interviewees included young men who had volunteered as suicide bombers, organizers and trainers of the bombers, and the families of successful bombers. Young men are not so much recruited for martyrdom as selected from a flood of applicants that rises with every Israeli military incursion against Palestinians and with every Mossad (Israeli secret service) assassination of Palestinian militant leaders. Those selected must be over eighteen, unmarried, and without family responsibilities. Until recently the bombers were all male, but this barrier fell in January 2002 with the first suicide bombing carried out by a female, Wafa Idris, a 27-year-old nursing-aide from a refugee camp near Ramallah in the West Bank. Hassan reported:

> None of the suicide bombers—they ranged in age from eighteen to thirty-eight—conformed to the typical profile of the suicidal personality. None of them were uneducated, desperately poor, simpleminded, or depressed. Many were middle class and, unless they were fugitives, held paying jobs. More than half of them were refugees from what is now Israel. Two were the sons of millionaires. They all seemed to be entirely normal members of their families. They were polite and serious, and in their communities they were considered to be model youths. Most were bearded. All were deeply religious.

Except for the beards, this description might equally be a description of the 9/11 attackers.

Each Palestinian martyr is prepared for his mission by a 'trainer' and accompanied everywhere during his last week by two 'assistants' to support his resolve. A member of HAMAS described the preparation to Hassan.

A GROUP OF HAMAS SUICIDE BOMBERS PARADE WITH FAKE DYNAMITE STRAPPED TO THEIR CHESTS. SUICIDE IS DISCOURAGED IN MUSLIM TEXTS, BUT MARTYRDOM MAY BE ACHIEVED IF ONE DIES FIGHTING THE ENEMY. *(AP/Wide World Photos/Mohammed Zatari. Reproduced by permission.)*

> We focus his attention on Paradise, on being in the presence of Allah, on meeting the Prophet Mohammad, on interceding for his loved ones so that they, too, can be saved from the agonies of Hell, on the houris, and on fighting the Israel occupation and removing it from the Islamic trust that is Palestine.

With the exception of specific reference to Israel and Palestine, this might equally be a summary of the content of Atta's manual. Thus the motivation of Palestinian volunteers is very similar to that represented in the "manual": a promise of immediate reward in heaven and remission of punishment for sin.

Again as in Atta's manual, intention is crucial. Hassan quotes the spiritual leader of HAMAS, Sheikh Ahmen Yassin, as follows: "But these rewards are not in themselves the goal of the martyr. The only aim is to win Allah's satisfaction. That can be done in the simplest and speediest manner by dying in the cause of Allah. And it is Allah who selects the martyrs." When Hassan asked whether martyrs might act from feelings of personal revenge, a trainer responded that if personal feelings alone motivate the candidate, "his martyrdom will not be acceptable to Allah." This response is consistent with the lesson of Ali ibn Abi Talib: the martyr must strike, not from personal feelings, but for Allah.

The similarities linking Atta's manual to the preparation of Palestinian martyrs suggest a reconsideration of the origin of the manual. In its combination of religious and psychological sophistication, the manual points, not to Muhammad Atta, an architecture student, but to someone with considerable experience in preparing young martyrs. If not from among the trainers of Palestinian martyrs, the writer is likely to have come from a similar background in preparing martyrs in Afghanistan, Algeria, Chechnya, Kashmir, Lebanon, Pakistan, or Yemen. Although little noted in the Western press, all of these countries have seen martyrdom operations organized by radical Islamic groups since the dissolution of the Soviet Union in 1989. Perhaps best known is the suicide bombing in Afghanistan that assassinated the leader of the Northern Alliance, Amad Shah Masud, just prior to 9/11.

Perpetrators Versus Supporters

Our discussion of the manual began with the question of whether the 9/11 attacks can be understood as a result of hatred, in particular hatred for the United States. Close examination of the manual does not support this interpretation, and neither does Hassan's description of the preparation of Palestinian martyrs. The martyr is not encouraged toward anger and hatred and indeed is explicitly warned against these feelings as incorrect intention. Although it seems plausible that one emotion can overwhelm another, that anger or hatred can be so strong as to overwhelm fear of death, the evidence suggests that this popular interpretation is simply not correct. It is not hatred of the enemy that conquers fear, it is love of God and the promise of paradise.

A paradox still remains in this understanding. There is no doubt that many Muslims feel shamed and humiliated by Western policies, including not only Western actions in Saudi Arabia, Iraq, and Israel but also support for corrupt governments in the band of mostly Muslim states that extend from Morocco to Indonesia. After every Israeli provocation, for instance, Palestinian militants in HAMAS and Islamic Jihad are pressured for action. Hassan (2001) quotes a militant leader: "Fending off the crowds who demand revenge and retaliation and insist on a human bombing operation—that becomes our biggest problem!" The paradox therefore is that there is great anger in the street but not in the hearts of the martyrs.

This statement of the paradox is already the key to its resolution. The motivation of the martyrs is not the same as the motivation of the people they come from. The anger of Muslims against the West is the background that brings martyrs forward and remembers them as heroes, but anger does not suffice to drive out fear. The peculiar result is that the Muslim in the street feels more anger than the Muslim giving his life.

This interpretation is consistent with what is known about men who risk their lives as combat soldiers. Interviews with men directly from the front lines of World War II (WWII, 1939–45) found that only about 20 percent mentioned hatred of the enemy as helping them "when things got tough." Most often mentioned as helping were "thoughts of God" and "not wanting to let my buddies down."

Sentiments of civilians at home during WWII seem to have been much more blood oriented. From her reading of memoirs and letters from WWII, Bourke (*An Intimate History of Killing*, 1999, p. 148) argues that, compared with those in combat, "Civilians were more prone to articulate virulent hatred toward the enemy, leading many commentators to conclude that reading or writing about killing was more likely to stimulate hateful feelings than actual participation in the slaughter." Bourke offers examples of civilians who wrote to their friends and relatives in combat about 'brutal Huns' and enemy 'devils,' only to be rebuked by return mail from soldiers who found patriotic talk and hatred of the enemy to be a naïve glorification of the depressing realities of combat. Similarly, surveys in England during the blitz found that reprisal bombing of German cities was more popular in unbombed rural areas than in London and other cities that actually suffered the bombing.

The psychology of this negative correlation between sacrifice and hatred must await a different essay than this one. Here it is only important to note that there is evidence to support the idea, however paradoxical, that those sacrificing the most for a cause are least motivated by hatred. The attacks of 9/11 are not to be understood, at least for the attackers, as a form of hate crime.

Islamic Martyrdom

The critical concern with intention, both for the martyrs and their trainers, requires explication. The issue at the bottom of this concern is the distinction between martyrdom and suicide. Suicide is forbidden to Muslims, and Hassan's interviewees in Palestine would speak with her only on condition that she did not refer to suicide bombers. The partisan nature of the term, *suicide bomber,* is apparent in the fact that Europeans, who generally sympathize more with the Palestinians than Americans do, more often refer to Palestinian bombers as *kamikaze bombers.* A suicide bomber is linked to the psychopathology of suicide, whereas a kamikaze-bomber is linked to the desperation of World War II Japanese attacks on U.S. forces in the Pacific.

Both Mneimneh and Cook, in their discussion of Atta's manual, show that suicide—taking one's own life—is if anything more discouraged in Islamic texts than in Christian texts. A Muslim martyr does not take his own life, but loses his life in fighting and trying to kill the enemy. Although massacres of prisoners and civilians can be found in the early history of Islam, even under the direction of the Prophet Muhammad, later commentaries and interpretations developed Islamic prohibitions against killing prisoners or civilians.

Mneimneh (in press) cites a reaffirmation of these prohibitions, issued by the Islamic Research Council at the Al Azhar University in Cairo on 4 November 2001. "Islam provides clear rules and ethical norms that forbid the killing of non-combatants, as well as women, children, and the elderly, and also forbids the pursuit of the enemy in defeat, the execution of those who surrender, the infliction of harm on prisoners of war, and the destruction of property that is not being used in the hostilities." More recently, however, Arab reactions to Israeli operations in the West Bank have begun to undermine the prohibitions of the Islamic Research Council. Sheikh Tantawi, the leading cleric of Al Azhar University, changed his mind to support martyrdom operations against Israeli children, women, and teenagers until the people of Palestine regain their land.

The Islamic Research Council in Cairo is often considered to be the highest moral authority in Sunni Islam, but Muslims, like Protestants, recognize no central teaching authority such as the pope provides for Catholics. As Protestant authority is the Bible, Muslim authority is the Qur'an. As Protestant church leaders influence their followers by their scholarly status in interpreting the Bible, so Muslim leaders influence their followers by their scholarly status in interpreting the Qur'an and the Hadith. This status is subject to challenge, and the interpretation offered by the Islamic Research Council is challenged by an interpretation published by anonymous Muslim scholars under the title of "The Islamic Ruling on the Permissibility of Martyrdom Operations" (www.minna.com/ html/aarticlesmartyrops.htm). Cook (in press) translates the key passage as follows.

> "These examples, all based upon the *hadith* 'Verily, actions are only according to intentions . . . ' clearly support the notion that the verdict concerning the *shahid* [martyr] does not differ based upon who the killing party is, provided the intention is pure. So, one who has a bad intention and is killed by the enemy is deserving of the Fire, as would be the case if he kills himself out of pain. And one who has a sincere intention will be in Heaven, whether he is killed by the enemy or kills himself in error. And, one who helps in killing himself for the good of the religion will be in heaven.

In the end, the authors of the Permissibility Ruling conclude that classical Islamic texts imply approval for martyrdom operations so long as the act is based in correct intention and will inflict losses and fear on the enemy while strengthening the hearts of Muslims. The key to martyrdom is intention, and the emphasis on correct intention in Atta's manual is consistent with and likely flows directly from the Permissibility Ruling.

Comparison of Islamic and Christian Understandings of Martyrdom

The Ruling justifies suicidal attacks, including attacks on civilians, in a way that is likely to seem strained and illogical to non-Muslims, as indeed it seems to the majority of Muslims whose views are represented by the Islamic Research Council. In fairness, however, it must be recognized that Christianity has had its own problems and divisions in defining martyrdom.

Jesus put himself in harm's way by going to Jerusalem at the Passover holiday and challenging the Jewish authorities by calling the Pharisees and scribes "blind guides" and "whitened sepulchres" and by driving the moneychangers from the temple. The account, however, of his last night has him sweating and praying "Father, save me from this hour." Betrayed and accused before the Sanhedrin, Jesus is asked whether he is the Son of God and answers only elliptically: "You have said so." Pilate asks him if he is a king and he answers that his kingship is not of this world.

Although the original meaning of martyr is "witness," Jesus is surprisingly unassertive as a witness. Instead he makes his enemies work to convict him.

In the first few centuries after Jesus's death, some of his followers showed more enthusiasm for suffering than Jesus had. St. Ignatius, on his way to Rome to be executed (117 CE), wrote Roman friends to ask them not to intercede for him. St.

IT IS DIFFICULT FOR MANY PEOPLE TO UNDERSTAND THE MOTIVATIONS BEHIND USING ONESELF AS A HUMAN EXPLOSIVE. YET SUICIDE BOMBINGS SUCH AS THIS ONE ON AN ISRAELI BUS HAVE OCCURRED THROUGHOUT HISTORY. *(AP/Wide World Photos/Jerome Delay. Reproduced by permission.)*

Perpetua (203 CE) is described guiding the sword to her throat. St. Euphus (304 CE) rushed into the Roman prefect to declare that he was a Christian and wanted to die. Whether these stories are literally true is less important than the attitude toward death that they convey; the early Christian martyrs were not just indifferent to death, they reached for it. The understanding behind their enthusiasm was much like the compact described in Atta's manual: although others might be saved, only the martyr could be sure of Paradise. According to Tertullian, the early third century Christian theologian, "The only key that unlocks the gates of Paradise is your own blood."

Christian enthusiasm for martyrdom was later seen to need tempering with recognition that death should be God's call rather than human pride; martyrdom had to be better distinguished from the pride and sin of suicide. According to St. Cyprian (257 CE), "Since our discipline forbids anyone to surrender voluntarily," Christians "may not give themselves up. But if they are sought out by you, they will be found." Clement of Alexandria, an early third century bishop, found it necessary to teach actively against volunteering: "who does not avoid persecution, but out of daring presents himself for capture, becomes an accomplice in the crime of the persecution."

Perhaps the clearest expression of the Christian balance was the martyrdom of St. Thomas More at the hands of Henry VIII. Henry wanted an annulment of his childless marriage to Catherine of Aragon, but the pope wouldn't agree. Henry proclaimed himself supreme head of the English church, and an obliging Parliament declared Henry's marriage annulled. All English subjects were required to swear an Oath of Succession that recognized the annulment. Thomas More, Henry's friend, ghostwriter, and Lord Chancellor, refused the oath and was subsequently beheaded.

In the manner of his refusal, however, More did everything he could to avoid death. His was a silent witness. He did not argue the oath was wrong, or immoral, or indeed tell anyone that he rejected the oath. He only refused to sign it. He argued that in the law, silence is construed as consent. In the end, his lawyerly defense was not enough to save him, but his effort to make his enemies work to convict him was notable. In his reluctant approach to death, he was more Christ-like than the eager martyrs described in the centuries immediately after Jesus.

In sum, the Christian idea of martyrdom has undergone some fluctuation over the centuries, and the distinction between martyrdom and suicide has sometimes been not very different from that urged in the Permissibility Ruling. Similarly, Christian warfare has not always distinguished civilians from enemy warriors; examples go back at least to the massacre that accompanied the crusaders' capture of Jerusalem in 1099, and extend into the twentieth century with the deaths of millions in city bombing during WWII. Even today, the primacy of intent over effect is invoked for military actions that kill civilians; the current description of such casualties, as in the bombing of Slobodan Milosovec's Serbia or the Taliban's Afghanistan, is "collateral damage."

RECENT HISTORY AND THE FUTURE

The 9/11 attacks are not to be understood as the product of individual pathology or pathological hatred. Polls suggest that only relatively few Muslims may hate the United States, but even if the 9/11 attackers came from among those few, the attackers themselves, as judged by Atta's manual, did not act out of hate. Rather they understood themselves to be doing God's will; they gave their lives in a rush for paradise rather than for the satisfaction of punishing their enemies. This may be a common pattern, in which those not personally at risk feel more animosity toward the enemy than those actually fighting and dying against the enemy. Finally, the crucial difference between suicide and martyrdom is, for both Muslims and Christians, a matter of intent. Most Muslims do not agree that intent can justify taking one's own life or killing civilians, but, for both Christians and Muslims, it is an old and difficult question as to when good intention can justify killing one's self or others.

This question signals what is usually understood as a sophisticated level of moral judgment, in which actions are judged by intention rather than by effect. Most adults would agree that mistakes and accidents do not deserve punishment or reward, or at least deserve less punishment or reward than choices made on the basis of foreseeable consequences. The difficult case is one in which a choice, such as the choice made by the 9/11 attackers, has multiple foreseeable results, some evil and some good. Gaining paradise is positive, as is discouraging the enemy and heartening one's friends. Killing women, children, and the elderly is negative, as is taking one's own life.

The success of the 9/11 attacks reinforces the justification of suicide terrorism. Quite simply terrorism works. It *does* hurt the enemy and it *does* encourage the terrorists' friends. The increase in Palestinian suicide bombings against the Israelis, including in early 2002 the novelty of female suicide bombers, indicates how widely this justification is appreciated. Even this novelty is only local. The Tamil Tigers, in their fight for an independent Tamil state carved out of Sri Lanka, have for years been famous for their female suicide bombers. One of whom killed Rajiv Gandhi, former prime minister of India and another of whom nearly killed the prime minister of Sri Lanka.

There is no mystery about why and how people kill others for political causes; the mystery is to understand how people can be ready to kill themselves for such causes. Most of us who are living comfortable lives cannot take the first step in being ready: we cannot imagine killing ourselves. Recent examples, however, make this kind of imagination easier. All of us are going to die; 9/11 means that more will be willing to die sooner for a cause that can give meaning to life. As the strong get stronger, the warfare of the weak will try to match high-tech weapon systems with more human weapons.

BIBLIOGRAPHY

Bennett, W. J. "Americans for Victory over Terrorism," *New York Times*, March 10, 2002, p. 7.

Bourke, Joanna. *An Intimate History of Killing: Face to Face Killing in Twentieth Century Warfare.* New York: Basic Books, 1999.

Cook, David. "Suicide Attacks or 'Martyrdom Operations' in Contemporary Jihad Literature," *Nova Religio,* in press.

Hassan, Nasra. "An Arsenal of Believers." *New Yorker,* November 19, 2001, pp. 36–41.

McCauley, Clark, and M. Segal. "The Social Psychology of Terrorist Groups." In Clyde Hendrick, ed., *Review of Personality and Social Psychology,* vol.9. Beverly Hills, CA: Sage, 1987.

Miller, J. "Arafat's Wife Endorses Suicide Attacks Against Israelis." *International Herald Tribune,* April 16, 2002, p.4.

Mneimneh, Hassan. "Raid on an Indefinite Path," *New York Review of Books,* in press.

Mneimneh, Hassan and K. Makiya. "Manual for a 'Raid,'" *New York Review of Books,* January 17, 2002.

Pape, Robert A. *Bombing to Win: Air Power and Coercion in War.* Ithaca, NY: Cornell University Press, 1996.

Sarraj, E. "Why We Blow Ourselves Up," *Time,* April 5, 2002, p. 39.

Smith, Lacey Baldwin. *Fools, Martyrs, Traitors: The Story of Martyrdom in the Western World.* New York: Knopf, 1997.

Stouffer, Samuel Andrew, et al. *The American Soldier, Vol 2: Combat and Its Aftermath.* Princeton, NJ: Princeton University Press, 1949.

Telhami, Shibley. "Polling and Politics in Riyadh," *New York Times,* March 3, 2002, sec. 4, p. 4.

Clark McCauley

AL-QAEDA AND THE REACH OF TERROR

Al-Qaeda (Arabic for "the base") is a world-wide terrorist network of organizations and individuals dedicated to *jihad* ("struggle" or "holy war") for the cause of Islam. According to various estimates, there are anywhere from 5,000 to 15,000 individuals active in al-Qaeda cells in as many as 60 countries across the globe in Asia, Europe, the Middle East, North Africa, North America, and South America (see map). Terrorist and insurgency groups closely linked with al-Qaeda include the Egyptian al Jihad al Islami and al Gamaa al Islamiyya, Pakistan's Harakat ul Mujahidin, Algeria's Groupe Islamique Armée, the Phillippines' Abu Sayyaf, and the Islamic Movement of Uzbekistan. While most of the individual groups associated with al-Qaeda have local- or regional-specific goals to establish Islamic governments that would enforce *sharia* (Islamic law) in their countries of origin, the broader network of terrorist cells is responsible for acts of violence on an international scale, targeted primarily at the United States.

Much of the attention on al-Qaeda has centered on its founder and leader, Osama bin Laden. Information regarding bin Laden's involvement in international terrorism dates back as early as 1993, when the first terrorist attack on New York City's World Trade Center took the lives of six people and injured 1,042. Although there is no documented proof that bin Laden was involved directly in the planning of the attack, it was orchestrated by an associate of his, Ramzi Ahmad Yusuf, who had previously taken refuge with bin Laden. The U.S. government began to publicly identify bin Laden as an international terrorist in the mid-1990s, when revelations surfaced concerning his connection to attacks on U.S. military personnel

THE CONFLICT

The terrorist attacks in the United States on September 11, 2001, underscored the significance of and threat posed by the al-Qaeda terrorist network, comprised of individuals and groups in approximately 50 countries worldwide. The organizational sophistication of the simultaneous airliner hijackings is unparalleled in the modern history of terrorism, which includes a series of major terrorist attacks attributed to al-Qaeda dating back to 1993, and it was a testament to the network's strength and dangerous capabilities.

Political

- Osama bin Laden, the most prominent leader of al-Qaeda, has issued many statements indicating political grievances. These include the U.S. military presence in Saudi Arabia; U.S. sanctions against Iraq; and U.S. assistance to Israel.

- Bin Laden has also often employed more rhetorical language describing what he refers to as a history of "U.S. terrorism," including the atomic bombings in Japan during World War II, the treatment of native Americans during the settlement of the United States, etc.

- Bin Laden has not made specific demands to the United States or to any other country, but instead has issued accusations and complaints, giving the impression that justification for terrorist acts can always be created.

Ideological

- Al-Qaeda and Osama bin Laden have displayed a militant, cult-like ideology that employs Islamic religious ideas to justify the violence they propagate, albeit at the extreme fringes of this belief system and commonly unacceptable within Islam.

- Although the members of the group and associated organizations represent a number of politico-ideological backgrounds ranging from far-right nationalism to far-left communism, al-Qaeda members and associates share anti-West and anti-U.S. sentiments. Only through violence and terrorism, they believe, can they oust Western influence and cease U.S. support for their own governments that they wish to overthrow and replace with strict Islamic regimes.

CHRONOLOGY

February 26, 1993 The first bombing of the World Trade Center occurs in New York City. Six people are killed and 1,042 are injured.

October 3–4, 1993 Eighteen U.S. servicemen are killed by al-Qaeda-trained fighters in a firefight in Mogadishu, Somalia.

November 13, 1995 The National Guard Communications Centre in Riyadh, Saudi Arabia, is bombed. Two Indians and five U.S. servicemen are killed.

June 25, 1996 A bombing of the U.S. military housing complex, Khobar Towers, in Dhahran, Saudi Arabia, kills 19 U.S. servicemen.

August 7, 1998 Near simultaneous bombing of the U.S. embassies in Nairobi, Kenya, and Dar al Salaam,

Tanzania, kills 224 people, including 12 Americans and 38 Foreign Service Nationals. More than 4,585 people are injured.

October 12, 2000 A bombing of the USS *Cole* in the port of Aden, Yemen, results in the deaths of 17 U.S. servicemen.

September 11, 2001 Four suicide airline hijackings occur in the United States. Two planes are flown into New York City's World Trade Center, precipitating the collapse of all 7 towers. Another plane hits the Pentagon; the last, believed to be heading for Washington, DC, crashes in Pennsylvania due to a passenger revolt against the hijackers. Including those who died in the airplanes, an estimated 3,000 people are killed. Thousands are injured.

and assets in Somalia (1992) and Saudi Arabia (1995—96). In addition, bin Laden was tied to several unsuccessful plots to commit terrorist attacks, including plans to assassinate the Pope on a trip to the Philippines in 1994 and U.S. president Bill Clinton (1993–2001) on his visit there in 1995. Significantly, it was actually the United States that began identifying bin Laden's loose network as "al-Qaeda," a development that helped bin Laden to consolidate his organization under one umbrella. By bestowing upon this loose organization a name, the United States actually helped bin Laden achieve a level of fame and unit cohesion that might have otherwise been impossible.

On August 20, 1998, in the wake of the near-simultaneous U.S. embassy bombings in Kenya and Tanzania that killed 224 people and injured thousands, President Clinton amended Executive Order 12947 to include al-Qaeda as a "Foreign Terrorist Organization" (FTO). This order effectively banned U.S. financial transactions with bin Laden and al-Qaeda, allowed law enforcement to freeze any of their assets in the United States, and named bin Laden a "Specially Designated Terrorist" (SDT). On June 7, 1999, bin Laden was added to the Federal Bureau of Investigation's (FBI) "Ten Most Wanted List," with a $5 million reward offered for his capture. The U.S. government displayed his picture on wanted posters, matchbooks, and leaflets

distributed worldwide in nearly a dozen languages, making him a hero among his supporters internationally. It appeared that bin Laden was single-handedly taking on the most powerful country in the world, a perception that raised his profile significantly.

Several al-Qaeda suspects were arrested and tried for various terrorist attacks and plots both in the United States and abroad throughout the 1990s. On August 20, 1998, President Clinton, in response to the embassy bombings in Africa just 13 days prior, commanded air strikes against a bin Laden camp in Khost, Afghanistan, as well as what was believed to be an al-Qaeda chemical weapons facility in Sudan (although, in the end, there was no conclusive evidence of this). Nevertheless, bin Laden himself evaded capture and continued his campaign of terror from his base and safe haven as a guest to the tyrannical Taliban regime in Afghanistan. Attacks continued. Nineteen U.S. servicemen and women were killed when the USS *Cole* was bombed in the harbor of Aden, Yemen, in October 2000. Finally, on September 11, 2001, 19 al-Qaeda members committed the worst single terrorist atrocity in modern human history: the multiple suicide airliner hijackings in the United States killed approximately 3,000 people in New York, Washington, DC, and Pennsylvania combined.

HISTORICAL BACKGROUND

When the Soviet Union invaded Afghanistan in December 1979, Muslim scholars and leaders around the world were outraged and began to call for a jihad against the invading superpower. As a result, thousands of Muslim men primarily of Arab origin volunteered their service to assist the Afghan resistance fighters against Soviet troops. With logistical and material assistance from the United States (mainly through covert operations conducted by the Central Intelligence Agency), Saudi Arabia, and Pakistan, the Afghans and foreign fighters— or *mujahideen* (holy warriors) as they came to be known—eventually defeated the Soviet Union and it retreated in February 1989. This defeat was a catalyst for the collapse of the Soviet empire in 1991. The victory was celebrated as a triumph for God against the atheist superpower by the "Afghan Arabs" who had traveled to Afghanistan and joined the war in their duty to serve Islam. This motivation contrasts with the national and territorial defense motivations of the Afghans themselves and would later become significant in the development of al-Qaeda.

Rise of a Leader: Osama bin Laden

Osama bin Laden was among the thousands of mujahideen that fought in Afghanistan. From a wealthy and prominent Saudi family of Yemeni origins, bin Laden brought not only himself to the cause but also significant financial support. According to Abdullah Anas, an Algerian who knew bin Laden at the time, he was heralded among the mujahideen as one who had given up a luxurious lifestyle back in Saudi Arabia to commit his life to the jihad against the Soviet Union. And while the main organizer of Arab support for the Afghans, radical Palestinian scholar Abdullah Azzam, was focused on the single task of driving out the Soviet troops, Osama bin Laden had a grander scheme in mind that would eventually lead him to split with Azzam and develop his own recruitment and training camps, an important factor in the development of al-Qaeda.

Bin Laden believed that defeating the Soviet Union would be just the first step in a worldwide jihad campaign to eradicate the oppression of Muslims by repressive regimes everywhere. In Afghanistan, bin Laden's early jihad supporters included individuals from the radical militant Egyptian group, al Jihad al Islami, which was implicated in the assassination of Egypt's President Anwar el Sadat in 1981. One of al Jihad's prominent leaders, Ayman al Zawahiri, would later form part of al-Qaeda's leadership with bin Laden and

A BOY HOLDS UP A POSTER OF OSAMA BIN LADEN, LEADER OF THE AL-QAEDA TERRORIST NETWORK. A TRANSLATION OF THE TEXT ON THE POSTER READS: "THE LIGHT OF GOD WILL OVERCOME THE MARCH OF THE INFIDELS. THIS LIGHT WILL NOT BE EXTINGUISHED WITH A BLOW." *(© AFP/CORBIS. Reproduced by permission.)*

commit one of his lieutenants, Muhammed Atef, as a military commander to the organization. Significantly, al Jihad favored terrorism and violence as the means by which to wage this international jihad, a characteristic that influenced bin Laden's development.

Bin Laden's camp, referred to as al Masadah (the Lion's Den), developed into the base from which bin Laden recruited and trained his own fighters loyal to him and his cause. Living and training apart from the other Afghan fighters, bin Laden's initial group of about 50 mainly Persian Gulf Arabs operated entirely separate from Azzam's organization and headquarters, Makhtab al Khadimat (Office of Services). According to the Federation of American Scientists profile of al-Qaeda, other names attributed to the group have included: Islamic Army for the Liberation of the Holy Places, World Islamic Front for the Jihad Against Jews and Crusaders, Islamic Salvation Foundation (a charitable foundation set up to raise funds for the organization), and the Osama bin Laden Network. The president of the German Criminal Justice Ministry, Ulrich Kersten, stated in an interview with the daily *Die Zeit* that at least seventy thousand fighters from

AL-QAEDA LEADER OSAMA BIN LADEN, CENTER, SITS WITH HIS TOP DEPUTIES AYMAN AL-ZAWAHIRI, LEFT, AND MUHAMMAD ATEF, RIGHT. ATEF IS BELIEVED TO HAVE BEEN KILLED DURING A U.S. AIR STRIKE ON KABUL, AFGHANISTAN. *(© AFP/CORBIS. Reproduced by permission.)*

over 50 countries had been trained in al-Qaeda camps. Although this figure appears to be exaggerated and likely includes individuals who returned home to continue normal lives after the Afghan War, it depicts the influence that bin Laden and the al-Qaeda phenomenon have had.

Development of the al-Qaeda Network

Many "Arab Afghans" returned home after the retreat of the Soviet Union ready to spark jihad in their own societies. Groups formed and consolidated in Algeria, Egypt, Jordan, Saudi Arabia, Sudan, Syria, and Yemen, among other countries. Bin Laden returned home to Saudi Arabia for a short period but left the country in 1991 and was eventually stripped of his Saudi citizenship in 1994, due to his extremist views and attempts to radicalize Muslims there and in the region at large. He moved on to Sudan, where he set up a network of charitable organizations and businesses, including a bank, in order to raise finances for the jihad. Pressure on the government of Sudan to crack down on terrorist developments in that country forced bin Laden on the run again. He moved onto Afghanistan in 1996, where he was sheltered by the Taliban and set up training camps for militant recruits from all over the world.

In addition to the remaining loyal Afghan Arabs, young men were recruited from the Middle East; European countries such as Belgium, France, Germany, Italy, Yugoslavia, and the province of Chechnya in Russia; and Central, East, and South Asian states such as Indonesia, Malaysia, Pakistan, the Philippines, Singapore, Uzbekistan, and the Xinjiang province of China. Many flocked to bin Laden from what is called the "Arab street," which refers to poverty-stricken Arabs whose discontentment is ignored by oppressive governments. Some, however, were well educated, middle to upper class individuals raised in a variety of different societies and cultures, including the West. These intellectuals represented extremes of the political and ideological spectrum, from the right-wing nationalism associated with their lands of origin to left-wing communism.

A Radical, Militant Ideology

Although al-Qaeda members came from quite a variety of backgrounds, they all shared a belief that the West, especially the United States, was responsible for the power grip of illegitimate and oppressive governments in their homelands. By supporting governments that were either "comprising Islamic ideals or interests" or "oppressing and repressing their Muslim populace," the United States was an implicit enemy. Only through violence and terrorism, in their opinion, could they oust Western influence and overthrow those governments, replacing them with Islamic regimes that would uphold the sharia.

Bin Laden and al-Qaeda represent a militant, cult-like ideology that employs religious ideas, but remains at the extreme fringes of that belief system. Some scholars have linked al-Qaeda and Osama bin Laden's brand of Islam with Wahhabism, an austere, purist branch of Islam practiced in Saudi Arabia, which influenced bin Laden in his own religious development. In broad terms, Wahhabism seeks to create a society based on strict adherence to the Qur'an. Other views liken al-Qaeda to a religious cult. Indeed, the terrorists' versions of some of the fundamental Qur'anic teachings demonstrate a radical divergence from mainstream interpretations. For example, Osama bin Laden has misrepresented the concept of *fatwah* (a formal legal opinion), as it is devised in all Islamic schools of jurisprudence. In Islam, believers are encouraged to seek answers to questions they have about Islam by submitting them to an Islamic cleric, or teacher. The teacher, possibly in consultation with other Islamic teachers and scholars, issues a *fatwah* in response to the question, clarifying the issue based on the writings of the Qur'an. Bin Laden misused this concept by issuing his own "fatwas," which were neither responses to questions nor issued by Islamic leaders. The definition of jihad has also been tainted; it is in fact translated literally as "struggle," not "holy war." Above all, Islam teaches that individual human beings should struggle to be better Muslims for God. This is the greatest jihad to be achieved in life. Additionally, suicide is glamorized by al-Qaeda in spite of being forbidden by Islam.

Scholar Olivier Roy differentiates the Islamic radicalism embodied in al-Qaeda from that of other groups past and present. Roy argues that "there is a fundamental difference that marks a break between the activities of bin Laden's networks and previous Islamic radicalism: no political strategy whatsoever underlies these activities." Until the development of al-Qaeda, groups were primarily focused on achieving specific political goals. Roy maintains that al-Qaeda is "de-territorialized" and actually exemplifies the unprecedented globalization that began in the latter part of the twentieth century. Attracted to "the myth of the reconstruction of an imaginary *umma* (a Muslim community)," its followers have joined in bin Laden's jihad against the world without having a clear sense of purpose. In this way, the enemy is undefined with respect to a set belief system or political circumstances and may therefore shift over time. Most importantly, with no goal or set of goals to be

achieved, the terrorist remains perpetually disenfranchised and disgruntled. Reconciliation is not desirable and is, therefore, impossible. Terrorists act for the sake of terrorism itself, and al-Qaeda leaders continually fuel the flames of hatred.

Declaration of Jihad against the United States

Bin Laden has acted more as a symbolic figurehead, attracting individuals to himself and the network via his charismatic personality, than an actual commander of terrorist units. Still, he has enunciated a number of political ideas and demands which connect him and al-Qaeda to past terrorist phenomena. The U.S.-led Gulf War (1991) against Iraq and the establishment of U.S. bases in Saudi Arabia during that conflict formed the turning point at which bin Laden began to oppose his former ally in Afghanistan, the United States. In his view, the United States was "occupying" the holy land of Islam in Arabia, where the holy Islamic sites of Mecca and Medina are located. To add insult to injury, he increasingly saw the U.S. presence as a security force for the Saudi regime, which he viewed as inherently illegitimate as a representation of Islam.

On August 23, 1996, bin Laden issued his first "fatwa" identifying the United States as an enemy and urging Muslims to kill American military personnel abroad. As described in U.S. indictment S(2)98 Cr. 1023, he stated from his base in the Hindu Kush Mountains of Afghanistan: " . . . to His Muslim Brothers in the Whole World and Especially in the Arabian Peninsula: Declaration of Jihad Against the Americans Occupying the Land of the Two Holy Mosques [Mecca and Medina]; Expel the Heretics from the Arabian Peninsula."

He declared a second fatwa, this time in the name of the International Islamic Front for Jihad Against the Jews and Crusaders, on February 23, 1998, shifting his focus to include not only U.S. military personnel and assets but also civilians. According to *al Quds al Arabi*, bin Laden avowed:

> . . . for over seven years the United States has been occupying the lands of Islam in the holiest of places, the Arabian peninsula, plundering its riches, dictating to its rulers, humiliating its people, terrorizing its neighbors, and turning its bases in the peninsula into a spearhead through which to fight the neighboring Muslim peoples . . . .these crimes and sins committed by the Americans are a clear declaration of war on Allah, his messenger, and Muslims. And ulema [religious scholars] have throughout Islamic history unanimously agreed that the jihad is an individual duty if the enemy destroys the Muslim countries . . . On that basis, and in compliance with Allah's order, we issue the following fatwa to all

Muslims: The ruling to kill the Americans and their allies—civilians and military—is an individual duty for every Muslim who can do it in any country in which it is possible to do it . . . .

Bin Laden's "Policy Goals"

Through many statements to the press since his two fatwa declarations, bin Laden has enunciated a number of vague "policy goals" and complaints against the United States. They can be summarized as follows in order of assessed importance and specificity, according to his emphasis and repetition in statements:

- The United States must leave the Islamic holy land (the Arabian Peninsula).

- The United States is causing widespread suffering of innocent Muslims in Iraq through its continued sanctioning of that country.

- The United States supports Israel and is therefore responsible for the suffering of the Palestinians (a cause bin Laden began to champion only after September 11, when he received some support among the Palestinian population for the terrorist attacks on New York and Washington).

- The United States is a "terrorist nation." Bin Laden refers to past acts such as the U.S. atomic bombings in Japan during World War II (1939–45) as evidence.

- An "Islamic nation" must be established. This was alluded to in a reference to the Ottoman Empire (1281–1924) that stretched from Eastern Europe to Western Asia.

Bin Laden's political ideas and demands may be convoluted and vague, but taken as a whole they do add up to a kind of political platform. Still, many scholars question whether bin Laden would be satisfied and halt his terror campaign even if the United States were to change its policies or help to resolve some of the issues above in his favor. It is possible that al-Qaeda would only turn to other grievances and continue to find reasons to justify terror.

Operations and Capabilities

Al-Qaeda's operations and capabilities have proven to be complex and increasingly deadly—culminating, of course, with September 11. Many factors combined contributed to al-Qaeda's ability to achieve this sophistication, including fundraising and financial resources, organizational structure, technology and communications, and military training and innovation.

Perhaps even more significant than bin Laden's roles as figurehead and spokesperson for al-Qaeda has been his ability to establish a sophisticated financial system to raise funds. Bin Laden's personal wealth inherited from his father was alone estimated at US$250–300 million. In addition, he utilized his university business education and practical engineering experience to cultivate a wide range of businesses, charities, and wealthy individual contributors (including some government figures from countries such as Saudi Arabia and Sudan). Businesses that bin Laden built during his time in Sudan (1991–96), for example, included construction and transportation firms, manufacturers of sweets and honey, a tannery, banks, agricultural manufacturers, and camel breeders. In addition, he reportedly conducted business in diamonds in Tanzania and the semi-precious stone lapis lazuli in Uganda. In order to collect money under the guise of religious purposes, bin Laden also set up a number of Muslim charities around the world, including in the United States. Individuals, assuming that their money was used for benign charitable causes, often had no idea that they were in fact supporting a vast terrorist network. Lastly, al-Qaeda was heavily involved in the lucrative drug trade in Afghanistan, where the cultivation of poppies for this purpose was extensive. All of these elements together provided the organization with a considerable amount of wealth.

Along with the substantial financial resources available to al-Qaeda, its unique organizational structure allowed the network an upper hand vis-à-vis U.S. and other intelligence agencies. There was a vertical aspect to the organization, as Rohan Gunaratna has described, with bin Laden at the top of an hierarchy that included other primary leaders, including al Zawahiri and Atef. Below the main leadership was a *Shura majlis* (consultative council), to which four committees reported: military, religious/legal (to develop al-Qaeda positions on such matters), financial, and communications/media. While these were likely not as formal as one would find within a business corporation or an actual country, the very fact that bin Laden and the leaders organized along these lines reflects a sophistication of thought and planning.

More important was the horizontal nature of al-Qaeda. It is a worldwide conglomeration or network of organizations, cell groups, and individuals—a characteristic which makes it next to impossible to infiltrate and track down every al-Qaeda element. Gunaratna points out that "to preserve operational effectiveness at all levels, compartmentalization and secrecy are paramount." While military training was centralized within the camps in Afghanistan and apparently systematized

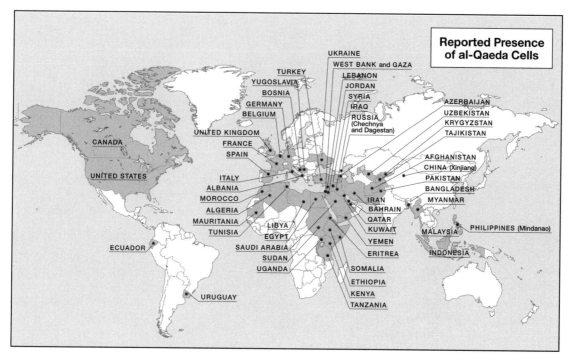

THE AL-QAEDA TERRORIST NETWORK HAS TERRORIST CELLS IN A NUMBER OF COUNTRIES AROUND THE WORLD. *(Gale Group.)*

according to a written manual (much of which was published by the U.S. Department of Justice on its website in January 2002), terrorist attacks were planned, organized, and perpetrated by very small groups of individuals. Most of these groups, referred to as "sleeper cells," remain dormant in the societies in which they live and operate for a substantial period of time. Some of the September 11 hijackers, for example, lived in the United States for several years, using the time to plan the attack and learn the skills they needed (in this case, piloting a commercial aircraft). It is highly probable that bin Laden himself most often had no prior knowledge about the logistics and timing of attacks. Many have also argued, for example, that the four (or possibly five) separate September 11 hijacking groups, consisting of four or five people each, were only connected through their leaders. By maintaining secrecy and group exclusivity and cohesion in this way, al-Qaeda has been able to operate underground and evade intelligence and law enforcement counterterrorism efforts.

In addition to organizational ingenuity, al-Qaeda has used modern technology and communications, including the media, in a limited but effective way. Although bin Laden's base and main training camps were located in countries lacking a sophisticated infrastructure (Sudan and then Afghanistan), important technologies were adapted

to the environment. Satellite communications have allowed al-Qaeda to speak with members and contacts throughout the world, to have access to modern computer technology and applications (including the Internet and electronic mail), to access international media (television, radio, etc.) in order to monitor current events in the world, and to maintain bin Laden and the group's international financial dealings. An official al-Qaeda press office reportedly existed in London until the man who ran it, Khaled al Fawwaz, was arrested in relation to the 1998 embassy bombings. Nonetheless, bin Laden has used the international media selectively to voice his beliefs and "policy goals" to the world and, most importantly, to gain attention for al-Qaeda and its jihad. Some have even alleged that bin Laden has employed hidden messages in media statements to communicate to al-Qaeda cells abroad awaiting instructions or information.

At the same time, the rugged and isolated terrain and lifestyle in Afghanistan—not to mention al-Qaeda's special "above-the-law" status in that country—provided the ideal, safe environment to train recruits and operate, despite its worldwide notoriety as a terrorist organization. Special terrorism training camps provided instruction in everything from military-style physical and weapons exercises to how to adapt to Western cultures so as to go undetected.

ALLEGED AL-QAEDA ATTEMPTS TO ACQUIRE WMD

October 31, 1997 The Arabic news magazine *al Watan al Arabi* reports that a "secret and dangerous meeting" took place in Sudan between bin Laden, Ayman al Zawahiri, Hasan al Turabi (leader of Sudan's National Islamic Front Regime), and others about the potential construction of a chemical and biological weapons (CBW) factory.

July 1998 The Italian newspaper *Corriere della Serra* alleges that members of bin Laden's "World Islamic Front for Jihad Against Jews and Crusaders" purchased three CBW factories in the former Yugoslavia in May 1998.

August 16, 1998 An Israeli military intelligence report is leaked that alleges bin Laden paid over £2 million to a middle-man in Kazakhstan, who promised to deliver a "suitcase" bomb to bin Laden.

September 25, 1998 A bin Laden aide, Mamdouh Mahmud Salim, is arrested in Munich, Germany, on charges of trying to obtain nuclear materials, particularly highly enriched uranium.

October–December 1998 Several reports surface that bin Laden was forging contacts with Iraqi intelligence officials, and that this contact potentially led to special Iraqi-sponsored al-Qaeda CBW exercises, such as training in the use of chemicals and toxins for assassination.

November 13, 1998 *Al Watan al Arabi* states that Osama bin Laden was engaged in a comprehensive plan to acquire nuclear weapons and reportedly gave a group of Chechens $30 million in cash and two tons of opium in exchange for approximately 20 nuclear warheads. This claim was uncorroborated.

December 24, 1998 In an interview with *Time*, bin Laden asserts that acquiring weapons of any type, including chemical and nuclear, is a Muslim "religious duty."

June 16, 1999 ABC News correspondent John McWethy writes that Osama bin Laden had constructed "crude" CBW laboratories in Khost and Jalalabad, Afghanistan.

February 2001 A key witness in the New York trial of the U.S. embassy bombing suspects, Jamal Ahmad al Fadl, testifies that Osama bin Laden tried to purchase uranium for nuclear weapons in Sudan in 1993–94.

November 15, 2001 The London *Times* reports that it discovered a blueprint for a "Nagasaki bomb" in files found in an abandoned al-Qaeda house in Kabul, Afghanistan. The U.S. government later reported, though, that such documents were not accurate and that al-Qaeda may have been "duped" into buying them.

March 23, 2002 The U.S. government reports that it discovered a biological weapons laboratory under construction near Kandahar, Afghanistan, which was abandoned by al-Qaeda when it was forced out of the area by the U.S. military. Allegedly it was being built to produce anthrax, but no biological agents were found in the facility.

Source: Monterey Weapons of Mass Destruction Terrorism Database.

Al-Qaeda has displayed a notable level of innovation in its military strategy and tactics. Simultaneously orchestrated attacks, such as the 1998 embassy bombings and the suicide hijackings of September 11, served to compound the effects—material and psychological—of each unique incident. September 11 witnessed a level of sophistication and originality previously unseen in the history of terrorism. The use of civilian airliners to destroy buildings was unprecedented and caused devastating results. Moreover, by striking both military and civilian targets, counterterrorism efforts were confused, and fear—both public

and governmental—increased all the more with each attack.

Last but not least, bin Laden's interest in weapons of mass destruction (WMD) has raised his profile internationally and boosted al-Qaeda's notoriety to new heights. Al-Qaeda has allegedly attempted to acquire WMD of all kinds: nuclear, radiological, biological, and chemical (see chronology). When asked in an interview with *Time* on December 24, 1998, whether he was seeking to obtain chemical or nuclear weapons, bin Laden replied that "acquiring weapons for the defense of Muslims is a religious duty. If I have indeed acquired these

A SUSPECTED INDONESIAN TERRORIST BELIEVED TO BE A KEY LEADER OF THE GROUP JEMMAH ISLAMIYYA, WHICH HAS CONNECTIONS TO AL-QAEDA, IS LED TO A HOLDING ROOM BY PHILIPPINE MILITARY POLICEMEN. THE GROUP ALLEGEDLY PLOTTED TO BLOW UP WESTERN EMBASSIES AND OTHER TARGETS IN 2002. *(AP/Wide World Photos. Reproduced by permission.)*

weapons, then I thank God for enabling me to do so." And in a November 7, 2001, interview with Pakistan's *Dawn* newspaper, bin Laden claimed that al-Qaeda possessed chemical and nuclear weapons as a "deterrent" against its enemies. While findings during the war against al-Qaeda in Afghanistan revealed that the network was in the beginning, experimental stages of attempting to develop biological and chemical weapons, there was no evidence that it had acquired any nuclear materials. Of course, many questions—including the unknown identity of the perpetrator(s) of the 2001 anthrax attacks in the United States—remain unanswered. In the end, the mere *possibility* that al-Qaeda had WMD was enough to spark widespread fear, as well as the diversion of significant amounts of resources to combat the threat of WMD terrorism.

Recent History and the Future

Since the attacks on the World Trade Center and the Pentagon on September 11, 2001, many new developments with regard to Osama bin Laden and al-Qaeda have taken place. On October 7, 2001, nearly a month after the attacks, U.S. president George W. Bush (2001–) directed military strikes against al-Qaeda camps and other targets in Afghanistan. As a result of this intensive interna-

tional military campaign, dubbed "Operation Enduring Freedom" by the U.S. Department of Defense, al-Qaeda was in large part forced out of its safe haven in Afghanistan, and the Taliban regime was forced from power. As of May 2002, an undisclosed number of al-Qaeda fighters were killed, and over 330 were captured and detained by the United States in a facility (first dubbed "Camp X-Ray" and then renamed "Camp Delta" after renovation of the facilities) at a military base in Guantanamo, Cuba. The United States believed that one of the primary al-Qaeda leaders, Muhammed Atef, was killed in Kabul during the fighting. Other leaders, however, including bin Laden and Ayman al Zawahiri, remain missing. Virtually all al-Qaeda camps in Afghanistan—including those located in caves in Tora Bora—were destroyed by aerial bombing.

While these developments have certainly damaged the cohesion and operational capabilities of al-Qaeda, there are many reasons to fear that this network will be difficult to eradicate entirely in the near future. These include:

• The loose, but internationally pervasive network character of the organization makes it difficult to keep track of the identity and whereabouts of al-Qaeda members.

- The fate of al-Qaeda leaders, including bin Laden and al Zawahiri, remains unknown.

- Individual cells worldwide are secret and self-sufficient.

- International financial assets potentially remain in the hands of al-Qaeda members and cells.

- Political and social conditions around the world continue to produce anger and resentment against the West.

Whether al-Qaeda can again mount a concerted and sophisticated campaign of violence depends on its ability to reconsolidate its capabilities and reestablish training camps and some sort of central base of operations. In this context, it is necessary that the United States and the international community work to eradicate the existence of lawless and failing states. Even though the Taliban has been ousted from power in Afghanistan, for example, the United States and its allies should support the creation of a viable and lawful government so that al-Qaeda (or other terrorist organizations) is not able to take root there again. Other unstable countries and regions such as Somalia and Chechnya could also prove to be future safe havens for al-Qaeda or other transstate terrorist organizations and networks.

While al-Qaeda has apparently had some contact with governmental officials from countries such as Iraq, Sudan, and possibly even Iran, there is no conclusive evidence that shows strong state involvement. Nonetheless, states looking to counter the United States or other countries might turn increasingly to terrorism in the future, given the relative success of al-Qaeda's operations. In light of the proliferation of WMD among hostile states, this could prove to be cataclysmic for the United States.

The degree to which al-Qaeda—or a potential future offshoot organization—will be able to surmount the ongoing U.S.-sponsored offensive against it remains to be seen. The following passage from a recent book attributed to Ayman al Zawahiri, however, indicates that these terrorists are not likely to give up easily:

> Liberating the Muslim nation, confronting the enemies of Islam, and launching jihad against them require a Muslim authority, established on a Muslim land, that raises the banner of jihad and rallies the Muslims around it. Without achieving this goal our actions will mean nothing more than mere and repeated disturbances that will not lead to the aspired goal . . . the dismissal of the invaders from the land of Islam . . . .This goal must remain the basic objective of the Islamic jihad movement, regardless of the sacrifices and the time involved.

BIBLIOGRAPHY

Bodanksy, Yossef. *Bin Laden: The Man Who Declared War on America*. Rocklin, CA: Prima Publishing, 1999.

Center for Nonproliferation Studies. *Terrorist Group Profiles: Al-Qaeda*. Available online at http://cns.miis.edu/research/wtc01/alqaida.htm (cited on March 1, 2002).

Cooley, John K. *Unholy Wars: Afghanistan, America and International Terrorism*. Sterling, VA: Pluto Press, 2000 (2nd edition).

Engelberg, Stephen. "One Man and a Global Web of Violence," *New York Times*, January 14, 2001.

Gordon, Michael R.. "U.S. Says it Found Qaeda Lab Being Built to Produce Anthrax," *New York Times*, March 23, 2002.

Gunaratna, Rohan. "'Blowback,'" *Jane's Intelligence Review* 13 (August 2001), pp. 42–45.

Mir, Hamid. "Osama Claims He Has Nukes," *Dawn* (Pakistan), November 10, 2001.

Orbach, Benjamn. "Usama bin Ladin and Al Qa'ida: Origins and Doctrines," *Middle East Review of International Affairs*, vol. 5, no. 4 (December 2001).

Pike, John. "Al Qaida (The Base), Islamic Army for the Liberation of the Holy Places, World Islamic Front for the Jihad Against Jews and Crusaders, Islamic Salvation Foundation, Usama bin Laden Network," Federation of American Scientists. Available online at http://www.fas.org/irp/world/para/ladin.htm (cited on March 24, 2002).

Al-Qaeda Training Manual, excerpts in translation. Released by U.S. Department of Justice, December 6, 2001. Available online at http://www.justice.gov/ag/trainingmanual.htm (cited March 25, 2002).

Reeve, Simon. *The New Jackals*. Boston, MA: Northeastern University Press, 1999.

Roy, Olivier. "Bin Laden: An Apocalyptic Sect Severed from Political Islam." *Internationale Politik* [International Politics], Deutsche Gesellschaft fuer Auswaertige Politik [German Society for Foreign Politics], December 2001.

"*Al Sharq al Awsat* Publishes Extracts from al Jihad Leader al Zawahiri's New Book," FBIS-NES-2002-0108, December 2, 2001.

Thamm, Berndt Georg. "Osamas ungezaehlte Gotteskrieger" [Osama's Unnumbered Holy Warriors], *Die Zeit*. Available online at http://www.zeit.de/2001/49/Politik/print_200149_gotteskrieger.html (cited on November 28, 2001).

Weapons of Mass Destruction Terrorism Database, Center for Nonproliferation Studies, Monterey Institute of International Studies, 2002.

Kimberly A. McCloud

SEPTEMBER 11, 2001: THE UNITED STATES IS ATTACKED ON ITS OWN SOIL

Tuesday, September 11, 2001, began as an unusually clear and bright late-summer day on the East Coast of the United States; yet before the day was over, the skylines of two of the nation's largest metropolises, New York City and Washington, DC, were obscured by ash and smoke from the largest terrorist strike in the nation's history. As officials tallied a death toll reaching into the thousands, all flights were immediately grounded by the Federal Aviation Administration (FAA); extra security precautions also shut down schools, shopping malls, and government buildings across the country. An attack unlike any other on American soil, the events of the day upended many common assumptions about the safety of its citizens and the ability of its government to respond to such a crisis. The day also marked a renewed scrutiny of the country's international relations; the world's lone remaining superpower after the collapse of the Soviet Union in the 1990s, the United States was now the primary target of terrorist objectives.

Although the terrorist attacks of September 11 ushered in fundamental changes in America's social, economic, and political terrain, the actual strikes took place in less than an hour, beginning with the midair hijacking of American Airlines Flight 11 from Boston's Logan Airport. At some point after the plane's 8:00A.M. departure as it climbed over upstate New York en route to Los Angeles, a team of five men, armed with box cutters and claiming to have a bomb on board, overpowered the 92 crew members and passengers and took control of the Boeing 767. Turning the plane south, the hijackers directed the plane toward their target: One World Trade Center (WTC) at the tip of Manhattan in New York City. At 8:45A.M., Flight 11 crashed into the skyscraper's north side

THE CONFLICT

On September 11, 2001, a group of 19 terrorists hijacked four passenger planes en route across the United States. Two of the planes under the hijackers' control crashed into the World Trade Center towers in New York City; a third plane crashed into the Pentagon building near Washington, DC. The fourth plane crashed in rural Pennsylvania after passengers attempted to retake control of the plane. The immediate death toll included 266 passengers on the four planes, 190 victims at the Pentagon, an estimated three to four thousand people at the World Trade Center disaster area, and the 19 terrorists.

Political

- Although almost every government in the world expressed unconditional outrage over the terrorist attacks of September 11, assembling a military coalition to respond to the events was a supreme challenge for the United States government. After intense negotiations with Pakistan, the neighbor of Afghanistan and one of the only countries to recognize the legitimacy of the Taliban regime, the Bush administration secured the country's support of a military effort against Osama bin Laden and his forces. Other nations in the region also agreed to allow U.S. troops to utilize their airspace or use their air bases for humanitarian relief operations.

Social

- The most devastating terrorist attack in history in terms of loss of life and property, the terrorist actions of September 11 also represented the largest loss of life on U.S. soil since the American Civil War. Concern over domestic security quickly became the most important topic of discussion in the United States.

Economic

- In addition to the devastating repercussion on the airline industry, other sectors of the economy were also affected by the terrorist attacks. Consumer spending dropped significantly, with the travel and tourism industries reporting some of the steepest declines. In October 2001, the first full month of reporting after the attacks, unemployment surged by a half a percentage point to 5.4 percent.

CHRONOLOGY

1993 Terrorists set off a bomb in a van parked in a World Trade Center basement garage. Six people are killed.

September 11, 2001 Two hijacked planes crash into the World Trade Center towers in New York City, which subsequently collapse; a third hijacked plane crashes into the Pentagon building near Washington, DC. A fourth plane hijacked by terrorists crashes in rural Pennsylvania.

September 12, 2001 The 19 members of the North Atlantic Treaty Organization (NATO) invoke Article 5 of the organization's charter and declare the terrorist attacks on the United States as acts of war against all NATO members.

September 14, 2001 The U.S. Congress approves US$40 billion in emergency spending and a $15 billion bailout of American airline carriers.

September 14, 2001 The Federal Bureau of Investigation releases names and photos of the 19 terrorists who commandeered the four airplane hijackings.

September 16, 2001 Pakistan publicly abandons its support of the Taliban regime in Afghanistan.

September 17, 2001 The New York Stock Exchange, closed since September 11, reopens.

mid-September 2001 An anthrax-laden letter is received in the offices of American Media, Inc., in Boca

Raton, Florida; one employee later dies from anthrax exposure.

September 21, 2001 President George W. Bush delivers his first major address to the American people in the wake of the terrorist attacks.

September 24, 2001 Executive Order 13224 is signed by President Bush to freeze terrorist funds.

October 2, 2001 The U.S. Federal Reserve cuts interest rates on overnight loans to banks from 3.0 percent to 2.5 percent.

October 7, 2001 Air strikes begin against Taliban forces in Afghanistan.

October 15, 2001 An anthrax-laden letter is found in U.S. senator Tom Daschle's office.

October 26, 2001 President Bush signs a counterterrorism bill increasing federal search and seizure powers.

October 2001 More than 30 anthrax exposures are verified in the United States during the month, with four deaths resulting from the attacks.

October 2001 Unemployment figure climbs to 5.4 percent in the United States during the month.

October 2001 The U.S. Commerce Department reports a 1.8 percent decline in consumer spending for the month of October 2001, the largest decline since 1987.

in the upper reaches of its 107 stories, setting off an intense fire with the twenty thousand gallons of jet fuel that it had carried for its intended cross-country journey.

With a daily population estimated at fifty thousand workers in the World Trade Center buildings, rescue efforts took on monumental proportions from the start. As firemen raced up the floors of the WTC North Tower, thousands of office workers who escaped the effects of the initial impact poured out of the building in an orderly fashion. Workers in the tower's twin at 2 World Trade Center also began to leave their building; some took to the stairs while others waited for elevators to take them to the ground. With imme-

diate reports suggesting that an air traffic control mistake might have sent the plane into its collision course, no one suspected that a second hijacked aircraft was set to attack the South Tower.

Also originating from Logan Airport, United Airlines Flight 175 was overpowered by a group of five terrorists as it ascended over New York State en route to Los Angeles. At 9:03A.M., as television networks began continuous coverage of the first air strike, Flight 175 crashed into the southeast corner of the upper floors of 2 WTC, killing its 65 passengers and crew members upon impact. As media commentators attempted to convey the scope of the crashes in their initial reports, emergency response teams poured into the WTC complex to locate survivors and assist in the evacuation of the area as other teams ascended into the buildings to fight the fires. Within minutes, the FAA shut down all air traffic at New York City area airports, and the Port Authority of New York and New Jersey closed all bridges and tunnels leading into the city. In an unprecedented move, the FAA also announced at 9:40A.M. that all flight traffic across the United States was suspended; all flights already in progress were ordered to land immediately at the closest airport.

Meanwhile, a third hijacked plane held hostage by a group of five terrorists directed American Airlines Flight 77—with 64 passengers and crew members aboard for a flight from Dulles International Airport in suburban northern Virginia to Los Angeles—into a collision course with the Pentagon, the headquarters of the U.S. military, in Arlington, Virginia, near Washington, DC. Upon impact at 9:43A.M., the plane ripped a 75-foot hole in the U.S. military building's west side and ignited an intense fire with its jet fuel. As an estimated twenty-three thousand Pentagon workers fled the building, staffers from the nearby White House also evacuated the area.

As the crisis on the ground unfolded, a struggle for control of a fourth hijacked plane, United Airlines Flight 93, traveling from Newark to San Francisco, took place between a team of four terrorists and the plane's 45 crew members and passengers. In the minutes since the hijackers seized control of the plane, several of its passengers had made phone calls to relatives and emergency officials and had learned of the fates of the other hijacked planes. Determined to prevent the plane from becoming another weapon of attack, a group of the passengers took a vote to overpower the terrorists. In the struggle to retake control of the plane, Flight 93 went down at 10:10A.M., crashing into rural Somerset County in southwestern Pennsylvania. Although everyone on board died upon impact, no lives were lost on the ground.

With the nation now on high alert, the earth shook around the WTC complex as the South Tower at 2 WTC began to list shortly before ten o'clock that morning. Although the building's innovative design by architect Minoru Yamasaki—with steel pillars serving as exterior supports for each of the building's four walls—had withstood the initial impact of the airliner collision, the intense jet fuel fire in its aftermath had softened the steel supports with an inferno estimated at 2,000°F. At 10:05A.M. the South Tower collapsed, sending tons of debris into the streets of lower Manhattan and taking the lives of hundreds of rescue workers

TWO AIRLINERS WERE DELIBERATELY CRASHED INTO THE TWIN TOWERS OF THE WORLD TRADE CENTER IN NEW YORK CITY. THE BUILDINGS COLLAPSED AN HOUR AFTER THE IMPACTS AND THOUSANDS OF PEOPLE WERE KILLED. *(AP/Wide World Photos/Patrick Sison. Reproduced by permission.)*

and office workers still trapped in the building. At 10:28A.M. the North Tower collapsed in similar fashion. The two tallest buildings on the New York City skyline had now disappeared in clouds of choking dust and debris.

Although the death toll fluctuated wildly as lists of victims were compiled and verified, an estimated 3,000 people died in the WTC attacks. Over 2,100 injured victims received medical treatment by emergency rescue teams in New York City. 190 victims perished at the Pentagon, as well as 266 airline passengers and crew members on the hijacked flights. For sheer loss of human life on American soil, nothing like it had been seen since the battles of the Civil War (1861–65). Adding to the physical damage of September 11, the 47-story building at 7 WTC also collapsed, joined by the 22-story Marriott Hotel at 3 WTC, two nine-story office buildings at 4 and 5 WTC, and an eight-story U.S. Customshouse at 6 WTC.

HISTORICAL BACKGROUND

Emergency Measures

At the time of the attacks, President George W. Bush (2001–) was holding a media event in a Sarasota, Florida, grade school to publicize his education initiatives. With the threat of more terrorist attacks hanging in the air, the commander in chief spent most of the day traveling back to the Washington area on Air Force One with a contingent of air force fighters accompanying the plane. When he finally returned to the White House shortly before seven o'clock that evening, President Bush prepared his remarks to the nation, which he delivered at 8:30P.M.

Although initial reports linked the terrorist groups on the planes to anti-American Islamic fundamentalists—with Osama bin Laden topping the list of suspected terrorist organizers—President Bush was careful to avoid any direct accusations in his address. Referring to the immense physical damage that had dominated media reports during the day, the president said, "Terrorist attacks can shake the foundations of our biggest buildings, but they cannot touch the foundation of America. These acts shatter steel, but they cannot dent the steel of American resolve." Explaining the motivation behind such acts, Bush added, "America was targeted for attack because we're the brightest beacon for freedom and opportunity in the world. And no one will keep that light from shining." In the rest of his brief remarks, the president announced that federal offices, which had been evacuated at 10:45A.M. that day, would reopen for essential business immediately and would carry on business as usual the following day. In his resolve "to find those responsible and bring them to justice," Bush also pledged that "We will make no distinction between the terrorists and those who harbor them."

The following day, the significance of the president's remarks became clearer as Osama bin Laden's name was firmly linked to the terrorist acts of September 11. Based in the Sudan from 1991 to 1996, the Saudi-born multimillionaire—who had his citizenship revoked by his homeland in 1994 for actively supporting global terrorist networks—was now operating out of Afghanistan. Bin Laden had previously fought with Afghan rebels in their war against Soviet occupiers in the 1980s and returned to Afghanistan in May 1996. Putting his considerable wealth and military experience behind the Taliban faction of Afghan rebels, bin Laden helped the group secure control of most of the country's territory in the civil war that followed the Soviet withdrawal. For the next several years bin Laden conducted additional terrorist operations from the sanctuary of Taliban-controlled Afghanistan.

Suspected in several bombings against U.S. military posts in Saudi Arabia and Somalia in addition to the U.S. embassy attacks in Dar es Salaam, Tanzania, and Nairobi, Kenya, on August 7, 1998, bin Laden was indicted by the U.S. Justice Department on 238 criminal counts in November 1998. In February 1999 U.S. intelligence agencies reported that bin Laden had gone into hiding in the mountains of Afghanistan; telephone intercepts indicated that his operatives were planning a series of attacks at several tourist sites, particularly places with special religious significance. Not that bin Laden hid his intentions; at a February 1998 meeting in eastern Afghanistan, bin Laden had openly called for a holy war against all Americans through the terrorist efforts of the World Islamic Front for Jihad Against the Jews and the Crusaders.

Security measures had reached a peak in the United States in anticipation of the millennium, which passed without any significant disruptions. The need for further domestic anti-terrorist measures remained unfulfilled, despite the obvious need for increased vigilance. Only approximately ten cities in the country had carried out any sort of drills to prepare for attacks by terrorists using weapons of mass destruction by 1999, and fewer than 50 cities had even instituted classroom training of emergency response crews to such an event. Even in the WTC twin towers—WTC 2's parking garage was the site of a bombing by Islamic terrorists in 1993, which killed six people and injured another thousand—security measures were lax. As Eric Darnton wrote in his 1999 book *Divided We Stand: A Biography of New York's World Trade Center*, "In the aftermath of the bombing, entry to the towers is preceded by a process of security clearance that ranges from perfunctory to elaborate . . . . but this process is ultimately of more psychological than actual deterrent value."

Of course, even the most rigorous measures on the ground at the WTC could not have prevented the tragic events of September 11. The failure of airport security measures, however, the weaknesses of which were a long-standing open secret among government and airline industry officials, outraged many Americans in the wake of the attacks. As Malcolm Gladwell wrote in his review of aviation safety in the *New Yorker* in October 2001, "Even as the number of terrorist acts has diminished, the number of people killed in hijackings and bombings has steadily increased. And, despite all the improvements in airport security, the percentage of

A MILTARY HELICOPTER FLIES IN FRONT OF THE PENTAGON, WHICH WAS SEVERELY DAMAGED WHEN A HIJACKED COMMERCIAL AIRLINER WAS FLOWN INTO THE BUILDING. MORE THAN ONE HUNDRED PEOPLE WERE KILLED AS A RESULT. *(AP/Wide World Photos/Ron Edmonds. Reproduced by permission.)*

terrorist hijackings foiled by airport security in the years between 1987 and 1996 was at its lowest point in thirty years." Indeed, the two airlines subjected to the September 11 attacks—American Airlines and United Airlines—had received 645 security fines from the FAA from 1998 through the end of 2000, with penalties amounting to over US$5.2 million. The performance of many private security firms hired by airlines to check passengers and baggage in airports was not much better. In one widely publicized case, Atlanta-based Argenbright Security, Inc., one of the nation's largest airport security firms with over 25,000 employees, was fined $1.2 million in 2000 by the FAA for falsifying training records, failing to perform background checks on employees, and hiring numerous employees with criminal records that included violent offenses; the investigation also revealed that at Philadelphia International Airport, more than 1,300 untrained Argenbright employees manned security check points.

Building a War Coalition

As scrutiny intensified over domestic security measures in the wake of the attacks, the Bush administration concentrated on assembling a coalition of nations to fight back against terrorist operatives. As bin Laden's two decades of rebel fighting and terrorist activity demonstrated, how-

ever, his forces were elusive targets. With numerous training camps within Taliban-controlled Afghanistan and active terrorist cells in countries around the world, bin Laden operated beyond the jurisdiction of any legitimate international tribunal and seemingly out of the reach of conventional military weapons. As former National Security Advisor Anthony Lake wrote in his prophetic 2000 book *Nightmares: Real Threats in a Dangerous World and How America Can Meet Them*, "Acting alone or in shadowy groupings like those of Osama bin Laden, these terrorists are harder to identify before they strike and to apprehend after they do." He goes on to say that, without any clear ties to foreign governments, such groups are unlikely to be affected by threats of retaliation. Additionally, without clear political goals, Lake asserts, the groups are unconcerned with popular reaction to their deeds. "The new terrorists are haters, not self-annointed heroes. Their aim is to lash out, to kill. And how better to kill than using weapons of mass destruction?"

The attacks of September 11 added an immediacy to anti-terrorist measures that the Bush administration used to build a coalition of nations for a long-range effort. On September 12, in an unprecedented move, the nineteen members of the North Atlantic Treaty Organization (NATO) invoked Article 5 of the organization's charter to declare the terrorist attacks on the United States as

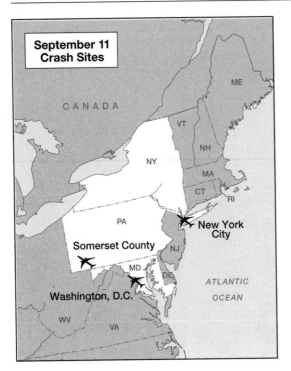

THREE OF THE FOUR PLANES INVOLVED IN THE
SEPTEMBER 11, 2001, TERRORIST ATTACKS TARGETED
THE WORLD TRADE CENTER IN NEW YORK CITY AND
THE PENTAGON NEAR WASHINGTON, DC. THE
FOURTH PLANE CRASHED IN A PENNSYLVANIA FIELD
BEFORE IT COULD REACH ITS DESTINATION, WHICH
REMAINS UNKNOWN. *(Gale Group.)*

acts of war against all NATO members. Even more
pivotal than NATO's support in building a coalition, however, was the crucial participation of
Afghanistan's neighbor, Pakistan, against bin
Laden. Although Pakistan was one of the few nations to recognize the Taliban as the legitimate ruling government of Afghanistan, its military chief
and president, Pervez Musharraf, offered his support to the United States on September 16. In exchange for significant financial aid and the promise
of eliminating sanctions against Pakistan, Musharraf's support also hinged on an American pledge
not to endorse the Northern Alliance—a rebel
coalition of militia groups that controlled about ten
percent of Afghanistan's territory—as the country's
next legitimate government. In addition to keeping an arm's length from the political tensions between Pakistan and the Northern Alliance, the
Bush administration also had to tread warily to
keep India, another regional rival of Pakistan, from
exploiting the political situation for its own ends.

The day after Musharraf abandoned the Taliban, a Pakistani delegation traveled for one last effort to convince the Afghan rulers to deliver bin
Laden to international authorities. The diplomatic

mission failed; one week later, on September 24,
Pakistan's entire diplomatic corps pulled out of Afghanistan. The Taliban lost another key ally when
the Saudi Arabian government cut all of its remaining ties with the regime on September 25.
Despite its increasing isolation, however, Taliban
authorities remained defiant and pledged to resist
any military efforts by the international coalition.

As the coalition grew in number, President
Bush solidified American support for what
promised to be a lengthy military effort. In one of
the most significant presidential addresses in recent
generations, Bush spoke to the American people in
a joint session of Congress on the night of September 21. In addition to announcing specific
counter-terrorist measures, including the establishment of a cabinet-level Homeland Security Office
under Pennsylvania Governor Tom Ridge, Bush
pledged to "pursue nations that provide aid or safe
haven to terrorism." He continued, "Every nation,
in every region, now has a decision to make. Either
you are with us, or you are with the terrorists. From
this day forward, any nation that continues to harbor or support terrorism will be regarded by the
United States as a hostile regime." Careful to distinguish between fundamentalist Islamic terrorists
and the overwhelming majority of peaceful followers of Islam, Bush was also careful to outline the
effort as a fight between civilization and barbarism.
In one of the most stirring moments of his address,
Bush declared, "By sacrificing human life to serve
their radical visions, by abandoning every value except the will to power, they follow in the path of
fascism, Nazism, and totalitarianism. And they will
follow that path all the way, to where it ends: in
history's unmarked grave of discarded lies."

An overwhelming majority of Americans had
already taken the president's message to heart.
Although one anti-Muslim murder against a gas
station owner in Arizona made national headlines,
violent actions directed against Muslim and Arab
communities in the United States did not reach the
high levels initially feared, though they did still occur. According to the Council on Arab-Islamic
Relations, a non-profit organization established to
promote a positive image of Arabs and Muslims in
the United States, a total of 1,717 incidents were
reported between September 11, 2001 and February 8, 2002. After September 11, however, most
citizens were far more interested in learning about
the religion of Islam than in speaking or acting out
against it. Bookstores across the country reported
selling out of world atlases and books related to
Islamic history; media coverage consistently portrayed the Islamic terrorists as non-representative

of their faith; and community events sponsored by interfaith organizations found an upsurge in attendance. While some Arab-American leaders were concerned that the detention of more than 1,000 individuals in the wake of the terrorist attacks may have heightened suspicion of their community, others voiced appreciation at the ongoing efforts of the Bush administration to portray Arab-Americans in a positive light.

Economic Aftershocks

With a 91 percent approval rating for his actions in the weeks after the September 11 attacks, President Bush received the broadest support of any president in modern American history. For an official who had taken office as a result of a contentious Supreme Court decision less than a year before, the political transformation was remarkable. Despite Bush's initial success at guiding American foreign policy, however, significant challenges remained for his administration on the home front. One of the most pressing concerns related to the economic catastrophe that faced American air carriers. In the four-day grounding of all flights within U.S. airspace, American carriers lost about $1.4 billion, according to industry estimates; however, considering the anticipated losses that the airlines expected to suffer in a sluggish economy, the actual losses were more likely between $850 million and $1.1 billion. Through the end of 2001, economists estimated that the airline industry in the United States would lose a total of between $2 billion and $4.5 billion as a result of the terrorist attacks.

In conjunction with a $40 billion emergency spending bill approved by Congress on September 14 to deal with the immediate needs of rescue operations, legislators also passed a $15 billion handout to American passenger and cargo carriers to forestall the potential collapse of the industry. The deal included $5 billion in emergency aid and a government guarantee of airline industry loans amounting to an additional $10 billion. In light of the aggressive lobbying by airline representatives so soon after the attacks, however, the bailout raised a storm of controversy. Industry observers noted that most domestic carriers were in abysmal financial shape before September 11, with most airlines operating at extremely high debt-to-capital ratios. Further, union officials noted that the bailout bill provided no relief for laid off airline workers, a crucial consideration in light of the massive layoffs announced by airline company officials within a week of the terrorist attacks. Finally, a sense that the airline industry had contributed to the tragedy by subcontracting crucial security duties to other companies—responsibilities that they were man-

PRESIDENT GEORGE W. BUSH EMBRACES A NEW YORK CITY FIREFIGHTER ON SEPTEMBER 14, 2001. MORE THAN FOUR HUNDRED EMERGENCY RESCUE PERSONNEL, INCLUDING FIREFIGHTERS AND POLICE, WERE KILLED IN THE SEPTEMBER 11 ATTACKS. *(AP/Wide World Photos. Reproduced by permission.)*

dated to perform by the FAA—caused many to question the integrity of the entire industry.

While the airline industry faced tough questions about its standard operating procedures in the wake of the September 11 attacks, its problems were made even worse by deteriorating economic conditions in general. After the unprecedented economic growth of the Clinton years—which witnessed the longest uninterrupted economic expansion in the modern era—the American economy sputtered throughout 2001. A growing number of economists before September 11 were predicting that the United States would be in a recession before the end of the year, and the terrorist attacks added to their gloom. Indeed, after the New York Stock Exchange reopened for trading on Monday, September 17, the following business week saw the worst Dow Jones average decline since the Great Depression (1929–39). Although the stock market made up some ground during the rest of the month, only about half the losses from that week were recovered.

Considering that two-thirds of the American economy was generated by consumer spending, economists were also worried about the possible disruption in consumer habits by the September 11

Reported Incidents Against Arabs and Muslims in the United States, by Category September 11, 2001–February 8, 2002

Type of Incident	Number
Airport Profiling	191
Bomb Threats	16
Deaths	11
Death Threats	56
Discrimination at Schools	74
Discrimination at Work	166
Hate Mail	315
Intimidation by Law Enforcement	224
Physical Assault/Property Damage	289
Public Harassment	372
Total Incidents	**1,717**

ARABS AND MUSLIMS WITHIN THE UNITED STATES FACED DISCRIMINATION AND SOMETIMES VIOLENCE AFTER THE TERRORIST ATTACKS, WITH 1,717 INCIDENTS REPORTED BETWEEN SEPTEMBER 11, 2001, AND EARLY FEBRUARY 2002. *(Gale Group.)*

attacks. When the figures for the month were released, it was not good news: according to the U.S. Commerce Department, personal spending plummeted 1.8 percent during the month, a drop that had not been seen since 1987. To make matters worse, unemployment during the month leapt to 5.4 percent, a half-point increase from the prior month. Although the results of consumer confidence surveys had been erratic throughout the year, they now showed that American consumers were decidedly pessimistic about the economy's direction.

Admitting that the economy had contracted for the third quarter, the Bush administration suggested that an economic stimulus package—including another tax cut in addition to the one the president had championed earlier in the year—might be submitted to Congress. In the meantime, however, the Federal Reserve Board took immediate action to reduce interest rates in the hope of reviving consumer spending. Announcing its ninth rate cut of the year in a meeting on October 2, the board's Federal Open Market Committee (FOMC) reduced the

rate charged to banks for overnight loans to 2.5 percent from 3 percent. In its press release, the FOMC stated, "The terrorist attacks have significantly heightened uncertainty in an economy that was already weak. Business and household spending as a consequence are being further dampened. Nonetheless, the long-term prospects for productivity growth and the economy remain favorable and should become evident once the unusual forces restraining demand abate."

Despite the FOMC's cautious optimism, others predicted that a return to normal economic conditions was wishful thinking. With U.S. borders at Mexico and Canada utilizing tighter security measures that delayed shipments into the country, American factories that had implemented "just in time" deliveries of components for immediate assembly faced serious obstacles to maintaining their production schedules. In the week after the attacks, DaimlerChrysler and the Ford Motor Company closed a half-dozen of their factories because of supply shortages caused by delays at the borders. With many countries in Latin America and Asia already in a recession, the U.S. economy also faced a more competitive global environment; economists noted that with consumer demand so low, industrial capacity in late 2001 had reached its lowest point since the Great Depression. Some experts even spoke of a global slowdown and predicted that the risk of a long recession in the United States was significant.

Public Health Concerns

While fears of a recession added to the country's long-term worries, public health scares triggered by anthrax exposures were a more immediate concern. A disease that could be introduced through the skin, by inhalation, or by eating meat from an animal tainted with the disease, anthrax was an easy bacteria to manufacture and transmit. Its spores were unusually resistant to heat and light and could survive for an indeterminate amount of time in the environment. Although skin anthrax had a 20 percent mortality rate if left untreated, inhaled anthrax was thought to be fatal over 90 percent of the time. Considered one of the most dangerous weapons of mass destruction, large stores of anthrax were known to be produced by Iraq in the 1990s. Heightening the suspicion, Iraq's leader, Saddam Hussein, refused to let United Nations weapons inspectors search suspected arsenals of biological weapons in 1998.

The first report of an unusual anthrax case in the United States was reported in early October, when Bob Stevens, a photo editor at tabloid pub-

BACKLASH: POST-SEPTEMBER 11 VIOLENCE AGAINST ARAB AND MUSLIM AMERICANS

Following the terrorist attack on the United States on September 11, 2001, immediate reports confirmed that Arab and Muslim hijackers were responsible for the airplane crashes into the World Trade Center in New York City and the Pentagon in Washington, DC, and speculated that Saudi exile and Islamic extremist Osama bin Laden was the mastermind behind the attacks. As the day went on, Muslim and Arab Americans braced themselves for possible attacks on their communities by fellow Americans in "retaliation" for the bombings. They were right to do so. By the end of the Wednesday, September 12, 2001, thirty reports of violence had been confirmed by the American-Arab Anti-Discrimination Committee. From September 11, 2001, to early February 2002 more than 1,700 crimes against Muslim and Arab Americans have been reported, ranging from verbal harassment and discrimination to murder.

In Illinois a group of more than 300 people descended on a mosque in a demonstration, chanting "USA! USA!" A Molotov cocktail was fired into an Arab-American community center in Chicago. Several cab drivers across the United States were pulled from their cabs and verbally and physically harassed. One man drove his car into the largest mosque in Ohio. Muslim women wearing *hijabs,* the head scarves that many Muslim women choose to wear as part of their faith, were verbally assaulted in the streets.

The violence, unfortunately, was not limited to Arab or Muslim Americans; nor was it limited to the United States. Stereotypes based on skin color and dress, especially turbans similar to those Osama bin Laden was seen wearing in footage from news broadcasts, were enough to trigger hateful acts toward non-Muslims, such as Sikhs, and people who are not actually from Arab nations, such as Pakistanis or Indians. An Indian

Sikh man operating a gas station in Arizona was shot and killed. Those close to the situation, including his family, believe he was shot because he wore the turban required by Sikhism. Three men were shot in Texas because of their appearance, apparently by a man who thought they "looked Muslim." The first victim, a naturalized U.S. citizen from India who was a Hindu, was killed by the gunshot. The other two victims were Pakistani—one died, the other was wounded.

Attacks occurred outside of the United States as well. A mosque was firebombed in Montreal, Canada, and verbal assaults towards children with Arabic-sounding names were also reported in the country. In Australia, too, there was an attack on a school bus, while a Lebanese church was vandalized with swastikas and an attempt at arson was made.

U.S. president George W. Bush made repeated efforts in speeches to the American people after September 11, to emphasize that Islam is a peaceful religion and that Muslims and Arabs should not be persecuted because of these acts by Islamic extremists. The reality, however, is that fear and anger from a shocking event such as the attacks of September 11 often result in a backlash on those associated with the group responsible, as was the case during World War II after Japan attacked Pearl Harbor and Japanese Americans were subjected to internment camps within the country.

People of all races, religions, and nationalities were killed in the September 11 attacks, including Arabs and Muslims. According to the U.S. Department of State, more than eighty countries suffered casualties from the attacks, including Argentina, Belarus, China, Egypt, Ghana, Iran, Kenya, Malaysia, Pakistan, Russia, Sweden, Turkey, Ukraine, and Yemen.

lisher American Media in Boca Raton, Florida, was hospitalized with flu-like symptoms. In a fortunate coincidence, Florida health officials had recently undergone training to spot anthrax exposure; however, Stevens was treated too late to save his life, and he died on October 5. While the Federal Bureau of Investigation (FBI) initially reported that Stevens was probably exposed to anthrax while on vacation in rural North Carolina, it soon became apparent that his exposure was deliberate. After a

second American Media employee, mail worker Ernesto Blanco, was diagnosed with anthrax, the company's offices were closed and all of its employees were tested. The source of the exposures was a letter sent to American Media.

One week after Stevens's death, another anthrax exposure was reported in the New York offices of the NBC television network when the assistant to news anchor Tom Brokaw was diagnosed with a skin exposure to the disease. Again, the

ANTHRAX: A WORLDWIDE SCARE

In October 2001, not long after the terrorist attacks on the United States, anthrax threats, both real and hoaxes, plagued the country. The fear of the deadly disease and possible infection, however, was international. People all over the world were in fear of contracting the deadly bacteria that had killed three in the United States. There were alerts and threats in Sweden, Germany, Switzerland, France, the United Kingdom, Australia, Brazil, and Israel.

People around the world were as panicked about the germ as those in the United States—with good reason. In Sweden four suspicious letters were found, echoing the manner of infection that occurred in the United States, where the germ was spread by a white powder inside a mailed envelope. German officials found suspicious white powder in the mailroom of the Chancellor's office. White powder was also found in a plane bound for Brazil from Germany. Suspicious mail was ultimately found in Australia, Israel, Switzerland, France, and Canada. In the United Kingdom a man was seen sprinkling a white powder in Canterbury Cathedral. All of these scares, unlike some of the U.S. incidents, proved to be either hoaxes or cruel jokes—not one of these instances of white powder turned out to be anthrax.

Even though there had been no confirmed anthrax infection reported outside the United States, people around the world were fearful of the possibility of the bacteria spreading around the world. The World Health Organization (WHO), in response to the alarming number of anthrax threats globally, insisted that people should not panic, but exercise caution and stay calm. The advice echoed that of health authorities and government officials in the United States.

source of the exposure was traced to an anonymous letter sent to the NBC anchor. With two media outlets now under biological attack, a stream of stories heightened the public's concern over the possibility that the assaults were related to a larger terrorist plot. When an anthrax-laden letter was discovered in the office of Senator Tom Daschle's office in the Hart Senate Office Building on October 15—resulting in the closure of several Congressional buildings for decontamination—it seemed clear to many that the exposures were indeed related. By the end of the month, traces of anthrax were also found in U.S. Postal Service (USPS) facilities in Kansas City, Indianapolis, Trenton, and Washington, D.C.

Although medical intervention had allowed more than half of those with inhaled anthrax exposure to survive, the outbreaks weakened the public's confidence in the Bush administration's ability to deal with an attack using biological weapons of mass destruction. First, the conflicting reports issued by public health authorities demonstrated that even experts knew little about how anthrax could be transmitted. Second, once fears of contamination were confirmed, government officials had responded with measures that were considered far too ineffective to deal with the contamination; by the end of October, after four USPS facilities were contaminated, unions representing postal workers filed suit against the USPS for endangering the lives of its employees by keeping the facilities open after anthrax cases were reported. Finally, critics noted that emergency efforts to evacuate and decontaminate affected areas had been uncoordinated and understaffed, pointing to a significant failure of the public health system to deal with such an attack.

Air War Begins

While the anthrax scares pointed to a weakness in the Bush administration's response to the terrorist assaults in the weeks after September 11, Americans continued to support its military efforts against the Taliban and bin Laden. By September 27, an estimated 1,000 airborne troops had settled into Uzbekistan and Tajikistan to prepare for the incipient air war against the Taliban regime and bin Laden's forces. On October 7, the coalition's air war in Afghanistan began against a force estimated at 40,000 Taliban members. In addition to about 90 active-duty American units, over 20,000 British troops amassed in the region to begin the assault against Taliban strongholds and terrorist training camps. Establishing control of Afghanistan's airspace almost immediately, a series of bombing raids during the month struck sites throughout the country, including the capital of Kabul and the Taliban centers of Jalalabad and Kandahar. Meanwhile, Northern Alliance forces slowly expanded their control over more of northern Afghanistan, coming within about 25 miles of Kabul by the end of October.

Coalition members insisted that civilian targets were avoided during the raids, and the Bush administration pledged an additional $320 million in humanitarian aid for Afghanistan as a goodwill gesture. The U.S. also sent 35,000 food rations to the country in air drops each day. Despite the concern for civilian fatalities, however, the air war carried on relentlessly; with a ground invasion almost impossible to conduct during an Afghan winter, coalition forces had a narrow window of opportunity to take control of the country. Although some Muslim leaders asked for a halt to the bombings during the holy month of Ramadan, beginning in mid-November, U.S. Secretary of Defense Donald Rumsfeld noted in an interview with the Voice of America that "history is replete with instances where Muslims have fought Muslims and Muslims have fought non-Muslims throughout all of the various holy days, including Ramadan."

RECENT HISTORY AND THE FUTURE

By November 2001, as the massive excavation of the WTC site proceeded, officials revised the final death toll from the attacks downward to between 2,950 and 4,167 victims in New York City. Together with the 266 airline passengers and crew members, 190 Pentagon employees, and nineteen hijackers, the final death toll from September 11 was well under the initial estimates from the tragedy. While the effective emergency responses in New York City and Washington, DC, helped thousands of potential victims survive the attacks, however, other losses were harder to control. In light of the continuing slide in consumer confidence and spending, the FOMC announced a tenth rate cut for the year on November 4, bringing interest rates to their lowest point in 40 years.

In addition to the long-range military efforts in Afghanistan, U.S. officials also unveiled a number of other initiatives to blunt the reach of terrorist organizations. As U.S. State Department Coordinator for Counterterrorism Francis X. Taylor remarked in a speech before the National Foreign Policy Conference for Leaders of Nongovernmental Organizations on October 26, "Our efforts include gathering and increased sharing of intelligence, rooting out terrorist cells, assisting countries to tighten their border security, good law enforcement, and identifying and disrupting terrorist flows." That same day Congress passed a counterterrorist bill that gave increased search and seizure powers to federal investigators. In addition to allowing the seizure of suspects' voice mail messages, the new law gave judges the authority to issue nationwide search warrants to obtain email transmissions from Internet service providers. Federal agents were given more latitude to search homes and businesses without giving notice to their owners. Federal authorities also began to search out financial holdings linked to terrorist networks and froze dozens of assets under Executive Order 13224, signed by President Bush on September 24. During the following month, at least $300 million in funds linked to bin Laden were frozen by the U.S. government.

While some critics looked upon the enlargement of federal powers as an infringement upon civil liberties, others continued to call for a greater federal response to the aftermath of September 11. In addition to the public health anxieties over anthrax, many Americans continued to worry about the safety of airline travel, particularly after persistent reports of lax procedures by security personnel. Placing airline security operations under federal control came under serious discussion in Congress, with several members pledging support to such a measure. As the *Economist* noted in an October 27 review of the American scene, "People realize that, after September 11th, there is no alternative to government action to deal with the problems being unleashed by terrorism."

BIBLIOGRAPHY

Adler, Jerry. "Ground Zero." *Newsweek*, September 24, 2001, p. 72.

"Airline Civil Penalties for U.S. Carriers." About Air Travel. Available online at http://www.airtravel.about.com/library/security/nsecurityfines.htm (cited November 6, 2001).

"America the Sensible." *Economist*, October 27, 2001, p. 34.

Arndt, Michael, et al. "An Airline Bailout—with Strings Attached." *Business Week*, October 8, 2001.

"Avoiding a Dark Winter." *Economist*, October 27, 2001, p. 29.

Barnaby, Wendy. *The Plague Makers: The Secret World of Biological Warfare*. London: Satin Publications, Ltd., 1999.

Begley, Sharon. "Protecting America: The Top 10 Priorities." *Newsweek*, November 5, 2001, p. 26.

———. "Unmasking Bioterror." *Newsweek*, October 8, 2001, 20.

"Big Government Is Back." *Economist*, September 29, 2001, p. 35.

"Blair: Key Quotes," BBC News, October 2, 2001. Available online at http://news.bbc.co.uk/hi/english/uk_politics/newsid_1575000/1575434.stm (cited November 2, 2001).

Bush, George W. "Address to a Joint Session of Congress and the American People," Washington, DC: September 21, 2001. *Guardian Unlimited*. Available online at http://www.guardian.co.uk/Print/0,3858,4261868,00.html (cited October 30, 2001).

———. "Address to the American People," Washington, DC: September 11, 2001. CNN. Available online at http://www.cnn.com/2001/US/09/11/bush.speech.text/ (cited November 6, 2001).

Curry, Tom, et al. "Bush Signs Counterterrorism Bill." MSNBC.

Darton, Eric. *Divided We Stand: A Biography of New York's World Trade Center.* New York: Basic Books, 1999.

Federal Reserve Press Release, October 2, 2001. Available online at http://www.federalreserve.gov/boarddocs/press/general/2001/20011002/default.htm (cited November 5, 2001).

Fernea, Elizabeth Warnock, and Robert A. Fernea. *The Arab World: Forty Years of Change.* New York: Anchor Books, 1997.

Fineman, Howard. "'Over There' is Here." *Newsweek,* October 22, 2001, 24.

Gay, Kathlyn. *Silent Death: The Threat of Biological and Chemical Warfare.* Brookfield, CT: Twenty-First Century Books, 2001.

Gladwell, Malcolm. "Safety in the Skies." *New Yorker,* October 1, 2001.

Halberstam, David. "Who We Are." *Vanity Fair,* November 2001, 2.

Herzberg, Hendrik, and David Remnick. "The Trap." *New Yorker,* October 1, 2001.

Hoveyda, Fereydoun. *The Broken Crescent: The 'Threat' of Militant Islamic Fundamentalism.* Westport, Connecticut: Praeger Publishers, 1998.

Hudson, Mike. "Fed Banks on 9th Rate Cut to Spur Consumer Spending." *Detroit News,* October 2, 2001.

Hudson, Mike. "Fed Expected to Cut Rates 10th Time." *Detroit News,* November 4, 2001.

Lake, Anthony. *Nightmares: Real Threats in a Dangerous World and How America Can Meet Them.* Boston: Little, Brown and Company, 2000.

"Last World Trade Center Bombing Conspirator Sentenced," CNN: April 3, 1998. Available online at http://www.cnn.com/US/9804/03/wtc.bombing/ (cited November 3, 2001).

Lynch, Jack, and Michael Brick. "Fed Makes 9th Rate Cut This Year in Effort to Revive Economy." *New York Times,* October 2, 2001.

Miller, Judith, et al. *Germs: Biological Weapons and America's Secret War.* New York: Simon and Schuster, 2001.

Remnick, David, et al. "From Our Correspondents." *New Yorker,* September 11, 2001.

"The Risks Are Worsening." *Economist,* October 20, 2001, p. 12.

Roy, Olivier. *The Failure of Political Islam.* Cambridge: Harvard University Press, 1994.

Song, Sora, and Cathy Booth Thomas. "Osama Will Pay. This Time in Cash." *Time,* October 12, 2001, p. 22.

Taylor, Francis X. "Remarks before the National Foreign Policy Conference for Leaders of Nongovernmental Organizations," October 26, 2001. U.S. Department of State, Bureau of Public Affairs. Available online at http://www.state.gov/s/ct/rls/2001/5773pf.htm (cited October 30, 2001).

"Trade Center Death Toll 'Lower'." BBC News, October 26, 2001. Available online at http://news.bbc.co.uk/hi/english/world/americas/newsid_1620000/1620835.stm. (cited November 5, 2001)

Updike, John, et al. "First Reactions." *New Yorker,* September 24, 2001.

U.S. Department of Defense. "Interview with Donald H. Rumsfeld," October 23, 2001. Available online at http://www.defenselink.mil/news/Oct2001/t10232001_t1023voa.html (cited November 8, 2001).

"U.S. Personal Spending Drops." CNN-Money Magazine, November 1, 2001. Available online at http://money.cnn.com/2001/11/01/economy/economy/ (cited November 5, 2001).

U.S. Senate Joint Economic Committee, Democratic Staff. "Assessing Losses for the Airline Industry and Its Workers in the Aftermath of the Terrorist Attacks." United States Senate Joint Economic Committee, October 3, 2001.

Weaver, Mary Anne. "The Real bin Laden." *New Yorker,* January 24, 2001.

White, Norval, and Elliot Willensky, eds. *American Institute of Architects Guide to New York City.* New York: Three Rivers Press, 2000.

"The World Trade Center New York." The World Trade Center New York Web Site. (cited November 5, 2001).

Zakaria, Fareed. "Time to Save 'Just in Time'." *Newsweek,* November 12, 2001, p. 38.

———. "Why Do They Hate Us?" *Newsweek,* October 15, 2001, p. 22.

Timothy G. Borden

STATE SPONSORED TERRORISM

In his State of the Union address on January 29, 2002, President George W. Bush added a new concept to the international terrorism lexicon by coining the phrase "axis of evil"—a specific reference to North Korea, Iran, and Iraq. After referring to weapons of mass destruction in relation to North Korea, Iran, and Iraq, as well as other difficulties with these nations, President Bush stated, "States like these, and their terrorist allies, constitute an axis of evil, arming to threaten the peace of the world."

"Terrorism is premeditated, politically motivated violence perpetrated against non-combatant targets by subnational groups or clandestine agents, usually intended to influence an audience." This definition, in U.S. Code, Section 2656f(d), sees terrorism as the actions of individuals or groups or organizations designed to instill fear or terror for the purpose of seeking a change in the perception or the policy of individuals, groups, or states. Terrorism, which has taken numerous shapes and forms, has grown to include radical states that sponsor or support terrorist activity as tools of their own foreign policy. A state sponsor is a government that supports an actor in the performance of an act or acts of terrorism.

Terrorism has become a tool of some states. A state determines that its interests are served by the actions of terrorist groups or organizations. The state then provides the means for the terrorist organization to pursue its objectives that will, in turn, facilitate the objectives or goals of the state. State sponsored terrorism seeks to achieve state ends or objectives through means other than the use of traditional force, namely war. Why terrorism rather than war? The state sponsor makes a decision that the use of conventional armed forces

THE CONFLICT

Terrorism has grown beyond extremist groups to also include radical states that sponsor or support terrorist activity as tools of their own foreign policy. A state sponsor is a government that supports an actor in the performance of an act or acts of terrorism. U.S. President George W. Bush stated in his 2002 State of the Union address that "States like these, and their terrorist allies, constitute an axis of evil, arming to threaten the peace of the world." Such words indicate the seriousness of and renewed attention directed at terrorism and those who sponsor it. In the wake of the September 11, 2001, attacks, the international community is placing intense scrutiny and pressure on state sponsors to end their support of terrorism. Iran, Iraq, Syria, Libya, Cuba, North Korea, and Sudan are the seven states currently designated by the United States as state sponsors of international terrorism.

Political

- A nation, or state, may determine that its interests are served by the actions of terrorist groups or organizations and will provide means for the terrorist organization to pursue its activities with the intent that such activity will also facilitate the state's objectives or goals.

- Each year the U.S. Secretary of Commerce, in consultation with the Secretary of State, provides Congress with a list of countries that support international terrorism, and getting off the list is difficult.

- Actions against states that sponsor terrorism can be difficult to implement and there is often debate about their efficacy.

Economic

- Condemnation of state sponsors' actions by individual states or the international community may take the form of economically harmful boycotts or embargoes.

Military

- In the wake of the September 11, 2001, attacks, there has been growing sentiment in the U.S. administration that military action be taken against state sponsors. This controversial action is under much debate within the United States and the international community.

CHRONOLOGY:

April 1, 1979 The Islamic Republic of Iran is declared.

November 4, 1979 American hostages are seized in the U.S. embassy in Tehran.

November 14, 1979 U.S. President Jimmy Carter freezes $12 billion in Iranian assets.

April 15–16, 1986 U.S. planes bomb Libya in reprisal for Libya's role in the bombing of a Berlin disco in which two American servicemen were killed.

October 29, 1987 U.S. president Ronald Reagan imposes the ban on Iranian imports.

July 1988 The United States mistakenly shoots down an Iranian airliner over the Persian Gulf, believing it to be a military aircraft.

December 21, 1988 A bomb explodes on Pan Am Flight 103 bound from London to New York. All 259 people aboard and 11 on the ground are killed as wreckage crashes on Lockerbie, a small town in Scotland. The United States first suspects Iran as having a hand in the explosion, then Syria.

November 13, 1991 Britain and the United States charge two Libyan agents, Abdel Basset Ali Megrahi, and Lamen Khalifa Fhimah with the Pan Am bombing.

January 21, 1992 UN Security Council Resolution 731 urges Libyan leader Muammar Qadhafi to comply with requests for the extradition of suspects in the Lockerbie bombing.

March 31, 1992 The UN Security Council imposes an air travel and arms embargo on Libya, in an effort to pressure Libya to extradite the Lockerbie suspects.

February 26, 1993 An explosion occurs at the World Trade Center in New York City.

August 19, 1993 Sudan is put on the U.S. list of states supporting terrorism.

December 1, 1993 The UN Security Council adds sanctions on Libya, freezing its foreign assets and banning sale of oil industry equipment. Libya, however, continues its refusal to hand over the Lockerbie suspects.

August 5, 1996 Congress passes the Iran and Libya Sanctions Act (ILSA).

May 23, 1997 Mohammed Khatami, a moderate, is elected president of the Islamic Republic of Iran.

August 24, 1998 The United States and Britain make a formal offer to Libya for a trial of the two suspects in the Netherlands under Scottish law. Libya later accepts the offer.

September 18, 1998 The Netherlands and Britain sign an accord allowing the trial to be held at Camp Zeist in the Netherlands.

April 5, 1999 The United Nations suspends sanctions against Libya.

January 2002 President George W. Bush identifies North Korea, Iraq and Iran as an "axis of evil."

April 1, 2002 U.S. Secretary of Defense Donald Rumsfeld focuses on Iran, Iraq, and Syria as terrorism sponsors and supporters.

is inappropriate, unlikely to achieve the objective, too risky, too costly, or too difficult for one reason or another. The support of a group to attack the enemy through terrorist acts then becomes the more appropriate choice. It is a "cost-effective" method of using force to accomplish a goal. Those that are sponsored by states gain additional capability to carry out larger scale and more deadly attacks than other terrorists because of the additional resources at their disposal.

What Do State Sponsors Do?

State sponsors are enablers that provide the terrorists (whether individuals, groups, or organi-

zations) with the ability to carry out their acts. State sponsors provide a range of support. To continue their activities and perform their operations, terrorists require funding, sometimes small amounts, oftentimes more substantial amounts of money. Some terrorist organizations have engaged in illegal activities to obtain the necessary funds, e.g., robberies, extortion, ransom, etc.; others have resorted to the siphoning of funds from related charitable organizations, sometimes creating organizations whose primary purpose is to raise funds for the terrorist activities. When their own techniques prove insufficient, or when they determine it is to their advantage, the terrorists can, and often do, turn to state sponsors for the funding they need to continue their operations. States, in turn, can utilize their financial leverage to convince terrorist groups to perform the actions the states deem desirable.

Training and training facilities are required by terrorists and a state sponsor can readily arrange the necessary facilities and those that will train the terrorists. The state can also provide offices and other facilities required by the terrorists in which they can plan, prepare, coordinate, and generally ensure the success of their operations. The sponsor can provide a refuge or safe haven to avoid rule of law before and after the attack, help raise or provide the funds necessary for the terrorists in preparation for and in carrying out the terrorist operation, and provide access to other sponsors and groups or individuals willing to endorse or assist the terrorists. Additionally, state sponsors supply a source of weapons and a means to transport them, such as through the diplomatic pouch and the use of state airlines. States have broad and ready access to essential equipment, including weapons that the terrorists can employ to their benefit. In addition, logistic support is often essential as terrorists seek to move to their targets and may require assistance to move themselves or their weapons to an appropriate location. Travel and identification documents required for international movement are essential to the terrorist as well and the state sponsor can readily provide these as needed.

In many instances the actions of the terrorist would have been difficult if not impossible without the aid and support of the state sponsor. An example was the use by Iran's government of young militants to take the U.S. embassy and seize hostages in 1979. Similarly Nizar Hindawi's effort to plant a bomb on a plane at Heathrow airport in London, England, in 1986 would have been impossible without Syrian government assistance.

Sponsorship Motivation

State sponsors are motivated by a number of factors, some of which intersect. There are often political, and sometimes ideological and religious factors, involved in the determination to sponsor terrorism. Defeat by an enemy in conventional war might trigger a desire to retaliate through terrorism, such as Syria supporting attacks against Israel because of defeat in the Arab-Israeli wars. A desire for a state to seek to recoup losses in combat with the terrorist target—an example being Syria supporting groups to get a response from Israel in regaining the Golan Heights lost by Syria to Israel in the 1967 Arab-Israeli War.

Often state sponsorship is to achieve political objectives after a failure to do so through conventional political, diplomatic, or military means. Thus, terrorists are cheaper than the military. There is also a series of specific reasons that prevail, such as ideological, religious, state security, regime security, and various tactical and strategic objectives.

HISTORICAL BACKGROUND

United States Designation of State Sponsors

Each year, under the provisions of Section 6(j) of the Export Administration Act of 1979, as amended, the U.S. secretary of commerce in consultation with the secretary of state provides Congress with a list of countries that support international terrorism. Each determination under Section 6(j) of the Act must also be published in the Federal Register. Section 6(j) stipulates that a validated license shall be required for the export of goods and technology to any country on the secretary's list and that the secretary of commerce and the secretary of state must notify the House of Representatives' Committee on Foreign Affairs, the Senate Committee on Banking, Housing, and Urban Affairs, and the Senate Committee on Foreign Relations at least 30 days before issuing any validated license required by this act.

Paragraph 6(j)(4) further states that once a country is put on the terrorist list, the determination may not be rescinded unless the president submits a report to the committees mentioned above. The president's report must certify that there has been a fundamental change in the leadership and policies of the government of the country concerned (this means an actual change of government as a result of an election, coup, or some other means); the new government is not supporting acts of international terrorism; the new government has provided assurances that it will not support acts of international terrorism in the future. When the same government is in power, the president's report must justify the rescission and certify that the government concerned has not provided support for international terrorism during the preceding six-month period; and the government concerned has provided assurances that it will not support acts of international terrorism in the future. Congress can then either let the president's action take effect or seek to block it, perhaps over the president's veto. Congress could also pass a joint resolution against the action, but this would also require the president's signature to have effect.

FIDEL CASTRO SPEAKS DURING A RALLY AGAINST
TERRORISM IN HAVANA, CUBA, ON OCTOBER 6, 2001.
CUBA IS INCLUDED ON THE U.S. GOVERNMENT'S LIST
OF STATE SPONSORS OF TERRORISM. *(AP/Wide World
Photos/Jose Goitia. Reproduced by permission.)*

The congressionally mandated designation of
state sponsors of terrorism by the United States—
and the imposition of sanctions—is a mechanism
for isolating states that use terrorism as a means of
achieving political objectives. The criteria are not
clear-cut for listing a state. The U.S. Department
of State determines the listing (or delisting) of a
state sponsor based on the broad determination of
a significant threat to the U.S. national interest.
Clearly this involves assessments and judgments of
that state's various policies and activities. U.S. policy seeks to pressure and isolate state sponsors so
that they will renounce the use of terrorism, end
support to terrorists, and bring terrorists to justice
for past crimes. The United States is committed to
holding terrorists and those who harbor them accountable for past attacks, regardless of when or
where the acts occurred. There is no "statute of limitations." States that choose to harbor terrorists are
seen as accomplices and will be held accountable
for the actions of the terrorists.

Getting off the list is difficult and, to date, only
Iraq has been able to achieve that end, though it
was later relisted. The United States is committed
to removing countries from the list of state sponsors once they have taken necessary steps to end
their link to terrorism. For example, in 2000–01,

and subsequently, the Department of State was engaged in ongoing discussions with North Korea and
Sudan with the goal of getting those governments
to end their support of terrorism and hence to be
removed from the state sponsors list.

Iran, Iraq, Syria, Libya, Cuba, North Korea,
and Sudan are the seven states that the U.S.
Secretary of State has designated as state sponsors
of international terrorism. Iran remained the most
active state sponsor of terrorism in 2000, but each
has involved itself with various terrorist groups either through providing financial support, weapons,
training bases, or safe havens for terrorists. State
sponsorship has decreased over time. Nevertheless,
the United States continues actively researching
and gathering intelligence on other states that will
be considered for designation as state sponsors. If
the United States deems a country to "repeatedly
provide support for acts of international terrorism,"
the U.S. government is required by law to add it
to the list.

Cuba

Following the collapse of the Soviet Union in
1989, Fidel Castro has been slowly trying to re-
suscitate the ailing communist Cuban economy,
which had been heavily reliant on Soviet subsidies.
Although Cuba remains a one-party state with a
command economy, it has benefited greatly from
increased revenues due to tourism and growing foreign investment in its petroleum sector. Foreign oil
companies doing business with Cuba, however, are
subject to the sanctions in the Helms-Burton Act
of 1996 and its restrictions on trade and investments with Cuba.

Cuba has served as a refuge for a number of
U.S. fugitives, as well as Basque and Colombian
terrorists. More serious regional security issues,
however, revolve around issues of illegal immigration and the country's use as a transshipment point
for narcotics to the United States. Havana also
maintained ties to other state sponsors of terrorism
and Latin American insurgents.

The United States has had a unilateral embargo on Cuba since the administration of John F.
Kennedy (1961–63). A unilateral embargo is one
in which the international community is not required to participate. Relations between the United
States and Cuba have varied over this period but
they have not risen to the level of warm or cordial
relations, in part due to the U.S. perception of Cuba
as a terrorism sponsor. Cuba, primarily for economic reasons, has sought to improve relations in
recent years with the clear objective of being removed from the U.S. terrorism sponsors list. Some

of the efforts to move in that direction include Cuba's government being unusually conciliatory about the U.S. using its naval base at Guantanamo Bay, which is rented by the United States from Cuba and long sought by the Cuban government to have its return to Cuban control, for Taliban and al-Qaeda prisoners. Cuba has even promised some cooperation with regard to the incarceration of those prisoners. Cuba was also quick to condemn the attacks of September 11, 2001, and indicated that it supports the principle of the war against terrorism, although it does not fully agree with the conduct of that war. Despite these and other positive signs Cuba remains on the terrorism sponsor list and the U.S. sanctions remain in place.

The continuing rationale for Cuba's retention on the list was provided by the Acting Coordinator for Counterterrorism Edmund J. Hull on April 30, 2001: "Our problems with Cuba relate to its continuing provision of safe haven to wanted terrorists. . . . They also have some associations with terrorist groups, like the ELN and the FARC in Colombia. Then finally I would point out that Cuba's position on terrorism is just very equivocal."

Iran

Iran is an Islamic republic that is politically divided between reformists and conservatives. Despite the victory for moderates in Iran's recent presidential and parliamentary elections, aggressive countermeasures by hardline conservatives have blocked most reform efforts. Iran remained the most active state sponsor of terrorism in 2000. Its Revolutionary Guard Corps (IRGC) and Ministry of Intelligence and Security (MOIS) continued to be involved in the planning and the execution of terrorist acts and continued to support a variety of groups that use terrorism to pursue their goals.

Iran's involvement in terrorist-related activities remained focused on support for groups opposed to Israel and groups oppposed to peace between Israel and its neighbors. Statements by Iran's leaders demonstrated Iran's unrelenting hostility to Israel. Supreme Leader Ali Hoseini-Khamenei continued to refer to Israel as a "cancerous tumor" that must be removed; President Mohammad Khatami-Ardakani, labeling Israel an "illegal entity," called for sanctions against Israel during the intifada (uprising); and Expediency Council Secretary Mohsen Rezai said, "Iran will continue its campaign against Zionism until Israel is completely eradicated."

Iran has long provided Lebanese Hizballah and the Palestinian rejectionist groups (those that reject negotiation or peace with Israel)—notably HAMAS, the Palestine Islamic Jihad, and the Popular Front for the Liberation of Palestine-General Command (PFLP-GC)—with varying amounts of funding, safe haven, training, and weapons. This activity continued at its already high levels following the Israeli withdrawal from southern Lebanon in May 2000 and during the Palestinian intifada in the fall of 2001. Iran continued to encourage Hizballah and the Palestinian groups to coordinate their planning and to escalate their activities against Israel. Iran also provided a lower level of support—including funding, training, and logistics assistance—to extremist groups in the Persian Gulf, Africa, Turkey, and Central Asia.

Despite the fact that Iran is a signatory to the Nuclear Non-Proliferation Treaty, the United States is still concerned about the upcoming completion of the Bushehr nuclear power plant, partly due to Iran's parallel efforts to develop long-range missiles. Aided in this endeavor by the North Koreans, Chinese, and the Russians, U.S. intelligence estimates expect the Iranians to possess an intercontinental ballistic missile in the next few years. Iran is also suspected of maintaining chemical and biological agents in order to strike a balance against those of Iraq.

Although the Iranian government has taken no direct action to date to implement Ayatollah Ruhollah Khomeini's fatwa against Salman Rushdie, calling for the writer's death, the decree has not been revoked, and the bounty for his assassination has not been withdrawn. Moreover, hardline Iranians continued to stress that the decree is irrevocable. On the anniversary of the fatwa in February 2000, the IRGC released a statement that the decree remains in force, and Ayatollah Mohammad Yazdi, a member of the Council of Guardians, reiterated that "the decree is irrevocable and, God willing, will be carried out."

The United States sees Iran as continuing to provide support—including arms transfers—to Palestinian rejectionist and terrorist groups. More recently Iran has failed to move decisively against al-Qaeda members who have relocated from Afghanistan to Iran.

Iraq

Under the leadership of President Saddam Hussein, Iraq has been involved in two major wars, the Iran-Iraq war (1980–88) which resulted from Iraq's invasion of the Islamic Republic under the Ayatollah Khomeini, and the 1991 Gulf War, which followed Iraq's invasion of Kuwait in the summer of 1990 and led to the ousting of Iraqi forces from Kuwait in early 1991. At the end of the Gulf War strict United Nations (UN) sanctions were imposed to pressure Iraq to relinquish its weapons of mass destruction (WMD). This, as well as the destruction of oil facilities and 90 percent of the power grid, left Iraq in a state of economic upheaval from which it has yet to fully recover. In comparison to pre-Gulf War levels, Iraq's GDP, per-capita income, and living standards have fallen sharply.

In the aftermath of Iraq's invasion of Kuwait in 1990 and the ensuing Gulf War, the international community, acting through the United Nations, imposed a series of requirements and sanctions on Iraq that took form in various UN Security Council resolutions. On April 3, 1991 the Security Council adopted Resolution 687, establishing a ceasefire on the basis of Iraq's acceptance of conditions deemed essential to the restoration of peace and stability in the area. It required Iraq give up its weapons of mass destruction (WMD), return Kuwaiti property, account for detainees, and renounce terrorism, as well as accept the United Nations demarcation of the Iraq-Kuwait border. Other resolutions, including 688, 715, and 833, were subsequently adopted to further the implementation of the terms of 687.

The United States has continually stressed Iraq's need to comply with the UN resolutions and has sought to enforce sanctions against Iraq until full compliance is met. A series of measures were adopted to enforce the resolutions, including UN economic sanctions against Iraq, a multinational interdiction force to police the sanctions regime at sea, no fly zones over portions of northern and southern Iraq, and multinational protection of the security zone in northern Iraq.

The overall objective of the United States has been to ensure that UN resolutions are implemented. The United States has been especially concerned that Iraq has sought to preserve its weapons of mass destruction capability by avoiding appropriate international inspection and monitoring. The goal is to prevent Iraq from reacquiring weapons of mass destruction and the missiles to deliver them. Though Iraq has not been especially active in terrorism since 1991, it was linked to a 1993 plan to assassinate former president George H. Bush (1989–93) in Kuwait.

The United States purports that Iraq has a long history of supporting terrorists, including the provision of sanctuary to the Abu Nidal organization. Iraq did plan and sponsor international terrorism in 2000. Although Baghdad focused on anti-dissident activity overseas, the regime continued to support various terrorist groups, but has not attempted an anti-Western terrorist attack since its failed plot to assassinate former president Bush in 1993. There

have, however, been reports that the Iraqi Intelligence Service (IIS) might retaliate against Radio Free Europe/Radio Liberty (RFE/RL) for broadcasts made by Radio Free Iraq critical of the Iraqi regime. To intimidate or silence overseas Iraqi opponents of the regime, the IIS reportedly opened several new stations in foreign capitals during 2000. Various opposition groups joined in warning Iraqi dissidents abroad against newly established "expatriates' associations," which, they asserted, were IIS front organizations. Opposition leaders in London contended that the IIS had dispatched women agents to infiltrate their ranks and was targeting dissidents for assassination. In Germany an Iraqi opposition figure denounced the IIS for murdering his son, who had recently left Iraq to join him abroad. Dr. Ayad 'Allawi, secretary general of the opposition group Iraqi National Accord, stated that relatives of dissidents living abroad are often arrested and jailed to intimidate activists overseas.

The Iraqi regime rebuffed a request from Riyadh for the extradition of two Saudis who had hijacked a Saudi Arabian Airlines flight to Baghdad, but did promptly return the passengers and the aircraft. Disregarding its obligations under international law, the regime granted political asylum to the hijackers and gave them ample opportunity to ventilate in the Iraqi government-controlled and international media their criticisms of alleged abuses by the Saudi Arabian government, echoing an Iraqi propaganda theme.

Several expatriate terrorist groups continued to maintain offices in Baghdad, including the Arab Liberation Front, the inactive 15 May Organization, the Palestine Liberation Front (PLF), and the Abu Nidal organization (ANO). PLF leader Abu 'Abbas appeared on state-controlled television in the fall to praise Iraq's leadership in rallying Arab opposition to Israeli violence against Palestinians. The ANO threatened to attack Austrian interests unless several million dollars in a frozen ANO account in a Vienna, Austria, bank were turned over to the group.

Additionally, the Iraq-supported Iranian terrorist group Mujahedin-e Khalq (MEK) regularly claimed responsibility for armed incursions into Iran that targeted police and military outposts, as well as for mortar and bomb attacks on security organization headquarters in various Iranian cities. MEK publicists reported that in March 2002 group members killed an Iranian colonel working in intelligence. A MEK claim to have wounded a general was denied by the Iranian government. The Iraqi regime also deployed MEK forces against its domestic opponents.

Libya

Following decades of economic isolation due to Muammar Qadhafi's anti-Western rhetoric, Qadhafi appears to have changed his view of the world and is now increasingly seeking international acceptance. Libya's political system, however, is Qadhafi's own creation, a mix of socialism and Islamic values, and he essentially runs the country as a military dictator. In the early 1990s Qadhafi refused to surrender two Libyan intelligence agents suspected in the 1988 bombing of Pan Am flight 103. This led the UN Security Council to pass Resolutions 748 and 883, which imposed stiff economic sanctions on Libya, particularly on its petroleum sector. By 1999 Qadhafi acquiesced and handed over the terrorist suspects in exchange for a suspension of UN sanctions. Since then, he has continued to seek a rapprochement with the United States and European countries in order to encourage foreign oil companies to reinvest in the oil fields that were abandoned following the passage of the Iran-Libya Sanctions Act (ILSA) in 1996.

Libya remains the primary suspect in several past terrorist operations, including the La Belle discotheque bombing in Berlin, Germany, in 1986 that killed two U.S. servicemen and one Turkish civilian and wounded more than 200 persons. It has also provided sanctuary to terrorist groups opposed to the Middle East Peace Process, including the Palestine Islamic Jihad and the Popular Front for the Liberation of Palestine-General Command, and has actively supported various African rebel and terrorist factions in Liberia, Sierra Leone, Guinea, and Eritrea in the past.

Recent developments show that Libya has not been engaged in recent terrorist activities and is trying to move toward reintegrating itself in the world community. By 1999 it had expelled the Abu Nidal organization and distanced itself from Palestinian rejectionist groups. That same year Libya released for trial two Libyans accused of the Pan Am bombing over Lockerbie, Scotland. The trial court issued its verdict on January 31, 2001, concluding that Abdel Basset al-Megrahi had caused an explosive device to detonate on board the airplane, resulting in the murder of the flight's 259 passengers and crew as well as 11 residents of Lockerbie, Scotland. Co-defendant Al-Amin Kalifa Fahima was released after the court concluded that there was insufficient evidence to satisfy the high standard of "proof beyond reasonable doubt" that is necessary in criminal cases.

Also in 1999, continuing its push for international reconciliation, Libya paid compensation for the death of a British policewoman who was killed

LIBYAN LEADER MUAMMAR QADHAFI SPEAKS OUT AGAINST LIBYA'S ALLEGED INVOLVEMENT IN THE 1998 BOMBING OF PAN AM FLIGHT 103 OVER LOCKERBIE, SCOTLAND. A SCULPTURE OF A HAND CRUSHING A U.S. WARPLANE STANDS IN THE BACKGROUND. *(AP/Wide World Photos/Amr Nabil. Reproduced by permission.)*

when gunmen in the Libyan People's bureau in London fired on an anti-Qadhafi demonstration outside their building in London, a move that preceded the reopening of the British embassy in Libya. It also paid damages to the families of victims in the bombing of UTA flight 772. Six Libyans were convicted *in absentia* in that case, and the French judicial system is considering further indictments against other Libyan officials, including leader Muammar Qadhafi.

Libya played a high-profile role in negotiating the release of a group of foreign hostages seized in the Philippines by the Abu Sayyaf Group, reportedly in exchange for a ransom payment. Many believe that Libya's behavior and that of other parties involved in the alleged ransom arrangement served only to encourage further terrorism and to make that region far more dangerous for residents and travelers. Additionally, Libya has yet to comply fully with the remaining UN Security Council

AL-QAEDA

Al-Qaeda ("the base") is an international terrorist network that seeks to purge Muslim countries of Western secular influence and to replace their governments with fundamentalist Islamic regimes. Led by Saudi exile Osama bin Laden, al-Qaeda operates worldwide and is the primary suspect in the September 11, 2001, attacks on the World Trade Center in New York City and the Pentagon, near Washington, DC. It is believed to have cells in some 60 countries, with several hundred to several thousand members organized in underground cells.

Although its attacks on the Pentagon and the World Trade Center were its most spectacular attacks and resulted in the largest number of casualties, there were previous attacks on U.S. interests, including a car bomb outside the Saudi Arabian National Guard building in Riyadh, Saudi Arabia, in 1995, as well as the bombings of the U.S. embassies in Kenya and Tanzania in 1998 and the attack on the USS Cole in Yemen in 2000, all of which are suspected to be linked to Osama bin Laden and al-Qaeda.

Al-Qaeda was formed, probably in 1988, in Afghanistan by Osama bin Laden and grew out of the anti-Soviet units that were formed in the 1980s. In the 1980s bin Laden and his colleagues recruited, trained, and financed thousands of mujahideen (holy warriors) from dozens of countries who opposed the Soviet invasion of Afghanistan. Subsequently he sought a broader mission for his fighters and found it in war against the West.

In Afghanistan the Taliban established their control over the regime and the country. In Taliban-controlled Afghanistan there developed a symbiotic relationship between Osama bin Laden and al-Qaeda on the one hand and the Taliban regime on the other. The Taliban-regime provided refuge for bin Laden and the al-Qaeda movement—as well as facilities for training personnel and for stockpiling equipment in preparation for terrorist actions worldwide. Al-Qaeda operated from Afghanistan from about 1996 until the collapse of the Taliban administration in 2001. Bin Laden and al-Qaeda are believed to have provided financial aid and political support for the Taliban until that time.

requirements related to Pan Am 103—accepting responsibility, paying appropriate compensation, disclosing all it knows, and renouncing terrorism. The United States remains dedicated to maintaining pressure on the Libyan government until it does so. Qadhafi stated publicly that his government has adopted an antiterrorism stance, but it remains unclear whether his claims of distancing Libya from its terrorist past signify a true change in policy.

In early 2000 there were indications that the Bill Clinton administration (1993–2001) was beginning to ease its policy stance in order to indicate to Libya and other state sponsors that there were benefits of cooperating with U.S. sanctions policies. The U.S. perception of Libya is changing in response to evidence that Tripoli has ended its support for international terrorism and is willing to cooperate with investigations into past terrorist acts. Most notable in this perception change is a possible lifting of the ban on U.S. citizens traveling to Libya (actually a ban on the use of U.S. passports for travel to Libya), which was first imposed in December 1981 and renewed most recently in November 1999.

North Korea

The Democratic People's Republic of Korea (DPRK) is a communist state under the authoritarian control of Kim Jong Il, who took control in 1994 after the death of his father Kim Il Sung. The DPRK devotes upwards of 30 percent of its GDP to military expenditures, in order to sustain a one million-man army, and its ongoing long-range missile development program. Initially a signatory to the Nuclear Non-Proliferation Treaty, the DPRK withdrew in 1993, while continuing to pursue graphite nuclear reactor technology, capable of producing fissionable material. The following year the DPRK froze its nuclear program in exchange for two light water nuclear reactors being provided by the United States, the first of which will not be operational until 2008.

The DPRK is not known to have sponsored any terrorist acts since 1987, when Korean airliner KAL 858 was bombed in flight. In 2000 the Democratic People's Republic of Korea engaged in three rounds of terrorism talks that culminated in a joint DPRK-U.S. statement on October 6, 2000 wherein "the two sides agreed that international terrorism poses an unacceptable threat to global security and peace, and that terrorism should be opposed in all its forms." The United States and North Korea agreed to support the international legal regime combating international terrorism and to cooperate with each other to fight terrorism. The DPRK, however, continued to provide safe haven to the Japanese Communist League-Red Army Faction members who participated in the hijacking of a Japanese Airlines flight to North Korea in 1970. Some evidence also suggests the DPRK may have sold weapons directly or indirectly to terrorist groups during the year; Philippine officials pub-

THE UNITED STATES BOMBED A PHARMACEUTICAL FACTORY IN SUDAN IN 1998, IN REPRISAL FOR THE BOMBINGS OF U.S. EMBASSIES IN KENYA AND TANZANIA THAT YEAR. THOSE RESPONSIBLE FOR THE BOMBINGS WERE SUSPECTED TO HAVE LINKS TO SUDAN. *(AP/Wide World Photos/Sayyid Azim. Reproduced by permission.)*

licly declared that the Moro Islamic Liberation Front had purchased weapons from North Korea with funds provided by Middle East sources.

Sudan

While Sudan has been cooperative with the United States on many fronts in the war against terrorism, it is not in full compliance with UN Security Council resolutions passed in 1996, which mandate an end to all Sudanese support for terrorism. Khartoum also still had not complied fully with UN Security Council Resolutions 1044, 1054, and 1070, passed in 1996—which demand that Sudan end all support to terrorists. They also require Khartoum to hand over three Egyptian al-Gama'a al-Islamiyya fugitives linked to the 1995 assassination attempt on Egyptian president Hosni Mubarak in Ethiopia. Sudanese officials continued to deny that they had a role in the attack. Sudan has yet to prevent elements of Osama bin Laden's al-Qaeda organization, the Palestinian Islamic Jihad, HAMAS, and the Egyptian al-Gama'a al-Islamiyya from operating on Sudanese soil.

The United States and Sudan in mid-2000 entered into a dialogue to discuss U.S. counterterrorism concerns. The talks were constructive and obtained some positive results. By the end of the year Sudan had signed all 12 international conventions for combating terrorism and had taken several other positive counterterrorism steps, including closing down the Popular Arab and Islamic Conference, which served as a forum for terrorists.

Sudan, however, continued to be used as a safe haven and refuge by members of various groups, including associates of Osama bin Ladin's al-Qaeda organization, the Egyptian al-Gama'a al-Islamiyya, Egyptian Islamic Jihad, the Palestine Islamic Jihad, and HAMAS. Most groups used Sudan primarily as a secure base for assisting compatriots elsewhere.

Syria

Syria has been on the U.S. State Department's list of state sponsors of terrorism since the list was established in 1979. The State Department's annual report on terrorism, *Patterns of Global Terrorism*, notes that Syrian government officials have not been personally involved in terrorist activities since 1986 when the then head of the Syria Air Force intelligence was held responsible for masterminding Nizar Hindawi's attempt to blow up an El Al Airliner. The Syrian government, however, has continued to provide safe haven, training facilities, and political support, among other items, to numerous Palestinian radical nationalist and Islamic terrorist organizations in Syria and in Syrian-controlled portions of Lebanon. It has also facilitated the shipment of weapons from Iran through Syria, by land and air, to Hizballah in Lebanon. It is likely that, as late as

TERROR ATTEMPT AT HEATHROW

In 1986 Syrian agents participated in an attempted terrorist operation that marked Syria as a state sponsor. The event involved an Irish chambermaid, Ann-Marie Murphy, who attempted to board an El Al Flight from London to Tel Aviv, Israel, on April 17, 1986, with a powerful plastic explosive in a false bottom area of her bag. Murphy, who was unaware she was carrying an explosive, was ostensibly going to meet her Palestinian fiancé's family. Nizar Hindawi met and romanced the Irish woman, who had become pregnant. Hindawi proposed and suggested that she travel to the Middle East to meet his family.

Hindawi placed the explosive in her bag and prepared it to go off during the flight from London to Tel Aviv. The bomb was detected before she boarded the flight. Hindawi dropped Murphy off at the airport and then returned to London to a hotel room reserved for Syrian Arab Airlines personnel. After she was stopped he went to the Syrian embassy, where he was provided with a hiding place. He later confessed to his role in the matter and clearly implicated Syria in the effort. Syria's involvement clearly marked it as a sponsor of the event. The support Hindawi received is well-documented and was at the core of his British government trial.

In a statement on October 24, 1986, the British Foreign and Commonwealth Secretary, The Rt Hon Sir Geoffrey Howe MP, announced that, in view of conclusive evidence of Syrian involvement in the attempt by Nizar Hindawi to place a bomb on an El Al aircraft at Heathrow airport, London, on April 17, 1986, the British government had decided to break diplomatic relations with Syria. In a statement to Parliament he noted:

> There is conclusive evidence of Syrian official involvement with Hindawi . . . .Certain facts are undisputed: Hindawi traveled on an official Syrian passport in a false name; Hindawi's visa applications were on two occasions backed by official notes from the Syrian Foreign Ministry; Hindawi met the Syrian Ambassador, Dr. Haydar, in his Embassy after the discovery of the bomb; . . . .We have therefore decided to break diplomatic relations with Syria.

2001, Syria was providing not only safe haven for political offices of various terrorist organizations, but also allowing operational planning and other activities to take place in the country.

Syria has been involved in terrorism since the 1950s, when it provided support for Palestinian *fedayeen*. *Fedayeen* are Palestinians who infiltrated into Israel to commit sabotage or terrorism in the period prior to the 1967 Arab-Israeli War. In the 1950s and 1960s Syria allowed Palestinian groups to use Syrian territory to stage attacks against Israel. In the 1970s it formed its own groups (Palestinian groups) as alternatives to the PLO, which operated independently of the Syrians in the 1970s. In the 1980s Syria began to use both state agents and surrogate groups to conduct acts. The year 1986 was the last for which there is confirmed involvement of Syrian state agents in an actual terrorist operations. Subsequently, in the 1990s and beyond Syria was especially active in providing support to various Palestinian, Lebanese, and Turkish (Kurdish) groups.

Syrian sponsorship of and support for terrorism seemed to reach its heights in the 1980s and involved a number of targets, not just Israeli. Between 1983 and 1985 Syrian-sponsored groups were responsible for attacks in some 15 countries, including 30 attacks in 1985 on a variety of targets including Arab, U.S., British, Palestinian, Jordanian and Israeli targets. Terrorism has been a useful tool for Syria with regard to Israel by shifting the conflict to a different arena of activity—away from the military sector to the arena of terrorism where Israel did not enjoy the significant advantages it did in the military sector. It would allow a weaker Syria to confront and "hurt" a stronger Israel by inflicting civilian and non-combatant casualties and perhaps leading to a change in Israel's strategy and policy.

Syria agreed in the 1990s to enter into peace talks with Israel, beginning after the Gulf War, in which Syria was a member of the coalition allied against Saddam Hussein and Iraq. When the Madrid Conference was convened in the fall of 1991, Syria participated, and later entered into a series of other negotiations. These talks involved the United States at the most senior levels and included substantial high-ranking delegations visiting Damascus to further the peace efforts, including a visit by U.S. President Bill Clinton in 1994. At the same time Clinton met with Syria's foreign minister in Shepherdstown, West Virginia, and then later with President Hafez al-Assad in Geneva in March 2000. In 2001 Syria sought membership on the UN Security Council and to that end launched a major campaign to change its image as a terrorist haven. Syria formally backed the U.S. campaign against the Taliban after the September 11 attacks on New York City and Washington, DC. Despite these actions, however, Syria remains on the list of state sponsors of terrorism.

As is the case with other state sponsors, Syria has been adamant in declaring that there is no

Syrian government complicity in terrorism. Formally Syria has noted its opposition to terrorism and condemns it in all its forms. Syria argues further that it distinguishes between terrorism and those who are struggling to restore their occupied land and usurped rights. Clearly Syria sees Israel as a terrorist state and has even suggested to Washington that Israel be added to the U.S. government's list of state sponsors. Its arguments continued to stress that there were double standards for terrorism, with terrorism being linked to Islam while Israel's terrorism against the Palestinians was tolerated.

Syria has continued to provide safe haven and support to several terrorist groups, some of which maintained training camps or other facilities on Syrian territory. Ahmad Jibril's Popular Front for the Liberation of Palestine-General Command, the Palestine Islamic Jihad (PIJ), Fatah-the-Intifada, and the Popular Front for the Liberation of Palestine (PFLP) maintained their headquarters in Damascus. The Syrian government allowed HAMAS to open a new main office in Damascus in March 2002, although the arrangement may be temporary while HAMAS continues to seek permission to reestablish its headquarters in Jordan.

In addition, Syria granted a variety of terrorist groups—including HAMAS, the PFLP-GC, and the PIJ—basing privileges or refuge in areas of Lebanon's Bekaa Valley, which is under Syrian control. Damascus, however, generally upheld its agreement with the Turkish government in Ankara not to support the Kurdish Workers' Party (PKK). Although Syria claimed to be committed to the peace process, it did not act to stop Hizballah and Palestinian rejectionist groups from carrying out anti-Israeli attacks. Damascus also served as the primary transit point for terrorist operatives traveling to Lebanon and for the re-supply of weapons to Hizballah. Damascus appeared to maintain its longstanding ban on attacks launched from Syrian territory or against Western targets.

Additionally, under President Hafez al-Asad, Syria used state agents and terrorist surrogates to commit acts of political violence designed to further its foreign policy objectives. Some of this was directed against non-combatants and civilians. Part of the reason for these actions is Syria's recognition that it cannot achieve its strategic policy objectives by conventional diplomatic or military means. Syria sought to hurt its regional adversaries—primarily Israel—by sponsoring acts of terrorism, and to achieve its policy objective of regaining the Golan Heights, taken by Israel from Syria in the Six Day War of 1967.

Syria's use of terrorism (originally by direct state-controlled and mounted organizations and later sponsored) has permitted it to achieve some of its goals and objectives. It has killed and injured individual Israelis, helped to solidify its presence in and control of Lebanon, and thwarted some regional plans for peace, including the May 17, 1983 agreement brokered by the United States between Israel and Lebanon. Nevertheless, despite these and other achievements Syria failed in its primary goal to regain the Golan Heights from Israel.

Its "failures" in the terrorism sphere resulted from a number of interrelated factors, including the fact that terrorists often have their own agendas in addition to those of the state sponsor and thus the two may not move in the same direction. Also, retaliation by a terrorist target, such as Israel, against the state sponsor is often an objective easier to achieve than against the sponsored group.

Syria's role in sponsoring anti-Israel actions by terrorist groups was amply demonstrated over time by the triangular relationship among Israel, Lebanon, and Syria with regard to the Palestine Liberation Organization (PLO) in the 1970s and 1980s, and with regard to Hizballah in the 1990s and subsequently. During U.S. Secretary of State Colin Powell's Middle East visit in April 2002 this was again demonstrated by Powell's sudden visit to Beirut and Damascus after Hizballah forces shelled Israel from Lebanon at the same time that Israel was engaged in a deadly exchange with the Palestinians in Israel and the West Bank.

The Status of Afghanistan

Why wasn't Afghanistan designated as a state sponsor of terrorism when it clearly meets the conditions for such a listing? In recent years the Taliban controlled regime in Afghanistan has emerged as the "sponsor" of the al-Qaeda movement and the operatives of Osama bin Laden. Although not formally listed as a "state sponsor" the Taliban-bin Laden connection in effect created a state-sponsored terrorist operation. That is terrorism supported by a state mechanism—Taliban Afghanistan. The relationship among the Afghan state, the Taliban regime, and the al-Qaeda terrorist organization (as well as Osama bin Laden himself) was a complex one and difficult to precisely define. It was a variant of state-sponsored terrorism, because it clearly differed from the usual pattern due to the very close and extensive links between Osama bin Laden and his al-Qaeda organization and the Taliban-controlled government of Afghanistan.

The problem with Afghanistan being listed as a state sponsor is that the United States saw

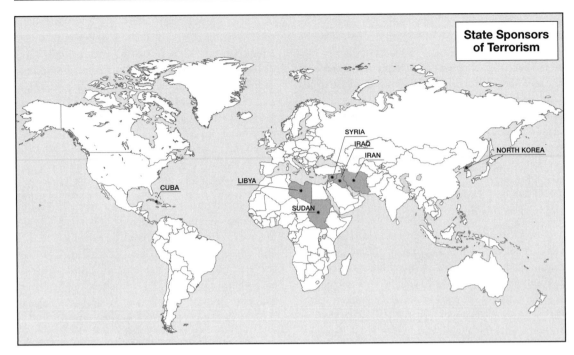

THE UNITED STATES LISTS SEVEN NATIONS AS BEING STATE SPONSORS OF TERRORISM—CUBA, LIBYA, SYRIA, IRAN, IRAQ, SUDAN, AND NORTH KOREA. *(Gale Group.)*

Afghanistan as a country where "there is no functioning central government" (*CIA Factbook,* 2001) but was instead seen as divided among various fighting factions. As of October 2001, the Taliban controlled about 90 percent of the country including the capital, Kabul, and virtually all the major urban areas.

A Taliban edict had renamed the country the Islamic Emirate of Afghanistan and installed Taliban leader Mullah Mohammed Omar, its supreme leader, as Head of State and Commander of the Faithful. He held all ultimate authority. A rival regime known as the Islamic State of Afghanistan (also known as the United Front or Northern Alliance) was nominally headed by Burhannudin Rabbani, mostly in the northeast area of the country. The Northern Alliance controlled most Afghan embassies and retained Afghanistan's seat in the United Nations. The UN recognized the Islamic State of Afghanistan, as headed by Burhanuddin Rabbani, which controlled about 10 percent of the country as of October 2001. Pakistan, Saudi Arabia, and the United Arab Emirates (UAE) were among the few who recognized the Taliban regime in 1997. Saudi Arabia and the UAE withdrew recognition following the September 11, 2001 attacks.

The recent decades of Afghanistan's history have been marked by warfare, which occurred in the 1980s following the Soviet invasion of the country and in the 1990s between and among various Afghanistan warlords of diverse ethnic backgrounds and political preferences and the various militias they controlled. Tribal and other loyalties were often quickly switched by both warlords and their fighters. The fighting was marked by numerous casualties, as well as displaced persons and refugees. The country sank into anarchy with various leaders and local warlords controlling various sections of the country with no overall, acceptable functioning authority.

In response to the anarchy and the role of the warlords a movement of *mujahideen* (holy warriors) arose. Many of the Taliban had been educated in *madrassas* in Pakistan and were largely from rural Pashtun backgrounds (and were severely underrepresented in the government in Kabul under Rabbani). The name "Talib" means pupil. The new group dedicated itself to removing the warlords, creating order, and imposing Islam throughout the country.

This effort generated substantial support from Pakistan. In 1994 it captured the city of Kandahar and proceeded to expand its control throughout Afghanistan, occupying Kabul in September 1996. By the end of 1998 the Taliban occupied about 90 percent of the country. Efforts by the UN and others who sought to end the conflict failed, usually because of Taliban intransigence. The Taliban imposed an extreme interpretation of Islam on the entire country and committed massive human rights violations and atrocities in the process. Since the mid-1990s the Taliban provided sanctuary to Osama bin Laden and provided a base for his and other terrorist groups. The United Nations Security Council sanctioned the Taliban for these activities on various occasions.

On October 7, 2001, the United States and its partners in the anti-terrorist coalition began a campaign in Afghanistan, targeting terrorist facilities and various Taliban military and political assets within the country. In part, this was in response to the Taliban's refusal to expel bin Laden and his group and end its support for international terrorism.

Measures Against States Involved in Sponsorship of Terrorism

Actions against states that sponsor terrorism can be difficult to implement and there is often debate about their effectiveness. Among the mechanisms available are: warnings of actions by individual states or the international community against the perpetrator if the actions do not cease and identified terrorists are not brought to justice; condemnation of their actions by individual states or the international community; boycotts or embargos of various sorts and types can be threatened or implemented. These might include limited actions such as selective boycotts or more significant actions such as diplomatic and/or economic embargoes or boycotts. Additionally, legal steps, usually at the international legal level, are possibilities. There is also the possibility of the use of force.

Internationally Imposed Sanctions (United Nations)

In the case of Libya the United Nations imposed sanctions under the terms of UN Security Council Resolution 748 of March 31, 1992. The Security Council has utilized a procedure of review and renewal it had routinely followed since the adoption of the sanctions in 1992 and continued until the Lockerbie trial.

Sanctions and Actions by Individual States—The United States, Iran, and Libya

The United States has adopted a special approach to various states, state sponsors, and others, when deemed appropriate for U.S. foreign policy. Sanctions were applied to Cuba in the form of an embargo during the administration of John F.

Kennedy (1961–63). In 1986, after the disclosure of Libyan involvement in various terrorist acts including actions against U.S. forces, the United States bombed Libya, specifically the cities of Bengazi and Tripoli. It also struck targets in Sudan and Afghanistan after the bombings of the U.S. embassies in Kenya and Tanzania. In addition, it attacked Taliban and al-Qaeda targets in Afghanistan after the September 11, 2001, attacks on the Pentagon and the World Trade Center. In the case of Libya and Iran the United States imposed the Iran-Libya Sanctions Act (ILSA) in 1996, which was renewed by Congress in 2001.

The Iran and Libya Sanctions Act of 1996 imposes sanctions on foreign companies that engage in specified economic transactions with Iran or Libya. The act was intended to help deny Iran and Libya revenues that could be used to finance international terrorism; to limit the flow of resources necessary to obtain weapons of mass destruction; and put pressure on Libya to comply with UN resolutions calling for it to extradite for trial the accused perpetrators of the Pan Am 103 bombing.

The law sanctions foreign companies that provide new investments over US\$40 million (later reduced to \$20 million) for the development of petroleum resources in Iran or Libya. The law also sanctions foreign companies that violate existing United Nations prohibitions against trade with Libya in certain goods and services such as arms, certain oil equipment, and civil aviation services. In the event of a violation the president is to impose sanctions against the violating company. The sanction choices include denial of Export-Import Bank assistance; denial of export licenses for exports to the violating company; prohibition of loans or credits from U.S. financial institutions of over \$10 million in any 12-month period; prohibition on designation as a primary dealer for U.S. government debt instruments; prohibition on serving as an agent of the United States or as a repository for U.S. government funds; denial of U.S. government procurement opportunities (consistent with World Trade Organization obligations); and a ban on all or some imports of the violating company.

The primary intent of the sanctions was to affect negatively the economies of the two state sponsors. Implementation of the law and the sanctions contained therein are essentially at the discretion of the administration in power. Officials generally examine each foreign investment deal as it is proposed to see if it warrants action under the act. Since these are unilateral sanctions the administration may often be reluctant to antagonize friendly countries who wish to invest in either Iran or Libya.

Various countries and the European Union (EU) have often spoken out against the ILSA. The EU in particular has commented on the fact that unilateral sanctions have extraterritorial effect and thus create unnecessary and unhelpful differences between the United States and the European Union.

In the summer of 2001 the U.S. Congress voted overwhelmingly on the ILSA Extension Act of 2001 (Public Law No. 107–24) to extend the sanctions against Iran and Libya for an additional five years. The sentiment of Congress was clearly that these two states were among the most dangerous of outlaw states. The sanctions renewed those first put in place in 1996 and were intended to discourage foreign energy firms from investing in Iran and Libya. If they did, sanctions could be applied to them.

RECENT HISTORY AND THE FUTURE

In the wake of the September 11, 2001 terrorist attacks in New York City and Washington, DC, the United States reassessed its global response to terrorism and, in so doing, suggested that further action against state sponsors of terrorism would be considered. The reference to an "axis of evil" clearly connected state sponsors with broader concerns on such issues as weapons of mass destruction and the need to ensure that these would not be used against the United States. At the same time the United States suggested possible links between these sponsors and attacks against the United States. Although not all of the state sponsors were linked to the September 11, 2001 attacks, there were some connections made, such as Iran's links to al-Qaeda. At the same time all seven state sponsors were retained on the United States' state sponsors list.

Using Force Against State Sponsors?

In the case of Iraq, although there was little evidence of a direct connection between Iraq and the September 11 attacks, there was growing discussion of a potential U.S. strike against the regime of Saddam Hussein. This was, in part, seen as a need to change a regime that is engaged in developing weapons of mass destruction and remains a state sponsor of terrorism. The George W. Bush administration (2001–) increasingly indicated its preference to use force to remove Saddam Hussein after the failure of the UN Security Council to modify its sanctions against Iraq into "smart sanctions" that would help to focus the sanctions' impact on the Iraqi regime and not on its people. The

idea of the use of force was increasingly associated with the U.S. Department of Defense and Secretary of Defense Donald Rumsfeld.

The idea of utilizing force to deal with the Iraqi regime had been broached on a number of occasions and emerged in 2002 as a major element in the relationship between the United States and its allies, especially in Europe. The United States worked to generate a coalition of support for its potential actions in Iraq, similar in many respects to the coalition it formed in 1990–91 for the Gulf War and to the coalition against terrorism formed in the wake of the September 11 attacks against the United States. The issues at hand and the discussions between the United States and Britain, a crucial and close ally on issues relating to terrorism and Iraq, were highlighted during a visit by British Prime Minister Tony Blair to President Bush in Crawford, Texas, in April 2002.

At a joint press conference on April 6, 2002, President Bush noted:

> . . . [T]he Prime Minister and I, of course, talked about Iraq. We both recognize the danger of a man who's willing to kill his own people harboring and developing weapons of mass destruction. This guy, Saddam Hussein, is a leader who gasses his own people, goes after people in his own neighborhood with . . . chemical weapons . . . .I explained to the Prime Minister that the policy of my government is the removal of Saddam and that all options are on the table.

Meanwhile, Tony Blair noted: " . . . [T]he President is right to draw attention to the threat of weapons of mass destruction. That threat is real. How we deal with it, that's a matter we discuss. But that the threat exists and we have to deal with it, that seems to me a matter of plain common sense."

Should the decision to use force against a state sponsor of terrorism be made, it will certainly change the position of all those listed on the state sponsors list.

BIBLIOGRAPHY

Byman, Daniel. "A Farewell to Arms Inspections," *Foreign Affairs*, no. 1, 79:119–132 (January/February 2000).

Christopher, Warren. *American Hostages in Iran: Conduct of a Crisis*. New Haven, CT: Yale University Press, 1985.

Combs, Cindy C. *Terrorism in the Twenty-First Century*. Upper Saddle River, NJ: Prentice Hall, 1997.

Hoffman, Bruce, "Recent Trends and Future Prospects of Iranian Sponsored International Terrorism," in Yonah Alexander, ed., *Middle Eastern Terrorism: Current*

Threats and Future Prospects. New York and Toronto: G.K. Hall, 1994.

Kegley, Jr., Charles W., ed. *International Terrorism: Characteristics, Causes, Controls.* New York: St. Martin's Press, 1990.

Kemp, Geoffrey. *America and Iran: Road Maps and Realism.* Washington, DC: The Nixon Center, 1998.

O'Ballance, Edgar. *Islamic Fundamentalist Terrorism, 1979–95: The Iranian Connection.* Washington Square, NY: New York University Press, 1997.

Satloff, Robert B., ed. *War on Terror: The Middle East Dimension.* Washington, DC: The Washington Institute for Near East Policy, 2002.

Zimmerman, Tim, "The American Bombing of Libya: A Success for Coercive Diplomacy?," *Survival,* vol. 29, pp. 195–214 (May/June 1987).

Bernard Reich, Jennifer B. Reich,
Michael Buczek

THE UNITED STATES VS. TERROR: A NEW KIND OF WAR

THE CONFLICT

The September 11 attacks on U.S. targets by al-Qaeda agents brought about the first war between a state and a transnational terrorist network. Al-Qaeda erased the difference between the battlefield and the home front by striking from the inside on a wide array of civilian targets and by hiding its battle detachments—the cells—among civilians. The war against terrorism thus poses an enormous challenge: how to go to war and overcome an enemy that has no territory, no army, and no government—and an enemy that has almost no recognizable political and military demands. Past attempts at waging large-scale conventional warfare on militants have fallen short of solving conflicts in a military sense. Recent initiatives are reshaping the U.S. military to be able to deal with unconventional threats of the twenty-first century.

Political

- The war against terrorism is one of the few wars of modern times that is not constructed by Cold War policy; this is not the "limited" warfare of Korea and Vietnam, dictated by the balance of power and weapons.

Religious

- While al-Qaeda has hinted at some political goals, such as the removal of U.S. troops from the holy lands of Islam, its war is empowered by a radical brand of Islamic fundamentalism and fanatical hatred of Western—particularly American—ideals and institutions. Accordingly, it perceives the world apocalyptically, as an arena of the eternal and uncompromising struggle between "true believers" and "infidels" ending in the unavoidable ultimate destruction of the latter.

On January 29, 2002, U.S. president George W. Bush (2001–) gave his State of the Union address. In the globally televised speech he once again committed the United States to expanding its campaign against international terrorism. Referring to Iran, Iraq, and North Korea as the "axis of evil" that supports international terrorism, he let it be known that these countries could become the objects of military and political pressure in the U.S.-led war on terrorism. After the initial success of the war on terrorism—the routing of al-Qaeda and the removal of the Taliban from power in Afghanistan—the president's lean toward expanding the war is not surprising, but it has raised controversy throughout much of the world. Whether the United States will or should expand its anti-terrorist campaign to other countries must be examined in a very different light than has been used in other recent conflicts. This is a new kind of war for the United States and the first war of its kind in history between a state and a transnational terrorist network.

The war against terrorism began with the unprecedented terrorist assault on the United States on September 11, 2001, when 19 trained and highly determined terrorists hijacked four California-bound U.S. civilian passenger planes in three East Coast airports (Boston, Massachusetts; Washington, DC; and Newark, New Jersey) in suicide attacks. Two of the hijacked airliners flew into the World Trade Center (WTC) towers in New York City, prompting their collapse, the death of thousands of people, and the destruction or severe damage of dozens of nearby buildings. Another plane hit the Pentagon in Arlington, Virginia, near Washington, DC, destroying a part of the building's west side. The last plane crashed near Shanksville, Pennsylvania, probably missing its target due to the passengers' resistance to the hijackers.

CHRONOLOGY

July 17, 1973 A military coup overthrows Afghani king Mohammad Zahir Shah and sets up a republican government.

April 28, 1978 A military coup leads to the establishment of a pro-Soviet regime and the beginning of a civil war in Afghanistan.

December 25, 1979 Soviet troops invade Afghanistan under the pretext of the Soviet-Afghan Friendship and Cooperation Treaty following a split within the leftist government and increasing civil strife in the country.

February 3, 1989 Soviet troops withdraw from Afghanistan.

April 16, 1992 Opposition forces take Kabul and form a new government, which soon collapses due to factional fighting.

September 26, 1995 The Taliban, a militant Islamic movement formed in 1994, captures Kabul after bitter fighting and declares Afghanistan an Islamic emirate. The Taliban harbors international Islamic terrorists. The remaining government and its forces retreat to the north, form an alliance with local warlords (the Northern Alliance), and continue their struggle against the Taliban.

September 11, 2001 Two hijacked airplanes crash into the World Trade Center in New York City, while a third plane hits the Pentagon in Washington, DC. A fourth plane crashes into a field in Pennsylvania.

September 20, 2001 In a speech to Congress, President Bush condemns the Taliban regime and blames them for allowing terrorists to train in their country. Bush also demands that the Taliban turn over all members of al-Qaeda.

October 7, 2001 The U.S.-led military campaign (Operation Enduring Freedom) begins.

October 19, 2001 U.S. ground forces battle in Afghanistan after nearly two weeks of air strikes. The ground battles open a new phase in the war.

November 9, 2001 Anti-Taliban forces capture the city of Mazar-e-Sharif.

November 13, 2001 Kabul is liberated from the Taliban.

December 6, 2001 Taliban forces surrender the southern city of Kandahar, marking the final collapse of the regime.

December 17, 2001 After days of bombing, air strikes over the Tora Bora mountains come to a close.

January 4, 2002 Sgt. Nathan Ross Chapman, a Green Beret, is the first American soldier killed by enemy gunfire.

March 4, 2002 One American helicopter is shot down in the Operation Anaconda assaults. Another helicopter is attacked while on the ground. Seven American troops are killed and at least 10 are injured in the two events.

The nation rapidly took urgent contingency measures. The White House, the Capitol, the Pentagon, and other government buildings were evacuated. More than 4,000 commercial airliners scrambled to find places to land. Many flights coming from overseas were diverted to Canada. Security was dramatically increased throughout the country. The armed forces were put on high alert. The aircraft carriers USS *John F. Kennedy* and USS *George Washington*, accompanied by seven other warships, took up battle positions off of the East Coast.

On September 12, 2001, President Bush described the terrorist attacks as acts of war. The evidence gathered by the U.S. and British intelligence services revealed that the majority of the perpetrators of the attacks were closely connected with the transnational Islamic terrorist network called al-Qaeda, led by the high-profile Saudi terrorist leader Osama bin Laden. In his speech to Congress on September 20, 2001, President Bush laid out the aims of the United States in the new war: to rally worldwide support in a coalition against international terrorism, to destroy the global terrorist infrastructure, and to wage war against the regimes that harbor terrorists. The president also stressed the immediate focus of U.S. retaliation: the al-Qaeda network and the fundamentalist Islamic regime in Afghanistan, the Taliban, which provided the terrorists with safe haven.

For the first time since the 1990 Kuwait crisis and the Gulf War of 1991, the United States was set on war footing. Reservists were called up in the first major mobilization in ten years. The Pentagon moved hundreds of planes to bases in southwest Asia and assembled three aircraft carrier groups in the Persian Gulf and the Arabian Sea. Congress passed a resolution allowing the president to use all necessary and appropriate force against any individual, organization, or country that played any role in the terrorist attacks on the United States. The context of this resolution echoed the Tonkin Gulf resolution, which was passed in 1964 after alleged enemy attacks on U.S. Navy ships off the coast of Vietnam and was the subject of great controversy. But there was little hesitation to pass such a measure in the days after the September 11 attacks. It was clear that domestic and particularly international circles held widespread sympathy for the United States and supported U.S. retaliation against the terrorists.

On October 7, 2001, the U.S.-led assault on Afghanistan began with air strikes accompanied by the cruise missiles launched from U.S. warships and one British submarine in the Arabian Sea. By October 9, 2001, U.S. air power had destroyed the weak air defense of the Taliban and achieved uncontested dominance in the skies over Afghanistan. Then the campaign moved to the next phase, in which the air war supplemented the ground operations, mounted by the U.S. Special Forces and anti-Taliban Northern Alliance troops.

In several weeks, using the combination of precision strikes on Taliban military targets and communication systems across Afghanistan and carpet-bombing the enemy front lines, the United States effectively broke the Taliban army. Additionally, since October 16, 2001, U.S. and British commandos systematically conducted "hit-and-run" raids to gather intelligence and destroy the enemy command and control facilities, particularly in the Kandahar area—the stronghold of the Taliban. The commando raids were also instrumental in securing areas within southern Afghanistan in which U.S. troops could land safely and carry out their "search and destroy" mission. The combination of precision air strikes with the guerrilla-style warfare, the concentration of massive firepower on decisive points of the front line, and the coordination of air strikes with the local allies by U.S. servicemen on the ground finally paralyzed the Taliban as a fighting force and created conditions for dramatic changes in the course of the war.

From November 9 to November 16, 2001, most major cities of Afghanistan were liberated from Taliban control, with the city of Kandahar liberated in December. Having achieved this, the U.S.-led forces went after the retreating remnants of the Taliban and al-Qaeda forces, successfully eliminating them in the caves and underground tunnels of the eastern part of Afghanistan. By the end of December 2001 the immediate aims of the campaign had been accomplished: the hub of the al-Qaeda network was destroyed and Afghanistan was liberated from the Taliban regime.

HISTORICAL BACKGROUND

The terrorist attacks on the United States were in keeping with some trends that had developed well before September 11, 2001. Since the late 1960s there have been some 500 hijackings of planes by terrorists. Additionally, during World War II (1939–45), in one year alone Americans faced about 4,000 aerial kamikaze (suicide attack) strikes. Although the United States had never seen deliberate strikes on its cities and population comparable to what occurred on September 11, the country did have an experience with terrorism. At the local level, in New York in 1919, when the government was cracking down hard on Italian radicals, about 60 militants rose up in a campaign of terrorism in which they targeted politicians, judges, and other officials. Among other terrorist acts, they bombed the attorney general's home in 1919 and a Wall Street location in 1920. These and other acts, however, did not in and of themselves prompt a war.

On September 11, 2001, however, for the first time in history, the acts of terror became the leading acts of war itself, inflicting a severe blow on the only global superpower of the early twenty-first century.

A New Kind of War

The United States had repeatedly proved its military strength in the last decade. The Gulf War of 1991, the 1995 North Atlantic Treaty Organization (NATO) intervention in the Bosnian War, and the NATO-Yugoslav War of 1999 proved the military preponderance of the United States as well as the futility of challenging it in conventional ways. Thus, U.S. adversaries had to find a new way to fight. Instead of confronting the United States with like forces—that is symmetrically, with weapons, strategy, and tactics, such as the fighting that occurred during the world wars—they developed a new, asymmetric approach to fighting the United States. The essence of this approach was to avoid U.S. strengths and to focus on its weaknesses, and also to try to turn the very attributes that put the United States in the forefront of the world stage into its vulnerabilities. The openness and technological complexity of the modern Western—particularly American—society makes it a soft target

VIDEOTAPE FOOTAGE RELEASED BY OSAMA BIN LADEN SHOWS MILITARY TRAINING SCENES FROM AN AL-QAEDA CAMP IN AFGHANISTAN. THE UNITED STATES CONNECTED THE SEPTEMBER 11, 2001, ATTACKS TO AL-QAEDA AND RETALIATED WITH THE "WAR ON TERROR." (© AFP/CORBIS. Reproduced by permission.)

for sudden, well-coordinated, and savage attacks. The September 11 attacks demonstrated that an adversary with radically different cultural priorities and values than the United States can obtain an advantage using the element of surprise and exploiting values such as the appreciation of human life and sensitivity to civilian casualties—that is, by hitting the United States asymmetrically.

One more tendency that contributed to the development of terrorism as a new kind of warfare was the evolution of terrorism itself. Terrorism, which is the use of systematic politically and/or ideologically motivated violence primarily against civilians, is well suited to be a main tool of asymmetric warfare. Traditionally, terrorist movements have had concrete demands and a distinct political agenda, which did not threaten the very existence of a society. Throughout the ages there have also been fanatical religious sects and cults that used violence in an attempt to achieve their goals, but their activity and impact were usually localized to particular countries or regions.

Since the 1970s, however, there has been a resurgence of militant Islam, which has a long history of anti-Western hostility. Militant Islam is the faith of the Islamic religion turned into ideology, with a political or government responsibility to society. It takes certain features of the religion to an extreme, resulting in something far different from what is practiced by faithful, peaceful believers. Thus, adherents to militant Islam are often referred to as "extremists." New power has been given these groups due to a number of factors: the paramount strategic importance of the Middle East; the growing and multifaceted instability in the region and around it, particularly after the end of the Cold War and the collapse of the Soviet Union; and the increasing wealth of local elite, including those sympathetic to extremist ideas. The ideological, political, and financial conditions for the development of terrorist networks were in place—through extremism, unstable or repressive political regimes, and depressed economic conditions—and the networks branched out throughout the Middle East, North Africa, Central Asia, and among the world's growing Muslim diasporas.

Al-Qaeda

When Soviet troops entered Afghanistan in 1979, Osama bin Laden, the son of a Saudi billionaire, joined the Islamic resistance in Afghanistan and became one of the battlefield commanders of the Afghan Islamic guerrillas, fighting the pro-Soviet regime and Soviet troops in the country. When the war ended with the Soviet defeat, bin Laden continued to use his inheritance to promote Islamic extremism throughout the world and

MAJOR TERRORIST ATTACKS AGAINST WESTERN INTERESTS BY ISLAMIC EXTREMISTS

November 4, 1979 Islamic radicals capture the U.S. embassy in Tehran, Iran, and hold 52 hostages for 444 days.

April 18 and October 23, 1983 Suicide bombers blow up the U.S. embassy and Marines Corps barracks in Beirut, Lebanon, killing 258 Americans.

September 20, 1983 The bombing of U.S. and French embassies in Kuwait leaves 5 dead and 86 wounded.

September 20, 1984 A bomb explodes at the U.S. embassy in Lebanon, killing 16 people and wounding a U.S. ambassador.

June 14, 1985 and 2 April 1986 Two TWA airliners are hijacked; five Americans are killed during the incidents.

September 5, 1986 The hijacking of a Pan Am plane out of Pakistan results in 20 people killed when security forces storm the plane.

1992—2001 Over the course of these nine years several terrorist plots were uncovered. They include: plots to assassinate President Bill Clinton and Pope John Paul II, attempts to kill U.S. military personnel in Yemen and Bosnia and American tourists in Jordan, a plot to blow up the Eiffel Tower and 11 American passenger planes over the Pacific, and plots to bomb Los Angeles International Airport, the cathedral and market in Strasbourg, NATO headquarters in Brussels, the British embassy in Bosnia, U.S. and Israeli embassies in Paraguay and the

Philippines, and U.S. embassies in Uruguay, Bosnia, and France. Most of these thwarted incidents were linked to al-Qaeda.

February 26, 1993 The first bombing of the World Trade Center occurs in New York City. Six people are killed and more than 1,000 are injured.

October 3, 1993 An ambush and attack on U.S. troops in Somalia results in the deaths of 18 Americans. This attack is linked to al-Qaeda.

November 13, 1995 A U.S.-run military training facility in Riyadh, Saudi Arabia, is bombed, with 7 people killed, including 5 Americans.

June 25, 1996 A housing complex in Dhahran, Saudi Arabia, is bombed, resulting in the deaths of 19 U.S. Air Force personnel and injuries to more than 500 Americans and Saudis.

August 7, 1998 The U.S. embassies in Nairobi, Kenya, and Dar es Salaam, Tanzania, are bombed; 301 people are killed, including 12 Americans. Some 5,000 are wounded. The attack is linked to al-Qaeda.

October 12, 2000 An attack on the USS *Cole* in Aden, Yemen, kills 17 sailors and injures more than 30. An investigation by U.S. officials connects the attack to al-Qaeda.

September 11, 2001 Attacks on the World Trade Center in New York City and the Pentagon near Washington, DC, result in the deaths of more than 3,000 people. The acts are attributed to al-Qaeda.

recruited devoted Arab veterans of the Afghan war as well as young Muslim radicals to join him in campaigns aimed at the expulsion of Western influence from the Middle East. He organized a global network of terrorist groups known as al-Qaeda ("the base" in Arabic).

The major innovation of al-Qaeda was its decentralized structure. It consisted of self-contained and widely dispersed cells (usually composed of four to five people), which operate independently in 40 to 60 countries, frequently intermingling with local terrorists and maintaining contact between themselves through modern communication systems (such as cellular phones, satellite phones, and email). The main task of al-Qaeda is to provide cells with global support infrastructure such as weaponry, propaganda, communications, training, and financial resources, including money from Muslim charities and profits from the drug trade and other criminal activities. During the 1990s bin Laden and his devoted supporters aggressively expanded their activity, transcending borders between states and exploiting every hot spot of the Muslim world: Yemen, Sudan, Egypt, Eritrea, Somalia, Bosnia, Chechnya, the Philippines, and Indonesia, to name a few.

The successful expansion of transnational terrorism was very much indebted to the important transformation of the Cold War geopolitical landscape: the emergence of so-called "failed states" like Afghanistan or Somalia, due to the combination of political and social disintegration, fierce civil strife, and lack of interest and support from the international community. The transnational terrorists can use the paramount anarchy in the "failed states" to obtain safe haven and to set up their training camps and communication centers, exploiting the remains of local infrastructure. Al-Qaeda's infrastructure in Afghanistan included some 40 training camps in which it trained, according to Western intelligence estimates, from 20,000 to 70,000 terrorists. Moreover, due to its profound organizational and financial resources, al-Qaeda managed to obtain a decisive control over the Taliban, an Islamic movement that installed a rigid, fundamentalist regime in Afghanistan. This led to a new phenomenon: a terrorism-sponsored state, instead of the state-sponsored terrorism widely known in modern history.

Throughout history, terrorists have constantly tried to acquire more lethal weapons. This is particularly true with respect to weapons of mass destruction (WMD). It is believed that the Japanese religious cult Aum Shinrikyo, which committed the first use of WMD in a terrorist act during its 1995 gas attack on the Tokyo subway system, also planned to use biological weapons against U.S. troops in Japan. Using sanctuaries in Afghanistan, al-Qaeda planned to launch chemical or biological attacks on U.S. and European targets. Hiding in the "failed states," terrorists can also try to overcome the technological and political difficulties of building their own WMD.

The profound transformation, both in scale and complexity, of operations that terrorists could mount produced an absolutely different kind of warfare. Powerful, well-organized, and devoted groups and associations transcended states, having enough financial and logistical resources and obtaining global reach capability. These terrorists are able to endanger international security profoundly.

Over the years, al-Qaeda demonstrated adherence to asymmetric warfare, developing its mobility and flexibility based on the cellular and decentralized structure of the network. For example, al-Qaeda orchestrated a complex system for surprise attacks, secretly infiltrating a large number of its operatives into other countries, including the United States, and creating so-called "sleeper cells," which could be positioned within a country for some time and then suddenly become active and strike from the inside. The organization used psychological warfare techniques extensively to promote its extremist ideology. Al-Qaeda also persistently sought to maximize the lethality and destructiveness of its attacks, deliberately targeting civilians and high-profile symbolic targets.

The September 11 attacks brought about the first war between a state and a transnational terrorist network. They also signaled the re-emergence of total warfare on a global scale for the first time since World War II. The post-1945 wars and conflicts, with very few exceptions, were not about physical survival of antagonists and were limited by strategic, political, and humanitarian considerations. The terrorist war that al-Qaeda waged is different from those wars in some important respects.

Ideologically, al-Qaeda's war was empowered by a fanatical hatred of Western—particularly American—ideals and institutions. Accordingly, it perceived the world apocalyptically, as an arena of eternal and uncompromising struggle between "true believers" and "infidels," with the unavoidable ultimate destruction of the latter. Strategically, the aim of al-Qaeda is to expel the non-Muslim presence from the lands of Islam through terrorism and the destabilization of pro-Western regimes and to ensure the worldwide expansion and preponderance of militant Islam. By its emphasis on strikes from the inside on a wide array of civilian targets, as well as by hiding its battle detachments—the cells—among civilians, al-Qaeda erased the difference between the battlefield and the home front in its traditional meaning. Tactically, al-Qaeda tried to achieve greater lethality of its actions by employing suicide attacks, converting conventional tools such as civilian airliners, into extremely destructive weapons (so-called "weapons of mass effect") and persistently seeking access to WMD.

Al-Qaeda developed an unrealistic and unachievable "grand design" for the world, based on re-making the history of the past 14 centuries. It sought to place Islam in a dominant role, and even to expand into a militant Islamic empire stretching across the planet. With these goals the al-Qaeda leaders had no interest in conventional politics. Despite the fact that the September 11 attacks hit important strategic objects (the Pentagon and a major business and communications hub at the World Trade Center), the terrorist actions pursued by the perpetrators were predominantly aimed at civilians and symbolic objects and served no practical military purpose in the traditional sense, except in their ability to create chaos and panic. The destruction of those objects and the killing of as many people as possible were the war aims in themselves.

AN ANTI-WAR PROTESTOR DEMONSTRATES AGAINST U.S. MILITARY ACTION IN AFGHANISTAN IN OCTOBER 2001. (*AP/Wide World Photos/David Longstreath. Reproduced by permission.*)

Thus there was no room for peace negotiations and compromises, or for concessions and cease-fires in this "war against terror." There was also not much possibility of obtaining an organized, unconditional surrender from al-Qaeda terrorists due to their extremism and their dispersed structure. Conversely, for the United States and its allies there is no natural point of conclusion to the war other than total victory, which is the complete eradication of transnational terrorist networks and the toppling of the regimes that support them.

Certainly the concept and practice of total war is not something new for the United States. Many historical campaigns of the U.S. Army against Native Americans witnessed elements of extreme destruction on both sides. Basic elements of modern total war emerged during the American Civil War (1861–65), and in both world wars.

Yet the strategic realities of the war against terrorism posed an enormous challenge: how to go to war and overcome the enemy, which has no territory, no army, and no government, nor any recognizable and well-defined political and military demands. The challenge is also complicated by the fact that aside from the relatively recent exceptions of the Russian and Israeli armies, the major world militaries—American, British, French, German, Spanish, and Italian—that have had extensive experience in counterterrorism, usually defined the struggle against terrorism as a lower level of conflict than formal warfare.

Moreover, attempts to apply large-scale conventional warfare to Islamic militants, such as the

Israeli campaign in southern Lebanon and the Russian campaign in Chechnya, have fallen short of solving the conflicts in either country even in a military sense. Similarly, on August 20, 1998, after the deadly bombing of U.S. embassies in East Africa masterminded by al-Qaeda, the U.S. Navy launched Operation Infinitive Reach. Six warships and one attack submarine fired 76 cruise missiles on suspected terrorist targets in Sudan and Afghanistan. As the subsequent events demonstrated, the retaliation did nothing to deter terrorists from further strikes and achieved little beyond expressing revenge.

While having a global reach, the military operations in the war against terror need to be limited in scale. This war, unlike any other in American history, involves simultaneous and coordinated activities of many nations on many fronts: diplomatic, financial, law enforcement, economic, social, and cultural. Such a multifaceted approach is the major application of asymmetric warfare on terrorism: it turns the decentralized and loose transnational nature of the militant Islamic terrorism into its weakness and exploits it through well-coordinated strikes, both military and non-military.

The U.S. military is still mainly designed to confront a Cold War reality. Recent initiatives are reshaping it to deal with unconventional threats in the twenty-first century. The ongoing transformations include the strengthening of its mobility, enhancement of logistics, and the improvement of the range and precision of its firepower. Yet, as with the attack on Pearl Harbor during World War II, the September 11 attacks challenged the U.S. military to adapt and embrace a new kind of warfare while simultaneously fighting a new enemy on a new battlefield.

A Victory by Christmas: The Strategy and Tactics of the 2001 Afghan Campaign

Operation Enduring Freedom was the name given to the American campaign against the terrorist forces that struck on September 11, conducting air assault and cruise missile strikes on sites in Afghanistan. While it resembled the 1991 Gulf War and the NATO-Yugoslav War of 1999, the overall U.S. campaign demonstrated a new approach. As the former NATO Supreme Commander General Wesley K. Clark (Ret.) noted: "This isn't the war we trained to fight. It requires a fresh strategy, enhanced forces, new weapons and changed attitude."

From the very beginning the strategic conditions in the Afghan theater challenged the planners from U.S. Central Command, led by Gen. Tommy R. Franks, with a number of daunting peculiarities and complexities. The difficult mountainous terrain of the country and its miserable infrastructure, shattered by more than 20 years of war, would complicate the logistics and enormously limit the maneuverability of any modern military force. At the same time these very conditions enabled light and mobile Taliban forces to engage and exhaust the invaders in sudden ambushes and attacks. Afghans had a history of successfully repelling invaders, particularly the British Empire in the nineteenth century and more recently the Soviet Union. From 1979 to 1989 the Soviets, using massive forces, tried to fight the Afghans in a conventional war, but they became bogged down in a savage and finally unsuccessful guerilla war, frequently referred as "Soviet Union's Vietnam."

Given the harsh conditions of the theater and the fanatical character of the enemy, some military observers and analysts foresaw a long and bloody campaign in Afghanistan. According to some estimates it would take some 100,000 U.S. troops to occupy and control the country. Such a large-scale operation would be put under additional risk by the approaching winter, which limited the time available for the operation. The Taliban, for its part, expected that the U.S. would follow the Soviet example of a massive ground invasion. It therefore prepared to outmaneuver the Americans, using its key tactical methods—highly mobile strike squads mounted on pickup trucks.

The general strategic scheme of the U.S. operation in Afghanistan was designed to avoid a Vietnam-style gradual escalation and involvement in a long and bloody war on the ground. Instead of committing a large number of U.S. ground troops, the Americans approached the operation with a combination of air strikes and special operations, closely coordinated with the U.S.-backed ground assault by the anti-Taliban Northern Alliance forces. While air strikes in concert with the ground assault by local proxy forces resembled the Kosovo campaign of 1999, the American war in Afghanistan also had important new elements, which reflected distinct Afghan realities and the intention of the U.S. command to engage the enemy asymmetrically, exploiting its vulnerabilities and reverting and outmaneuvering its strengths. The dispersed nature of warfare in the Afghan deserts and mountains as well as the decentralized structure of the Taliban and al-Qaeda forces demanded special operations to take the fight to the enemy, keeping it off-balance as well as seizing and maintaining the initiative on the battlefield. In coordination with an intense bombing campaign and military pressure from the Northern Alliance, this swiftly reshaped the situation on the ground.

The political dimension of the war was of much importance as well. The United States actively exploited the unpopularity of the Taliban inside and outside Afghanistan, due to its violent character and extreme interpretation of the Islamic laws. To isolate the Taliban further the United States publicly emphasized the just and defensive character of its war on terrorism and stressed the puppet role of the Taliban under al-Qaeda. U.S. representatives established contacts with the exiled Afghan king Zahir Shah, then living in Rome. Zahir had some influence in the country, particularly among the Pushtuns, the largest ethnic group in Afghanistan. Additionally, the military campaign was the first in history to be paralleled by a large-scale humanitarian effort, with U.S. cargo planes conducting massive food drops for the starving Afghans.

The United States also successfully managed the tremendous logistics problems of waging a war over such a long distance and in a landlocked country. The measures undertaken included gaining access to bases in Bahrain, Oman, Pakistan, and Uzbekistan and obtaining flight rights over these and some other countries. The air assault on Afghanistan was carried out by use of cruise missiles—50 missiles were launched during the first strike—as well as by B-1 and B-52 bombers, flying from the Island of Diego Garcia in the Indian Ocean, and B-2 Stealth bombers, which half-circled the globe, flying from their base in Missouri. The tactical F-14 Tomcat and F/A-18 Hornet aircraft flew from

AFGHANISTAN, 2001: ORDER OF THE BATTLE

U.S. forces:

- Three aircraft carrier battle groups with cruisers, destroyers, attack submarines, frigates and support ships

- More than 400 aircraft

- Some 50,000 sailors, airmen, marines, and soldiers, including Special Forces (about 4,000 U.S. troops were deployed inside Afghanistan by the beginning of 2002)

U.K. forces:

- 3 Royal Navy attack submarines, 1 support aircraft carrier and a naval task group

- 4,200 military personnel, including sailors, marines and Special Forces

Northern Alliance (anti-Taliban)

- 12,000–15,000 troops

- 60-70 tanks and armored vehicles

- 3 cargo planes and 8 transport helicopters

- Some 25 surface-to-surface and short-range ballistic missiles

Taliban forces:

- 25,000–45,000 troops (plus 400–600 al-Qaeda militants)

- 650 tanks and armored vehicles

- 15 combat planes, 40 cargo planes, 10 transport helicopters

- Some 20 missiles (old Soviet SA-7 and American-made Stingers)

air carriers in the Arabian Sea. The electronic warfare aircraft EA-6B and the E-2C early warning radar planes provided reconnaissance support. KC-10 and KC-135 air tankers were used to refuel combat planes in midair.

The strikes, which hit air defense systems, weapons depots, and training camps of the enemy, were relatively modest in comparison with those of the Gulf War of 1991 and the NATO air campaign against Yugoslavia in 1999. In contrast there was no center of gravity on the enemy side in Af-

ghanistan to knock out, nor were there many important military, political, and economic targets. In the first strike on Afghanistan 40 aircraft were involved. By the end of December 2001 the number was increased to 60–100 planes per day. In the Persian Gulf in 1991 some 2,500 coalition aircraft were used per day, while in the first strike against Yugoslavia some 300 allied planes participated, with NATO later increasing the number to 1,000 planes per day.

At the same time, U.S. air power, using precise guided munitions (PGM), succeeded in taking out the enemy air defense, communications, and control facilities, eliminating some top commanders of the Taliban and al-Qaeda forces, isolating the battlefield, and demoralizing and paralyzing the enemy. As one top-ranking Taliban commander, quoted by Scott Peterson in a December 4, 2001 *Christian Science Monitor* article, admitted later, "All ways were blocked, so there was no way to carry food or ammunition to the front. All trenches of the Taliban were destroyed, and many people were killed."

The launch of ground operations in Afghanistan was also unconventional by U.S. standards. Small groups of U.S. Special Forces flew into Afghanistan on helicopters and MC-130 transport planes, supported by Apache combat helicopters, F-16 fighters, and A-130 gunships from bases in Oman. The commandos raided Taliban and al-Qaeda facilities, disrupted communications, and engaged enemy forces. The U.S. Special Forces demonstrated a great deal of tactical flexibility and adaptability to the conditions and terrain. Following traditions of warfare in Central Asia, U.S. soldiers sometimes rode on horseback. As strategic areas near Kandahar and Kabul were secured, U.S. Marines and light infantry detachments were deployed to complete the destruction of Taliban and al-Qaeda forces.

While the terrorists' success in the September 11 attacks obviously signaled a major failure of U.S. intelligence, intelligence operations were an important factor in the success of American war efforts in Afghanistan. The covert operations of the Central Intelligence Agency (CIA) had played a decisive role in supporting the anti-Soviet resistance of the Afghans in 1979—1989. It was the largest paramilitary program in CIA history, with total estimated costs at US$3 billion. During the 2001 campaign in Afghanistan, U.S. intelligence operations encouraged divisions between the Taliban and its ethnic base—the numerous Pushtun tribes—by restoring old and establishing new contacts with influential warlords.

Despite profound U.S. successes in the air and ground operations in Afghanistan, no tactical element was decisive alone. Only a combination of tactics and close coordination among U.S. services and local proxy forces led to the victory. Moreover, while the main elements of the U.S. military strategy in Afghanistan were more or less familiar, they were frequently combined in nontraditional and innovative ways, strengthening the U.S. ability to challenge the new enemy asymmetrically.

The U.S. Navy contributed significantly to the U.S. air assault by firing cruise missiles and by launching a huge share of air strikes (some 70 percent) from aircraft carriers. It also provided its own commandos for special operations and an aircraft carrier, the USS *Kitty Hawk,* as a floating base for Special Forces. The mobile units of the Marines were of great importance in occupying and controlling military bases and objects deep inside Afghanistan as the campaign proceeded. The U.S. Air Force supported the ground operations decisively, providing air mobility and cover for commando raids as well as using extremely effective 5000-pound bunker-buster bombs and 15,000-pound gravity bombs to assist the subterranean warfare in the caves and underground tunnels in the eastern part of Afghanistan. The carpet-bombing of the well-entrenched Taliban forces on the northern front helped the Northern Alliance's thrust into Kabul, avoiding a World War I-style bloody stand off of armed enemies facing each other's firepower.

Intelligence-gathering was a key asymmetric advantage of U.S. forces and an important asset in combined operations in Afghanistan. New technologies helped to get a real-time view of the battlefield from remote and safe locations. Of particular help were drones (also known as radio-controlled unmanned air vehicles or UAVs) which were able to fly deep into hostile territory and take continuous video footage of the ground. As a result, the time lag between the detection of a ground target and its attack from the air was dramatically reduced, almost completely eliminating confusion and uncertainty (the so-called "fog of war").

While UAVs had been used earlier for real-time reconnaissance by the Israelis in southern Lebanon and the Gaza Strip as well as by U.S. forces in the Balkans, in Afghanistan the drones debuted in direct combat missions, launching Hellfire guided missiles on the enemy. This foreshadowed a new era of the automated battlefield. At the same time, U.S. Special Forces, acting as scouts on the ground, doing intelligence-gathering, and marking targets with lasers, dramatically increased the effectiveness of the use of PGM in Afghanistan.

A KABUL RESIDENT SHOWS THE DAMAGE DONE TO A HOUSE AFTER IT WAS HIT DURING AN ALLIED BOMBARDMENT IN OCTOBER 2001. *(AP/Wide World Photos/Amir Shah. Reproduced by permission.)*

According to some estimates, it took only 2 bombs to hit a target in Afghanistan, compared to approximately 10 bombs in the Gulf War.

Innovative strategic reconnaissance on the ground was of particular importance in the final phase of the campaign due to the relatively limited use of satellites (unlike in the Gulf War) to find the enemy, who were by then hiding in caves and tunnels. Also, the revolutionary combination of air and ground operations, called "synergistic warfare" by some experts, was enormously effective in the destruction of moving targets in Afghanistan. Thus, the combination of familiar strategic and tactical approaches, including the use of overwhelming air power, stealthy commando raids, and support of proxy ground forces, allowed the United States to avoid committing a large number of its own troops in combat, while creating necessary conditions for the swift and decisive destruction of terrorist sanctuaries in Afghanistan.

RECENT HISTORY AND THE FUTURE

Defending the Homeland

The chairman of the U.S. Joint Chiefs of Staff, Gen. Richard B. Myers, called the military operations in Afghanistan "only the beginning of a global campaign and perhaps the most visible component" in the long war against terrorism (as quoted by Eric Schmitt in the *New York Times*, November 18, 2001). By its very nature, a war in which U.S. civilian losses will very likely outnumber combat losses emphasizes homeland security as the vital front of the struggle.

Although a new federal agency—the Office of Homeland Security, headed by former Pennsylvania Governor Tom Ridge—was created on September 20, 2001, in the aftermath of the terrorist attacks, the problem of homeland defense is not new in U.S. history. Acts expanding the security prerogatives of the Federal Executive as well as restricting the rights of suspected aliens and alleged domestic saboteurs were passed by Congress during the hostilities with France in 1798, in the Civil War and its aftermath, during World War I, following the anarchist bombing campaign in New York of 1919–20, and during World War II. In 1916, after Mexican revolutionary and bandit Pancho Villa raided U.S. territory, National Guard troops were mobilized to secure the border with Mexico. Homeland security measures were effective in defeating German sabotage campaigns during both world wars. At the same time, the defense preparations for possible Japanese invasion in 1942 led to security measures that were responsible for the deportation of more than 100,000 West Coast Japanese-Americans who were loyal to the United States.

In the war on terrorism, domestic security emerges as a pivotal component of U.S. anti-terrorist strategy. Yet the United States, by virtue of being the largest open society in the world, is extremely vulnerable to transnational terrorism. In 2000 more than 350 million non-U.S. citizens entered the country. The ability of the Immigration and Naturalization Service to monitor the process and investigate possible violation of immigration laws was and is rather limited; it has only 2,000 agents. U.S. Customs processed per day in 2000 an average of 1.3 million people, 348,000 private vehicles, 38,000 trucks and railcars, 16,000 containers on 600 ships, and 2,600 aircraft. In total, more than 2 billion tons of cargo ran in and out of U.S. ports in 1999. Also, about 7.5 million passengers got on and off cruise ships in American and Canadian ports in 2001.

Inside the United States there are 86 stadiums with more than 60,000 seats each, 10 motor speedways with more than 100,000 seats each, and some 50 percent of the world's tallest buildings, any one of which could be targeted by terrorists. Additionally, the intensity of modern communications complicates the anti-terrorist measures on the home front. In 1999 Americans made 5.2 billion phone calls overseas. Before the 2001 anthrax scare, the U.S. Postal Service processed 680 million pieces of mail per day, while FedEx and UPS handled about 5 million and 13.6 million packages respectively. Given all the difficulties and complexities of fighting terrorism domestically in an open and dynamic society, there is no alternative to a coordinated effort by various federal agencies and services.

After September 11, the United States increased security on U.S. strategic objects—including nuclear power plants, transport facilities, and other elements of infrastructure in cities and public places—and stockpiled vaccines against possible biological attacks. The protection of the 95,000-mile U.S. shoreline is being strengthened, and border control is being improved. (Historically American enemies have viewed Mexico and Canada as potentially safe bases for hostile activities against U.S. territory.) There are also proposals to radically change the role and functions of the U.S. military in homeland defense.

With the new war being simultaneously waged both internationally and domestically, and often mainly on the home front, the traditional distinction between the military and the National Guard is becoming vague. New developments may include the creation of a single U.S. military command in charge of defending the nation's territory, instead of relying on separate services such as North American Airspace Defense Command (NORAD) in Colorado Springs, the Coast Guard, the Pentagon's Joint Command in Norfolk, and the National Guard. The possibility of anti-terrorist operations by U.S. military on U.S. soil calls for close coordination of actions with law enforcement agencies and may entail reconsideration of legal norms that bar military personnel from police work. (Those limitations—*The Posse Comitatus Act*—were introduced after President Ulysses S. Grant used troops as federal marshals in the South during the controversial 1876 presidential elections.)

Despite the enormous complexity of the problems that homeland defense efforts need to address, the war that began at home must be won at home.

BIBLIOGRAPHY

America's New War: History, Insight, Analysis. A special edition of *Military History Magazine* and *MHQ: The Quarterly Journal of Military History*, 2001.

Bergen, Peter L. *Holy War, Inc.: Inside the Secret World of Osama bin Laden.* New York: Free Press, 2001.

Clark, General Wesley K. (Ret.) "How to Fight the New War," *Time,* September 24, 2001, p. 47.

Flynn, Stephen E. "America the Vulnerable," *Foreign Affairs* 81, February 2002, pp. 60–74.

Hoffman, Bruce. *Inside Terrorism.* London: Victor Gollancz, 1998.

Klare, Michael T. "Waging Postindustrial Warfare on the Global Battlefield," *Current History* 100, December 2001, pp. 433–437.

Laqueur, Walter. *The Age of Terrorism.* Boston, Toronto: Little Brown & Co., 1987.

Peterson, Scott. "A View Behind the Lines of the U.S. Air War," *Christian Science Monitor,* December 4, 2001.

Rappoport, David C. "The Future Wave: September 11 in the History of Terrorism," *Current History* 100, December 2001, pp. 419–424.

Peter Rainow

CONTRIBUTORS

Mohammed Abu-Nimer is an associate professor of peace and conflict resolution at the School of International Service, American University, Washington, DC. He is the author of *Nonviolence and Peacebuilding in Islam* (University Press of Florida, forthcoming 2003) and *Reconciliation, Justice, and Coexistence* (Lexington Press, 2001).

ENTRIES: The Muslim World Reacts to September 11

Gary Ackerman, a Research Associate at the Center for Nonproliferation Studies at the Monterey Institute of International Studies, researches terrorism, especially terrorism involving Weapons of Mass Destruction (biological, chemical, radiological and nuclear weapons) and mass-casualty terrorism in general. Mr. Ackerman received his Master's degree in International Relations from Yale University. His work includes research on terrorism theory, empirical analysis of trends in WMD terrorism, threat assessment and government response and prevention programs.

ENTRIES: Chemical Terrorism Threats; Money for the Cause: Financing Terrorism

Craig Allen is an associate professor and the coordinator of broadcast news at the Walter Cronkite School of Journalism and Mass Communication at Arizona State University. His two books include *News Is People: The Rise of Local TV News* (2001) and *Eisenhower and the Mass Media* (1994). He has written extensively on the mass media and television news and has contributed to documentaries on international mass communication. Prior to receiving his Ph.D. at Ohio University in 1989, he was a newspaper reporter at the *Oregon Journal* in Portland and a news director and producer at television stations in Denver, Colorado Springs, and Spokane.

ENTRIES: The Media's Relationship with Terrorism

Gerry Azzata is a former lawyer and law librarian. She has researched and written extensively in the areas of human rights and international law. A freelance writer with the Gale Group and other reference publishers during the past six years, she continues part-time work as a reference librarian. Her specialties are legal issues, biographical material, and bibliographies.

ENTRIES: Prosecuting Terrorism

Navin A. Bapat graduated with a B.A. in Political Science from the University of Michigan in 1998 and received his M.A. from Rice University in 2001. He is currently a third year graduate student at Rice, focusing on political conflict and violence, specifically conflict between states and sub-state actors. The focuses of his current projects are how states bargain with terrorist groups during the course of attacks, how terrorist attacks may trigger international disputes, and how terrorist campaigns terminate.

ENTRIES: The European Union's Response to 9/11 and its Aftermath

Timothy G. Borden holds a doctorate in history from Indiana University and received his A.B. in international relations and economics from Brown University. He has taught at the University of Toledo and Indiana University at Bloomington, and his work has appeared in *Labor History, Michigan Historical Review, Polish American History, Northwest Ohio Quarterly*, and *Organization of American Historians Magazine of History*. Dr. Borden has received grants to study and teach history and economics in Romania, Bosnia-Herzegovina, Argentina, and Paraguay.

ENTRIES: Air Security and Terrorist Threats; Biological Threats of Terrorism; Civil Rights Suspended; Homeland Security: Guarding Against Terrorism; The Olympics Confronts Terrorism; September 11, 2001: The United States is Attacked on its Own Soil

Morten Bremer Maerli is a researcher at the Norwegian Institute of International Affairs, Oslo, Norway. He is a physicist by training with both practical and research experience in the fields of nuclear safety and security. From 1995 to 2000 he served as a Senior Executive Officer at the Nuclear Safety Department of the Norwegian Radiation Protection Authority, with physical protection and accountancy of nuclear materials as his prime responsibility. Through his work he has gained regional knowledge and hands-on experience of the current situation and practices concerning the handling, storing, and security of nuclear materials in northwest Russia. In addition to his degree in physics (Master's of Science, MSc), he holds a Bachelor of Arts degree from the Institute of Media and Communication, University of Oslo, focusing on risk communication and perceptions of the risk of radiation. In 1999 Bremer Maerli published the book *Atomterrorisme,* assessing the intentions and the capabilities of sub-national groups to perform acts of nuclear and radiological terrorism. He has acted as a technical consultant to the Norwegian Ministry of Foreign Affairs, e.g. at the Conference on Disarmament, Geneva, on discussions on the Fissile Materials Cut Off Treaty. Bremer Maerli was a technical advisor to the Norwegian delegation to the 2000 Review Conference of the Parties to the Treaty on the Non-Proliferation of Nuclear Weapons, New York. During the 1999/2000 academic year Bremer Maerli was a Science Fellow at the Center for International Security (CISAC) at Stanford University, working on nuclear nonproliferation and the prevention of nuclear terrorism. In August 2000 he started his Ph.D. studies, focusing on Russian nuclear naval fuel and the risk of proliferation. During the 2000/2001 academic year he was a Visiting Research Scholar at Sandia National Laboratories, California, and affiliated with the Center for International Security and Cooperation of Stanford University.

ENTRIES: Nuclear Terrorism: Threats, Challenges, and Responses

Michael Buczek holds a BA in International Security from George Washington University.

ENTRIES: The PLO and Yasser Arafat—From Terrorism to Statesmanship to Terrorism

Charles Hauss teaches comparative politics and conflict resolution at George Mason University. He is also Director of Policy and Research at Search for Common Ground, the world's largest conflict resolution non-governmental organization. He has written seven books and numerous articles on aspects of comparative politics, international relations, conflict resolution, and the impact of technology on political life. He lives and works in the Washington, DC, area.

ENTRIES: Osama bin Laden—A Face of Terrorism

Amal Khoury is a doctoral candidate at the School of International Service at American University, Washington, DC. She is completing her dissertation on conflict resolution and development.

ENTRIES: The Muslim World Reacts to September 11

Lynn M. Kunkle is a doctoral candidate at the School of International Service at American University, Washington, DC. She is completing her dissertation on Christian-Muslim reconciliation strategies and dialogue.

ENTRIES: The Muslim World Reacts to September 11

Cheryl A. Loeb has a Master's degree in International Studies from the University of Northern British Columbia in Canada, where she focused her research on the 1972 Biological Weapons Convention, infec-

tious diseases, and biological weapons terrorism. She currently works as a research associate at the Monterey Institute of International Studies, the Center for Nonproliferation Studies. She conducts research on weapons of mass destruction proliferation, domestic terrorism, and on the status of the Biological Weapons Convention. Prior to her joining the Washington, DC, office of the Monterey Institute of International Studies, Cheryl worked in Bonn, Germany, at the Bonn International Center for Conversion. In Bonn she worked on a variety of projects that looked at chemical weapons destruction activities in Russia, biological weapons threats, military expenditures, and surplus weapons disposition.

ENTRIES: Domestic Terrorism: Oklahoma City to Anthrax and Beyond; Hostage Taking and Terrorism: The Human Bargaining Chip

Mark M. Lowenthal is an internationally recognized expert in intelligence, with more than 26 years of experience in both government and the private sector. In his government career, Dr. Lowenthal served as a Deputy Assistant Secretary of State for Intelligence and as Staff Director of the House Permanent Committee on Intelligence. From 1997–2002, Dr. Lowenthal worked in the private sector providing consulting and intelligence support to government agencies and private sector corporations. He returned to government service in 2002, and is currently the Counselor to the Director of Central Intelligence. Dr. Lowenthal is also an Adjunct Professor at the School of International and Public Affairs, Columbia University. He is the author of *Intelligence: From Secrets to Policy,* a widely used textbook on the subject. The views expressed in this article are his own and are not attributable to any government agency.

ENTRIES: U.S. Intelligence in the Twenty-first Century

Cynthia Keppley Mahmood is Senior Fellow at the Joan B. Kroc Institute for International Peace Studies, University of Notre Dame. She received her Ph.D. in Anthropology from Tulane University in 1986, and is Director and Editor of the book series on *The Ethnography of Political Violence* at the University of Pennsylvania Press. Her own research focus is religious militancy in South Asia; she has published three books and many articles on Sikh, Muslim, and Hindu nationalism on the subcontinent. Dr. Mahmood also serves as consultant to governmental and non-governmental agencies in the United States, Canada, and the United Kingdom on issues relating to South Asia, human rights, and terrorism.

ENTRIES: Extremism—The Fundamentals

Nancy Matuszak has a Bachelor's in Political Science from Oakland University. She is the editor of several reference books, including *History Behind the Headlines* volumes 3 and 5, and is a published writer.

ENTRIES: Living with Terrorism: Everyday Life and the Effects of Terror

Clark McCauley is a Professor of Psychology at Bryn Mawr College and Co-Director of the Solomon Asch Center for Study of Ethnopolitical Conflict, University of Pennsylvania. He is the editor of *Terrorism*

Research and Public Policy (Frank Cass, 1991) and has written in recent years about the psychology of ethnic group conflict and the psychological foundations of genocide.

ENTRIES: (Psychology) Understanding the 9/11 Perpetrators: Crazy, Lost in Hate, or Martyred?

Kimberly A. McCloud joined the Center for Nonproliferation Studies at the Monterey Institute of International Studies in July 2000, after completing the Master of Arts degree in National Security Studies at Georgetown University. She is a Research Associate at the Chemical and Biological Weapons Nonproliferation Program, where she conducts research and writes on the connection between weapons of mass destruction terrorism and ethnic and religious radicalism, as well as the potential chemical and biological warfare capabilities and intentions of Iran. From 1996–98, Ms. McCloud worked for the Permanent Mission of Japan to the International Atomic Energy Agency, where she was responsible for assisting in the operation of the Point of Contact for the Nuclear Suppliers Group. In 1995, she received her BA in History from the University of California at San Diego.

ENTRIES: Al-Qaeda and the Reach of Terror

Frederic S. Pearson is Director of the Center for Peace and Conflict Studies and Program on Mediating Theory and Democratic Systems at Wayne State University. Dr. Pearson received his Ph.D. in 1971 from the University of Michigan and has become a recognized authority in the fields of international military intervention, arms transfer effects on wars, and ethnic conflict analysis. He has twice been senior Fulbright research professor (Netherlands and UK), having written on arms trade and crisis behavior in both countries. Dr. Pearson's complete *vitae* are available on the Community of Science web site. Among his six books are *Arms and Warfare: Escalation, De-escalation, Negotiation* (1994, with Michael Brzoska) and *The Global Spread of Arms: Political Economy of International Security* (1994). He and John Sislin completed *Arms*

and Ethnic Conflict (2001, from Rowman and Littlefield). He is editor for the special issue of the *Journal of Peace Research* on "Identity-based Disputes and Conflict Management" (no. 3, 2001). His relevant recent articles include "Patterns of Arms Transfers to Ethnic Groups in Conflict," *Security Dialogue* (vol. 29, December 1998, with Sislin, J. Boryczka, and J. Weigand) and "Arms Trade: Economics of," in the *Encyclopedia of Violence, Peace, and Conflict* (with Sislin and M. Olson). In 2000 Dr. Pearson was designated a conflict resolution consultant to the U.S. Commission on National Security/21st Century in Washington, DC.

ENTRIES: Fighting Terrorism with Force

Peter Rainow, Ph.D., is author and co-author of four books and more than forty chapters and articles on military and international history, published in the United States, the United Kingdom, Italy, Russia, and Ukraine. In 1996–97 he was a Visiting Scholar at Hoover Institution, Stanford University; in 1991–92 he also participated in the Consensus Project on the future of International Relations at John M. Olin Institute of Strategic Studies, Harvard University.

ENTRIES: The United States vs. Terror: A New Kind of War

Bernard Reich is Professor of Political Science and International Affairs at George Washington University in Washington, DC. His latest book is *Government and Politics of the Middle East and North Africa,* fourth edition, co-edited with David E. Long.

ENTRIES: The PLO and Yasser Arafat—From Terrorism to Statesmanship to Terrorism; State Sponsored Terrorism

Jennifer B. Reich is currently studying Law at George Washington University Law School. She holds a BA degree in History and Psychology from George Washington University and an MA degree in Applied Psychology from Columbia University.

ENTRIES: State Sponsored Terrorism

GENERAL BIBLIOGRAPHY

This bibliography contains a list of sources, primarily books and articles, that will assist the reader in pursuing additional information on the topics contained in this volume.

A

Abilek, Ken, with Stephen Handelman. *Biohazard: The Chilling True Story of the Largest Covert Biological Weapons Program in the World.* New York: Random House, 1999.

Alexander, Yonah. "Commentary: Terrorism in the Twenty-first Century: Threats and Responses," *The World and I,* June 1999.

Alexander, Yonah, and Michael S. Swetnam. *Usama bin Laden's al-Qaida: Profiles of a Terrorist Network.* Ardsley, NY: Transnational Publishing, 2001.

Amstutz, Mark R. *International Conflict and Cooperation: An Introduction to World Politics.* New York: McGraw-Hill Companies, 1998.

Anderson, Sean, and Stephen Sloan. *Historical Dictionary of Terrorism.* Lanham: Rowman & Littlefield, 2002.

Antokol, Norman, and Mayer Nudell. *No One a Neutral: Political Hostage Taking in the Modern World.* Medina, OH: Alpha Publications, 1990.

Arendt, Hannah. *The Origins of Totalitarianism.* reprint, New York: Harcourt Brace Jovanovich, 1973.

Arrighi, Giovanni. *The Long Twentieth Century.* New York and London: Verso, 1994.

Avruch, Kevin. *Culture and Conflict Resolution.* Washington, DC: U.S. Institute of Peace Press, 1998.

B

Bairoch, Paul. *The Economic Development of the Third World since 1900.* Berkeley: University of California Press, 1975.

Barkan, Steven E., and Lynne L. Snowden. *Collective Violence.* Boston: Allyn and Bacon, 2001.

Bartlett, C. J. *The Global Conflict: The International Rivalry of the Great Powers, 1880–1990.* New York: Addison-Wesley Longman, 1994.

Bercovitch, Jacob and Richard Jackson. *International Conflict: A Chronological Encyclopedia of Conflict Management, 1945–1995.* Washington, DC: Congressional Quarterly, 1997.

Bradbury, Jonathan, and John Mawson. *British Regionalism and Devolution: The Challenges of State Reform and European Integration.* Regional Policy and Development Series 16, London: Jessica Kingsley Publishers, 1997.

Brown, Michael E. *The International Dimensions of Internal Conflict.* Cambridge: MIT Press, 1997.

Buck, George. *Preparing for Terrorism: An Emergency Services Guide.* Albany: Delmar Learning, 1998.

C

Chang, Nancy, Center for Constitutional Rights (ed.), and Howard Zinn. *Anti-Terrorism Measures Threaten Our Civil Liberties.* New York: Seven Stories Press, 2002.

Collins, Joseph J., and Gabrielle D. Bowdoin. *Beyond Unilateral Economic Sanctions.* Washington, DC: Center for Strategic and International Studies, March 1999.

Cox, Matthew, and Tom Foster. *Their Darkest Day: The Tragedy of Pan Am 103 and Its Legacy of Hope.* New York: John Wiley and Sons, 1995.

Crenshaw, Martha. "Terrorism and International Violence," in Manus Midlarsky, ed. *Handbook of War Studies II.* Ann Arbor: University of Michigan Press, 2000.

D

Darton, Eric. *Divided We Stand: A Biography of New York's World Trade Center.* New York: Basic Books, 1999.

Dempsey, James X., and David Cole. *Terrorism and the Constitution, Sacrificing Civil Liberties in the Name of National Security.* Washington, DC: First Amendment Foundation, 2002.

Deudney, Daniel H. and Richard A. Matthew, eds. *Contested Grounds: Security and Conflict in the New Environ-*

mental Politics. Albany: State University of New York Press, 1999.

Diehl, Paul, and Nils Gleditsch, eds. *Environmental Conflict.* Boulder: Westview Press, 2000.

Dieter, Fleck, Michael Bothe, and Horst Fischer. *The Handbook of Humanitarian Law in Armed Conflict.* New York and London: Oxford University Press, 2000.

Dobkin, Bethami A. *Tales of Terror: Television News and the Construction of the Terrorist Threat.* New York: Praeger Publishers, 1992.

Drezner, Daniel W. *The Sanctions Paradox: Economic Statecraft and International Relations.* Cambridge: Cambridge University Press, 1999.

Dudonis, Kenneth J., David P. Schulz, and Frank Bobz, Jr. *The Counterterrorism Handbook: Tactics, Procedures, and Techniques,* 2d ed. CRC Press, 2001.

E

Encyclopedia of World History. New York and London: Oxford University Press, 1999.

Enders, Walter, and Todd Sandler. "Is Transnational Terrorism Becoming More Threatening? A Time Series-Investigation." *Journal of Conflict Resolution,* vol. 44, no. 3, 2002, pp. 307–332.

F

Falkenrath, Richard A., Robert D. Newman, and Bradley A. Thayer. *America's Achilles' Heel: Nuclear, Biological, and Chemical Terrorism and Covert Attack.* Cambridge: MIT Press, 1998.

Fukuyama, Francis. "Rest Easy. It's Not 1914 Anymore," *New York Times,* 9 February 1992.

G

Gall, Susan B., ed. *Worldmark Chronology of the Nations.* Farmington Hills, MI: Gale Group, 2000.

Gall, Timothy L., ed. *Worldmark Encyclopedia of Cultures and Daily Life.* Farmington Hills, MI: Gale Group, 1997.

Ganguly, Rajat and Raymond C. Taras. *Understanding Ethnic Conflict: The International Dimension.* New York: Addison-Wesley Longman, 1998.

Gilbert, Allison, Robyn Walensky, Melinda Murphy, Phil Hirschkorn, and Mitchell Stephens, eds. *Covering Catastrophe: Broadcast Journalists Report September 11.* Chicago: Bonus Books, 2002.

Gilpin, Robert, and Jean M. Gilpin. *Global Political Economy: Understanding the International Economic Order.* Princeton: Princeton University Press, 2001.

Goldscheider, Calvin. *Cultures in Conflict: The Arab-Israeli Conflict.* Westport: Greenwood Publishing Group, 2002.

Goldstone, Jack A., Ted Robert Gurr, and Farrakh Mashiri. *Revolutions of the Late Twentieth Century.* Boulder: Westview Press, 1991.

Gottlieb, Gidon. *Nation Against State: A New Approach to Ethnic Conflicts and Sovereignty.* Washington, DC: Council on Foreign Relations Press, 1993.

Gunaratna, Rohan. *Inside Al Qaeda: Global Network of Terrorism.* New York: Cambridge University Press, 2002.

Guyatt, Nicholas. *The Absence of Peace: Understanding the Israeli-Palestinian Conflict.* London: Zed Books, 1998.

H

Haass, Richard N. *Conflicts Unending: The United States and Regional Disputes.* New Haven: Yale University Press, 1990.

Haass, Richard N., and Meghan L. O'Sullivan, eds. *Honey and Vinegar: Incentives, Sanctions, and Foreign Policy.* Washington, DC: Brookings Institution, 2000.

Hahnel, Robert. *Panic Rules!: Everything You Need to Know about the Global Political Economy.* Cambridge: South End Press, 1999.

Hall, John R., with Philip D. Schuyler and Sylvaine Trinh. *Apocalypse Observed: Religious Movements and Violence in North America, Europe, and Japan.* London: Routledge Press, 2000.

Heskin, Ken. *Northern Ireland: A Psychological Analysis.* New York: Columbia University Press, 1980.

Heymann, Philip B. *Terrorism and America: A Commonsense Strategy for a Democratic Society.* Cambridge: MIT Press, 1998.

Hodgson, Marshall G. S. "World History and a World Outlook." In *Rethinking World History: Essays on Europe, Islam and World History.* New York: Cambridge University Press, 1993.

Hoffman, Bruce. *Inside Terrorism.* New York: Columbia University Press, 1998.

Hoffman, Stanley. *World Disorders: Troubled Peace in the Post Cold War Era.* Lanham, MD: Rowman & Littlefield Publishers, 2000.

Hoge, Jr., James F., and Gideon Rose, eds. *How Did This Happen?: Terrorism and the New War.* New York: Public Affairs, 2001.

Homer-Dixon, Thomas F. *Environment, Scarcity, and Violence.* Princeton: Princeton University Press, 1999.

Hoveyda, Fereydoun. *The Broken Crescent: The 'Threat' of Militant Islamic Fundamentalism.* Westport: Praeger Publishers, 1998.

Hudson, Christopher, ed. *The China Handbook: Prospects Onto the Twenty-first Century.* Chicago, IL: Glenlake Publishing Company, 2000.

Hunter, Shireen T. *Turkey at the Crossroads: Islamic Past or European Future?* Brussels: Centre for European Policy Studies, 1995.

K

Kakar, Sudhir. *The Colors of Violence: Cultural Identities, Religion, and Conflict.* Chicago: University of Chicago Press, 1996.

Kaplan, Robert D. *The Ends of the Earth: From Togo to Turkmenistan, from Iran to Cambodia—A Journey to the Frontiers of Anarchy.* New York: Vintage Books, 1996.

Kanet, Roger E. *Resolving Regional Conflicts.* Urbana: University of Illinois Press, 1998.

Katz, Richard S. *Democracy and Elections.* New York and London: Oxford University Press, 1998.

Keegan, John. *A History of Warfare.* New York: Vintage Books, 1994.

King, Anthony D., ed. *Culture, Globalization and the World-System: Contemporary Conditions for the Representation of Identity.* Minneapolis: University of Minnesota Press, 1997.

Kohn, Hans. "Nationalism," *International Encyclopedia of the Social Sciences,* 11: 63–39.

L

Laqueur, Walter. *The New Terrorism: Fanaticism and the Arms of Destruction.* New York: Oxford University Press, 2000.

Lake, Anthony. *Nightmares: Real Threats in a Dangerous World and How America Can Meet Them.* Boston: Little, Brown and Company, 2000.

Lal, Brij V., and Kate Fortune, eds. *The Pacific Islands: An Encyclopedia.* Honolulu, Hawai'i: University of Hawai'i Press, 2000.

Lambert, Richard D., Alan W. Heston, and William Zartman. *Resolving Regional Conflicts: International Perspectives.* London: Sage Publications, 1991.

Lesser, Ian O., Bruce Hoffman, John Arquila, David Ronfeldt, and Michele Zanini. *Countering the New Terrorism.* Santa Monica: RAND Corporation, 1999.

Lifton, Robert Jay. *Destroying the World to Save It.* New York: Henry Holt and Company, 1999.

Linenthal, Edward Tabor. *The Unfinished Bombing: Oklahoma City in American Memory.* New York: Oxford University Press, 2001.

M

Mayall, James, ed. *The New Interventionism, 1991–1994: United Nations Experience in Cambodia, Former Yugoslavia, and Somalia.* Cambridge: Cambridge University Press, 1996.

———. *World Politics: Progress and Its Limits (Themes for the 21st Century).* Cambridge: Polity Press, 2001.

McNeill, William H. *Plagues and Peoples.* New York: Anchor Books/Doubleday & Co., Inc., 1998.

McRae, Rob, and Don Hubert, eds. *Human Security and the New Diplomacy: Protecting People, Promoting Peace.* Montreal: McGill-Queen's University Press, 2001.

Miall, Hugh, and Tom Woodhouse, et al. *Contemporary Conflict Resolution: The Prevention, Management and Transformations of Deadly Conflict.* Cambridge: Polity Press, 1999.

Mitchell, C. R. *The Structure of International Conflict.* New York: St. Martin's Press, 1990.

Miller, Judith, et. al. *Germs: Biological Weapons and America's Secret War.* New York: Simon and Schuster, 2001.

N

Nacos, Brigitte L. *Terrorism and the Media.* New York: Columbia University Press, 1994.

Nash, Gary B., Charlotte Crabtree, and Ross E. Dunn. "In the Matter of History," in *History on Trial: Culture Wars and the Teaching of the Past.* New York: Alfred A. Knopf, 1998.

National Commission on Terrorism. *Countering the Changing Threat of International Terrorism.* Washington, DC: U.S. Congress, 2000.

El-Naway, Mohammad, and Adel Iskander. *Al Jazeera: How the Free Arab News Network Scooped the World and Changed the Middle East.* Cambridge: Westview Press, 2002.

Nye, Joseph S. *Understanding International Conflict: An Introduction to Theory and History.* New York: Addison-Welsey Longman, 1999.

O

O'Brien, Patrick K. *Atlas of World History.* New York and London: Oxford University Press, 1999.

Osborne, Milton. *The Mekong: Turbulent Past, Uncertain Future.* New York: Atlantic Monthly Press, 2000.

P

Paris, Erna. *Long Shadows: Truth, Lies, and History.* Bloomsburg, 2001.

Prendergast, John. *Frontline Diplomacy: Humanitarian Aid and Conflict in Africa.* Boulder: Lynne Rienner Publishers, 1996.

R

Ramsbotham, Oliver, Cliver Ramsbotham, and Tom Woodhouse. *Humanitarian Intervention in Contemporary Conflict: A Reconceptualization.* Oxford: Blackwell Publishers, 1996.

Ramsbotham, Oliver, and Tom Woodhouse. *Encyclopedia of International Peacekeeping Operations.* ABC-CLIO, 1999.

Rashid, Ahmed. *Jihad: The Rise of Militant Islam in Central Asia.* New Haven: Yale University Press, 2002.

———. *Taliban: Militant Islam, Oil and Fundamentalism in Central Asia.* New Haven: Yale University Press, 2002.

Ratcliffe, Peter. *Race, Ethnicity, and Nation: International Perspectives on Social Conflict.* London: UCL Press, 1994.

Rayner, Caroline, ed. *Encyclopedic World Atlas: A–Z Country-by-Country Coverage.* New York and London: Oxford University Press, 1994.

Regis, Ed. *The Biology of Doom: The History of America's Secret Germ Warfare Project.* New York: Henry Holt and Company, 1999.

Reeve, Simon. *The New Jackals: Ramzi Yousef, Osama Bin Laden, and the Future of Terrorism.* Boston: Northeastern University Press, 1999.

Reich, Walter, ed. *Origins of Terrorism: Psychologies, Ideologies, Theologies, States of Mind.* Washington, DC: Woodrow Wilson Center Press, 1998.

Rehnquist, William H. *All the Laws But One: Civil Liberties in Wartime.* New York: Alfred A. Knopf, 1998.

Rochards, Andrew. "Meaning of 'Genocide'" *Times Literary Supplement,* 15 May 1998.

Rothchild, Donald, and David A. Lake, eds. *The International Spread of Ethnic Conflict: Fear, Diffusion, and Escalation.* Cambridge: Harvard University Press, 1994.

Roy, Olivier. *The Failure of Political Islam.* New York: Columbia University Press, 1998.

S

Sachs, Wolfgang. *Global Ecology: A New Arena of Political Conflict.* London: St. Martin's Press, 1993.

Sargeti, Lyman Tower, ed. *Extremism in America.* New York: New York University Press, 1995.

Schiavo, Mary, with Sabra Chartrand. *Flying Blind, Flying Safe.* New York: Avon Books, 1997.

Schlesinger, Arthur Meier. *The Disuniting of America: Reflections on a Multicultural Society.* New York: W.W. Norton, 1998.

Schnaiberg, Allan, and Kenneth Alan Gould. *Environment and Society: The Enduring Conflict.* New York: St. Martin's Press, 2000.

Shawcross, William. *Deliver Us from Evil: Peacekeepers, Warlords and a World of Endless Conflict.* New York: Simon and Schuster, 2000.

Simmons, Aan G., and Ian G. Simmons. *Changing the Face of the Earth: Culture, Environment, History.* 2d ed. New York and London: Oxford University Press, 1993.

Smith, David A., Dorothy A. Solinger, and Steven Topik, eds. *States and Sovereignty in the Global Economy.* New York: Routledge, 1999.

Snooks, Graeme Donald. *The Dynamic Society: Exploring the Sources of Global Change.* New York: Routledge, 1996.

Spencer, Metta, ed. *Separatism: Democracy and Disintegration.* Lanham, MD: Rowman & Littlefield Publishers, 1998.

Staub, Ervin. *The Roots of Evil: The Origins of Genocide and Other Group Violence.* Cambridge: Cambridge University Press, 1992.

Stearns, Peter N. "Nationalisms: An Invitation to Contemporary Analysis," *Journal of World History* (Spring 1997): 57–74.

Sulimann, Mohamed. *Ecology, Politics and Violent Conflict.* New York: St. Martin's Press, 1998.

T

Tucker, Jonathan. *Toxic Terror: Assessing Terrorist Use of Chemical and Biological Weapons.* Cambridge: MIT Press, 2000.

V

Von Hippel, Karin. *Democracy by Force: U.S. Military Intervention in the Post-Cold War World.* Cambridge: Cambridge University Press, 2000.

W

Walter, Barbara F. *Civil Wars, Insecurity, and Intervention.* New York: Columbia University Press, 1999.

Weart, Spencer R. *Never at War: Why Democracies Will Not Fight One Another.* New Haven: Yale University Press, 2000.

Weaver, Frederick Stirton, and Ron Chilcote. *Latin America in the World Economy: Mercantile Colonialism to Global Capitalism.* Boulder: Westview Press, 2000.

White, Jonathan R., and Todd R. Clear. *Terrorism: An Introduction.* Belmont, CA: Wadsworth Publishing Co., 2001.

Wilkinson, Paul. *Terrorism Versus Democracy: The Liberal State Response.* London: Frank Cass, 2001.

Wippman, David, ed. *International Law and Ethnic Conflict.* Ithaca, NY: Cornell University Press, 1998.

Worldmark Encyclopedia of Nations. Farmington Hills, MI: Gale Group, 1998.

Wolfe, Patrick. "Imperialism and History: A Century from Marx to Postcolonialism," *The American Historical Review* 102 (April 1997): 388–420.

Worsley, Peter. *The Three Worlds: Culture and World Development.* Chicago, IL: University of Chicago Press, 1989.

Z

Zhang, Wei-Wei. *Transforming China: Economic Reform and its Political Implications.* New York: St. Martin's Press, 2000.

Zinn, Howard, and Anthony Arnove (ed.). *Terrorism and War.* New York: Seven Stories Press, 2002.

General Bibliography

Index

Page numbers in boldface refer to a topic upon which an essay is based. Page numbers in italics refer to illustrations, figures, and tables. A number followed by a colon refers to the volume in which you will find the given page reference(s).

A

Abankwah, Adelaide, 3:112
Abdel-Rahman, Sheik Omar, 3:283, 5:269
Abduction. *See* Kidnappings
Abduh, Mohammed, 5:218
ibn Abi Talib, Ali, 5:278
Abkhazian, 1:263
Abu Nidal (ANO), 5:314
Abu Sayyaf (extremist group), 5:132, 140–141
Abyat, Hussein, 3:177–178
Acadians, deportation of, 3:17
Accra Acceptance and Accession Agreement and Accra
      Clarification (1994), 1:180
Aceh flag, 3:*164*
Aceh province. *See* Irian Jaya and Aceh
Aceh Security Disturbance Movement. *See* Free Aceh
      Movement (GAM) (Indonesia)
Achille Lauro hijacking (1985), 5:138, 203
Act of Union (1707, U.K.), 3:321
Act of Union (1801, U.K.), 2:226
Act of Union (1841, U.K.), 3:18
Acteal Massacre (1997, Mexico), 1:68, 69
Activism and activists
      Belo, Carlos Filipe Ximenes, 2:92–93
      Dai Qing, 4:68
      Dodson, Michael and Patrick, 4:33, 35
      Freitas, Terence, 2:69–70
      Gay, Lahe'ena'e, 2:69–70
      indigenous activists, Australia, 4:30, 34
      Internet use, 2:193
      Mandela, Nelson, 2:257
      Menchú Tam, Rigoberta, 2:*125*
      Native Americans, 2:210–211
      Peltier, Leonard, 2:207
      Suu Kyi, Aung San, 2:189, *194*
      Tutu, Desmond, 2:258
      Washinawatok, Ingrid, 2:69–70
Ad hoc tribunals, effectiveness of, 4:130–131
Adams, Gerry, 2:232, 5:*170*
Adams, James, 5:102
Addis Ababa Agreement (1972), 1:272
"Adivasis." *See* Scheduled castes and tribes, India
Advertising
      anti-female circumcision, 3:*117*

cigarettes, 4:283–284, 286–287
diamonds, 3:66
AFDL (Armed Forces for the Liberation of Congo-
      Zaire), 1:82
Afeworki, Issayas, 1:108
Afghan-Soviet conflict (1978-1989), 1:3–4, 4:3,
      5:174–176, 290
Afghanistan
      civil war, 1:4–5, 4:3–4
      commercial enterprises linked to al-Qaeda, 5:98
      Communism, 1:3–4
      demography, 1:2
      drug trade, 1:9
      economic sanctions, 3:78, 4:10
      ethnic groups, 1:2, 4:3–4
      future of, 4:12–13
      maps, 1:*7, 8, 9, 10*
      Muslims, 1:2–3
      non-recognition of Taliban government, 4:10
      state sponsored terrorism, 5:319–321
      tunnels, 5:*277*
      war destruction, 1:*4*, 5:*333*
      warlords, 5:320
      westernization, 1:3
      See also Northern Alliance; Taliban; "War on terror-
          ism"
AFL (Armed Forces of Liberia), 1:179–180
AFRC (Armed Forced Revolutionary Council) (Sierra
      Leone), 4:272–273
African Americans, 1:174–176, *176*
African Association for the Defense of Human Rights in
      Congo-Kinshasa (ASADHO), 1:87
African National Congress (ANC), 2:253, 254–256, 258,
      261
African Union, **4:172–185**
"African World War," **1:78–88**
Africanizing, Congo, 1:80
Agrarian reform. *See* Land reform
"Agreed Framework" (1994, U.S.-North Korea), 4:233
Agreement on Agriculture (GATT), 4:291
Agreement on Textiles and Clothing (GATT), 4:291,
      292–293
Agriculture
      Amazon rainforest, 1:16–17, 20
      Chinese communes, failure of, 3:45–46

Index

I

M

Index

Q

Index

Sierra Leone colony, 4:267–268
Somalia colony, 3:244, 245–246
Sri Lanka colony, 2:264
See also Northern Ireland
United Liberation Movement of Liberia (ULIMO),
     1:179–180
United National Party (Sri Lanka), 2:264–265, 269
United Nations Conference on Trade and Development
     (UNCTAD), 4:290–291
United Nations Conventions, Declarations, and
     Resolutions
     Convention on International Trade in Endangered
          Species of Wild Fauna and Flora (CITES)
          (1989), 4:133, 134, 136, 143–144
     on criminalization of terrorism, 5:165, 167
     Declaration of Principles of International Law
          Concerning Friendly Relations Between States
          (1971, UN), 5:162
     Declaration on the Granting of Independence to
          Colonies, Countries and Peoples (1960), 5:162
     Draft Declaration of the Rights of Indigenous
          Peoples, 4:35–36
     Framework Convention on Climatic Change (1992),
          4:161, 162–163
     Intergovernmental Panel on Climate Change (1988),
          4:161, 162
     International Convention for the Suppression of the
          Financing of Terrorism (1999), 5:99
     Resolution 181 (1947), 2:144
     Resolution 731 (1992), 4:189–190
     Resolution 748 (1992), 4:191, 194, 5:321
     Resolution 808 (1993), 4:125–126
     Resolution 827 (1993), 4:126
     Resolution 955 (1994), 4:128–129
     Resolution 1192 (1998), 4:194
     Resolution 1261 (1999), 4:57
     Resolution 1368 (2001), 5:70
     Resolution 1373 (2001), 5:101, 169
     Resolution on the Situation in Bosnia and
          Herzegovina, 1:36
     Universal Declaration of Human Rights (1948),
          4:304
     Universal Declaration on the Rights of Indigenous
          Peoples (1995), 2:106
     women's rights declarations, 3:113
     See also International law
United Nations Human Rights Commission, loss of U.S.
     seat, **4:299–309**
United Nations Interim Force in Lebanon (UNIFIL),
     2:286
United Nations Mission in East Timor (UNAMET),
     2:95, 97
United Nations Observer Mission to Sierra Leone, 4:274
United Nations Peace Keeping Force in Cyprus (UNFI-
     CYP), 2:82, 84
United Nations peacekeeping missions, **2:283–291**
     Angola, 2:15
     Bosnia-Herzegovina, 1:29
     Cambodia, 3:10
     controversial missions, late 1990s, 4:307
     Cyprus (UNFICYP), 2:82, 84
     East Timor (UNAMET), 2:95, 97
     history of, 4:303–304
     Korean Peninsula, 2:152
     Kosovo, 2:166, *287*, 4:210

Lebanon (UNIFIL), 2:286
Macedonia, 4:210
Mozambique, 2:186
Rwanda, 1:231–232, 235
Sierra Leone, 2:*288*, 4:267, 274
Somalia, 3:252
United Nations Security Council, 4:196
United Nations Special Commission (UNSCOM),
     1:147–149
United Nations Special Committee on Palestine, 2:144
United Nations Temporary Commission for Korea
     (UNTCOK), 2:151–152
United Nations Terrorism Prevention Branch, 5:170–171
United Nations Transitional Administration in East
     Timor (UNATAET), 2:96
United Nations Troop Supervision Organization
     (UNTSO), 2:285
United Nations (UN)
     Angola, 2:14–15, 19
     arms control agreements, role in, 4:306–307
     Bosnia-Herzegovina, 1:29
     Cambodia, 3:1
     Committee on the Rights of the Child (2000),
          4:57–58
     Conference on Trade and Development, 4:290–291
     Congo, 1:86, 87
     Croatia, 1:244–245
     Cyprus, 2:86
     decolonization assistance, 4:306
     defining terrorism, 5:107–110
     demand for Laden's handover, 4:9–10
     East Timor, 2:95–96
     economic sanctions, 3:78, 82
     Eritrea-Ethiopia border dispute, 1:109
     fear of American isolationism, 4:308
     female circumcision, 3:116–118
     formation of, 4:302–303
     General Assembly, 4:304–305
     General Protocols I and II (1977), 4:57
     goals of, 4:303
     human rights promotion, 4:304
     international humanitarian law, 4:124–125
     involvement, 1950s, 4:306
     involvement, 1960s, 4:306–307
     involvement, 1990s, 4:307
     Iraq embargo, **1:143–150**, 1:*147*
     Jerusalem, 2:143–144
     Liberia, 1:179–180
     New World Order conspiracy theory and, 5:59
     Optional Protocol to the Convention of the Rights
          of the Child (2000), 4:57, 58
     organization of, 4:304–305
     Palestine partition, 1:114–115, 5:250
     Security Council, 4:304–305
     on September 11 attacks, 5:168
     Special Representative for Children and Armed
          Conflict, 4:57–58
     "War on terrorism" support, 5:104
     withdrawal from Afghanistan, 4:8
     women's rights declarations, 3:113
     Yugoslavia arms ban, 1:31
United Somali Congress, 3:249
United States
     aid to Europe after World War II, 2:113–114
     AIDS and HIV, 3:256–257, 268

Index

X

Y

Index